THE *CHRONICA MAIORA* OF THOMAS WALSINGHAM 1376–1422

Translated by
DAVID PREEST
with introduction
and notes by
JAMES G. CLARK

THE BOYDELL PRESS

First published 2005
The Boydell Press, Woodbridge

ISBN 1 84383 144 9

The Boydell Press is an imprint of Boydell & Brewer Ltd
PO Box 9, Woodbridge, Suffolk IP12 3DF, UK
and of Boydell & Brewer Inc.
668 Mt Hope Avenue, Rochester, NY 14620, USA
website: www.boydellandbrewer.com

A CIP catalogue record for this book is available
from the British Library

Library of Congress Cataloging-in-Publication Data
Walsingham, Thomas, fl. 1360–1420.
  [Chronica maiora. English]
  The Chronica maiora of Thomas Walsingham, 1376–1422 / translated by
David Preest ; with annotations and an introduction by James G. Clark.
     p. cm.
  Summary: "First complete translation of detailed chronicle of medieval England,
one of Shakespeare's most important sources" – Provided by publisher.
  Includes bibliographical references and index.
  ISBN 1–84383–144–9 (hardback : alk. paper)
  1. Great Britain – History – Henry V, 1413–1422. 2. Great Britain – History –
Henry IV, 1399–1413. 3. Great Britain – History – Richard II, 1377–1399.
I. Preest, David. II. Clark, James G. III. Title.
  DA240.W35 2005
  942.03'8 – dc22   2004030861

This book is printed on acid-free paper

Printed in Great Britain by
Athenaeum Press Ltd, Gateshead, Tyne & Wear

Contents

Acknowledgements

I would like to thank Caroline Palmer for her invitation to become involved in this project and for her patient forbearance as it neared completion. I am also grateful to my colleagues at Bristol, Brendan Smith and Rachel Gibbons, for sharing their knowledge of the kings, courts and courtier-knights of fourteenth- and fifteenth-century England and France.

JAMES G. CLARK

I was lucky enough to obtain from the Oswestry Town Library a mint copy (pages uncut) of the two volumes of Thomas Walsingham's *Historia Anglicana* in the Rolls series, edited by Henry Thomas Riley and published in 1863 and 1864. His marginal summaries and generously detailed 108-page index made the task of translation much easier. It was also a pleasure to work from the edition of Walsingham's *The St Albans Chronicle* published by V. H. Galbraith in 1937, using the copy that belonged to the library of Thomas's own St Albans abbey. Of more modern works I have benefited greatly from being able to consult Christopher Given-Wilson's *Chronicles of the Revolution*, published in 1993, and volume 1 of *The St Albans Chronicle*, edited and translated by John Taylor, Wendy Childs and Leslie Watkiss and published in the Oxford Medieval Texts series in 2003. My aim has been to produce a translation which, while reproducing all Walsingham's content, stays readable throughout the long journey through his pages.

Andrew Rossabi kindly helped with the translation of difficult passages and John Siswick with the computer problems presented when integrating the text and notes. I would especially like to thank my wife Verity for her valuable IT support day-by-day and for reading through the entire translation, removing obscurities and suggesting many a happier turn of phrase.

DAVID PREEST

List of Abbreviations

AC	*Anonimalle Chronicle, 1333 to 1381 from a MS written at St Mary's Abbey, York and now in the collection of Lieut.-Col. Sir William Ingleby Bart.*, ed. V. H. Galbraith, Publications of the University of Manchester, Historical Series, no. 45 (Manchester, 1927)
CA	*Chronicon Angliae, ab anno domini 1328 usque ad 1388 auctore monacho sancti Albani*, ed. E. M. Thompson, Rolls Series, 64 (1874)
CCR	*Calendar of Close Rolls preserved in the Public Record Office, 1374–1422*, ed. W. H. Stevenson et al., 14 vols. (London, 1913–32)
CPR	*Calendar of Patent Rolls preserved in the Public Record Office, 1374–1422* ed. J. G. Black et al., 12 vols. (London, 1895–1911)
EETS	Early English Text Society
Emden, *BRUC*	A. B. Emden, *A Biographical Register of the University of Cambridge to AD 1500* (Oxford, 1963)
Emden, *BRUO*	A. B. Emden, *A Biographical Register of the University of Oxford to AD 1500* (3 vols, Oxford, 1957–59)
Froissart, *Chroniques*	*Chroniques de J. Froissart*, ed. S. Luce (14 vols, Paris 1869–)
FCBuchon	*Les Chroniques de Sire Jean Froissart*, ed. J. A. C. Buchon, 3 vols (Paris, 1835)
Gesta abbatum	*Gesta abbatum monasterii sancti Albani a Thomas Walsingham regnante Ricardo secundo eiusdem ecclesiae precentore compilata*, ed. H. T. Riley, 3 vols, Rolls Series, 28/4 (1867–69)
Gesta Henrici	*Gesta Henrici Quinti: The Deeds of Henry the Fifth*, ed. F. Taylor and J. S. Roskell, Oxford Medieval Texts (Oxford, 1975)
HVRS	*Historia Vitae et regni Ricardi secundi*, ed. G. B. Stow (Philadelphia, 1977)
Knighton	*Knighton's Chronicle, 1337–96*, ed. G. H. Martin, Oxford Medieval Texts (Oxford, 1995)
MRH	*Medieval Religious Houses in England and Wales*, ed. D. Knowles and R. N. Hadcock (London, 1971)
RP	*Rotuli parliamentorum ut et petitiones et placita in parliamento*, ed. J. Strachey (6 vols, London, 1767–77)
Saul, *Richard II*	N. Saul, *Richard II* (New Haven and London, 1997)
Scotichronicon	*Scotichronicon, by Walter Bower, in Latin and English*, ed. A. B. Scott and D. E. R. Watt 9 vols (Aberdeen, 1993–6)
John Streeche	F. Taylor, 'The Chronicle of John Streeche for the Reign of Henry V, 1413–1422', *Bulletin of the John Rylands Library*, xvi (1932), 137–87
Trokelowe	*Johannes de Trokelowe et Henricus de Blaneforde Chronica et Annales*, ed. H. T. Riley, Rolls Series, 28/3 (1866)
Usk	*Chronicon Adae de Usk, AD 1377–1421: Chronicle of Adam Usk, 1377–1421*, ed. C. Given-Wilson, Oxford Medieval Texts (Oxford, 1997)
WC	*Westminster Chronicle, 1381–94*, ed. L. C. Hector and B. F. Harvey, Oxford Medieval Texts (Oxford, 1982)
Wylie, *Henry IV*	J. H. Wylie, *History of England under Henry the Fourth* (4 vols, London, 1884–98)
Wylie and Waugh, *Henry V*	J. H. Wylie and W. T. Waugh, *The Reign of Henry the Fifth* (3 vols, London, 1914–29)

Introduction

The chronicle compiled by Thomas Walsingham, monk of the Benedictine abbey of St Albans, is one of the most valuable and vivid narrative histories to survive from later medieval England. No other author produced such a detailed account of the events of his own time over so long a period; Walsingham continued to compile his chronicle for forty-six years, from the closing months of the reign of Edward III until shortly after the sudden death of Edward's great-grandson, Henry V, in August 1422. In contrast to many of his contemporaries, Walsingham's chronicle was also a completely independent narrative, founded for the most part on first-hand reports from a host of high-profile informants. He used documents sparingly, but as precentor of his monastery he understood the power of written records and those examples he did choose to transcribe are among the most significant royal and papal *acta* of the period and in several cases they are preserved uniquely in his text. He did not borrow from other chroniclers although they undoubtedly borrowed from him. In fact Walsingham's chronicle contains a number of incidents and insights that are not recorded in any other contemporary source. It is largely to him that historians owe their knowledge of the course of key events such as the peasants' revolt, the appellant crisis and the conquest of Normandy and – perhaps more especially – their understanding of the character of the kings: the dissipation of the elderly Edward III, the brittle, unpredictable personality of Richard II and the transformation of Prince Henry of Monmouth into the mighty Henry V.

Walsingham was also one of the only English chroniclers in this period to record in detail events in continental Europe. The opening of the papal schism and the resumption of the Anglo-French conflict projected the European powers into a period of profound political instability. France descended into civil war. Portugal and the Spanish kingdoms suffered dynastic struggles. The Low Countries became a battleground as Burgundy, England and the counts of Flanders contended for control of their burgeoning cities. Meanwhile a fugitive Roman pope could find no permanent sanctuary in the Italian peninsula as papal authority fast evaporated. Writing at some distance from these events but with a watchful eye for detail, Walsingham presents a unique if partisan perspective on the European scene.

But there is another dimension to Walsingham's work beyond this blend of candid political commentary and reportage. By the standards of the fourteenth century, the *Chronica maiora* was also an accomplished work of Latin literature. To a far greater degree than any other annalist of his day, Walsingham aimed to write a history that engaged and entertained the reader with the high drama of its scenes and the high rhetoric of its speeches. His writing reflects a knowledge not only of scripture and the liturgy – as might be expected of any experienced monk – but also of the work of many ancient and medieval historians, of academic theology and even a smattering of canon law. In his use of imagery, vocabulary and the sheer vigour of some of his dramatic set pieces, Walsingham also shows himself to be a very knowledgeable student of the Classical poets and prose authors. In his chronicle we catch a glimpse of the cultural world of English monks in the later Middle Ages.

It was this learned, literary quality which recommended Walsingham's work to later writers and it should be remembered that in reading the *Chronica maiora* we discover the source of much Renaissance history, of the chronicles of Edward Hall, Raphael Holinshed and John Stow, and, of course, of the historical dramas of William Shakespeare.

St Albans Abbey and the Writing of Chronicles

Thomas Walsingham was one of a succession of celebrated chroniclers to have emerged from St Albans Abbey in the Middle Ages. St Albans was counted amongst the greatest monasteries in medieval England. It was set apart from the mainstream by its antiquity, its royal status, its size, and by its wealth, which was exceeded only by the greater abbeys of Glastonbury and Westminster.[1] But more significant than any of these distinctions was its reputation as a place of learning. From the time of its post-Conquest recovery under the rule of the Norman Paul of Caen (1077–93), St Albans was celebrated as 'a school that was master to other schools'.[2] In the early years of the twelfth century Nicholas Breakspear – later to become Pope Hadrian IV, the only English pontiff – received his education at the abbey and in the generations that followed many famous scholars fought, and sometimes failed, to gain admission.[3] At a time when a number of the greater Benedictine abbeys and priories in England were distinguished for their artistry in the copying and decorating of manuscript books, the scriptorium of St Albans won international renown for the quality of its work.[4] When the monastic writers of Clairvaux and St Victor sought the means to publish their work in England, it was to St Albans that they made their first recourse.[5] The reputation of the abbey, its scholars, and scholarly books remained intact for the next three centuries. In the lifetime of Thomas Walsingham, St Albans was still regarded as an exemplar of monastic education and formation and its contribution to the education of the laity – through its almonry and endowed grammar school – had also come to be recognised.[6] The country's most able scholars, many of them now university graduates, continued to seek admission to the convent, abandoning an academic career for a share in its learned and literary heritage.[7] The conventual library, which in the course of the fourteenth and fifteenth centuries may have expanded to hold as many as three or four thousand books, continued to attract eager readers, borrowers and bibliophiles from England and continental Europe.[8]

Over the course of four centuries St Albans nurtured original scholarship in a wide range of fields. In the twelfth century the monks were known for their interest in exegesis, hagiography and patristic theology.[9] In the early fourteenth century it was the scientific advances of Abbot Richard of Wallingford that attracted wider attention.[10] In the generation after the Black Death – Walsingham's generation – it was the talented team of academic theologians at the abbey who preached against the heresies of Wyclif that was prominent in public life.[11]

---

[1]   For St Albans and its place in English monastic history see V. H. Galbraith, *The Abbey of St Albans from 1300 to the Dissolution of the Monasteries*, Stanhope Essay (Oxford, 1911); L. F. R. Williams, *The History of the Abbey of St Alban* (London, 1917) and now J. G. Clark, *A Monastic Renaissance at St Albans: Thomas Walsingham and his Circle, c.1350–1440* (Oxford, 2004), pp. 1–41. See also M. D. Knowles, *The Monastic Order in England* (Cambridge, 1940), pp. 117–18, 123–5, 187–8; D. Knowles, *The Religious Orders in England* (3 vols, Cambridge, 1948–59), i. 292–8; ii. 39–48.

[2]   *Gesta abbatum*, ed. Riley, i. 58–9.

[3]   *Gesta abbatum*, ed. Riley, i. 196. Alexander Nequam was one notable scholar who failed to gain admission to the convent. See R. W. Hunt, *The Schools and the Cloister: The Life and Works of Alexander Nequam*, ed. M. T. Gibson (Oxford, 1984), pp. 1–5.

[4]   R. M. Thomson, *Manuscripts from St Albans Abbey 1066–1215* (2 vols, Woodbridge, 1982), i. 20–69. In cultural and intellectual terms, Thomson argues, it was during the abbacy of Geoffrey Gorron (1119–46) that the abbey made 'the great leap forward'.

[5]   Ibid., i. 41, 44, 66.

[6]   It was the claim of the monks of Walsingham's generation that whenever a devout, well-disciplined monk was encountered it was declared that he must be 'de usu sancti Albani': *Gesta abbatum*, ed. Riley, iii. 410; Clark, *Monastic Renaissance*, pp. 75–8.

[7]   Ibid., pp. 15–16, 44.

[8]   Ibid., pp. 79–123. See also R. W. Hunt, 'The Library of the Abbey of St Albans', in *Medieval Scribes, Manuscripts and Libraries: Essays Presented to N. R. Ker*, ed. A. G. Watson and M. B. Parkes (London, 1978), pp. 251–77.

[9]   Thomson, *Manuscripts from St Albans*, i. 20–41; Hunt, *Schools and Cloister*, pp. 1–5, 7.

[10]   *Gesta abbatum*, ed. Riley, ii. 182. See also J. D. North, *Richard of Wallingford*, 3 vols (Oxford, 1976).

[11]   Clark, *Monastic Renaissance*, pp. 239–53.

But there is no doubt that throughout the period the monks were best known for the writing of history. The English monasteries had been committed to the compilation of chronicles since the Anglo-Saxon period and the restoration of monastic life after the Conquest had given renewed stimulus to this work. The greater Benedictine abbeys and priories, the Canterbury convents (of Christ Church and St Augustine's), Bury St Edmunds, Durham, Glastonbury, Evesham, Westminster and Worcester all witnessed periods of chronicle writing between the twelfth and the fifteenth centuries but there was none that was either as continuous or as copious as that at St Albans. According to Thomas Walsingham, who did more than any other monk of his house to commemorate the chroniclers of earlier times, the tradition of historical writing at St Albans could be traced as far back as the mid-twelfth century when Adam Lyons the Cellarer had compiled a contemporary history and Abbot Ralph Gobion (1146–51) had composed a more ambitious history of Alexander of Macedon.[12] Their work was continued by a succession of contemporary chroniclers in the thirteenth century, Roger Wendover (d. 1236), John of Wallingford (d. 1258), William Rishanger (d. 1312) and, of course, Matthew Paris (d. 1259).[13] Walsingham also recovered the names of several monks who continued to compile chronicles in the early years of the fourteenth century, amongst them Simon Binham, Henry Blaneford, Richard Savage and John Trokelowe.[14] Probably the last named was no more than an amanuensis of another but the fragments of historical texts preserved in the manuscripts of this period do attest to the presence of a number of anonymous compilers, not only at St Albans but also at its dependent priories.[15]

Walsingham was not the only monk to continue this work in the centuries before the dissolution. During his lifetime there were at least three compilers of annals at St Albans whose names have not been recorded.[16] One of these may have been the abbot's chaplain and almoner, William Wintershill, who was remembered as a compiler of administrative records and who commissioned copies of chronicles by other authors.[17] The writing of history continued in the generation after Walsingham's death with the work of Abbot John Wheathampstead, who wrote on both contemporary and classical history, and of his own amanuensis, John Amersham.[18] Even at the end of the fifteenth century an anonymous monk continued to compile summary accounts of the most recent abbots to fill the last leaves of the *Liber benefactorum*.[19]

Thomas Walsingham and the other monks who lived and wrote at St Albans in the century after the Black Death were profoundly conscious of the tradition in which they worked. Walsingham himself chose to present his own histories – in the *Chronica maiora* and *Gesta abbatum* – as a continuation of his illustrious predecessor Matthew Paris, and his approach to the recording of contemporary events, his reading of the sources, and his refinement of his own prose

---

12 For Adam the Cellarer see *Amundesham*, ed. Riley, i. 435, ii. 313; *Gesta abbatum*, ed. Riley, iii. 390. Ralph Gobion's *Historia* survives in Cambridge, Gonville and Caius College, MS 154, fos 1r–156v and Cambridge, Corpus Christi College, MS 219, fos 1r–64r. See R. Sharpe, *A Handlist of the Latin Writers of Great Britain and Ireland to AD 1540* (Turnhout, 1997), p. 428. In this same period an anonymous monk composed a life of Christine, prioress of Markyate, which incorporated portraits of many contemporary political figures. See *The Life of Christina of Markyate*, ed. C. H. Talbot (2nd edn, Oxford, 1987), pp. 1–5, 8–10.
13 For the work of these writers see A. Gransden, *Historical Writing in England I. c. 550–c. 1307* (London, 1974), pp. 356–79, 485–6. See also V. H. Galbraith, *Roger Wendover and Matthew Paris*, David Murray Lecture (Glasgow, 1944); R. Vaughan, *Matthew Paris* (Cambridge, 1956).
14 BL, Cotton MS Claudius E IV, fo. 334r; *Amundesham*, ed. Riley, ii. 304–5. See also *St Albans Chronicle*, ed. Galbraith, pp. xxvii–xxxvi.
15 J. G. Clark 'Thomas Walsingham Re-considered: Books and Learning at Late Medieval St Albans', *Speculum*, 77/2 (2002), 854–82 at 844; Clark, *Monastic Renaissance*, pp. 155–7.
16 For the anonymous annalists who wrote alongside Walsingham see Clark, 'Thomas Walsingham Re-considered', 854–82.
17 For Wintershill and his books see Clark, 'Thomas Walsingham Reconsidered', 843–6; Clark, *Monastic Renaissance*, pp. 88, 157.
18 For Wheathampstead see A. Gransden, *Historical Writing in England II. c. 1307 to the Early Sixteenth Century* (London, 1982), pp. 371–86.
19 BL, Cotton MS Nero D VII, fos 35r–48r, 114r–117r, 155v–57v.

style reflected his deep engagement not only with the work of Brother Matthew but also with the whole literary culture which had flourished at St Albans for so long.

Thomas Walsingham: Life and Work

While Walsingham's chronicle is familiar to many historians as an authority for the reigns of Richard II, Henry IV and Henry V, the figure of Thomas Walsingham himself remains obscure. Walsingham revealed very little of himself in his own work. He did not write a prologue to the chronicle and in the whole course of the text he does not address the reader on more than a handful of occasions.[20] He never refers to himself by name. In fact in a number of the earliest surviving manuscripts of the chronicle there is no mention of Walsingham at all and it would appear (as discussed below) that he himself never settled on a title that might be attached to his work and it was left to the compositors (or scribes) of the early manuscripts to compose a colophon of their own.[21] Walsingham's reticence was in keeping with monastic tradition but not with many of his fourteenth-century contemporaries, including other monastic authors, who increasingly sought recognition for their work.[22]

Curiously, Walsingham is also almost invisible in the institutional records of St Albans Abbey. The period in which he was writing was one of the best documented in the monastery's history, but in the sixty years between 1360 and 1420 – the likely extent of his monastic career – there are barely half a dozen references to his presence in the community.[23] These scant references to one of St Albans' most significant authors have aroused the suspicion that the record of Walsingham and his work was deliberately suppressed after his death, either because of the provocative nature of his political commentary – which seems unlikely since the chronicle itself was repeatedly copied – or because the chronicler himself had fallen foul of the factions that fractured the community in the fifteenth century. By English standards, St Albans was a large monastery, numbering as many as seventy monks, novices and lay brothers during Walsingham's lifetime. These men were drawn from a variety of backgrounds, but the senior officers came from a clique of families of the lower gentry and burgess class, while the rump of the community came from lesser stock living on the abbey's outlying estates.[24] Walsingham himself was a member of this second constituency and he may have always struggled for recognition from the first.

One of the few certain dates in Walsingham's biography is his ordination to the priesthood on 21 September 1364 at the hands of the (then) bishop of London, Simon Sudbury, and from this

---

[20] See below, pp. 50, 330, 339.

[21] See, for example, the copies of parts of the *Chronica maiora* preserved in Dublin, Trinity College, MSS 510 and 511 (*s.* xv *med.*) and London, College of Arms, Arundel MS 7 (*s.* xv *in.*), one of the two principal manuscripts used for the text published in the Rolls Series as the *Historia Anglicana*.

[22] See, for example, the *Polychronicon* of Ranulf Higden, into the opening lines of which the Chester monk wove an acrostic identifying himself as the author. There were many other monastic chroniclers of the period who, in prefaces and prologues, willingly assumed the mantle of author and identified themselves with their work. See especially John of Glastonbury, Richard Cirencester of Westminster Abbey, and Thomas Elmham of St Augustine's Abbey, Canterbury: Gransden, *Historical Writing in England II.*, pp. 157, 206–10, 345–55, 399–400.

[23] The principal sources for the history of St Albans in the fourteenth and fifteenth centuries are the continuation of the *Gesta abbatum*, an anonymous biography of Abbot Thomas de la Mare (1349–96), an anonymous annal of the first decade of the first abbacy of John Wheathampstead (1420–41), and a complete account of the abbacy attributed to John Amersham. All of these narratives were printed in the Rolls Series, but they have not been edited or translated subsequently. See *Gesta abbatum*, ed. Riley, ii. 113–418, iii. 3–372 (*Gesta abbatum* continuation); iii. 375–535 (biography of Abbot de la Mare); *Annales monasterii sancti Albani a Iohanne Amundesham*, ed. H. T. Riley, 2 vols, Rolls Series, 28/5 (1870–1), i. 3–69 (anonymous annal), i. 73–408; ii. 3–247 (annals attributed to John Amersham). The account rolls of the abbey, which might afford much valuable biographical information about Walsingham and his generation, have not survived.

[24] For the size and social composition of the monastic community in Walsingham's lifetime see Clark, *Monastic Renaissance*, pp. 12, 14–17.

piece of evidence it possible to sketch the probable outline of his early life.[25] In late medieval England it was customary for every monk to be ordained and the ceremony of priesting had come to be regarded as the formal conclusion of the training period that began with the noviciate.[26] Canon law decreed that no man be ordained before the age of twenty-four although in the decades following the Black Death (1348–51) many English monasteries sought dispensations from this because of a severe shortage of priests. Taking into account both the necessary period of monastic training prior to ordination and the possibility of a premature priesting, it may be that Walsingham was no more than twenty-four years old in 1364 and that therefore he was born around 1340, making him, incidentally, almost an exact contemporary of both Geoffrey Chaucer and Jean Froissart.

Like the majority of monks of his generation, Walsingham probably entered the cloister in his late teens or early twenties. Given his toponym it is possible that he began his monastic career at one of St Albans' two dependent priories in Norfolk, progressing to the motherhouse before his ordination.[27] Before his ordination, and perhaps for some years afterwards, Walsingham was sent to study at Oxford, a formative experience that he recalled with real feeling in his chronicle when describing the spread of Wyclifism at the university in 1378.[28] The English Benedictines had maintained a *studium* at Oxford – Gloucester College – since the end of the thirteenth century, and under the statutes of their General Chapter reinforced by the papal canons *Summi magisti* a selection of the ablest monks from every abbey and priory was sent there to study for a higher degree in either theology or (less commonly) canon law.[29] The canons required a ratio of one monk in every twenty to be sent to the university, but St Albans always sent a higher proportion and perhaps as many as four or five of its monks were at Oxford at any point in the fourteenth and fifteenth centuries.[30] It remains unclear whether Walsingham did complete a degree or whether, like many of his monastic contemporaries, he returned to the cloister empty-handed after only a short period of study. His criticism of the academic community's apparent support for Wyclif might suggest that he cast himself in the mould of an orthodox *magister theologiae*. He does appear to have been remembered at Oxford as a distinguished *alumnus* of Gloucester College.[31]

Apart from his academic studies, nothing is known of Walsingham's early years at St Albans. His name does not appear in the records of the abbey until 1380 – perhaps as many as twenty years after he made his profession – when he is identified as the compiler of the *Liber benefactorum*, a register of all the benefactors and benefactions that had supported St Albans since

25 *Registrum Simonis de Sudbiria dioceses Londoniensis, AD 1362–1375*, ed. R. C. Fowler, 2 vols, Canterbury and York Society, 34, 38 (1927–38), ii. 28.
26 See B. F. Harvey, 'A Novice's Life at Westminster Abbey in the Century before the Dissolution', in *The Religious Orders in Pre-Reformation England*, ed. J. G. Clark (Woodbridge, 2002), pp. 51–73. For customs at St Albans see Clark, *Monastic Renaissance*, pp. 41–51.
27 St Albans maintained dependent houses at Binham and Wymondham and held many estates in eastern and northern Norfolk. See *MRH*, pp. 59, 81.
28 See below, p. 50.
29 For the presence of the Benedictines at Oxford in the later Middle Ages, and for Gloucester College in particular, see V. H. Galbraith, 'New Documents about Gloucester College' in *Snappe's Formulary and other records*, ed. H. E. Salter, Oxford Historical Society, lxxx (1924), pp. 338–86; *Documents illustrating the activities of the General and Provincial Chapters of the English Black Monks, 1215–1540*, ed. W. A. Pantin (3 vols, Camden 3rd ser. xlv, xlvii, liv, 1931–37), i. 75; ii. 55–8; R. B. Dobson, 'The Religious Orders, c.1270–1540', in *The History of the University of Oxford, II. Late Medieval Oxford*, ed. J. I. Catto and T. A. R. Evans (Oxford, 1992), pp. 539–79. For the student monks of the greater abbeys and priories see also B. F. Harvey, 'The Monks of Westminster and the University of Oxford', in *The Reign of Richard II: Essays in Honours of May McKisack*, ed. F. R. H. Du Boulay and C. M. Barron (London, 1971), pp. 108–30; J. Greatrex, 'Monk Students from Norwich Cathedral Priory at Oxford and Cambridge, c.1300–1530', *EHR*, cii (1991), 555–83; *id.*, 'English Cathedral Priories and the Pursuit of Learning in the Late Middle Ages', *Journal of Ecclesiastical History*, xlv (1994), 396–411.
30 Clark, *Monastic Renaissance*, pp. 12, 14–17.
31 *Survey of the Antiquities of the city of Oxford composed in 1661–66 by Anthony Wood, II. Churches and Religious Houses*, ed. A. Clark, Oxford Historical Society, xvii (1890), p. 259.

6   *Introduction*

its first foundation.[32] Here Walsingham is also named as precentor, one of the principal officers of the monastery responsible for the direction of the monks in the choir – including their musical performance – and the supervision of the abbey chancery, where charters and other documents were composed, copied and recorded under the seal of the convent, and the custody of the seal itself. In the greater monasteries – such as St Albans – the precentor was also responsible for the work of the scriptorium (writing room) and the supervision of the scribes, illuminators and binders engaged there in the production of manuscript books.

There is no doubt that Walsingham assumed this role: an undated passage in the anonymous life of Abbot Thomas de la Mare (1349–96), perhaps the most significant contemporary reference to Walsingham, describes how he worked alongside Abbot Thomas in the creation – the writer uses the phrase 'a fundamentis', literally, 'from scratch' – of a new scriptorium where, with fellow compiler and scribes (*suos conscripti*), he supervised the production of many manuscripts.[33] It was once believed that because the most significant products of the St Albans scriptorium were manuscripts containing chronicles that the office of precentor must have carried with it a particular responsibility for the writing of chronicles and that Walsingham was the abbey's 'official' (and only) historian in the same way that a single monk at the French Benedictine abbey of St Denis always held the office of 'historiographer royal'.[34] But there is no evidence to support this. In his capacity as precentor Walsingham may have been responsible for the compilation of some important collections of abbatial and conventual documents, including the *Liber benefactorum*, but he did not hold a monopoly on historical writing and as already noted there were a number of other monks of his generation who compiled chronicles and other historical texts of their own.

Walsingham's service as precentor shaped his outlook as a writer, giving him a sensitivity not towards the historical record *per se* but rather towards the raw materials on which it depends, the charters, letters and other documents which come into the chronicler's hands, and the language, style and often strikingly different context in which they were compiled. His eye for the detail of a document is evident throughout his chronicle. He draws attention to the demands of the St Albans rebels regarding the abbey's charters and describes in detail the damage done to the conventual archive.[35] Whenever he gives a digest of a document rather than a full transcription, he is careful to preserve its key diplomatic features, and when a document is deficient in some way – such as the parliament roll of which he appears to have had only a partial transcript – he tells the reader so.[36] The importance of his own abbey's archive is a constant preoccupation and it is in the proprietorial tone of the exemplary former office-holder that he reports the theft of the precentor's roll in 1414.[37] His love of the scriptorium, of the mechanics of book and document production, never left him. In a passage towards the end of the chronicle (1417) he describes vividly the cache of Lollard tracts discovered near St Albans, noting features of their script and decoration and number of blasphemous annotations that filled their margins.[38]

Whether Walsingham was appointed precentor in 1380, or whether he had already held the office for several years, remains unclear and it may be only coincidental that he began to compile his chronicle in 1376. But there is no doubt that he continued to hold the office for another fourteen years until he was appointed prior of the monastery's dependency at Wymondham in 1394.[39] It is difficult not to see this appointment as a demotion for Walsingham: he was trans-

---

[32] The St Albans *Liber benefactorum* is now BL, Cotton MS Nero D VII. The colophon naming Walsingham as the first compiler of the book is at fo. 82r.

[33] *Gesta abbatum*, ed. Riley, iii. 393.

[34] This was the view of Sir Thomas Duffus Hardy in his *Descriptive Catalogue of Materials Relating to the History of Great Britain and Ireland to the end of the Reign of Henry VII*, 3 vols, Rolls Series, 26 (1862–71), p. xxxvi. See also C. Jenkins, *The Monastic Chronicler and the School of St Albans. A Lecture* (London, 1923), pp. 29–31; Galbraith, *Roger Wendover and Matthew Paris*, pp. 9–10.

[35] See below, pp. 134–7.

[36] See below, p. 330.

[37] See below, pp. 395–6.

[38] See below, pp. 426.

[39] *Gesta abbatum*, ed. Riley, iii. 425, 436.

ferred from a position of influence at the heart of the mother house to one of its satellites, a priory of no more than a dozen monks.[40] The last years of Abbot Thomas de la Mare appear to have been troubled by infighting at St Albans and Walsingham was one of several senior monks to be sent away, perhaps because they had pressured the aged and increasingly incapacitated abbot to stand aside.[41]

According to the anonymous continuator of the *Gesta abbatum*, Walsingham was unhappy at Wymondham and one of the first acts of de la Mare's successor, John Moot, after his election in 1396, was to release the former precentor 'from his worldly cares' and recall him to St Albans.[42] It has been suggested that his two years at Wymondham represented a fundamental turning point in Walsingham's life that also provides the key to interpreting his work as a chronicler.[43] It is true that it brought an end to his career as precentor and removed him from his position at the centre of book – and document – production at St Albans, but it does not appear to have had a significant effect on his approach to historical writing. There are some stylistic differences between the earliest and latest passages of the chronicle – notably in the number of references to classical literature – but its scope and structure remain remarkably consistent throughout.

Already a man of sixty on his return from Wymondham, Walsingham did not hold office again. He remained active at St Albans for another twenty-five years or more and appears to have been regarded as a figure of some authority and seniority; at the election of John Wheathampstead in 1420 it was Walsingham who led the monks into the chapter house to conduct the ballot.[44] This was his final appearance in the abbey records, but he lived on for another two years at least to record the death of Henry V in August 1422. It is possible that he was still living – in his mid or late eighties – at the end of the decade.[45]

The *Chronica maiora* was the product of a monastic career which spanned more than sixty years, as much as a third of which Walsingham passed as the presiding officer of the monastery's chancery and scriptorium. But it was not the only outcome of his long years at St Albans. Walsingham was a prolific writer and his chronicle can only be properly understood when set alongside the many other works that he is known to have composed or compiled. He was not only a committed chronicler of contemporary events but also of the changing fortunes of his own monastic community and alongside the *Chronica maiora* he compiled a continuation of Matthew Paris's great *Gesta abbatum*. He was not the first to continue Matthew's work but his narrative was more comprehensive and more colourful than those of his predecessors and it provided a proper appreciation of the recovery of the abbey after the Black Death under the direction of Abbot Thomas de la Mare.[46] He also composed dozens of brief biographies of past abbots and priors, episcopal, royal and seigniorial benefactors for the *Liber benefactorum*, reflecting extensive

---

40 For Wymondham Priory see *MRH*, p. 81; *VCH Norfolk*, ed. H. A. Doubleday, W. Rye and W. Page (6 vols, London, 1909–14), ii. 336–43.

41 *Gesta abbatum*, ed. Riley, iii. 411–12, 415–21, 436. See also Clark, *Monastic Renaissance*, pp. 21, 25–6.

42 Ibid., iii. 436.

43 For this suggestion see *St Albans Chronicle*, ed. Galbraith, pp. xl–xli. For its reiteration see Gransden, *Historical Writing in England II.*, pp. 118–56; J. Taylor, *English Historical Literature in the Fourteenth Century* (Oxford, 1987), pp. 63–6. G. B. Stow challenged Galbraith's dating of the earliest manuscripts but otherwise confirmed his outline of Walsingham's career: 'Bodleian Library, MS Bodley 316 and the Dating of Thomas Walsingham's Literary Career', *Manuscripta* 25 (1981), 67–76.

44 Cambridge, Clare College, unclassified binding fragment, fol. 1rb.

45 Many of Walsingham's monastic contemporaries lived to an advanced age: Abbot Thomas de la Mare died in 1396 at the age of 87. See *Gesta abbatum*, ed. Riley, iii. 422; Clark, *Monastic Renaissance*, p. 15.

46 Walsingham's continuation of the *Gesta abbatum* is preserved in BL, Cotton MS Claudius E IV, fos 98r–321r and was printed in *Gesta abbatum*, ed. Riley, ii. 371–466, iii. 3–372. For other fourteenth-century continuations see Clark, 'Thomas Walsingham Reconsidered', 844–6; Clark, *A Monastic Renaissance*, pp. 155, 169.

47 The *Liber benefactorum* is now BL, Cotton MS Nero D VII. The manuscript has suffered in post medieval rebindings and the folios are now badly misplaced. The passages to which Walsingham contributed are at fos 1r–24v, 49r–72v, 75v–77v, 81v–108r. An abridged copy of the text was made in the early fifteenth century, now Cambridge, Corpus Christi College, MS 7, pp. 202–22 (fos 102r–111v).

research into the earliest cartularies and chronicles in the abbey's collection.[47] He returned to these early sources to compile a series of short narratives recalling the re-foundation of St Albans after the Norman Conquest and its rise to prominence in the twelfth century.[48] Walsingham may also have been the author of the original account of the life and martyrdom of Saints Alban and Amphibel, the *Tractatus de nobilitate, vita et martirio sanctorum Albani et Amphibali* that appears in the same manuscript as his *Gesta abbatum* continuation. The colophon claims that the text is a translation from a French original but no such source is known to survive and the Latin style of text is strikingly similar to Walsingham's own *Chronica maiora*.[49] He may also have been the compiler of the collection of miracle stories celebrating the shrine of St Alban that also appears in this manuscript.[50]

These works of domestic history and hagiography were the staple diet of English monks in the Middle Ages and as a monk of St Albans, a monastery with a centuries-old tradition of historical writing and an unrivalled archive, it was almost inevitable that Walsingham – like many of his colleagues – would continue this work. What set him part from his contemporaries was that he also read, researched and wrote on a wide range of subjects rarely seen in contemporary cloisters. It was presumably in his capacity as precentor that he composed a treatise on musical notation, the *Regulae de figuris compositis et non compositis et de cantu perfecto et imperfecto et de modis significandi* which survives in one fifteenth-century manuscript unconnected with St Albans.[51] It is perhaps the only work on the subject to have been written by an English monk in the post-Conquest period and it provides one of the earliest English witnesses to the new forms of polyphonic notation first developed in fourteenth-century France.[52] It is possible that Walsingham was also the author of a philosophical treatise known only from its incipit as 'Natura est duplex' that is preserved in two fifteenth-century manuscripts.[53] A university-educated monk in a community of graduates, there is no doubt that Walsingham did develop an interest in academic topics, and among the unattributed essays that were sketched into the manuscript BL, Royal MS 13 E IX, compiled under his supervision, was a study of the controversial Oxford theologian, Richard Fitzralph.[54]

---

[48] Arranged under the heading, *De fundatione et meritis monasterii sancti Albani* these essays appear at the end of Walsingham's continuation of the *Gesta abbatum*: BL, Cotton MS, Claudius E IV, fos 331va–332v. See also *Amundesham*, ed. Riley, ii. 296–306.

[49] Two copies of this text survive in St Albans manuscripts, the earliest of which is the Claudius manuscript which also contains Walsingham's *Gesta abbatum* continuation and was probably compiled under his supervision: BL, Cotton MS Claudius E IV, fos 334va–336vb. The second copy, Oxford, Bodl., Bodley MS 585, fos 1r–9v, may have been made for Abbot John Wheathampstead. The text was printed from the Claudius manuscript in J. E. van der Westhuizen, *The Life of Saint Alban and Saint Amphibel* (Leiden, 1974), pp. 277–85. For its authorship see D. R. Howlett, 'A St Albans Historical Miscellany of the Fifteenth Century', *Transactions of the Cambridge Bibliographical Society*, vi (1974), 195–200; W. McLeod, 'Alban and Amphibel: Some Extant Lives and a Lost Life', *Speculum*, 42 (1980), 407–30; J. G. Clark, 'The St Albans Monks and the Cult of St Alban: The Late Medieval Texts' in *Alban and St Albans: Roman and Medieval Architecture, Art and Archaeology*, ed. M. Henig and P. Lindley, The British Archaeological Association Conference Transactions, xxiv (Leeds, 2001), pp. 218–30 at 225–26.

[50] BL, Cotton MS Claudius E IV, fos 59ra–70vb. See also Clark, 'The St Albans Monks and the Cult of St Alban', pp. 218–30 at 222.

[51] BL, Lansdowne, MS 763, fos 98v–105r (Waltham Abbey); a post-medieval copy is preserved in BL, Additional MS 4912. See also *Johannes de Hothby. Opera omnia de musica mensurabili*, ed. G. Reaney, Corpus scriptorum de musica, 31 (Neuhausen, 1983), pp. 74–98. The appearance of the text in a manuscript without a St Albans association would suggest that it circulated beyond Benedictine circles.

[52] For the background to these developments see *The New Oxford History of Music III. The Ars noua and the Renaissance*, ed. A. Hughes and G. Abraham (Oxford, 1960), pp. 6–7. See also F. L. Harrison, *Music in Medieval Britain* (London, 1958), pp. 42–3; R. Bowers, 'The Performing Ensemble for English Church Polyphony', in *Studies in the Performance of Late Medieval Music*, ed. S. Boorman (Cambridge, 1983), pp. 161–92 at 171–8.

[53] London, Lambeth Palace Library, MS 456, fos 136r–141r; Oxford, Bodl., Bodley MS 676, fos 149v–162r. The attribution to Walsingham was made by the early seventeenth-century antiquarian, Gerard Langbaine. See also Sharpe, *Latin writers*, p. 690.

[54] Clark, 'Thomas Walsingham Reconsidered', 850.

But the most remarkable – and in many ways, un-monastic – of Walsingham's other writings were those on classical literature. In the course of his career, Walsingham produced no fewer than four major studies – their structure is so idiosyncratic it is difficult to call them commentaries – of classical authors and texts. Possibly the earliest of these was the *Historia Alexandri magni principis*, in which he recounted the story of Alexander of Macedon and his conquests by weaving together the narratives of both classical and early medieval authors, explaining points of etymology, literary devices and mythological references wherever necessary.[55] He adopted the same approach for in his *Dites ditatus*, a study of the Trojan War based on the *Ephemeris belli Troiani* of Dictys Cretensis but which also drew on dozens of other classical Roman authors, many of them rarely seen in fourteenth- and fifteenth- century England.[56] Walsingham was also the author of the *Archana deorum*, a more conventional commentary upon the fifteen books of the *Metamorphoses* for which again he drew together a diversity of authorities from the earliest commentators of Christian antiquity (Fulgentius, Lactantius) to the work of contemporary scholars such as John Ridevall and Pierre Bersuire.[57] He also compiled a collection of *accessus* (critical introductions) and short commentaries for readers of thirty of the greatest classical poets, including Lucan, Ovid, Seneca, Terence and Virgil. Some of these were culled from earlier sources, but several, such as his précis of Lucan's *Civil War* and his study of Seneca's *Tragedies*, may have been his original compositions.[58] As a Classical scholar, Walsingham had no obvious counterpart in fourteenth-century England; indeed his work recalled an earlier age – of William of Malmesbury, or even earlier, of Bede – when Latin literature formed the foundation of the monastic curriculum. The range of his reading testifies to the riches that were still to be found in the library of St Albans Abbey even after 1350, although the rarity of some of his sources would suggest that he also made contact with scholars beyond the convent walls.[59]

Walsingham's immersion in classical culture had a considerable impact on his writing of contemporary history. Throughout his chronicle, but especially in the later sections of the text, he cultivates a classical style of narration in which even the most commonplace events – the sailing of another expedition to France, another dispute in parliament over the subsidy – are reported as moments of great passion and high drama. The four ships that founder off the coast of [King's] Lynn in 1406 in Walsingham's hands fall victim to an Ovidian sea stirred up by Scylla and Charybdis.[60] The routine arguments between Archbishop Arundel and the commons over the royal subsidy are similarly redrawn with Arundel cast into the role of Argus.[61] It was perhaps also Walsingham's reading of the classics which sharpened his wit and encouraged him to explore the comic potential of contemporary events, whether in the sharp satire of his treatment of Richard and his courtiers, or the bawdy burlesque of the Welsh women and their outrages in the Glyn Dŵr war.[62] In the later sections of the chronicle, Walsingham's use of language and imagery becomes increasingly inspired by, if not directly borrowed from, the Latin classics, to the extent that some

---

55 The text is preserved uniquely in Oxford, Bodl., Douce MS 299.

56 The text is preserved uniquely in Oxford, Bodl., Rawlinson B 214, fos 1r–106r.

57 The *Archana deorum* is preserved in two manuscripts of the first half of the fifteenth century, in both of which the text is differently arranged and bears a different colophon: BL, Lansdowne, MS 728, fos 16r–158v and Oxford, St John's College, MS 124, fos 12r–124r. The text was printed from the St John's College manuscript in *Thomas Walsingham De Archana deorum*, ed. R. A. Van Kluyve (Durham, NC, 1968). For an analysis of the text see Clark, *Monastic Renaissance*, pp. 163–208.

58 BL, Harley MS 2693, fos 177v–202v. The colophon naming Walsingham appears at the beginning of the collection at fo. 177v, but there are additional colophons for the epitomes of Lucan and Seneca. The epitome of Lucan also appears in an anthology compiled for Abbot Wheathampstead, Oxford, Bodl., Rawlinson MS D 358, fos 102r–104v.

59 For Walsingham's use of sources from the conventual library, and from other collections, see Clark, *Monastic Renaissance*, pp. 176–86.

60 See below, pp. 347–8.

61 See below, p. 335.

62 See below, p. 322 (1402).

set pieces – such as the English victory at Agincourt in 1415 – read as if they have been entirely relocated in a classical landscape.[63]

The Making of the Chronica maiora, 1376–1422

Walsingham's chronicle was his life's work and the scope, structure and style of the text evolved over the course of his long career. But the precise nature of this process of evolution is not readily recovered from the surviving manuscripts. There is no autograph copy of the complete chronicle, although there are two manuscripts of portions of the text (down to 1392) which may have been copied directly under Walsingham's supervision and which may contain his own directions to the compositor.[64] The most complete manuscripts, from which the printed editions have been derived, were made in the mid fifteenth century, and with no obvious connection to St Albans or one of its satellites, they stand at some distance from any lost original.[65] Walsingham's own intentions for the text, his method of working and the extent of his revisions, must therefore be teased out from beneath the layers of improvements and interventions made by subsequent generations of compositors, readers and scribes.

Structure

Walsingham probably first planned his chronicle as a continuation of the *Chronica maiora* of his St Albans predecessor Matthew Paris, compiled in the middle years of the thirteenth century.[66] This is how the text was presented in the two surviving manuscripts connected with Walsingham, BL, Royal 13 E IX and BL, Royal 14 C VII: the Royal manuscript was in fact first compiled by Matthew and Walsingham simply added a quire of his own narrative at the end. Later compilers working in contexts where Matthew Paris was less well known preferred to treat the chronicle as a continuation of Ranulf Higden's contemporary *Polychronicon* but at St Albans it seems the *Chronica maiora* was always pre-eminent.[67] It is possible that Walsingham was inspired to continue Paris's chronicle in response to the political tensions that attended the accession of Richard II in 1377, in the same way that Matthew himself had written against the background of the baronial wars. But he was also aware that other writers had already continued the *Chronica maiora* to the beginning of the fourteenth century and he was eager to extend their work into his own day. He was sensitive towards the traditions of his own house and in compiling his own *Chronica maiora*, his aim was as much to continue the commemoration of St Albans and its monastic community as it was to develop a critical commentary on current events. Indeed for his own monastic colleagues, Walsingham probably intended his contemporary history to be read alongside his continuation of Matthew Paris's *Gesta abbatum*, the two texts serving as complementary narratives of the struggles of monastic religion in the secular world.

The original portion of Walsingham's chronicle, that is the portion written for the most part in his own words, begins in 1376, although he – or possibly a colleague or co-compiler of one of the early manuscripts – used extracts from other histories to connect his own narrative with those, including the continuators of Matthew Paris, covering the period from 1272.[68] Although

---

[63] See below, pp. 410–11.

[64] BL, Royal MS 13 E IX and BL, Royal MS 14 C VII. For the evidence for Walsingham's supervision of these compilations see Clark, *Monastic Renaissance*, pp. 105–8.

[65] The manuscripts used for the first printed text published in 1574 and for the Roll Series edition in 1863 were respectively Cambridge, Corpus Christi College, MS 195 and Cambridge, Corpus Christi College MS 7 together with London, College of Arms, Arundel MS 7. For these editions see below, p. 21.

[66] For Matthew Paris's *Chronica maiora* see *Chronica maiora*, ed. H. R. Luard, 7 vols, Rolls Series, 57 (1872–84). See also Vaughan, *Matthew Paris*, pp. 49–77, 110–58.

[67] For manuscripts in which Walsingham's chronicle appears as a *Polychronicon* continuation see, for example, Oxford, Bodl., Bodley MS 462 and Oxford, Bodl., Rawlinson MS B 152. For the contribution of his *Chronica maiora* to the descent of the *Polychronicon* text see J. Taylor, 'The Development of the *Polychronicon* continuations', *EHR*, lxxvi (1961), 20–36.

[68] The evidence of this retrospective connection of Walsingham's chronicle and the earlier continuations of

the most complete manuscripts of the chronicle compiled after Walsingham's death give the impression of a seamless narrative between 1376 and 1422, there is no doubt that the text passed through several distinct phases of compilation at his own hands. The first dozen years of the chronicle (1376–88) were composed as a discrete narrative during the years that it described and in its earliest form gave fuller treatment to the key events of the first two years, the Good Parliament and following it the turbulent relations between John of Gaunt, the commons and the city of London. During these years it appears that Walsingham recorded events as they occurred and even in the later, revised text translated below the chronicle retains something of its early spontaneous character. His reporting of foreign affairs, such as the revolt of the Ghentois (1378–82) and the troubles of Urban VI (1378–88), is often confused and sometimes repetitious as he struggles to assimilate the snippets of news that have found their way to St Albans.[69] This first recension of the chronicle was notable not only for the level of detail in the narrative – which Walsingham never reproduced in the later portions of the chronicle – but also for its outspoken criticism of Gaunt whose ambition and appetite for power Walsingham presented as the principal cause of the political instability.[70] Whether by design, or simply because of the permeable nature of the St Albans scriptorium, this 'scandalous' (as it has been called by some historians) recension of the chronicle began to circulate almost as soon as it was compiled, reaching other monasteries – Norwich and possibly Westminster – if not much further afield.[71] By the end of the 1380s the suspicions surrounding Gaunt had been eclipsed by new anxieties about the behaviour of the king himself. In the aftermath of the appellant crisis, Gaunt emerged as something of an elder statesman, a guarantor of stability, guarding the realm from the worst excesses of the crown. Walsingham responded to the change in the political climate with the wholesale revision of the 'scandalous' chronicle, substituting the more moderate and nuanced narrative that appears in the translation below. It is possible that he came under pressure from his abbot who was now anxious to ally himself with the Lancastrian dynasty. Generally the chronicles composed at the abbey do not appear to have been regarded as the official voice of the monastery, but at the end of the 1390s Abbot John Moot had become closely (and perhaps covertly) associated with the critics of Richard II and it may be that he turned to Walsingham's text as a timely source of propaganda.[72] Walsingham did not entirely eschew political commentary but never again did he express such bitter resentment towards any political figure, reserving his most splenetic outbursts instead for universal enemies, the French, the mendicant friars and John Wyclif.[73]

The 'scandalous' recension of the chronicle was not the only portion of Walsingham's chronicle that appears to have been compiled as a discrete narrative. He also treated his account of the

---

Paris is preserved in four of the earliest manuscripts, not only BL, Royal MS 14 C VII and BL, Royal MS 13 E IX but also BL, Cotton MS Faustina B IX and Oxford, Bodl., Bodley MS 462. For the compilation of these connecting passages see *St Albans Chronicle*, ed. Galbraith, pp. li–liii.

69   See below, pp. 64, 73–7, 81–3, 93, 110–11, 116, 180–1, 187–94.

70   For Walsingham's systematic assault on Gaunt see *CA*, pp. 73–5, 92, 103–7, 111–18, 120, 127–30. For an analysis of the text see also *St Albans Chronicle*, ed. Galbraith, pp. xii, xvi, l–li; Gransden, *Historical Writing*, pp. 129, 138–9.

71   Given the sensitive nature of the text it is surprising that several copies still survive. BL, Harley MS 3634, originally one part of a codex that also contained Oxford, Bodl., Bodley MS 316, is connected with Norwich Cathedral Priory since it bears the arms of the house on an opening leaf. BL, Cotton MS Otho C II, may have been at Westminster Abbey since Walsingham's chronicle is bound together with a copy of Matthew of Westminster's *Flores historiarum*. V. H. Galbraith drew attention to the signs of alteration in the text of BL, Royal MS 13 E IX, and conjectured whether political expediency had been the motive: *St Albans Chronicle*, ed. Galbraith, p. li and n.

72   When Thomas, duke of Gloucester was interrogated at Calais in November 1397 it was claimed that he had confessed to a conspiracy against King Richard in which the abbot of St Albans, amongst others, had been complicit. Whether the conspiracy was of recent origin or whether it had been formed at the time of the appellant crisis in 1387 was never clearly established, but it is worth noting that neither Abbot Moot, nor his predecessor, Abbot de la Mare, had been particular Ricardian loyalists and they, and their convent as a whole, were closely connected to Gloucester and the other appellants through ties of patronage. See Saul, *Richard II*, pp. 371–2.

peasants' revolt of June 1381 as a self-contained text and reproduced a portion of it verbatim in his continuation of the *Gesta abbatum*.[74] This was one of the most carefully structured sections of the whole chronicle. Walsingham offers his readers a complete 'history' of the revolt, framing his account with his own reflections on its origins and its wider significance for the ecclesiastical and seigniorial authorities. Rather than the general report of the whole episode presented by other contemporary commentators, he provides parallel narratives of the revolt in the city of London and in the provinces, in Cambridgeshire, Kent, Norfolk, Suffolk and, of course, at St Albans itself.[75] If not writing at the actual time of revolt, Walsingham surely began work on this narrative shortly afterwards since he was able to gather a greater body of documentary evidence than in many other sections of his chronicle: not only copies of the charters and letters issued by the crown and the abbot of St Albans but also the vernacular broadsides of the peasant leaders themselves.[76]

The later sections of the chronicle, covering the final decade of Richard II and his deposition, and the reigns of Henry IV and Henry V, have a uniform character that would suggest that the text was carefully edited, perhaps at the close of each reign. Here there is no obvious repetition and Walsingham appears to be writing with the benefit of hindsight when he reports the uprisings against Henry IV and the campaigns and conquests of Henry V.[77] His accounts of the political situation in France and of the resolution of the papal schism also suggest foreknowledge of the consequences of each episode: in the case of the Council of Constance he worked directly from the official *acta*.[78] Whether Walsingham alone was responsible for this work, or whether a subsequent compiler should be credited as editor remains open to question. How long he remained active at St Albans after 1422 may never be known. The chronicle ends abruptly at the summoning of Henry VI's first parliament in 1422.[79] Perhaps this was Walsingham's chosen conclusion to his work, but even by his standards it is somewhat understated. We might not expect a lengthy *envoi* from a writer who preferred to conceal himself, but it is surprising that he did not leave his readers with one of the stern homilies he had used so often before. There must be a strong possibility that Walsingham died with the chronicle unfinished and that it was one or more of the compilers and copyists who came after him who brought it to a close. It is worth noting that another late work of Walsingham's, his history of Normandy, the *Ypodigma Neustriae*, also appears to have been hurriedly finished by another hand; from its prologue, which Walsingham addressed to Henry V, the *Ypodigma* purports to be a polemical account of the duchy and its relationship with the kingdom of England, but this aim is soon forgotten and the text becomes just another general history of the post-Conquest period.[80]

The translation of the chronicle that appears below reproduces the text found in the most reliable of the early manuscripts compiled during Walsingham's lifetime or within a generation of his death.[81] This is generally regarded as the most complete version of the text, as revised by Walsingham and (very probably) the first generation of copyists and compilers who came after him. It has been suggested that Walsingham also wrote a shorter version of the text, recalling his

---

[73] See below, pp. 321–3, 330–1, 341, 348, 372, 397, 399.

[74] For the narrative of the peasants' revolt in the *Chronica maiora* see below, pp. 00–00. For the parallel narrative in the *Gesta abbatum* see *Gesta abbatum*, ed. Riley, iii. 285–372.

[75] See below, pp. 140–5, 150–1.

[76] See below, pp. 133–6, 138, 140–1, 147–8, 162–3.

[77] See below, pp. 321–2, 326–9, 336–8, 358–9, 405–12, 422–8, 430–3.

[78] See below, pp. 344–8, 350–5, 361–72, 375, 381–2, 419–22, 429–30, 433–4.

[79] See below, p. 447.

[80] The *Ypodigma Neustriae* survives in a single, somewhat meagre manuscript copy made in the middle years of the fifteenth century, now Cambridge, Corpus Christi College, MS 240. The text was printed in the Rolls Series, *Ypodigma Neustriae*, ed. H. T. Riley, Rolls Series, 28/7 (1876). See also Clark, *Monastic Renaissance*, pp. 168, 265–6.

[81] Specifically, BL, Royal MS 13 E IX, Cambridge, Corpus Christi College, MS 7, London, College of Arms, Arundel MS 7, and Oxford, Bodl., Bodley MS 462. Both the Royal and the Cambridge manuscripts were compiled and copied at St Albans; Royal 13 E IX may have been produced during Walsingham's precentorship, Corpus 7 was in the possession of William Wintershill, Walsingham's contemporary and also apparently a compiler of chronicles. For these manuscripts see also Clark, *Monastic Renaissance*, pp. 105–10.

predecessor Matthew Paris who precised his own *Chronica maiora* as a *Historia minor* or *Historia Anglorum*.[82] A number of the manuscripts do contain passages that appear to have been abridged from the most complete version of the text and on this evidence it has been conjectured that there was once an entirely separate *Chronica minora* circulating alongside Walsingham's *Chronica maiora* but that no copy of the text has survived. But it is dangerous to develop an argument on the basis of manuscripts whose very existence is only speculative. There is abundant evidence that Walsingham's chronicle was repeatedly copied and extracted, both during his lifetime and immediately after his death, under the direction of a number of different compilers and it is surely possible that the abridgement of the text can be explained simply in terms of their successive interventions.

Scope

Walsingham was not the first to continue Matthew Paris's *Chronica maiora* and in the interests of creating a single, seamless narrative he adopted the same format as his predecessors. He made no attempt to divide his text into books or chapters but as in any of the earliest monastic annals he arranged his material according to the regnal year. His only concession to his readers was to provide running heads for the reigns of Richard and the Henries although these were not always reproduced in the later manuscript copies.[83] Like his predecessors, the routine events of each year – the meetings of parliament, the notable obituaries, the king's keeping of Christmas – provided a framework for the rest of the narrative. For much of the chronicle, Walsingham also closed the account of the year with a summary of events, frequently including a summary weather report. Within this framework, Walsingham addressed a very wide range of subjects. The outlook of many other contemporary chroniclers – monastic and secular – was limited by their own pre-occupations. The anonymous monk of Westminster who compiled a chronicle of the years 1381–88 described the events that directly affected his abbey – such as the sudden death of Sir William Ufford in St Stephen's chapel and the proceedings of the Merciless Parliament (1388) – in disproportionate detail, but was indifferent to, or uninformed about, matters beyond the capital.[84] In the same way, although Adam Usk offered a number of important insights into high politics that were beyond the reach of cloister-bound commentators, his concentration on his own career progression through continental Europe meant many significant events received only the most cursory notice.[85] Certainly Walsingham was preoccupied with the affairs of his own abbey. He was prepared to juxtapose a report of national importance with stories of the miraculous intercession of his patron saint at a nearby church, or the visitation to the monastic community by representatives of the Benedictine General Chapter.[86] Like many monastic commentators there were times when he viewed matters of national and international importance as if through an inverted telescope, seeing only the enormous significance of his own house. His account of the peasants' revolt is one of the most accurate and comprehensive of all contemporary accounts, but it is also badly imbalanced with the anarchy in the city of London attracting barely half the number of pages devoted to the tenants and townsmen of St Albans.[87] But this tendency was tempered by a genuine fascination for the world beyond his convent walls. Witnessing profound upheavals over a period of forty years, Walsingham became deeply engaged in the debates and dramas of national political life. His discussions of the downfall and deposition of Richard II and the rise of the Lancastrian regime have none of the customary detachment of a monastic chroni-

---

[82] The possibility of a shorter chronicle was first proposed by V. H. Galbraith in 1937: *St Albans Chronicle*, ed. Galbraith, pp. xlvi–vii. See also Gransden, *Historical Writing*, pp. 118–56; Taylor, *English Historical Literature*, pp. 63–6. For Matthew Paris's *Historia Anglorum* see also Vaughan, *Matthew Paris*, pp. 49–77, 118–24, 152.

[83] See BL, Royal MS 13 E IX, fos 177r–326r.

[84] *WC*, pp. 22–3, 235–639.

[85] See *Usk*, pp. 269–70.

[86] See below, pp. 272, 360.

[87] See below, pp. 131–42, 151–2, 156–71, 163–7.

cler but demonstrate a genuine understanding of the dynamics of personal monarchy and magnate power.[88] Unusually for an English writer of this period, Walsingham was also a enthusiastic observer of foreign affairs and his interest extended beyond the familiar territories of Flanders and the kingdom of France to the German territories, Hungary, Naples and, perhaps most notably, the Iberian kingdoms.[89] His account of the dynastic conflict between Castile and Portugal and the uneasy but enduring Anglo-Portuguese alliance is more detailed than any other non-Hispanic authority.[90] But Walsingham's wider interests were not purely political. He also cultivated an interest in the cultural and social mores of his time and made space in his chronicle to describe changing patterns of dress, gender relations, language and even sexual behaviour.[91]

Walsingham addressed this wide array of subjects in roughly chronological order except where the complexity of the issue – such as the conflict over the crown of Naples, or the simultaneous military campaigns of Henry V and his captains – made it impossible for him to maintain it.[92] His aim was always to maintain a balance between national and international affairs, to the extent that his coverage of some episodes, such as the momentous parliaments of 1376 and 1388, was necessarily foreshortened. But there were a number of themes to which he attached a particular priority, and for which he created space in the chronicle for an especially extended treatment. Perhaps the most important of these was the ongoing struggle of the orthodox Church against John Wyclif, his teachings and their supporters. In the earliest section of the chronicle, Walsingham devotes dozens of pages to the first condemnation of Wyclif in 1378, and although he was generally reluctant to reproduce documents unedited, he transcribes in full the identical bulls dispatched to the archbishop of Canterbury, the king and the university of Oxford and also appends the official list of condemned opinions.[93] Walsingham returns to this theme on a number of occasions between 1382 and 1415, each time engaging in a lengthy digression and giving a full transcript of condemned opinions and other documents.[94]

Of equal importance to Walsingham was the story of corruption and crisis in the Roman papacy, which he traced from its beginnings at the election of Urban VI in 1378 to the final, consensual election of Pope Martin V in 1417. Here too Walsingham was at pains to present the documentary record without any of his usual paraphrasing.[95] The story of the schism presented Walsingham with a vehicle for his own anti-papal prejudice which appears to have pre-dated the schism and was fuelled both by traditional English resentment of papal provisions and contemporary Benedictine suspicions of the promotion of (mostly mendicant) papal chaplains.[96]

Another recurrent theme also reflected these corporate rivalries. At regular intervals throughout the chronicle, Walsingham went out of his way to report incidents which cast suspicion on the mendicant friars, whether through their supposed support for political conspiracy, popular sedition or even outright heresy.[97] In these passages more than any other in the chronicle, Walsingham speaks directly to his monastic readers, reporting these slanders apparently for no better reason than to add to the burden of sin that he and his colleagues already attributed to the mendicant order.[98]

These matters were the preoccupation of the clerical (if not exclusively monastic) community in which Walsingham had passed the greater part of his life, and, for which, primarily, he was

---

[88] See below, pp. 298–311.
[89] See below, pp. 278, 282, 314, 380 (German territories including Prussia); 285 (Hungary); 173–4, 183, 210–11, 224–5, 354–5 (Naples).
[90] For Walsingham's account of Anglo-Portuguese relations see below, pp. 119–20, 194–5, 231–4, 275–6.
[91] See below, pp. 29, 322, 331, 341, 382–3.
[92] See below, pp. 173–4, 224–5, 354–5 (Naples), 406–13, 422–25, 430–3 (Henry V).
[93] See below, pp. 49–61, 174–82, 372–4.
[94] See below, pp. 174–82, 372–4.
[95] See below, pp. 74–7, 419–21.
[96] See below, pp. 119, 249, 294.
[97] See below, pp. 29, 149–50, 204, 321–3.
[98] See below, pp. 321–3, 149–50.

writing. But he also developed a number of secular themes that reflected the preoccupations of the community of magnates and upper gentry upon which his monastery was increasingly dependent. Between 1376 and 1388 he followed the fortunes of the city merchants as they fought for confirmation of their liberties. Over the forty years of the chronicle he also observed closely the deepening crisis in crown finance, the growing burden of taxation and – not without a degree of sympathy – the mounting anger amongst the elected commons.[99] But these were subordinate to his enthusiastic reporting of the French war that runs throughout the text. Perhaps like the aristocratic patrons of St Albans themselves, Walsingham preferred to focus on the daring exploits of English armies in the field than on the political stalemate that their diplomats found frequently at the negotiation table. He was also more inclined to celebrate the martial prowess of the English captains – from Sir Hugh Calveley in the 1370s and '80s to Thomas, duke of Clarence after Agincourt – than to measure their moral worth.[100] When the army of Sir John Arundel ran riot while waiting to embark from Southampton in 1379, Walsingham's expressions of outrage are mitigated by the level of lively detail and dialogue that he lends to the story.[101] In these passages the sober, sterile moralising of his monastic education was eclipsed by his exposure to the secular culture of chivalry that surrounded him.

Sources

The scale and scope of Walsingham's chronicle reflect his access to a wide variety of sources. The second half of the fourteenth century witnessed the wider circulation of official documents, newsletters and other digests of royal and parliamentary *acta* as the English government began to recognise the political benefits of disseminating information.[102] Even in the provinces it was now possible for chroniclers to piece together a more or less complete record of public affairs and many of the most authoritative accounts of the period – the anonymous chronicles of the monk of St Mary's York (the so-called *Anonimalle Chronicle*) and Westminster Abbey, and the history of the Leicester canon Henry Knighton – were founded on extracts from the rolls of parliament, newsletters reporting on the progress of the war or other notable happenings, royal proclamations and other ephemera.[103] St Albans Abbey was better placed than most to intercept the trail of parchment that now issued from Westminster, Windsor, Kennington and other places of government. Not only did the abbot and convent maintain their own collection of public records – to which Richard II himself had recourse – but they also played host to the officers of state themselves on more than one occasion; it was to St Albans that the keeper of the realm, Edmund, duke of York, retreated in 1399 in the dying moments of the regime.[104] Walsingham is therefore likely to have been able to lay his hand on copies of almost any of the *acta* of the period as well as many of the unofficial records: not only newsletters but also popular broadsides and other suspect or seditious texts. But in comparison to his contemporaries, he made limited use of this material in his own writing. He rarely transcribed documents in full, preferring to paraphrase or précis their contents, or to transform them into reported speech.[105] It was only those documents he regarded as the most significant or unusual that he reproduced verbatim in the chronicle and in this his judgement differed markedly from many other chroniclers. To some extent his selection reflected his own technical interest in scriptorial practice; the products of continental chanceries aroused greater interest than their domestic counterparts, and the cryptic vernacular correspondence of

99 See below, p. 29.
100 See below, pp. 48–9, 62, 66–7, 79–80, 86–90, 197 (Calveley); 406–7, 424–5, 426–7, 430–1 (Clarence).
101 See below, pp. 96–101 at 97–9.
102 See G. L. Harriss, 'Political Society and the Growth of Government in Late Medieval England', *Past and Present*, 138 (1993), 28–57; W. M. Ormrod, *Political Life in Medieval England, 1300–1450* (London, 1995), pp. 6–7, 56–60.
103 For the use of these documents in these texts see *Knighton's Chronicle*, pp. xxxii–xl, *WC*, pp. xliii–xlvi.
104 See also *Monastic Renaissance*, p. 36.
105 See below, pp. 147–8, 153.

Jack Straw and his colleagues was too strange not to be transcribed.[106] But he also prioritised the documents that expounded his principal themes. Thus the text of the bulls, decrees and other documents concerning the condemnation of Wyclif (1377–78) and the summoning of the Councils of Pisa and Constance (1409, 1414–17), and even the archbishop of Bordeaux's circumlocution before Henry IV (1414) on the subject of the schism, were each faithfully transcribed.[107] However, many of the key documents of Ricardian and Lancastrian politics, such as Richard II's questions to the justices at Nottingham (1387), the proceedings of the Merciless Parliament (1388) and the articles of deposition themselves (1399), were reported only sketchily, or even omitted entirely.[108] Indeed when it came to domestic concerns, such as the regular sessions of parliament, Walsingham was apparently disinclined to consult the official record and reported only what he had been able to learn at first or second hand. When parliament removed from Westminster to Gloucester in 1378, he had almost nothing to say at all.[109] To what extent Walsingham was dependent, as other commentators were, on newsletters and other public records for his reporting of military campaigns and other affairs overseas is difficult to determine. In a number of cases – Cambridge's expedition to Portugal (1381–2), Despenser's crusade (1383) – his account appears to match those known to have been derived from these sources, but the language, imagery and a number of incidental details are his own.[110]

Walsingham was equally selective in his use of the work of other historians. There is no doubt that he did draw on a number of the anonymous chronicles of the mid-fourteenth century – such as the continuation of Adam Murimuth and the earliest of the *Polychronicon* continuations – to connect his own contemporary history with the earlier continuations of Matthew Paris.[111] But he does not appear to have continued to consult these works for the period after 1376, when he began to write his history in his own words. There is no correspondence between the text of Walsingham's chronicle and the continuations of the *Eulogium historiarum* – a chronicle that originated at Malmesbury Abbey – and the *Polychronicon* that circulated widely at the end of the fourteenth century.[112] Nor is there any evidence that Walsingham was either aware of, or borrowed from the contemporary chronicles composed during his own lifetime at a number of other greater Benedictine houses, Glastonbury, Westminster Abbey and St Mary's Abbey, York.[113] He had much to gain from reading both the anonymous Westminster chronicle and the *Anonimalle Chronicle* compiled at York: both authors were at times better informed than he about court ceremonial and the proceedings of the commons, but in spite of connections between their monasteries and his, there is no evidence of contact.[114] There is no doubt that the anonymous monk of Evesham who composed the *Historia vitae et regni regis Ricardi secundi* at the turn of the fifteenth century became dependent on Walsingham's chronicle for his account of the king's last decade and deposition, but the relationship was only one-sided.[115] Walsingham was more

---

[106] See below, pp. 162–3.

[107] See below, pp. 49–54 (Wyclif), 350–4 (Pisa), 400–2, 419–22 (Constance), 362–9 (Archbishop of Bordeaux).

[108] See below, pp. 251–2 (1387), 261–3 (1388), 310–12 (1399).

[109] See below, pp. 72–3.

[110] See below, pp. 119–20, 194–5, 199–211. For the use of newsletters by other chroniclers see *Knighton's Chronicle*, pp. xxii–xli, lxi, 55n, 326n; *WC*, pp. xliii–xlvi, li–liv.

[111] *St Albans Chronicle*, ed. Galbraith, pp. lii–liii; Gransden, *Historical writing*, p. 124; Clark, 'Thomas Walsingham Reconsidered', 844.

[112] For these chronicles and continuations of chronicles see Gransden, *Historical writing*, pp. 56, 157–8; Taylor, *English Historical Literature*, pp. 20–1, 77–89, 105–6, 133–53.

[113] At Glastonbury, John Seen compiled the *Cronica sive antiquitates Glastoniensis ecclesie*, and was also said to have written a work of classical history, now lost; at Westminster, Richard Cirencester composed the *Speculum historiale* and, at St Mary's York, an anonymous monk produced the *Anonimalle Chronicle*. For these works see Gransden, *Historical Writing II*, 110–13, 157, 399–400; Sharpe, *Latin writers*, 312–13, 464.

[114] For the accounts of the *Anonimalle* author and the anonymous Westminster monk of the coronation of Richard II and other ceremonies see *AC*, pp. 107–15; *WC*, pp. 235–369.

[115] For the Evesham monk's use of Walsingham's chronicle in the composition of the *Historia vitae et regni regis Ricardi secundi* see Stow, 'Bodleian Library, MS Bodley 316 and the Dating of Thomas Walsingham's

familiar with the work of past historians. His passing reference to the return of Thomas Becket from exile in 1170 betrays his knowledge of Herbert of Bosham's *Life*.[116] The comparison of the unfortunate murdered Bury monk, John Cambridge, to the legendary King Beldgabred can only have come from the *Historia Britonum* of Geoffrey of Monmouth.[117] His preference for the archaic names of peoples and places – Britons and Gauls, Armorica and Neustria – suggests that he was well versed in other early histories, not only Bede's *Historia ecclesiastica* and William of Malmesbury's *Gesta regum* but also William of Jumièges' *Gesta Normannorum*.[118]

But for Walsingham, as for Matthew Paris before him, written sources, whether in other chronicles or official documents, were subordinate to the first-hand accounts he was able to acquire from his own circle of friends and informants.[119] The tone and the telling details of many of his narrative passages, of the ceremonies and proceedings of court and parliament and the many military campaigns of the period, would suggest that they were derived from those who had witnessed them for themselves. Walsingham does not identify any of his informants by name, but many of the public figures that feature in his chronicle were familiar faces at St Albans. Abbot Thomas de la Mare had been a councillor of Edward III and cultivated a close friendship with Edward the Black Prince and his princess, Joan of Kent.[120] After the deaths of both king and prince, Countess Joan entered into a close personal (and possibly political) alliance with Abbot Thomas, and through her intercession many prominent courtiers were introduced to the abbey.[121] It may have been under the influence of members of the countess's household that Walsingham developed his suspicions of John of Gaunt in the months following the Good Parliament. It was at her insistence that Sir John Chandos, Sir Lewis Clifford, and Sir Richard Sturry were admitted to the abbey confraternity in 1381, a ceremony which must have been witnessed by Walsingham and may have exposed him to the whisperings already current about their suspected sympathy for Lollardy.[122] Many of the greater knights and magnates were also well known at St Albans: the celebrated campaigner Sir Robert Knolles was listed among members of the confraternity, and Henry Percy, Gaunt's ally and earl marshal was described in the *Liber benefactorum* (which Walsingham compiled) as a 'great defender of our house'.[123] If Walsingham had access to him or his retainers, it might explain his detailed documenting not only of the ongoing border battles, but also of the political tensions provoked by Percy and Gaunt in the months following Richard's accession. Thomas, duke of Gloucester, was also benefactor of the abbey, and this might explain Walsingham's sympathetic treatment of him and his fellow appellants: it is worth noting that Gloucester is also known to have possessed a copy of the earliest 'scandalous' recension of Walsingham's chronicle his private library.[124] During the decade of Richard's tyranny, St Albans drifted away from the political mainstream perhaps as a result of the ageing Abbot De la Mare's

---

Literary Career', 67–76; *id.*, 'Thomas Walsingham, John Malvern and the Vita Ricardi Secundi, 1377–1381: A Reassessment', *Mediaeval Studies*, xxxix (1977), 490–97; *Historia vitae et regni regis Ricardi secundi*, ed. G. B. Stow (Philadelphia, 1981), pp. 12–20.

116 See below, p. 36.
117 See below, p. 142.
118 For examples of Walsingham's use of these names see below, pp. 330, 387, 434.
119 For Matthew Paris's reliance on a network of friends and informants see Vaughan, *Matthew Paris*, pp. 13–17, 135–6.
120 Both Walsingham himself and the anonymous biographer of Abbot de la Mare testify to his friendship with the prince and princess: *Gesta abbatum*, ed. Riley, ii. 403–4 , 408–9 (Walsingham); iii. 382–3, 395, 403–4 (anonymous).
121 The evidence for this is preserved in the *Liber benefactorum*, where the admission of large groups of courtiers is recorded between 1377–81, on each occasion 'ad instanciam comiti Johanni': BL, Cotton MS Nero D VII, fos 128v–130v.
122 BL, Cotton MS Nero D VII, fos 129r–v.
123 Ibid., fo. 111r.
124 Gloucester's contributions to the abbey were commemorated in the *Liber benefactorum*: BL, Cotton MS Nero D VII, fo. 110r. A portion of an early manuscript containing the 'scandalous' recension of Walsingham's chronicle, Oxford, Bodl., Bodley MS 316, bears the *ex libris* of Gloucester's book collection at his castle at Pleshy, Essex. For Walsingham's treatment of the appellants, see below, pp. 254–63, 298–302.

retreat from public life but their early support for the Lancastrian cause projected the convent back into the court circle at the accession of Henry IV. From the moment of the deposition, the monks were called upon to serve in the settlement of the new regime. They became the captors of a prominent political prisoner, Bishop Thomas Merke of Carlisle, who had remained with King Richard to the end.[125] Richard's body passed through St Albans before its burial at King's Langley and it was Abbot John Moot (1396–1401) who presided over the funeral.[126] Walsingham must have learned much from both these experiences and when Moot was succeeded in the abbacy by the well-connected William Heyworth, he secured a permanent correspondent in the Lancastrian court.[127] Indeed it may be that this succession of abbots proved to be Walsingham's most important informants. Their position in parliament, and, on occasion, at court or in meetings of the king's council, made it possible for Walsingham to receive regular dispatches from the very heart of royal government.[128]

Style

Walsingham's preference for personal testimony shaped his writing style. As if to preserve something of the character of the original reports, wherever possible he worked dramatic dialogues into his narrative, drawing the speeches of the protagonists either from the supporting documents, or, probably more frequently from his own imagination.[129] Even in passages of pure narrative he adopted a highly personal tone, employing expressions that were colourful and confiding and at times colloquial to the point of vulgarity.[130] Here he also demonstrates an eye for high – and low – comedy that may owe as much to his exposure to secular culture as it does to his interest in classical satire.[131] It appears he was conscious of the contrast this offered to the other chroniclers of his own day and at one point he was moved to express the hope that his readers would not be scandalised by what he had written.[132] But at the same time there was also a sober and studied – though no more conventional – dimension to his work. Juxtaposed with the passages of vivid and sometimes violent expression were those in which Walsingham was determined to display his scholarly credentials. Here the narrative is woven together from fragments of classical poetry and prose, Lucan's *De bello civili*, Ovid's *Metamorphoses*, Statius' *Thebaid*, the satires of Juvenal and Persius and Virgil's *Aeneid*.[133] There was more to these references than scholarly conceit. Walsingham recycled these fragments to fashion an authentic classical style for his own prose, correct even down to the detail of the terms used for different forms of weaponry on the battlefield.[134] As the writing of the chronicle progressed he became ever more obsessed with this enterprise to the point that his descriptions of the exploits of Henry V, and in particular the Agincourt battle, depart some way from the historical reality of the events they purport to represent.[135] This technique set Walsingham far apart from his contemporaries, monastic and secular and anticipated the classically-inspired histories of subsequent generations.

Walsingham and his contemporaries: the influence of the *Chronica maiora*

Walsingham wrote in a period that has been seen as the Indian summer of the medieval monastic chronicle. The second half of the fourteenth century saw a return to historical writing in many of

---

125 *Gesta abbatum*, ed. Riley, iii. 454.
126 *Trokelowe*, ed. Riley, p. 331.
127 For the patronage of St Albans under Heyworth see *Gesta abbatum*, ed. Riley, iii. 493–502.
128 An anonymous account of the attendance of the abbot at parliament at the end of the fourteenth century is preserved in a *quaternus* bound into BL, Harley, MS 3775, fos 126v–127v. See also *Amundesham*, ed. Riley, i. 414–17.
129 See, for example, below, pp. 74, 334.
130 See, for example, below, pp. 322, 372.
131 See below, p. 322.
132 See below, pp. 410–11.
133 For echoes of, or extracts from, these classical authors see below, pp. 328, 410–11.
134 See, for example, below, pp. 410–11.
135 See below, pp. 410–11.

the greater abbeys and priories in England, in some case for the first time since the golden age of the twelfth century. The stimulus for this was derived in part from the success of Ranulf Higden's *Polychronicon*, the first major English history to appear for more than two centuries, which inspired many houses to customise and continue it with their own domestic and regional interests centre stage.[136] But like Walsingham himself, it was also true that in the aftermath of the Black Death a new generation of monks had emerged with an academic education and a taste for scholarship. In the period during which Walsingham was writing there were new contemporary histories in production at many of the Benedictine monasteries in the orbit of St Albans, not only Evesham, Westminster and York, but also Bury St Edmunds, St Augustine's Abbey, Canterbury and Reading.[137] There is also evidence of a wide variety of historical writing alongside Walsingham at St Albans itself. He was not the only monk of his generation to continue the *Gesta abbatum*, and an anonymous author – perhaps his exact contemporary, the abbot's chaplain William Wintershill – composed a biography of Abbot Thomas de la Mare.[138] The same author may also have composed the account of the period 1392–1406 which was printed in the Roll Series under the title of the *Annales Ricardi secundi et Henrici quarti*.[139] Another anonymous monk compiled an annal of the first decade of the abbacy of John Wheathampstead,[140] while two other named monks collaborated on an epitome of Bede's *Ecclesiastical History*.[141] To a contemporary observer Walsingham would have appeared as only one of a whole monastic community committed to the writing of history.

To what extent Walsingham himself was aware of these other writers, even those active in his own convent, is unclear. He did maintain scholarly contacts within, and possibly beyond, St Albans, but these were directed towards his interest in classical scholarship rather than contemporary history. The example of Matthew Paris has shown that it was perfectly possible for a prolific scholar to remain in splendid isolation for much of his career even when part of a much patronised, politicised community such as St Albans.[142] But what is beyond question is that – whether or not he was aware of it himself – Walsingham's own work did have a considerable impact upon them. From the end of the 1380s, when the 'scandalous' recension of the first decade of the narrative was complete, Walsingham's chronicle reached a wide readership not only at St Albans and its sizeable network of dependent houses, but also, it seems, in many other monasteries and secular communities elsewhere. It is unlikely that readers were aware of Walsingham's name, but in several of the surviving manuscripts the colophon did connect the chronicle with St Albans. It is possible that the text was deliberately disseminated – published – from the scriptorium as other original compositions were in this period although if this was the case it was a process over which Walsingham himself appears to have had little control given the number of different forms – a continuation of Matthew Paris, of the *Polychronicon*, the earlier scandalous narrative or subsequent recensions – in which it was reproduced.[143] It may be more plausible to suggest, however,

---

136   For the composition and circulation of the *Polychronicon* see J. Taylor, *The Universal Chronicle of Ranulf Higden* (Oxford, 1966). See also his 'Development of the *Polychronicon* continuation', 20–36.

137   Gransden, *Historical Writing II*, pp. 55, 105, 206–10, 343, 345–55, 403.

138   The anonymous biography is preserved uniquely in Cambridge, Corpus Christi College, MS 7, fos 91r–102v, and was printed as a continuation of the *Gesta abbatum*: *Gesta abbatum*, ed. Riley, iii. 375–423. See also Clark, 'Thomas Walsingham Reconsidered', 846–7.

139   The *Annales* was printed in the Rolls series in a composite collection of St Albans chronicles, *Iohannes de Trokelowe et Henrici de Blaneforde monachorum Sancti Albani Chronica et Annales*, ed. H. T. Riley, Rolls Series, 28/3 (1866), pp. 155–420. For discussion of its authorship see Clark, 'Thomas Walsingham Reconsidered', 844–5.

140   The annal was printed in the Rolls Series as a preface to the longer annals attributed to John Amersham: *Annales monasterii sancti Albani a Iohanne Amundsham conscripta*, ed. H. T. Riley, 2 vols, Rolls Series, 28/5 (1870–71), i. 3–69.

141   These were John Bebseth, prior of the St Albans dependency of Hatfield Peverell, Essex, and William Wrightley, who may also have been the scribe. Their work survives in Oxford, Bodl., Rawlinson B 189, fos 119r–72v; the names of the monks are recorded on fol. 119r.

142   For Matthew Paris at St Albans see Vaughan, *Matthew Paris*, pp. 1–20 at 3.

143   For evidence of the production and possible publication of original works at St Albans see Clark, *Monas-*

that it was an *ad hoc*, unplanned process that bypassed the St Albans authorities and reflected the preoccupations and priorities of individual scribes.[144] Either way, there is scarcely a single contemporary history composed in the last quarter of the fourteenth and the first quarter of the fifteenth century that does not bear the imprint of Walsingham's work. The greater part of the anonymous St Albans *Annales* was derived directly from the *Chronica maiora* to the extent that historians have often assumed that it represented nothing more than another recension of Walsingham's own work, although there is both codicological and textual evidence that disproves this.[145] The anonymous Evesham monk who composed the text known as the *Historia et vita regni regis Ricardi secundi* also borrowed extensively from Walsingham and thus provides a valuable early witness to the extent of its circulation.[146] A number of the anonymous continuations of the mid-fourteenth- century chronicles, not only the *Polychronicon* but also of the chronicle of Adam Murimuth and the *Eulogium historiarum* also drew material from the *Chronica maiora* to the extent that the descent of these texts in manuscript in the later fourteenth and fifteenth centuries can only properly be understood in terms of their relationship to Walsingham.[147] Only the anonymous chronicles composed at Westminster and York (i.e. the *Anonimalle Chronicle*), both of which appear in unique manuscripts connected with their respective houses, appear to have remain insulated from the influence of St Albans.

These works were completed before 1422, but it is clear that the influence of Walsingham's chronicle endured at least for a generation after his death. The early fifteenth-century chronicler Thomas Otterbourne reproduced many of Walsingham's stories of Richard II and the Lancastrians, refracted through the anonymous *Annales* of which he appears to have possessed a now lost copy.[148] Chroniclers of Otterbourne's generation, such as John Streeche of Kenilworth and the author of the lost life of Henry V which served as the source of the English life of 1513, also appear to have been aware of the later portion of the *Chronica maiora*, perhaps through the medium of a *Polychronicon* continuation.[149] It is possible that Walsingham's work was also known to the Augustinian friar John Capgrave, a prolific historian and author of another history of Henry V.[150] From the middle years of the fifteenth century there was something of a slump in the production of manuscripts of medieval Latin chronicles and Walsingham's work, like that of Matthew Paris, was eclipsed by works written in the English vernacular such as the Brut and the various London chronicles.[151] There were echoes of Walsingham, and other St Albans works, in the 'Cronicles of England' published almost simultaneously by William Caxton and the St Albans printer between 1480 and 1485, but it was to be another ninety years before Walsingham's own Latin text first appeared in print.[152]

---

tic Renaissance, pp. 97–123. For a general survey of monastic book production in this period see also A. I. Doyle, 'Publication by Members of the Religious Orders', in *Book Production and Publishing 1375–1475*, ed. D. Pearsall and J. Griffiths (Cambridge, 1989), pp. 190–213.

[144]   For the personal compilations and private commissions produced at St Albans during Walsingham's lifetime see Clark, *Monastic Renaissance*, pp. 110–11.

[145]   For the relationship between the two texts see Clark, 'Thomas Walsingham Reconsidered', 846–7.

[146]   For the monk's debt to Walsingham see note 115 above.

[147]   Taylor, 'Development of the *Polychronicon*', 20–36.

[148]   Gransden, *Historical Writing II*, p. 196 and n.18.

[149]   For Streeche see F. Taylor, 'The Chronicle of John Streeche for the reign of Henry V, 1414–1422', *Bulletin of the John Rylands Library*, xvi (1932), 137–87. For the First English Life see *The First English Life of King Henry V*, ed. C. L. Kingsford (Oxford, 1911). The story of St Vincent Ferrier's sermon may owe something to a reading of Walsingham: see pp. xxxiii–vi.

[150]   For Capgrave see *John Capgrave's Abbreviacion of Cronicles*, ed. P. J. Lucas (EETS, OS 285, 1983), pp. lxxx–lxxxiv.

[151]   For these developments see Gransden, *Historical Writing II*, pp. 220–48.

[152]   Caxton's *Cronicles of England* was first printed in 1480 [STC 9991]. The edition of the St Albans printer appeared in 1485 [STC 9995].

Editions and Translations

Given its obvious importance and influence upon subsequent generations of historians, printed editions of Walsingham's chronicle have proved remarkably scarce. The first printed text was produced under the supervision of Matthew Parker, archbishop of Canterbury, in 1574 and although it was derived from early manuscripts then in his possession it did not represent a critical edition.[153] In the same period the antiquarian John Stow and other scholars began to collaborate on a translation of the earliest scandalous recension of the text, working directly from the surviving manuscripts. Only a fragment of this translation now survives and there is no evidence that it was printed, although Stow's reading of the text undoubtedly informed his own chronicle compilations.[154] A portion of Walsingham's text was printed a second time by William Camden in 1603 as part of his *Anglica, Normannica, Hibernica Cambrica et veteribus scripta*.[155] These first two editions of the chronicle do not appear to have enjoyed a wide circulation and were never reprinted; it is likely that Elizabethan and Jacobean audiences read Walsingham only at second or third hand through the writings of those – such as Edward Hall, Raphael Holinshed and John Stow – who had worked directly from the manuscript copies. It was another two hundred and fifty years before a scholarly edition was attempted under the auspices of the Rolls Series and the editorship of Henry Thomas Riley and Edward Maunde Thompson.[156] Riley and Thompson were conscious of the confusion caused through the repeated reproduction of the chronicle in manuscript and their main concern was to disentangle its different recensions. Their decision to print the principal recensions as separate volumes in the series was a reasonable one but they created more confusion than they resolved by ascribing to them different (and wholly spurious) titles, the *Chronicon Angliae* for the earliest 'scandalous' text covering 1376–88 and the *Historia Anglicana* for the complete, revised text that continued down to 1422. The virtue of these texts was that they were transcribed from the earliest and most valuable of the extant manuscripts of the chronicle, BL, Cotton MS Faustina B IX, BL, Cotton MS Otho C II and BL, Harley MS 3634–Oxford, Bodl., Bodley MS 316, for the 'scandalous' recension and BL, Royal MS 13 E IX, Cambridge, Corpus Christi College, MS 7, and College of Arms, Arundel MS 7 for the subsequent revision. It is for this reason that modern historians have continued to refer to them. In 1937 V. H. Galbraith sought to elucidate some of the problems that Riley and Thompson had failed to resolve with the publication of another recension of the last portion of the chronicle preserved (as part of a *Polychronicon* continuation) in Oxford, Bodl., Bodley MS 462.[157] The Bodley manuscript provided new evidence of the significant expansions and revisions that had been made in the text of the chronicle between 1406 and 1420, such as the introduction of new political anecdotes – the story of Sir Robert Waterton and the curry-comb, for example – and a number of new document transcripts. Recently, John Taylor, Wendy Childs and Leslie Watkiss have embarked on a new critical edition of the complete text which incorporates (but does not always question) the discoveries and interpretations made by the Rolls Series editors and V. H. Galbraith.[158]

---

153 *Historia breuis ab Edwardo primo ad Henricum quintum* (London, 1574) [STC 25004]. See also M. McKisack, *Medieval History in the Tudor Age* (London, 1971), pp. 41–2.
154 BL, Harley MS 6217, fos 3r–20r, a paper booklet of twenty folios wrapped in a vellum bi-folium; according to a note on the wrapper the translation is from the Latin text in BL, Harley MS 3634. See also McKisack, *Medieval History*, pp. 111–14.
155 Printed at Frankfurt in 1603.
156 *Thomae Walsingham quondam monachi sancti Albani Historia Anglicana*, ed. H. T. Riley, 2 vols, Rolls Series 28/1 (1863–64); *Chronicon Angliae, ab anno domini 1328 usque ad annum 1388, auctore monachi quodam sancti Albani*, ed. E. M. Thompson, Roll Series, 64 (1874).
157 *The St Albans Chronicle, 1406–1420*, ed. V. H. Galbraith (Oxford, 1937).
158 *The St Albans Chronicle: The Chronica Maiora of Thomas Walsingham, I. 1376–1394*, ed. J. Taylor, W. Childs and L. Watkiss, Oxford Medieval Texts (Oxford, 2003).

The Translation

The text printed below is a translation of Walsingham's chronicle from 1376, the date at which he began to work independently and to write – with the exception of documents – in his own words, down to 1422, the date at which the narrative ends in the most complete of the extant manuscripts. The translation has been made from the text printed by Riley as the *Historia Anglicana* and transcribed by him from the Royal and College of Arms manuscripts, collated together with the chronicle from 1406–1420 printed by Galbraith as *The St Albans Chronicle*, in turn transcribed from the manuscript Oxford, Bodl., Bodley MS 462. Thus it represents the fullest and most fully revised text of Walsingham's *Chronica maiora* that is known to have circulated in fifteenth-century English manuscripts and might have been accessible to readers in the later Middle Ages.

The *Chronica Maiora* 1376–1422

The Reign of King Edward III

[1376]

The parliament, often called The Good,[1] is held at London

In 1376 in the fiftieth year of the reign of King Edward III,[2] the king had a full parliament held at Westminster at the beginning of the month of May,[3] at which, in his usual fashion, he asked the commons to grant him a subsidy for the defence of his kingdom. The commons in reply said they had been perpetually harassed by many such demands, and declared that the truth was that they could not sustain such burdens for long without the greatest harm to themselves.[4] For they were agreed that the king plainly had sufficient resources for the defence of his realm, if his kingdom was governed sensibly and honestly; but as long as his kingdom was in the hands of untrustworthy officials, as under the present regime, it would never have an abundance of supplies or money. And so they offered to prove this to be the case, and said that if after such proof the king was found to be in need of anything, they would help him according to their means.

During the parliament many accusations were made against the king's household and various other officials of the king, particularly against Lord Latimer,[5] his chamberlain, who had exercised a very bad influence and control over the king. And so the duke of Lancaster,[6] Lord Latimer and

---

There is no evidence to suggest that Walsingham intended the Chronica maiora to be subdivided into books, chapters or other distinctions, and formal headings for sections of the text appear only intermittently in the earliest manuscripts. Where section headings are attested by the earliest manuscripts, they have been incorporated into the translation. For ease of reference headings have also been added where there was none and these have been enclosed in square brackets to identify them as the translator's interventions. See also above, pp. 4, 10–13.

1 Walsingham was the only contemporary authority to record the name popularly given to this protracted and turbulent parliament. The author of the *Anonimalle chronicle*, who described its proceedings in equal detail, called it the 'great parliament'; the same title (maximum parliamentum) was used by John Malvern in his continuation of the *Polychronicon* and by the author of the English Brut (the grettest that has seen many yere afore). Walsingham's name was adopted by the Elizabethan historian, John Stow, in his *Annal or General Chronicle of England*. See also J. Taylor, 'The Good Parliament and its Sources' in J. Taylor and W. Childs (eds.), *Politics and Crisis in Fourteenth-Century England* (Gloucester, 1990), pp. 81–96. For the political significance of the Good Parliament and its proceedings see G. A. Holmes, *The Good Parliament* (Oxford, 1975).
2 Edward III (b. 1312), son of Edward II (b. 1284, reigning from 1307–27) and Isabella of France, proclaimed king in 1327 but only assuming personal rule in October 1330.
3 In fact the parliament opened on 28 April 1376. It sat for nine weeks: *RP*, ii. 321; Holmes, *Good Parliament*, pp. 147–54.
4 Since the re-opening of the French war in 1369, the crown had pressed for subsidies in every parliament. In 1373 the assembly had refused to agree to a grant before their demands were met and the temper of the commons had persuaded the Edwardian government not to seek a parliament in the years 1374–75.
5 William, 4th baron Latimer (c. 1329–81), had served Edward III for almost twenty years, first in Gascony and then as governor of Bécherel in Brittany. He was invested as a knight of the garter in 1361 and became chamberlain of the king's household in 1369. He owed his promotion to the favour of the king's mistress, Alice Perrers. Latimer was accused of profiting from the recent unsuccessful military campaign in Brittany; it was alleged that he had extorted excessive ransoms from a number of Breton towns whilst at the same time surrendering others to the enemy – including Bécherel and Saint-Sauveur – in return for bribes. It was also suspected that he had profited from the removal of the wool staple from Calais. In the longer, 'scandalous' version of his narrative Walsingham added that as overseer of the Breton campaign Latimer – together with the veteran campaigner, Sir Robert Knolles – had sanctioned the severe oppression of the people, the cities, towns and castles of the region (*CA*, pp. 76–78).
6 John of Gaunt (1340–99), duke of Lancaster, third son of Edward III, created duke in 1362 having succeeded to the Lancaster estates through his first wife, Blanche, daughter of Henry of Lancaster (d. 1361). Gaunt served alongside his elder brother in the Spanish campaign of 1367 and conducted further campaigns in France in 1371 and 1373 in his capacity as lieutenant of Aquitaine.

many other high officials of the king were removed from their posts and others appointed in their place. Also at the request of the commons it was decreed that certain bishops and earls and other lords of praiseworthy morals should be in control of the king and the kingdom from now on, seeing that the king was now on the verge of senility and had need of such counsellors.[1] But this body lasted barely three months because of interference by those who had been removed from the king's side, as I have described above.

Also the knights in parliament made serious complaints about a very forward woman called Alice Perrers, who had become too friendly with King Edward.[2] They accused her especially of very many scandals in the land for which she and her cronies were responsible.[3] For she had gone far beyond the limits set for women, and forgetting her femininity and her frailty, she had on some occasions sat besides the king's justices and on others placed herself next to the doctors in the ecclesiastical court,[4] and had not been in the least afraid of urging her point of view in defence of the accused or even of making demands which were contrary to the laws. The result of these scandals was that the king was getting a very bad name not only in his own land but also abroad, and the knights demanded that she be sent right away from him.

Also in this parliament some noteworthy lapses of Richard Lyons and Adam Bury, citizens and merchants of London, were brought into the light of day.[5] The first of these two very shrewdly, and in fact sensibly, escaped the due punishment with the help of money.[6] The second of them, who was stunned by the penalties imposed upon him, fled at once from England to Flanders, so that he might find salvation there.

The man who had acted as speaker of parliament for all the knights and had put forward these demands of them all was called Peter de la Mare. As he was intelligent and a very able speaker, a man of experience and good sense and discretion, such matters had been deservedly entrusted to him before all the rest.[7] Acting on the instructions he had received, he had spoken out against Alice and various other members of the council of King Edward, and so at the instance of the said Alice, he was sentenced to life imprisonment at Nottingham [Castle]. Although his friends often pleaded for his release, he stayed in prison there for two years.[8]

---

1   The episcopal advisers were the bishops of Norwich, Rochester, London and Carlisle. They were joined by Henry Percy, Richard Stafford, Guy Brian and Roger Beauchamp together with Edmund Mortimer, earl of March, Thomas Beauchamp, earl of Warwick, William Ufford, earl of Suffolk and Hugh, earl of Stafford. See *CA*, pp. 69–70.

2   Alice Perrers (d.1400) entered the service of Queen Philippa of Hainault before October 1366. In his longer, 'scandalous' narrative, Walsingham records that she was of 'infamous origin', a native of the town of Henneye: *CA*, p. 95.

3   Walsingham elaborates on these scandals in the longer version of his chronicle. He claims that Perrers had concealed from the king her marriage to the courtier Sir William Windsor, and that she maintained her influence over the king through her exercise of the 'magical arts': *CA*, pp. 96–7. See also W. M. Ormrod, *The Reign of Edward III: Crown and Political Society in England, 1327–77* (New Haven and London, 1990).

4   This allegation, of particular concern to a clerical commentator such as Walsingham, does not appear in other contemporary accounts.

5   Both Bury and Lyons were London merchants and had both served terms as the city's sheriff (1349–50, 1374–5), with Bury also being mayor in 1364–5 and 1373–4. C. M. Barron, *London in the Later Middle Ages. Government and People, 1200–1500* (Oxford, 2004), pp. 138, 143, 271, 303, 331–3. Like Latimer, both were accused of profiting from the recent English campaigns in France. In the longer, 'scandalous' account, Walsingham claims that Lyons had embezzled at least 10,000 marks that had been destined for the crown: *CA*, p. 78.

6   In the longer, 'scandalous' narrative, Walsingham complained that Lyons was not sent to the Tower but continued to enjoy a life of luxury: *CA*, pp. 93–4.

7   Peter de la Mare was knight of the shire of Hereford. Walsingham's enthusiasm for him may be connected with his alleged kinship with the Abbot of St Albans, Thomas de la Mare.

8   In the longer version of his chronicle, Walsingham alleged that Gaunt had wished to see de la Mare executed (*CA*, p. 105). As it happened, he remained incarcerated for only twelve months and was released following the very public reconciliation between John of Gaunt and Bishop Wykeham. In the longer version of the chronicle, Walsingham compared the moment to the return from exile of another antagonist of royal authority, Thomas Becket: *CA*, p. 151.

A chapter on the death of the Prince

On 8 July, while parliament was still in session at Westminster, Edward, prince of Wales, first-born son of King Edward, died in the king's palace.[1] It was in fact the feast of the Trinity [8 June], a day which the prince, in his reverence for this great festival, had always been accustomed each year to celebrate with the greatest solemnity, no matter where he happened to be. While he was alive and safe, all nations, both Christian and pagan, had gone in deep dread of his good fortune in war, just as though he was a second Hector.[2] And so when he died, all the hopes of the English died with him. As long as he survived, they feared no enemy's invasion, and, while he was in the field, no shock of war. While he was present, the English had never suffered the disgrace of a campaign that had been badly fought or abandoned. He attacked no nation that he did not conquer. He besieged no city that he did not capture.[3] And so, with the extinction of the prince, the efforts of the current parliament were also assuredly extinguished. For the commons of the parliament, whose side the prince had taken, did not obtain the outcome that they had hoped would improve things.[4] Lord Richard of Bordeaux,[5] the son of Edward, prince of Wales, was made earl of Chester in this parliament, and a few days later received the whole of his father's principality.

[The people of Warwick attack the abbey of Evesham]

In this year at the beginning of the month of June, the people and tenants of the earl of Warwick[6] made an evil and wicked attack on the abbot and monks of Evesham and their tenants.[7] In their efforts to destroy the abbey and the town they beat and thrashed unmercifully the abbot's servants and even cruelly strangled some of them. They also invaded the manors of the monks, breaking

---

[1] Edward of Woodstock (b. 1330), eldest son of Edward III, created prince of Wales in 1343, popularly known (even in his own lifetime) as the Black Prince, had suffered poor health since his return from Spain in 1367 and although he continued to campaign in the early 1370s his condition continued to deteriorate. The nature of the sickness has still not been confidently diagnosed. In the earlier, 'scandalous' recension of the chronicle Walsingham recalled that his final illness coincided with the opening of this parliament: *CA*, pp. 88–92. The *Anonimalle Chronicle* reports that he fell into decline before Pentecost (1 June): *AC*, p. 92. He died at Westminster on Trinity Sunday, 8 June. Froissart describes how his body was embalmed and placed in a lead coffin to preserve his remains until the feast of St Michael when the funeral finally took place. He also reports that Charles V ordered obsequies for the prince at the Sainte-Chapelle in Paris: Froissart, *Chroniques*, viii. 224–5, FCBuchon, i. 707.

[2] In the longer version of his chronicle, Walsingham prefers to compare the Black Prince with Alexander the Great: *CA*, p. 91.

[3] The Black Prince had been a key contributor to some of the greatest victories of his father's reign including the pitched battles at Crécy (1436) and Poitiers (1356) and had commanded the Anglo-Castilian army that prevailed over the usurper Enrique of Trastamara at Najera in 1367. Walsingham omits to mention his brutality at the siege of Limoges (1371), which brought an ignoble end to his military career. For a contemporary account of these exploits see *Life of the Black Prince by the Herald of Sir John Chandos*, ed. M. K. Pope and E. C. Lodge (Oxford, 1910). See also R. Barber, *Edward, Prince of Wales and Aquitaine. A Biography of the Black Prince* (London, 1978).

[4] Walsingham here surely exaggerates the likely influence of the Black Prince, whose infirmity had been public knowledge for several years.

[5] Richard of Bordeaux (b. 6 January 1367), son of Edward of Woodstock (1330–76), prince of Wales, known as the Black Prince, and Joan of Kent.

[6] Thomas Beauchamp, (d. 1400), had campaigned in France with Gaunt in 1373 and during the Good Parliament had been a member of the committee of magnates that directed the proceedings against Latimer and Lyons. He joined Thomas, duke of Gloucester and Richard, earl of Arundel as an appellant against Richard's councillors in 1387–88, a role for which he was finally deprived of his title and estates in 1397.

[7] Walsingham added this account to his chronicle after the earliest 'scandalous' narrative had been completed. The Benedictine abbey of Evesham was one of the handful of wealthy houses exempt from episcopal or seigniorial jurisdiction and thus a natural focus for envy and resentment. An entry in its own chronicle from 1379 stated that it was 'full of all good things' (*Chronicon abbatiae de Evesham ad annum 1418*, ed. W. D. Macray, Rolls Series, 29 (1863), p. 303). However, the chronicle does not record this episode and the identity of the 'friends' who brought its resolution is unknown; there is no record to be found either in the anonymous *Historia et vita regis Ricardi secundi*, also the work of a monk of Evesham. The abbot in this period was John de Omberseley (d. 1379).

down the fences around their enclosures and burning them in fires. They killed their game and in the end, as they vented their fury, they were doing all the harm which chance suggested to their cruel minds. Not even content with this, they broke down the banks of the fishponds, allowing the water to run out, and caught the fish and took them away with them. They did much other damage as well to the abbey and inflicted the gravest injuries on the monks. It certainly seemed likely that they would have destroyed the abbey and its lands beyond possibility of recovery, had the king not speedily given a helping hand by sending a letter with his commands to the earl and giving him strict instructions to suppress such malefactors and disturbers of the peace. And so the fear of the king and the mediation of friends restored peace between the parties, although the injured party did not obtain full satisfaction, as the losses inflicted were too great for it to be possible for them to be made good.

Some people say that it was because of this conflict that the king was no longer willing to be guided by the lords appointed by parliament. Instead he took back his son, the duke of Lancaster, to look after himself and his kingdom, and the duke remained in control and direction of affairs right up to the death of the king. He immediately allowed the king, contrary to the decrees of parliament, to restore to favour Lord Latimer and Richard Stury[1] and several others who by the judgement and sentence of parliament had been banned from his presence forever. The king also recalled to his side his concubine, Alice Perrers, whom parliament had judged should be removed from his palace because of the shameful scandals occasioned by her forwardness. This was contrary to the oath sworn by the same Alice and ratified by the king himself that she would not under any circumstances come into the king's presence. In fact she stayed with him until he died.

Florentines entering England appeal to the king

In the same year some Florentines were excommunicated by the pope on account of their rebellion against the Roman church and unheard-of acts of disobedience. Among their other crimes and awful deeds of cruelty they had tortured with red-hot iron hooks a monk, sent to them by the pope with papal commands, while he was still alive, and had buried him in the ground before he was actually dead. Some of the Florentines later came to England. They asked for the king's peace and stayed in England, until the pope in his bulls revealed the enormity of the crimes in which they had been involved. When that happened, they actually became servants of the king, just as though they were English, with all their goods and chattels. This was because of the decision contained in a letter from the pope, that they should either do this or hurry back to the curia and hand themselves over to the mercy of the pope and his curia. The Florentines therefore chose what seemed to them to be the lesser of the two evils, namely to serve the king of England like his countrymen rather than to submit themselves to the judgement of the Romans.[2]

On 22 July Simon Langham, an English cardinal, died.[3]

---

[1]   Latimer was pardoned on 8 October: *CPR, 1374–7*, pp. 353–4. Stury, a chamber knight who was Captain of Hammes, in the Pays de Calais, had been expelled from the court for his duplicity. See also, *CA*, p. 87.

[2]   Pope Gregory XI had placed Florence under interdict during the so-called War of the Eight Saints. The refugees in England initially had been arrested but were released on 30 January 1377 and with the status of King's serfs were permitted to trade: *CCR, 1374–7*, p. 422.

[3]   Simon Langham was a Benedictine monk of Westminster Abbey. He was appointed bishop of Ely in 1362 and bishop of London in 1363, the same year he served as Edward III's chancellor. In 1366 the king translated him to Canterbury but he was archbishop for only two years, forced by the king to resign in September 1368 when Urban V created him cardinal of S. Sisto. Employed to effect a rapprochement between England and the Papal Court, Langham died on 22 July 1376. See Emden, *BRUO*, ii. 1096.

The abundance of both wine and water in England after Christmas

In 1377, the fifty-first year of the reign of King Edward III, the great quantities of wine imported into England were such as few past ages had ever seen.

Around Christmas there were such great floods in parts of Northumberland, caused by the melting of the snows which had previously carpeted the ground to a great depth, that, as the water came down from the mountain tops together with pieces of ice, it overthrew farmhouses and carried away in its onset the possessions of the peasants which they had piled up on the ground, namely coals, mill-stones, timbers and harvested crops. And then the floodwater, making its way down to the sea, put out of action or sunk completely various ships, as the pieces of ice collided with the ships with terrific force.[1]

A Parliament in which novelties are sought

At the feast of the purification of the Blessed Virgin [2 February] a parliament was held in London, summoned by the duke of Lancaster.[2] He was acting for the king, who was now ill beyond hope of recovery. At this parliament both clergy and laity were asked for subsidies for the king. He was granted the following unprecedented taxes:[3] on each lay person of either sex older than fourteen, with the exception of acknowledged paupers who begged in the streets, he could levy one groat or four pennies, and from all members of religious orders of both sexes and from any beneficed churchman he could levy twelve pence, and one groat each from the others who were not beneficed, with the exception of the brothers of the four mendicant orders [i.e. the Dominican, Franciscan, Augustinian and Carmelite friars]. They were not scourged by this tax, because they are not with men in the labour of men.

Also in this parliament the statutes of the previous parliament, deservedly called the Good, were annulled, and, since the king wished it, persons who had suffered by its judgements were restored to their former positions.

John Wyclif and his works

About the same time there came to prominence in the university of Oxford a man of the north, called Master John Wyclif, a doctor of theology.[4] In the schools and elsewhere[5] he publicly asserted mistaken, heretical doctrines, which were quite absurd and an attack on the position of the universal church. They also contained a particularly poisonous tirade against monks and other property-owning people in religious orders. He did take the precaution of cloaking his

---

[1]   This may be the same storm recorded by the author of the *Historia vitae et regni Ricardi secundi* as occurring around the feast of St Martin (11 November) 1377 which caused great damage to the fleet assembled by Thomas, earl of Buckingham: *HVRS*, p. 49. Walsingham did not mention the episode in the earliest, 'scandalous' recension of the chronicle.

[2]   In fact parliament met on 27 January: *RP*, ii. 361. Although at Gaunt's suggestion the session was opened by the nine-year-old Prince Richard of Bordeaux taking his late father's seat (as Walsingham recorded in the earliest, 'scandalous' recension of the chronicle: *CA*, p. 111), there was no doubt that Gaunt himself was in control. The committee of magnates appointed to advise the commons in their deliberations were Lancastrian loyalists and Gaunt succeeded in reversing the measures undertaken in the Good Parliament against Latimer, Lyons, Adam Bury and Bishop William of Wykeham whose temporalities were now restored. The session was dissolved on 2 March.

[3]   King Edward's grant of a general pardon for all civil and criminal offences in honour of his jubilee helped to persuade the commons to be open-handed on this occasion.

[4]   In the earliest, 'scandalous' recension of the chronicle, Walsingham introduces Wyclif as the instrument of John of Gaunt and the spread of his heretical teachings as another of the evils conjured by the duke: *CA*, p. 115. Wyclif was born in West Yorkshire probably in the 1330s and was an established scholar at Oxford by the mid-1350s. He was elected to a fellowship at Merton College in 1356. He completed Book I of his *De dominio civili* in 1376 and books two and three the following year. See also A. Hudson, *Premature Reformation: Wyclifite Texts and Lollard History* (Oxford, 1988) pp. 65–7.

[5]   According to the Anonimalle chronicle Wyclif had been preaching in London: *AC*, p. 103.

heresy, and at the same time spread it more widely under choice colours, by assembling followers and members of one party from among his associates at Oxford and elsewhere and dressing them in ankle-length garments of russet, as a sign of their greater perfection.[1] They were to go around barefoot, spreading his heresies among the people and preaching them openly and publicly in their sermons.

Among other errors they held to the following propositions as completely certain. That the Eucharist on the altar after the sacrament is not the real body of Christ but its symbol. That the church of Rome is not the head of all the churches more than any other one church, and that greater power was not given by Christ to Peter than to any other apostle. That, as regards the keys of the church, the pope at Rome does not have greater power than any other ordained priest. That, if there is a God above, temporal lords can legally and rightfully take away the property owned by a church that transgresses. That, if a temporal lord knows of a church that has transgressed, he is bound under threat of damnation to remove its temporal possessions from it. That the Gospel is sufficient guide in this life for any Christian, and that all the other rules of the saints, which are observed as rules of life by the various religious orders, do not add any more perfection to the Gospel than does whitewash to a wall. That neither the pope, nor any other prelate of the church, should have prisons to punish sinners, but that any sinner should be able to go freely wherever he wants and do what he likes. These and many other such doctrines were preached and promulgated so widely by these heretics to the subversion of our faith, that lords and magnates of the land and many of the people warmed to their words and gave support to the preachers of these heresies, particularly because their arguments gave such power to laymen to take away from churchmen and men in religious orders their temporal possessions.

When these doctrines and ravings had been read and made known to the pope, he condemned twenty-three of them as heretical folly, and sent bulls to the archbishop of Canterbury [Simon Sudbury, 1375–81] and the bishop of London [William Courtenay, 1375–81], telling them to use their authority to get John arrested and carefully examined concerning these doctrines. This was done and after John had made a pronouncement on the subject, though it was all lies and empty talk, the archbishop, in the presence of the duke of Lancaster [i.e. John of Gaunt] and Lord Henry Percy,[2] enjoined silence upon Wyclif and all his followers with regard to these matters, and banned him from any future handling and treatment of the subject and from allowing others to spread it abroad.[3] So for a time both Wyclif and his followers were silent. But in the end it was not long before they dared, with the approval of some of the lords of the land, to take up and spread again before laymen the same opinions and others far worse than the ones they had spread previously.

Discord, originating in the church of St Paul, between the clergy, the duke, Lord Henry Percy and the people of London, over John Wyclif

On the very day on which all this took place in London, the citizens of the town, because of a harmful, insolent remark made against the bishop of London by the duke of Lancaster, at once rose up as a body, took up arms, and had it in mind to kill the duke.[4] But the bishop put a

---

[1]   The russet-coloured clothing of Wyclif's supporters was also remarked by the Leicester chronicler, Henry Knighton (vestibus de russeto utebantur) although he interpreted it as indicative of the 'simplicity of their hearts'. He makes no mention of their garments being ankle-length: *Knighton*, pp. 298–301.

[2]   Henry Percy, 1st earl of Northumberland (1341–1408), was created earl and appointed earl marshal in 1377.

[3]   Wyclif was examined at St Paul's Cathedral on Thursday 17 February. The presence of Percy, who held the office of marshal, may represent a move by Gaunt both to intimidate the bishops and to undermine the civic autonomy of the city of London. Walsingham's confidence in the examination process was misplaced. The palpable hostility between Gaunt, Percy and the two bishops brought it to an end before any sanctions against Wyclif could be properly promulgated.

[4]   The unrest occurred on day after Wyclif's examination (18 February) when it was alleged that Percy had exercised his right as marshal to arrest suspected supporters of Wyclif within the city walls. Percy and Gaunt were said to have been dining with Sir John Ipres, and, forewarned of the mob's intent, they made their escape by the river steps and took a boat to the palace at Kennington.

complete stop to this happening. Indeed, if he had not then halted their attempt, these citizens, who were only just held in check by the intervention of a bishop, would have burnt the house of the duke at the Savoy in that moment of madness.[1] In the end they quietened down at the bidding of the bishop, although, among other insults aimed at the duke, they had reversed his arms in the public market place.

But the duke and Henry Percy, whom the citizens had looked for in the duke's house to murder him, had been warned about this great uprising, and had left their meal and fled to the manor of Kennington, where Richard [of Bordeaux], son of the prince of Wales, then happened to be staying with his mother.[2] There, with their hands held up in horror, they made their complaints about the vicious attacks made on them. For these and many other reasons the people of London fell out of favour with the duke, who even got the mayor and the senior officials of the time discharged and deposed from office and had others elected in their place.[3]

The capture of John Misterworth and his death[4]

During these same days the knight John Misterworth, a traitor and deserter, was captured at Pamplona in Navarre and brought to London.[5] He was first drawn and hanged and then beheaded. Finally his body was quartered and sent to four famous cities of England, while his head remained fixed upon London bridge for a long time afterwards. Ambitious, wicked, and a dissimulating liar, he had been disloyal to his king and country and in his greed had converted to his own use huge sums of money which he had received from the king to pay the troops. Because of this and other charges laid at his door, or which should have been laid there, he became afraid that he would at last pay the penalty and die the death he had deserved, and so ran away to the king of France, as I have described earlier.[6] He pledged his loyalty to this king and promised that he would bring up the Spanish fleet for an invasion of the kingdom of England. But a just God justly allowed him to be intercepted and punished, rather than that he should be such a traitor as to fulfil his wicked purpose of criminally making a treacherous and underhand attack on his lord, the king, and on his native soil. [7]

At the same time the envoys, who had departed for France to make peace, brought back to England nothing but rumours of war.[8]

At this time King Edward, during the festival of St George the Martyr [23 April] at Windsor, conferred a knighthood upon Richard of Bordeaux, his heir and the son of his own son, Edward, prince of Wales.[9]

---

[1] The threat to burn Gaunt's Savoy palace, located outside the city on the western border of Fleet Street, was realised twelve years later during the Great Revolt of 1381: see below, pp. 122–3.

[2] Joan, countess of Kent, princess of Wales and Aquitaine, known as the 'fair maid of Kent' (b. 1328). She had married the Black Prince in 1361.

[3] The Londoners were also required to make recompense by displaying Gaunt's arms, in gilt, on a marble pillar at Cheapside.

[4] Walsingham is the only contemporary authority to record the fate of Misterworth (or Miusterworth), a Gloucestershire knight. His earlier exploits and his dispute with Sir Robert Knolles, were recorded in the *Chronica maiora*, under 1370 (*CA*, pp. 65–6) and were also reported by the *Anonimalle Chronicle* (*AC*, pp. 63–5).

[5] Pamplona was the capital city of King Charles II of Navarre.

[6] Misterworth had been a member of the 1370 campaign under the command of Sir Robert Knolles and had blamed the celebrated captain for its shortcomings. Accused of embezzling funds assigned to him for the raising of troops he fled and sought sanctuary in the French court.

[7] In the earliest, 'scandalous' recension of the chronicle, Walsingham reports that Misterworth pledged his loyalty in a letter to the king, but it was suppressed by Gaunt and Percy: *CA*, pp. 135–6.

[8] The truce negotiated at Bruges in 1375 had been maintained for two years but was now perilously close to being broken.

[9] According to the Anonimalle author on this occasion Richard also knighted Thomas of Woodstock, Henry of Derby (the future Henry IV), the heirs of Beaumont, Mowbray, Oxford, Percy, Stafford and even the son of Alice Perrers: *AC*, p. 106.

The death of the king, and those who assembled around the deathbed

On 21 June King Edward died in his palace at Sheen after reigning for almost fifty-one years.[1] It is shameful to record that at his bedside during the whole period of his illness was that unspeakable whore, Alice Perrers, who in his middle age had always satisfied all his desires of the flesh. She did absolutely nothing for the salvation of his soul, nor did she allow others to do anything, but kept continually promising him that he would recover, until she recognised in the closure of his voice the unmistakable signs of death. Then, unbelievably, when she saw that he had lost his powers of speech, that his eyesight was growing dim and that his bodily heat was leaving his extremities, the shameless hussy at once snatched the rings from his fingers and left. Only a priest then sat beside the dying king, since the others were intent on seizing what they could, and, as the king could not speak or make his confession with his lips, this priest persuaded the king to ask forgiveness for his sins by means of a crucifix which he held out and put into his hands.[2] The king took it with the greatest reverence, and kissed it in deep devotion, at one moment stretching out his hands as best he could as a sign that he wished for forgiveness, and at another pouring forth floods of tears from his eyes and kissing the feet of the image over and over again. At last, when at a nod from the priest he had asked for forgiveness for his sins, with such movements and signs as he could make, from God first and foremost and secondly from all creatures whom knowingly or unwittingly he had offended, he gave up the ghost. His body was buried at Westminster with all reverence.[3]

Among all the world's kings and princes he had been a glorious king, benevolent, merciful and magnificent. His nickname was 'the man of grace', on account of that singular grace in which he excelled. In this gift of grace of exceptional quality given him by heaven, he surpassed all his predecessors. He was big-hearted, for, although he sometimes saw that he was about to suffer unfortunate setbacks or forthcoming troubles, he never grew pale or changed his countenance. He was also famous and fortunate in war; in all his battles, by land and sea, he always won the day and triumphed gloriously.[4] He was friendly, unassuming and gentle to all men, whether strangers or acquaintances. He had a warm love for all his subjects, promoting their interests and ruling them with piety. He was a man of God, often going on pilgrimage and reverencing and honouring the ministers of his Church. In the concerns of his kingdom he showed foresight, flexibility and judgement. He was softly spoken and courteous in the pleasant manner of his speech, and restrained and adult in his behaviour and gestures. He was like a father to orphans. He shared the sufferings of the afflicted and the sorrows of the sad. He lifted up the oppressed and gave help at the right time to all the needy. Indeed in his bestowing of benefits he was always readily generous beyond all living men. He set a limit to the abundance of his possessions. He was not puffed up or proud, but always self-controlled. To his inferiors he behaved as an equal, and among the rulers and princes of the world he showed himself the master.

He took care and trouble to get buildings put up, and in various places in his kingdom several buildings of outstanding craftsmanship and elegant structure were completed on most beautiful

---

[1]   The king had been seriously ill for sometime. The cause of death appears to have been a stroke. At the time of his death, Edward III was celebrating his jubilee year. Proclaimed king in 1327, he did not assume personal rule until 1330. He had reigned longer than any of his predecessors except Henry III (1216–72). At his passing contemporary commentators celebrated his achievements; Froissart described him as second only to King Arthur in the annals of English history: Froissart, *Chroniques*, viii. 230; FCBuchon, i. 709.

[2]   Walsingham is the only contemporary authority to claim that the king was deserted at the last and the only one to record the presence of Alice Perrers. A fuller account of her avarice appears in the earliest 'scandalous' recension: *CA*, pp. 142–3. The king's surgeon, Adam Raise, was well known at St Albans and perhaps provided these details.

[3]   The king's body was carried from Sheen to London in a procession lasting three days. According to the Anonimalle author the burial took place on Sunday 5 July: *AC*, p. 106. Froissart describes the procession of the coffin through the city of London, accompanied by 24 knights clothed in black: Froissart, *Chroniques*, viii. 230–1; FCBuchon, i. 709.

[4]   Edward's most notable victories were the naval battle at Sluys in 1340, and the pitched land battles at Crécy and Poitiers (1346 and 1356).

sites at great expense.[1] He showed restraint when he experienced joys and he sat lightly to losses. His recreations were hawking and hunting, on which he spent a lot of time, whenever he was free and the season of the year allowed. He was a cheerful and generous giver, and a big spender. His body had an elegance about it and in height he neither exceeded the norm nor sank into short-ness. His face was like an angel's and more worthy of reverence than a human face usually is. So marvellous a grace shone from it that, if someone looked at it in actuality or dreamed about the king at night, he would certainly expect that cheering comforts would come his way that day. And because Edward was famed for the general goodness of his behaviour, to live under him was to be a king, or so his subjects thought. Indeed so far had his fame spread among distant, foreign nations that those who were subject to his dominion or in some alliance with him thought them-selves happy to be so. For they believed there was no kingdom under heaven which had brought forth such a noble, eminent and fortunate king or which, on his death, would produce one in the future.

However even in his old age he did not cease from excessive, wanton sexual couplings, that aforesaid whore A. P. [Alice Perrers] being shameless enough to lead him on, so men said. Indeed it was thought that he ended his life the sooner because of this excess.

At this point I must briefly note that, just as at the beginning of his reign all the popular successes one after another made him renowned and famous, so, as he moved towards old age and went down the sky to his sunset, the happy events were gradually driven out by his sins and grew fewer, while many unfortunate and unlucky disasters mushroomed in their place. I am sad to say that these diminished his fame.[2]

---

[1]   Edward's most significant building work was at Windsor which he remodelled during the 1350s and '60s: his clerk of works was William Wykeham, later bishop of Winchester, and one of the ministers at the centre of the allegations in the Good Parliament. See also Ormrod, *Edward III*, pp. 56–7.

[2]   The last five years of his reign were marked by a succession of military failures; plagued by illness, the Black Prince made an ignominious return from his final campaign in 1371; in his and his father's absence many of the lands annexed in earlier phases of the war were lost to the French whilst the chevauchées of John of Gaunt and other captains failed to draw the enemy into a further pitched battle. In 1372 the English fleet under the command of the earl of Pembroke was destroyed by Castilian galleys off the coast of La Rochelle. See also Ormrod, *Reign of Edward III*, pp. 28–9.

The Reign of King Richard II

The Londoners invite the future king to come to London

In 1377, upon the news of the death of King Edward III on 21 June, which was the eve of the feast of St Alban, first martyr of the English [22 June], the citizens of London sent some of their more prominent members to Kennington, where both the prince and his mother the princess were then staying, to pay the respects of the city and citizens of London to them. John Philipot, a citizen of London, who had been chosen to speak on behalf of his fellow citizens, made the following speech:[1]

> 'Our news, your excellency, is such that we cannot bring it without great sadness. For there is no doubt that death is at hand for our invincible king Edward, who, I might say, has governed and ruled us and this kingdom for many decades in unbroken peace, and who now, with the signs of death clear upon him, ceases to be our ruler. So on behalf of the citizens and city of London we ask that you, our next king and the only one we recognise as king, will show your highness's approval of your city, which is your chamber. We shall be subject to the commands and directed by the decisions of you alone, in obedience to your lordship and as servants of your person and your words. And, so that we may make the other pronouncements required of our embassy, your highness should know that your city is distressed beyond words that you have long withdrawn your presence from the city which is known to be so devoted to you that it is ready on your behalf to give up not only its possessions but also, if necessary, its life. So we come before you to make our prayer that you may be willing to stay among us, as a comfort for the citizens as well as for your own safety and solace. We also beseech you, most illustrious prince, to agree to put an end to the discord which the quarrels of certain people have recently caused to arise between our citizens and our lord, the duke of Lancaster, and which has brought losses to many and gain to nobody. Such a settlement would be profitable both for the duke himself and for our citizens.'

When these and similar requests had been made, the prince and his council replied that he would try to satisfy their desires on all these points. So, sent away with this answer, the envoys took back the happy news to their fellow citizens.

The peace made between the duke [of Lancaster] and the Londoners

On the following day, the feast of St Alban [22 June], the king sent to London [William] Lord Latimer, Sir Nicholas Bond,[2] Sir Simon Burley[3] and Sir Richard Abberbury.[4] They greeted the citizens in the name of the new king (for, as I have said, King Edward had died the previous day),

---

[1]   Philipot (d.1384) was a member of the city's Grocers' company and served as mayor and sheriff (1372–3, 1378–9). This episode, including Philipot's speech, is not recorded by other contemporary authorities. See also Barron, *London*, pp. 333–4.

[2]   Sir Nicholas Bond had been a chamber knight of the Black Prince since at least 1361 and shortly before his death became a member of the household of Joan of Kent. He was one of three knights – the others being Sir Richard Abberbury and Sir Simon Burley appearing alongside him here – who had served as master of Prince Richard, that is to say as his custodian and guardian. Bond remained close to the young king in the opening days of the reign and is said to have carried the exhausted ten-year-old in his arms after his coronation.

[3]   Sir Simon Burley (c. 1336–88), had passed his early career as a knight in the service of the Black Prince, fighting alongside him at Najera in 1367. Like Sir Nicholas Bond (see above) he served as master to Prince Richard and now held the office of under chamberlain in his household. He remained a close confidant of the king for the first decade of his reign.

[4]   Like Sir Nicholas Bond and Sir Simon Burley, Sir Richard Abberbury began his career in the service of Edward the Black Prince and like them he served for a time as master to Prince Richard. At his accession, he became a knight of the chamber.

bringing to them both sad tidings of the death of the old king and happy news about the disposition of the new king: for he promised that he would show his affection for them and their city by coming to it and living in it, as they had asked.[1] And, discharging further commands from the new king, they said that the king had spoken to the duke on their behalf, and that the duke had submitted to all his wishes on this matter. And so, they said, it was the king's will that the citizens also should themselves make submission to him in the same way, and he would then work out how peace might be established between them, to the honour of the citizens and the advantage of their city.

But the citizens were alarmed at this method of peacemaking, and answered that they completely refused to do what he asked, particularly as they knew that the king was a boy and too weak to act as their champion in such an important matter, and that their case would not be heard by the king but by their own enemies and deadly foes, who would inflict punishment upon them by their decisions, if they, the citizens, agreed to the commands of the king on this issue. At last, after they had discussed the matter for six hours or more, they came to this agreement, that, if the knights who had come as envoys were willing to swear to the citizens that their submission would result in no loss of goods or physical injury for any citizen or in any decision prejudicial to their city, they, the citizens, would willingly acquiesce in the king's demands. And these knights, in their eagerness to satisfy the wishes of the king and to work for the peace of the citizens, solemnly promised them on their oath of loyalty as knights that, if they submitted to the king as the duke had previously done, this would not be to their harm but to their advantage.

After receiving this assurance, the citizens made their way to the king's manor at Sheen, where they found the new king, his mother, the duke of Lancaster and his brothers, the sons of the late king and several bishops all congregated around the body of the dead king. When Richard heard of their arrival, he immediately gave orders for them to be summoned to his presence, and they, as before, begged him to use his best efforts to bring about peace between the duke and themselves. For their part, they were ready to submit to the king's judgement in all matters but not as though they were people who were confessing that they had wronged the duke in any way. They had come at this time to establish peace and to honour both the king and the duke by soothing the spirits and allaying the wrath of both men

When the duke saw that the citizens had made this form of submission to the king, he was highly delighted by it. He put aside all the bitterness he had felt against them, and, rushing to the feet of the king, he begged him to undertake their case in the form in which they had expressed it, and asked that those who had been imprisoned for some crime imputed to them should be released by the king's grace, and that if there were any who were in danger of losing a limb or life for a reason of this kind, that the king of his grace should restore to them their life and limbs.

The duke himself also pardoned the citizens for any wrong they had done to him in any matter, and received them into the fullness of his grace, declaring under oath in the presence of the king that he would be their friend and would look after their interests as though they were his very own. And as a sign that this was not a simulated peace, he there and then in the presence of the king kissed each one of them individually. And so the citizens were sent away to their homes in peace.[2]

And on returning there, they praised God for the miracles he had done and gave thanks to Alban, blessed protomartyr of the English, that on the anniversary of his passion this unexpected peace had been given to them, and confessed that it was their prayers to him which had brought them help in their urgent need. For they had previously on this matter sought his support with the most heartfelt supplications. Who would have believed that the same duke, who yesterday had been in control of the whole land, could today have been brought to such humility without a manifest miracle?

---

1   In the earliest, 'scandalous' recension of the chronicle, Walsingham cites the text of the king's message in full: *CA*, pp. 147–8.
2   For the quarrel between Lancaster and the Londoners see above, pp. 30–1.

On the following Friday the duke and the commons of the city of London met at Westminster, and it was proclaimed by the voice of a herald that the duke and the citizens had entered upon a period of peace and concord. When this had been done, all returned rejoicing to their homes.

The young king makes peace with many and releases Sir Peter de la Mare from captivity

Indeed the young king, prompted by his innate goodness, desired peace among all his subjects and at the beginning of his reign restored peace, harmony and unity to the relationship between the duke and the bishop of Winchester.[1] But also whenever he found out that some dispute had arisen in his kingdom, he took the quarrel into his own hands, promising an outcome that would be advantageous and profitable to both parties. It was a happy augury in such a young boy that of his own accord and at no one's instigation he was so concerned about peace, and that he should be aware of the blessings of peace for his people without anyone teaching him this lesson!

Nor must I forget to mention that as soon as he was honoured with the name of king he took the decision to release Sir Peter de la Mare. He had been imprisoned in Nottingham castle and was being kept in safe custody there because of the loyalty he had shown to his king and his kingdom, when, in the parliament held at Westminster in the last year of King Edward, as the knight chosen to be their speaker by the commons on that occasion, he had refused to consent to the taxes demanded during that parliament. And so that Sir Peter might be completely protected from the attacks of his enemies, the king publicly freed and released him from all those things which could be demanded of him or imposed upon him in the name of the king. Sir Peter immediately hurried to London to give his thanks to the king.

You could have seen the people in every town and village going out to greet him with great joy and saying with no less enthusiasm than once they had said to the blessed Thomas[2] when he returned from exile, 'Blessed is he, who comes in the name of the Lord.'[3] And the Londoners themselves also greeted him and showed with various gifts and presents how highly they regarded him.

The town of Rye is captured and burned by the French

At dawn on the feast day of the apostles Peter and Paul [21 June] about five thousand Frenchmen with fifty ships of different sizes attacked the town of Rye. After just a short struggle they captured the town, although the citizens, confident in their own strength, had declared and made a firm promise that no one would take away any of their moveable property from the town. So that because of their love of possessions they at least put up a brave show in the battle. But like the sons of Ephraim they bent and shot the bow[4] but turned tail on the day of battle, and the result of this folly was that the town of Rye with all its property was taken by the French.

But when the abbot of Battle[5] heard this sad news, he collected together his able-bodied men and held a council to discuss how to prevent the French from sacking and looting the towns and

---

[1]   William Wykeham, (b. 1324) was bishop of Winchester from 1366 until his death in 1404. He had a distinguished career in royal service, holding the office of keeper of the Privy Seal from 1364 and serving for two periods as chancellor, the first from 1368–71.

[2]   i.e. Thomas Becket, archbishop of Canterbury from 1162 until his assassination in 1170. From 1164 Becket spent six years and one month in exile, returning on 30 November 1170, barely four weeks before his assassination. According to his biographer, Herbert of Bosham, a crowd gathered to greet him when he landed near Sandwich; shortly afterwards his party was confronted by hostile officers of the king, but as he approached Canterbury on the following day, they were said to have been met by celebratory processions from every village on the route. Walsingham may have derived this reference directly from Herbert's text. See above, p. 17.

[3]   Psalm 118: 26.

[4]   Zechariah 9: 13.

[5]   The Benedictine abbey of Battle was barely a dozen miles from Rye and a little over half that distance from Winchelsea. By far the largest religious house in the region, the abbot and convent were bound to assume responsibility for the defence of the coastal towns. The abbot was Haimo of Offington (d. 1384), who had held office since 1364. See also below, pp. 46, 109.

fields and to stop them from roaming any more widely over the countryside. Such questions had kept the abbot awake all one night when one of the Frenchmen sent out to forage was taken prisoner by one of the abbot's servants. The abbot asked him about the plans of the French, and he said that they intended to hold on to Rye for ten days.

In his efforts to prevent the French from doing any more damage to the neighbouring towns and those situated on the coast, the abbot took himself and his men to the town of Winchelsea, which is near Rye, on the very day on which, according to the prisoner, the French intended to make an armed attack on the town. But when the French saw the abbot and his men assembled in Winchelsea, they gave up hope of advancing any further into the countryside and began to set fire to all parts of the town of Rye. In five hours they had reduced the whole town to ashes, including its wonderfully beautiful church. They took away four of the richer citizens as prisoners, and killed sixty-six of the townsmen, while only losing eight men themselves. After they had burned Rye, they returned to their ships a little before sunset, taking with them on their ships forty-two casks of wine that they had found in the town. And so leaving Rye a wasteland, they entrusted themselves to the deeps of the sea with the plunder which they had taken.

On 5 July the body of the illustrious King Edward was honourably buried at Westminster.

The anger of the Londoners against the justiciar, [Sir] Robert Bealknapp[1]

During these same days the king, remembering his promise, had made an appearance in London. The citizens welcomed him with generous gifts of different kinds, and they deserved to be greeted by him with the honour that was fitting. And soon afterwards, by a universal decree of lords and magnates, [Thursday] the 16 July, that is the seventeenth day before the first of August, was appointed as the day for the king's coronation. Invitations to it were sent to both ecclesiastics and laymen, in order that so important a ceremony should be carried out with all due solemnity.[2]

Meanwhile those high-ranking men, who by ancestral right were concerned in various aspects of the administration of the coronation, asked that their duties should be assigned to them. The judges carefully considered the hereditary rights of each one of them and sensibly appointed to each man his duty, so that no disputes should arise on a day of such solemnity. And if there was a dispute which could not be settled at that time, they postponed it until after the coronation, and appointed certain persons to carry out the duties concerned properly, with the rights of both parties being safeguarded.

The Londoners demanded the office which belonged to them, namely that of being butler. But Sir Robert Bealknapp, the king's chief justice in the Court of Common Pleas, replied to them rather tactlessly and said, 'Sirs, butlers perform many duties. Some draw off the wine, some bring it to the banquet, some pour it out when it has been brought, some carry it to the guests sitting around the hall, while yet others wash up the vessels concerned, namely the pots, the ewers and the bowls. And so there is no point in you asking to be assigned the office of butler, unless you specify which duty it is you want.' When the citizens heard this, they at once angrily replied that it was not their duty to wash the dishes, and that they had better dishes of their own than he did, which they wanted to test out on his head. And so the citizens departed in great anger with threats against Sir Robert, and they would have killed him, if afterwards he could have been found in the city. But because they were not able to seize him, they made an effigy of his head as an insult to his

---

1   Sir Robert Bealknapp (d. c.1400) was chief justice of common pleas from 1366. He was involved in the suppression of the peasants' rebellion in the summer of 1381 and later served as commissioner for the defence of the Kent coast. He was knighted in 1385 but two years later he was forced into exile in Ireland for his opposition to the parliamentary process against Michael de la Pole, earl of Suffolk. He was pardoned and returned in 1397. Walsingham is the only authority for the episode recounted here.

2   According to Froissart, there was a determination amongst the councillors that Richard should be crowned as soon as possible so that under his authority the government might act decisively against the French: 'they declared with one accord "We must make haste to crown our king and then go against the French, before they do us any further damage" ': Froissart, *Chroniques*, viii. 232; FCBuchon, i. 710.

person and placed it above the aqueduct in Cheapside, so that it would be pouring out wine from its mouth on the arrival of the king and the people.

The magnificent cavalcade of the king on the day before his coronation[1]

On the day preceding the king's coronation, magnates and a large number of people from the kingdom had flocked into London, as I have mentioned above, and a little after three o'clock in the afternoon the nobles of the land with the Londoners and many others whom their love for the king had brought to town, mounted on high-stepping steeds, hurried to the Tower where the king was then staying.

And when they had then arranged there who should go in front and who should follow, they began to ride to Westminster through the streets of the city packed with people. The city indeed had been decorated with so many banners of gold and silver and silk and with so many other devices to delight the minds of the onlookers that you might have thought you were seeing in London the actual triumphs of the Caesars or looking upon the surpassing splendour of Rome as it once was. So many people had gathered there that the packed streets could not hold them all, but, as I might say,

> On steps ascending to the cross on high
> Stand crowds, while others keen to see their king
> The high walls crown in hours of patient waiting.[2]

In this great procession first came the citizens of Bayeux, with at their head a group of musicians playing flutes, trumpets, drums and other tuneful instruments.[3] These were followed by one of the districts of the city which they call 'wards', and they were in their own party with loud music. There followed them the German mercenaries of the king, who were themselves different in their dress from the others. Then there followed another ward of the city, like to the first in its appearance. It was followed by Gascons, whose splendidly colourful clothes were different from those of the previous groups. Soon also the citizens of London, who had been left waiting, followed the Gascons in a cavalcade so long that it numbered about three thousand, seven hundred in one company. These were followed by the earls and barons of the kingdom, with their knights and esquires, in clothing similar to that of their king. For they were all dressed in white, a colour symbolising the king's innocence. The Captal de Buch[4] with his men rode proudly in his company between the king and the lords. Then came the marshal of England, who at that time was Lord Henry Percy [earl of Northumberland], and the duke of Lancaster [John of Gaunt], steward of the Kingdom Surrounded by the same knights, and riding on tall, noble steeds they went in front to make a safe passage for the king through the crowds. And it actually happened that, although they had previously been objects of dread not only to the common people but also to the very magnates of the kingdom because of their great riches and the numbers of their attendants, on this ride they behaved so courteously and bade the crowds to make way with such good-tempered eloquence that neither on that day nor the next did a single person in that huge crowd receive any verbal or physical abuse of any kind. The result was that they won the favour of almost the whole people, who previously had regarded them with hateful suspicion.

The king followed behind them, riding on a great warhorse fit for his majesty and regally caparisoned. [Sir] Simon Burley carried the king's sword in front of him, holding it high in his hands. And [Sir] Nicholas Bond, walking on foot, led the king's horse by its bridle. Behind the king came his knights and contemporaries, and the members of his royal household. Nor were great numbers of clarions and trumpets missing from this large company. For any procession has

---

1   It was the tradition that a procession was made on the eve of a coronation from the Tower to Westminster, but for this, the first coronation for more than fifty years, the route was extended to include Cheapside, Fleet Street and the Strand.
2   Walter of Châtillon, *Alexandrais*, PL, ccix, 518.
3   Walsingham appears to be in error here. It was more likely that the men of Bayonne (Gascony) led the procession.
4   Jean Grailly (d.1377) was Captal de Buch (Gironde). He was succeeded by Archambaud.

its own trumpeters going along in front, and trumpeters had also been stationed by the Londoners on the aqueduct and on a tower in the same marketplace which had been raised in honour of the king, in order to blow their trumpets as the king passed by. All of them blew their trumpets in unison at the same moment, and produced a marvellous sound for the listeners. That day was a day of light-hearted gladness and of the braying of trumpets, a day long awaited which brought back to our land the peace and the laws which had now for a long time been in exile owing to the sloth of an old king and the avarice of his toadies.

And to honour the king still further, the citizens had decided that wine in abundance should flow through the pipes of the aqueduct,[1] and that the flow should be continuous for the whole three hours or more of the procession. Also a castle with four turrets had been built in the higher part of the marketplace that is called Cheapside, and wine in abundance flowed down from this as well in two directions. Also on its turrets had been positioned four beautiful girls, of the same stature and age as the king,[2] one on each turret. As the king approached from afar, they blew down golden leaves on to his face, and, as he came nearer, they threw down flowers seemingly made of gold on to him and his warhorse. And when he reached the front of the castle, they were given gilt cups, and, filling them with wine at the pipes of the fort, they offered them to the king and his lords. On the top of the castle, which had been raised high inside its four turrets like a dice, was positioned a gold angel, holding a crown. It had been fashioned with such cleverness that, as the king approached, it leaned forward and held out the crown to him. And there were many other things devised in the king's honour in London on that day, which it would take a long time to mention one by one. For throughout its streets and squares individuals were competing to see who could show the most enthusiastic reverence to the king. So, amid the great jubilation of the people and citizens and to the great joy of the lords and nobles, the king was escorted to the palace near the monastery at Westminster, where he spent that night.

The ceremony of the king's coronation

On Thursday 16 July, the eve of the feast of St Kenelm, once a king, the archbishop and bishops and the nobles of the kingdom assembled at Westminster very early in the morning. A procession of monks [of Westminster Abbey] wearing copes was drawn up, and the bishops with the monks came to the door of the king's chamber. There they found the king had been made ready at the hands of his attendants, and they conducted him to the church of St Peter, while they chanted the antiphon in honour of the apostle together with a suitable prayer and also this prayer, 'O god, you who visit the humble and comfort us with your mercy, extend that mercy to your servant, our king, so that in him we may experience your coming among us.'

As soon as the king arrived at the altar, he knelt down on the pavement before the altar, which had been covered with cloaks and carpets.[3] After the prayer I have mentioned had been said, the archbishop and those bishops who were present knelt on the floor around the king, while two bishops reverently chanted the litany. When this was finished, the king was raised up and led to his chair, while the choir sang this antiphon, 'Let your hand be strengthened.' Then the bishop preached a sermon to the people on the subject of the king and his kingdom, showing how the king should behave towards his people, and in what ways the people owed him obedience.

After the sermon, the king took his oath before the archbishop and the magnates who were present in the abbey, since they alone were able to hear his oath. He swore that he would allow the church to enjoy her liberties, that he would respect her and her ministers, that he would keep to the true faith and that he would put a stop to plunder and all acts of injustice in all classes of people. Secondly he swore that he would ensure that the good laws of the land were everywhere upheld (particularly the laws of King Edward the Confessor [1042–65], now a saint, who lay

---

1   The *Anonimalle* author records that the wine was both red and white: *AC*, p. 108.
2   Walsingham is the only authority to have observed the age of these girls.
3   According to the *Anonimalle* author a scaffold had been constructed from where the monks and priests might perform the office: *AC*, p. 109.

buried in that very church), and that the bad laws were repealed. Thirdly he swore that he would be no respecter of persons but would judge fairly between man and man, and take special pains to show mercy, just as a forgiving and merciful God was then granting him the favour of his mercy.[1]

Next the archbishop, preceded by the marshal of England, Lord Henry Percy, turned to all parts of the church, repeating the king's oath to the people, and asking if they were willing to make submission to such a prince and ruler and to obey his commands. And the people replied with a mighty shout[2] that they were willing without any compulsion so to obey him. Then the archbishop blessed the king in these words of prayer,

> Almighty and everlasting God, bless, O Lord, this our king. You who govern all earthly kingdoms, so bless and glorify him that he may wield his sceptre with the loftiness of King David, and that he may be found gracious, when glorified with his merits. Grant him with your inspiration to rule his people with gentleness, just as you enabled Solomon to rule over his kingdom in peace. May he always have for you the fear of a subject and serve you with a quiet mind. May your shield protect him and his nobles, and by your grace may he emerge the victor everywhere. Honour him before all the kings of the nations. May he happily rule over his peoples, and may the nations happily reverence him. May his life among the companies of all peoples be marked with magnanimity. May he be unparalleled for the equity of his judgements and enriched with the abundance of your grace, as the ruler of a prosperous country. Bestow blessings upon his children and give to his years length of life, so that in his days justice may arise among us. Enable him to keep his royal throne secure, and in the eternal kingdom to be justly and happily proud.

This benediction was sung by the archbishop after the first prayer by way of a preface, and, after it was sung, he said another prayer over the king, namely 'O ineffable God,' with its antiphon, 'Be comforted and be a brave man, etc.'

Then the archbishop approached the king and undressed him apart from his vest, ripping his garments from the top right down to the bottom with his hands. The wardens of the Cinque Ports by virtue of their office held over the king a large, blue screen of silk, attached to four spears at its four corners. This they kept in position throughout the ceremony, in the procession to the abbey as well as during the anointing and the mass, and, after the mass, on the return to the palace from the church. But despite this screen, just before the archbishop divested the king of his garments, the earls brought up a cloth of gold, under which the king was concealed as he received the sacrament of anointing.[3] As I have said, the archbishop stripped him of his clothing and then anointed his hands with the holy oil, saying as he did so, 'Just as Samuel anointed David king, so may these hands of yours be anointed with the holy oil that anointed the hands of the kings and prophets, so that you may be blessed and made king in this kingdom and over this people, given to you by the Lord God to rule and govern.' He also said the prayer, 'Look down, Almighty God.'

After this, the archbishop anointed his head, and his chest and his shoulders, and both his elbows, saying 'May this head of yours, chest, shoulders and elbows be anointed with the holy oil, etc,' as above. While this was happening, the choir sang the antiphon, 'Zadok the priest and Nathan the prophet anointed Solomon king at Gihon [1 Kings 1: 45], and the people going up joyfully shouted, 'Long live the King. Alleluia.' Then the archbishop added the prayer,

> O God, may the son of God, Jesus Christ, our Lord, who was anointed by the Father with the oil of exultation before his fellows, himself pour upon your head through this present pouring of the holy oil the spirit of the Paraclete, and may he cause its blessing to penetrate to your inmost heart, so that you may be judged fit to receive invisible gifts by means of this gift that can be seen and touched, and to reign for ever with him in heaven, when you have finished your just rule over your earthly kingdom.

---

[1]   This was substantially the same oath taken by his grandfather some fifty years before, but according to the official record, Richard also undertook to uphold such laws as his subjects 'justly and reasonably' (juste et rationabiliter) should choose.

[2]   The *Anonimalle* author has 'ils ove graunde crye et noyse responderent': *AC*, p. 110.

[3]   The *Anonimalle* author records that Lord Furnival held his right hand as the archbishop anointed him: *ibid.*

Then, when the prayer was finished, the archbishop with the bishop began the hymn, 'Come Creator, Spirit,' while the king knelt in a long plea for pardon, with the archbishop and his suffragans around him.

When the hymn was finished, the king was lifted to his feet by the archbishop, who put on him first the tunic and then the dalmatic of St Edward[1] with a stole arranged around his neck, while saying appropriate prayers. Then the archbishop with the bishops handed him the sword, with these words,

> Receive this sword, given to you as king, from the hands of your bishops, which, though unworthy, are hands consecrated with the powers and authority of the holy apostles. Through the office of our benediction it is ordained by God for the defence of his holy church. Remember the words of the prophecy of the Psalmist, 'Have your thigh girt ready with your sword, warrior king,' [Psalm, 45: 3] so that with its aid you may exercise the power of righteousness, forcibly destroy the weight of wickedness, and fight for and protect the holy church of God and its faithful people, while cursing and destroying those who are no more true to their faith than the enemies of Christianity. Armed with this sword, may you mercifully help and defend widows and children, restore the desolate places, preserve those that are restored, avenge injustice and reinforce what has been done for good, so that in doing this, as an illustrious champion of justice glorious in the triumph of your virtues, you may deserve to reign without end together with the Saviour of the world, whose image you bear in your name.

Then two earls girded him with the sword.

Next the archbishop delivered to him the bracelets, saying, 'Receive the bracelets, badge of uprightness and wisdom and of God's embrace, so that you may know that all your operations against enemies, visible and invisible, are able to be well-armed.' Afterwards the archbishop invested him with the royal pallium, saying, 'Receive the pallium, decorated with the four angels, so that from it you may take the knowledge that the four quarters of the world are subject to the divine power, and that no one can rule successfully on earth, unless the power of ruling has been given to him from on high.'

And while the archbishop was blessing the royal crown, two earls, whose office it was, put on his spurs.[2] When the crown was blessed, the archbishop put it on his head, saying, 'May God crown you with the crown of glory and justice and with the honour that comes from deeds of bravery, so that, through the office of our benediction, with a firm faith and abundant fruit of good works you may arrive at the crown of the everlasting kingdom.' Then the archbishop gave him the ring with these words, 'Receive the ring of royal dignity. Just as through this ring, the token of the life of the Catholic faith, you are today ordained head and prince of this kingdom and people, so through it you will continue to be the author and stabiliser of Christianity and the Christian faith, and, successful in your works and rich in your faith, will reign in glory with the king of kings.'

Immediately after this Lord Furnival[3] came up and as his office offered him the red glove, which the archbishop blessed and placed on the king's hand. Then he gave him the sceptre while he said these words, 'Receive the sceptre, the sign of royal power, the proper staff of kingship, the rod of virtue, so that with it you may first rule yourself well, and by your royal virtue defend from attacks of wicked people that holy church, which is Christ's people entrusted to you. With it may you make straight the crooked and bring peace to the good and with your help direct them so that they can keep to the right path. Thus may you pass from your earthly kingdom to the kingdom of heaven.' Then the archbishop put in the king's other hand the rod, which had a dove on its top (the sceptre, which he had received and was holding in his gloved hand, rose up from a round

---

[1]   A wide-sleeved vestment with vents in either side, commonly worn by priests, but since the reign of Edward the Confessor (1042–65) customarily worn by English monarchs at their coronation.
[2]   According to the *Anonimalle Chronicle* both Lord Furnivall, recorded here by Walsingham, and Edmund Mortimer, earl of March, were in attendance during these rites: *AC*, p. 111.
[3]   William, lord Furnival or Furnivall (1326–83). His title was inherited by Thomas Neville (d.1407) who married William's daughter and heir, Joan, in 1379.

golden ball and had an image of the cross on its top). The king received the rod to the accompaniment of these words, 'Receive the rod of virtue and equity, so that you may know how to comfort the good and frighten the bad. Teach the path to those who stray, offer your hand to those who fall, bring down the proud and lift up the humble, so that our Lord, Jesus Christ, may open the door to you.'

After this the king was blessed by the archbishop with these words, 'God bless you and keep you. Just as he has wished you to be king over his people, so may he grant you to be the fortunate consort of his eternal felicity in this world below.' When this had been done, the king kissed the bishops and abbots, who then immediately led him to the royal throne, while the bishops began the hymn, 'We praise you, O Lord.' When the hymn was finished, the archbishop spoke these words, 'Stand firm and from now on keep the place, which you have now inherited by right of succession from your father. I declare that it has been assigned to you by the authority of Almighty God and by being handed to you by all us bishops and other servants of God here present. You must remember that, as a cleric is nearer to the sacred altars, the greater is the honour you are to pay him in appropriate places, so that the mediator between God and men may confirm you as the mediator of your people as you sit on your kingdom's throne, and so that our Lord, Jesus Christ may make you reign in his eternal kingdom.'

The Coronation Mass

When this had been done, the Mass appropriate for the king's coronation was begun. Its office was, 'Look down, O God, our protector etc.,' its epistle, 'Submit yourselves to every human creature for the sake of God etc.' [1 Peter 2: 13], its gradual, 'Lord, direct my prayer,' the Alleluia, 'O Lord in virtue,' its gospel, 'The Pharisees going away' [Matthew 12: 14], and its offertory, 'Listen to my prayer, my king'.[1] The gospel was read by the bishop of Ely [Thomas Arundel, 1374–88] and the epistle by the bishop of Worcester.[2]

When the gospel had been read, the king was escorted from his royal throne to make the offering. So first he offered his sword which he had received to the archbishop, and then as much gold as he pleased, though, as the custom was, not less than a mark: for he can offer more to God and St Peter, if he so wishes. After the offering of the money, he offered the archbishop the bread and the wine, following monastic custom, from which the archbishop and the king himself were afterwards communicated. Next the earl, whose office it was to carry the sword in front of the king, bought back at a given price the sword which the king had offered up, and, receiving it, carried it in front of the king.[3] When the Mass had been celebrated up to the point of communion, the king was conducted to the altar, and kneeling down before the archbishop said, 'I confess.' After his absolution the king received communion and was escorted back to this seat.

Events at the coronation banquet

Meanwhile a knight called Sir John Dymock had been making himself ready.[4] He proclaimed that he had the right of defending the rights of the king on that day and even, if necessary, fighting a duel, if anyone should dare to assert that the king had no right to the kingdom of England. Indeed Sir Baldwin Freville had previously claimed this same office but with no success. So Sir John Dymock came to the doors of the church at the end of the Mass, wearing splendid armour and sitting on a warhorse with very beautiful trappings and with its head and chest also covered in armour. Sir John had taken the horse from the king's stable, using over the horse the same ancient

---

1   Amidst all these liturgical details, Walsingham omits the Collect, 'Quaesimus omnipotens Deus'.
2   Henry Wakefield, Bishop of Worcester from 1375 until his death in March 1395.
3   The *Anonimalle Chronicle* identifies this as Henry of Bolingbroke, earl of Derby (b.1366), the eldest son of John of Gaunt and the future King Henry IV: *AC*, p. 114.
4   It was customary for the king's champion to issue a formal challenge to his opponents at the close of the coronation ceremony. Sir John Dymock (d.1381) was a Lincolnshire knight who had represented his county in the parliaments of 1372, 1373 and 1377. His claim to the title of king's champion was derived from the ancient rights of the manor of Scrivelsby, which he held.

custom that he had used in choosing arms from the king's treasury. For in order to perform his office he had chosen according to his wishes the best horse except one and the best set of armour except one. So he came to the door of the monastery, preceded by two horsemen who carried his spear and his shield, and waited there for the Mass to end. But the marshal, Lord Henry Percy, who was about to make a way in front of the king, came up to Sir John, accompanied by the steward of England, that is the duke, and the constable, Sir Thomas Woodstock, and the brother of the same marshal, Sir Thomas Percy,[1] all riding on great warhorses, and said that Sir John should not have come at that hour, but should have put off his arrival until the royal banquet. So he advised him to come back later, and to take off his vast load of armour and rest until then. The knight went away, intending to follow the advice of the marshal.[2]

Immediately after the departure of Sir John, the king was carried on the shoulders of his knights all the way to the royal palace, preceded by the lords riding on their warhorses and also by a great crowd of players of different types. He was carried right into his chamber, where he rested for a short while, as he was feeling weak from his efforts and had eaten little.

Later he went to the Hall, where he created four new earls before he took his place at table. His uncle, Sir Thomas [of] Woodstock, he made earl of Buckingham, with a grant of one thousand marks a year from the royal treasury, until his own lands provided him with a similar revenue.[3] Also Sir Giuchard d'Angle, once his tutor, he made earl of Huntingdon, also with a yearly grant of one thousand marks until his own revenues provided him with a similar sum.[4] Lord [John] Mowbray he made earl of Nottingham, and Lord Henry Percy earl of Northumberland. He also created nine knights on that day.[5]

After this ceremony, he took his place at table, joined for this splendid banquet by bishops, earls and barons and a vast crowd of commoners who had gathered together from all quarters of the kingdom. Indeed so great a throng of citizens had streamed into that enormous Hall that if the duke of Lancaster, steward of England, the earl of Buckingham, constable of the land, Lord Henry Percy, the marshal, and many others, on their tall horses, had not made a path in the Hall for the servants, those carrying the dishes would hardly have reached the banqueters. If I were to try to itemise the preparations for the banquet, the costliness of the utensils and the wealth of courses provided, the reader would perhaps be bowled over by the cost and the extent of all this splendour and be afraid to believe in it. I think I should leave out everything else and tell you of just one thing which had been arranged to display the munificence of the king. In the middle of the king's palace a hollowed out marble column had been erected on a stepped base with a huge, winged eagle standing on its top, and from under the feet of the eagle on the capital of the column wines of different kinds flowed down in four directions throughout the whole day of the king's coronation, and no one stopped any person, even the poorest, from drinking his fill. Such was the coronation, which took place when the king himself was ten.

Events on the day after the king's coronation

On the next day there was a public procession on behalf of the king and the peace of the kingdom. All the prelates, that is to say the archbishop and the bishops and abbots present at the coronation,

---

[1]   Sir Thomas Percy (c. 1344–1403), brother of Henry Percy, 1st earl of Northumberland. He was created earl of Worcester in 1397.

[2]   The *Anonimalle Chronicle* records another challenge made by the earl of Arundel to the mayor of London: *AC*, p. 115.

[3]   Thomas of Woodstock (b.1355) was the seventh son of Edward III. He was created earl of Buckingham in 1377.

[4]   Giuchard d'Angle's elevation to the peerage was in recognition of his long service to the crown. A knight of Lower Poitou he had fought with the French at Poitiers in 1356 but changed his allegiance after the Treaty of Calais (1361) and after the collapse of that settlement he was deprived of his estates and settled in England. He was granted £1000 for life for his services to Edward III, the Black Prince and to Richard. He died in 1380.

[5]   John Mowbray (1366–83) was elder son of John Lord Mowbray (d.1368). At his death his brother Thomas, later duke of Norfolk, succeeded in the earldom. Froissart also records these new creations and like Walsingham fails to name the nine new knights: Froissart, *Chroniques*, viii. 232–3; FCBuchon, i. 710.

dressed up again and took part in this procession, as did the duke himself and the magnates, together with a vast crowd of commoners. During the progress of the procession the bishop of Rochester [Thomas Brinton, 1373–89] addressed the people, making the plea that the quarrels and arguments between people and lords, which had continued uninterruptedly for a long time since their beginning, be put to sleep. He also urged the lords not to embarrass the people in the future by imposing huge taxes for which they gave no reason. But he also gave the advice that, if there was some good reason that made it absolutely essential for the people to help the king and the kingdom, they should put up with what was required of them and do it without complaints or seditious objections. And then he urged all of them alike, as subjects of a king who was an innocent boy, to give up the vices to which they had been slaves, namely fornication in brothels and adultery, and to make an effort to emulate his purity and innocence. He said that such behaviour towards the father of their country was altogether fitting, and that it was all too easy for the king to stray from the right path and for kingdom and country to be in peril, if those who were constantly in attendance on the king with their advice were such evil livers. When this address was finished, all the Lords and prelates went to their own homes.

The actions of the duke of Lancaster after the coronation[1]

After a few days the duke of Lancaster departed for his estates. With his father now dead and a new king in place, he saw that his position in the kingdom would be completely different and that the new counsellors would regard his own careful efforts with total contempt. He was afraid that he himself would get the blame, if any harm befell the king or his kingdom, and that he would receive little or no thanks for any successes. And so he obtained permission from the king and left for his own estates, having promised the king that if his help was ever needed, he would come with larger forces than any other lord of England, whether to help the king or to do something else which would redound to his advantage or honour. Men said that he was red with vexation because the king had taken from him his castle at Hertford. He had intended to make this castle his chief home, and for this reason had asked all the neighbouring landowners roundabout for timber to fortify his castle, and those he asked had indeed suffered great losses, as they had not dared to oppose his wishes at the particular time at which he had made them clear. And so he retired from court but to his castle at Kenilworth.[2] But before he departed, selection was made through his agency of those who were to attend the council of the king and to some extent to act as his guardians. Those selected were these good, sensible men of repute, William Courtenay, bishop of London, Edmund Mortimer, earl of March,[3] and several others who were very well thought of by the common people. But because the bishop of Salisbury[4] and Lord Latimer were also included, a groundswell of complaint began among the masses.

At the same time the marshal of England, Lord Henry Percy, earl of Northumberland, handed in his staff of office and left for his home. Appointed in his place was Sir John Arundel,[5] brother of the earl of Arundel. Sir John stoutly resisted the French when they attacked the town of Southampton. He bravely kept them from entering the town and sent them back to the sea.

---

1   Walsingham's preoccupation with Gaunt and his plans in this period was not shared by the other principal chroniclers of this period; the author of the *Historia vitae et regni Ricardi secundi* turns directly from Richard's coronation to comment on the campaigns in Scotland: HVRS, p. 47.

2   Here Walsingham embroiders the facts in order to present Gaunt in the worst possible light. He withdrew from court for pragmatic reasons; the Scots were threatening the border country and he advanced north to assist, among others, Henry Percy, earl of Northumberland. He left in conciliatory mood and appears even to have been reconciled with Bishop Courtenay with whom he had clashed over Wyclif only months before: Saul, *Richard II*, pp. 29–30 and n. 17.

3   Edmund Mortimer II, 3rd earl of March (1351–81), son of Roger Mortimer V, 2nd earl of March. He succeeded to the earldom in 1360 and married Philippa, daughter of Lionel, duke of Clarence, second son of Edward III. He was marshal of England from 1369–77 and was appointed lieutenant of Ireland in 1379.

4   Ralph Ergom, bishop of Salisbury from 1375–88, when he was translated to Bath and Wells.

5   Sir John Arundel (c.1348–1379), second son of Richard Fitzalan II, 3rd earl of Arundel, appointed marshal in 1377.

The earl of Northumberland attacks the Scots

At about this time a quarrel arose for some trivial reason between the English and the Scots at Roxburgh on a market day.[1] People on both sides were killed, but the Scots suffered the greater losses. And so, roused to anger, they shortly afterwards returned to the same town, led by the earl of Dunbar,[2] and got possession of it in a night attack. They killed some citizens, looting their property with grasping hands and setting fire to the town with devouring flames. When the new earl of Northumberland [Henry Percy] heard of this, he was deeply pained in his heart especially at the death of the townspeople, and determined to exact retribution from the enemy and to remove the shame from the land of his own people. So he crossed into Scotland with ten thousand men[3] and plundered the lands of the earl of Dunbar, who had been totally responsible for the disaster. For three days he burnt all that stood in his way, and after repaying the enemy with this suitable piece of revenge returned with all his forces to his own land.

The French capture the Isle of Wight

In order that the English might not be the only ones to meet with triumphs unmixed with disasters, in the same year on 21 August the French took the virtually impregnable Isle of Wight, though more by guile than valour.[4] If it had been properly defended by the garrison it would not have fallen to anyone. But the careless watch kept by the islanders led to destruction for themselves, an unexpected triumph for the French and disgrace and heavy losses for the English. What happened was that the French were driven to its coasts by a storm, and then tried to invade the island, believing that the islanders were unaware of their arrival. In fact the French intention was picked up by the inhabitants, who allowed them to make a landing on their territory, thinking that, when a certain number had landed whom they thought they could handle, they would keep the rest from landing. But it turned out differently from their expectations. A few were let in, as planned, but when the inhabitants tried to stop the rest from landing, their efforts were in vain, since the French poured from their ships in such numbers that time after time they drove back the islanders from their defence of the coastline. In the end the islanders, who had previously believed that they could capture the French pretty well just as they liked, were compelled to flee and look for hiding places, as the French, having got possession of the island in this fashion, roamed everywhere, killing the inhabitants, burning some of their towns and making off with their belongings. The French at last reached the castle on the island. They imagined that they could capture it with little trouble, but they found there in Sir Hugh Tyrrell, the castellan, a person able to inspire an unbelievably fierce defence. He boldly met the French near the castle, and inflicted great slaughter upon them. So they stopped attacking the castle, and, thinking it unsafe to live alongside such a dragon in the future, they collected as much booty as they could from the island and forced the inhabitants to beg their friends outside the island for a thousand marks [£666] of silver to save their houses from fire and to secure the rest of their possessions. And they only departed after

---

[1]   Walsingham's chronology is incorrect here: the skirmish that arose at the Roxburgh fair occurred in 1378. It sparked a series of border raids that continued, sporadically, into the next decade.
[2]   George Dunbar, 9th earl of Dunbar (c.1336–1416x23), also called earl of March, held lands in the Scottish eash march, in Annandale and Berwickshire.
[3]   The author of the *Historia vitae et regni Ricardi secundi* confirms the size of Northumberland's force: *HVRS*, p. 47.
[4]   While the peace negotiations continued at Bruges (see above, p. 31), the French maintained a presence in the Channel with a fleet of Castilian galleys, harrying not only the English coastline but also the enemy's fortifications at Calais and on the coast of Aquitaine. Froissart records that since troops had been sent to protect the principal ports of Dover and Pevensey, the French pushed their attacks further west towards the coastal towns of Hampshire, Dorset and Devon including Southampton, Dartmouth and Plymouth, where they seized several rich notables as their prisoners (Froissart, *Chroniques*, viii. 233–4; FCBuchon, i. 710). At the end of June the fleet returned briefly to Harfleur, and the assault on the Isle of Wight was perhaps its first action after leaving harbour. The author of the *Historia vitae et regni Ricardi secundi* confirms both the date of the assault on the island and the sum demanded by the invaders: *HVRS*, p. 47. See also Saul, *Richard II*, p. 33.

they had received an oath of good behaviour from the islanders and a promise that for a whole year they would not keep out the French, whenever it pleased them to land on the island.

The French attack Winchelsea

After their seizure of the Isle of Wight, the French went back to their ships and sailed around the coast until they came to their objective of the town of Winchelsea.[1] When they discovered that the abbot of Battle [Haimo of Offington] had hurried there to protect it, they sent envoys and asked him to ransom the town. But the abbot refused to buy what he had not lost, and even warned them to give up their attack on the town with threats of the losses that could befall them. This reply angered the French, and they asked the abbot, if he wanted a fight, to send a champion or even champions to meet theirs in combat, while both armies looked on. But the abbot said no to this petition as well, on the grounds that he was a man of religion, and so could not accept such proposals: he himself had come to Winchelsea, not for a fight, but to look after and preserve the peace of his country. When they heard this reply, the French judged that the abbot and his men were fainthearted, and soon moved up their engines of war, especially the missiles of which they enjoyed a good number, and made a fierce attack on the town. The battle lasted from three o'clock right up to the evening, but the French achieved very little, thanks to the praiseworthy determination of the abbot and his men.[2] And while they were fighting at Winchelsea, they sent a detachment from their fleet against the town of Hastings. The French found the town almost empty and set fire to it. But then, seeing that they were making no progress at Winchelsea, they withdrew.

The prior of Lewes is captured in battle

In the same year the French got into Rottingdean, near Lewes, where they were met by the prior of Lewes,[3] with a small band of men. But the French force defeated them and the prior was captured and taken to their ships, together with two knights who had supported him, Sir John Fawsley and Sir Thomas Cheyne, and one esquire called John Brocas.[4] And another esquire who, although he was French by birth, had long been in the service of the prior of Lewes, fought with such courage and bravery in this battle against the French, that in the end his entrails were hanging down to his feet, and, a terrible tale to tell, in his charges against the enemy he at first dragged his entrails after him for a considerable distance until finally he left them behind altogether. The English lost about a hundred men in this battle.[5]

The French, through treachery, capture the town of Ardres

As I have said the French went back to their own country with their whole fleet, whose numbers had increased to 37 galleys, 8 Spanish cockboats and some barges. Soon after landing, some of them set out to join the siege of Ardres, which was then taking place.[6] The governor of the town's

---

1   The contemporary accounts do not agree on the chronology of these coastal attacks, and it may be that these skirmishes in Sussex occurred before, or at the same time as, the assault on the Isle of Wight. The author of the *Historia vitae et regni Ricardi secundi* recalled that these were the worst attacks to be witnessed on the English coast for more than forty years (*HVRS*, p. 47). Froissart reported that it was from the hostages captured in Sussex that the French forces first learned of the death of Edward III (FCBuchon, i. 711).

2   The author of the *Historia vitae et regni Ricardi secundi* reported the 'vigorous resistance' (viriliter arcuit) of Abbot Haimo: *HVRS*, p. 47.

3   John de Cariloco or Cherlewe, prior from c.1366–96.

4   Both Cheyne and Fawsley were veterans of the continental campaigns; Fawsley had the further distinction of having captured the constable of France, Bertrand du Guesclin, at the Battle of Navarre in 1367. Brocas, correctly Bernard, may be identified with an esquire who held the Hampshire manor of Barton Peverell. He was Captain of Calais in 1377: *CPR, 1377–81*, pp. 38, 420.

5   The monks of Lewes Priory, situated on the banks of the Rother estuary, were forced to pay a ransom for the release of Prior John and also suffered the destruction of their demesne crops and the flooding of their sea defences. Later, they appealed to the pope for licence to appropriate churches to help recover their losses. In the earliest, 'scandalous' recension of the chronicle Walsingham blamed the debacle on the earl of Arundel who had left Lewes castle undefended: *CA*, p. 168.

6   The French attack on Ardres was part of an offensive intended to isolate the English garrison at Calais.

castle, a German called the Lord Gomenys[1] surrendered the town with the treason that was always a familiar feature of their world, and the French seized first the town, and soon its defences. Because of his treachery this same castellan was captured by Sir Hugh Calveley,[2] the governor of Calais, sent to England and handed over to the prison authorities.

Thomas Felton is captured in Aquitaine

While this was happening in France, an incident that brought sorrow to the whole of England took place in Aquitaine.[3] That excellent knight, Sir Thomas Felton,[4] who had been entrusted with the governorship of the province of Aquitaine, very rashly attacked a larger French force with a small band of men, and was overwhelmed and captured by their great numbers, together with many noblemen of the land who supported the English party. This misfortune happened near the place called Le Réole.

A parliament at London

At this same time a parliament met in London, which lasted from Michaelmas right up to the feast of the blessed apostle Andrew [30 November].[5] Present at this parliament together with Sir Peter de la Mare were almost all the knights, who, in that parliament rightly called 'the Good', had so nobly stood firm for the advancement of the land and the welfare of the kingdom. And so they took up their demands in the very place in which they had formerly put them down[6] and insisted on the banishment of Alice Perrers, since she, in contempt of the statute of parliament and the oath she had taken, had been bold enough to go to the king's court to urge him to grant her whatever it was she happened to want. Although she had bribed several of the lords and all the lawyers of England, who defended her publicly as well as in private, she was convicted out of her own mouth, thanks to the wisdom and care shown by the knights I have mentioned, and sent into exile, with all her property, moveable and immoveable, being assigned to the royal treasury.[7] A grant of two tenths was made by the church and clergy to help the king, payable in the current year on condition that in future the king refrained from burdening his people with such demands

Forces under Philip, duke of Burgundy, focused their attacks on the outlying forts of which Ardres was perhaps the most significant. It fell on 7 September 1377, but shortly afterwards the French began a surprise retreat, anxious, it appears at the onset of the autumn rains, and the English captain Calveley was able to mount something of a counter-offensive. Gomenys, the governor, was tried in parliament and condemned to death. Froissart offers a detailed account of the French assault. Of all the English strongholds in the pay de Calais, he suggests that Ardres was the most poorly defended and that the castellan, John Lord Gomenys, had been all but neglected. By his reckoning, Philip of Burgundy mustered a force of 2,500 lances to lead against the garrison. He also reports that Gomenys himself blamed the enfeeblement of Edward III for the failure to fully garrison the town and castle: Froissart, *Chroniques*, viii. 241–7; FCBuchon, 712–15 at 715.

1 John, Lord Gomenys. See also *CPR, 1377–81*, pp. 241, 260–1, 265.

2 Sir Hugh Calveley (d.1393), a professional soldier, had served as a mercenary commander supporting Enrique of Trastamara's conquest of Castile in 1366 but entered the service of the Black Prince in 1367. He was deputy of Calais from 1377–79 and governor of Brest in 1380.

3 Forces under the command of the duke of Anjou had advanced from the south seizing English possessions in the Dordogne valley including Bergerac, Candat and Castillon. Froissart reports this episode in greater detail: at Ymet, between Le Riole and Bergerac, Felton attacked a French column of some 600 lances, accompanied by a siege engine and other artillery intended for Bergerac. There was much hand-to-hand fighting and in spite of their numerical disadvantage Felton's men fought well but were finally defeated and Felton himself was taken prisoner by Sire Jean de Lignac: Froissart, *Chroniques*, ix. 7–10; FCBuchon, ii. 4–5.

4 Sir Thomas Felton, lieutenant of Aquitaine, had begun his career as a knight in the service of the Black Prince. In the Rolls Series edition of the earliest, 'scandalous' recension of the chronicle his name is given incorrectly as Sir Thomas Helton: *CA*, p. 170.

5 This, the first parliament of the new reign, began on Wednesday 13 October 1377. The commons were dispersed on 28 November but according to the rolls of parliament the magnates remained in session for another month during which Alice Perrers was subject to examination: *RP*, iii. 3–29.

6 Sir Peter de la Mare and his allies succeeded in punishing Alice Perrers but other, politically sensitive demands – for a role in the nomination of officers for the king's household and for no statute to be repealed except under the authority of the commons – were refused.

7 Perrers' property was valued at a staggering £2,626 8s 4d.

and extorting money from his subjects, but instead lived on his means and carried on the war from them.[1] As had been said in the previous parliament, his own resources as king were quite enough for him both to maintain his royal house and to continue with the war, provided that suitable servants were chosen to manage these resources. Two citizens of London, William Walworth[2] and John Philipot,[3] were deputed to look after this money.[4]

The English take to the sea but achieve nothing

About this time the English heard that a large fleet of Spanish ships were being kept at Sluys for lack of a wind, and so, collecting together a force of armed men, they planned to take to the sea with a big fleet, wishing to repay the Spaniards for the damage which they had inflicted upon the English, when they had given help to the French the previous summer.[5] In command of this fleet were Lord Thomas Woodstock, earl of Buckingham, the duke of Brittany,[6] [William] Lord Latimer, Lord Fitzwalter,[7] Sir Robert Knolles[8] and several other stout hearts with them. But they experienced cruel fortune when they put to sea. For a strong wind and damaging storm arose and soon the ships were separated from each other and scattered in different directions, their masts broken off and their sails torn to shreds, while several of the smaller vessels which were present to carry supplies for the expedition were sunk. The sailors who had gone aboard these smaller vessels abandoned them in their fear of the storm and got on board the larger ships or those that in their opinion were stronger. At length the divine mercy intervened, and the ships were brought back together and returned to the English coast. They were refitted, given a new force of fighting men and put to sea again.[9]

The memorable deeds of Sir Hugh Calveley

During an expedition against Boulogne made at that time, Sir Hugh Calveley had the good fortune to find in the harbour a barge named after the town, another belonging to the king of France[10] and

---

1   According to the *Anonimalle* author, a sum of 400,000 marks had been demanded by the crown: *AC*, p. 116.

2   William Walworth (d.1385) was a member of the fishmongers' company in the city of London; he served as alderman in 1368, sheriff in 1370 and 1380–1 and mayor in 1374–5. He sat as a member for London in the parliament of 1383. See Barron, *London*, pp. 333–4. For his role in the peasants' revolt of 1381 see below, pp. 129–30.

3   For John Philipot see p. 34 above.

4   Walsingham does not mention perhaps the most important business of this parliament, the appointment of a new council to govern during the king's minority; several existing councillors were reappointed, including the bishops of London and Salisbury, and Edmund Mortimer, earl of March, but some such as Lord Latimer and Lord Cobham were dismissed, their position having been damaged in the aftermath of the Good Parliament. See Saul, *Richard II*, p. 30.

5   Preparations for this expedition had been in hand since the summer and a fleet of 100 ships sailed on 1 November. The raising of this force marked a return by the new regime to the old strategy of undermining the enemy through a succession of chevauchées on their castles and coastal fortifications. The storm occurred around 10 November.

6   Jean IV de Montfort (1339–99), duke of Brittany; he inherited the dukedom at the age of six (1345) and the duchy was cast into a twenty-year war of succession. With the support of English troops, Duke Jean defeated and killed the rival claimant Charles of Blois, himself supported by the French, at the battle of Auray in 1364, but the loyalties of the Breton magnates were divided and he was forced into exile in 1373. He settled in England where he married the king's daughter, Mary. He returned to Brittany in 1379: see below, pp. 87–8; Jones, *Ducal Brittany*, pp. 85–7.

7   Walter, 4th baron Fitzwalter.

8   Sir Robert Knolles (d.1407), was perhaps the most celebrated of all English captains in this phase of the Hundred Years War and one of only a handful of professional soldiers to have secured wealth, political and social status through his successes on the battlefield. He began his career as a lowly archer but was knighted in 1351 and took a leading role in subsequent campaigns. He captured Bertrand du Guesclin, constable of France, in 1359, served with the Black Prince in Spain in 1367 and commanded the expedition to France in 1370.

9   The fleet embarked again in mid-December and did succeed in seizing Brest in early January.

10   Charles V (1338–80), son of Jean II and his queen Bona of Luxembourg, sister of Emperor Charles IV, acceded to the throne in 1364.

twenty-six bigger and smaller ships.[1] All of these he suddenly set fire to and burnt by hurling flaming torches, as he did to a great part of the suburbs of Boulogne. On the very same day he had mass celebrated by his chaplain here, and in his bold way heard it through to the end. When the mass was over, he sacked this part of the town and made off with whatever desirable items he found there, together with some prisoners who had fallen into his hands in an unlucky hour for them.[2] He also drove along in front of him a great number of sheep and cattle, which he had found in the pasture near the town, and which were sufficient to supply Calais properly with food for a long time.[3]

He must also be praised for this reason. There was no place which was a bigger danger to Calais than the castle of Marck, if it took sides with the enemy, and one day this castle was actually lost to the enemy because of the carelessness of its garrison.[4] But on the very same day on which the French took possession of it, Sir Hugh vigorously recovered it and made it obey its previous master. This is how it happened. The commander of the castle, Sir Robert Salle, who was no ordinary knight but among the more famous ones for his energy, had gone to England for various reasons, having entrusted the guarding of the castle to certain careless individuals. In Sir Robert's absence, they had not done their duty properly but enjoyed themselves with games and archery, and one day, when they had begun their archery just outside the castle, some mercenaries in the garrison, who came from Picardy, reputedly the most treacherous people in France, noticed that all the English had left the castle. Immediately they shut the gates, took up positions on the walls and, treacherously supporting the French, they let them into the castle and by this trick kept out those Englishmen to whom its defence had been assigned. But, as I have said, when Sir Hugh discovered what had happened, he made an assault and captured the castle, taking as prisoners the French who had entered the castle and beheading all the men of Picardy as being guilty of treachery.

The conclusion of the year

Thus finished a year of mixed fortune, for, although there was a good corn harvest, the fruit harvest had been almost non-existent. As far as peace was concerned, the English had experienced a disturbed and uneasy year, caused as much by the treachery of their own citizens as by their fear of the French. For the French the year had been a costly one. They had spent a huge amount of money for a minimal return, as from Easter right up to Michaelmas they had paid out a thousand marks a day on the upkeep of the thirty-seven galleys and eight cockboats. Undoubtedly the paying out of such a sum over so long a period could have exhausted the resources of the richest kingdom.

[1378]

In 1378, the first year of the reign of king Richard II, the king kept Christmas at Windsor.

A papal bull sent to England to restrain the heresiarch, Master John Wyclif[5]

A few days before Christmas the pope [Gregory XI] sent a bull to the university of Oxford, using

---

[1]   According to Froissart, at this time Calveley, Sir John Harleston, captain of Guines and Lord Gomenys, captain of Ardres, led many assaults in the pays de Calais of which the attack on Boulogne was the most productive: Froissart, *Chroniques*, viii. 241. According to the *Anonimalle Chronicle*, thirty-four vessels were captured, amongst them 'niefs et batels de vitelers et des peschours': *AC*, p. 117.
[2]   The *Anonimalle* author reports that five hostages were captured: *AC*, p. 117.
[3]   The *Anonimalle* author claims that the livestock was sold at a rate of a cow for 4 'soldes' and a sheep for sixpence: *AC*, p. 117.
[4]   The castle at Marck had been granted to the English under the terms of the Treaty of Bretigny (1360). For the commander or keeper of the castle at this date, Sir Robert Salle, see *CPR, 1377–81*, pp. 64, 201, 590.
[5]   It appears that Wyclif's teachings had been first brought to the attention of Pope Gregory by a party of English scholars present at Avignon, and in particular by the Benedictine, Adam Easton, who had presented to

the services of Master Edmund Stafford.[1] Like a father he rebuked and corrected its manifest lack of action in having allowed for so long the heretical opinions of that disciple of the Antichrist himself, Master John Wyclif, to take root in its midst, while there had been no one who would bother to take up the spade of Catholic doctrine in order to uproot the deadly, poisonous plant which Wyclif had planted. It can easily be seen how far the modern day provosts or rectors of this university have departed from the good sense and wisdom of their predecessors, if I tell you that when they heard the reason for the arrival of the pope's envoy, they debated for a long time whether they should honour and accept the pope's bull or do him the dishonour of completely ignoring it. O university of Oxford, how far have you tumbled and fallen from the heights of wisdom and learning which were yours! Once it was your custom to make clear to the whole world tangled masses of uncertainty, but nowadays, when darkened by clouds of ignorance, you are not afraid to express doubt on matters on which no Christian layman should have any hesitation. I am ashamed to recall such folly, and so I pass over any detailed treatment of this incident, lest I appear to be biting with my teeth my mother's teats, which once gave me to drink the milk of learning.[2] The wording of the pope's bull, which he sent to the university of Oxford,[3] was as follows:[4]

'Gregory, bishop, servant of the servants of God, to our beloved sons the members and chancellor of the university of Oxford, in the diocese of Lincoln, greetings and apostolic blessing. We are compelled to be surprised and pained at your behaviour. On account of the favours and privileges granted to your university by the apostolic see and on account of your knowledge of the Scriptures, over the sea of which you row so happily by the gift of the lord, you should have been champions willing to fight for the orthodox faith, without which there is no salvation of souls. Instead your inactivity and idleness allow tares to spring up among the genuine wheat in the fields of your famous university, and, what is more pernicious, to go on growing without you taking any trouble to pull them out, according to what we have recently heard. Such behaviour darkens the brightness of your reputation, endangers your souls, shows contempt for the Roman church and harms the orthodox faith.

'And what causes us still more bitter anguish is that the discovery of the growth of the tares was made in Rome rather than in England, although it is in England that the remedy of pulling them up has to be applied. For many trustworthy people have whispered into our ears the news which had quite upset them that John Wyclif, rector of Lutterworth in the diocese of Lincoln, professor of holy scriptures[5] but also, alas, a master of mistakes, has broken out into a fit of such hateful madness that he is not afraid to assert as matters of dogma and publish abroad – or, as we might put it, to spew up out of the poison-ridden heart of his cloister – various mistaken, false propositions, which in the wickedness of their heretical cleverness are an attempt at undermining and weakening the state of the whole church and even the secular realm. Some of his views, though in rather different terminology, seem to echo the wicked opinions and foolish doctrine of

---

the Curia an apparently lengthy list of conclusions attributed to Wyclif that were considered suspect. From this schedule, Gregory selected eighteen for special censure and drafted bulls directed to the chancellor and masters of Oxford, to the archbishop of Canterbury and the bishop of London. The publication of the bulls was delayed probably in response to the news of the death of Edward III; they did not reach England until the end of the year. See also M. Harvey, 'Adam Easton and the Condemnation of John Wyclif', *EHR*, 113 (1998), 321–34.

1   An Oxford scholar, Stafford was also a canon of Lichfield. He was presented to the see of Exeter in 1395 and died in 1419. See also Emden, *BRUO*, iii. 1749–50.

2   This is the only reference Walsingham makes to his own educational background, and whilst there is no documentary evidence to support it, this would seem to prove that he did study at Oxford either before or after his profession as a monk. See introduction above, p. 5.

3   The bull was not well received by the university authorities. The chancellor publicly declared in favour of Wyclif in the Schools.

4   For the background to the bull and another recension of the text see also *Fasciculi zizaniorum*, ed. W. W. Shirley, Rolls Series, 5 (1858), 242–4.

5   'sacrae paginae professor' was the customary title for all those who held the doctorate in theology.

Marsilius of Padua and John of Jandun of hateful memory, whose book has been condemned and banned by pope John XXII [1316–34] of happy memory, our predecessor.[1] And this has all happened in the kingdom of England, which is famous for its glorious power and its great wealth, but still more famous for the ruddy piety of its faith and its clearness of exposition of holy scripture, as it habitually produced as defenders of the Catholic faith men of mature weight of character conspicuous for their piety, who won recognition for their orthodox knowledge of holy writ. And he has infected other faithful Christians with the contagion of his opinions, leading them away from the straight path of faith to the precipice of perdition.

'We cannot ignore and pass over, nor ought we be willing to do so, this deadly pestilence. If it is not stopped and rooted out in its early stages, any cure for it can only be applied when it is too late, as by then it will have spread its contagion far and wide. And so we strictly instruct and command your university in this apostolic document, relying on your holy obedience and under the threat of loss of all favours, indulgences and privileges granted to you and your university by the said apostolic see, not to allow in the future the assertion or promulgation of these Conclusions and Propositions, which have a bad influence upon good works and the faith, however much their supporters try to defend them with a certain twisted cunning of language and terminology. We also order you with our authority to arrest the said John or give instructions for his arrest, and to hand him over in safe custody to our venerable brothers, the archbishop of Canterbury and the bishop of London, or to one of them. Should any from the said university who are under your jurisdiction object to this, supposing there are, which God forbid, others infected with errors of this kind, you are to take strict and resolute measures to arrest and hand over them as well and to do anything else which seems to you necessary. If you show a proper care, which up to now has been missing, in the carrying out of these orders, you will thereby win the gratitude and goodwill of ourself and of the said see, besides being payed your deserved reward by God. Given at Rome in the church of St Maria Maggiore, 22 May, in the seventh year of our papacy.'

Papal bulls sent to the archbishop of Canterbury and the bishop of London, that they should warn the king and magnates of England not to give any support or allegiance to John Wyclif

'Greetings to my reverend brothers, the archbishop of Canterbury [Simon Sudbury] and the bishop of London [William Courtenay]. As for the extremely dangerous errors contained in some dreadful Propositions and Conclusions aimed at weakening the whole position of the church, which John Wyclif, rector of Lutterworth church in the diocese of Lincoln, and called a professor of theology is said to have impiously and rashly dredged up, for the moment they are outlined in the enclosed document, but we are writing you a fuller account than this present bull in other letters patent of ours, which we are sending together with the present bull. So it is our wish and command for you two brothers that you and other masters who are learned in Holy Scripture and not infected by errors of this kind but sincere and fervent in their faith, should carefully ensure that our most distinguished son in Christ, Edward illustrious king of England [i.e. Edward III], and our beloved sons, the noble sons born to King Edward, and our beloved daughter in Christ, the noble lady Joan, princess of Aquitaine and of Wales, and the other magnates of England and counsellors of the king, are fully informed and told of the shameful damage that can be done to the holy kingdom of England by the doctrines of Wyclif, and warned that the Conclusions are not only heretical in matters of the faith, but that, if favourable notice is taken of them, they mean the destruction of the whole system of government. Also, you are most urgently to require of them that with all their powers they give help and support as Catholic princes and champions of the

---

[1]   The controversial writings of Marsilius of Padua (1275x80–1342x43) and John of Jandun (d.1328) had been central to early-fourteenth-century arguments over the independence of secular monarchs from papal authority. Jandun's conclusions were condemned by John XXII in 1327 together with selected conclusions of Marsilius. The contention that Wyclif had drawn on Marsilius' *Defensor Pacis* was unfounded and may have come directly from Adam Easton. It was typical of the early response to Wyclif that his conclusions were treated as nothing more original than a restatement of these earlier opinions.

faith to the rooting out of these errors, out of their reverence for God, the apostolic see and ourself, and for the rewards given by God and the honours of men. Given at Rome in the church of St Maria Maggiore 22 May, in the seventh year of our papacy.'

'Greetings to our venerable brothers, the archbishop of Canterbury [Simon Sudbury] and bishop of London [William Courtenay]. Not without great perturbation of spirit have we lately learnt from the accounts of several trustworthy people that John Wyclif, rector of Lutterworth in the diocese of Lincoln, professor of holy scripture but, alas, a master of mistakes, has broken out in a fit of such hateful madness that he has not been afraid to assert as matters of dogma and to publish abroad in the kingdom of England some mistaken, false Propositions and Conclusions which are not consonant with the faith and which are an attempt at undermining and weakening the state of the whole church. Some of his views, though in rather different terminology, seem to echo the wicked opinions and foolish doctrine of Marsilius of Padua and John of Jandun of hateful memory, whose book has been condemned and banned by Pope John XXII of happy memory, our predecessor. And he has evilly infected other faithful Christians with these doctrines, leading them from the pathway of the Catholic faith, without which there is no salvation.

'Considering that it was our duty, as it still is, not to conceal and neglect so harmful an evil, which could spread far and wide, destroying men's souls with its deadly infection, in another bull of ours we secretly informed you of the declaration of the said Propositions and Conclusions, a copy of which we sent enclosed with our bull, and entrusted both of you together, or one of you, with the task of getting, on our authority, the same John arrested and put in prison, if you found the facts were as we had stated them, and keeping him imprisoned under safe custody until you received further instructions from us on this matter, as we said at greater length in the first bull.

'But realising that the said John could possibly get wind of the proposed arrest and imprisonment and, God forbid, make his escape or, through the protection of a hiding place, nullify our command, to the greatest detriment to the faith, we now in this papal bull, so that such damnable Propositions and Conclusions should not remain undiscussed or their hasty proposer remain unpunished to the greatest detriment to the faith, instruct and command you two brothers that both of you together, or one of you, should, if you cannot arrest and imprison the said John, see to it that you yourselves, or some other person or persons, on our behalf peremptorily warn and summon the said John, by means of a public edict made in the university of Oxford in the Lincoln diocese and in other public places, where it is a likely guess the information could come to the knowledge of the said John, to appear before us within the space of three months, reckonable from the day of this summons, wherever we then happened to be, and in person before us to make his reply concerning these Propositions and Conclusions, and to hear and carry out whatever verdict concerning them we shall have decided upon and the application of reason dictated. Moreover in the notice of this summons you are to warn him that, whether he appears or does not appear within the stated time, we shall take action on the case and proceed against him comprehensively right up to the punishment which is due to him and demanded by his faults and which seems right to us as we follow God and preserve the faith.

Also it is our wish and our decision expressed in this bull that this summons, carried out by you according to our orders, should bind the same John just as firmly as if it had made its way and been delivered to him in person, with no obstacle being placed in its way by any contrary ruling whatever. Make sure that you give us accurate information as soon as you can in a sealed letter, containing a detailed account of the affair, recording the date, the wording of the summons and your actions in the matter. Given at Rome at the church of St Maria Maggiore 22 May, in the seventh year of our papacy.'

'Greetings to our venerable brothers, the archbishop of Canterbury [Simon Sudbury] and bishop of London [William Courtenay]. The kingdom of England, which is indeed glorious for its power and its great wealth, but still more glorious for the piety of its faith and its brilliantly clear exposition of holy writ, has habitually produced as defenders of the Catholic faith men of mature weight of character, conspicuous for their piety and equipped with a correct understanding of Holy Scripture, who in their truthful writings instructed and brought on to the pathway of the commands of the Lord not only their own people but also those of other lands. And as is known from the results of what happened in olden times, those named as bishops of the kingdom and placed on their watchtowers of responsibility, kept careful watch themselves and did not allow any heresy to spring up which could infect their sheep, but immediately tore up any tares which did come forth as the result of the sowing by some enemy, so that year after year there grew up pure grain for storage in the granary of the Lord.

'But, alas, how different things are now in this same kingdom! The appointed guardians are slothful and careless and keep no watch over the state, while enemies enter it, seeking as plunder that most precious treasure of souls. Their hidden entrance, or rather open attack, was reported to us at Rome, despite the long distance which separates us, before any resistance was made to it in England. Indeed it was not without great perturbation of spirit that we lately learnt from the accounts of several trustworthy people that John Wyclif, rector of Lutterworth church in the diocese of Lincoln, professor of holy scripture but, alas, a master of mistakes, has broken out in a fit of such hateful madness that he has not been afraid to assert as matters of dogma and to publish abroad in the kingdom of England some mistaken, false Propositions and Conclusions which are not consonant with the faith and which are an attempt at undermining and weakening the state of the whole church. Some of his views, though in rather different terminology, seem to echo the wicked opinions and foolish doctrine of Marsilius of Padua and John of Jandun of hateful memory, whose book has been condemned and banned by Pope John XXII of happy memory, our predecessor. And he has evilly infected other faithful Christians with these doctrines, leading them from the pathway of the Catholic faith, without which there is no salvation. These propositions which sprang up in this manner have not been uprooted, or at least no resistance has been made to them that we know of, but have been overlooked and tolerated. You and the other bishops of England, who should be pillars of the church and named as watchful defenders of the faith, because of your shutting your eyes to what was happening and carelessly allowing it to go on, should now, if justice is done, be a red mass of shame with your own consciences eaten away in guilt.

'And so since it is not our wish, nor should it be, to conceal and neglect so harmful an evil, which, if not cut down or torn up by the roots, could spread far and wide, destroying men's souls with its deadly infection, which God forbid, in this apostolic bull we give you, our brothers, the command and order that, on receipt of the bull, both of you, or one of you, in the matter of the declaration of the said Propositions and Conclusions (a copy of which we send to you enclosed in our bull, giving you secret information of it), should get the said John on our authority arrested and put in prison, if you find the facts were as we have stated them. You are also to seek to obtain his confession in the matter of these Propositions and Conclusions, and you are to send to us by trusty messenger a sealed document, revealed to no one, which contains his confession, anything he may have said or written when introducing and giving proof of his Propositions and Conclusions, and an account of your own actions so far. You are to keep this John in prison under safe custody until you receive from us further instruction on the matter.

'Opponents, etc. Summoned, etc.[1] No obstacle to our decision is to be found in the constitutions of our predecessor, Pope Boniface VIII [1294–1303] of happy memory, in which he laid down that no one should be summoned to justice outside his own country or diocese, except in certain cases in which a man could not be summoned to travel more than a day's journey from the boundary of his diocese, and that judges appointed by the apostolic see should not presume to summon defendants, who would have to travel more than one day's journey from the boundary of their diocese, while it was a matter of a two day journey for the General council, and in a ques-

---

[1] Here formulae from the original document have been abbreviated by Walsingham, an editorial convention he employs in his transcriptions of other papal and royal *acta*.

These were the propositions, or rather the ravings, of Wyclif that reached the ears of the pope. He was understandably disturbed by them, and so sent to the bishops the bulls that I have quoted, in order to deal with this important matter which affected the state of the universal church. But it is better to pass over in silence than to describe the slackness and the unconcern of the bishops in carrying out the commands entrusted to them.[1] The only fact that I have decided to hand down to the notice of posterity is this. Although the bishops themselves had been suitably roused when they received the honour of such a mark of favour and had declared that no prayers, threats or bribes would stop them from pursuing the path of justice in this matter, even if their lives were in danger, when the day arrived for the trial of that renegade, they were smoother than butter through their fear of a reed shaken by the wind, to the public loss of their own dignity and the harm of the whole church. And men who had vowed not to obey even the very lords and princes of the kingdom until they had punished the excesses of the heretic himself according to the commands of the pope, were completely terrified by the appearance, not of some noble knight or man of power, but of a fellow from the court of Princess Joan [of Kent] called [Sir] Lewis Clifford, who was not even a noble, powerful knight, but who arrogantly forbade them to presume to pronounce any sentence of condemnation against John [Wyclif].[2] Such was their terror that you would think they were lacking all manhood, and had become as one who does not hear and who has no rebukes ready in his mouth.

Also I do not think I should fail to report that, when the bishops and that heretic met in the chapel of the archbishop at Lambeth, the riff-raff of the town whom I would not even call citizens of London, dared to burst impudently into that chapel and to interfere in the matter by making speeches on behalf of Wyclif, trusting, I suppose, in the previous lack of concern shown by the bishops.[3] Thanks to such chances or devices, on that occasion a false prophet and genuine hypocrite got away. He was not to appear again before the bishops this side of the death of Pope Gregory [XI], a death which greatly saddened the faithful, but which brought cheer to those false to the faith like Wyclif himself and his followers.

The declarations of John Wyclif[4]

In the first place I declare publicly, as I have often done at other times, that I intend and wish with my whole heart, helped by God's grace, to be a genuine Christian, and, as long as breath remains within me, to proclaim and defend to the best of my ability the law of Christ. And if through ignorance or some other cause I fail in this attempt, I ask my God for pardon, and now, as before, I revoke and retract my errors, humbly submitting myself to the correction of holy mother church. And as the statement of faith which I made in the schools and elsewhere has been spread abroad by my pupils and even carried by them as far as the Roman Curia, I wish to state in writing the opinion for which I have been attacked, so that Christians may not find in me a cause for stumbling. I am willing to defend my beliefs to the death, as I believe all Christians ought, but especially the Roman pontiff and the other priests of the church. I base my Conclusions on the sense and meaning of the words of scripture and the holy doctors, which I am prepared to expound. And should it be that my Conclusions are contrary to the faith, I am willing unhesitatingly to revoke them.

---

1   Walsingham is unduly critical here. Wyclif had refused an initial summons from the bishops to appear before them at St Paul's in January and it may be that he only appeared in March because by then he had mobilised the support of key courtiers, as Walsingham suggests.
2   Sir Lewis Clifford (b. c.1335) had been in the service of the Black Prince for almost twenty years. Waslingham is the only contemporary authority to identify him at this stage as a sympathiser of Wyclif's; later, notoriously, he would name him as one of the so-called 'Lollard knights'. See below, p. 250.
3   It is worth noting that Wyclif's second examination before the archbishop ended exactly as had the first in February 1377, with a riot in the city of London. See above, pp. 30–1.
4   This text is what is recorded in the *Fasciculi Zizaniorum* as Wyclif's speech before the October parliament of 1377: *Fasciculi zizaniorum*, ed. Shirley, pp. 258–71.

1. THE FIRST CONCLUSION:[1] *If the whole human race since Christ assembled together, not one of them would have the power of directly ordaining that Peter and all his successors should have political power over the world in perpetuity.*
Now it is clear that it is not within men's power to stop the coming of Christ for the last judgement, since we must believe in that article of faith, 'Then he will come to judge the quick and the dead.' For from then on, according to our belief in scripture, human governments will cease. My understanding is that political power, or civil, secular power, is given by the Lord to lay people while they are alive and on the road of their earthly pilgrimage. Philosophers discuss such political power. And although it is referred to as 'periodical' and sometimes as being 'in perpetuity', since it is the case that in holy scripture, church usage and the books of the philosophers 'in perpetuity' is commonly taken to be a clear synonym for 'for ever', I propose from now on to understand the word in that more usual sense. For the church takes in that sense when it chants, 'Glory be to God the father, and to his only Son and to the Holy Ghost, both now and for ever.' So the obvious conclusion for the principles of faith is that it does not lie within the power of men to decree that the pilgrimage of the church is forever.

2: *God cannot give to a man civil dominion for himself and his heirs in perpetuity.*
By civil dominion I mean, as I meant above, power which is political and which lasts forever. As above, it is because scripture understands that there are resting places for ever in the beatitude of heaven that I then said, in the first place, that God cannot, when power is ordained, give a man civil dominion for ever. I said in the second place that it seems probable that God, even with his absolute power, cannot give a man such dominion for ever, because it seems that it is not possible for God always to imprison his bride in this transitory life, and so always postponing her final fulfilment in the beatitude of heaven.

3: *Many documents devised by men granting inheritance of civil power forever are invalid.*
The validity is only in some documents. For if all documents were accepted as Catholic, it would not then be possible to remove possessions granted by them from an unjust owner. And if such an unjust owner received backing from the authority of the church, he would be given an acceptable reason for trusting in his possessions and in a permission to sin. For just as all that is true is necessary, so we can suppose that all that is false is impossible, as is clear from the testimony of scripture and the holy doctors who talk about the necessity of the future.

4: *He who possesses the grace that bestows grace to the end does not have merely the appropriate justice, but appropriate rights to all the gifts of God in his lifetime.*
It is clear from our belief in scripture, Matthew 24, that the divine Truth promises to any one entering into his joy, 'Truly, I say to you all, he will put this man in charge of all his goods.'[2] For the rights of the communion of saints on earth are founded objectively on the universality of the gifts of God.

5: *Only as a minister can a man give to his natural or adopted son both earthly and heavenly authority in the school of Christ.*
This is clear from the fact that every man in all his works should recognise that he is a humble servant of God, as is shown from our belief in the scripture, 'A man should regard us as being servants of Christ' [1 Corinthians 4: 1]. Indeed Christ himself so ministered to us and taught his chosen apostles to do likewise. On earth indeed the saints will give to their brothers dominion over the good things there, as is clear when we think of their bodies and the lesser goods of the natural world, according to that text in the sixth chapter of Luke, 'Good measure, pressed down, shaken together and running over will be poured into your lap' [Luke 6: 38].

---

[1]   The first five conclusions concern the concept of dominion, the seven following focus on the issue of excommunication. See also *Fasciculi zizaniorum*, ed. Shirley, pp. 245–57.
[2]   In fact, the reference is to Matthew 25: 21.

6: *If God exists, temporal lords can legitimately and deservedly take away the possessions of a church that falls into error.*

This conclusion is tied up with the first article of faith, 'I believe in God, the father all powerful.' Now I understand 'powerful' in the sense of that scripture which concedes that God is powerful enough to raise up sons for Abraham from stones [Matthew 3: 9; Luke 3: 8]; for otherwise all Christian princes would be heretics. To prove that conclusion, let the reasoning be set out as follows: if God exists, he is all powerful. If he is all powerful, he is able to command temporal lords to take away the goods of a church in error. If he gives this command, temporal lords have been able from the first legitimately to remove the goods of the church in this way. And so relying on this logic Christian princes have put into practice this opinion. But nobody should suppose that it is my intention to argue that secular lords have the right to remove the goods of the church whenever and however they like or on their own bare authority. They must be supported by the authority of the church, and it must be done in cases and in a manner defined by law.

7: *We know that it is not possible for the Vicar of Christ by means of his bulls, or by them together with his own wish and consent or together with the wish and agreement of his College to qualify anybody for heaven or disqualify him.*

This is clear from the Catholic faith, since it is necessary for the Lord to take the first place in all actions carried out by his subordinates. For this reason, just as in all cases of qualifying a man for heaven, first of all grace and authority are demanded for that qualification, so in all cases of disqualification authority is demanded for disqualification because of a man's faults. It follows that such qualification or disqualification does not come purely from the office held by the Vicar of Christ, but also from above.

8: *It is not possible for a man to be excommunicated to his own damnation, unless first and foremost he has been excommunicated by himself.*

This is clear, seeing that it is necessary for such excommunication to originate in the sin of the condemned man. And so Augustine says in his *Concerning the words of the Lord, Sermon 21*, 'Do not trample on yourself, and no man will conquer you.' And the faith of the church still sings, 'No adversity can harm the man over whom wickedness has no dominion.' This is the substance of this eighth conclusion. But every excommunication is to be feared for many reasons, even though excommunication from the church, for a man who receives it humbly, is not life-destroying but life-saving.

9: *No one ought, unless in the cause of God, to excommunicate, suspend from office, lay under interdict or proceed to punish anyone according to any other penalty of the church.*

This is obvious, since every just cause is the cause of God, and so the reasoning behind it ought to be weighed very carefully. Indeed, love for the excommunicated person should be more important than zeal for punishing or greed for temporalities of any kind. For a person who excommunicates for any other reason damns himself by his own action. This is the substance of the ninth conclusion. But it is consistent with this that a prelate can, following reason, excommunicate a man, principally because of a wrong done to his God. This is clear from the fourth question on the thirteenth case [of Gratian's *Decretum*].[1]

10: *Anathema or excommunication is not binding of itself, but only so far as it is imposed upon an enemy of the law of Christ.*

This is clear, since it is God who binds completely each man that is bound, and he cannot excommunicate unless his law has been violated. This is the substance of the tenth conclusion. But it is consonant with this that ecclesiastical censure does not bind completely, for it has also to be considered why it is being used against an enemy of a member of the church.

---

[1]   In fact the correct reference is Gratian's *Decretum*, Part II, Causa XIII, Quaestio 4.

11: *There is no example of Christ giving power to his disciples to excommunicate a subject, where it is a matter of depriving them of their earthly possessions. Just the opposite.*
This is clear from our faith in scripture, where the belief is stated that God, and our neighbour and our enemy are to be loved above all things, and more than all the possessions of this world. And it is a necessary truth that the law of God cannot contradict itself.

12: *Disciples of Christ do not have the power to demand temporalities by means of the civil enforcement of their decisions.*
This is clear from our belief in scripture, Luke ch. 22, where Christ banned his apostles from exercising civil rule with the words, 'Kings rule over their peoples, but for you it is not so' [Luke 22: 26]. And the verse is explained in this way by the blessed Bernard, the blessed Chrysostom and other saints. This is the substance of the twelfth conclusion. But it is not contradicted by the fact that disciples of Christ can by ecclesiastical censure make demands on temporalities, if it is to aid a punishment being inflicted by their God.

13: *It is not possible for the pope or any other Christian, if he claims to have some means from the absolute power of God to release or bind, to have that means of loosing or binding.*
The opposite of this would destroy the whole Catholic faith, since it would mean he was a blasphemer misusing this absolute power of the Lord. This the substance of the thirteenth conclusion. By this conclusion I do not intend to diminish the power of the pope or of any other prelate of the church, by claiming that they cannot in virtue of their position bind and release. But I do believe that the conditional claim is to be rejected as impossible in the sense required. It is not possible for the pope or any other Christian to claim that he has some means of loosing or binding unless he looses or binds because of the thing itself. Then he cannot be sinful.

14: *We must believe, that only then does the priest of Christ bind or release completely, when he does so in conformity with the law of Christ.*
This follows from the fact that it is not possible for him so to do, unless in virtue of that law, and therefore not unless in conformity with that law.

15: *It ought to be Catholic belief that any priest, properly ordained according to the law of grace, has sufficient power for properly performing any sacrament in its kind, and therefore of absolving any repentant sinner from any sin.*
This is clear from the fact that priestly power in its essence does not have greater or lesser degrees. Admittedly the powers of lesser priests are now sensibly restricted, but on other occasions, when there is some overwhelming need, the restrictions are removed. This is the substance of the fifteenth conclusion. And so, according to the doctors, it is possible in the case of a prelate to bestow a double power, both the power of ordination and the power of jurisdiction or rule, and they are priests in accordance with this double power, as being men of a higher majesty and position.

16: *It is possible for kings, in cases defined by law, to take away temporalities from churchmen, if they habitually misuse them.*
This is clear from the fact that temporal lords ought to labour for the richer fruit of spiritual almsgiving than for the almsgiving that benefits the body. This is necessary because there would be a need of spiritual almsgiving in punishing in certain cases clerics, who damn themselves in body and soul, by taking away their temporalities. A case defined by law would be the failure of the person in charge to provide spiritual chastisement, and especially the failure to correct the faith of a cleric. This is clear from the seventh question on the sixteenth case, beginning 'To sons' [of Gratian's *Decretum*, Part II, Causa XVI, Quaestio 7, cap. 31, 'filus'], and from the third section of the fortieth chapter beginning 'If the pope' [of Gratian's *Decretum*, Part I, Distinctio xl, Pars, 'Si Papa'].

17: *Whether it is temporal lords or any others that have endowed the Church with temporalities, nevertheless it is legitimate under certain circumstances to guard against sin and to effect a cure by*

depriving the Church of its temporalities, unvetoed by excommunication or any other ecclesiastical punishment, seeing that temporalities are only given to the church with this condition implied.
This is clear from the fact that nothing ought to be an impediment to special works of charity. It is also necessary, seeing that in every human action the condition of the divine pleasure ought to be taken into account, and necessarily so in making civil law. See the *Sermons* of Corradius, ch. 5, at the end of the Tenth Sermon. This is the substance of the seventeenth conclusion. God forbid that its words should give any opportunity to temporal lords to take away its goods of fortune to the detriment of the church.

18: An ecclesiastic, even the Roman pontiff, can under these conditions be rebuked by his subjects, and for the good of the church even brought to trial by clergy and laity.
This is clear from the fact that the pope himself is susceptible to sin, short of the sin against the Holy Ghost, a suggestion that is put forward in the holiness, humility and reverence which we owe to so great a father. Consequently, since our brother is susceptible to sin, he lies under the law of brotherly correction. And since his whole college can fail to correct him through considering the prosperity of the church which it is bound to further, it is clear that the rest of the body of the church, which it is possible to consider according to most people consists of the laity, is able to effect a cure by correcting him and bringing him to trial, and thus leading him back to the fruits of a better life. This possible situation is alluded to in the fortieth distinction of Gratian's Decretum, Part 1, Distinctio xl 'If the pope deviates from the faith . . .' For just as such a lapse on the part of the pope is not to be alleged without clear evidence, so he ought not to regard the allegation of a possible lapse with such obstinacy that he refuses humbly to receive healing from his superior, that is God. The practice of this conclusion is attested by many chronicles. Let the condemnation of the truth have no place in the church of Christ, as being uncomfortable for sinners or the ignorant. For then all our faith in scripture would be open to condemnation.

So that crafty fox, John Wyclif, displaying his intellect in his wicked Propositions in the way I have described above, with the determined support of the people of London tricked his examiners, mocked the bishops and got away. All his Propositions, when understood in their completeness in the way which he put them forward in the schools and in his public preaching, undoubtedly smack of heretical wickedness. But when he dropped them into the ears of the laity, he did not add a dose of circumlocution, but taught them in an unadorned and open fashion, as described above. By this means he captured the support of the people, who willingly listen to outrageous talk, especially when it is about the church and vicars, and are willingly led to inflict harm and injury upon monks and priests, whenever some opportunity turns up, as that is just the sort of thing they long and pray for.

And although he had been commanded by the bishops not to repeat such Propositions in the schools or his sermons as they were a scandal to the laity, that celebrated hypocrite ignored the instruction of his archbishop and in his obstinate disobedience did not omit to put forward some new Conclusions which sounded just as bad or worse than his original ones, as is clear from what follows.

1. Civil lordship is lordship over property. It is carried out by a wayfarer over goods which are all held in accordance with human laws.
2. It is not possible for a professional cleric to exercise civil lordship and be free from mortal sin. And by 'professional cleric' he understands the pope, cardinals, bishops, deacons and other priests.
3. The pope, just like any other professional cleric, cannot make dispensations that go against the apostle, so that he may have civil possessions.
4. Civil lordship, formally stated, is inseparably bound up with sin.
5. Civil action is the action of a creature possessing reason, carried out according to human law.
6. Just as God cannot perform civil actions, nor man in a state of innocence, so it is not lawful for anyone who any professional cleric to perform civil actions.

7. Any college of clerics whatever, that acquires goods of fortune, revenues or income in order to exercise civil dominion by means of them, commits mortal sin.

8. It is impossible that Christ with the absolute power of god should have been a civil king.

9. Monks, just like Christ's apostles, should have no civil possessions, as can be clearly elicited from the rule and professions made by all monks.

The major part of the accumulation of the goods of fortune in the hands of the religious would have been removed from them, if the laws of the kingdom of England had been properly put into effect – and by the term 'religious' in this Conclusion he means bishops, priests, monks, canons, and all professional clerics.

The English fleet returns

About that time the English fleet returned to France. As I have already described, it met with great dangers from wind and wave at the moment of its first setting out,[1] but at this second attempt it experienced still greater ones, though not so much from storms as from the treacherous mutiny of its sailors, whom it could have expected would do their duty. This mutinous spirit was very clearly seen among the sailors commanded by [Walter] Lord Fitzwalter. At the moment when the fleet of Lord Thomas Woodstock, earl of Buckingham, had decided to attack the Spanish fleet, these very sailors, to whom Lord Fitzwalter should have been able to give orders, not only refused to go to the help of Thomas, but even forcibly held back Lord Fitzwalter when he wanted to hurry to bring relief to Thomas. Indeed when he roundly abused them for refusing this help, they would have gone so far as to kill him, had he not taken the precaution of slipping away. In the end he escaped in a sloop with one or two companions, joined up with the earl and gave him all the help he could. As a result eight Spanish ships were taken in the sea off Brittany near the harbour of the castle of Brest, and possibly more would have been captured if those deserters from their duties of attack and defence had been present to help. And so the achievement was less praiseworthy than it might have been. The fleet returned to England after Christmas. From the moment it assembled, it had been so hindered, impeded and battered by adverse rainstorms, snow, gales, tempest- blasts, and then by mutiny, that it seemed as though divine support had been missing.

Only Sir Thomas Percy of this expedition had remained behind, to repair his fleet, when the rest had set sail a second time, and he deservedly not only avoided the misfortunes of the voyage but also, with the help of God, won a great triumph for himself and the whole kingdom. For after he had patched up his weakened vessels, he set out with one large ship, two barges and a few other smaller vessels, and came across fifty ships laden with French merchandise, some of which were Flemish, some Spanish. He boldly attacked this squadron after first warning the Flemish ships to separate themselves from the Spanish. When the Flemish ships refused to leave their companions, as they were aware that they were carrying provisions for themselves as well as for France, Sir Thomas attacked the whole squadron without making any distinction, and they, seeing his fierce determination and expecting great reinforcements to arrive for him at any moment, stopped putting up any resistance. Very soon twenty-two of them surrendered, although twenty-eight of them managed to escape. And so only Sir Thomas, through this exploit, returned home with a success. The others brought back nothing besides a blackened reputation. It was said of them that their expedition failed because they had dared to take with them for their wars at sea not only common prostitutes but even wives of their countrymen to satisfy their adulterous lusts.

[Sir] Robert Knolles

At the same time [Sir] Robert Knolles, who had been entrusted with the command of the castle of Brest, learned from the information of scouts that in a few days time some Bretons would be arriving to plunder the country round about so that he himself would be roused by this to leave the castle in a rash attempt to drive them off; and then, if fortune favoured them, the Bretons were confident of killing Robert himself. But their plans were in vain; for he foiled their cunning

---

[1]   See above, p. 48.

scheme by getting in first, and, following the lead of the divine grace, he used against them the scheme they had devised against him and they fell into the pit which they had made, and eighty of them were captured and thrown in prison.[1]

Sir Hugh Calveley and his men despoil the merchants of Boulogne

A few days after Christmas, Sir Hugh Calveley, who regarded idleness as damaging to himself, and who was unwilling for the enemy to spend days at a time doing nothing, called together all his people round about who followed the English flag and all his mercenaries. After he had given them a great feast and could see that the wine had made all of them rather merry, he asked them whether, if necessity demanded it, they were willing to follow him in a joint enterprise which could involve loss or profit. They assured him with an oath that they were ready to follow his banner wherever he wanted. For the time being he merely thanked them individually and sent them back to their homes, but just three days later he asked them to turn up with their weapons. They obeyed his summons, and Sir Hugh in person told them what he had in mind and what he had decided to for their mutual benefit.

And soon, when all of them agreed to carry out his wishes, he led out his armed band in secret and hurried as fast as he could to the town of Étaples. It was market day in the town, and there had flocked there merchants from Boulogne, Montreuil, Amiens, and Paris, together with many others who had come to sell their goods with no fear of danger. Sir Hugh and his men passed the night in hiding, and in the morning he waited for a suitable time and entered the town with his troops. They immediately rushed upon the unarmed crowd, killed several and put many in chains, to be ransomed as captives. Then in enemy fashion they plundered all the merchandise and set fire to and burnt the town, apart from a few places that were protected from the flames and saved by the care of their owners.[2] The wines, and other bulkier items which they were not able conveniently to take with them, Sir Hugh threatened to pour out or throw into the sea, unless the merchants intervened by pledging him their word that to preserve their goods they would pay him as tax a sum of money to be decided upon at his own pleasure. Having tied up all the loose ends, he marched back unharmed to Calais with his men, bringing with him from the market goods which could be expected to be of use to his people in Calais for many a year.

The men of Winchelsea recover spoils taken from them

During these days the men of Winchelsea and Rye collected a force together, embarked on barges and sailed towards Normandy to see if they could obtain any reparation for the losses of the last year inflicted on them by the enemy and wishing to do them some harm. They landed at night and made an armed entry into the town called St Pierre-en-Port.[3] Killing any they came across at sword point, they roamed the streets, and brought back bound to their vessels those whom they thought worth taking prisoner, in other words those able to pay a worthwhile sum of money as ransom. They sacked churches as well as houses, in all of them meting out the same measure with which they had been previously meted at Rye, and at length they found many spoils which had been taken from Rye, and especially the bells removed from the church, together also with the lead stripped from it by ill-omened hands. In the end, committing the whole town to the care of Vulcan, they hurriedly descended to the nearby town of Veulettes, and, doing the same thing there, they returned home with hugely valuable booty.

---

[1]   Under the terms of the agreement with Duke Jean IV de Montfort of Brittany, Brest had been leased to the English in April 1378 and Sir Robert Knolles had assumed the captaincy. The success of Franco-Breton forces had left Brest somewhat exposed but wth a garrison of almost 300 Knolles's position was secure. See also M. Jones, *Ducal Brittany, 1364–99: Relations with England and France during the Reign of John IV* (Oxford, 1970), pp. 147–8.
[2]   It is disingenuous of Walsingham to suggest that this destruction was the 'enemy fashion'. It was also a characteristic of the chevauchée that the English forces had frequently conducted on the French mainland.
[3]   To the north east of Fécamp.

The request of the duke of Lancaster

At the same time John [of Gaunt], duke of Lancaster, made an urgent request that the money should be entrusted to his charge which had been previously granted to the king by clergy and laity in the last parliament, claiming that with this same money he would keep back the enemy from the coasts of England for a whole year, and besides this would also confer upon the people some great benefit.[1] The nobles, although unwillingly, agreed to this importunate request with, it is said, some bitterness of heart. They already knew that fortune was against them and that the duke held such power in the kingdom that it was extremely inadvisable for them to go against his wishes. So a plan was decided upon and it was arranged that on the first day of March all the individuals who were part of this expedition should assemble at the coast with all their preparations made. And so that the sea should not be unguarded in the meantime, they hired nine ships from the people of Bayonne to protect both sea and land from invasion and pillage by the French. When these ships had been equipped with an adequate force of marines, they soon ploughed a furrow over the waves and met a fleet of Spanish merchantmen. They joined battle by making a fierce attack on the Spanish fleet, and in a short time they had captured fourteen ships loaded with wine and other provisions, and returned to England to announce the glad news. However they gave the first fruits of their spoils, a hundred casks of choice wine, to [Sir] Robert Knolles, governor of the town of Brest, since they had crossed the channel back to England under his protection.

Enrique the Bastard prepares a fleet

Meanwhile Enrique the Bastard, who calls himself 'king of Spain',[2] was given a great fright when he heard that the people of Bayonne had inflicted so many losses on his men and that the duke of Lancaster had assembled a great force to sail the seas.[3] He judged that the duke would be sailing not only in defence of the sea but also in an attempt on his kingdom, seeking to claim it by force on behalf of his wife, who was the lawful heir of the kingdom of Spain. And so Enrique ordered a fleet to be got ready from the whole land, so that he might either manfully prevent the duke from entering his country, or, if fortune favoured him and Mars was on his side, take him prisoner.

And perhaps this would have happened, if the king of Portugal had not got in his way. For some disagreements arose between the two of them and the king of Portugal with a well-nigh innumerable force of Christians and Saracens made a hostile attack on the Spanish kingdom, just at the moment when the Bastard had made preparations to start his journey against the duke. This happening rattled the Bastard, and he judged it safer to stay in his land to drive out those who had now occupied his kingdom, rather than to make a hasty exit from it of doubtful validity in search of men who had not yet arrived at his borders.

While these matters that concerned the duke of Lancaster were proceeding in the way I have

---

[1] In the earliest, 'scandalous' recension of the chronicle, Walsingham claimed that Gaunt deliberately delayed this campaign and he condemned him for it: *CA*, pp. 195–6.

[2] Enrique of Trastamara (c.1333–79), from 1366 King Enrique II of Castile, was the illegitimate son of Alfonso XI (d.1349) of Castile by his mistress Leonor de Guzman. The crown of Castile had been inherited by Alfonso's legitimate son, Pedro I, (known as 'the cruel'), but Trastamara attracted magnate support and made an abortive attempt to depose his half-brother in 1354. He fled to France where his claim also attracted support since Pedro was suspected of the murder of his French queen Blanche of Bourbon. With the support of both the French and Free Lances, Enrique invaded Castile in 1366 and successfully deposed Pedro who now sought succour from the English, the enemies of Enrique's French allies. English forces under Edward the Black Prince defeated Enrique at Najera in 1367 but within two years Pedro was again deposed and Enrique recovered the kingdom. See also P. E. Russell, *The English Interventions in Spain and Portugal in the time of Edward III and Richard II* (Oxford, 1955), pp. 46, 96–105, 147–8, 152, 167–9, 195–8, 217–20.

[3] Enrique had been forced into an ignominious retreat two years before when his invasion of Gascony foundered at the walls of Bayonne, where the English garrison under the command of the experienced captain Sir William Elmham, presented spirited resistance. See also Froissart, *Chroniques*, ix. 69; FCBuchon, ii. 30.

described, and he himself, so the story goes, was not hurrying down to the sea but delaying his departure from day to day, the commanders of the western fleet were stirred into action, and, without waiting for the duke, made for the high seas with a force of high-spirited warriors, intending to wait for his arrival there: they thought it more glorious to live on spoils taken from the enemy while at sea than on provisions looted on land from the inhabitants. When they had ploughed the pathways of the sea for several days, they were met by an armed force of Spaniards. Both fleets soon engaged in combat, and, led on by a desire for booty, fought a battle without further delay. But our men, driven apart by adverse weather conditions, conceded victory to the enemy, some of them escaping in flight but some falling prisoner into the hands of the enemy. Sir Hugh Courtenay, a knight with an outstanding reputation, was captured in this conflict.[1] His misfortune was ascribed solely to the duke of Lancaster because he had kept his presence from them for so long. But I do not know whether the duke was to blame, for the angry crowd does not always get it right.

The pope dies

At the same time, around the feast of St Ivo bishop [24 April], on 26 March came the death of Pope Gregory [XI].[2] He was a particularly good and just man, who had been greatly troubled by the losses suffered by the kingdoms of both England and France and had worked hard to bring about peace between them. Also, on account of his affection for Simon Langham, cardinal and bishop of Palestrina and one time archbishop of Canterbury,[3] he had himself, when pestilence raged in this land, given a complete indulgence from the Church's treasury through his bulls to all who died at that time, provided that they had repented and confessed. The only exceptions were those who were weighed down by debt. This was a massive benefit, most worthy of everyone's acceptance, and quite the greatest that he could have given to our people.

He was succeeded by Bartholomeo [Prignano], archbishop of Bari, who suffered many tribulations at the hands of the cardinals because of his promotion of justice.[4] Indeed the cardinals themselves tried to disgrace him by depriving him of the papacy, as I shall explain later on in the proper place.

John Mercer plunders ships at Scarborough

About this time, while John, duke of Lancaster, was still busy on land, the son of John Mercer, a Scot by birth, collected together a large band of French and Scots and even some Spanish and attacked some English ships near Scarborough.[5] They were off their guard, so he captured them

---

[1] This cannot refer to Hugh Courtenay, earl of Devon, who died, aged 73, in May 1377, or his grandson, Hugh, who died in 1374. Perhaps Edward (c.1357–1419) Courtenay, earl of Devon is intended.

[2] In fact Gregory XI died on 27 March. Rome was in a state of high tension even before Gregory expired and the civic authorities placed a guard on the city gates and prepared the piazza of St Peter's for public executions in an effort to maintain order and pressure the cardinals into proceeding to the election of a Roman successor.

[3] For Langham see note above, p. 28.

[4] The sixteen cardinals, ten of whom were French, and two Roman, present in Rome (five others were at Avignon and one in Tuscany) entered the conclave on 7 April as the Roman mob clamoured outside for the election of a Roman 'or at least an Italian'; under pressure, they proceeded to an election on the morning of 8 April but fearing the anger of the mob at their preference for a candidate who was neither a Roman nor a cardinal, they concealed the true candidate until they had made their escape. The next day the uproar had abated and Prignano, who had also been acting Vice-Chancellor of the Curia, was proclaimed as Urban VI; he was elected on 8 April 1378 and installed ten days later.

[5] The attack on Scarborough, led by Andrew Mercer, a Perth merchant, was a reprisal for action taken by the English two years before. Andrew's father, John, had been shipwrecked off the Northumbrian coast and in spite of the Anglo-Scottish truce, his cargo was seized and he himself had been imprisoned in Scarborough castle. John had been released in the summer of 1377 after partial payment of his ransom, but his son Andrew had still sought revenge. Walsingham's claims as to Mercer's character and connections with the French are characteristic embroidery, although there is no reason to doubt that Andrew Mercer's squadron included both French and Spanish ships; the chronicler evidently disapproved of John's release and suspected that a greater

with little trouble and took them with him out to sea, having first killed some of those who were in command of these ships and taken others prisoner. His most important reason for inflicting this harm on our shipping was his wish to avenge the shame suffered by his father, who had previously been captured by the English and on the king's order put under guard in Scarborough castle. The father was as Scottish as the son, by both birth and country, and had been a great favourite of the French king because of his great wealth. He was a crafty, shrewd individual, and it was not without good reason that the king himself and all the French followed his advice in matters affecting the English. By chance the men of Northumberland had intercepted him with some of his ships and handed him over to their earl [i.e. Henry Percy]. As I have said, he was given into custody in Scarborough castle, but had soon afterwards been set free, to the great loss of the whole kingdom and all its inhabitants. For if he had been ransomed in the usual way of prisoners, his uncountable wealth would have enriched king and kingdom. And his son, after inflicting the losses on our ships at Scarborough, was boasting about fortune smiling on him, and not only planning to do still greater damage to England, but even openly threatening it. But He who brings low the proud and lifts up the humble put paid to his attempt himself.[1]

For then indeed God raised up against him one of the citizens of London, who brought him low and freed the kingdom of England from its fear of him, as will become clear to those willing to read the following account. John Philipot was a citizen of London, a man endowed with a good brain and very powerful because of his wealth.[2] He noted carefully the deficiencies, not to say the treachery, of the duke of Lancaster and the other lords, who should have been defending the kingdom, and, as he was sorry for the sufferings of his countrymen, out of his own pocket he hired about a thousand marines to take back from the son of John Mercer the ships and the goods which he had seized by his piracy, and to guard the kingdom of England from such raids. And it happened that the Almighty, who always listen to holy prayers, provided such a successful outcome for him and his men that, in a short time, his mercenaries captured the son of John Mercer by right of war and all the ships he had so violently seized at Scarborough, together with the fifteen Spanish ships, laden with much wealth, which had on that occasion assisted Mercer, though at an unlucky hour for themselves.[3] There were celebrations up and down the land, as everybody praised and marvelled at the great goodwill and affection that John Philipot had shown towards the king. Indeed at that time it was Philipot alone whose praises were on everybody's lips as an object of admiration, whereas the fickle commons, in its usual way, hurled bitter words of scornful invective against our nobles and the campaign which they had been engaged in for so long.[4] Criticism came especially from the citizens of London, who said that now there were very few hearts who were on the king's side, and that they alone were faithful to him. In fact some of the nobles, although speaking ironically, had called Richard the Londoners' king, because they had helped him so much at his coronation.

ransom might have been expected for so grand a prize. The author of the *Historia vitae et regni Ricardi secundi* records that fifteen Spanish vessels were involved: *HVRS*, p. 50

1   Walsingham's optimism here is misplaced: although orders were issued for the Mercer and his son to be surrendered to Henry Percy, and their imprisonment in Alnwick Castle was anticipated, they had still not been imprisoned in the following spring.

2   For Philipot, who was mayor of London in 1378, see above, p. 34. Like the Londoners themselves, Walsingham regarded him warmly as a champion of the city's liberties.

3   Walsingham is the principal authority for Philipot's revival but there is no reason to doubt his accuracy even if the size of his force may be exaggerated.

4   Walsingham was an ardent admirer of Philipot, a reflection of the close affiliation between the monastic community at St Albans and the cultural and political community in the city of London. But on this occasion his enthusiasm was echoed elsewhere; even as far off as the Midlands, the Evesham monk responsible for the *Historia vitae et regni Ricardi secundi* considered Philipot 'ciuis egregius Regis et regni specialis amator': *HVRS*, p. 50.

The jealousy of the nobles towards John Philipot[1]

The leading men of the kingdom of England, that is the barons and earls, when they saw that John Philipot's action had received such praise, were conscience-stricken and took it badly. Although they could see that their guilt and culpability were such that their idleness was now obvious to the people, they began not only to plot against John Philipot in secret but also to reproach him in public, claiming that it was not lawful for him to do such things without the consent of the council of the king and the kingdom.[2] It was just as if they had said that it had not been lawful for John to aid the king or the kingdom without the consent of the earls and barons. When they had made such speeches, with their principal spokesman being Hugh, earl of Stafford, even though he was almost the youngest of them,[3] it is said that John made this answer. 'You can know,' he said, 'without any doubt, that I did not expose myself and my money and my men to the dangers of the sea, just so as to steal from you and your colleagues for my own gain a good name for fighting. It was rather that I felt sorrow for the troubles that had fallen on my people and their land, which, thanks to your sloth, has now fallen from being the noblest of kingdoms and the mistress of nations into such a pit of misery that it lies open to the plundering attacks of the lowest tribe. None of you was willing to lift a finger in its defence. So I risked my own life and possessions to save the people to whom I belong and to set free their country.' The earl had no answer to make to this.

The earls of Salisbury and Arundel come to an agreement with the people of Cherbourg about the town

The duke of Lancaster still lingered in England, refusing to try his fortune at sea in the limited time available of spring and early summer. It was not known what obstacles detained him. But at his persuasion the two earls of Salisbury[4] and Arundel[5] did set sail. They were to examine the places for possible future naval expeditions of the enemy and their allies, and to report that there was no danger. Indeed the earl of Salisbury, Sir William Montagu, who had vigorously practised the profession of arms from his youth up, soon after setting sail, landed his ships on the coast opposite in order to inflict some damage upon the enemy. As his staying on there was proving harmful to the enemy, he made an agreement with the citizens of Cherbourg (which belonged to the king of Navarre, who by then had become an enemy of the king of France [Charles V])[6] to the

---

[1] This is not a suggestion made by other chroniclers.

[2] In the earliest, 'scandalous' recension of the chronicle, Walsingham suggests that John of Gaunt was the instigator of the murmuring against Philipot: *CA*, pp. 199–200.

[3] Hugh (c. 1342–86), 2nd earl of Stafford, who had been a member of the Black Prince's circle before 1376, was one of six new members of the king's council appointed in October 1377. He was also one of a committee of ten appointed to examine the state of the King's finances in April 1379.

[4] William Montagu, 2nd earl of Salisbury (1328–97), served with Edward III on the Crécy (1346) and Poitiers (1356) campaigns, latterly as the king's constable.

[5] Richard Fitzalan (1346–97), 4th earl of Arundel. For his later career see below, pp. 245–8, 253–4, 263.

[6] Caught between the more powerful, rival monarchs, Charles II 'the Bad' of Navarre had held the French at bay while courting the English, but in the spring of 1378, Charles V of France had intercepted two Navarese envoys, apparently en route for England, and had retaliated with the seizure of Charles the Bad's Norman possessions, including Cherbourg. His lieutenant Bertrand du Guesclin (c. 1320–80, Constable of France, 1370–80) siezed Evreux and the Cotentin, but when it came to Cherbourg he was outmanouevered by Navarre. Charles appealed to the English for assistance, and attended upon Richard in person at Windsor. He was granted a force of 1000 men-at-arms for a period of four months on the condition that, when recovered, Cherbourg to be placed under English control. As Froissart recounts in greater detail than Walsingham, the English undertook command of the castle and town for a period of three years, placing a garrison there under Sir John Harleston while sovereignty remained in the hands of King Charles. From the point of view of Navarre this arrangement soon paid dividends when an advance on the town led by du Guesclin's brother Olivier was repelled by Harleston with reinforcements under Sir John Arundel. The younger du Guesclin was captured: Froissart, *Chroniques*, ix. 61–2, 95–8. See also Henneman, *Olivier de Clisson*, p. 89; R. Vernier, *The Flower of Chivalry: Bertrand du Guesclin and the Hundred Years War* (Woodbridge, 2003), pp. 179–82.

effect that the town should pass to the control and government of the king of England, provided that he took upon himself the defence of the town against the French, to the advantage of the king and kingdom of England and the harm of the French. When this had been done, the earls of Salisbury and Arundel [Richard Fitzalan] sent back messengers to the king and council of the realm, informing them about this pleasing success, and asking them to send out from England men who would guard the town. The number of men that seemed sufficient to guard the town were sent out, and soon after the earls returned to England.

Sir Hugh Calveley captures the castle of Marck

About this same time, a period which it is a blessing to remember, Sir Hugh Calveley would not allow the French to fall asleep while he was in the area, and he captured the castle called Marck, and razed it right down to the ground, together with a church, which was near the castle and a great stronghold for the French. After a short time he set off for St Omer, and, capturing a countless host of animals of different kinds, took them all the way to Calais. No one dared to oppose his ventures, because God was with him and directing all that he did.

Sir Hugh must also be praised for this exploit: the captain of the castle of Ardres had planned to play a crafty trick on him, but Sir Hugh in person justly tricked the captain, shrewdly using this opportunity to push the captain into the pit which he had dug. The captain had asked for reinforcements from the French king, some soldiers and weapons, siege engines and artillery and the other things by which the defences of the enemy can be weakened or completely destroyed. He promised that with these he would do great damage to our towns, especially those situated near Calais. A day had been fixed for transferring all these things to the town of Ardres, but the captain was afraid of the watchful Hugh, who hardly ever, if at all, allowed the French and their equipment to pass anywhere near him without attacking them. So to keep Hugh too busily engaged to hinder the plans he had made, the captain sent him a message, saying that he wanted to discuss certain matters with him. The captain had worked it out carefully so that the discussion would be on the very day on which all the equipment mentioned was due to arrive. But Hugh was no fool. He realised that it was not for nothing that the captain had so carefully appointed this particular day for their discussion, but he agreed to be given a safe conduct for that very day to discuss whatever the captain had in mind. But he sent a secret message to his own men, instructing them to block the crucial road, and led them out in secret from Boulogne to the town of Ardres, in case the captain was plotting further harmful schemes against the English. And by the will of God it happened that all this equipment was successfully captured by Hugh's men and taken to Calais, together with all the weapons and other belongings of the soldiers, before the captain himself had even left for the conference, which he had cunningly devised to trick Hugh. So when he saw everything going to Calais, he was shaking in his shoes in terror, and withdrew, shaking his head and lamenting. He admitted the trick, which he had dreamed up, declaring that he had been ingeniously outwitted and outmanoeuvred in his own stratagem.

The English defeated

About this time the English suffered a great defeat, which brought disgrace to the whole kingdom, because of the folly of the arrogant Northumbrians.[1] It is characteristic of them that they talk in lofty language and impetuously attempt grand schemes, while being very prone to collapsing and very easily brought low. On this occasion they put their trust in their own strength and, with hardly any consultation at all, they burst from their western borders into the land of Scotland, thinking that there they could make the mountains level with the valleys and grind the rocks to powder without any help from their neighbours. But the Scots were well informed of the attack, assembled an adequate force and went out to meet them. Without great losses of their own men

---

1   This was one of a number of skirmishes that occurred in the borders after the incident at Roxburgh fair. Walsingham is the only English authority to record this in detail and there is no evidence to corroborate his suggestion that it was a great battle or that the losses on the English side were significant.

return to Spain, the count regarded the pledge he had given to his captors as a light matter, although his son, as I have said, was left behind as a hostage in England.[1]

Well, after the two famous Edwards, the king the father [i.e. Edward III] and the prince the son, had paid their dues owed to nature, the counsellors of the new king arrogantly interfered in the matter. Some think that this was done to please the duke of Lancaster, for he had a claim to the kingdom of Spain, and with such an important count on his side, would find it easier to get possession of the kingdom. But others declared that it was done on behalf of the Lady Maud, the sister of the king and the widow of Sir P. Courtenay [i.e. Hugh, lord Courtenay, d.1374], in order that her betrothal to such an eminent man might lead to the growth of peace and friendship between the kingdoms as the result of such a marriage. But the king and the duke were completely unable to free the son from the grasp of the esquires, who had hidden him far away from their control. So the esquires were arrested and thrust into the Tower of London. But they escaped from their imprisonment there and took refuge in the court of Westminster.[2] The duke and their enemies, the counsellors, took this badly and they decided upon an unheard of remedy:[3] ignoring all the sanctions laid down by a line of holy kings and confirmed by a host of high pontiffs, scorning the threats of all the decrees which forbade such terrible behaviour and showing no fear of God or reverence for holy mother church, they finally decided to drive them from their sanctuary, bring them all the way back to the Tower, and to guard them more carefully there – or, as was thought, to put them to such suffering that death was the unavoidable result. So fifty of the king's courtiers were sent armed to Westminster to put into effect an action that paid no regard to man or God or the church. The counsellors sent them in secret.[4] They were afraid of the citizens, and thought that a rising might take place among the people.

The armed men entered the sanctuary of St Peter [i.e. the abbey church], cunningly surrounded the first man, John Shakell, and dragged him from his freedom in the church, and immediately took him back to the Tower. But when on the same day they approached the second man, Robert Hawley, they found him attending a celebration of the Mass on the morrow of St Laurence's day [11 August].[5] They called upon him to make amends to the king for the offences he had committed against his majesty, in that, although he was the liege-man of the king, he had shown contempt not only for the king's requests but even for his prayers, and had dared to turn his back on him in this shameless fashion. While Hawley struggled to accuse not the king but his counsellors of injustice, greed and false testimony, the armed men laid hands upon him to drag him forcibly from the church and one of them drew a dagger. But Hawley, though unarmed himself, forced the armed men to take to their heels and in his desire to save his skin, he twice ran for refuge around the choir of the monastery, until finally in the choir itself he was completely surrounded by the soldiers. In short they assailed him on all sides with daggers and shouted to him with dreadful cries to give himself up. Their shouts disturbed that most holy assembly of monks as well as the priest, who was standing by the holy altar after reading the words of the holy gospel, and their madness blazed still higher until not only were they polluting the house of God but even as agents of wickedness turning their weapons against the very servants of Christ (who, as I said, were serving the Lord in the choir at that moment) fixing their sword-points on the

[1]   In fact on his return to Spain, Denia sought the intercession of King of Aragon for a reduction of the ransom sum.
[2]   Hawley and Shakell were arrested and imprisoned in October 1371; almost seven years later, in August 1378, they made their escape. They sought sanctuary in Westminster Abbey which, under canon law, should have ensured them exemption from any secular jurisdiction.
[3]   Walsingham reflects the opinion widespread at the time that Gaunt was responsible for this whole episode in spite of the fact that he was campaigning in Brittany throughout the summer and autumn of 1378.
[4]   This force was led by Sir Alan Buxhill, Constable of the Tower, together with Sir Ralph Ferrers, a chamber knight and councillor. For his career see CPR, 1377–81, pp. 19, 39, 40, 45, 142, 449. In his earliest 'scandalous' account of this episode Walsingham claimed that Gaunt was behind the decision to seize Hawley and Shakell, but here he is content to follow other contemporary commentators and lay the blame more generally, at unnamed counsellors of the king. See, for example, HVRS, p. 51.
[5]   The date is confirmed by the Anonimalle author: AC, p. 122.

breasts of all of them, and forbidding them on the pain of frightful death not to help the man whom they themselves were struggling to destroy. By now they had surrounded Robert Hawley, while he for his part was seeking the peace of the church and asking the reason for such outrage and with crossed arms commending himself to God and the church with these words, 'I give myself up to God, the avenger of wrongs such as these, and to the sanctuary of holy mother church', and, as he was saying these words, one of them cruelly struck his head with his sword and dashed out his brains, as he stood in the choir, close by the altar. At the same moment another ran through his body with his sword-point from behind. And one of the servants of the church, who had tried to stop the occurrence of such a crime by admonishing and warning them not to besmirch that holy temple, miraculously dedicated by the chief of the apostles and unpolluted up to that day, soon had a sword driven through his ribs by one of them on that very spot, and in his death, so we believe, gained a martyr's crown.[1] The agents of the sacrilege, heralds of Antichrist, not content with such accursed deeds of evil, got hold of the lifeless corpse of Robert Hawley by the feet, and dragged that loathsome object through the most sacred place of the choir and through the church, bespattering everything with his blood and brains, until finally they threw it contemptuously out through the doors. They were like raving bacchanals, neither fearing God nor showing reverence to men.

And so a sanctuary is profaned, Zion is in mourning, the holy church of St Peter sits in sadness.[2] The seat of kings, the leading church of the land has been treated with contempt and derision, the roads of Zion are in mourning because all its gates are destroyed, its priests uttering laments and the church itself overcome with bitter sorrow. Enemies have been placed at its head, its foes enriched, because the Lord had made a pronouncement about it. And what did the Lord say? As we have been told by our elders, the Lord prophesied this sacrilege when he foretold that vengeance for the murder of St Thomas [Becket], archbishop of Canterbury, would be delayed until the shrine at Westminster was polluted by human blood. Such vengeance should have been feared, and we must pray to the Lord for the coming of peace and truth in our time.

The first sentence of excommunication pronounced against the malefactors by the bishops

After these murders had been carried out at Westminster, the shepherds of the church met together and for some time were uncertain how to act: should they strike with the fear inspired by actual swords, or with the spiritual sword, or should they entrust everything to the power and strength of St Peter? At last, though late in the day, they plucked up courage, and the archbishop of Canterbury [Simon Sudbury] with five suffragans went before the people, and with thunder and lightning pronounced sentence of excommunication against all who had taken part in this criminal enterprise or who had given advice or help to the murderers. The bishops singled out by name Sir Alan Buxhill and Sir Ralph Ferrers, who had been the leading spirits among the malefactors, but at the end of their words especially excepted from excommunication the king, his mother and the duke of Lancaster. On Sundays, Wednesdays and Fridays at St Paul's, the bishop of London for a long time continued in awesome fashion to pronounce this sentence of excommunication against the malefactors, with the result that several of them, struck and scorched by this terrible thunderbolt, rapidly turned in repentance to the peace offered by the church.

The duke [of Lancaster] increases the ill-feeling against him

At the same time a council was held at Windsor.[3] The duke of Lancaster had now returned thither, together with the other nobles who had accompanied him to the sea as described above, since he had used up his money without achieving any success, according to what everybody said about

---

1   This was the sacristan of the abbey. His name is not recorded. See also *AC*, p. 122.
2   The *Anonimalle* author reports that after the killing of Hawley no mass was celebrated in the church until Christmas: *AC*, p. 122.
3   The council was convened between 13 and 16 September: *AC*, pp. 122–3; Saul, *Richard II*, p. 469.

him. When, on his arrival at Windsor, he heard about the terrible thunderbolt being launched daily from the lips of the bishop of London [William Courtenay], he was very angry and said that he particularly abhorred the impudence of a prelate, who, on receiving letters from the king begging him to desist or to defer the pronouncement of the excommunication, had totally ignored the prayers of the king and persisted in his preconceived stubbornness. And what was still more bizarre, he claimed, was that the bishop had haughtily turned down an invitation from the king to attend the council at Windsor.[1] This being so, the duke declared that he was willing to hurry to London, should the king command it, and drag the contumacious bishop to the council by main force, however opposed to this those 'rascal' Londoners (as he called them) might be. Also people were saying that it was on his order and with his connivance that all the wicked events at Westminster, which I have described had taken place, so that many people were moved to think badly of him in their hearts and to speak ill of him.

A parliament at Gloucester

On the festival of St Luke the Evangelist [18 October] a parliament was held at Gloucester,[2] at the instigation of some awkward people who were always contriving to do the priesthood or the kingdom some new mischief. Their chief reason for choosing Gloucester was their belief that in such a distant spot the bishops, the common people of the realm and the citizens of London would be less daring in opposing or speaking against their wishes. For the story got abroad that their intention, if they had achieved their perverse purpose, had been to mulct the kingdom for a limitless sum of money and even to deprive holy church of many of her possessions.[3] And so they had chosen Gloucester for their scheme, fearing that if the parliament was held in London, the citizens might use their influence or power to hinder their plans in some way.[4] But God who brings to nought the wisdom of the wise and with just a nod rejects the intelligence of the intelligent smashed their scheme. Indeed it is believed that the hearts of the archbishop and the other bishops were comforted and visited by the Lord, who gave them such strong assurance that they decided among themselves not to agree to anything which might be prejudicial or harmful to the church. Their decision became known to the mischief makers, who, being themselves worried about suffering a shameful defeat, transformed themselves into angels of light and decided for the time being not to put into effect any of their plans but to do everything which the archbishop and his suffragans might decree or order.

But so that they should not leave their country completely unscathed, they passed a measure that for the present year merchants should pay one mark for each sack of wool. They also decreed that for each pound of silver, obtained from imports from abroad that were then passed on to a buyer, sixpence should be paid to the king.[5]

---

[1]   Given his earlier confrontations with Gaunt over John Wyclif (see above, pp. 30–1) it is not surprising that Bishop Courtenay seized this new opportunity to publicly condemn the duke.
[2]   In fact parliament convened on Wednesday 20 October; *RP,* iii. 31.
[3]   Unusually, Walsingham expressed his fears and suspicions more moderately than some commentators; the Evesham monk who composed the *Historia vitae et regni Ricardi secundi,* and who was perhaps, better placed to recall the atmosphere of the assembly, recalled how 'princes and lords came together as one' to conspire against the Church: *HVRS,* pp. 52–3.
[4]   The location of this parliament might also account for Walsingham's cursory treatment of its proceedings, both in this text and in the earlier 'scandalous' narrative. In particular he appears unaware of the presence of John Wyclif, 'une graunde clerke a Oxenford' as the *Anonimalle* author describes him, to contribute to a debate on the privilege of sanctuary, a direct response to the Hawley-Shakell affair, in which Abbot John Litlington of Westminster was also involved: *AC,* p. 123.
[5]   In fact the Gloucester parliament was marked by the resistance of the commons towards granting any further financial assistance to the crown. They refused the request for a subsidy, expressing not only their concern at the council's failure to use of the 1377 grant for a new co-ordinated campaign against the French but also their suspicions that Gaunt had interfered with the work of the two treasurers for war. It was in this atmosphere of antagonism that the assembly was dissolved on 16 November: *RP,* iii. 37.

New nuncios from the pope

To this same parliament there came eminent papal envoys from Italy, asking for help from the king and his noblemen for the pope, who was in a tight spot. They outlined the injuries and the losses which the pope had suffered at the hands of his overweening apostate cardinals in their attempts to weaken and overthrow himself and the whole church. Envoys also arrived from these same cardinals, bringing ten dispatches with seals affixed, and in person speaking out strongly for the cardinals and asking for help to be given. But through the support of the Lord God who orders all things justly, the cardinals' envoys were sent away and the papal envoys were received favourably and promised that help would gladly be given to the pope, as soon as a suitable opportunity arose.

The archbishop of Canterbury [Simon Sudbury] indeed, when he weighed up the lies and mistakes included openly and publicly in the dispatches, in which the cardinals themselves were willingly implicated, powerfully cursed their wicked deeds and suddenly impelled by the spirit of God began to preach on the text, 'We shall have one shepherd' [Ezekiel 3: 23]. For he had discovered in the dispatches that they had held an election for a new pope, and he now so clearly expounded their heresy to the people in many arguments and making particular use of their own words that their wickedness was obvious to all and their accursed error exposed.

At that time one of the cardinals was absent from Rome. He had once been bishop of Amiens,[1] and he had recently been ordered by Pope Gregory [XI] of blessed memory to settle some disagreements that had arisen at Pisa between the pope and the citizens of the town. When he heard of the death of Pope Gregory and the election of Urban [VI] as the new pope, he decided to stay in Pisa for the time being, until he got news from his fellow cardinals or the pope. So he stayed in Pisa, but being soon afterwards summoned by apostolic letter he hurried to the curia to obey the papal commands. After his arrival, the new pope, on entering the council chamber, began to speak on many moral issues, and his sermon included an attack on the greed of the cardinals: for they, he said, corrupted by the gleam of gold and blinded by money, pursued wealth more than they did peace among the nations of the world, even though that was their mission.

The pope attacks the cardinals[2]

The pope also in more detail openly expressed his abhorrence and condemnation of the perfidy of the bishop of Amiens [Jean de la Grange].[3] The charge against him was that when he had been sent on frequent missions by Pope Gregory [XI], his predecessor, to establish peace between the kingdoms of England and France by whatever means he could, although he had pocketed the vast sums of gold and silver paid by both countries on the orders of the pope for the expenses of his journey, he had done nothing about the purpose of his mission and had taken no steps to bring about peace between them. He had rather made sure that the quarrels and hatred existing between

---

1   Jean de la Grange, bishop of Amiens from 1373 until 1375, the year he was raised to the cardinalate. He died in 1402. At the time of Urban's elections he was at Sarzana.
2   The cardinals had chosen Bartolomeo Prignano to be a cipher whom they might manipulate for their own ends but after his election he turned against them, attacking them for their corruption and prodigality. Walsingham here conflates into a single scene the events of three months. As tensions mounted at the end of May, the cardinals left the heat of Rome for Anagni, while Urban removed to Tivoli from where he summoned the cardinals to join him. The cardinals now compounded the breach by raising a force of Breton and Gascon mercenaries and made it permanent with their declaration on 20 July that Urban's election had been invalid; they also called for the four Italian cardinals who remained with Urban to join them in opposition. Urban sent envoys to Anagni to negotiate, but the rebel cardinals were now seeking support from further afield and on August 9 Charles V of France, Louis of Anjou and Queen Johanna of Naples all declared their support for the cause of the anti-Urbanists. Urban retaliated on 18 September with the appointment of twenty-eight new cardinals and two days [20 September] later the rebels completed their secession with the creation of Robert of Geneva (b.1342), cardinal archbishop of Cambrai, as Pope Clement VII. He was indeed 'high born' being the son of Count Amadeus III.
3   Jean de la Grange had been absent from the election of Urban on legaline business with the Florentines at Sarzana. Urban is said to have called him a liar when he attempted to pledge his loyalty.

bitter fighting, fortune smiled upon our men and the castle was recaptured in miraculous fashion, for all the lords, who as I have said had taken up position around it, forced their way in at one and the same moment, each one at the section that he had been given to take by storm.[1] Only two of the English were killed. Very many were wounded. On the Scottish side about forty-eight were trampled on and finished off with the sword, with only one of them being kept back to live so that he might tell us of Scottish plans.[2] And so with the help of God those workers of iniquity fell into the pit which they themselves had made, and almost all these villains of the March were crushed at the very moment when they were proudly beginning to think that they had completely driven out the English as a result of this one success.[3]

Just when the first break into the castle had been reported to the earl of Northumberland, he sent a messenger to the earl of Dunbar [George, 9th earl], who is the warden of the marches on the Scottish side, to ask if it was with his connivance or on his advice that the truce had been broken in this fashion and all these deeds done. The earl of Dunbar asserted that he had had absolutely no involvement in the affair and no knowledge of it before it happened; in fact he willingly gave his promise to hurry with the earl of Northumberland to Berwick and give all the help he could in wrenching the castle from the hands of the traitors. He came as he had promised, and asked the Scots by virtue of the treaty to give back the castle, which they had unjustly seized, either to the king of England or the earl of Northumberland or to the king's representative. The Scots in typical fashion gave the brief but impudent reply that there was no chance of them giving the castle back to the king of England or the king of Scotland; in fact they intended to hold it for the use of the king of France [Charles V] against all men, as long as they lived. And this boast was fulfilled. For they held it for eight days and on the ninth, as I have said, they were put to the sword.

The dispute between the king of France and the Bretons

During these days the king of France [Charles V] summoned a parliament at Paris, and compelled the nobles of Brittany who had come to the meeting to swear to give up the walled towns and fortresses that they had in their possession either to himself or to his representative, whenever it should please him to ask for them.[4] When some refused to bind themselves with such an oath, he frightened them with threats of death and forced many to swear. But the Bretons, when the parliament was over, hurried back to their homes and fortified their strongholds, bringing in corn and other necessities to stock them. The king of France soon sent Bertrand du Guesclin[5] with a large force to seize these strongholds from the hands of the Bretons and to garrison them with his Frenchmen. But the Bretons, who had known they were coming, resisted them bravely. With a strong band of armed men they kept the French out of their territory and compelled them to retreat. This was the occasion of war breaking out between the king of France and the Bretons.

---

[1]   Froissart agrees that the fighting was long and hard, lasting 'almost all day' but the *Anonimalle* author suggests it was a swifter action, the castle being regained within two hours: Froissart, *Chroniques*, ix. 36; FCBuchon, ii. 14–15; *AC*, p. 126.

[2]   Froissart identifies this prisoner as Alexander Ramsey: *Chroniques*, ix. 37.

[3]   Froissart describes the chevauchée that Northumberland now undertook in the border country as far as Melrose Abbey: *Chroniques*, ix. 37–47; FCBuchon, ii. 15–16.

[4]   For almost a decade Jean IV, duke of Brittany, had resisted the authority of the French crown, frequently lending support to the military endeavours of its English enemies. By the close of 1378 Charles V had been pushed to breaking point and in the December meeting of the Paris parlement John was formally accused of treason and his estates were declared confiscate. Du Guesclin, who was himself a Breton, moved to take control of the duchy's key fortifications. See Jones, *Ducal Brittany*, pp. 84–6; Vernier, *Flower of Chivalry*, pp. 178–9.

[5]   Duke Jean IV of Brittany had been summoned to Paris to face charges of conspiring with the English against the crown of France and at the same time the French Constable Du Guesclin, himself a Breton, Olivier de Clisson (1336–1407), a leading magnate in the Duchy, and other Breton lords loyal to Charles V attempted to tighten their hold over the duchy. However, the greater part of the Breton magnates now came together in opposition to the threat from the king's men and formed a league for the defence of Brittany. See Henneman, *Olivier de Clisson*, pp. 92–6; Vernier, *Flower of Chivalry*, p. 179.

Thus passed a year which had seen rich, abundant harvests; but in church matters it had been a year of disturbances on account of increasing heresies among the clergy, and a sad year because of the death of Pope Gregory [XI]; in England, France, Scotland and Brittany it had been a year full of suspicion, troubles and disturbances on account of various events and tumults.

[1379]

In 1379, the second year of the reign of Richard II, that outstanding knight Sir Robert Rous, the governor of Cherbourg, who had caused trouble to the French on several occasions and taken as prisoner Olivier, the brother of Bertrand du Guesclin, returned to England, after a governorship of many other useful achievements for his kingdom, and Sir John Harleston was sent out to take up the post.[1]

[Sir] Hugh Calveley recalled from Calais

During the same period Sir Hugh Calveley was recalled from Calais. His energetic governorship had brought profit and honour to the whole of England, and he was now made admiral of the seas. He was given as a colleague Sir Thomas Percy, to watch over the paths of the sea for one year. Lord William Montagu, earl of Salisbury, replaced Sir Hugh Calveley at Calais. Soon after his arrival his raids into France restocked Calais with great numbers of different kinds of animals and beasts of burden.[2]

The deeds of Hugh Calveley and Thomas Percy on the seas[3]

At the same time Sir Hugh Calveley and Sir Thomas Percy put to sea with large numbers of armed men. Sailing up and down the seas off Brittany they came across seven merchantmen, loaded with wine, and one warship. They overpowered them with little trouble, took possession of them and had them taken to Bristol. But when they got to the coast of Brittany, some of the men of Hugh and Thomas disembarked to raid the neighbouring country. And a French knight, called Sir Geoffrey de Charny [the Younger],[4] who was lying in ambush with a great force of soldiers, rushed out upon them, unaware as they were of any such ambush, and took as prisoner all who had gone up from the coast. But he had given his men instructions not to do injury to any of them, but to preserve them completely unharmed. And this was done. So Sir Geoffrey, taking with him the men whom he had captured with the rights of war, hurried under safe conduct to Sir Hugh Calveley and returned his prisoners without ransom, promising him that if he wanted to go up into the region, he would find the knights and citizens of the area very much on his side, and ready with their own hands to surrender their walled towns and fortresses to him. But if he wanted to delay in order to make sure of the country, Geoffrey, in the name of the princes of the land, offered him supplies and a thousand horses for his army, if he wished to ride over the land. But Sir Hugh excused himself from any delay or horse riding and said that he had another enterprise to finish which he had undertaken, and that for the present he could find no time at all to grant their wishes.

1   Sir Robert Rous had been a household knight from the outset of the reign and was a member of the king's second council (from October 1377–October 1378). He also served as acting marshal before being appointed to Cherbourg in 1378. Walsingham's chronology is incorrect here: according to Froissart the garrison there was reinforced by Sir John Arundel shortly before the skirmish which led to the capture of Olivier du Guesclin, but by that stage Rous appears already to have given way to Sir John Harleston. For Harleston's appointment see *CPR, 1377–81*, p. 495.
2   For Montagu as Captain of Calais see *CCR, 1377–81*, p. 193.
3   This episode is not recorded by other contemporary authorities.
4   For Charny's career see Henneman, *Olivier de Clisson*, p. 215.

tage if they were able to pick up any spoils from the enemy as they sailed home, and so refused to go back for the time being, but said they preferred first to return to their home town and then come back when they had gained new strength from new supplies of food and equipment.

To cut a long story short, they set sail for home while the knights with their troops proceeded to the policing and guarding of the seas. Sailing rapidly they were soon far apart from each other, out of sight and out of earshot, when the Cornish sailors came across a Flemish ship, loaded, packed, crammed and filled with armed traitors, cruel men of no religion. The Flemings knew that our guard-ships had gone off in the other direction and when they saw the Cornish ship sailing on its own, they began playing their usual game. Trampling and treading underfoot loyalty and honour, they boldly attacked our vessel. But the sailors saw that it was a matter of life and death, and got themselves ready to resist like men. A fierce fight followed, our men fighting for their ship and their lives, the Flemings on the other hand exerting themselves to ensure that their treacherous falseness on this occasion was not revealed, should they fail to emerge on top as victors. But what could a few tired sailors achieve against a large force of fresh men? Our men for a long time had been experiencing the hardships of life at sea and so were not equal to an enemy who outnumbered them and who had suffered minimal fatigue from the waves. So victory passed to bloodthirsty men of an inhuman cruelty. They took possession of the ship. Our sailors were laid low, killed and thrown overboard. No one was spared. No exceptions were made. There was nobody preserved, once chance had exposed him to their cruelty. In the end, when they thought that all had been killed, they sent the ship to the bottom, so that the English should never find out about their deceitful treachery and their treacherous deceit.

But a boy from the ship was still alive. While both sides were going at it hammer and tongs, he had seen that our men were losing and had crossed over into the Flemish ship. He had gone down into the hold and had stayed in hiding there, unnoticed by anybody, until the Flemings reached an English port. He had stuck it out for three days without food, but when he heard the Flemings talking to Englishmen and recognised the language of his countrymen, he suddenly sprang forth from the depths of the ship and began loudly calling for some loyal assistance from the English. They ran to his aid. The Flemings were thrown into confusion. No one knew exactly what was going on. But in the end, as the lad's shouts grew louder, the truth of the matter was revealed to the English. They soon took the Flemings prisoner and dispatched them to prison to receive a suitable reward for their crimes.[1] The ship and its goods were confiscated for the use of the king.

The mighty knight, Sir John Clerk, is laid low by a wound in the thigh

But with English losses it never rains but it pours and in the same year they suffered a heavy loss that was lamented throughout the whole island. This loss was that of Sir John Clerk,[2] a powerful fighter, intelligent and strong and the ally and colleague of that most energetic knight, Sir Hugh Calveley. He had gone to Brittany and was staying in a castle there. A galley entered the harbour, apparently bent on setting fire to the castle's ships. When Sir John's men saw it, they armed themselves and rushed down to the ships, to defend them in person from fire and pillage. Sir John was never lacking in the qualities befitting a leader, and when he saw his men hurrying so determinedly to save the situation, he too lightly armed himself and hurried down and boarded his ship, crying that he wanted to share the fortunes of his men, whether good or bad.

When the men from the galley saw things happening just as they wanted and our men attacking them without proper caution, they pretended to be fleeing in terror and by throwing javelins and other missiles they egged on our men until they came to the entrance to the harbour itself. So both sides made their way out of the harbour, the enemy pretending to flee and our own soldiers in hot pursuit, but it was not long before our men realised that they had been tricked. For

---

[1]   The author of the *Historia vitae et regni Ricardi secundi* reports that the Flemish prisoners were despatched to London to be imprisoned: *HVRS*, p. 54.
[2]   Sir John Clerk of Ewell had served as king's escheator in Essex, Hertfordshire and Surrey: *CPR, 1377–81*, pp. 445, 463, 482, 496.

they suddenly saw that they were surrounded by five galleys, which had been lurking in ambush. They did not know what to do or where to turn. But Sir John, summoning up his courage, suddenly, like a giant, charged into the enemy, overthrowing some and driving off others, so that it seemed that he on his own was sufficient to deal with so many. The enemy marvelled at the brave spirit of the man, and turned their hostile attentions and the weight of their weapons against him alone. Meanwhile some of his men at his urging had gone back to the harbour, and they were saved from danger, protected and defended by the shelter given by his strong right arm. Finally seeing that all his men could be saved, he thrust out those who were still in the ship before he himself left it, and stood as a wall against the enemy, until they should reach land. Nor did he grow weary until he had seen all his men reach land safe and sound before himself. Then, when at the very end he wanted to leave the ship himself, he was just jumping down from it when he was wounded in the thigh by somebody's axe. He collapsed to the ground and was taken prisoner on the spot. His thigh was broken by the blow and his leg almost separated from his body. He was a man of transparent goodness and bravery, who left to posterity the memorials of many excellent achievements.

A barge of York is sunk together with its crew

To add to the pile of woes at this same time a fine barge of York was lost.[1] It had made an over-rash attack on enemy galleys and was suddenly surrounded on all sides by the host of galleys and captured together with its crew. But the joy the enemy took in this splendid plunder turned sour. For when the foreigners had managed to make their way on board and the barge was full with the foreigners and our sailors whom they were now holding captive, it suddenly and unexpectedly plunged to the bottom of the fathomless ocean and was sunk together with all the English and the foreigners who had boarded it and all the goods which they had carried on to it. Its hull had been holed during the fighting between the two sides, but neither our men nor the enemy noticed it until they realised they were in fact dying by drowning.

The duke of Brittany is warmly welcomed by his people[2]

It was during these days that the duke of Brittany [Jean IV], whom I have mentioned before, was recalled by his people to take up his dukedom, from which he had been practically expelled many years ago. Having received hostages and reasonable security, he crossed the seas to his own land and landed at the harbour by St Malo on 4 August. When they met him, his lords, knights, esquires, merchants and citizens could scarcely contain themselves for joy at the sight of their proper master. So great was the common joy and happy delight of all, that you could have seen the very princes of the people, splendidly armed and wearing the most costly garments, in their longing to see and welcome with honour the object of their souls' affection, compete in regarding their adornments as things of lowest worth as they threw themselves headlong into the waves of the sea, and in their devotion made their way to the ship carrying their duke, as far as was possible genuflecting even amid Neptune's waters.[3] Some of them, in their efforts to pay honour to their lord as he approached, got completely drenched, with the waves of the sea reaching their knees, or the breasts of some, or right up to the chin of very many of them. Among the others who met him

---

[1]   It is surprising that Walsingham, who usually gave scant attention to matters of regional interest, should record this loss, especially since the author of the *Anonimalle Chronicle*, who was himself writing from York, makes no mention of it. It is not mentioned by any other authorities.

[2]   Jean IV, duke of Brittany had been in exile in England since 1373. Envoys from the Breton lords had travelled there in the summer of 1379 to persuade him to return to the duchy. After concluding an alliance with Richard II on 3 August, he embarked, according to Froissart, accompanied by Sir Robert Knolles and an army of 200 archers and 200 men-at-arms. He landed at Guérade and progressed to Vannes before meeting the Breton magnates at Nantes: *Chroniques*, ix. 205–6; FCBuchon, ii. 83–5.

[3]   Froissart confirms the 'grant joie' that greeted the duke on his return: *Chroniques*, ix. 207; FCBuchon, ii. 84.

at this harbour from Dinan were Charles de Dinan, lord of Montafilant[1] and Beaumanoir,[2] Pierre, lord of Tournemine and Hunaudaye,[3] the vicomte de Dinan,[4] the governor of Dinan and Selidort, the lord of St Gilles,[5] the lord of Ferrières,[6] the lord of Plessis,[7] the lord of Montauban[8] and several other knights, whose names I have not bothered to record. Attending them were as many as three hundred and sixty esquires, or lances, to use the common expression, whose names are too many to record.

On 7 August he was joined by the constable of Rennes[9] and several others, to the number of sixty lances, and on 8 August by the lords of Laval,[10] Chatillon[11] and Montfort[12] with several other knights and esquires amounting to ninety lances. On 10 August he was joined by the vicomte of Rohan,[13] who once had been his bitterest and most powerful enemy, but who now came with several other knights and esquires of his dukedom, amounting to as many as four hundred lances. All these recognised and honourably welcomed him as their proper and rightful lord and made peace with him as he wished.

There is one strange fact to record. After the many quarrels in his country, the thunders and lightnings of countless wars, the looting by his enemies and the thefts of public property by brigands, all of which the region had experienced continuously over many years, the duke still found all the furniture and treasures in his house, in fact his whole property which he had left behind when quitting his country, so intact and unharmed that it was as if he in person had preserved them with all his courage and strength. The common people had been enflamed with such constant love for their master, and had so vigorously persisted in continuing to show him loyal affection that they had much, much rather allowed their own property to be sacked and looted than for anything to be stolen from those things which their own rightful lord had left in their care. Even the taxes of the region, which they had always collected in peacetime for the uses of their duke, had still, amid devastation wrought by the enemy, been collected and taken to a safe place, so that whenever, as actually happened, he returned to treat them with his gentle kindness, he would find vast treasures which surpassed his hopes.

When the duke thought how all this had happened contrary to his expectations, he was filled with an indescribable happiness, and thanked the God, who, whenever he wishes, transfers and changes the ownership of kingdoms and regions, and gives them to whomever he wishes, and then again, when the time for his showing pity arrives, restores them to those who fear his name. Then the duke returned the most heartfelt thanks to his people for the unbelievable loyalty and gratitude that he had found among them, and he promised that in the future, just as in the past, he would rule them not with the rages of a tyrant or enemy but with the justice and love of a prince.

A memorable exploit of Sir Hugh Calveley

There is one notable exploit that I do not think should pass through the waters of Lethe into oblivion. It is an exploit that deserves praise no less than record, and it was performed by Sir Hugh Calveley, that exemplar of bravery and the virtues and gleaming mirror of military worth. It was his decision, carried out with fierce courage, which saved the duke himself and the people

1   Charles de Dinan (d. 1418), sire de Montafilant and Beaumanoir.
2   Jean IV, sire de Beaumanoir (d. 1385).
3   Pierre II, de Tournemine (d. 1383), sire de Hunaudaye.
4   Jean Raguenel, vicomte de Dinan et de la Bellière (d. 1401).
5   Perhaps Georges de Saint-Gilles, son of Jean, sire de Betton.
6   Perhaps Silvestre de la Feuillée, subsequently marshal of Brittany (1384–5).
7   Perhaps the sire de Plessis.
8   Olivier IV, sire de Montauban (d. 1388).
9   Thomas de Fontenay (d. 1379).
10 Guy XII, sire de Laval and Vitré (d. 1412).
11 Jean de Laval, sire de Chatillon (d. 1398)
12 Raoul, sire de Montfort (d. 1394).
13 Jean I, vicomte of Rohan (d. 1396).

who were his subjects from the mocking insults of the enemy, when he protected from looting and attack by the barbarians the contents of the duke's castle, that is the public and private wealth stored in his treasury, the weapons of war, the vessels of gold and silver, and all the furnishings of the duke.[1]

The duke of Brittany [Jean IV] and Sir Thomas Percy and other nobles had gone ahead and occupied the harbour. Sir Hugh was also of their number. But the supply ships carrying the provisions and the other equipment I have mentioned had not yet anchored, since all the ships could not enter the narrow, dangerous harbour at the same time, when all of a sudden, to their dismay, some French and Spanish rogues sped to the scene in their galleys, thinking they would have everything their own way, as our ships which had already gained the harbour would not be able to return to bring help. They thought this for two reasons, the adverse winds and the suspect and dangerous nature of the place. Without delay they got ready their customary instruments of war, namely the weapons commonly called 'guns', and made such a fierce attack and sustained assault on the battered fleet, that both the men in the fleet and those now on land lost all hope of saving the supply ships. Sir Hugh Calveley lamented loudly when he saw this. His heart beat faster in his breast and oblivious to all the dangers he told the ship captain to turn the ship, which was carrying him, back towards the enemy, since, as he said, 'It is shameful for us to suffer the double disaster of seeing our men and boats destroyed while being unable to bring them help. Sooner should we embrace death than sustain such damaging losses amid the jeers of the enemy. So let them not say that we refused or did not dare to bring relief to our comrades when sore beset. Let them know the power of our God, let us show them that we are not without brave hearts.'

When the ship captain persisted in his reluctance to obey, giving as his excuse the impossibility of returning to the supply ships, and detailing the dangers they would incur if they did manage to do so, Sir Hugh threatened him with punishment unless he attempted the return. And so with very great difficulty they made the return journey and got as far as the enemy. On arrival, Sir Hugh at once got ready his own weapons and commanded the archers to show the enemy what their hands and arms could do with their bows and arrows. They eagerly obeyed his orders, and shot a fierce, dense volley of arrows at the enemy, just like the hailstorm that tends to occur in the early days of spring. No place, no corner was safe from the flying arrows. Wherever the enemy took up position, they were wounded, or pierced, or at least halted in their tracks by the arrows. So while our 'swordsmen', the archers, fought this battle from a distance instead of hand to hand, an opportunity and means of escape was provided for the supply ships. Nor did Sir Hugh stop until he had seen all the ships safely anchored. Then finally he himself followed them, manfully keeping the pursuing enemy from his own ship, baffling their attempts as much by courage as by craft, until he too with his men safely re-entered the harbour.

The Bretons and their duke had been witnesses to all this from one side of the harbour. The brave deeds of Hugh and his Englishmen caused such love to blaze up in their hearts that they thought it a fine thing to swear an oath to lay down their lives for them, should some necessity require this. Indeed the duke himself scarcely ever stopped giving thanks, at one time praising God for his grace and goodness, at another extolling and lauding Hugh as one who had made him rich instead of poor, seeing that to his disgrace and shame he would have lost his wealth and property, had not the courage and energy of the good Sir Hugh saved the day.

On the other side of the harbour the French with their captain, Bertrand du Guesclin, were standing on the walls and towers of St Malo. They experienced the same emotions as the Bretons, praising the daring deeds of the champion, but also, in the typical manner of a crowd, being afraid that the hero would be killed or captured, and, although they were the enemy, they prayed to the Lord for his safety. Bertrand du Guesclin even publicly proclaimed that he would have preferred all the French to have perished in that battle than for such a man to have suffered any adversity. Such praise was deserved by Hugh, for he saved his own men by losses inflicted on the enemy, but

---

[1]   For a parallel account of Calveley's exploits at St Malo see Froissart, *Chroniques*, viii. 165–70; FCBuchon, ii. 84–5. See also Jones, *Ducal Brittany*, pp. 84–5; Henneman, *Olivier de Clisson*, pp. 47–9.

at the same time won warm praise from the enemy by his bravery. It is a fact that in our day there is not to be found among the company of knights any one who obeys the laws of the Most High as well as did Hugh. My opinion is that all these extraordinary things happened to him so that future generations might learn how much could be achieved by devotion to God, love for his saints, reverence for mother church and a burning passion for doing the just thing. In truth, no one at all in our time could easily have been found who placed a higher value on sanctity or was more given to prayers and almsgiving.

A rich Genoese merchant is assassinated by English merchants, through jealousy

At the same time there came to England a well-born, wealthy merchant of Genoa.[1] He promised the king and his kingdom several advantages if the king would agree to allow him to occupy a newly built warehouse at Southampton and to store his goods there. But he was suddenly assassinated by English merchants, to the great detriment of the people and the kingdom. For he had promised (and it was said that he would have kept his promise, if he had obtained his wishes and not been suddenly deprived of his life) to make the port of Southampton so influential that no port in western Europe could have been its equal.

Indeed all the goods from the East which formerly Genoese merchants had been accustomed to take to Flanders, Normandy and Brittany would have been brought to our lands. And so foreigners would have been forced to get their goods from Englishmen, who had been accustomed to get money out of foreigners only with great danger to themselves. But such advantages were knocked on the head by the wickedness of our merchants, who boiled over with uncontrollable rage against an innocent man who was bent on doing us some good. They thought that all his schemes for the public advantage would result in losses for themselves, and, so the story goes, a man suspecting no treachery was suddenly surrounded by night and murdered in a London street before the door of his lodging by criminals who had been hired to do the deed.[2]

And so the loathsome wickedness and accursed greed of our merchants won for us the hostility of our friends, the citizens of Genoa, and of the other nations round about us, and the treacherous behaviour of a few made suspect the reliability of all our people. For no foreigner will be bold enough to put his trust in our promises, when we are known to have been capable of such a breach of faith and such inhuman cruelty. Everyone will fear our cunning and curse our name. And besides all this there is the fear of God. So wantonly are we offending him by our crimes and by our total disregard of his commandments that we are not now sinning through negligence, but, like servants who know the will of their master but do not do it, we are deliberately going against his laws. For we know that God warns us by his commandment, 'You are not to kill the innocent and the just' [Exodus 23: 7] but our greedy avarice pays no attention to divine commands and our lust for worldly goods shuns the decrees of natural law. For inhuman men the gain of earthly wealth is more important than the affection and friendship found in our life together, which makes us all brothers. So we ought to fear that reproachful, threatening saying of an angry God avenging the murder of a brother, 'The voice of your brother's blood is crying to me from the ground, and because of your deed the ground is accursed, which has opened its mouth and received the blood of your brother' [Genesis 4: 10]. For what brother of the flesh was ever working to bring greater benefits to his brothers than the murdered man was devising for us? For it was actually reported that he would have sold a pound of pepper for four pence, and made similar reductions with all other kinds of spices. This over a period would have brought indescribable profit to our people.

[1]   The Genoese merchant was Janus Imperialis. He had entered England two years before in the spring of 1377 as an envoy of the duke of Genoa to negotiate a treaty with the English government. He had been granted a safe conduct by the king, and in April 1379 had, with others, registered a recognizance worth 40,000 francs to be levied in England.
[2]   Two London merchants, John Algore, a grocer, and John Kirkby, a mercer, were held responsible for the murder. They were committed to Nottingham Castle on 24 June 1380. Even without Walsingham's lengthy lamentation, the episode was undoubtedly an embarrassment for the English government.

A great pestilence in northern parts, and the Scots' invasion of the same

In the summer of the same year under an evil star a plague broke out in the north of England, which was greater than any that had ever been seen before. The death rate was so high that in a moment it had robbed almost the whole area of its noblest men. And as for the middle classes all that can be said is that there was practically no home that was not emptied of people so that only the building itself was left. The plague in its maw swallowed up the largest families, and left not just one survivor but no survivor. But these are just a few details to explain what follows.[1]

So heavy was the hand of the Lord upon them that towns and cities, which once had been filled with men notable for war, wisdom and wealth as well as with the tenants themselves, were stripped of their inhabitants and reduced to an unpeopled wasteland. To cap it all the Scots, enemies of the human race as we all know, did not learn any compassion from the countless deaths of their neighbours or any sympathy from this widespread destruction of an unhappy people. Finally without any fear for the hand of the Lord which was so near to them, but showing more inhumanity than brute beasts and more savagery than wild animals and regarding the occasion as just right for their cruel practices, they struck in a frenzy at a people, which had already been struck down by the Lord and was wasting away through plague and pestilence, and added to the pain of their injuries. They cut down with the mouth of the sword those men able to fight who had not yet caught the infection of the plague. They cut off the heads of most of them and, carried away by a spirit of madness, did not shrink from kicking them with their feet to each other over and over again, as though they were having a game of football. When they saw that no one made any opposition or resistance to all these enormities, they grew bolder. Thinking they could do absolutely anything they liked, they roamed through the land, sacking towns, carrying off the wealth and driving before them animals and beasts of burden and even the very herds of pigs, although they were an animal which no Scots had ever tried to drive off before.

Now, when the Scots had been planning the sacking of the north before the actual invasion, they had summoned some of the inhabitants and anxiously asked them why such a pestilence had fallen only on them rather than on the Scots and their other neighbours as well. Their simple reply was that they did not know the reason for the great pestilence, seeing that divine judgements were kept from their eyes. But one thing they did repeatedly assert, namely that the whole calamity of the plague and in fact all the misfortunes which had befallen them, had happened through the special grace of God for them. Sometimes they had happened so that the Northumbrians might pay for the sins that they had wrongly committed in this life and, though given to evil works, might stop what they had begun through fear of death. Sometimes it had been so that they might have a greater faith in God through the exercise of righteousness, as it is written, 'The righteous will both fear the Lord and place their hopes in him' [Psalm 40: 3] And on other occasions it was for many unrevealed reasons, which it is not right for you to know. When the Scots heard from these people that the pestilence had been sent them by the grace of God, they trembled with fear where there was no fear, just as if they were feeling the terror that the beasts of the field feel. And so, both before and after they had invaded the north, each morning they crossed themselves, using the following blessing, which had been composed with much thought and was regarded by them as very necessary.

The senior by position or the eldest in age among them began by saying, 'Bless us', and they all replied, 'O Lord'. Then the elder continued, 'May God and Saints Kentigern,[2] Romanus and Andrew keep us safe today and every day from the divine grace and foul death which is destroying the English.' And after this blessing, they thought they were sufficiently protected and sheltered

---

1   This was the fourth outbreak since the Black Death of 1348–51. Here Walsingham dates it to the summer of 1379, but the *Anonimalle* author, writing from York, records it under the year 1375: *AC*, p. 79. The author of the *Historia vitae et regni Ricardi secundi* agrees with Walsingham that it was the worst such outbreak witnessed in the north of the country: *HVRS*, p. 55.
2   Kentigern (d. 612x614) was patron saint of Glasgow. The Gaelic pet-form of his name was 'Mo-Choe' from which the Cumbric 'Mungo' descended.

from all the evil chances that could befall them. This blessing sounds much more ridiculous in their own language than it does in Latin, which is the reason why I think it worth recording here. It goes as follows: 'Gode and Seynt Mango, Seynt Romayne and Seynt Andreu, schild us this day fro Goddis Grace, and the foule deth that Ynglessh men dyene upon.' It must be hoped that one day, if not now, the Scots will get their prayers answered, and that by way of a proper punishment they will themselves experience the inhuman cruelty which they inflicted upon a people who had been brought low by the scourge of God and were struggling to deal with the plague. For the divine wrath advances with slow step, but it makes up for its slowness by its severity.

John Shakell is restored to his former liberty

At the same time through the intervention of men of authority, who had rightly and justly felt a deep grief for the wrongs inflicted long ago on Robert Hawley and John Shakell in the church at Westminster, John Shakell was pardoned and set free. As I have recorded earlier [see above, pp. 69–71], he had been irreverently pulled from the church, dragged to the Tower of London, and there committed to prison. At the request of these venerable men it was agreed between the king and John Shakell that John should reveal to the king that his captive was the son of the count of Denia, who only recently on the death of his father had himself inherited the dukedom. For men did not yet know who the prisoner was or what he was like or where he had been hidden away for so long. It was also laid down that the king, in return for his getting possession of the prisoner, should give John lands with an annual return of a hundred marks and five hundred marks in money; and that the king from his own revenues should found a chantry chapel to last for ever, to be served by five priests for the souls of those who had been killed by his servants in the church at Westminster.[1]

Once these conditions were agreed on, the prisoner was restored to the king and John Shakell to his former liberty. And when John was commanded to reveal the prisoner, to everybody's amazement he produced that servant of his who had stood by him and served him as a valet throughout all his tale of woe, both before the persecution which had been inflicted on him in prison and outside the prison; and had so faithfully stuck to his task that it had been impossible to recognise him; he had served John so zealously that people could have been excused for thinking he was his hired man. You could have observed the Englishmen present deeply overcome with shame at the outstanding loyalty shown by the count, seeing that each of them, though living in the greatest of ease, lacked the qualities which they realised the count had possessed when his whole kingdom was in a state of great confusion and upheaval. They all asked one another who among them could be found like the count, who, when he could have changed his status so as to be recognised as a lord deserving honour by the king and the nobles of the land, did not do so. Out of regard for the loyalty which he owed to his captors he had scorned to do all this, and in the end during the attacks made on them he had almost offered up his head to the sword because of his faithfulness to them.

The tale of the young man's integrity is one worth the telling. Although he was exposed to hostile attacks, no change of fortune could break his spirit. He was found to be without a flaw, unshakeable in adversity, untroubled amid uncertainty, meeting setbacks with loyalty to his captors. Any Englishman, whoever he is, who is plotting to betray his country for ill-gotten gain or enticed by other gifts, should look at the example of utter loyalty given by this foreigner. He was not a native Englishman, but, regarded rightly, an enemy from other lands. And yet he kept the faith and observed the oath by which as it were he had joined himself to his masters with such bold steadfastness that in his loyalty he chose to become poor and needy and a servant to his captors in their troubles rather than break his faith, betray his principles and, to the detriment of his captors, enjoy the gay life of abundant plenty, to which his birth had accustomed him, in the company of the king and the nobles of England. I have told this story that present and future

---

[1]   The king's 'spiritual' recompense is also reported by the author of the *Historia vitae et regni Ricardi secundi*: HVRS, p. 55.

Englishmen, who have at their fingertips in this Spaniard an example of an unfeigned loyalty carried through to the end, may be ashamed of the disgrace of treachery, and learn of the glorious praise that is won by faithful goodness and, on the other hand, the shameful reputation and bad name that accompanies traitors.

The count of Flanders, while imposing new constitutions upon his subjects, is driven out by them

About the same time the count of Flanders [Louis II, de Maële] with all his family and household and his whole council was forcibly driven from his land by his subjects. They had risen against him, as he had imposed new duties on them, asked for new taxes and foolishly placed new burdens on them, all of which demands were unheard of and contrary to their liberties.[1] And a people's army of twenty thousand men or more chosen from the community was soon assembled to guard the frontiers of the land against invasion by the supporters of the count, their natural lord, and to assail or capture the count if he thought to persist in such attempts. In the meantime the usual sacking and looting of the property of the count and his followers took place, along with the burning of buildings and killing of servants and all the customary things that go on because of the hatred felt for the aristocrats or the vindictiveness of the victors.

Some losses also befell Waleran [of Luxembourg], the count of St Pol, who had come to the area about this time to strengthen his castles situated there.[2] For when the people discovered that he took the side of their own count, they soon in a spirit of furious anger all transferred their attentions to a manor of his. The whole estate, which exceeded all his other estates in the number of its buildings and its beauty, was levelled to the ground. Not a beam was left on a wall, or stone on stone by the people, so that it might be clear and obvious to everybody that they were pursuing with a deep, heartfelt hatred both their own count and all who were close friends of his.

After many days had now gone by, the count saw them still persisting in their stubborn attitude, preferring to die rather than lose their ancestral practices. He himself was thoroughly fed up with the damage being done to his lands while this was going on and sent messengers to find out if by any chance their minds had been changed in the meantime, or if they had lost heart because of the labours or heavy cost of military service. But when he found that they were absolutely firm in their determination and had not been exhausted by any of their exertions, he decided to climb down and give his people what they wanted. So he announced to them that he would be ready to rule them as a mild master, if they themselves in other respects would submit to him as usual. But they replied that they would in no way be subject to him unless he got rid of his whole council and was willing to accept only councillors chosen by the decisions of the people. Also that he should put into the people's hands those who had been the cause of this disturbance and upheaval. So as the count saw no other way to recover his power, he decided, though against his will, to grant their requests and so in the end was restored to his countship.

Edmund Broomfield acts fraudulently in obtaining the abbacy of [Bury] St Edmunds[3]

About the same time Edmund Broomfield, a monk of the church of Bury St Edmunds [i.e. the Benedictine abbey of St Edmund at Bury], arrived back from the Roman Curia. He brought with

1 This marked the beginning of the revolt which over the course of the next three years saw Ghent and other cities rise against the count and which caused Count Louis to call upon the French crown for military aid. Froissart provides a detailed account of the origins of troubles: *Chroniques*, ix. 158–70. As Walsingham describes below (see pp. 110–11) the tension turned to violence in September 1379 when the Ghentois murdered the count's bailiff, Roger d'Autrive.
2 Waleran of Luxembourg, count of St Pol (1355–1415), had returned to Flanders following the payment of his ransom to Richard II, for which payment he had received support from Count Louis de Maële. His connection with the count now made him a target for the Flemish rebels: Froissart, *Chroniques*, ix. 153–7.
3 Walsingham gives extended coverage here to what was, ostensibly, a conventional case of a disputed election. It was not simply that the monks of Bury St Edmunds were fellow Benedictines well known to the monastic community at St Albans. This was one of the first opportunities to test Edward III's statute of provisors that sought to place ecclesiastical appointments under the sole authority of the crown. It was

him bulls, in which he asserted that by the gift and ordinance of the pope he had been confirmed as abbot and pastor of that very church. Now this Edmund, with his fees paid by the monastery, had reached the top of the academic tree, but, whenever he was recalled to the monastery from the university [of Oxford], he had invariably caused trouble, sowing discord and stirring up hatred between the brothers.[1] So his fellow monks, growing tired of his frequent trouble making, with the advice of John Brinkley, their father and pastor at the time [i.e. the abbot], had decided to rid themselves of his presence by some means or other, right or wrong, so that one sick sheep might not infect the whole flock of the monastery. And so that their design might be effected with some degree of caution and secrecy and without scandal to the monks or the place or Edmund himself, they offered him the job of proctor of the monastery at the Roman Curia.[2] Once he got there, he would be kept permanently there, dealing with the needs of the abbey, and so the house would be freed of his presence, and for the future the monastic peace would suffer the minimum disturbance from his trouble making.

But before they allowed him to depart from them and set out on this mission, they thought to themselves that as a general rule the different climate of a foreign land does not change men's natures,[3] for the Ethiopian cannot change the colour of his skin, and so they required him to swear an oath that he would not acquire or procure some benefit for the house which might turn out in some way or other to be prejudicial to the abbey. Edmund took the oath, and in public. Later indeed, at the instance of the presidents of the Chapter General, he was given the responsible post of proctor for the whole order of Black Monks [i.e. Benedictines], and, so that the high pontiff might receive him more favourably, he was given letters of recommendation to the pope both from his own abbey (though these went somewhat against the grain) and from the presidents of the Chapter.[4] All this caused considerable damage to the monastery, as I shall describe below.

He arrived at Rome, and had stayed there for a long time without obtaining any benefice from the pope, when he heard of the death of John Brinkley, his former abbot.[5] Fortune, he thought, had now smiled upon him, and to effect and bring about his long cherished ambition, he went to see a Flemish lawyer, called master John Shipdam, who was staying in the Curia, and promised him a large sum of money annually, if he could bring it about that somehow or other he was made abbot of Bury St Edmunds. If it happened that he had no success with this appointment, he was to acquire for him one of the vacant bishoprics. Or if this was impossible, he was to try to get him made prior of Deerhurst.[6] Whichever it was, Edmund gave him his word that he would have the one sum annually for his efforts. John won over some of the cardinals to his side, as they never refuse money, so that with their intervention and support he might successfully carry out Edmund's business. Sure of the help of these cardinals, he put Edmund's case before the pope,

---

further complicated by the fact that Bury was one of the few houses to claim exempt status. An account of the dispute was also compiled by a Bury monk, Andrew Aston, at the end of the 1420s: *Memorials of St Edmund's Abbey at Bury*, ed. T. Arnold, 3 vols., Rolls Series, 96 (1892–6), iii. 113–37.

1   Broomfield had been a monk at Bury for some fifteen or twenty years. He had studied at Oxford, securing his doctorate in theology six years before, in 1373. For a summary of his career see Emden, *BRUO*, i. 275–6.

2   There is no documentary record of Broomfield's presence in Rome before his appointment as Proctor for the Benedictine General Chapter (see below) in 1375, and it may be that Walsingham here is making his own embellishments to the story.

3   This phrase, 'the different climate of a foreign land . . . ', recalls Horace, *Epistles*, 1. 11. 27, 'caelum non animum mutant qui trans mare currunt'.

4   The General Chapter was the governing council of the English Benedictines. Broomfield was appointed its proctor in 1375. The Chapter was led by two presidents, representing the northern and southern provinces of the English church: in this period the southern president was Thomas de la Mare, abbot of St Albans, Walsingham's own superior. His implied criticism of the Chapter and its promotion of Broomfield therefore would surely have angered Abbot Thomas, but it was at least consistent with Walsingham's treatment of those Benedictines who courted papal patronage. See, for example, his condemnation of the monks of his own order who accepted papal chaplaincies: see below, pp. 119, 249.

5   John de Brinkley had held the abbacy at Bury since 1361. He died on 31 December 1379.

6   Deerhurst Priory in Gloucestershire was a dependent cell of the great French Benedictine abbey of St Denis and as such, during the war with France, a likely target for interference of this sort. See *MRH*, p. 64.

asserting that Edmund was the actual choice of the chapter, and that all the monks had desired and wished him to be in charge of their church. The pope, for his part, was well aware of the evils of the times and of the daily increase in strength of his adversary, the antipope, and he considered that Edmund would be of great help to him, if he was made abbot there, and so was easily persuaded to confirm his appointment, or, if his election had not yet been properly carried out, to grant him freely this benefice. To cut a long story short, with the support of the pope and at his gift Edmund realised the ambition on which he had set his heart, and in high excitement got ready to return to his country with his bulls.

Edmund and his partisans are committed to the tower of London

But the monks at Bury had met for an election immediately on the death of their abbot, and had unanimously chosen as abbot John Timworth, the sub-prior of the monastery. He was suited to the post and a zealous member of their order. When the brothers heard that Edmund had fore-stalled them as I have described, they soon hurried to send two monks to the Roman Curia to assure the pope that Edmund's claims were false and to seek ratification for their own choice as abbot. The two messengers took with them letters of appeal from the king and several of the nobles, asking for the confirmation of the monks' choice and the deposition of Edmund. But for the time being the pope favoured Edmund rather than the monks, and permitted the envoys to waste a lot of time at Rome, which did harm to their chances.

Edmund in the meantime, well aware of the dangers involved in delay and that 'Plans post-poned are always spoiled',[1] hurried to Bury St Edmunds. Once there, he won over to his side men from the lands round about, and soon assembled a large force in his support. Escorted around by his many supporters, he got his bulls read in the parish churches. The people, as usual in such circumstances, being always keen and eager for something new, believed his claims and supported his candidature, especially as he was their neighbour and countryman. Edmund saw that things had begun just as he wished, and now hoped to unite earth and heaven, flesh and the spirit, cloister and marketplace, in fact to bring together monks and laity and make them one. He entered the chapter house surrounded by a large crowd and sent clerks to invite the monks to the chapter house at the bidding of the pope, and, on pain of disobedience, to listen to his commands. The more simple-minded brothers took fright at such a disgrace and entered the chapter house. But there were others who had considered the dangers and disadvantages which could accrue to the monastery from such an appointment, and who did not join the crowd in the chapter house.

So Edmund from his seat in the chapter house easily won over to his side the monks who were present. Some were influenced by fear of rebuke, others by affection for Edmund and others by lust for power, especially those who were gripped by a longing for secular positions of power. So after his own business had been stated and he saw that he had a party in his support, he chose new obedientiaries and deposed the old ones. But he did restore John Timworth, their choice as abbot, to his old post of sub-prior, in the hope that, although John had been elected as abbot himself, he might consider agreeing to his own election and obeying his orders. Then, with those monks who had come to the chapter house and been persuaded by his arguments, he entered the church, and putting on the pontifical vestments, he solemnly celebrated Mass as abbot. Amid a packed crowd he celebrated a festival day, not one that ended with prayers before the horns of the altar, but one that ended in feasting and revelling, attended by large, cheering numbers of both sexes.

But that joyful beginning did not last long, but ended prematurely in upset and sorrow. For a little while later knights and esquires of the king with their attendants came to Bury St Edmunds and without great difficulty took Edmund off to answer to the king for what had happened. Those monks who had supported him, some eighteen of them, left with him and followed him to London.[2] When he arrived at Westminster, he was asked by the chancellor, Sir Richard

---

1   Lucan, *De bello civili*, ii. 27.
2   According to the author of the *Historia vitae et regni Ricardi secundi* shortly after his return to Bury, Broomfield had secured the support of thirteen monks (*HVRS*, p. 55), but Walsingham's higher figure for

news of this atrocity heaped quite dreadful curses on the heads of the knights and implored God to send upon them all the misfortunes and calamities within his power.[1]

While all this was going on, Sir John Arundel himself paid no attention to the outcry and all the curses or the shame of such infamy, but piled sin upon sin and added atrocity to atrocity. In fact he allowed his men to ransack the countryside as they liked and to impoverish the people. While they collected food supplies and other items they needed by force, Sir John did not compel them to make payment, but rather backed up their violent methods and so shared in the results of their wrongdoing himself. As a result of all this the people of the area protested that they had preferred the coming of the enemy to their land, apart from the burning of their homes, to that of Sir John himself and his crew.

These are just a few unimportant things compared to what followed. For on the day on which they were about to set sail, a newly-married bride, who on that very same day had been joined to a man of the district by the hands and prayers of a priest and who was returning from the church after a Mass and the marriage service, was violently snatched by Sir John and his men from the midst of the hands of those escorting her home and actually taken onto their ships, where they intended to have their wicked way with her after they had set sail.[2] They never thought or considered that such enormities would be quickly punished. It is said that they even carried off from the nunnery married women, widows and young girls and put them on board their ships.

And still they were not saturated by sin, for some of them turned their hands to sacrilege. They had listened to a mass, with little devotion apparently, and before the priest could take off his chasuble, they went up to the altar and stole a chalice. They ran off to the ships with it with top speed, as happy as though they had seized some booty, with the priest following them, still in his vestments of alb, stole and maniple, threatening them with punishment in his efforts to get back the chalice. Although all he succeeded in getting was derision and bloodcurdling threats of what would happen if he did not go away, not even so did he decide to take it lying down. He called together the neighbouring priests and went right down to the shore with them, carrying lit candles, bells, books and those other things needed for pronouncing a sentence of this kind. And there he asked on pain of excommunication for the stolen goods to be restored. Not even under these circumstances did the soldiers bother to make amends, and so he hurled upon them a terrible, public sentence of excommunication, extinguishing the candle by throwing it into the sea.

Sir Hugh Calveley and Sir Thomas Percy and various others who knew nothing of the exploits of Arundel's men had it proclaimed publicly throughout the district before they embarked on their ships that those who had suffered any trouble from their men, either through injuries caused or for any other reasons or incidents, should come to their camp before the day of sailing, and there they would receive adequate compensation for any misdeeds they wished to complain about. The result was the people followed them down to the sea with heartfelt prayers, while, just the opposite, they had accompanied Sir John Arundel with the direst of curses.[3]

A few hours later, when the wind began to blow a little more strongly, Sir John gave orders for all to embark and for the ship captains, with the sails spread and set for the deep, to commit their vessels to the winds. But the captain in whose ship Sir John himself was a passenger, one Robert Rust of Blakeney,[4] foresaw the storm that was to come, and urged Sir John not to put to sea at that time: there would soon be a storm, he said, which undoubtedly would endanger their ships and perhaps even be a cause of shipwreck. But Sir John, 'the victim of his destiny', refused to lend an ear to the captain's words, but all the more pressed him to set sail.

[1]   The story is corroborated both by the author of the *Historia vitae et regni Ricardi secundi* (*HVRS*, p. 57) and the *Anonimalle* author, who describes how Arundel's men 'pristrent dames et damoisels encontre lour volontes et les pargiserent et defoulerent vilaynesment': *AC*, p. 131. The episode must have occurred before 26 October when a committee of enquiry was appointed to examine the evidence: *CPR, 1377–81*, pp. 420–1.
[2]   This allegation is unique to Walsingham's account.
[3]   The author of the *Historia vitae et regni Ricardi secundi* also contrasts Arundel's conduct as a commander with that of Calveley and Percy, whom he describes as 'milites, satis deuoti, pii et beneuoli' (*HVRS*, p. 58)
[4]   For Rust see *CPR, 1377 81*, p. 365.

So seeing his words could not persuade Sir John that he ought to delay his departure, the captain entrusted the ships to Neptune and after a short time reached the deeps of the sea. And, to quote the poet, 'After the ships reached the deep, soon the winds massed together and menaced the waters. Above their heads a dark storm of rain brought on the night and a tempest at the same time, and the waves hissed in the darkness. Straightaway the winds upturned the seas, and great waters arose. The ships were tossed and scattered over the expanse of the sea. The clouds wrapped up the daylight and soon the rain obscured the sky. They wandered blind over the waters and everything around them threatened them with immediate death.'[1]

And, so it is said, what was more terrible than death itself was a vision or sight of the devil that appeared before them, and which they could see with their own eyes was leading down to hell those who had gone aboard the ship of John Arundel. It is difficult to describe all the cries, tears and woeful groans of the women who were on the ships either through force or of their own accord, in those moments when the force of wind and wave lifted them right up to the heavens and then plunged them down to the depths, and when they now saw before them not a picture of death but death itself, and did not doubt that they would be destroyed at any moment. As for the anguished, agonised thoughts and guilty consciences and the great remorse filling their frame that overcame those men, who had dragged the women to face the perils of the sea just to satisfy their lust, they would know best how to describe it who were partners in their crimes but who at length through the mercy of God were thought worthy of reaching safety's harbour.

In this situation, buffeted on this side by winds and storm blasts and on that by waves and women's shrieks, they were not sure what to do. They first tried to lighten the vessels by throwing unimportant things overboard, and then by throwing all their valuables, to see if even in this situation some hope of safety for them might emerge. But when they saw that this made their situation no less desperate but rather worse, they poured the blame for their misfortunes on to the women, and with the same hands with which they had coaxingly touched them and the same arms with which they had lustfully stroked them they picked them up and threw them in to the sea. It is said that they did this to about sixty women, who became food for the fishes and the creatures of the deep. But even after this the storm, instead of stopping, grew still worse, so that all the men lost all hope of escaping the dangers of death.

But after several days and nights passed in the greatest dread, not merely in danger of death but in her very jaws, at last they saw the coastline of Ireland and an island situated in the waves of the sea near to the coast. Overcome with sudden joy at this, Sir John Arundel at once ordered the sailors to make for the shore, to see if they might be given the chance of touching land. But the sailors were reluctant to do this and declared that it would be safer, amid such huge seas, to stay in deep water than to be dashed on to the beach or the rocks by the strength of the winds as they approached the land. At this John rushed upon them in a frenzy and, so it is said, cruelly murdered some of them.

Even Robert Rust, whose ship it was, was afraid that John might attack him, and so promised, that if luck was with him, he would drive the ship aground not far from land. John said to him, 'Don't you see that island near to the land? For the time being let us find safety on that. We can at least clamber up its shore and refresh our tired limbs. Perhaps the people on the mainland will see us and take pity on our misery and bring us food, or take us on to the mainland, or at least, heavy blow though this seems, take us shipwrecked men prisoners. But suppose we are prisoners for a time. That is not so bad as dying a thousand deaths at sea before we actually die, finding it impossible in the end to escape from unlovely death. Or suppose they are enemies on the mainland. I would far sooner choose to be killed by the hands of the enemy (our bodies, perhaps, will be granted a burial) than to be drowned like cattle in the waves of the sea and become food for the monsters of the deep.'

When Robert, the captain of the ship, heard this, he made every effort to drive the ship

---

1   This passage 'After the ships reached the deep . . .' is a prose paraphrase of Virgil's *Aeneid*, i. 82–91, iii. 192–200.

aground between the mainland and the island, hoping that the island could protect the ship from the winds, and judging that there would be an easy scramble up on to the mainland. But when the ship got there, Robert saw that there were cliffs of an amazing size on both shores and that he himself was suddenly caught in the middle of them. Like one who knows he is going to die, he at once gave a terrific shout and advised his comrades to make their confessions, urging all of them to prepare themselves for death, 'Since,' he said, 'there is now no place left for our escape.' But when for a long time they had been tossed here and there in this terrible danger, and the ship, which had been driven on to the rocks, was now letting in the waves, all of a sudden they spotted a way up on to the island, steep and difficult though it was because of the rocks and the sand. Robert put forth all his strength and drove the ship on to the sand so that, even though the ship was broken, this at least might give them a chance of escaping. And when he had driven the ship out of the waves of the sea as far as he could, he himself was the first to leap on to the sand, and then many after him jumped from the ship and reached the island.

Finally Sir John Arundel himself also jumped and reached the sand. But, so it seemed, he was too sure that he was safe. For, as if nothing remained to be feared, although standing on quicksand he began to shake the water from his clothes, which had been drenched by sea water while he was on board the ship. Robert Rust saw this, and realising the danger which John had not yet escaped from, he went back down to the quicksand and, grabbing his hand, tried to drag him away from the dangerous spot. But in his concern for another's safety he was less cautious than usual and, oblivious of his own safety, he lost his life. While he was trying to pull John away with him, the sea at that moment poured in, piled up in a dangerous wave, which drove the other waves further in, knocked them both over and as it ebbed pulled both of them out in to the deeper parts of the sea. And this was the end of them.

The most famous esquire of John's was one Musard, a very worthy gentleman who stood out even in the company of great men and who was the bravest and boldest of all the English. He had also leaped on to the sand and was clinging to a rock with his hands. But as the sea flowed in, its wash tore him violently from his rock, and threw him further out to sea so that he was carried here and there, now on his front, now on his back until the sea dashed him on to the rocks with its surge and broke him to pieces. Another esquire called Denyok met a similar fate. When that noblest knight Sir Thomas Bannister, Sir [John] Trumpington[1] and Sir Thomas Dale[2] jumped from the ship, they each tried to run in front of the others, but they got in one another's way, so that as the sea rose into a crest again it swept them and several others away and took them down into the abyss. The few who emerged out of the sea and reached the island found it uninhabited and died of the cold. For most of them had no clothes, and for the few that perhaps did have them, the clothes were full of sea water and made them still colder. The survivors struggled to combat the cold by various means including running and wrestling. They stayed on the island in great distress from a Thursday until the afternoon of the following Sunday, at which hour the Irish, with the sea now being calm, got into their boats, sailed to the island, brought them to the mainland and gave them a light meal. For they had been almost dead with hunger.[3]

Sir John, besides losing his life in this storm, also lost all his belongings and all his wardrobe, which in its splendour was fit to be ranked above that of a king. For it is said that for his own use he had fifty-two new outfits, either of gold or with gold thread, and all of these were swallowed up by the sea, together with his horses and his warhorses which were valued at ten marks. Also twenty-five other ships of his fleet met a similar fate and were lost with men, horses and other

---

[1] For Sir John Trumpington, a Lancastrian retainer, see S. Walker, *The Lancastrian Affinity, 1361–99* (Oxford, 1990), p. 28 and n.
[2] For Thomas Dale, a Bedfordshire knight, see *CPR, 1377–81*, pp. 38, 46.
[3] Froissart offers a similar but markedly more sober account of the storms, saying the ships were first drawn towards the Cornish coast before being driven into the Irish sea. He reports that as many as 100 men-at-arms were drowned along with Arundel and Bannister and also tells of Calveley's escape and observes that reports of the celebrated captain's death had reached London before he had to disprove them: *Chroniques*, ix. 209–11; FCBuchon, ii. 94.

valuables. Sir John's body and the bodies of those who shared his end were found after three days by the survivors and buried in an Irish abbey.

The celebrated campaign of Sir Thomas Percy

Sir Thomas Percy, Sir Hugh Calveley, Sir William Elmham and some others had been scattered over a wide area of sea, but they ploughed their furrows through the deeps and deservedly escaped death because of their upright lives and their great faith. Then the following miracle happened to them. After such a tempest when for hour after hour he had been faced with the awful prospect of death, Sir Thomas Percy was more in need of a hammock or some softer couch on which to rest his limbs, which had been weakened and exhausted by lack of food and sleep and the toil of so many hardships, when he was suddenly attacked by a Spanish ship, full of armed men, who thought they would easily overpower him after all he had been through.

But this knight, who had never known defeat, did not need to consider what to do. It was not the place or the time for such consideration, and he immediately made up his mind to use up on the enemy that modicum of energy and fighting spirit that remained to him, and in this way at least to end his life nobly, if victory was denied him. But fortune, or rather the Almighty brought Sir Thomas and his men strength, courage and a welcome victory over the enemy. The conflict was not a momentary one or speedily settled, but lasted continuously for three hours before the surrender of the enemy. The sea then calmed down and Sir Thomas returned with the very ship which he had overpowered and captured and his prisoners, bringing to the country the double joy of the preservation of his own safety and the taste of victory. And as soon as he had been able to enjoy a discussion with the inhabitants, he received from them a hundred pounds of silver, and left behind the ship which he had captured as security for it. With this money in his pocket he at once bravely set sail again and made his way to the castle of Brest (of which he was the joint governor together with Sir Hugh Calveley) to stop that fortress incurring any misfortune at enemy hands through being without a governor any longer. And soon, with God leading the way, he happily arrived at the place desired.

Soon after this Sir Hugh Calveley, Sir William Elmham and various others made landfall at various points in England and Ireland. The remarkable thing here is that, while the others were barely able to escape with their lives, Sir Thomas Percy and Sir Hugh Calveley not only lost none of their men but none of their horses either. There is pleasure in seeing in this affair an obvious punishment by God's anger and also the manifest mercy of his goodness. But as I do not want to be accused of showing partiality or hatred for those whose fortunes, good and bad, I have described, I am leaving the reader to interpret these events as he likes. I will just assure the reader of this, that there is no added emotional colouring, no lies, no rhetoric, but my whole narrative is just the truth itself, as I have learnt it from those who were present at all these events and whom I have no warrant for disbelieving.

About the same time the Spanish and the French assembled a large force of ships from the whole of France, Spain, Portugal and the areas under their control, to hinder our expedition as it sailed to Brittany, or rather, by engaging with our men, to weaken them or even capture them and so force them to give up their enterprise. But so that our enemies should not be given an increasing freedom to rejoice at our misfortunes, they felt the same hand of the Lord on them as well, though not the same hand, but, so it is said, a far heavier one. For in the storm which I have described above they lost a greater number of ships and more men.

So ended a year of good harvests and quite good fruit crops. For the Roman church it was a mixture of happiness and sadness. The French kept quiet but gave cause for suspicion. For the English a mixture of the rough and the smooth made it a year of distress as well as success. It was a happy, joyful year for the Bretons as they welcomed back their natural master. For Flanders the expulsion of their count meant anxiety and infamy. The Scots had a good year, as the plague did damage to the north of England.

[1380]

In 1380, the third year of the reign of Richard II, at Christmas time William Montagu, [2nd] earl of Salisbury, returned from Calais, where he had been governor of the town for the year. He was succeeded by Sir John Devereux, a knight who all his life had practised the profession of arms.[1]

During the same period that noble knight, Sir John Harleston, returned from the governorship of the town of Cherbourg and was followed in the post by the energetic knight, Sir William Windsor.[2]

A Parliament at London

After the octave of Epiphany in that year [13 January] a parliament was assembled in London, which sat continuously until 1 March.[3] During it the commons of the land asked for one of the barons to be appointed as guardian for the king. They wanted a man of formed character and decisive action, approachable and discreet, who would know how to make sensible replies to questions in public. So they elected unanimously Sir Thomas Beauchamp, earl of Warwick,[4] to spend all his time with the king, and to draw annually from the king's treasury a sum of money appropriate to his duties. In the previous year various bishops, earls, barons, justiciars and many others had been appointed to this task, to assist his council and to be free to do the king service. All of them for the year had drawn a vast sum of money from the king's treasury, and had done little or nothing for it. So now, as I have said, the commons asked for these numbers to be reduced to one man, who could sufficiently well perform all the various individual things that the whole body had previously done.[5]

Also in this parliament Sir Richard Scrope[6] relinquished the office of chancellor, and Simon Sudbury, archbishop of Canterbury [1375–81], took over the duties of that office, though very many protested that it was illegal for one who was archbishop. But whether Simon got the office for himself, or willingly received it when offered, God alone knows.

Proceedings against Edmund [Broomfield], abbot of Bury [St Edmunds]

There also came to that parliament envoys from the Roman Curia, not sent directly by the pope but by the Cardinal de Agapito.[7] They brought with them letters from the cardinal, in which he stated that he had been instructed by the pope to write to the archbishop of Canterbury, to the

---

1   During the winter of 1379–80 Montagu had led raids in the Pays de Calais reported in England only by the *Anonimalle* author: *AC*, pp. 130–1. Sir John Devereux (d.1393), a Buckinghamshire knight, had begun his career in the service of the Black Prince and, like a number of the prince's knights, had entered the young king's household in 1377. He was a member of the second continual council and later (1388–93) served as steward of the household: Saul, *Richard II*, p. 74.

2   Sir William Windsor (d.1384) was the husband of Alice Perrers, former royal mistress. Under Edward III he had served as lieutenant and later viceroy of Ireland (1369–76); he was appointed governor of Cherbourg in 1379.

3   Parliament opened on 16 January; the session was dissolved on 3 March: *RP*, iii. 71.

4   Beauchamp (1337x1339–1401), 12th earl.

5   Walsingham here misinterprets the measures undertaken in this parliament. Warwick was not appointed governor of the realm as he implies but assumed the role of protector of the king's person. Walsingham's concentration on Warwick conceals the more significant ministerial changes made in this session. Dissatisfaction at the continual council's direction of the campaigns in France had grown steadily over the preceding months and the loss of Arundel's fleet (see above, pp. 99–101) had proved the final straw for many in the commons. When the parliamentary session opened, and Chancellor Scrope began his customary plea for financial aid, such was the state of royal finance that he was compelled, for the first time, to admit the council's culpability. The response of the commons was immediate and uncompromising: they called for an end to the continual council and demanded the right to appoint only five ministers of state, i.e. chancellor, treasurer, keeper of the privy seal, chamberlain and steward of the household and also sought the appointment of a new commission of enquiry to investigate the administration of the council. Their demands were accepted although in the event, whilst the councillors were dismissed, only one of the principal ministers was replaced, Scrope making way for Archbishop Sudbury.

6   For Scrope see above, p. 96.

7   Agapito Colonna (d.1380), cardinal deacon of Santa Prisca, bishop of Lisbon.

chapter of the abbey of Bury St Edmunds and to the papal collector, ordering them individually and as a unit, when they had seen and read his letters, to write back immediately individual letters, informing him whether Edmund Broomfield, whom I have mentioned earlier, had been received into the king's favour and admitted to peaceful possession of the abbey of Bury St Edmunds.

The reason for this legation is said to have been as follows. After Edmund's departure from the Curia, the pope heard and saw so many letters asking him to confirm the choice of abbot made by the monks, that he realised that the provision he had made himself of appointing Edmund abbot was displeasing to the king and the nobles of the land. So he was greatly troubled in his mind. And thinking of the immense help the king and his nobles would be able to give him against his enemy, the antipope, if he enjoyed their friendship, and how much damage they could do him if they were on the other side, he secretly decided, not indeed to depose Edmund, but, because he was a priest and his follower, to transfer him to an Irish bishopric which was then vacant.

But that smooth speaker, master John Shipdam, whom I mentioned earlier, heard of this. And, without wasting time, on the next day, when the proctors of the abbot chosen at Bury St Edmunds had an audience with the pope in the consistory and were asking for that choice of abbot to be confirmed, John Shipdam turned up and declared that it was completely improper for this to happen, for the very reason that the Edmund concerned had already been received into the king's favour and invested with his temporalities. To prove that this was so, he brought in a Cistercian monk and also a priest, who had just arrived from England, and whom he had hired to swear before the pope that they knew for certain that Edmund had been admitted to the king's favour, and in fact had not only been admitted into his favour but also summoned to the council of his household and invested with his temporalities. And to increase the belief in their story, they swore that before their departure from England they had seen Edmund with their own eyes processing in splendour through London, surrounded by the huge entourage that was only proper for an abbot and preceded by an escort of twelve esquires. The officers from Bury St Edmunds consistently refuted this account, saying that it was all a fabrication.

So the pope postponed proceeding with the case until he had received further, more accurate information about the matter. So, as I have said, this was why the cardinal had written such a letter.

The archbishop's reply informing the pope

The archbishop of Canterbury hurried to reply at once to the pope with information about the matter that was causing him concern. After a declaration of the obedience and reverence which he owed to the pope, he said that on account of his reverence for the pope he had pressed the king and the nobles for a decision about Edmund, asking that they should allow Edmund peacefully to enter the church assigned to him by the previous decision of the pope. But a little later in the course of the letter the archbishop said that he had definitely understood from the reply of the king and the nobles of the land that they would never, through fear of the intervention of some other person, allow Edmund to become abbot of Bury or even to leave prison, unless it happened - and this was the sole exception – that they were persuaded to do so by urgent, anxious prayers from the pope himself. He also explained that the pope from the beginning had contravened the rights of the king and the customs of the land by making such provisions. And among other matters he begged the pope to consider the evils of the present time, and in view of the dangers that were looming up on all sides to agree to the wishes of the king by confirming the abbot chosen from Bury according to the wishes of the king and the nobles of the land. With fitting humility he also urged the pope to put no trust or belief in the letters or words of anybody who in a letter or by word of mouth should say to his holiness anything different from what he himself had put in this personal dispatch of his own.

In the same parliament a grant was made to assist the king of a tenth from the church and of a fifteenth from the laity, with the added condition that from the present time of the beginning of March up to Michaelmas in that year no other parliament should be held. But that condition, as I shall describe later, was not kept.

The marriage [of Johanna Courtenay]

In the same year in the octave of Easter [1 April] a wedding took place at Windsor, celebrated with a great crowd of trumpeters and actors. It gave joy to few and advantage to nobody, and indeed most people were upset by it and found it hateful. Lord Waleran, count of St Pol, a foreigner from overseas, was so much loved by Lady Johanna Courtenay [correctly, Maud or Matilda], the sister of the king, that she thought no Englishman's embraces worth having compared to his, and so he married her at the time and place given above. Because she had presumed to do this against the advice of her own mother, once a princess and now the mother of the king, and all her friends, she was deprived of their assistance, and justly incurred their indignation. She also suffered reproaches from her own people, which were not likely to die away easily.[1] But, because she was his sister, the king on the advice of his counsellors gave them his town and manor of Byfleet, thinking to honour his sister and to incline the mind of the count towards greater loyal service to himself.

The duel between John Annesley and Thomas Catterton

About this time a new spectacle was seen in England. Its very unusualness was what drew so many spectators to it, as human nature delights in the unusual as much as in the different. In the parliament rightly called 'the Good' held in the time of king Edward III, a knight called John Annesley accused the esquire Thomas Catterton of treason. Thomas had once been governor of the castle of St Sauveur,[2] built by Sir John Chandos[3] of happy memory in France on the Isle de Contentin, and John Annesley asserted that Thomas had sold the castle to the French for a vast sum of money, at a time when he lacked neither the means of defence nor provisions.[4] He offered to fight a duel with this Thomas over the matter according to the law of combat. For as his wife had at the time an inheritance due from John Chandos who was a very close kinsman of hers, the possession of this castle would have come to him, if it had not been treacherously lost by the false behaviour of Thomas. Because of this accusation Thomas was taken captive and put in prison.

But soon after, at a time when the duke of Lancaster [John of Gaunt] was allowed to do whatever he liked in the last days of his father the king [Edward III], Thomas was released on the intervention, so it was said, of Lord Latimer, for whom he had previously fought in peace and war, whether the causes were just or unjust, true or false. But John Annesley had not found any way to put his challenge into effect right up to that time, as certain people claimed that it would be against the laws of the land for a subject of that land to fight a duel in that country for any reason under the law of combat. The people most opposed to the duel were those who were afraid of being attacked by a similar accusation. But in the end at an assembly of legal experts and the

---

1   The lady who 'so much loved' Lord Waleran was Matilda or Maud Courtenay (d.1392) half-sister to Richard II, the daughter of Joan of Kent by her first husband, Thomas Holland. Maud's first husband had been Hugh Courtenay, grandson of the earl of Devon. Walsingham's disapproval of this marriage was echoed by other commentators (see, for example, the *HVRS*, p. 58). Waleran of Luxembourg, count of St Pol had distinguished himself in recent campaigns against the English and his capture at Ardres in 1375 had represented something of a coup. He had remained in captivity in England until July 1379 and his marriage formed part of the terms of his release, for which a ransom of 100,000 francs was also paid. Froissart reported that St Pol now became an object of suspicion in France and he and his bride were refused entry to the country (Froissart, *Chroniques*, ix. 133). Walsingham had observed him at first hand since he was amongst many members of the court circle admitted to the confraternity of St Albans abbey in 1379–80: BL, Cotton MS Nero D VII, fo. 80r.

2   St Sauveur-le-Vicomte, Normandy.

3   Sir John Chandos (d.1370) was one of the most celebrated knights in the first decades of the Anglo-French conflict. He had served at the siege of Cambrai (1337), Crécy (1346) and was credited with saving the life of the Black Prince at Poitiers (1356). Later he served as constable of Guienne and seneschal of Poitiers. It was his anonymous herald who composed the celebrated *Life* of Edward, the Black Prince.

4   The French had besieged St Sauveur for ten months between August 1374 and May 1375 before they persuaded Catterton to agree a surrender if he received no further reinforcements by 3 July. No forces were sent and the surrender occurred. The loss of the castle was much criticised in England and was one of the complaints levelled at Sir Thomas Latimer at the Good Parliament in 1376.

senior knights of the region, it was decreed that in an overseas matter like the present one, which had not arisen inside the boundaries of the kingdom but was over the possession of a foreign castle, it was completely legal for anyone to fight a duel, if the constable and marshal of the kingdom had been informed of the case beforehand, and if the duel was taken up by the parties in their presence.

So a day was appointed for the duel, and in the meantime the necessary preparations were made for it in the court at Westminster; these are the barriers which are known as 'lists', which are made of great strength from timber, as though they were going to last for ever. When the appointed day arrived, men came together for this novel spectacle from all parts of the kingdom in such great crowds that the number of people flocking into London, on the evidence of many, far exceeded the multitude of those who a few years previously had come together for the coronation of the king. On the day itself very early in the morning first the king with his nobles and the commons entered the place, and then, according to the custom, the knight entered, armed and sitting astride his warhorse with its gorgeous trappings. For the challenger must enter the lists first and await the arrival of the accused. Then, after an interval, the esquire was called to defend his cause in the following words, 'Thomas Catterton, the accused, you must appear to defend yourself in the case which Sir John Annesley, knight and accuser, has publicly and in writing brought against you.' The herald for the duel cried aloud this proclamation three times. When the third summons had been completed, the esquire appeared, also armed, sitting on a warhorse royally caparisoned with cloths bearing Thomas's arms. When he arrived at the lists, Thomas at once dismounted, so that the constable, according to the rules of the duel, should not punish him for entering the lists. But his forethought did no good. For his horse, which was running up and down near the lists, sometimes put his whole head and chest inside the lists. So the constable, Lord Thomas of Woodstock, claimed the horse, swearing that he wished to have its head, as that was how much of it had been seen inside the lists. And so the horse was awarded to him. But I will tell the story of this later. Now I must return to the story of the duel.

After the esquire had entered the lists on foot, the marshal and the constable brought forward the indenture, made in their presence with the willing consent of the parties, in which was previously contained the points laid against him by his opponent, the knight. But the esquire was pricked by his conscience to try to make exceptions, so that he might somehow avail to make his case more acceptable. But when the duke of Lancaster saw him delaying matters and heard that he now wanted to make exceptions, he publicly swore that unless the esquire was willing to admit all the points in the indenture which had been drawn up according to the rules for the duel and the laws of combat and which had not been completed without his assent, he would soon be dragged away to be hanged as being guilty of treason. By this action the duke won for himself the favour of many and wiped out some of his previous bad reputation.

But when the esquire heard this, he declared that he dared to fight with the knight not only over this matter but over any matter in the world, especially as he had more trust in his physical strength and the support of his friends than in the case which he had undertaken to defend. For he was tall of stature, whereas the knight even among men of average height appeared short. And he numbered among his powerful friends [William] Lord Latimer and Lord Basset[1] and several others, (whose names I do not give to protect them), and he hoped to be supported by their intervention, if by chance he happened to suffer some injury. Encouraged by these advantages he entered the lists. His opponent, the knight, took the customary oath, and then Thomas himself boldly swore that the cause for which he was about to fight was a just one, that he was not aware of any magic practices by which he could gain a victory over his enemy, and that he was not carrying about his person any herb or stone or any kind of amulet, by which evil-doers are accustomed to triumph over their foes.

After these preparations, they both poured forth heartfelt prayers and began the duel, fighting at first with lances, then with swords and finally with daggers. The duel lasted a long time, until

---

1   Ralph, Lord Basset of Drayton, a partisan of John of Gaunt.

the esquire had had all his weapons taken from him. Then at last the knight with great power knocked Thomas to the ground and gathered himself together to assault him, but the sweat running down through his helmet partially blinded him, so that, when he thought he was throwing himself on top of Thomas, he in fact missed the esquire and fell at his side. Although Thomas was now almost breathless from the exertion involved, when he saw Sir John's fall, he turned towards him and, seizing hold of him, he lifted himself up over the body of the knight and threw himself completely upon him. When they saw this, the spectators interpreted it in different ways. Some said the knight was now losing and would at any moment be completely defeated. Others claimed that the knight would soon be on his feet and win the victory over the esquire. Meanwhile the king gave orders for a truce to be sounded and for the knight to be lifted from the ground. To cut a long story short, men were sent to lift up the esquire, but when they came up to the knight, he earnestly begged that the king should allow him to go on lying on the ground as I have described. He claimed that all was well with him and that he would be the winner, if the esquire was put back on top of him as he had lain before.

But when this request was refused, Sir John at last allowed himself to be lifted from the ground, and, as soon as this was done, he hurried off to the king without anyone supporting him, whereas Thomas, after he had been lifted up, had not been able to walk at all or even to stand without the assistance of two men, who placed him on a chair where he tried to get back his breath. When Sir John came before the king, he asked him and his nobles to grant him the grace of being put back into his original position with the esquire on top of him; for he realised that Thomas was now just about to breathe his last, owing to the immense exertion and heat and weight of his armour which had almost killed him. When the king and the nobles saw Sir John seeking to renew the fight with such spirit and determination, and also publicly promising a huge sum of gold if this was done, they decided that the knight should be put back again with the esquire on top of him in exactly the same positions in which they had lain on the ground before. But meanwhile Thomas lost consciousness and suddenly fell from the chair as if dead into the arms of those standing around him. Many rushed to his aid and poured on him wine and water, but they achieved nothing at all until they took off his armour and all his clothing and he was naked right down to his skin. So this showed that the knight had won and the esquire had lost. But after a long delay Thomas recovered a little consciousness and, opening his eyes, he began to lift his head and to glare terrifyingly on all those standing around. When the knight was told of this, he approached still in his armour (for he had taken none of it off since the start of the duel) and addressing Thomas and calling him a lying traitor, he asked him if he dared restart the duel. But Thomas had neither the understanding or the breath to reply to this, so it was proclaimed that the duel was over and that all should return to their homes. But the esquire, as soon as he was carried to his bed, began to be delirious and his delirium lasted until about three o' clock the following afternoon when he breathed his last. This duel took place on 7 June, an event enjoyed by the crowd of the commons but a source of worry to traitors.[1]

An English army rides through France without meeting any resistance

About this time the king of England and his council assembled a strong force and sent it to the help of the duke of Brittany [Jean IV], who had lost almost all hope of resisting the French, once he had heard that Sir John Arundel and his army had met the terrible fate at sea which I have described.[2] In charge of this force were Lord Thomas of Woodstock, earl of Buckingham and uncle

---

[1]   The date is corroborated by the author of *Historia vitae et regni Ricardi secundi* (*HVRS*, p. 58). Annesley was rewarded for his pains with an annuity in recompense for the loss of his interest in the castle.

[2]   The need to safeguard English commercial interests and also to support Duke Jean IV of Brittany had convinced some, if not all of the king's councillors, to mount another continental campaign. The plan was discussed in the January parliament and Thomas, earl of Buckingham, the king's uncle, was chosen to command this force, perhaps because of the persuasive powers of his retainer, Sir John Gildesburgh, who was the speaker in this session. Buckingham was to be accompanied by some of the country's most experienced captains – such as Calveley and Knolles – and a force of five thousand was assembled in May and June.

of the king, Sir Thomas Percy, brother of Lord Henry Percy, earl of Northumberland, Sir Hugh Calveley, Sir Robert Knolles, [Ralph] Lord Basset, Sir John Harleston and Sir William Windsor. Without a doubt they were all of them men who could justifiably have taken individual command of an army, such was their wisdom, bravery and skill in fighting. Because it was not safe to sail straight from England to Brittany because of the galleys guarding the pathways of the sea and the small numbers of their own ships, which could not transport several of them at the same time, they chose to ferry their forces from Dover and Sandwich to Calais, and from there to ride through the whole of France until they came to Brittany. They were afraid that if they were scattered over a vast expanse of sea, the numbers of their men might be diminished through the attacks of pirates.[1]

John Philipot, a citizen of London, deserved praise and honour for his help to that expedition. He both hired the ships for it through his own efforts and, when the men were burdened with debt through the usual long delay on shore waiting for the ships and leaders to arrive, he paid their debts, satisfying the creditors and restoring the objects pawned to their owners. For the men had pawned jerkins, breastplates, helmets of metal and leather, bows, lances and other kinds of weapons in order to get food, and either they would not have crossed the channel at all owing to the lack of armour, which had been disposed of as I have described, or at least would have set out completely unarmed. I have heard from the lips of John Philipot himself that he redeemed from the hands of creditors a thousand of the breast-coverings or tunics commonly called 'jackets'.[2]

Having set out on the expedition, our men rode in circles over the whole of France, looting and laying waste the country as enemies do, burning the towns and estates, and putting the people to the mouth of the sword without any thought of mercy, until they reached the borders of Brittany.[3] Not one person from that famous kingdom had taken it upon himself to put a stop to their daring. The French themselves had been so completely terror-stricken that although they lived in a kingdom so huge that one man from the English army could always have been opposed by a thousand Frenchmen, they quickly chose, like women, to look for hiding places in which they could skulk rather than to meet the squadrons of the English as an army. These, O Christ, are your works, these, O good Jesus, are your miracles. You have the power to fight and to win with a few just as much as with a multitude. You provide for your servants a safe path through the thickest ranks of the enemy and you visit our foes with the punishment which is their due. For it was you, Lord, who made the French as motionless as stones, until your people, the army of the English, had passed through their land. Nor was it in wanton arrogance that our troops toiled to subjugate the kingdom of France, but trusting in the just rights and the innocence of their king, the true heir to the kingdom of the French.[4]

Froissart provides a full list of the English captains, naming Sir Thomas Percy, Sir Thomas Trivet, Sir William Clinton and Sir John Harleston, amongst others: *Chroniques*, ix. 238–9; FCBuchon, ii. 95–6. See also Jones, *Ducal Brittany*, pp. 90–1; Saul, *Richard II*, p. 52.

1   It was the absence of available shipping that necessitated a crossing at the Dover straits and an approach to Brittany across French soil. It appears that an advance guard may have landed at Calais by 19 July, but the main force did not leave England until five days later.

2   Walsingham is the only authority to draw attention to Philipot's role in the preparations for the campaign.

3   Buckingham seized the opportunity to conduct a chevauchée through the Pays de Calais, Champagne and southern Burgundy. Froissart describes in detail his assaults on the fortified towns of Ardres, St Omer, Thérouannes, Arras, and St Quentin: *Chroniques*, ix. 238–54; FCBuchon, ii. 96–109. Philip the Bold, duke of Burgundy assembled a large army at Troyes to engage the English as they passed but Charles V ordered him not to draw them into a pitched battle (Froissart, *Chroniques*, ix. 259–62; FCBuchon, ii. 106–9). Walsingham describes this stand off below when reporting the events following the death of Charles V, see below, pp. 111–13. The king's death on 16 September finally removed any prospect of an engagement and Buckingham had reached Rennes before the end of the month.

4   Walsingham regarded this episode as indicative of the righteousness of the English cause, but the *Anonimalle* author reminded his readers of the political reality, that the duke of Brittany had begun to seek a rapprochement with France (*AC*, p. 132). The duke sought to distract Buckingham and his men by persuading them to besiege the pro-French fortress at Nantes, whilst secretly he negotiated a treaty with the French themselves. After five months, Buckingham was compelled to return to England.

A Scottish ship is captured

About this time the men of Hull and Newcastle upon Tyne went on a joint expedition aimed at eliminating the large numbers of wicked pirates of those days. By chance they met a Scottish ship and, discovering that there were enemy aboard her, they fiercely attacked her and, killing or capturing her crew, they towed the ship back to their own area. It contained goods estimated to be worth seven thousand marks.[1]

As soon as the earl of Northumberland, Lord Henry Percy, heard of this success, he hurried to the scene and in his wish to obtain part or whole of the booty ordered them in the name of the king not to take it upon themselves to make any division of the goods of this ship without some approval from himself. But the men of the North in typical fashion were soon wildly breathing fire from their nostrils. With faces distorted with anger and nostrils filled with a tempest of fury and barking like dogs in their extreme indignation, they angrily replied that they had exposed themselves to the dangers of death for the good of the king and his kingdom, and that it was with their own hands that they had killed great numbers of the enemy and seized their goods. It was not right for them, who had done all the work, to accept a portion of the spoil assigned by the earl. Rather any decision about the division of the spoils should be taken by the very men who had had the danger of obtaining them. And so their orders were for the earl to withdraw with all speed, so that they were not forced to turn their weapons on him in defence of their own property. They again declared that they would more gladly and speedily put themselves at risk in defence of their plunder than have its division decided by one who had played no part at all in the obtaining of it.

When the earl heard this, for all his greedy thirst for the plunder, he went away very angrily, with the intention of thinking up some obstacle for people whom he knew were unwilling to leave the decision to him. So he obtained writs for the seizure of the captors, as rebels against himself and so against the king, seeing that he was the representative of the king in that area. But in the meantime neither the earl himself nor the men of Newcastle, who had done the most to oppose him, got any enjoyment from the booty. On the contrary they were cheated of their desired booty and had a laughable trick played on them. For they were again deprived of their possessions, when they were craftily taken from them and shipped off to other parts.

This is how it happened. After the earl had failed to get the division of spoils which he had demanded, one of the men from Hull who had shared in the labour of the expedition asked his companions to give him the share due to his efforts. For he was afraid that if matters were delayed any longer neither he nor his companions would have any joy of the booty. But his friends from Newcastle and neighbouring places replied that it was not yet time to do a share-out, especially as they did not yet know what the earl of Northumberland was likely to devise against them. The verbal argument over this led to a quarrel, and when the end result was that they refused to give the man from Hull any of the booty, he went back home, returned unexpectedly after a few days with an armed force and made off with the captured ship and all its booty. Nobody dared to oppose him, and he returned to Hull, having robbed his disloyal allies and laughing at the mocking way in which he had spoilt the plans of the count.

Enemy troops are captured in Ireland

The French and Spanish had made frequent attacks on the coasts of England and had seized several ships, but on the feast day of St Margaret the virgin [20 July], while they were endeavouring to continue with their usual works of wickedness, they were forced by a sudden attack by men from the west of England to put into an Irish port called Kinsale [Co. Cork] by the natives.[2] While they were there, a brave, spirited attack by the English and the Irish led to the

---

[1] Walsingham is the only contemporary commentator to record in any detail the capture of the vessel and the subsequent struggle with Northumberland.
[2] Castile and France agreed upon a combined campaign against the English in February 1380 although the fleet launched in the summer, which Walsingham describes here, was only a small one of about twenty

seizure of the following generals, Jean de Vienne, admiral and governor of France,[1] Juan Perez of Berriz and Juan his brother, Gonzalo Martinez of Motrico, Turgo lord of Morauntz, the lord of Reych, Perez Martinez of Bermeo, Juan Medite of Bermeo, the steward of Belle Île, the steward of Vergara, Juan the steward of Santander, Cornelius of San Sebastian, Pascal of Biscay, Juan Martinez Coporgorge of San Sebastian and several other famous men.[2] Also several were killed, amounting to four hundred men. Twenty-one vessels of different size which they had captured from us were recovered there, and from the enemy fleet our men captured four barges and one sloop. Four Spanish generals escaped capture at our hands, namely Martin Grauntz, Juan Perez Montago, Juan Ochoa of Guetaria and Garcia of San Sebastian.

The Scots capture the market town of Penrith

During this summer the Scots, who were upset at the seizure of their ship, were eager to pay back the Northumbrians for this and to give them tit for tat.[3] So with a huge mob of wild tribesmen they crossed our borders into Westmorland and Cumberland, looting and killing. Going further south, they drove back to Scotland from Inglewood forest, so it is said, about four thousand beasts of different kinds, raging and slaughtering wherever they went and burning whatever they could. Not content with this they marched by night and suddenly and unexpectedly burst into Penrith, where the marketplace happened at that time to be thronged with a great crowd of people. Very many were killed, several taken prisoner and all the rest put to flight. The Scots collected and carried off enough wealth to satisfy the cupidity of the greediest army. Then returning home via Carlisle, they decided to attack that. But they were alarmed by the news that on the previous night a well-nigh innumerable host had secretly flocked to the defence of the town from the neighbouring counties. So they decided to travel on, driving the captured cattle around the town, fearing that, should they stay on there, they might perhaps be outwitted by some trick and compelled to release the booty, which they had taken in Penrith and the surrounding countryside. So this was done, but even so in going around the town they lost some of their men to archers of Westmorland and Cumberland, the result of this being that they moved off and retreated in a fearful hurry, driving the captured cattle before them and herding them into Scotland.

The earl of Northumberland was greatly disturbed by the damage they had done. On the earl himself they had inflicted losses amounting to more than a thousand fairs, but while he was preparing to drive them out and to return damage for damage, he was suddenly stopped from doing anything against them by a rescript from the king. So the earl hurried up to London to the king's council and asked how it could be that he was actually forbidden by the writ of the king and the realm to fight against these monstrous enemies. But he soon received a reply, being gently told to wait for the march-day that the English and the Scots keep each year at the same time, and returned home, with no plans to take action before that day.

The town of Winchelsea is captured

In this same summer enemy galleys that were continually roaming the seas inflicted much damage on many places along the coast. For whenever the villains on their ships saw an unguarded place, they disembarked and frequently carried off booty scot-free and sometimes even set fire to and burned the towns. But like sea birds, whenever they saw soldiers approaching, they would hurriedly dash back to the water. On occasions chance put them in the hands of our men, so that once a group of eighty and once a group of a hundred were cut off before they could reach the sea, and, being pierced by arrows, were compelled to stay behind.

---

galleys. It appears the English captains were well prepared and watched the ships pass the Dorset and Devon coast before pursuing them: Russell, *English Intervention*, pp. 243–5.

1   Jean de Vienne, sire de Roullans, had been appointed admiral of France in December 1373.
2   The companions of Jean de Vienne have not been identified.
3   The author of the *Historia vitae et regni Ricardi secundi* confirms the attack on Penrith was a reprisal for the capture of the Scottish ship; *HVRS*, p. 59.

Among the shameful losses inflicted on our land was their capture of the town of Winchelsea. On that occasion they put to flight the abbot of Battle [Haimo de Offington] and all his men who were attempting to bring help to the town, and captured one of his monks who had put on armour and joined the abbot's force.[1] Richard [Fitzalan], earl of Arundel, a man who had been raised to his high position by his father's wealth and his descent from a long line of earls, postponing the fame to be gained from a display of military action, decided to do absolutely nothing to check these raids, lest he should bring harm upon the stubborn monks. For when the French rogues made their way up to his estate, he came out against them with the remarkably unsuitable household for such a person of one lance, to use the common expression, his purpose being not to cause them terror but to fill their minds with contempt for the position of earl and the nobility of the English knighthood! For what they saw or were told about was one of the richer and more powerful noblemen of the district advancing towards them with the tiniest of households, not intending to give battle to the raiders or to give his country hope of resisting the enemy, but rather, so it was said, to strike fear into his own men who were lesser than himself but better, and who of course would have boldly kept the enemy at bay, if Richard himself had not timidly taken a hand in the matter!

Thomas Felton is freed from prison

About the same time Sir Thomas Felton, having arranged his ransom, was freed from prison in Aquitaine. As he was returning home he met up with the English army, which, as I have said, had been sent to France to help the duke of Brittany [Jean IV]. All the nobles in the army received him with great joy and kept him with them for several days. During his stay with them he gave them much helpful advice and warned them of many dangers. All this was seen to be of great significance later on.

The cruelty of the count of Flanders

About the beginning of September a dispute arose between the count of Flanders [Louis II, de Mäele] and the commons of Ypres and Ghent.[2] The people of Ypres had assembled to discuss the matter with the magnates of the count, when the count himself unexpectedly arrived with a vast horde of armed men, charged in to the citizens of Ypres and killed eight thousand of them, perhaps having assayed a deed for which he himself was to receive a still bitterer punishment. Then, obeying the instincts of his cruel mind, he immediately laid siege to the town of Ypres, and, on capturing it, he at once burnt part of it and left part of it untouched by the flames as evidence of his victory. He ordered the execution of forty of the leading men of the town and he sent the same number to Bruges to be put under prison guard. Having committed these atrocities, he summoned the people and haughtily proclaimed that he was to be their master. So he ordered them to be careful not to oppose him in the future, lest they all suffered the same punishment as those whom I said had been executed. He asserted with an oath that he would punish all who ever thought about resisting him by striking them down with the same sentence of mass execution as

---

[1]   The *Historia vitae et regni Ricardi secundi* (*HVRS*, p. 60) reported that it was the Prior of Lewes and his monks who were driven from the town, but the abbot of Battle, which was nearer to Winchelsea, seems more likely.

[2]   The tensions between the Counts of Flanders and their subjects in the cloth towns of Ypres and Ghent were long-standing. When Count Louis I chose to support the French cause at the outbreak of the Hundred Years War the English halted the flow of raw wool into the Flemish markets casting the whole region into an economic crisis. The commons of Ghent rebelled and under the leadership of Jacques van Artvelde the three towns (including Bruges and Ypres) formed an autonomous union and forced Count Louis to flee into France. In the winter of 1379–80 these events threatened to be repeated: on 6 September 1379 the Ghentois murdered Count Louis's bailiff, Roger d'Autrive and on 8 September the rebels burned the count's castle of Wondelghem. Within a month Ypres had also fallen to the rebels and siege had been laid to Oudenaarde: Froissart, *Chroniques*, ix. 177–85; FCBuchon, ii. 134–6. See also E. Perroy, *The Hundred Years War* (London, 1960), pp. 188–9. Later the Ghentois chose Philippe van Artvelde, Jacques's son, and the revolt continued until Artvelde's death at the hands of a Franco-Burgundian army at Roosebeke on 27 November 1382. See below, p. 193 and n.

he had just inflicted on their fellow citizens. And then when he was assailed by the cries of the widows whose husbands he had killed, he asked who these women were and why they were making such an outcry. When he discovered that they were the widows of the men he had punished with death, so that he might leave no stone of cruelty unturned, he at once ordered them to be executed also, instructing his men to send them to their husbands, so that they might not be compelled to endure their widowhood any longer with all its vain floods of tears.

After this, he surrounded and besieged Ghent with its one hundred thousand people. For he was planning to overwhelm that city, not only because he judged it to be rebellious, but also particularly because the people of Ghent had set fire to the town of Dendermond, for showing that it gave excessive support to the count. But the men of Ghent were not at all frightened and terrified of the count and his army. They lifted the town gates off their hinges and carried them into the middle of the market-place, thus making a broad avenue for the count and his soldiers, if they should dare to enter Ghent.

The king of France

In this summer came the death of Charles [V], who was said to be the king of France but who had obtained the kingship unjustly by perjury, and who had been the bitterest opponent of the king of England and of Pope Urban [VI]. It is said that he was poisoned by his own people, and so paid a full repentance for fomenting an unjust war with England and for his support of the anti-pope.[1] On the advice of his nobles, before his death he appointed his younger brother, the duke of Burgundy [Philip the Bold], as regent of the kingdom of France, and entrusted him with the care of his little son and all his household, the little boy not yet being of an age to become king.

But after the king's death the duke of Anjou [Louis I, b.1339, duke from 1360–84], Charles's elder brother, was upset that his younger brother had been preferred to him (for, so he claimed, by reason of his age the regency of the kingdom should have belonged to him) and began to oppose him openly, assisted by [Olivier] the lord of Clisson and some other nobles of Anjou.[2] The quarrel between them became so public and notorious that they were almost each more afraid of the cruelty of the other than of the power and numbers of our English army, which was then riding up and down their lands with impunity.[3] But the duke of Burgundy, aiming to show himself a worthy regent, did not think it was the right time to fight with his brother when he could see our soldiers killing Frenchmen on all sides and laying waste the countryside with fire and sword. So he assembled at the city of Troyes as large a force as he could of about four thousand armed men from the whole country except from the lands of the duke of Anjou and [Olivier] the lord of Clisson, which he knew would refuse to follow him because of the dispute I have mentioned, and he was also joined by a large body of men from the commons. With all these he decided to block our line of march by getting in front of our army and forcing it by some means or other to engage in battle.

When our men learned of this, they decided to get ahead of the French without delay, fearing that some obstruction could be placed in their path if the French got ahead of them. They carried

---

[1]   Charles V died on 16 September 1380. Froissart also reported the suspicion that he had been poisoned, suggesting the king of Navarre as a likely conspirator: *Chroniques*, ix. 280; FCBuchon, ii. 113.

[2]   Six years before in 1374, Charles V had issued an ordinance outlining the arrangements for government in the event of his death, in which a regency would be established under his eldest brother Louis of Anjou until his own heir had reached the age of thirteen but at his death it was ignored. Walsingham's claim that Philip of Burgundy was created regent in his place was unfounded. Froissart describes how Charles summoned his brothers, Burgundy, Berry, Bourbon and Anjou, to his deathbed to discuss the government of the realm and how he urged them to crown the Dauphin Charles as soon as possible, but Anjou absented himself leaving the direction of government to the three remaining royal princes: *Chroniques*, ix. 280–4, 287–8; FCBuchon, ii. 113–14, 116–18. A bitter dispute ensued. Anjou attempted to seize power but was compelled to submit to a settlement in which his brothers Burgundy and Berry would join him on a permanent council of twelve to govern in the young king's name, with Anjou recognised as *primus inter pares* but without the title of regent.

[3]   The dispute over the regency occurred in the closing months of 1380 coinciding with Buckingham's chevauchée: see above, pp. 106–7 and n.

this out, rapidly assembling in front of the French, who were very puzzled as to how their plan could have become known to our troops so quickly. Our men chose a definite position and stationed their troops, arranged fairly and in good order, squadron by squadron. They also placed the carts (which we call the 'baggage-train') in the rear. To their amazement some of the French moved out and crossed a newly-made ditch, which they had constructed for the greater safety of their army, in order to fight our men. But in no time at all a few of our soldiers got possession of the ditch, killing many of the French in the process, and without any great difficulty forced the rest to abandon the ditch and to retreat to their lines. This deed struck such great fear into the French army that they did not dare any longer to go beyond their ditch, while the people of Troyes were so terror-stricken that they at once collected together their most precious possessions and departed in a panic for other places, believing that the English would soon be attacking them and their city, which they saw no possibility of defending against them.

Our men waited in their position for a few hours after the skirmish, but when they saw that the French were unwilling to make any further assaults and attacks on them, they withdrew without great losses but with the glory of a victory. They were wary of remaining in the same place, particularly because they did not know the situation of the duke of Brittany [Jean IV], whom they had been sent to help, although, if they had decided after the skirmish to attack the French or make an assault on Troyes, they might have gained great benefit from this. But their love for the duke and the strict orders they had received of hurrying to his help kept them from proceeding with such a plan. However on their approach to and arrival in Brittany they discovered, that, although they had passed through many perils on their route as they made their way through hostile territory and closely massed bands of the enemy, they now had not finished their immense labours but only begun them.

For the duke, out of love for whom they had attempted all this, had been induced by fear or enticed by money to go over to the enemy before their arrival. This was obvious to many of the wiser heads among them when they saw the duke giving them his thanks and favour more out of fear than out of love (if they can be called 'thanks' and 'support' when they are somehow extorted by force from an unwilling giver). Now at last the English can at least acknowledge how rash was their undisciplined folly and their hot-headed stupidity. They placed their trust in all men alike, and thus scattered to the four winds any sensible policy along with their forces and their wealth. Fearing, it would seem, that their own land would devour its inhabitants, they sent them out to perish on the seas or in foreign lands, when they could have been its defence, shield and help! And so our troops abroad, while they are more concerned with keeping an eye on other peoples dangers, suffer losses from which there can be no recovery and expose themselves to different dangers, just like those who, avoiding Scylla's whirlpool, dash themselves on Charybdis.[1]

No one could tell the extent of the loss and the sorrow which the death of Sir John Arundel and the destruction of the nobles who met the same fate as him brought to their fellow countrymen. There was no quarter of England, no district, no city or town that did not lose someone on that unlucky expedition. The leading men from the whole kingdom had been members of it and I think there was practically no corner in all the land which was free from mourning, where a mother did not grieve for her son lost in that shipwreck, or a wife for her husband, or some person for a kinsman or relative. I have decided to keep silent about the quantity of valuables that were lost, leaving out the money to maintain the expedition, the seizure of which pauperised the poor and impoverished the land. For the soul is more important than food and the body than raiment, and the irreparable loss suffered by our land was the destruction and loss by drowning of so many good and brave noblemen.

And yet, despite all these past disasters, England was still so senseless that she was not afraid to go through all the business again of choosing knights, finding the money and committing to an uncertain fate her best and most experienced men. Incredibly almost all her nobles were sent out on a joint expedition to Brittany, dispatched to deal both with open, public enemies as well as

---

1   Ovid, *Metamorphoses*, xiii. 730.

possible secret ones. Indeed this expedition would perhaps never have seen home again, if it had not been better looked after by the watchful eye of God than by the loyal support of its country, especially as it was surrounded on one side by the unmistakably hostile French and on the other by the wavering or secretly hostile Bretons, who between them plotted evil tricks and cunning ambushes and were trying their hardest to betray it or bring it down.[1] For it would be too long a story to tell of the obstacles, both open and concealed, which the English encountered at the hands of the French, as they boldly rode through the whole kingdom of France, laying waste its lands with fire and the sword and doing exactly as they pleased on their march towards Brittany.

When at last they stole into Brittany, they found everything in confusion. The duke was wavering and uncertain, tending now this way now that, and the Bretons themselves untrustworthy and full of deceit. No one could doubt that they were in an extremely dangerous position. And what was worse than all this was that that they had suffered betrayal by their own people. For, as soon as they had left England, English hearts had forgotten about them as if they were dead. Immediately agreements had been broken, promises not kept and almost all hope of help removed. So if God had not protected them because of the pre-eminent purity of life and innocence of heart of their leaders, they would never have re-entered their own land. For the generals of this expedition, unlike most previous generals, did not allow their troops on their way to the channel to ravage their own country or let a mass of people heading for the battlefield deserve the curses of the poor of England. On the contrary, they were careful to win by their actions the support, thanks and goodwill of the whole English people, before they embarked on the deep waters of the sea. And then, after landing in France, when they had had the great, good luck to pass unharmed through almost the whole kingdom of France against the wishes of its people and without losing a single man on the whole journey, in no way did they forget their God in their great good fortune, but said the most devout prayers for the king and his nobles, and for all the religious in England, asking that they should think it right to be steadfast in prayer and to hold processions and perform other religious acts for their welfare. The result was that, although they suffered from plots both in their own territory and in enemy lands, God in his goodness showed that he was pleased with their works, and brought the whole expedition to a happy conclusion, by graciously leading them back to their homes with honour and in safety.

And indeed their return was a work of grace: at the beginning they thought they had found friends, but they soon discovered that their Breton friends were their enemies, even the duke himself. For it was out of love for him, as I described earlier, that England had lost so many powerful noblemen. And it was to bring help to him that they themselves, forgetting all the previous losses, had undergone such perilous travels. And yet the moment they arrived at his court, he held a conference with them at which his one concern was to discuss not their stay but their withdrawal. They weighed up the duke's fickleness in their minds. They foresaw the dangers which were being prepared for them, for they had been warned by certain men in the opposition's ranks, who were very well-disposed towards the English, that unless they speedily took more care and thought about their own position they would all be betrayed and either killed or at least handed over alive to their enemies. At this point the duke offered them no small amount of gold on condition that they withdrew. They accepted his offer and so by the will of God and with his right hand protecting them they returned home, without any loss or hurt to themselves or their possessions, with two exceptions. They lost all their horses, either in Brittany or while recrossing the channel, and in their unsuccessful attempt to take the town of Nantes by siege they lost several leading men including that most eminent knight, Sir Hugh Tyrell, whom they saw succumb to cruel fate when he was pierced by a bolt from a crossbowman.

---

1   For Jean IV, duke of Brittany's secret negotiations with the French see above p. 107 n.
2   Tyrell had served as a commissioner of array for Wiltshire: *CPR, 1377–81*, p. 38.

The coronation of the king of France and the uprising of the people of Paris

In the November of this year the son of Charles, the former king of France, was crowned king. He was still quite young, only ten or eleven years old.[1] At the celebrations after his coronation, when almost the whole nobility of France had gathered together in Paris, there broke out among the common people a sudden great uprising and disturbance. There was an increasing flood of complaints against the nobles, because by means of various taxes called 'gabelles' they had not so much made their country poor as stripped it bare. Already, it was claimed, these taxes had been used for oarsmen and sailors who had contributed nothing to the kingdom, for various mercenaries, hired to guard the French and harm the English, whose achievements had also been nil, and for the lords and nobles of the kingdom, whose efforts too had been in vain. For these very nobles, who ought to have been a defence for the poor, had themselves been in need of protectors, seeing that, when they saw the English army riding through the whole kingdom and laying everything to waste with fire and sword, there had not been one of them who dared to block the English advance or even to look at them, but they all like women had shut themselves away in their cities or castles. The lords, they asserted, should be ashamed that in this vast kingdom where the numbers of nobles, magnates, knights and soldiers should have been so many that in consequence they could easily have put ten Frenchmen in the field against one man of the English army, none out of all of them had dared to oppose the English for the sake of his kingdom or for the sake of the people. They said the nobles ought also to be ashamed that they had so many times deceived the people with false promises. For they had promised that they would subjugate the English, if now this and now that tax was paid, and that they would bring peace, if only the people would contribute so much, but none of their words had become true. Why, at this very moment, when the English had come into their midst, the French nobles were fearfully staying in their homes and doing absolutely for their country while everything was left for the English to plunder.

So the nobles should know that there was no chance of the people being willing to be taxed or to agree to taxation, but that they would prefer to abandon their king and his nobles, who ever only had an eye to their poverty, and take themselves off to the English, whom they knew would rule them more peacefully than would the French, their natural masters. And as they shouted out such words they could scarcely restrain themselves from laying hands on some of the king's household and advisers. So the leading men and the magnates, being afraid that they would be assaulted when they saw the people so angry, tried to calm them down with all manner of soothing words, but they were barely able to check their anger and make them quiet again for even a short time.[2]

In this situation the king and the chief men of the kingdom retired to a fortified place to await the outcome of events, putting into practice the advice of the poet, 'When frenzy runs amok, give way to frenzy.'[3] The people indeed kept up this frenzy throughout the night following and completely destroyed the house of a Parisian nobleman, whose advice, so they thought, had been responsible for them being so often troubled by taxes. They also, as they roamed through all the different quarters of the city, killed without pity all the Genoese sailors that they could find, since, as they themselves said, these sailors had almost exhausted all the funds of the city without any success. And indeed the total of their daily pay was so great that as the days went by it increased to £750, this being divided equally among twenty-five galleys. Besides, this pay had gone on for a

---

[1]   Charles VI (b. 3 December 1368) was crowned at Rheims on 4 November 1380. He was eleven years old.
[2]   Here Walsingham conflates events in France that occurred in the years immediately following the death of Charles V. The repeated demands for taxation met growing resistance in the closing months of 1380 and in November the French government was forced to suspend all levies and even to abandon the collection of arrears. But these concessions came too late and revolts erupted in a number of provincial cities. On 1 March 1382 there was an uprising in Paris after the burgesses attempted to levy a merchandise tax (maillot); a mob (maillotins) broke open the arsenal and massacred the tax collectors and a settlement was only reached after the burgesses agreed to abandon the levy.
[3]   Ovid, *Remedia amoris*, 119.

long time, from the beginning of the month of May, which is when ships first dare to plough the western ocean, right up to the end of August, after which ships are afraid to linger in our sea owing to storms and gales.

The duke of Lancaster marches against Scotland and impoverishes his kingdom

John [of Gaunt], duke of Lancaster, whom I have often mentioned, was at this time sent to the north with a very adequate force to attack the perfidious and rebellious Scots, and to cause as much disturbance as he could to the whole Scottish kingdom. The occasion for this expedition was the violent raid made by the Scots during which, as I have described, the enemy acting like savages had invaded the lands of Cumberland and Westmorland and the town of Penrith. But you will be able to guess the achievements of the duke and the success of his expedition from all his previous expeditions. For after the duke's efforts those rascally, deceitful Scots, although the duke had worked as hard as possible to make a peace binding them as well as us, inflicted still more irrecoverable losses on the kingdom of England. As I have said many times before, they not only deceived us but laughed at us.

During the duke's expedition almost the whole province of Northumberland was laid waste in providing hospitality for our army, so much so that the people swore with an oath that they had put up more patiently with the arrival of the Scottish army, whom they could legally and lawfully resist, than their replacement by the arrival of the English, whom they could not punish out of consideration for their kinship and fatherland, not to say their fear of the laws. So, after impoverishing Northumberland and after the expenditure of the incredible sum of gold of eleven thousand marks previously collected from the commons, the duke's army returned home, bringing back with it nothing good for their country, except the horses which they had got from the Scots on that occasion and taken up for their own use.

Letters are found incriminating Ralph Ferrers

During these days in which our soldiers achieved nothing, a certain poor man brought to John Philipot some sealed letters, which he had found. John summoned some fellow citizens, opened one of the letters, and read in it treason against his country. When he examined the seal on the outside, he recognised it as being the seal of the knight Ralph Ferrers, who held almost the first place among the counsellors of the king.[1] At once he took four other letters as well, sealed in the same way, first to the lord chancellor and then to the king. When they had looked at them, recognised the seal as Ralph's and saw to whom the letters were addressed, the king and such of his council as was then present were completely amazed that such an aged knight, in whom his country had placed the greatest hope, should turn traitor. For one of the letters was addressed to Bertrand du Guesclin, another to Bureau de la Rivière, one indeed to [Olivier] the lord of Clisson and one to the admiral of the fleet and the general of the French and Spanish armies, who at this time were sailing around our coasts and in different places doing great damage to our country.[2] The letters contained such secret plans of the king and his kingdom that no one could doubt that only Ralph Ferrers or someone like him who sat in on the private council of the king, could have imagined or known about or laid bare such information.

So in the greatest haste some knights were sent with John Philipot to the duke of Lancaster, who, as I have said, had then gone to the north to deal with the Scots, and who had also Ralph Ferrers with him at that time. The impressions of the seal were shown secretly to the duke. Ralph Ferrers was summoned and ordered to show his personal seal. When the two were compared, they

---

1   Ferrers, a chamber knight, and a member of the first continual council of Richard's reign, had been one of those responsible for desecrating the sanctuary at Westminster and the murder of the squire, Robert Hawley. See above, p. 71.
2   Du Guesclin was constable of France until his death in July 1380. Clisson succeeded him. For their place in French government see above pp. 66, 79, 89, 111. Cardinal Bureau de la Rivière of Amiens had been a councillor of Charles V but he was banished from the court at the accession of Charles VI, which might cast doubt on the veracity of these letters.

were found to be identical. To add still more weight to their suspicions, Ralph admitted that for the past three years he had not entrusted the keeping of his seal to anyone else. All this evidence showed those who were there that Ralph was pretty clearly guilty. The duke ordered him to be arrested and imprisoned in Durham castle. But when the envoys who had sought out the duke on this matter had returned to the king, the duke sent Ralph some comforting words, telling him not to be cast down by this event, but to be of a brave heart in the knowledge that he would certainly suffer no harm for what had happened. As soon as this became known to the people, they made many verbal attacks on the duke, full of bitter abuse. But how Ralph escaped will become clear when I write an account of the following parliament. Four barons, who were present at this next parliament, went bail for Ralph Ferrers, until he had more convincingly demonstrated his innocence.

The expulsion of the count de St Pol

Waleran [of Luxenburg], count of St Pol, with his wife, Johanna [correctly, Maud or Matilda] Courtenay, the sister of the king, had recently left England, or more accurately had been banished to his own land for his crimes, but quietly to avoid the king's person being disgraced by someone who had such a close connection with himself. Like all his race, as soon as Waleran began breathing his own air, he was willing to declare that he had not walked with the English out of heartfelt sympathy, but rather out of a feigned cunning. Indeed, once he was home, he soon found an opportunity of going to those French magnates who stood at the right hand of the new king, the young son of Charles, to get them to promote his interests before the king and his council. With no delay he was welcomed by all of them, made chamberlain of the king, and publicly showed himself an enemy of England, so that it was obvious to all that England had nursed a viper in her bosom.

The Flemings make peace

The Flemish people of Ghent, after long, ruinous litigation, after a lengthy but unsuccessful siege of their city, after deaths and killings of their own people and by them of their countrymen on the count's side, in all of which they continually held the upper hand, at last made peace with the count, when he lifted the siege and asked for peace. But it was of short duration.[1]

A parliament at Northampton

About the feast of St Martin [11 November] a parliament assembled at Northampton on the orders of some of the council.[2] It was against the wishes and without the consent of almost all the nobles of the kingdom, and especially against the wishes of the citizens of London.[3] Everybody thought it a very bad idea because winter was coming on, and it would be held in Northampton, where it was not easy to find an adequate supply of firewood or lodgings suitable for such a crowd of people. The reason why a few councillors had decided the parliament should be held there was their appetite for the revenge, which they were panting to take on John Kirkby who had murdered the merchant from Genoa [i.e. Janus Imperialis], a story I have touched on earlier in this book [see above, p. 90]. They had correctly estimated the passions of the Londoners and calculated, as

---

[1]   Walsingham here refers to the truce agreed between Count Louis of Maële and the Ghentois who had been in rebellion against him for more than a year. After a protracted siege at Oudernaarde, at the intervention of Philip, duke of Burgundy, the rebel forces had been persuaded to withdrew and made a temporary peace with the count, who after further negotiations, made a triumphal return to Ghent. Froissart traces the dispute from its first beginnings with the death of the popular champion of the Gantois, Jean de Lyon: *Chroniques*, ix. 158–232; FCBuchon, ii. 51–5, 65–77. See also R. Vaughan, *Valois Burgundy* (London, 1975), pp. 19–22.
[2]   Parliament opened on 5 November although the session was immediately adjourned until the following Thursday (8 November), since so many of the prelates, lords and commons had not yet arrived on account of the flooded state of the roads; even then many of the magnates were absent on Gaunt's Scottish campaign. The session was dissolved on 6 December: *RP*, iii. 88.
[3]   The Londoners lamented the loss of trade that such a relocation would mean.

would have been the case, that if the parliament was in London, there was no way that its citizens would allow John Kirkby to be executed for the murder of the Genoan. Rather, if they tried to achieve this in London, danger was hanging over their own heads.[1]

So, taking counsel beforehand, they got the parliament held at Northampton and during this parliament, of course, they got Kirkby dragged away and hanged, with the people of London reduced to being spectators of all that was happening. They also forced through the collection of a new tax to help the king and particularly those who had recently been sent through France to Brittany with Lord Thomas of Woodstock. The tax which it took dire threats to get levied[2] was half a mark on each male religious who was a priest and the same amount on each female religious and also on secular priests, and also a twelve pence poll tax on men, both married and unmarried, and also on women. This tax was the cause of unheard-of trouble in the land, as will become clear from what follows.[3]

[1381]

The new year

In 1381, the fourth year of the reign of King Richard II, after the joyful celebrations of the feast of Christmas, a council assembled in London, at which Lord Thomas Brantingham, bishop of Exeter[4] was dismissed from the office of treasurer and his place was taken by Sir Robert Hales,[5] master of the Hospital [i.e. prior of the order of Hospitallers in England], as high-minded and energetic a knight as any, but who was not pleasing to the commons.

About the same time there arrived at Southampton some galleys, which others usually call 'carracks'. They were laden with spices and wines of many kinds and other valuable items, and brought great profit to the inhabitants of the whole land during the season of Lent.

The ravings of John Wyclif

At the same time the old hypocrite himself, the angel of Satan and forerunner of the Antichrist, who should not be called 'John Wyclif' but the heretic 'Weak-belief', was continuing his ravings and seemed to be drinking up the river Jordan and plunging all Christians into the abyss. Indeed he took up the heretical views of Berengarius and Ockham[6] and struggled to prove that after the priest had consecrated the elements at a mass they then remained actual bread and wine just as they had been before the consecration, and that Christ merely 'stood by' as he did everywhere

---

1   The summoning of parliament to Northampton may have been in response to renewed tensions between the government and the city of London, itself smarting at the failure (and expense) of Buckingham's expedition and the suspicions surrounding the murder of the Genoese merchant Janus Imperialis (see above, p. 90). Walsingham is surely right to suggest that it would have been difficult for the government to punish the murderer, Kirkby, in the presence of the city's mercantile community.

2   Walsingham here exaggerates the struggle to secure a grant of taxation; in this session the commons proved less obdurate than they had been in the previous two years. They demanded to know the precise sum sought by the crown (£160,000) but they set no other conditions on their agreement to the grant.

3   Typically, Walsingham emphasises the cost to the regular religious, masking the real significance of this tax. It was the third polltax to be levied in four years. For the first levy, of 1377, the rate had been set at 4d and in 1380 there had been an attempt – albeit unsuccessful – to establish a graduated rate of tax. But now the rate was raised to 1s without any distinction being made between rich and poor.

4   Thomas Brantingham was bishop of Exeter from 1370 to his death in 1394.

5   Sir Robert Hales (d.1381) entered the order at Rhodes and was amongst the 100 hospitallers who joined the Cypriot crusaders who took Alexandria in 1365. He was appointed prior of the order in England in 1371 and was a member of the third continual council from 1378.

6   Berengar of Tours (d.1088), a pioneer in the use of logical method in the analysis of Christian doctrine, was condemned at the Second Lateran Council (1059) for his teaching that bread did not change its nature in the sacrament of the eucharist, remaining bread in both form and substance. William of Ockham (1280–1349), a Franciscan theologian and philosopher who favoured nominalism, aroused suspicion for his analysis of the *Sentences* of Peter Lombard, the standard theological textbook in northern European universities; fifty-seven of his propositions were censured by Pope John XII in 1323 and five years later he was also condemned for his teaching on apostolic poverty. He fled to the court of Lewis of Bavaria but was never formally condemned as a heretic.

though in a more special way, while the consecrated bread had no more value than any other bread, apart from the one fact that it had been blessed by a priest. Furthermore if it was the body of Christ, he asserted that when he broke it he could be breaking the neck of his God. He also declared that Christians were wrong to venerate that sacrament, since it was, he claimed, merely bread and inanimate matter, and they rather ought to venerate a toad or any living creature you like rather than that bread, seeing that his argument was that a living thing was more important than something which lacked life. With such ravings as these he won over many into belief in the same heresy.

A knight's ghastly attack on the body of Christ

A Wiltshire knight whose name was Laurence of St Martin and who lived near Salisbury was similarly won over by Wyclif's preaching.[1] When the Easter festival was at hand at which it was his duty to receive the life-giving sacrament, he asked his priest to give him holy communion on the eve of that festival, and in accordance with his request after the celebration of the mass was given what he had asked for. But after he had been given the host by the priest and had got it in his hand, he immediately stood up and hurried home, carrying the body of our Lord.

When he saw the knight behaving in this untypically crazy fashion, the priest ran after him, shouting and adjuring him not maltreat the sacrament in this way, but to give it back to him or to behave like a Christian and respectfully consume it. But neither his prayers nor his shouts did any good at all. The knight locked his doors against him, found some oysters and divided up the host, gulping down part of it with the oysters, part with some onions and part with wine. He stoutly asserted that any bread in his own house was as valuable as that which he was glad to have eaten in such a manner. His servants were horror-stricken by this dreadful, unheard of act, and told the whole story to people outside.

The parish priest, who was suffering great anguish of mind from this atrocious crime committed by the knight, gave the bishop of Salisbury, master Ralph Ergom, a full, orderly account of this order-breaking performance, and the bishop at once ordered the knight to be summoned. Even in front of the bishop the knight refused to recant, but because of Sir Laurence's high reputation in those parts the bishop told him to go home, gather together the various priests that he knew and discuss the matter with them. It might be that heaven would look upon him and give him the grace to think more healthily about the sacrament in the interval before the appointed day on which he was to appear again before the bishop. He did all this and returning on the appointed day, he followed the instruction of the priests who had flocked to his house to deal with the matter, and confessed that he had had a wrong view about the sacrament of the altar and that he had sinned greatly in doing it dishonour. And so he humbly begged pardon of the bishop and all who were present.

Seeing his change of heart and hearing his humble confession, the bishop ordered him as part of his repentance to erect a stone cross in a public place in Salisbury, on which was to be carved the full story of his action in all its details. And every Friday of his life he was to come to the cross, bareheaded and barefoot, dressed just in his vest and pants, and kneeling before it to make a full, public confession of all that he had done. The bishop enjoined other acts of repentance, both public and private, but it would take too long to put them down on the page.

I have told this story in more detail than usual so that all might see the huge crop of evils sown in the ground by that beast come out of the abyss [Revelation 11: 7], that colleague of Satan, John Wyclif or Weak-belief.

---

[1]   Sir Lawrence of St Martin had served as JP in Wiltshire in 1380: *CPR, 1377–81*, p. 512.

A cardinal arrives in England

At this time there arrived in England a cardinal priest of the church of St Praxedes called Pileus.[1] He came with the duke of Teschen[2] and many nobles from the retinue of the emperor, to speak about the conditions for drawing up a marriage between the emperor's daughter [Anne] and the English king – and to empty the kingdom of a vast sum of money. For, so he claimed, he brought with him an unheard of power, and in a short time he got the whole kingdom flocking to him to obtain various favours. And indeed he did confer different benefits on different people. He personally granted indulgences which only the pope had been in the habit of granting. To anybody who would pay he willingly gave 'confessional letters' for two or three years. He admitted to the papal chaplaincies rich as well as mendicants, nor did he refuse the gold of those who begged to be made public notaries. Nor did he refuse portable altars to anyone offering him money. Instead of rejecting the £40 together with other gifts offered him by the Cistercians, he graciously granted them a general permission to eat meat outside the monastery, as they were accustomed to do inside; it made no difference. He sold the grace of absolution to the excommunicated. He only remitted vows made to go on pilgrimage to the thresholds of the apostles, to the Holy Land or to St James when he had received as much money as the pilgrims, according to an accurate reckoning, would have had to have spent in making the pilgrimages. To sum it all up in a few words, there was no request at all which he did not think it right to grant, provided money played its part.

When the English asked him by what power he did all this, he got very angry and said that, if they wanted to know about his power, he would give them an answer in Rome. And in fact his collecting bags were already so full of English silver, that new arrivals got no response from his servants unless they brought gold. 'Bring us gold,' they were told, 'we're already full up with your silver.' And when it was time to depart, he was not willing to leave any of the gold or silver behind, but got it all carried down to the Channel with him on mules. The sum was bigger than England had ever been accustomed to pay at one time in tax or tallage.

A voyage or expedition to Portugal[3]

At the same time through the contrivance of the duke of Lancaster a large force was collected to be sent to the help of the king of Portugal [Fernando I 1367–83] against the king of Spain [Juan I of Castile 1379–90], his enemy. For the duke maintained that it would be expedient for England to send to Portugal an army of soldiers together with a plentiful supply of gold, so that the king of Portugal [Fernando I], who had sent for them, might be bound with a greater love to the kingdom of England and its people. For he would then stop the sea passage through the pillars of Hercules by Cadiz, which moderns call 'the straits of Morocco', to ships which had to sail past him and his dominions, if they wanted to invade the Atlantic ocean in order to help the French and the

---

[1]   Cardinal priest Pileo de Prata, archbishop of Ravenna from 1370. He was papal nuncio to Urban VI and one of the Roman pope's closest counsellors. Pope Urban had promoted the prospect of a union between the English crown and the Imperial house – first mooted by Emperor Charles himself in 1378 – as a means of consolidating his own position in the schism. As early as December 1378 he had dispatched Pileo to Prague to secure the support of the Emperor's son, Wenzel, king of the Romans; there he met with the English envoys, Sir Simon Burley and Sir Michael de la Pole before the end of 1379. Negotiations continued into 1380 and according to the author of the *Historia vitae et regni Ricardi secundi* (p. 61 and n), this delegation arrived in England at the beginning of March.

[2]   Premislas, duke of Teschen, one of two deputies appointed to represent Anne of Bohemia in the marriage negotiations.

[3]   Preparations for this expedition began immediately after the Northampton parliament had been dissolved on 6 December 1380. Ships were detained from 7 January and the captains provided with the first portion of their expenses in February. The force of more than 2000 (a larger number than Walsingham suggests here) was assembled at Plymouth by 21 May 1381 and it sailed on or after 23 May. See also P. E. Russell *The English Intervention in Spain and Portugal in the Time of Edward III and Richard II* (Oxford, 1955), pp. 305–44.

Spanish in attacks on Brittany or England. If this happened, he declared, England would be safe and France and Spain, particularly France, would be frustrated.

The generals and leaders appointed to the expedition were Lord Edmund Langley, earl of Cambridge and the uncle of the king, Sir William Beauchamp,[1] Sir William Botreaux,[2] Sir Matthew Gournay[3] and several other knights whom there is no necessity to name.[4] They crossed the sea and indeed arrived without loss at the city of Lisbon, the capital of Portugal, and were warmly received by the king.[5] Although their small numbers meant they were not suitable to make an armed invasion of Spain, they were very useful to Portugal, being strong enough to defend the frontiers of the land and either stop the Spanish from invading Portugal or from doing the damage they wanted to its people.[6]

The Spanish thought that it would be a very good move to besiege Lisbon with our men inside it, so they got together ships and a great force of Spaniards and surrounded and laid siege to the city.[7] But they were then given an opportunity to experience the courage of the English. For when they had besieged the city for many days and had achieved nothing except bloody wounds and knocks, they at last shamefully abandoned the siege and went back home. So our men gained in confidence when they saw how feeble the Spaniards were, and frequently doing the damage to the Spanish that their strength and numbers allowed they bravely stayed on in Portugal, until further soldiers might perhaps be sent to join them.

The troubles that befell England during the revolt of the peasants and others of the common people[8]

About this time the kingdom of England experienced a sudden, great catastrophe which spread over all parts of the land. It had never been heard of before in their history and it was sent as a punishment for their sins.[9] If God, the Lord of mercies, with his wonted regard for goodness had not quickly checked it, the government of the land would have been completely wiped out and become a tale for laughter and mockery among all nations.

For in Essex the peasants, whom we call 'villeins' or 'bondsmen', together with the other coun-

---

[1]   Beauchamp (c.1343–1411) was the younger son of the earl of Warwick and had served with Gaunt in the Najera campaign of 1367.

[2]   Sir William Botreaux had served as a commissioner of array and JP in Cornwall: *CPR, 1377–81*, pp. 40, 307, 513, 569.

[3]   Gournay had served in the Spanish campaigns of the 1360s and knew well both the territory, and Pere II of Aragon: Russell: *English Intervention*, p. 303.

[4]   Sir Thomas Symond was another captain: Russell, *English Intervention*, p. 302.

[5]   The English ships arrived at Lisbon on 19 July; they had not experienced losses, but the Portuguese squadrons which had been sent out for their protection had been decimated by the Castilians a month before.

[6]   Walsingham greatly exaggerates the effectiveness of the English presence. Neither Cambridge nor Fernando showed any urgency to take offensive action against the Castilians, who, unopposed, continued their incursions across the border.

[7]   What Walsingham describes as an attempt to besiege Lisbon was rather an attempted assault on the English transport ships made by Castilian galleys approaching the mouth of the River Tagus. Cambridge mounted an effective defence, deploying troops and artillery from the shore, and the Castilians retreated: Russell, *English Intervention*, pp. 313–14.

[8]   Walsingham's account of the peasants' revolt of 1381 is perhaps the best and most detailed of all the contemporary narratives. In contrast to other chroniclers – the *Anonimalle* author, Henry Knighton – Walsingham was an eye witness to many of the events that he described. St Albans itself erupted in open rebellion and for much of the summer the monks must have been in fear of their lives. The drama at St Albans inevitably distorts Walsingham's coverage of events elsewhere and the chronology of his narrative is interrupted by his long excursus on the struggles of his own abbey. But even in his descriptions of the unrest in other parts of the country, in East Anglia, Kent and the city of London, he is a surer guide than any other source.

[9]   Walsingham regarded the revolt moralistically, but other contemporary chroniclers offered more wide-ranging interpretations. Froissart (*Chroniques*, x. 94–5; FCBuchon, ii. 150) believed it was the over-concentration of agricultural labourers in the south-eastern counties which had inevitably given rise to these tensions. The Westminster chronicler (*WC*, pp. 2–3) considered the trouble to have been caused by Kentish men who were renowned as 'mad dogs' (rabidissimi canes).

trymen there, taking on an enterprise beyond their strength and having hopes of subjecting all things to their stupidity, massed together in great numbers and began to revolt in order to gain their freedom. Their minds were set on becoming equal with their masters and never again being bound in servitude to any man at all. To give their plans a greater chance of fulfilment, men of just two villages, who were the originators and prime movers of this evil, began by getting messages sent immediately to every small village, asking all, old men as well as those in the prime of life, to put aside all excuses and to come to meet them, equipped with weapons as best they could.[1] Those who refrained from coming or ignored them or who despised the idea should realise that their goods would be ransacked, their homes burnt or knocked down, their heads cut off. Such frightening threats compelled all of them to run to join the leaders. They left behind the work of the plough and the sowing of seed in due season, their wives and their plots, and in a short time such a big number had been brought together that they numbered about five thousand of the poorest countrymen and peasants. These men who came together to seek a kingdom were armed, some with staves, some with swords thick with rust, some only with axes, others with bows of a venerable age, made redder than antique ivory from the smoke of the fire, and with a single arrow, most of which had just one feather. Among a thousand of such men it would have not been easy to see one properly armed, but, as they made a great number, they all believed that the whole kingdom could not resist them. And that they might be able to rejoice in the strength provided by additional troops, they sent messengers to Kent to inform them of their hopes and plans and to invite the men of Kent to join them in gaining their freedom, in considering the best course of action, and finally in bringing about change in the kingdom and its evil customs.[2]

When the men of Kent heard of a happening which they had often wished and prayed for in the past, they themselves also, putting aside all delay, collected together a large band of common people and peasants, using the same lies with which, as I have described, the men of Essex assembled their crowds, and in a short time had raised almost the whole county in a similar revolt.[3] Next they blocked all the roads used by pilgrims on their way to Canterbury, and stopping all pilgrims, of whatever class, they compelled them to swear an oath: first that they would stay loyal to king Richard and his commons, and accept no king who was called 'John' (this was owing to their dislike of John [of Gaunt], duke of Lancaster, who through his marriage to the daughter and heiress [Constanza] of Peter [Pedro 'the Cruel'], once king of Castile, called himself 'king of Castile'); secondly that they should be ready to come and join the rebels, whenever they should decide to send for them, and that they should persuade all their fellow citizens or villagers to favour the rebels; thirdly that they should not consent or agree to any taxes being levied in the kingdom in the future apart from the 15% tax which was the only one their fathers and forefathers had known and accepted.[4]

And so it happened that in a flash the news of this uprising was spread abroad into Sussex, the counties of Hertfordshire and Cambridgeshire, into Suffolk and Norfolk. The whole people were agog with expectation of what all this might mean for them and what would be the outcome of

---

[1]   According to the *Anonimalle* author, the trouble in Essex began when one of the collectors of the subsidy, John Bampton, attempted to raise the levy at Brentwood and surrounding villages. The inhabitants of Corringham, Fobbing and Stanford-le-Hope resisted, took up arms against him and marched 'from town to town inciting others to rise against their lords' (ils alerent de ville en ville pur exciter autres gentz de lever encontre les grandes seignours): *AC*, pp. 134–5.

[2]   The *Anonimalle Chronicle* corroborates the correspondence between the Essex and Kent rebels, claiming that letters were also sent to the commons of Norfolk and Suffolk: *AC*, p. 135.

[3]   The *Anonimalle Chronicle* reported that the Kent rising began on or shortly after 3 June (Whit Monday), the mob gathering first at Dartford, moving on to Rochester around 7 June, where the castle was attacked and its prison broken open, and finally arriving at Canterbury on 10 June. The chronicler records that three townsmen identified as traitors were summarily executed and then the mob moved out of the city and moved towards London: *AC*, pp. 133–40 at 135–6.

[4]   The *Anonimalle* chronicler also reports that the mob demanded the deposition of Archbishop Sudbury and his substitution by a monk of the Cathedral Priory: *AC*, p. 137

these bold attempts.[1] Many guessed there would be a better future, but some were afraid that the revolt would end in the destruction of the whole kingdom, prophesying that the result of such daring would be the division of the kingdom and its consequent desolation and destruction. As their hordes were increasing daily and their numbers had become almost uncountable so that they feared nobody's resistance, they began to put into practice certain of their schemes. Ignoring any claims of what was right, they punished with execution all the various lawyers they could seize, whether they were apprentices or senior justiciars, and all the country's jurymen, declaring that England could not enjoy the liberty of freemen until all these legal men had been killed. The peasants were highly delighted by this declaration, and, being led on to the greater by the lesser, they decided to consign to the flames all the rolls of the courts and the old records, so that, once the memorials of the past had been wiped out, their masters would be absolutely unable to make any claims on them in the future. And this they did. Their masters had not yet been willing to wake up and deal with this wickedness. They stayed motionless in their homes, sleeping and snoring, until the men of Kent and Essex met and joined their bands into one army of about one hundred thousand common people and peasants.

Indeed there ran to join them from all sides those who had been weighed down by debt or who were fearing the punishment of the law for their misdeeds, so that there was assembled in one place a collection of the commons bigger than anybody could remember seeing or had heard about. These vast numbers arrived at the place called Blackheath, where they decided to review the crowd they had collected and to count the numbers of their forces.[2] When they had taken up their position there, knights sent by the king came up to them, to ask the reason for this disturbance and the assembling in this place of such a vast crowd of people.[3] The reply was that they had come together to hold talks with the king on certain matters of business, and that the royal envoys should return to the king with the news that it was absolutely necessary for him to meet the rebels in order to hear the desires of their hearts.

This reply was reported to the king. Some of his councillors urged him to hurry to meet the rebels, but the archbishop of Canterbury, Master Simon Sudbury, then chancellor of the land, and Sir Robert Hales, master of the Hospital of St John and the treasurer of the day, stubbornly opposed such advice.[4] Their point was that the king was under no obligation at all to meet with such bare-legged rascals, and that something different should be done to check the arrogance of such wastrels. When the crowds heard what they had said, they became very angry and swore that they would seek out the traitors to the king, namely the archbishop and Robert, and take off their heads, as they believed they would then walk more safely. Hurriedly making their way towards London, they got to Southwark, and filled all the places there and in its neighbourhood.[5]

So the mayor of London [William Walworth] and the aldermen, fearing for the city, immediately decided to close the gates. But the ordinary people of the city, especially the poor, in their support of the rebels forcibly stopped the mayor from closing the gates, threatening him with death if he attempted to do it. And so it happened that for the whole of the following night, which happened to be the eve of the feast of Corpus Christi [12 June], the riff-raff enjoyed free entrance and exit. The common people of London, and indeed of the whole kingdom, had been encour-

---

[1]   The government itself was slow to respond and as the rebellion spread through Essex and Kent the king and his household were actually journeying away from the capital between Windsor and the upper Thames valley: Saul, *Richard II*, p. 63.

[2]   The *Anonimalle* author (p. 139) records that the mob arrived at Blackheath on the eve of Corpus Christi (12 June); the figures he gives (50,000 from Kent, 60,000 from Essex) are gross exaggerations but it may be that even Froissart's estimate of 60,000 in total was excessive (*Chroniques*, x. 104–6; FCBuchon, ii. 151–2).

[3]   The king had returned from Windsor to London at the beginning of the week and now retreated downriver to the relative safety of the Tower, accompanied by the chancellor, treasurer and the earls of Oxford, Salisbury and Warwick. He appears to have contemplated meeting the rebels right away as they requested but was advised by Chancellor Sudbury and Treasurer Hales to send envoys in his place.

[4]   For Hales and Sudbury see above pp. 39–43, 73, 117 and n.

[5]   According to the *Anonimalle Chronicle* when they reached Southwark on the evening of Wednesday 12 June the rebels attacked the Marshalsea, razing to the ground the house of the marshal, John de Imworth.

aged to support the rebels because they declared that their only plan was to search out traitors to the kingdom and then to stop. And what gave greater credence to their words was that they stole nothing at all but bought everything at a fair price, and, if they discovered one of their number thieving, they executed him, like men who had a special horror of thieves.

But on the morrow, which was the very feast of Corpus Christi [Thursday 13 June], as they went in and out of the city and began discussions with the ordinary common people of London about gaining their liberty and seizing the traitors, especially their pet hate the duke of Lancaster, they quickly and easily persuaded all the poorer people in the city to join in their conspiracy. And as the sun rose higher on that day and it grew warm and the rebels began drinking all the different wines that took their fancy out of the most expensive goblets, they became not so much drunk as mad[1] (for the wealthier citizens and the common people had left all their cellars open for them) and began to have long talks with the simpler elements in the city about the traitors. Besides other schemes they encouraged each other to hurry to the Savoy, the house of the duke of Lancaster [John of Gaunt], in its beauty and grandeur the fairest house in the kingdom, and to set fire to it and burn it to the ground.[2] This would be an act of defiance of the duke himself, whom they called a traitor, and would strike fear into the other traitors.

This plan won immediate acceptance from the people of London. They thought it particularly disgraceful that anyone other than themselves should do harm or damage to the duke, and so they at once rushed to the Savoy like madmen, set fire to it all round and gave themselves up to the destruction of the building. They wanted it to be clear to the people of the whole kingdom that they were not doing this out of greed, and so they ordered a proclamation to be made that no one, on pain of death, should dare to touch anything or keep any of the things found there for their own use. Instead they were to smash into bits with their axes the numerous gold and silver vessels of the house and throw them into the Thames or into the sewers. The gold cloths and mantles of silk they were to tear into pieces and trample them underfoot, and they were to grind in their mortars the rings and other pieces of jewellery set with precious stones, so that they would be henceforth completely unusable. These instructions were all carried out. Then, to ensure that they omitted no way of shaming the duke but did to him all the harm they could think of, they seized his most expensive personal garment, called a 'jacket', and stuck it on a spear which they set up as an archery target. And when they could not do enough damage to it by shooting arrows, they took it down and cut it to bits with their axes and swords.

They burn down Temple Bar and the house of the Hospitallers of St John

Besides these wicked enough deeds they also, in their anger against Robert Hales, Master of the hospital of St John, destroyed the place called Temple Bar, where the more well-to-do legal apprentices had their lodgings. A great number of records, kept in safety there by the judges, were destroyed in the fire.[3] And ranging wider in their mad career, they set fire to the grand buildings of the Hospital of St John at Clerkenwell, and had it burning for seven continuous days.

Friday dawned, a day of anger, of distress and trouble, of calamity and sorrow. Matins was still going on in St Albans, when men arrived from Barnet in a tearing hurry to announce that the commons had instructed them to gather together the common people of Barnet and St Albans

---

[1]   This is confirmed by the Westminster chronicler who recorded how they became 'wrought up to a state of sheer frenzy' (stimulata in rabiem: *WC*, p. 4–5).

[2]   In his continuation of the *Gesta abbatum*, Walsingham described the Savoy palace as the most beautiful building in England at that time (*Gesta abbatum*, ed. Riley, iii. 286). For Froissart it was 'un tres bel ostel': *Chroniques*, x. 108; FCBuchon, ii. 156.

[3]   Knighton also describes the destruction of books, charters and other documents. He records that the rebels now turned on anyone thought to be a lawyer or student of law (*Knighton*, pp. 216–17), whilst the Westminster chronicler maintained that the mob murdered anyone who was in their way (WC, pp. 4–7); both Froissart and Knighton report that Richard Lyons, one of the city merchants condemned during the Good Parliament, was sought out and put to the sword. Lyons was said to have been the former master of their leader, Walter Tyler. Froissart also reports the murder of Lyons and says that Flemings living in London were also a favourite target: *Chroniques*, x. 108; FCBuchon, ii. 156.

and to hurry to London at top speed, carrying the weapons with which they knew best how to defend themselves. If this was not done, twenty thousand insurgents would be turning up to set fire to Barnet and St Albans and to take the citizens with them by main force.[1]

The abbot [Thomas de la Mare] was immediately informed of this. He was frightened by the arrival of the messengers and the damage that could follow from it. He hurriedly summoned all the members of his household and some townspeople and asked them to hurry to London to dampen down the wicked spirit of the insurgents and to prevent their arrival in St Albans. The abbot's men and the townspeople immediately hurried to meet the rebels and eagerly set off on their journey to London.[2] But these two groups had different plans in mind, the abbot's men being bent on doing something useful, the townsmen on doing damage. For when they were not far from London near the estate of the master of the Hospital of St John [i.e. Robert Hales] called Highbury, they saw there a huge crowd of about twenty thousand peasants and common folk.[3] They had just set fire to some very tall houses, and, as the blaze was now past all control, they were also trying to raze to the ground with various tools the parts that could not be destroyed by fire. The people from St Albans were seen by a rebel leader called Jack Straw. He at once summoned and called them over and they gave him their pledge that they would support King Richard and the commons.[4]

By that time the squads of the peasants had split up into three parts. One of them, as I have described, was intent on destroying the estate at Highbury. Another was waiting near London, at a place called Mile End.[5] A third had actually seized Tower Hill. This crowd near the Tower showed itself to be so out of control and lacking in respect that it shamelessly seized goods belonging to the king which were being conveyed to the Tower. And besides this, it was driven to such a pitch of madness that it forced the king to hand over to them the archbishop [Sudbury], the master of the Hospital of St John [Hales] and others hiding in the Tower itself, all of whom they called traitors. They told the king that if he was unwilling to do this they would deprive even him of his life.

So the king, being in a very tight spot, allowed them to enter the Tower and search its most secret recesses, as their wicked wills dictated, since he himself could not in safety refuse any of their requests. At that time there were present in the actual Tower six hundred soldiers, equipped with weapons, all strong, experienced men, and six hundred archers. The amazing thing was that all of these were so lacking in fight that you would have thought them more dead than alive. For all memory of their former famous military career was dead among them, they had completely

---

[1]   Barnet was within the liberty of St Albans and therefore under the jurisdiction of the abbot and convent. According to the account Walsingham composed for the *Gesta abbatum*, the Barnet men arrived at St Albans at midnight (*Gesta abbatum*, ed. Riley, iii. 289).

[2]   According to the *Gesta abbatum*, the delegation from Barnet and St Albans amounted to 'almost 500': *Gesta abbatum*, ed. Riley, iii. 290.

[3]   According to both Knighton and the Westminster chronicler (*Knighton*, pp. 216–17; WC, pp. 4–5) the buildings of the Highbury manor of Robert Hales, master of the Hospital of St John of Jerusalem at Clerkenwell, had only recently been restored: Knighton called them 'a second paradise of elegance'. Given their opposition to Hales himself, the manor was an obvious objective for the mob after their successful assault on the hospital. The *Anonimalle* author observes that the rebels gorged themselves on the food and wine of the house as well as laying waste to the building itself: *AC*, p. 135.

[4]   Walsingham is the only authority to attest to the involvement of St Albans men in these events. The Westminster chronicler observes that there were 'disaffected' (dissidiosos) at St Albans but makes no mention of their presence in London: WC, pp. 14–15.

[5]   It was the Essex rebels who had assembled at Mile End. Early on Friday morning – the meeting was arranged for 7 a.m. – King Richard rode out from the Tower to meet them, accompanied by members of his household, although some, including his mother, Countess Joan, soon turned back. The rebels presented Richard with two principal demands, that he should surrender the traitors (meaning Hales, Sudbury and other hate-figures) into their custody, and that he should abolish serfdom and agree to a standard rate of rent for land of 4d per acre. The king responded carefully, consenting to the execution of all those convicted of treason, and confirming that rebels should have their freedom. But his concessions came too late to prevent the third splinter group of rebels – recorded here by Walsingham – storming the Tower: *Knighton*, p. 213; Froissart, *Chroniques*, x. 106; Buchon, ii. 156–7. See also Saul, *Richard II*, pp. 68–9. In Scotland it was reported that the king was captured by the rebels: *Scotichronicon*, vii. 391.

forgotten their previous strength and glory, and, in a word, in the face of these peasants from almost all of England all their military boldness had withered away.[1]

For who would ever have believed that not just peasants but the lowest of them and not several of them together but individuals on their own would have dared with their worthless staves to force a way into the bedroom of the king or of his mother, scaring all the nobles with their threats and even touching and stroking with their rough, filthy hands the beards of some of the most eminent of them? Or that they would have begun chatting about future possible socialising, about the nobles staying loyal to the riff-raff, and about them taking an oath that they would join the rebels in seeking out the traitors to the realm, when the rebels themselves were clearly not free from the taint of treachery, seeing that with their banners and little flags held aloft they had not feared to make this entry into the Tower with an armed force according to their own whim, as I have described. And, besides all this, several of them, who, as I have said, had gone on their own into the various rooms, had the effrontery to sit and lie on the bed of the king joking merrily, with one or two even asking the king's mother [i.e. Joan of Kent] for a kiss.[2]

Yet it is a remarkable fact that the several knights and esquires that were there did not dare to summons a single one of the rebels for such impropriety, or to lay hands upon them to stop them, or even to mutter about it beneath their breath. Men who had once been serfs of the lowest sort went in and out like lords, and swineherds, who were not even the swineherds of the knights but of the peasants, laid down the law to knights. All this, I believe, was because God wanted to show the English that a man will not be strong because of his own strength, putting his hopes in bow or sword, but because of Him who saves us from those who trouble us and who in his mercy and goodness ever confounds those who imprison us. But enough on this subject. Now let me write about what happened to the archbishop.

What happened to the archbishop

When the hour of destiny arrived which clearly showed that divine vengeance had fallen on the kingdom of England, those peasants, lowest of riff-raff and demoniacal wastrels, made their way, as I have described, in their bands through the streets yelling horribly, and, inspired by the devil, went in through the gates of the Tower, searching for the archbishop and primate, the common father of the whole people. They found one of his servants and furiously commanded him to lead them to the place in which the holy father (whom they called 'traitor') was hiding. The servant did not dare to disobey their command, and led them to the chapel, in which the archbishop, having celebrated Mass and received holy communion, was busy with his prayers. The archbishop indeed was well aware of their plan and imminent arrival, and had spent the whole of the preceding night in making his confession and saying his holy prayers. So with a mind completely freed from care he was fearlessly awaiting their arrival. Both during and after the Mass which he had celebrated he had berated their delay, saying such things as, 'When are they going to come? Good God, what are they waiting for? God willing, it's already time for them to be here.'

---

[1]   There were several knights with the king whose military careers were both 'famous' and 'glorious', although the best known, such as Sir Robert Knolles, had followed the king to Mile End. Other contemporary commentators also condemned the easy capitulation of the Tower garrison. Knighton condemns the 'womanish fear' of these 'worthless sons': *Knighton*, pp. 212–13. Froissart reports that the mayor sought to persuade Richard and his party to remain at the Tower: *Chroniques*, x. 109; FCBuchon, ii. 157–8.

[2]   Walsingham gives a more graphic account of the rebels in the royal apartments in his earliest, 'scandalous' narrative, observing how they besported themselves on the beds and (with obvious phallic symbolism) waved their 'filthy sticks': *CA*, p. 165. Of the other contemporary chroniclers, only Froissart also recalls the treatment of the king's mother, reporting that in fright she fainted and had to be carried from her chamber to a waiting river barge that removed her to the Tower Royal where she remained for a day and a night, 'like a woman half-dead'; FCBuchon, ii. 157–8. The rebels were also thought to have threatened John of Gaunt's son, Henry of Bolingbroke, earl of Derby, also present in the Tower. See also W. M. Ormrod, 'In Bed with Joan of Kent: the King's Mother and the Peasants' Revolt' in *Medieval Women: Texts and Contexts in Late Medieval Britain: Essays for Felicity Riddy*, ed. J. Wogan-Browne, R. Voaden, A. Diamond, A. M. Hutchison, C. M. Meale, L. Johnson, Medieval Women Texts and Contexts, 3 (Turnhout, 2000), 277–92.

When he heard them coming, he said to his household with great firmness, 'Let us now go calmly to meet them.[1] For when there is no pleasure in living, it is better to die. At no time previously in my life could I have met death with a clearer conscience.' After a little while his executioners entered and shouted, 'Where is the traitor to our land? Where is the plunderer of the common people?' But the archbishop was not at all troubled by these questions, and replied to their shouts saying, 'It's good that you have come, my sons. Here I am, the archbishop you are looking for, though no traitor or plunderer.' When they saw him, those limbs of Satan immediately laid their wicked hands upon him and hurried him out of the chapel, showing no reverence to the place or its holy altars, or to the image of the crucified which was carved on the top of his crozier, or even to the body of Christ which the priest was holding before the archbishop. Behaving worse than demons (for they fear and flee from the sacraments of Christ) and ignoring the presence of their saviour, they dragged the archbishop by his hands and his hood through different places until they came to their fellow accomplices outside the gates on Tower Hill.

When they brought the archbishop there, a devilish yelling went up, not like the usual shouts of men but worse than any human cries and beyond any imagining. The nearest comparison would be with the shrieks of the inhabitants of hell. As long as God allowed their wickedness to go unpunished, they yelled in this way whenever they executed anybody or destroyed houses. No words could be distinguished amid the horrific noise. Their throats were filled with many different kinds of bellowing or, more accurately, with the devilish cries of peacocks. The archbishop stood in their midst, surrounded by the scum of the earth in their thousands. When he saw the forest of drawn swords around his head threatening death, he is said to have asked his assailants, 'My dearest sons, what is it you are proposing to do? What sin have I committed against you that you wish to kill me? If you kill me, who am your pastor, priest and archbishop, beware of the wrath of the just avenger coming upon you, or at least of the whole of England being laid under an interdict for such a deed.'

He had barely finished these words when they shouted with ghastly shrieks that they were not frightened of any interdict or of the pope, and that all that was left for the archbishop was that he should bow his neck for his head to be cut off by their swords, seeing that he had been false to his people and a traitor to his kingdom. Realising that his certain death was at hand and that no way of escape remained, the archbishop, who was a man of great eloquence and incomparably wiser than all the wise men of England, followed up the many examples of encouragement to holiness and life-saving words, which I have described, by last of all forgiving as far as he could the sin of the executioner who was about to behead him, so that he might be fully seen in his death to follow his saviour who had pleaded with his father for his killers. Then he knelt down and bent his neck for the blow. The axe struck his neck, but not fatally. Putting his hand to the wound, the archbishop said, 'Ah! Ah! It is the hand of the Lord.' He had not yet taken his hand from the wound, when the axe struck him a second time, cutting off the tips of his fingers and some of his arteries, and he fell to the ground. But he was not put to death until his neck and head had been pitifully mutilated by eight blows, and then, so we believe, he died a death worth a martyr's crown.[2]

His body lay there unburied all that Friday, the feast day of St Basil [14 June], and all the next day, as no one dared to give it burial because of their fear of the mob who were past appeals to reason and who were behaving like madmen wherever they went.[3] But the archbishop's execu-

---

[1]   Other commentators confirm that Sudbury and his companions submitted to the mob when they confronted them at the Tower: Knighton records that they were 'summoned . . . to their deaths not by force or assault, not with the sword or the arrow . . . but by threatening words and the clamour of the crowd' (*Knighton*, pp. 212–15).

[2]   Walsingham's description of the execution, and the grisly observation of the eight blows, is more detailed than any other account. Other chroniclers offered more measured obituaries for Sudbury – Knighton calls him a 'luminary', (*Knighton*, p. 215) the Westminster author recalls his 'hallowed head' (*WC*, pp. 6–7) – and it is tempting to connect Walsingham's fulsome praise with the fact that as a young monk he had received ordination from the hands of the future archbishop, when bishop of London.

[3]   Sudbury's head was placed on the end of a pole and paraded through the streets before being set up on London Bridge, where a scarlet cap was nailed to it to identify it as the head of a prelate: *WC*, pp. 6–7.

tioner immediately experienced the divine vengeance, for he was driven insane and struck with blindness. Also one of the crowd of peasants, spurred on by greed, on the night after the archbishop's beheading, went up to the body without being seen so that he might secretly pull off the ring which was on his finger.

Also, a man who had been blind for many years and who for a long time had been supported by alms from the archbishop, on hearing of the death and the cause of it, in faith asked God for his sight to be restored through the archbishop's merits, and his sight was given back to him. At his grave a man of Dover, who had now been blind for two years and had been instructed in a vision to go to the body, that same night rejoiced that his sight had been restored to him. A pregnant woman who was completely unable to give birth, asked for the archbishop's help and on that day was delivered of three boys, who were all baptised. Many other miraculous signs were sent by God after his death, and there was clear evidence of the vengeance of God on those who had been responsible for his death or had willingly agreed to it. These I shall mention later, when it is the time and place to do so.[1]

Other victims of the rebels were Robert Hales, a most energetic knight and master of the Hospital of St John and treasurer of the kingdom, John Legg, one of the king's men,[2] and a brother of the Franciscan order. The last-named was killed because of the ill will and anger the rebels bore to John of Gaunt, duke of Lancaster, of whom the Franciscan had been a friend.[3] Several others, both Flemish and English, were beheaded on the same day, for no other reason than to sate the cruelty of the peasants who then held the upper hand. For if they could seize anybody who had not sworn them an oath of loyalty or who was unwilling to go along with them with the same enthusiasm, or if any of the rebels had a particular enemy, with all these they would play the frightening game of suddenly pulling off their hoods amid their usual cries, and immediately competing with each other in rushing to behead them in the public squares. They paid no respect to holy places, but murdered those they hated in churches and sanctuaries all over London. I know from a reliable eyewitness that thirteen Flemings were forcibly pulled out of the church of the Augustinian Friars in London, and beheaded in the public street, and seventeen from another London parish church, all of whom were similarly beheaded, as that accursed mob, who ignored the reverence paid to sanctuaries and the fear of God, had no respect for any man.[4]

When the king and his council saw these crimes being perpetrated, they hastily held a quick discussion, as the crisis did not allow long deliberations, especially as they were one and all confounded by the killing of the archbishop of Canterbury and of the treasurer of the kingdom, the most powerful men in the land, and as they were afraid that the rebels, having murdered the greater, would not spare the lesser. So the king consulted with those members of the council who were then present with him, and, in order to check the frenzy which was then running riot, offered peace to the rebels, on condition that they stopped burning and destroying buildings and murdering people and returned home without more ado, there to wait for the charters which would confirm this peace. The men of Essex gladly accepted this offer. They were now tired of their lengthy labours and felt some wish to see their homes, wives and children again. But they chose some of their number to stay behind and receive the royal charter, while the rest went home. But while the men of Essex went away, the men of Kent stayed in London all the following night.

---

1   Walsingham is the only contemporary authority to attribute miraculous powers to Archbishop Sudbury.
2   John Legg, a royal serjeant-at-arms, had been prominent in the collection of the poll tax.
3   This was William Appleton, a Franciscan, who was physician to John of Gaunt. The Westminster chronicler, who gives the greatest details on the executions, records one other victim who can be identified as a juror, Richard Somenour of Stepney: *WC*, pp. 6–7 and n. The *Anonimalle* author also records four victims, claiming two of them were killed 'longe temps apres', although Knighton says there were 'seven in all' (*AC*, p. 145; *Knighton*, p. 215).
4   In his earlier, longer narrative Walsingham identified the London parish church as St Martin-in-Vintry: *CA*, p. 162. The Westminster chronicler recalled that there were 'mounds of bodies' (*congeries corporum*); perhaps as many as 150–60 foreigners were killed: Saul, *Richard II*, p. 69. A marginal note in the Westminster manuscript also records that the royal treasury there was plundered (*WC*, pp. 8–9).

How the peasants planned to set fire to London

When the next day dawned, which was Sunday 15 June, the feast of Saints Vitus and Modestus in the octave of the feast of Corpus Christi, amazingly the men of Kent hardly slackened off at all from the previous day in their career of crime, but were still busy with murdering men and destroying and burning houses. But the king sent envoys to them to announce that their allies had left London and would be living in peace in the future, and that he wished to grant them the same terms if they were willing to accept them.[1] The chief leader of the rebels, called Wat Helier or Tyler (for they had made up such names for themselves from their jobs), an able fellow and very sensible, if only he had decided to put his abilities to good use, replied that he was willing to accept the peace, provided that he could dictate the conditions.[2] He had actually planned, as he seemed stronger than the king and the nobles, by quibbling to keep the king and his council in suspense until the next day, so that during the night he could more freely carry out his wicked plan. For because all the poor, common people of London were on their side, he had decided that night to kill the king and the nobles in attendance on him, to sack the city and, setting fire to it in four places, to burn it to the ground.

But God, who checks the proud and gives his gracious support to the humble, did not allow Tyler's sacrilegious plans and designs to be carried through to the end, but of his grace abruptly scotched his wicked scheme. Three successive charters were drawn up for him (I shall give the substance of one of them later), but not one of them could satisfy him. So in the end the king sent to him one of his knights called John Newton,[3] not so much to invite him as to beg him, as Tyler's arrogance was well known, to go to the king and discuss with him the articles which he was insisting should be inserted in the charter. I will include one of these articles in my history so that my readers may understand more clearly that the other articles would have been contrary to reason.

The arrogance of Walter Tyler

For above everything else Tyler wanted to obtain the commission for him and his men to execute all judges, confiscators, and all who were learned in the law or connected with the law and its administration. For he had conceived the idea that if those learned in the law were killed, all decisions in the future could be taken according to wishes of the common people, while there would actually be no such thing as law, or, if there were, it would be established as he decided. Indeed the story goes that the day before these things happened he had put his hand to his lips and arrogantly declared that before four days had passed all the laws of England would emanate from his mouth and lips. So when, as I have said, Sir John Newton was pressing him to hurry, Tyler angrily replied, 'If you are in so much of a hurry, go back to the king. I will come when I feel like it.' Then, as the knight rode back, Tyler followed him, riding on a horse, but a little more slowly, and when he had arrived near the place called Smithfield where the king was stationed, Sir John was sent to him a

---

[1] This is one occasion when Walsingham departs from the chronology agreed by other contemporary authorities. The events described here took place on Friday and Saturday during, and in the aftermath of the mob's assault on the Tower of London and the city. When it became clear to the king and his counsellors that their concessions at Mile End had appeased only one section of the mob the decision was taken to seek a similar meeting with the men of Kent, as described here. The envoy was dispatched to Tyler and his followers late on Friday with the proposal that they should come to the king at Smithfield the following day. Early on Saturday afternoon the king visited Westminster Abbey to seek succour at the shrine of St Edward and then made his way to Smithfield for the confrontation with the rebels which resulted in Tyler's death. Walsingham conflates this into a single episode, giving the envoy – whom he identifies as Sir John Newton – a greater role than may have been accurate. Froissart also dates Tyler's death to the Sunday although at some distance from the event his confusion is more explicable: *Chroniques*, x. 120–1; FCBuchon, ii. 162. See also *AC*, pp. 148–9.
[2] According to the *Anonimalle* author, Tyler had been chosen as leader of the Kentish rebels when the mob reached Maidstone on their way to London (*AC*, p. 137). He appears to have originated in Essex and the indictments of the jurors of Maidstone hundred describe him as 'of Colchester': Saul, *Richard II*, pp. 62–3.
[3] Sir John Newton was constable of Rochester. Walsingham is the only authority to identify him as the king's envoy. See Saul, *Richard II*, p. 69.

second time to hear his wishes and report back. And the knight came up to Tyler to hear what he was intending to say, seated on his warhorse. Tyler indeed was angry that the knight had come up to him riding on his warhorse and not on foot, and at once angrily cried that it was more appropriate for Sir John to approach his presence on foot than sitting on a horse. But the knight had not completely forgotten all his old knightly virtue, and at once said in reply, 'As you are sitting on a horse, there is nothing wrong in me approaching you as a knight on horseback.' This remark angered the rascal. He whipped out his knife, (commonly known as a 'dagger') and threatened to strike Sir John with it, while at the same time calling him a traitor. Sir John bristled at this word, stoutly asserted that Tyler was lying, and also took out a similar dagger to fight the rebel leader. For his part the rascal could not bear that he had been insulted amidst his peasants, and made ready to rush upon the knight.

The king saw that danger was imminent for the knight and, in order to cool the villain's anger for the moment, ordered Sir John to dismount and to hand over to the rascal the dagger which he had taken out. But Tyler was too far gone to be appeased even by this gesture. All he wanted to do, in whatever ways and by whatever means he could, was to rush in his fury upon the knight. So William Walworth,[1] mayor of London, and several other of the king's knights and esquires who were standing by, came up to the king and said that it would be an unprecedented, never to be forgotten disgrace if, in their presence, the king allowed a noble knight to meet so shameful a death before his face. So they should with all speed come to the help of Sir John and arrest the rascal.[2]

Although the king was just a lad of tender years, when he heard this, he summoned up his courage and commanded the mayor of London to make the arrest. Without any hesitation the mayor [William Walworth], a man of unparalleled courage and bravery, arrested him on the spot, aiming a blow at the head of the man who had caused him so much trouble.[3] Tyler was then at once surrounded by the other servants of the king, and run through all over his body by their swords.[4] He crashed from his horse on to the ground, for the first time giving hope to the nobles of England, who were almost down and out, that it was possible to resist the commons. When the commons saw his downfall, in their grief at his death they immediately cried out, 'Our captain is dead. Our leader has been treacherously killed. Let us stand together and die with him. Let us shoot our arrows and bravely avenge his death.'[5] So they drew back their bows and prepared to shoot. But amazingly the king, inspired by an ability unexpected in one so young and fired with

---

1   See p. 48 above.

See p. 48 above.

2   The contemporary chroniclers' accounts of the confrontation between Tyler and the king differ in their particulars but with the exception of Walsingham each agrees that it was only after the rebel leader had issued his demands – for an end to serfdom, the abolition of outlawry, the disendowment of the church and the equality of all men under the king – and the king had offered him concessions that violence erupted and Mayor Walworth and the knights intervened. None of these other authorities place Sir John Newton in the action, nor do they support Walsingham's suggestion that the king and his retinue had followed the envoy to Smithfield: Richard remained at Westminster Abbey until late on Saturday afternoon.

3   The authorities differ in their accounts of Tyler's demise: the *Anonimalle* author reports that when the discussion was concluded Tyler demanded a drink and dismounted to take it, at which point one of the king's esquires exclaimed that he was 'the greatest thief in the county'. Tyler turned on the esquire, but Mayor Walworth intercepted him and attempted to make an arrest. Tyler drew his dagger but the mayor drew his own sword and struck him in the shoulder (*AC*, pp. 148–9). Knighton maintains that Tyler had been toying with a dagger throughout the discussions and was struck down after he seized the reins of the king's horse apparently with the intention of stabbing him (*Knighton*, pp. 218–21). Froissart also depicts Tyler toying with the dagger: *Chroniques*, x. 120. The Westminster chronicler records only that Tyler was struck by Walworth as he resisted arrest (*WC*, pp. 10–11).

4   Knighton names one of the esquires who despatched Tyler as Ralph Standish. According to his and Froissart's accounts Standish and Walworth were both knighted by the king at the scene: *Knighton*, p. 221.

5   All of the authorities agree on the cry that came up from the rebels: Knighton added that there was a 'great wailing' from the crowd (*Knighton*, p. 221). There is also general agreement as to the courageous response of the king, although only Walsingham suggests that the rebels were prepared to fire on their monarch: Knighton maintains that 'the crowd slipped away'. He also records that Tyler's body was 'dragged roughly' to St Bartholomew's church (*Knighton*, p. 221).

courage, urgently set spurs to his horse and came up to the rebels. Circling round them on his horse, he said, 'My men, what is this? What are you doing? Surely you don't want to shoot your king? Don't be upset or sad at the death of a traitor and a rascal. I will be your king, your captain and your leader. Follow me to the open ground where you shall be granted all the requests which it shall please you to make.'

Now the king did this so that the peasants in their present anguish of mind should not set fire to the houses at Smithfield where they were when their leader, that traitor, was slain. And so the peasants followed the king and the knights who were with him to the open ground, not yet fully decided whether they should kill the king or quietly give up and return home with the royal charter.

Meanwhile the mayor of London hurriedly rode off with just one servant, and entering the city, began to cry out, 'You noblest of citizens, men who do what is pleasing and fear God, give help without delay to your king who is in danger of death. And help me, your mayor, for I am in the same danger. Or if, because of my faults, you decide not to help me, at least do not abandon your king.' When the magnates of London and those others, who kept a love for the king fixed in their hearts, heard these words of the mayor, in no time at all they formed a group of about a thousand well-armed men, and immediately took up their position in the squares of the city, ready for action and waiting for a knight who could lead them to the king.[1] Fortune brought along Sir Robert Knolles for several of them, who all asked him to be their leader, conscious that they could be more easily defeated if they approached the scene in a disorderly, straggling manner. Sir Robert happily took command of this section, the rest being commanded by other knights, and, their armour making a brilliant show, they were all led to the presence of the king.[2]

The king and his attendant knights and squires were greatly heartened by the unexpected arrival and help of these armed men. They suddenly encircled the whole host of peasants with troops on every side, just as though they were sheep being shut in a sheepfold, waiting for the hireling to decide which sheep he wished to send out to pasture and which he wanted to slaughter.[3] On that very spot you could have seen the remarkable change which the right hand of God can bring about, the peasants now throwing down their cudgels, choppers, axes, swords, bows and arrows, falling to the ground and humbly begging forgiveness, when a moment ago they had been boasting that they had the lives of the king and his royal ministers not just in their grant but in their power. The unhappy rebels hid in cornfields, ditches, caves and woods, only wanting now to save their skins by running away or hiding, when just previously they had held in their hands the power of life and death over the nobles of almost the whole of England. So the knights attendant on the king, whose desire was to revenge themselves on the rebels not so much for the harm they had caused as for the shame they had brought upon them, asked the king to allow them to take off the heads of at least a hundred or two hundred of the riff-raff, so that posterity might know that men from the class of knights had been able to do something against the peasants. But the king refused to agree to their requests. He said that several of the insurgents had only joined the mob out of fear, and that in such executions it could perhaps happen that the innocent would

---

[1] After two days during which the rebels had rampaged through London unopposed, the death of Tyler appears to have given the city authorities sufficient confidence to raise armed levies from the wards to rout them. Froissart reports that Nicholas Brembre raised his own retinue, nine city aldermen mustered a further 600 men-at-arms, and that the force amounted to 7–8000 in total; FCBuchon, ii. 162–3. Whatever the true numbers, the authorities all agree that the remaining rebels were rapidly surrounded and driven from the city: the Westminster chronicler observed that they were 'completely encircled' and 'threatened with annihilation' (*WC*, p. 13); Knighton reports that they were rounded up like sheep in a pen (*Knighton*, pp. 220–1), echoing the image employed here by Walsingham.
[2] As Walsingham suggests here, it is likely that Knolles also raised his own retinue of men-at-arms. See also Saul, *Richard II*, p. 72.
[3] Richard and his advisors were anxious to ensure that once dispersed from Smithfield, the rebels did not re-group elsewhere in the city. He called on them to gather at Clerkenwell where he confirmed the terms of their 'agreement' – reiterating the manumission conceded at Mile End – on condition that they disbanded and returned into Kent.

be punished and the guilty escape scot-free. But he gave orders for a proclamation to be made immediately to the people of London, bidding them not to communicate with the rebels in the future or to allow any of them in the city that night, but to permit them to spend the night outside in the open air. None the less he did give orders that the charter they had asked for should be handed to them written out and sealed, in order to avoid for the time being a still greater evil. For he knew that Essex had not yet been pacified or Kent brought under control, and that the people and peasants of these counties were ready to rise in rebellion, if their wishes were not speedily granted.[1]

The wording of the charter that was extorted by force from the king is as follows (the names of communities were changed, according to the different counties to which it was sent).[2]

The King's charter for the manumission of the peasants

'Richard, by the grace of God king of England and France and lord of Ireland, sends greetings to all his bailiffs and loyal subjects to whom this letter comes. We inform you that of our special grace we have manumitted each and every one of our bondsmen and subjects and others of the county of Hertford. We have freed absolutely all of them from all bondage, and we discharge them through this charter. And we also grant pardon to our same bondsmen and subjects for all crimes, treacheries, misdeeds and robberies committed and perpetrated in whatever way by them or any one of them. And we annul any act or acts of outlawry if any such have been promulgated against them or any one of them as a result of these happenings. We extend to each and every one of them, absolutely all of them our complete peace from this day forward. As testimony to this we have had these letters patent of ours written. Witnessed by myself in London, on the fifteenth of June in the fourth year of my reign.'

Having received this charter, the commons went back home, but without at all ceasing from committing their previous crimes, as I shall show below, as I give details of what the townsmen of St Albans did after their return from London. That the full facts may be better known, I shall go back a little in my story, beginning again with the day the townsmen left St Albans, that is the Friday preceding Sunday 15 June.

The story of the wicked crimes committed by the townsmen of St Albans against their abbot[3]

So when, as I have described previously, the townspeople of St Albans and the servants of the abbot arrived at the manor of Highbury on the Friday which was the day after the feast of Corpus Christi, and moved on from there and got to London, the townspeople soon separated from the abbot's servants and turned to deeds of wickedness.[4] For they went to the church of St Mary at Bow, which is situated in London, and there began to discuss their enslavement to the monastery and how they might effect the wishes which they had long harboured in secret. These were that they should enjoy new boundaries around the town in which they could graze their animals freely, have places assigned to them in which they could fish without blame and similar places assigned for hunting and hawking, and set up their hand-mills wherever they liked at their own wish and

---

1 According to the Westminster chronicler a force was now raised to rout the rebels still gathered in Essex (*WC*, p. 13).
2 Thus Walsingham reproduces the document addressed to men of Hertford which must have been in circulation at St Albans.
3 Walsingham's account of the actions of the rebels at St Albans given here follows closely the fuller account he incorporates in his domestic history, the *Gesta abbatum sancti Albani* (*Gesta abbatum*, ed. Riley, iii. 285–372) for which he also transcribed many of the abbatial and royal charters and letters relating to the rebellion. Some passages from the *Gesta* are reproduced verbatim in this chronicle.
4 In his account in the *Gesta abbatum*, Walsingham relates that when it became clear to the abbot's servants that the tenants and townsmen meant to join the uprising, they diverted from the main party and sought an audience with the earl of Warwick at Barnet, where they pledged their loyalty to the king. They rejoined the main party, but as Walsingham reports here, at least one of their number returned to the abbey to forewarn the monks. See *Gesta abbatum*, ed. Riley, iii. 297–8.

whim. They also wanted to suffer no interference from the bailiff of the liberty inside the town boundaries, and to claim back the bonds which their parents had once made to abbot Richard of Wallingford [abbot of St Albans 1327–35] of pious memory, any other charters which were prejudicial to them, and, in a word, all records in the abbey which were a support to them or involved loss for the monastery.

To attain their desired ends more quickly, some sang the praises of Wat Tyler and went to see this leader of the peasant riff-raff of Kent. They thought that there would never be any man in the kingdom greater than him, and that the laws of the land would have no validity in the future, as most of the judiciary had already been killed and the rest, so they thought, should be on the list for killing. So they would obtain authority from Tyler, go back home and demand what they wanted under the strictest conditions. Indeed, should the abbot decide to refuse their demands, they would immediately threaten his house with fire, the monks with death, and finally a demolition of the monastery so total that not one stone would be left upon another.

But others declared that it was safer to go into the king's presence, as at that time his presence was denied to no one, and to ask him for a letter addressed to the abbot, under the privy seal, which would instruct the abbot to return to them the liberties and rights possessed by their fathers and ancestors in the time of King Henry [III, 1215–72]. In fact the men of St Albans approved of both plans. They went to the king for a letter addressed to the abbot, and asked Wat to send some of his wastrels to help them destroy the monastery, if that should be necessary.

The principal negotiator of this business with the king was William Grindcobbe. He was much indebted to the monastery, because he had been educated, fed and maintained there, and he was closely related to some of the monks, past and present.[1] In the negotiations he genuflected six times before the king in the presence of the mob to obtain the letter they wanted. The king gave it to him. William was also the chief speaker in the negotiations with Wat, the peasants' idol, though he had with him several other companions in crime. They all heaped slander on the abbot, prior, and some of the monks, complaining about their unjust tyranny over the people round about, their oppression of the commons and their withholding of pay to the poor and their servants.

Wat, indeed, had not planned to leave London nor to send any of his followers on missions, but he was so moved by their words that he promised to go to St Albans to 'shave the beards' of the abbot, prior and other monks, in other words, to cut off their heads, accompanied by twenty thousand men if it was necessary or if they thought the business required them to be sent. This was on condition that the townsmen obeyed all his orders and did not ignore a single one of his commands. He also instructed them what they were to do as soon as they had arrived home, just as he had already done with groups and individuals who had left or who were about to do so, and they had to affirm under oath that they would leave none of his commands or instructions undone. This I shall describe below. So having received this promise of protection, the townsmen prepared to return to St Albans. But one of the abbot's servants, riding hell for leather, got there before them and reported the deaths of the archbishop, treasurer and several others, adding that the commons were so lacking in mercy or gratitude that they would pitilessly murder their enemies, and that the prior [John Moot] would be beheaded and the various other monks were in great danger, if they waited around for the forces of the commons to arrive.

---

[1]   The monastic community was recruited primarily from within the liberty of St Albans and thus many of the tenants and townsmen were, like William Grindcobbe, kinsmen of the monks. Walsingham's comments suggest that Grindcobbe had been raised in the precincts of the abbey, perhaps as one of the boys of the almonry, where the monks maintained a school for a small group of poor boys to learn grammar and to assist the monastic community in their liturgical duties. Of course, Walsingham's concern here is to cast the rebels in the role of ungrateful subjects wrongly resisting the rule of a just and paternalistic overlord, that is the abbot and convent. Like Grindcobbe himself, Walsingham conveys the impression that the St Albans rebels were all men of humble origin – 'peasant riff-raff' even – but the Westminster chronicler claims that the St Albans rising was led by 'nobiliores de villa' (*WC*, p. 14).

The flight of the prior

So the prior [John Moot] took to his heels, as did four of the monks and also some other servants of the monastery.[1] By long stages and through great dangers, some on horseback, others on foot, they at length arrived breathless at Tynemouth.[2] The townspeople are said to have returned not long after the prior's departure, though William Grindcobbe and William Cadington,[3] the baker, had hurried on ahead, so that they might be seen to have done at least something off their own bat before the arrival of their comrades. What they really wanted was that some special action could be ascribed just to them, so that they might win a great name afterwards. When their friends arrived, they told them that everything had turned out well, that in the future they would not be servants, as in the past, but masters, and that they had already set in motion important, astounding schemes against the abbey. The most important of these schemes for causing the abbot dismay were the destruction that very night of the sheepfolds which the abbot had set up in Falconwood and other woods, the speedy cutting down of the gates to Eywood and other woods, and also the immediate demolition by every possible means and methods of the sub-cellarer's house, which was on the opposite side of the road to the fish market. This house, they thought, blocked the view of the townspeople and was prejudicial to their nobility as citizens –for that was what they now called themselves. There was no delay. That very night before going to bed those foolish men, accepting the claims of fools, in a mood of great madness carried out all the plans I have mentioned, the destruction of the sheepfolds, the cutting down of the gates and the demolition of the house.

So ended this Friday in St Albans, the day that was the beginning of the subsequent troubles. So that posterity may better understand what happened, I will deal with these, partly in the next chapter, thus separating the Friday from the Saturday.

What happened on the Saturday[4]

So, early on the Saturday in St Albans the leaders got up, intending to investigate what had been accomplished, and the townspeople went out with them in great glee to Falconwood. A proclamation had already been made that no one who could bear arms should stay at home, but that as individuals and in a body, on pain of death, they were to follow the leaders immediately and to sally forth, carrying the weapons and tools which they knew how to use and with which they could best defend themselves. Moreover, if they were householders, their house would be destroyed and all the goods found there confiscated. These severe threats caused good and bad alike to hurry out, following on the heels of the instigators of the wickedness, William Grindcobbe, whom I mentioned before, William Cadington and others whose names I do not bother to record.

The huge crowd arrived at the appointed place. Their aims and actions and threats had been carefully worked out. As far as the sheepfolds and the gates in the woods were concerned, the decision was that anything which had been left untouched in the first attack, was now to be immediately destroyed, so as to be good for nothing in the future. This unholy plan was followed by evil action and so became fact.[5]

Then they went back with the same crowd to St Albans, where they now found awaiting their return peasants and country people from the surrounding villages and the lands of the monastery.

1   Prior Moot's companions are not named here or in the *Gesta abbatum*.
2   Tynemouth Priory, Northumbria, one of the dependent cells of St Albans Abbey. It might seem surprising that the prior and his companions felt compelled to flee so far from the scene of the rebellion, but the abbey's other principal cells were in Essex and Norfolk, counties which were also in rebellion.
3   Froissart also identifies a baker as one of the ringleaders of the revolt but names him Thomas Bacquier: *Chroniques*, x. 110; FCBuchon, ii. 165.
4   This passages reproduces verbatim the account in Walsingham's *Gesta abbatum*: ed. Riley, iii. 302.
5   In his *Gesta abbatum* account Walsingham adds that the mob attacked the abbot's warrens and made a grisly gesture of defiance by fastening a rabbit to a pillory: *Gesta abbatum*, ed. Riley, iii. 303.

In fact two thousand or more rascals had willingly assembled at their summons. For in their instructions to the men of the villages within the liberty of St Albans, they had told them to put aside all excuses and under the penalties already described to come together once and for all to demand and gain all those freedoms which the rebels had decided to ask for. Furthermore, they were to allow no gentlemen to stay at home but were to bring everybody with them to aid the rebel cause. If indeed any were unwilling to make common cause with them and show them loyalty, they were to cut off their heads and knock down or burn their dwellings; for such had been the teachings and instructions of Wat Tyler, their lord and master.

When the St Albans rebels saw the crowd which had gathered at their orders, they were greatly heartened, their spirits soared and they began regarding themselves as important people. At once they joined right hands and in turn received and gave oaths. In their great arrogance they hurried to the gates of the monastery, to make a demonstration of the immense powers which they had received from Wat.

When they arrived at the gates of the abbey, which were opened for them, with indescribable haughtiness they ordered the janitor to unlock the prison for them. Now the janitor was well aware of their scheme, and knew what orders they would give and what they were intending to do. For the abbot had been secretly informed about everything by some townspeople, whose hearts had been touched by God, and he had told the janitor what to do. So he hurriedly unlocked the doors of the prison. The rebels went inside, brought out all the prisoners and told them to go away as free men, the only condition being that in future they should owe a debt of loyalty and gratitude to the commons, and should attach themselves inseparably to the rebel cause.[1]

One prisoner indeed, whom they had brought out of the jail among the rest, they adjudged worthy of death and beheaded him on the large space of ground in front of the gates of the abbey, making themselves both judges and executioners. Uttering the diabolical yells which they had learned in London at the beheading of the archbishop, they carried the head to the pillory and fixed it on the top as a clear sign to all the people that they were now able to use new laws and depend on new privileges. Soon afterwards their confederate rebels from Barnet arrived, to swell the numbers of the wicked, and coming with the same designs against the abbey.

About 9 o'clock Richard of Wallingford, the leading townsman of St Albans, arrived from London, riding on the swiftest of horses.[2] He had remained behind to bring the letter which, as I have described, William Grindcobbe had so often requested from the king. According to the usage of the rebels who had committed all the crimes in London, Richard was carrying unfurled in front of him a banner or standard with the arms of St George. When the townspeople heard of his arrival, they hurried to meet him on a large piece of open ground, taking with them the crowd of the commons and peasants from the district around, who had arrived in the town at their summons. Richard dismounted, fixed his standard in the ground and commanded all the people to follow it closely, as in battle. After a short interval which he gave up to talk and plans with the townspeople about dealing with the abbot, he told the common people to stay by the standard and to wait until they should return with a firm answer from the abbot, saying what he had decided to do about the petitions presented to him on the part of the people. With several of the more important townspeople he went into the church and at once sent for the abbot to come and reply to the commons. For at this time the rebels so gloried in this name of 'commons' that they thought no other name more honourable. Nor in their foolish hearts did they think that in the future there would be any masters, except only king and commons.

The abbot indeed had long ago decided on a speedy death in defence of the liberties of the

---

[1]   This account of the opening of the prison reproduces verbatim the narrative found in Walsingham's *Gesta abbatum*: ed. Riley, iii. 304.
[2]   Wallingford, Oxfordshire, was the location of one of the abbey's larger dependent priories and some of its most valuable estates, and this may have been the origin of Master Richard. However, Richard of Wallingford was also the name of one of the monastery's most celebrated abbots, whose dealings with the tenants and townsmen in the early fourteenth century the rebels referred to repeatedly during the uprising; it is possible therefore it was a pseudonym assumed by the leader of the townsmen.

monastery rather than doing anything which would result in a harmful precedent against the abbey. But now he was assailed by the prayers, advice and arguments of his monks, who said that, even though he had completely made up his mind to die, his death at this point would do the monastery no good. For the irrational mob had firmly decided either to get what they wanted or to murder the abbot and his monks and burn the monastery. Thomas was at last won over by their arguments and went down to meet the deputation. He entered the church. Richard of Wallingford, after a brief greeting, handed over the royal writ which William Grindcobbe had recently obtained or rather extorted from the king. It read as follows.[1]

The letter of the king sent to the abbot about the royal charters

'Beloved in God, at the petition of our beloved subjects of the town of St Albans, it is our wish and command that you do cause certain charters in your keeping, written by our ancestor King Henry for the burgesses and the good people of the said town concerning common land, pasture, rights of fishing and certain other possessions outlined in the words of these charters, to be delivered up to the said burgesses and good people, according as law and right shall require, so that they may have no ground in the future for complaining to us on this matter. Given under our signet in London on the fifteenth of June in the fourth year of our reign.'[2]

Further events at St Albans on the Saturday[3]

The abbot received the letter with proper respect and read it through, but tried to inform and warn them that all such charters had come to an end in the times of their fathers and that this was recorded in the royal rolls at Westminster. Therefore he declared that, according to the laws of the kingdom of ancient usage, all their petitions ought to be devoid of any right or claim. But Richard of Wallingford, the spokesman of them all, said in reply to this that for the time being the commons had the whip hand. They did not care a straw for the laws and they refused to wait around for or accept answers of such a kind. 'So,' said Richard, 'I advise and urge you not to try exasperate the commons in any way. You will never quieten them down until in one way or another they obtain their hearts' desires.'

The abbot still did not give in, but only produced in his defence more reasons and excuses why he should not grant their requests. So Richard and the leading men of the town, who were present at that meeting, said further, 'You should think of the thousands of people at the doors of the monastery waiting for a speedy answer, who will no doubt turn their anger on to us if we delay any longer in this matter. For they have made up their minds either to get what they want immediately or to send messengers to Wat Tyler, asking him to come with twenty thousand men to destroy this place and put the lives of the monks in danger.'

The abbot indeed was touched with sorrow in his innermost heart when he heard these words, and said to them, 'For shame, good neighbours! It is now thirty-two years since I became your abbot and father, and never have I shown you hostility or caused you sadness.[4] Rather, as often as you were in trouble and distress, I have laboured to free you from the miseries by which you were beset. And you, for no reason, are doing all you can to overthrow me, your friend and peace loving lord.'

The rebels replied, 'We admit that you have been a fair and peace loving master towards us, and that is why we decided not to cause you any trouble during your abbacy in pursuit of our rights. Indeed we were waiting for the day of your death, so that the triumph of our cause might

---

1   Once again these passages reproduce verbatim the account found in Walsingham's *Gesta abbatum*, ed. Riley, iii. 305.

2   Walsingham transcribes the letter in its original French; the same text appears in the *Gesta abbatum* narrative: *Gesta abbatum*, ed. Riley, iii. 306.

3   Again, this account is the same as that appearing in Walsingham's *Gesta abbatum*, ed. Riley, iii. 306–7.

4   Thomas de la Mare was elected abbot in 1349, when the fortunes of the monastic community and the town, both ravaged by the Black Death were at their lowest ebb. More than forty monks had died from the pestilence including the then abbot, Michael Mentmore. See *Gesta abbatum*, ed. Riley, ii. 369–71 at 370.

be over your successor after your death. But now there is no further business between us, except for you to escape danger by yielding at once, and for us to return to the commons with one answer or another, so that our lives are not put at risk by delay.'

When the abbot considered the dangers hanging over his head, he chose to incur the lesser evil to avoid the greater and granted the rebels all they wished to obtain. The townspeople saw that the times were now smiling upon their wicked schemes and immediately itemised the demands I have described, asking for new charters of liberties to be drawn up and for the bonds which their fathers had made with the monastery to be returned to them at once. There was no delay. The abbot wanted to free himself from their troublesome presence, and so gave orders for the bonds they were demanding to be handed over, and promised to draw up charters at their dictation concerning the liberties which they wanted. The rebels imagined they would not be using civil or ecclesiastical law in the future, and so soon made a bonfire of these bonds near the cross in the marketplace, together with various records and rolls of the monastery which they had extorted from the archdeacon.[1]

But these concessions were not enough to appease the unruly mob. They also asked for an ancient charter of the townspeople's liberties, whose capital letters were one of gold and one of blue.[2] Without this, they declared, the wishes of the people could not be satisfied. But the abbot asserted that he knew of no such charter, nor had he ever heard mention of it. He asked them to be content with their present position: they had obtained from him all the concessions which he could give them, and he had refused none of the requests which they had thought it right to make: he was willing to search to see if the charter could be found anywhere among the records and to hand it over to them without any trickery, provided that they now ceased from their frenzy.

The delegates went back from the church to the rank and file and reported the answer of the abbot, namely that after 3 o'clock they would receive all the documents asked for, signed and sealed by the abbot and his monks, and that up to that time they should keep the peace. But in the meantime the rascals entered the cloister carrying tools and levered up from the outer parlour the millstones which had been placed in the floor of the parlour doorway as a record and memorial of the suit between the townspeople and the monastery in the times of the former abbot Richard [of Wallingford]. They carried them off, took them to the commons and in their presence broke them into small pieces. They gave a piece to each rebel, just like the custom of breaking the consecrated bread on a Sunday and taking it to the churches in the parish, so that the rebels could look at the pieces in their homes and remember that once upon a time they had got their revenge on the monastery in this matter.

So the monks were given a space of time in which to eat. But there was no enjoyment in their eating, for, in the presence of so much grief, anxiety, sadness and fear, their food was the bread of tears. Indeed, they ate the bread of sorrow and their drink was mixed with their tears. Could any sane, sensible man not have been compelled to weep during those days, as he saw the changed order of the times, when things were turned upside down and slaves so lorded it over their masters that everywhere life and death were in the hands of peasants who had no knowledge of ruling and no wish to show mercy. Who could hold back his tears when he saw London, the noble capital of the realm, ransacked for a whole day and night and subjected to the will of the

---

[1] St Albans was a monastic borough where the abbot and convent claimed both secular and spiritual jurisdiction. The archdeacon of the liberty remained a monastic officer right down to the dissolution. The rebels do not appear to have stolen the muniments and rolls mentioned here but the archdeacon unwisely had surrendered them to them for inspection. A similar carelessness with the monastic archive occurred thirty years later at the height of the Lollard insurrections: see below, p. 395.

[2] The demand for the ancient charter illuminated in blue and gold appears to have been at the centre of the rebellion at St Albans. In his *Gesta abbatum*, Walsingham explains that there was a long-standing belief amongst the townsmen of St Albans that in the remote past the town had enjoyed a whole host of privileges granted by Offa of Mercia the founder of the monastery and that these had been steadily eroded by the monastic community over subsequent centuries. In his *Recapitulatio* which concludes the *Gesta abbatum,* Walsingham re-examines the origins and early history of the town in an attempt to expose the falsity of these claims: *Gesta abbatum,* ed. Riley, iii. 365–72 at 365–6.

commons? Who did not tremble when he heard that the highest of clerical heads had been cut off by men of the lowest condition, yes, the archbishop cruelly killed at the heart of the kingdom, and the treasurer of the land beheaded side by side with him? Who had not felt pain when the king of England, the highest and noblest king in all the world, was so enchained by his serfs that he could do nothing without their permission, while the noble, battle-hardy knights of his land were silent in the presence of peasants and carried out their every wish?

The townspeople mass together at the gates of the monastery[1]

Finally, to return to St Albans, you can imagine the sadness that filled the hearts of the monks when they saw that their famous monastery would either now continue to exist because of the merciful feelings of their bondsmen, who know nothing of mercy or love for their masters, or be burnt down in the frenzy of their wrath. Anyway such were the dishes from which the monks ate on that day until the time came after 3 o'clock[2] when the townspeople came to get their charter of liberty. As they arrived, a huge crowd of more than two thousand rascals formed at the gate of the monastery. They all with one mind and voice shouted out that the townsmen must be given their charters or they would tear down the Great Gate[3] there and then.

Now the abbot had got a charter drawn up based on their requests and he sent it to the towns-people to read it out in their meeting; if they thought it right to accept it, he was ready to sign and confirm it with the seals of himself and the monastery. But he failed to please them, seeing that they had not drawn it up themselves. They were so arrogant that they dispatched one of his own esquires to the abbot with the demand that he should send his own clerk with inkhorn and parchment, who would write down what they themselves decided, and that afterwards the abbot and the monks should put their seals to the document. The abbot's reply was that he would sign everything they wanted, provided that they were his friends in the future and gave up their designs. The rebels got their clerk and a charter was drawn up, signed and sealed according to their wishes. But still they were not satisfied. They claimed that there still existed in the monastery a charter of their ancient liberties, and they swore that it must be returned to them or they would pull down the monastery. The abbot sent some respected, honoured esquires of the district to announce that he was willing, if they so wished, to celebrate Mass on the next day in their presence and to swear an oath over the sacrament, which he would receive with all his monks or with those whom they thought should take part, that he did not knowingly have any such charter in the monastery.

But not even so could he calm down the rebels: they were either determined to receive what could not be had or to abide by their previous opinion. What was the abbot to do? Difficulties hemmed him in on all sides, and anxieties overwhelmed him. So he sent the same messengers as before to tell the rebels that the abbot was willing to obey their wishes in everything: but that, as they were demanding the impossible, he asked them to give way to reason, and, as no such charter could be found, to draw up their own charter containing whatever liberties or conditions they liked, and to date it to the reign of King Henry [III] and the abbot of that day; he himself would then at once sign and seal it. But even then he could not satisfy those gannets. They shouted that they would put no trust in any oath, but that they wanted either to recover the irrecoverable charter or to burn down the monastery in flames.

But the rebels also planned to do a lot of damage to their neighbours, and as they could not fit in the destruction of the monastery and the damage to their neighbours at the same time, at long last, by the will of God, a kind of truce was made and it was agreed that the abbey should enjoy immunity until 3 o'clock on the following day, but that then it would be definitely pulled down, unless the charter, which did not exist, was shown to the commons. Even so, some fifteen hundred men of all sorts, peasants and bondsmen of the monastery, together with some townsmen and the

---

1   The passages following again reproduce Walsingham's *Gesta abbatum* account: *Gesta abbatum*, ed. Riley, iii. 310.
2   That is to say, after the office of None.
3   The main entrance to the abbey, on the northern edge of the precinct wall.

commons of the district, stayed on in front of the Great Gate, instigated solely by malice and saying that they were willing to pull down the whole building of the gateway, if somebody was willing to strike the first blow. The bondsmen[1] of the monastery were so hostile to their masters that even with the grant of charters of liberty they still preferred to destroy the monastery than to get their hands on the charters. We did send to the men at the gate abundant supplies of ale and huge baskets full of bread for anyone to drink and eat as much as he liked, in the hope that in return for the kindness shown the rebels might be won round.

But all this achieved nothing until one of the leading townsmen came up, induced by his conscience to expose himself to the danger in their midst. On his arrival he cautiously restrained them by saying, 'What are you rascals doing? What schemes have you got in mind? Surely you who are strangers and newcomers are not intending to strike the first blow in the overthrow of this building rather than we who are the burgesses and freemen of this town? So give up your schemes and follow the burgesses. You must do what they decide to do. For they will be your leaders, and take you to destroy buildings or carry out other plans.' These words caused them to withdraw from the gate and to hurry to join another gathering of similar rascals in the town. They spent the rest of the day in knocking down houses and breaking looms or other things found in them, behaviour learnt from Wat Tyler in London.[2]

Proclamation of the townspeople[3]

They also took it upon themselves to make proclamations under the unfurled royal banner about stationing large groups of men around the town to keep watch. They were afraid that some soldiers might come to the help of the abbey and might take them by surprise as they were watching the paths and streets around the river and St Germans,[4] or that some monks might get in or out. They gave orders that any persons they were able to capture should be executed or kept under close watch until the morrow. The result was that more than a hundred people were keeping watch at the various stations, so that if the prior or those who had got away with him had returned by the road which passed through the groups of rebels, they would have been beheaded. It was also announced that if anyone was owed money by the abbot, prior or other monks as payment or reward, he should come to ask for it the next day. The burgesses of the town of St Albans would see to it that they were paid out of the monastery's property, as far as that property was able to cope with all the demands made on it. The rebels made many other appointments, which it would take too long to list.

While the rebels were engaged in these fruitless tasks, a man armed with a sword and shield got into the abbot's court, and boldly asked the abbot to give him a hundred marks; if the abbot refused, he would without doubt immediately collect his gang of rascals and set fire to the grange of St Peter and the manor of Kingsbury, situated near the town.[5] For he had been a former tenant of the manor of Kingsbury, who, when he had been unable to repay a huge sum of money owed to the monastery, had run away into hiding in his fear of the punishment of the law. But now he had come back. His story was that he had been frightened of the prior, who was determined to get the money out of him. He had not run away, but had gone to friends so that they could help him repay this huge sum, unjust though it was. And now he was asking the abbot for one hundred marks as recompense for the losses caused by his sudden departure from the manor. He said that he had incurred these losses because of the prior, to whom he had in fact owed nothing when

---

[1]   That is to say the labourers bound under indenture to serve the abbot and convent.

[2]   Once again these passages are reproduced in Walsingham's *Gesta abbatum*, ed. Riley, iii. 311–12.

[3]   For this section see *Gesta abbatum*, ed. Riley, iii. 313–14.

[4]   The river Ver, which flows to the west of the town of St Albans. St Germans is a district to the north of the abbey church. See T. R. Slater, 'Benedictine Town Planning: The Case of St Albans', in *The Church in the Medieval Town*, ed. T. R. Slater and G. Rosser (Aldershot, 1998), pp. 155–76.

[5]   St Peter's was the largest of the three town parishes at St Albans. Kingsbury was an ancient royal manor to the west of the town and the north west of the monastic precinct; it had been developed by earlier generations of abbots and subsumed into the town: see Slater, 'Benedictine Town Planning', pp. 155–76.

everything was reckoned up, although there were one hundred marks owing to him according to the terms by which he had been a tenant of the manor. He intended now to get satisfaction for that sum, seeing that the times smiled on its recovery, or to set fire to the places concerned. For he had, so he claimed, two thousand men of the commons gathered nearby. So unless the abbot made speedy restitution, he would get his revenge for his injuries by burning the places down. To cut a long story short, the abbot, buffeted by this whirlwind, had no alternative but to comply with this fraudulent demand, although the rascal was persuaded by the prayers of many to take just twenty pounds of the hundred marks. He went away, swearing that he would prefer to get his hands on the prior even more than on the total sum, so that his revenge could be on the prior's person. In fact the prior had never done him any wrong, but had given him a lot of help and support until it became obvious that he would never repay his debts and was a liability to the monastery. Thus was one of the many terrible losses and injuries suffered by the abbot and the monks on that day.

The townspeople of St Albans riot

The monks spent a distressful night. They were at their wits end as to what to do on the next day about the conditions laid down by the townspeople, if the charter which it was impossible to find was not given back to them. Almost all of them had made up their minds to escape, now that the wicked people of the town were looking for an opportunity to destroy the monastery by imposing impossible terms. Sunday began to dawn, a day on which the divine consolation was to smile more favourably on men brought low by fear and worn out by anxiety. For the hubris of the townsmen suddenly met its nemesis, and their arrogance of the day before unexpectedly collapsed on the Sunday. For they were deeply saddened by the rumours spreading everywhere that their leader, that scab Wat Tyler of hateful memory, had most foully been done to death. The story was that he had been killed before the king, and that the commons of London had gathered in large numbers in the king's support and in united resistance to the commons of Kent and Essex and the others who were trying to raise them in revolt against the king. Also one of the king's knights had arrived in St Albans very early in the morning and had got read out a proclamation of peace from the king, which said that all subjects of the king were to keep the peace from that hour onwards on pain of forfeiture of life and limb. The king also sent a letter of protection to the abbot, which covered the monastery and all the places belonging to it.[1] It went as follows:

Letter of protection from the king for the abbot of St Albans[2]

'Richard, by the grace of God king of England and of France and lord of Ireland, to all our lieges and commons of the county of Hertford, and of all other counties adjoining and near to it. We do pray you, charge, and command, the most strictly that we may, and upon the faith and allegiance which unto us you owe, that unto our very dear in God, the abbot of St Albans, or unto our house and monastery of the said place (which is of our patronage), or unto any of the people, monks or others, or unto any of the goods within the said monastery and the enclosure thereof, and in any other places whatsoever of the said abbey, or unto it and its appurtenances, you do not nor suffer to be done as far as in you lies, any grievance, damage or molestation whatsoever, in body or goods, in any manner whatsoever: for if the said abbot, or any of his people, has offended towards you, we ourselves will make him give redress for the same, and make amends, as right shall demand. And this our command so take to heart, that it may behove us to congratulate you upon all the love and loyalty that unto us you bear. Given under our great seal at our city of London, the fifteenth of June, the fourth year of our reign.'

---

[1]   The Westminster chronicler claims that the king himself came to St Albans shortly after the events at Smithfield but there is no corroboration for this in the abbey's own records: *WC*, pp. 14–15.
[2]   Walsingham transcribes the letter in its original French and then gives the above translation: *Historia Anglicana*, ed. Riley, i. 480–1.

The wickedness of the townspeople of St Albans

When the townsmen of St Albans heard all that had happened, they realised that the news, which was frequently repeated, was a blow to their plans. But they still decided without sense or reason to continue on that Sunday to demand their liberties, while they were still supported by the crowd which had been summoned on their orders in the manner I have described from the towns of Luton, Watford, Barnet, Rickmansworth and Tring, and from the other villages and towns round-about. They did not want in the eyes of those they had summoned with such pride to appear too easily terrified or obedient to the commands and instructions of the king. They did not consider what might happen but fixed their minds completely on the present, and thought only of fulfilling the desires of their hearts, never imagining that any gains might one day be taken back from them again. So they made light both of the king's proclamation, which offered them peace if they ceased from their unjust acts of rebellion and extortion from Friday onwards, and of the perils and losses which awaited them in the future for such revolts and disturbances. And on Sunday, very early in the morning they gathered together in a large crowd to recover more fully on that day what they had demanded the day before. But they were less rowdy and headstrong than formerly, and tried to get the charters wearing masks of peace and tranquillity, with promises of the good relations which would arise between monks and townsmen and which would last for ever because of these charters. They did not think of the lines:

> From gains ill-gotten even grandsons get
> No joy, for unclean money turns out ill.[1]

And so that all these plans should seem to be proceeding with greater safety and be cloaked in a darker obscurity, they decided to conceal and hide from the commons the charter concerning the pardoning of their crimes, which some of them had obtained from the king the previous day for the county of Hertford and had brought to St Albans, and which, as I have said, promised a conditional pardon, forgiveness and freedom. They intended to conceal it until by fair means or foul they had succeeded in getting the abbot to grant their requests. So then, if they met with some future opposition to their gains, they would be able to use the strictly valid excuse that they had made their requests and had them granted before the publication of the charter, implying that they would not have been willing to disobey the king's commands if they had known about them, although everybody knew perfectly well that they had of their own free will and craftily not so much requested the charters as extorted them from the monks by terror and threats.

So, as I have described, at the appointed day and hour the leading citizens of the town entered the abbot's chamber, and forcefully demanded the charters of liberty according to the agreement of the day before. Their prayers were granted. They dictated their wishes themselves, sitting beside and standing over the clerk, until in their presence all the points had been inserted in the charter which they had decided upon to gain their liberty. This was bound to happen, seeing that the mob had not yet been completely calmed down and pacified, but violence and disturbance still reigned throughout the town. But once they had obtained the charter of their own devising, they demanded that charter concerning the liberties of the town, which, as I have often said, was not in the possession of the abbot or the monks. But as the boldness of the peasants on that day was less marked than on the previous day, they did not press their claims for this charter as urgently as before. But they did ask for a pledge of one thousand pounds sterling, signed and sealed by the abbot and the monastery, to be made to them, that if before the feast of the annunciation to the blessed virgin the abbot was able to find such a charter, he was to give it back to the townsmen without any trickery. And if no such charter could be found, he was to be ready, with twelve senior monks of the monastery, to swear upon the Eucharist that he did not knowingly have or keep in his possession any such charter. If all this was done, they were willing to declare the pledge invalid and of no account. Now the unreasonableness of the townspeople had long been causing the

---

[1]   The second line of the couplet is taken from Ovid, *Amores,* i. 10. 48.

abbot and his brothers great anxiety, but when they now saw that yesterday's wildness had died down, they were filled with joy and began to have hopes of saving the monastery. And there was the more cause for congratulation because they hoped to hear better news soon about the power of the king and the subjection of the peasants. This was mainly because on that very day the abbot had been greatly encouraged by receiving a letter from the knights, Sir Hugh Segrave, the king's steward,[1] and Sir Thomas Percy,[2] which instructed him to yield to all the demands of the crowd, in the certain knowledge that no losses or evil precedents for himself or his monastery would result from such concessions.

So the abbot granted the current petition of the townsmen. Just as they wished, he produced a written pledge in the form required, with his own seal and that of the monastery affixed, and handed it to them. While this was going on, the rebels walked about just as they pleased in the abbot's chamber, chapel and courtyard, behaving more like masters than his subjects. They were present at the writing of the pledge, in fact dictating what should be written, and watched the sealing with great curiosity. For at that time the seal of the abbot and the monastery were both there.

And a miracle occurred when it was time to seal the charter concerning the liberties for the town and townsmen. The wax was applied with all skilful care by experienced people to the common seal, on which had been depicted by the craftsmen of old the figure of Alban, glorious protomartyr of the British, holding a palm in his hand. But once applied, the wax could by no means be pulled off and removed from the seal, although they tried three times, this being a certain indication that the martyr had no wish for the rebels to be his masters, but that he, as previously, wished to be master over them. The townsmen went on their way, rejoicing that they had obtained their pledge and the charter of liberties for the town, and intending then at last to display publicly at the market cross the charter which they had obtained from the monastery, together with the royal charter, which, as I have said, seemed to forgive the subjects of the king for the crimes, acts of treason, misdeeds and extortions etc. committed by them, as well as promising bondsmen their freedom in the manner mentioned above. They also made a proclamation and displayed the charter of protection that the lord king had sent to the monastery. Outwardly their expressions were those of utter goodwill, but a mass of wickedness reigned in their hearts, as will be clear from what follows.

A charter is granted to all the bondsmen of St Albans

On the following Monday and Tuesday [17 and 18 June] the bondsmen of all the towns belonging to the monastery met together, declaring that they had instructions to put all their other tasks aside and to demand charters of manumission and liberty, according to the tenor of the royal charter. They all received similar charters, which read as follows:

> To all the sons of holy mother church who will read this letter, greetings in the Lord from Thomas, by permission abbot of the monastery of St Albans and of the monks of the same place. I must inform you that I have read a letter from the king which goes as follows, 'Richard, by the grace of God, etc.'. It is my wish and command that this letter is strictly observed in the town of N.[3] As witness to this fact, I append to this letter both my own seal and the common seal of our chapter.

All those who came in search of such charters had been summoned by the townsmen of St Albans to cause trouble for the abbot and monks and damage to the monastery. For as soon as the peasants received the charters, they thought themselves of higher birth than the line of the king and as released from all servitude and the performance of customary tasks. So they decided to perform no tasks at all, none of their customary duties and not even to pay or hand over any taxes.

---

[1]   Segrave, who had been a chamber knight since the beginning of the reign had been appointed acting chancellor on 16 June, succeeding the earl of Arundel who had held the office in the hours immediately following Archbishop Sudbury's death: Saul, *Richard II*, p. 77 and n.
[2]   Percy had been one of the handful of household knights and nobles who had been with the king at Mile End on the Friday and at Smithfield on the Saturday of the revolt: Saul, *Richard II*, p. 65.
[3]   This is a letter-form, with the name of the town unspecified.

This is what happened in St Albans, and the bondsmen committed similar crimes wherever in the land such disturbances broke out. Now I shall pass on to other places, in which abominable crimes were perpetrated. I shall begin again from the Saturday, so that I may give a more detailed account of the time and the day of wickedness.

Mad deeds in Norfolk

The disorderly sequence of my narrative is caused by the disorder of the events themselves. They happened in very many places, and because different sorts of crime were committed at the same time in a variety of places, it is hardly possible to maintain a chronological narrative. For what happens is that I start writing about the horrors and worse than horrors that took place in London on the Friday and Saturday, but I can barely bring this tragedy to its end before having to write of similar events occurring in St Albans, as I have described. Nor am I able to give the details of the unhappy story of St Albans before some equally dreadful or even more horrible and scandalous enormity happens elsewhere.[1]

For on the same Saturday [15 June], in order that the hurricane should seem to be widespread, God sent the anger of his wrath, his wrath and anger and the beginning of troubles upon the counties of Suffolk and Norfolk. He did this through messengers of wickedness, some men who were actually more dangerous than the treacherous messengers of Satan in Essex and who were to bring an innocent people living in peace and quiet to rise in a revolt similar to the ones which had already happened and to turn the hearts of the serfs against their masters.

Under the leadership of a wicked priest, called Jack Straw,[2] who had been in London in person the day before and had received instructions from that villain, Wat Tyler, they quickly and easily, acting more effectively than beneficially, brought together a crowd of common people, whose number was said to have exceeded fifty thousand. These followed the example of those who had rioted in London, and going on a general rampage, they destroyed the houses and estates of magnates and lawyers, killed the legal apprentices and caught and beheaded Sir John Cavendish, the chief justiciar of the kingdom, putting his head as an object of shame on the pillory in the marketplace of the town of Bury St Edmunds.[3]

They also rapidly arrested the prior of Bury St Edmunds, John Cambridge, a hard-working and quick-thinking monk, while he was trying to escape from before their face, and cruelly killed him by cutting off his head. John had been a musician, superior to Thracian Orpheus [in Greek Legend Orpheus's mastery of the lyre was said to charm beasts and move inanimate objects], Roman Nero and British Beldgabred[4] both in the sweetness of his voice and his knowledge of song. People were quite well aware why he had been killed. Being a careful and sensible man, he

---

[1] In fact Walsingham preserves the chronology of events as accurately as any other contemporary authority and his coverage is in greater depth than other observers. It was to be expected that he devote such a lengthy digression to the events at St Albans itself, to which he certainly must have been an eyewitness.

[2] In fact the leader of the rebels in this region was one John Wrawe who was, as Walsingham suggests, an unbeneficed priest and previously vicar of Ringsfield near Beccles, Suffolk. Walsingham's confusion is understandable given the prominence of the name 'Jack Straw' and the extent to which the rebels employed pseudonyms.

[3] Cavendish was murdered at the beginning of the uprising on Friday 14. His death is reported by the *Anonimalle* author (*AC*, pp. 150–1) and by Knighton (*Knighton*, pp. 224–5, 240–1), but not by the Westminster chronicler. Given St Albans' network of dependent houses in East Anglia, Walsingham and his colleagues were probably better informed of events in Suffolk and Norfolk than many of those close to the capital. The fact that lawyers and legal apprentices were targeted here, as they had been in London, is a further reflection of the coherence of the rebellion even across county and regional boundaries. An account of the rising in Suffolk, which describes the murder of Cavendish in some detail, was compiled by the Bury monk Andrew Aston at the end of the 1420s, perhaps drawing on the first hand recollections of his colleagues: *Memorials of St Edmund's Abbey*, ed. Arnold, iii. 113–37 at 125–30.

[4] According to Geoffrey of Monmouth in his *Historia regum Britanniae*, Beldgabred was a legendary king of Britain who 'surpassed all the musicians of ancient time both in harmony and in playing every kind of musical instrument so that he was called the God of minstrels'. See A. Griscom and R. E. Jones, *The Historia regum Britanniae of Geoffrey of Monmouth* (London, 1929), p. 300 and n.

had taken up and defended the cause of his monastery. And because in his loyalty to the monastery he had fought for its rights against the townspeople of Bury St Edmunds, he received his death sentence near the town of Mildenhall, which is recognised as being under the jurisdiction of this same monastery. Death was pronounced upon him by the judgement and decision of his own serfs and bondsmen rather than by that of his enemies, the townspeople of Bury St Edmunds. His body was stripped down to his vest and pants, and it lay unburied in a field out in the open for five days, with nobody daring to take it away or to give it the gift due to its nature because of the savagery of the peasants.

A note on Jack Straw, leader of the peasants

After this wicked crime had been carried out, the leader of this treason, the infamous Jack Straw [John Wrawe], hurried to the town of Bury St Edmunds with his treacherous commons, the crowd I have mentioned before. As no one offered any resistance, they made their way into the town, carrying the head of the prior aloft on a spearhead, as if processing around the town for the citizens to see it, until they came to the pillory. On arriving there, with complete absence of taste, they brought together the heads of the prior and [Sir] John Cavendish on the points of their spears, at one time as though one was listening to the other, and then as though they were kissing: this piece of mockery of both of them was supposedly a sign of their former friendship. Finally, when they had had their fill of such sport, they again placed both their heads upon the pillory.[1] They next showed their hatred of the prior by destroying a completely new house that he had built and constructed from the foundations upwards.

After these crimes, they entered the cloisters of the monastery and gave orders that John Lakenheath, the keeper of the barony, be handed over to them, with threats that they would burn down the monastery, unless this was done.[2] Then, when he stood among them, amazingly none of them recognised him. But they did all this, as the sequel will easily prove, at the instigation of the townspeople, who had secretly employed the commons to do this, while removing themselves from the mob, so that by this they might seem to have had no part in such heinous crimes. John's one thought was for the danger to his monastery, and he replied to the rebels that he was the man they were looking for, and asked the commons why they were seeking him. They answered him, 'You traitor, we are seeking you now to put you to death; for you will not prolong your life much longer.' 'I am ready for death,' said John, 'and I embrace it willingly, provided that this monastery suffers no harm because of me.' He was immediately dragged off by the commons, who, shouting loudly that they had found the false monk, brought the traitor to the marketplace where he was publicly beheaded, though it took eight strokes of the axe before his head was separated from his body. His head at once joined the head of the prior on the pillory. Not content with this the rebels sought another monk called Walter Toddington for the same punishment of death, but he hid himself so carefully that he could not be found and so avoided the danger of death.

After this they called out all the monks and said that for a long time now their allies, the burgesses of Bury St Edmunds, had been kept down by the power of the monks. Therefore they wished the monks now to hand over in the sight of the commons the bonds by which the townsmen had been bound to king and monastery, in case they might have opposed the abbey in some way. They also wanted the charters of the town's liberties which King Cnut, the monastery's founder, had once granted them, and which his royal successors right down to the present time had granted in support of the monastery.[3] The monks, indeed, feared for themselves and their

---

1   The *Anonimalle* author corroborates this and adds that another unnamed monk was also murdered alongside Cambridge, presumably meaning John Lakenheath as Walsingham describes here in the following passage: *AC*, p. 151.
2   Lakenheath was one of a number of monks charged with the administration of the abbey who exercised the baronial powers vested in the abbot as tenant-in-chief of the liberty. See also R. S. Gottfried, *Bury St Edmunds and the Urban Crisis, 1290–1539* (Princeton, 1982), pp. 168–72.
3   Like St Albans, Bury St Edmunds was a monastic borough, the abbot and convent maintaining secular and spiritual jurisdiction over the townsmen. Their complaints echo those of their St Albans counterparts,

house if they did not obey the will of the commons, and brought into the marketplace for all to see all the charters asked for which could strengthen the power of the townsmen or weaken their own, swearing that they could not find in the monastery any more charters which could be handed over to the advantage of the townsmen.

But the commons were scarcely willing to believe their words. They called the townsmen, who were putting on a show of gloom as though dissatisfied with what had happened, and instructed them to scrutinise and look over carefully the bonds and charters, and if they could not obtain their old liberties from these, they were to give details of those things which had been accustomed to make them happy. And the rebels also gave instructions that the abbot, Edmund Broomfield, who was being kept in prison in Nottingham[1] and whom they had decided to set free so that on the following feast of [the nativity of] John Baptist [24 June] he could properly celebrate the divine rites in his own monastery, should forty days after his arrival guarantee with his seal the charter that had by then been drawn up and that the monks also should not delay to do the same thing with their common seal.

The monks had been fearing the worst, and so they were pleased with these demands of the rebels, even though they used force and dictated what had to be done. In fact the monks as a pledge of their good intentions put into the hands of the townsmen the most valuable jewels of the monastery, a gold cross, a precious gold chalice, and several other jewels taken from the monastery, whose value exceeded a thousand pounds. These were all to be returned if Edmund Broomfield, once freed from prison and enjoying the office of abbot there, should within the time limit put his own seal to the liberties of the townspeople together with the general consent and seal of the monks. If this condition was not met with, the jewels were to stay in the hands of the townsmen forever.

So that was a strange state of affairs in Bury St Edmunds, with the commons demanding for the townspeople things that in no sense concerned them. Indeed the commons could not have known about them, or about the things they should not be doing, unless they had been told about it and put up to it by the townsmen. For who would ever have believed that the commons would have sought to kill an innocent monk, whom they had never seen or met, and whom they did not recognise when he stood by them, if they had not been put up to this by others? What business was it of the commons to demand liberties for the townsmen, when they did not even live in the town? Or if all that happened displeased the townsmen, why did they put off handing back what had been seized, when the commons went away and peace was restored? To me it seems completely inexcusable, as will become clear from the sequel.

Similar happenings in Cambridgeshire and the Isle of Ely

Now that I have described in part what happened in Bury St Edmunds, I shall pass over the crimes committed in Cambridge and Cambridgeshire and the Isle of Ely, which were not different from but exactly the same as the crimes of murder and the demolition of houses and the other horrors which I have described as happening elsewhere, and move to the events in Norfolk.[2]

So when a large crowd of rebels had gathered there, under the leadership of a dyer of Norwich called John Lister,[3] they too began to do what the commons had done everywhere else, leaving out nothing of all the things that they had heard the rebels had done in other places. In fact they dared to commit still greater crimes and began to turn their hands to pillage. So almost no place was able to be safe from this crowd of men, who were inspired by a common desire to cause trouble.

---

turning on privileges which may have been granted in the remote past when the abbey was first founded and the town first established. For an analysis of the disputes between the townsmen and the monks see R. S. Gottfried, *Bury St Edmunds and the Urban Crisis, 1290–1539* (Princeton, 1982).

[1]   For Broomfield and the reasons for his imprisonment see above, pp. 93–6.

[2]   At first it appeared that northern East Anglia might escape the rebellion, but violent demonstrations erupted on Friday 14 June when some of the Suffolk insurgents headed north.

[3]   In fact the leader's name was Geoffrey Lister and he was a dyer of Felmingham, Norfolk. Froissart names him as William Lister: *Chroniques,* x. 115.

And since their own authority seemed insufficient when such enormous crimes were being committed, they decided to attach Lord William Ufford, earl of Suffolk, to their rebel band, so that if it should be that later the lower classes were being accused of these happenings, they would be able to point to a magnate, indeed a peer, under whose umbrella and with whose connivance they had done these things. But the earl was warned that they were coming. He hastily got up from the table at which he had taken his seat, and journeying across country, avoiding the towns and the groups of rebels on either side, he arrived at St Albans and so to the king. He had disguised himself as the squire of Sir Roger de Boys, carrying a knapsack on his back.

Frustrated in this attempt, the commons suddenly seized the estates of other knights, and, finding the owners at home, they compelled them to swear the oaths they dictated and for their own greater safety to ride around the country with them. Had the knights not done this, they would rapidly have met an ugly death. The names of the knights forced to follow the rebels were Lord Scales,[1] Sir William Morley,[2] Sir John Brewes,[3] Sir Stephen Hales[4] and Sir Robert Salle.[5] This Robert did not last long in the rebel band, as, unlike the others, he did not know how to dissimulate but began publicly to condemn their deeds and to express his horror at them. As a result he was suddenly pierced through the brain by a peasant who was his own bondsman and died on the spot, though being a knight who, if he had had the chance of fighting against them in open combat, would have terrified a thousand rebels on his own.[6] His companions, learning from the danger that had overtaken Sir Robert, realised that they had to dissimulate or die a similar shameful death, and so decided to praise everything praised by the rebels and to pour scorn on what displeased them. And so when they were graciously received by that rascal, John Lister, who called himself 'King of the Commons', they found that they were judged suitable to be appointed tasters of his food and drink and to obey his commands on bended knee as he sat at meat. Indeed he specially chose out that honourable knight, Sir Stephen Hales, to carve his meat and to taste the food that he was about to eat, with other knights being appointed to other duties.

After many days had gone by and the commons were now beginning to grow tired, they decided to send two knights, Sir William Morley and Sir John Brewes, with three trusty men from their own number to the king in London or wherever he could be found, in order to obtain from him a charter of freedom and forgiveness. So that it might be a better charter than the ones which had been conceded or were to be conceded to other counties, they handed to the envoys a huge sum of money which they had taken from the citizens of Norwich on the pretext that this would keep the city safe from murder, fire and pillage, in order that they should gain by money a peace and a liberty which they had not deserved by their own actions.

The courage of the bishop of Norwich

So the two knights, with their companions from the assembly of the commons, hurried to carry out the commands laid upon them. And when they had reached the village of Icklingham, which is not far distant from the town of Newmarket, they unexpectedly encountered Henry Despenser, the bishop of Norwich, a man quite capable of bearing arms, and who was in fact armed to the teeth.[7] For when he was staying at his manor of Burley near the king's castle at Oakham in the Stamford area, he had heard news of the rebellion down in Norfolk, and had

---

1 Roger, Lord Scales (b.c. 1347–86).
2 For Sir William Morley see *CPR, 1377–81*, p. 494.
3 Brewes was a Norfolk knight: *CPR, 1377–81*, p. 509.
4 Hales had served as a JP in Norfolk: *CPR, 1377–81*, p. 513.
5 Salle served as governor of the castle of Merk, Calais, *CPR, 1377–81*, pp. 64. 201.
6 Salle's death is also reported by Knighton, who describes him as a knight 'famous for feats of arms' (*Knighton*, p. 225). He was murdered at Norwich on Monday 17 June. Walsingham maintains that Salle would have defended himself had he been given the chance; in Froissart's account he does just that until he is overcome by the rebels.
7 Despenser was Bishop of Norwich from 1370 until his death in 1406. His role in the revolt is reported also by Knighton (*Knighton*, pp. 224–7) but Walsingham's account is by far the most descriptive. Walsingham praises Despenser's martial prowess, describing him as a warlike bishop. See below, p. 146.

decided to go down there to see whether the rebels followed up their tumult with deeds or had already done so. He had no more than eight lances in his company at that time and a very small number of archers. But when he saw the knights together with some of the commons, he commanded the knights under their allegiance to him to say if any of the traitors to the king were present with them. Fear of the peasants had for a long time been entering deep into the hearts of the knights and their reply was a lie, for they thought that the bishop had uttered his ill-judged command in the boldness of his youth and that he did not have the men to help them if they did betray the traitors. But the bishop saw correctly how matters stood, and urged them to act boldly and hand over any traitors with them. Then the knights, wiping off their cowardice and plucking up their courage, replied that two of the rebel leaders were in their company, and that a third had gone off to buy food: and they gave the bishop full details of their mission.

The bishop at once got the two beheaded, and himself took on the job of tracking down the third, one of his own sheep, who indeed had been as good as dead ever since he had forsworn his loyalty to the king, and now was about to be killed in actuality by episcopal decree.[1] Their heads were nailed up at Newmarket, and the bishop speedily hurried with the knights to North Walsham in Norfolk, the town in which the commons had decided to await the king's answer and the return of their companions. The bishop's numbers continually increased as he crossed the countryside, since many knights and gentlemen of the district, who had been lying low in fear of the commons, joined his side when they saw that their bishop had become a knight and had put on a helmet of metal and a tough breastplate which arrows could not pierce and had snatched up an actual, double-edged sword.

So when the bishop, surrounded by a reasonable force, arrived at North Walsham,[2] he found that the peasants, just like soldiers, had surrounded the place in which they had gathered with a ditch, and in their defence had fixed a wall of tables, windows, doors and stakes above the ditch. But the bishop saw that their wagons and carts had been placed well in the rear, as though flight was the last thing in their minds. There was no delay. The warlike bishop, appalled by the audacity of these rascals, intended to meet them in open battle and ordered his trumpeters and buglers to sound the charge. He himself, snatching up a spear in his right hand, urged on his steed with sharp spurs and charged against the enemy with such dash and boldness that in his speedy gallop he got to the ditch more quickly than his men's arrows; not that there was any need for archers with their bows, for battle was joined at close quarters hand to hand. The warrior priest, grinding his teeth like a wild boar, spared neither himself nor his enemy. He directed his course to wherever he saw the greater danger, and running this man through with his sword, knocking that one to the ground and wounding another, he did not cease from fierce slaughter until the whole force following him had gained the ditch and were ready to fight.

The bishop's men fought fiercely, as did the commons, until, as usually happens, a weaker conscience struck terror into the side that was in the wrong, and deprived their minds of boldness and a willingness to die. Nothing is more disastrous than fighting wars with a bad conscience, for such people are always attacked by fear and confusion, and never end up winners. The cowardly commons turned tail, and because no other means of flight was left to them except their wagons and carts, which I have said they had placed in the rear, they struggled to get away through woodland. But the bishop, who throughout the affair acted like a shrewd commander, cut off such attempts. He stopped those who were thinking of fleeing by killing them and he killed them by stopping them, until finally a complete victory was won. The main leaders of the rebels, including their 'king' John Lister, were taken prisoner, while the bishop killed or spared the rank and file exactly as he pleased.[3]

---

[1]   These executions took place on 19 and 20 June. One of the victims is named by Froissart as John Hanchach: Froissart, *Chroniques*, x. 116–17.
[2]   On Monday 25 June.
[3]   The skirmish at North Walsham passed into popular Norfolk tradition as a scene of mass slaughter: R. B. Dobson, *The Peasants' Revolt of 1381* (London, 1970) p. 257.

The end of John Lister, king of Norfolk

So the bishop sentenced John, idol of the people of Norfolk, to be drawn, hanged and beheaded. The bishop listened to his confession, absolved him by virtue of his office and went with him in person to the gallows, showing he could do works of mercy and piety even on a defeated enemy. Indeed as John was being dragged off for his hanging, the bishop even held up his head so that it should not knock against the ground. Even after this the bishop did not rest until he had sought out all the rebels throughout his whole area and justice had been done on them. We should praise the goodness and applaud the boldness of the warlike bishop who in this way brought peace to his region and indescribable benefit to the whole country.[1]

A chapter proving that the rebels had conspired to destroy the church, the Christian faith and the king

Having described a few of the happenings in Norfolk, I shall refrain from describing the crimes committed in Suffolk and the destruction wrought in other counties by men who were possessed by the devil and who brought chaos upon the whole land. Unless they had been possessed by devils, they would never have conspired to destroy holy church and the Christian faith and to overthrow the government of the kingdom. Such conspiracy is proved by their deeds and the confessions of some who were later taken captive, as I will describe in the appropriate place. Their deeds are a judgement against them, seeing that they killed the father of all the priests and the head of the English church, namely the archbishop of Canterbury. What else did they do to harm the faith? They compelled teachers in the grammar schools to swear that they would never any more instruct the young in that subject. What more did they do? They were zealous in consigning old records to the flames. And to make it impossible for anyone to be found again who in the future had the ability or the knowledge to write down things old or new, they murdered likely candidates. It was dangerous to be recognised as a priest, but much more dangerous if you were found with an inkpot by your side. Such people rarely or never escaped the rebels' hands.

Their plans for the destruction of the kingdom were shown by the confession of John Straw, who, after Wat Tyler, was the most important rebel leader. When he was taken captive and sentenced by the lord mayor to be executed in London, after sentence had been passed, the mayor [William Walworth] said to him in public, 'John, think a bit. There is no doubt that your death is at hand.[2] You cannot hope for any means of escape. So, to help your end and for the salvation of your soul, tell us truthfully of the plans you formed among you, and your purpose in stirring up the host of rebels. He hesitated for some time and was reluctant to speak, so the mayor added, 'John, be completely clear about what I shall order to happen for the good of your soul, if you do as I say. I shall make sure that several masses are said to help your soul for thirty years.' And many of the citizens who were present promised to do the same thing, each one in person. So John, now encouraged by these fair promises, began to speak as follows:

The confession of Jack Straw

'This is not the occasion,' he said, 'when lying is appropriate or when it is right to utter falsehoods, especially as I realise that, if I lie, my spirit will be assigned to fiercer torments, whereas I hope to achieve a double benefit from telling the truth. For, if I speak without any discolouration of falsity,

---

1   Froissart reports that the execution took place at Stamford but there is no corroboration for this.
2   Walsingham is the only contemporary authority to describe such a scene as this, the apparent exchanges between Mayor Walworth and Jack Straw before his execution; and this and his so-called confession that follows this passage must be pure invention. Walsingham uses the confession to underline his own partial and highly prejudiced view of the revolt, the responsibility for which he lays firmly at the feet of his own pet-hate, the mendicant friars. Given their behaviour towards him at Mile End and Smithfield – which is well attested – it is unlikely that the rebels had ever intended to assassinate the king himself, but it may be that Walsingham does here give a fair representation of the rumours that circulated during and in the immediate aftermath of the revolt.

the reasons for the troubles. For the mendicants were not mindful of the profession they had made, and also forgot the purpose for which their orders had been instituted. The most holy men who formed their order had wished them to be poor and completely free of all temporal possessions, precisely so that they should not have what they might fear to lose if they spoke the truth. But nowadays the mendicants, in their envy of the landowners, justify the crimes of the nobles and also back up the common people in their wrongdoing, so that they approve the sins of both classes. So to acquire possessions and to amass money, these mendicants, who have renounced possessions and sworn to persevere in poverty, say that good is bad and bad good, leading the nobles astray by flattery and the people by lies, and leading both classes off the straight and narrow way together with themselves. By their perverse lives they have so spotted their profession of truth that in these days on anybody's lips the sentence, 'He is a mendicant, therefore he is a liar' is as good an argument, in subject matter as well as in form, as though one were to say, 'This is white, therefore coloured.'[1]

But so that I may not seem to have written the above out of rancour, let me admit that we are all at fault and let us correct for the better the sins we have knowingly committed, and let us pray to God more earnestly for the gifts of love and peace, so that peace and truth may come to be in our day.

The king raises a very large army against the men of Kent[2]

In the preceding pages I have written, not without effort, the tragic history of the uprising of the peasants, and the mad rioting of the commons and the bondsmen, so that future ages might know of these events and take precautions. Now it seems right to return to the description of the harvest that their courses reaped, when the king and his nobles reasserted their authority.

After the death of that most arrogant rascal Wat Tyler in the way I have described, the hopes and the confidence of the peasants collapsed. But because the minds of the king and his courtiers were still a mass of uncertainty as they saw the people bent on evil, they granted them charters of freedom and of pardon for their crimes and their consequences, and allowed them to depart.

After this, the king had an army mobilised from the citizens of London, and sent messages throughout the land that those who loved the king and his royal honour should quickly join him in London, equipped with armour and riding on horses: no one was to come unarmed or on foot, and those who had no weapons should remain at home, and likewise those who had no horses. And it happened that within three days the king had about him a force that amounted to forty thousand cavalry, all very splendidly armed. Every day he went out to Blackheath to count the

---

[1] The Franciscans' espousal of apostolic poverty had been a source of controversy, not only in England but throughout the western Church from the time of their foundation in the thirteenth century. Envious of the evident popularity of the order amongst the laity, the monastic orders alleged that the poverty of the friars was nothing more than a cloak used to conceal their acquisition of great wealth at the expense of the wider Church. The argument had recently resurfaced in England with renewed intensity when Richard Fitzralph, archbishop of Armagh, attacked the hypocrisy of friars in his treatise *De pauperie salvatoris*. Fitzralph attracted a strong following in English monasteries as his arguments lent scholarly substance to their anti-mendicant prejudices. Walsingham himself regarded Fitzralph as nothing short of a saint. When Wyclif emerged at the end of the 1370s, monastic commentators such as Walsingham connected the rise of this new brand of bitter anti-clericalism with the continuing cynical corruption of the friars. See K. Walsh, *A Fourteenth-Century and Primate: Richard Fitzralph in Oxford, Avignon and Armagh* (Oxford, 1981), pp. 446, 455.
[2] Of the principal authorities, only Walsingham offers a very detailed account of the suppression of the revolt, including transcripts of a number of the key royal proclamations. The Westminster chronicler suggests that Richard turned his attention first to the Essex rebels (*WC*, pp. 12–13) but Froissart supports Walsingham's claim that it was the Kentish rebels that were the focus of the royal forces. In fact the newly appointed council under the new chancellor, William Courtenay, who had replaced Sudbury at Canterbury, now embarked on royal visitations of both Essex and Kent supported by a significant force of arms. The size of this force is unclear: the 40,000 Walsingham suggests here is surely an exaggeration, but the wardrobe accounts show that the sum of 2000 marks was set aside for the payment of men-at-arms and archers: Saul, *Richard II*, p. 77.

number of arrivals, the king himself at the head of his troops, riding on a large warhorse, with the royal standard being carried in front of him. He rejoiced to be seen by his army and to be recognised by his men as their lord.

After this massive force had been assembled, a bigger army than had ever been seen in England before, the king heard that the men of Kent had revolted again, and had a second time gathered together their wicked bands to destroy the whole kingdom.[1] To put it briefly the king was indignant, the army was white hot with anger, and they decided to set out for Kent at once and to remove from the world of the living the whole race of Kentish men and Jutes.[2] But at the intervention of the lords and nobles of Kent, who went surety for the commons, the king and those with him changed their minds concerning the punishment which they had spoken of inflicting upon all those ignorant people. And then for the first time justiciars were sent to hold courts and to try the malefactors, and especially those who had been responsible for inflaming and rousing the Kentish mob. The whole county was silent in the sight of these judges, and there was great fear.[3]

Then the mayor of London [William Walworth], who was himself also sitting in judgement, arrested not only malefactors of London but also all who could be arrested from Kent, Essex, Sussex, Norfolk, Suffolk and the other counties where there were commons inside the liberty of the city of London. He bravely brought them to public trial and beheaded all those whom he found tainted with the treason I have described.

The execution in London of the leaders of the commons[4]

Then Jack Straw, John Kirkby and Alan Threader, the leaders of the commons, were beheaded. Then also John Starling of Essex, whose boast was that he had cut off the head of the archbishop [Simon Sudbury], was himself also beheaded.[5] After he had done that deed, the devil took possession of him and he began to go mad. He went home, hung a naked sword around his neck in front of his chest, and hung down his back a knife, also unsheathed, of the sort we call a dagger, and thus clad travelled around the marketplaces and villages like a madman, shouting and crying out that these were the weapons with which he had murdered the archbishop. And after spending a few days at home, he went back to London, declaring that there he would receive a reward for his achievement. But after his arrival there and constant pronouncements that he had beheaded the archbishop, the reward he received was his death sentence. But we should also notice the fact that all the men of Kent and Essex who had laid harmful hands upon the archbishop confessed to the deed in similar fashion, however unwillingly, so that the archbishop's murderers of their own accord came to London and there for the most part were beheaded.

A note on the bondsmen of St Albans

Also at that time the bondsmen of St Albans were given an omen of future trouble in their city. For some of those enrolled and sent by the abbot to swell the king's army refused – it is uncertain whether through wickedness or arrogance – to admit that they had been sent to the king by the abbot and put it about that they had come of their own accord. But they were seen in the city by Richard Perrers, one of the archbishop's esquires who was in the service of the abbot and wearing his livery. He recognised some of them as the malefactors who had instigated the troubles at St

---

1   Renewed unrest erupted in Kent at the beginning of July and it was at this point that a royal visitation was directed there: Saul, *Richard II*, p. 78.
2   The Jutes were the Anglo-Saxon settlers in the south-east of England.
3   Under the newly appointed chief justice, Sir Robert Tresilian, an assize had already been conducted in Essex to root out and try the insurgents. Tresilian now turned his attention to Kent.
4   As Walsingham recounts here, the ringleaders of the London mob were executed, but it is notable that many others involved in the rebellion, both in the capital and in the southern and eastern counties, received lesser punishments such as periods of imprisonment or fines: Saul, *Richard II*, pp. 73–4.
5   One John Starling was identified in the inquisitions of November 1382 as one of the rebels who had been 'traitorously entertained' in the city of London by Alderman John Horn on the night of 12 June, on the eve of the mob's rampage through the city. See Dobson, *Peasants' Revolt*, p. 214.

Albans. There and then he called up the bailiffs and had them put in prison. The death punishment no doubt would have awaited them the next day, if the abbot had not helped them by sending them a speedy deliverance. For, once committed to prison, the only safety they could hope for was to send messengers to tell their fellow-townsmen of the dangers they were in and to point out that unless they now took it upon themselves to go to the abbot to plead for their safety, they would without any doubt be put to death on the morrow. These things happened on the eve of the passion of the blessed Alban [22 June] the eighth day after that Friday on which they had first begun to cause trouble to the martyr.

To cut a long story short, the leading men of the town came to the abbey with sorrowful faces during the solemn matins celebrating the passion of the martyr, while the monks were singing the hymn of praise, the Te Deum Laudamus, intending to ask for help for their companions and hoping to get it from the abbot. When lauds and matins were over, they put the whole position before the abbot. He heaved a deep sigh, and in a sadness greater than usual cursed that esquire of his who had caused the trouble for the bondsmen, and swore that he would have preferred to have been run through by a sword himself than to have heard this story, especially as it was he who had sent the men to London and so was responsible for the calamity which had befallen them.

Without wasting a moment, the abbot called one of his monks and ordered him to make for London with all possible speed, not stopping or sparing his horse, until he had seen the prisoners set free and leaving the prison. The monk carried out his orders as quickly as he could and hurriedly rode to London through the night without any sleep. Richard Perrers was enjoined to give up his plan, if he loved the honour of the abbot, and he then swore an oath in the presence of the mayor that it was the abbot who had sent those men to increase the numbers of the king's army. So at last after their great fright, the men were set free actually on St Alban's day, after taking an oath of loyalty to King Richard and to their master, the abbot of St Albans. This was the beginning of the troubles that befell them.

Nor were the bondsmen of St Albans free from terrors for all the following weekdays and Sundays until the Friday on which, as I shall relate, the king came to St Albans to avenge the wrongs done to the angry martyr by the rebels. But I shall tell this story more fully in its proper place, in the meanwhile relating the deeds of the king up to that time.

So during this time the king with a very large force stayed now in London, now in Waltham, thinking what to do for the general good and peace of his kingdom. In the end the king's council decided to send writs of the following kind to all parts of the land.

Royal commission for the resistance to those disturbing the peace of the kingdom

'Richard, by the grace of God king of England and France and lord of Ireland, sends greetings to each and every one of his sheriffs, mayors and bailiffs and to our other loyal subjects of the county of N.[1] We have been given to understand that different groups of our subjects have risen in revolt in different counties of our kingdom of England, contrary to our peace and disturbing our people. They have gathered together in assemblies and meetings, and, doing much damage to our loyal subjects, they have given it to be understood by our people in the counties and are affirming that they have raised such gatherings and revolts and are still raising them and continuing to do damage, in obedience to our wishes and on our authority.

'In this present writ we inform you that revolts, gatherings and damage of this kind are completely opposed to our wishes and authority, just as all such happenings should be. On the contrary, they cause us the maximum amount of displeasure, and we regard them as a most harmful slur on our own person, injurious to the crown and damaging and disturbing to the whole of our kingdom. And so we give orders and commands to you as a body and as individuals that you get this writ read out publicly in whatever places you think it should be read in order that our peace in these days may be more speedily and securely restored. And that, using if necessary a strong hand and all your powers, you get such arrangements made that in the counties concerned

---

[1]   This is a letter-form to be used throughout England. Thus the county is unspecified.

the minimum harmful destruction from gatherings or revolts of this kind or from any other cause may result or be inflicted through any failure to build up resistance by means of this writ. And that you do not omit to do any of this under pain of forfeiting all those things which you are liable to forfeit to us. You must command each and every one of our liegemen and subjects to have nothing at all to do with such gatherings, revolts and destruction, but to go back to their homes and to remain there peacefully under pain of forfeit of life and limb and all those other things which they can forfeit to us. Witnessed by me, in London, on the eighteenth day of June, in the fourth year of our reign.'

This commission greatly heartened the loyal subjects of the king and his kingdom and justly disheartened the rebels, so that those who previously had sought the limelight were forced to search for hiding places, while the lawyers, and those who at the revolt's beginning had fled from the face of frenzy, now dared to come out of their holes. The rebels now waited in silence, quaking at the thought of the sentences and punishments which would be brought against them, while the loyalists wiped away the apprehension from their faces and joyfully rose to their feet to get revenge for the wrongs they had suffered.

Except that not all peasants everywhere were reduced to a similar state of terror. In Essex, where the madness had first begun to sprout, the peasants assembled a new force in the village of Billericay,[1] which is near the town of Hatfield Peverel,[2] and, putting too much confidence in their numbers and led astray by their over estimation of themselves, decided either to enjoy the freedom they had wrung from the king or to die fighting in its defence.

The Essex rebels send messengers to the king concerning their freedom

So they sent messengers to the king, who was then staying at Waltham,[3] to ask him if he was thinking of allowing them to enjoy their former freedom, and to make the further request that in this freedom they should be equal to the lords, and that they should not be summoned to the courts except twice a year to view their frank-pledge. Now the king and his council, who were then with him, were completely amazed at such boldness from the rebels, and for some time hesitated over what reply should be sent back, until the king in his own person replied as follows:

'You miserable people, hated on land and sea, who do not deserve to live, you are asking to be made the equals of your lords. There is no doubt that you would have been punished by a most shameful death, if we had decided not to observe the rights of envoys. But because you have approached us as envoys, for the time being you shall not die but shall enjoy life, as long as you report our reply truthfully to your fellow rebels. So give them this message from the king.

'Peasants you were and peasants you are. You will remain in bondage, not as before, but in an incomparably worse state. For as long as we are alive to achieve this and by the grace of God rule this kingdom, we shall work with our minds, powers and possessions to keep you in such subjection that the abject state of your servitude may be an object lesson to posterity, and that now and in the future men like you may always have before their eyes, as if in a mirror, your miseries, as a reason for cursing you and for fearing to commit similar crimes themselves.

'But you who have come as messengers, if, when you have fulfilled our command and the office of your embassy, you decide to return to us and to remain loyal in your allegiance to us, you shall live. So, when you have returned to your fellows and carried out our commands, do you then choose the course which you decide is the better.'[4]

---

[1] The Westminster chronicler claims that it was in the neighbourhood of Brentwood and the surrounding villages that the upheaval began again: *WC*, pp. 12–13.

[2] Hatfield Peverel, Essex, was the location of one of the abbey's dependent priories: *MRH*, p. 67.

[3] Responding to the rumours of renewed insurrection in Essex, Richard had travelled out of the city on 22 June and had reached Waltham the following day.

[4] This, of course, represents a marked change from the conciliatory tone adopted by the king at Mile End and Smithfield where he had promised manumission and equality of all his subjects under his sovereign authority: as Walsingham reproduces in the passages that follow, Richard soon confirmed this new policy with his letters. See above p. 124 and n.

When the messengers had departed, Thomas of Woodstock, earl of Buckingham, and Thomas Percy, brother of the earl of Northumberland [i.e. Henry Percy], were immediately sent with an armed force to crush the bold peasants, who, like their fellows in Norfolk described earlier, had completely barricaded themselves behind trenches, palisades and carts, except that the men of Essex enjoyed greater protection from woods and thickets. But, although there were a lot of them, they were easily scattered by only ten lances (to use the common term), who rode ahead of their commanders.[1]

The killing of the peasants

When the lords saw that the rebels had been routed like this, they put a cordon around the woods, so that none of them should escape, although it would have been dangerous to have hunted them down inside the woods. The result was that five hundred rebels were killed in different spots by the men of both lords, the remainder getting away alive through the protection afforded them by the woodland. And at the same time, eight hundred horses, which the peasants had brought with them to drag or carry their packs, passed into the use of the king's soldiers. But even after that victory no immediate stop was put to the wickedness of those rascals. Those who had been able to escape this mass killing dared to kick against the pricks a second time, and to do evil again. Indeed the ones who had got away reassembled and hurried to Colchester, where they began with vehement entreaties, powerful threats and arguments in plenty to stir up the townspeople to a new revolt and similar mad behaviour. But when they achieved nothing, they went on to Sudbury. But Lord [Walter] Fitzwalter and Sir John Harleston[2] heard of their movements and pursued them with an armed force, and, when the rebels were making the usual proclamations on behalf of the commons, they suddenly and unexpectedly charged among them, killed as many as they pleased and sent the remainder away alive or put them in prison.

The king proceeds to Havering in Essex

So this was how matters stood in Essex and Suffolk. Meanwhile the king, wishing to see justice done in Essex in person, moved to his estate called Havering-atte-Bower, and then to the town of Chelmsford, where he appointed Sir Robert Tresilian justiciar,[3] to sit in inquiry concerning the malefactors and disturbers of the kingdom and to punish the guilty according to the customs of the land. The men of Essex saw that fortune had turned against them, and five hundred or more of them, weighing up the evils that were imminent, came barefoot and with their heads uncovered to the king as suppliants, in order to ask for his pardon and mercy. Pardon was granted to them on condition that they betrayed and handed over to the king himself the leading malefactors who had started the revolt. The result was that many rebels were handed over to custody. To decide whether to set them free or put them to death, the justiciar appealed to the consciences of twenty-four of the informers to speak the truth concerning the actions and the behaviour of the accused, neither sparing anyone because they liked him, nor going after anyone because they hated him. The result was that, on the verdict of twelve of them, most of them were put to death by drawing and hanging, with in the end nineteen of them being hung from one gallows.[4]

Formerly those who had sat in judgement on the peasants in Essex, Kent and London had used execution, owing to the number of men to be put to death, but then they had decided that capital

---

[1]   After his meeting with the rebel leaders at Waltham the council immediately issued summonses to raise a force against the rebels; the troops were mustered at Great Baddow and Rettenden (Chelmsford) and advanced on the rebels on 27 June. Battle was drawn the following day and the mob rapidly routed.

[2]   Fitzwalter and Harleston were both experienced knights who had served with Buckingham on the abortive chevauchée of the previous year. See above, pp. 106–7.

[3]   Tresilian (d.1388), a Cornishman and a justice of king's bench since 1378, was appointed chief justice after the assassination of Sir John Cavendish at Bury St Edmunds.

[4]   The impact of Tresilian's justice is corroborated by the Westminster chronicler who reports that 'royal judges were now everywhere to be seen . . . giving the guilty short shrift. Gibbets rose where none had been before, since existing ones were too few for the bodies of the condemned' (*WC*, p. 15).

punishment did not fit crimes that were so heinous and so manifest, it being somehow too secret a punishment for so obvious a crime. For this reason they later decided that, according to the customs of the land, all those who were found to be chiefly responsible should be punished by drawing and hanging. This happened especially in Essex.

Meanwhile the king and his council decided to send the following letter to the different counties.

Letter for the revocation of liberties

'Richard, by the grace of God king of England and France and lord of Ireland, sends greetings to all to whom this letter has come. It is true that recently, during the hateful turmoil caused by the horrific actions of certain of our bondsmen and subjects who rose up in revolt against our peace, certain letters patent of ours were issued at the importunate insistence of those very rebels which stated that we manumitted all our bondsmen and subjects, both the commons and others of the other counties of our realm of England, and that we also freed and discharged from all bondage and servitude each and every one of the recipients themselves. And also that we granted to these same bondsmen and subjects of ours pardon for the revolts of every kind raised by them against us as they rode and marched all over our kingdom with armed men and archers and men equipped by other means and with standards and banners flying. And also that in respect of all the treacheries, thefts, crimes and robberies committed and perpetrated by them or some of them, and in respect of any act or acts of outlawry which might have been promulgated against them as a result of these happenings, our peace was firmly given to them as a body and as individuals. And that we wished that these same bondsmen and subjects of ours should be free to buy and sell in any of the cities, boroughs, market towns and other places inside the kingdom of England. And that no acre of land in the counties, which was held by bondsmen or serfs, should be held for more than four pence, and that if any had been held for less, the price should not be put up in the future.

'But in view of the fact that these letters were sent out improperly from our court and without full consideration, and weighing up the fact that the concessions contained in the letters have clearly caused the greatest harm to us and our crown, and have disinherited not only us and the bishops, lords and magnates of our kingdom but also the sacrosanct English church, while bringing losses and troubles upon the whole state, on the advice of our council we have revoked, quashed, invalidated, made null and void the said letters and anything which was done as a result of them, and we do hereby revoke, quash, invalidate and make null and void those letters. It is not our wish that anyone, of whatever class or condition, should in any way have or gain freedom or any benefit from these letters. For, however much our individual subjects have put themselves under massive forfeiture by acting against the terms of their bondship, it is our wish and intention, on the sensible advice of our council, to bestow upon them for the future such grace as shall be pleasing to God and useful to us and our kingdom and with which our loyal subjects will reasonably regard themselves as being content. In this present letter we give notice of this decision to all whom it may concern.

'Also, by the terms of this letter, we now give strict instructions to each and every one of the lords, nobles and our other faithful bondsmen and subjects, as well as to the sheriffs and other officials of the county of N., that they should themselves on our behalf get public proclamations made of our present letter, wherever they think it expedient and necessary, in the various cities, boroughs and other towns and places of the county, including towns both inside and outside liberties. Further it is our strict command that each and every freeman and serf should, without any argument or muttering and without making any kind of resistance or difficulty, carry out, just as they used to do, the customary works and tasks of bondage owed by them to us or their other lords, as they had been accustomed to do them before the troubles began. Also we give orders to these same people that, during these rebellious times, they are not to withdraw more than usual from doing the customary works and tasks of bondage mentioned above, or to make any excuses to us or their lords for delaying to do them. Nor are they to demand, claim or clamour for any other freedoms and privileges other than those they reasonably possessed before the troubles.

And that those who have in their possession and safe keeping our letters of manumission and pardon, should immediately return and restore them into our hands and those of our council so that they may be cancelled, under the loyalty and allegiance which they owe to us, and under the forfeiture of all things which can be forfeited by them in the future. As witness to this we have had written these letters patent. Signed by me, at Chelmsford, the second day of July, in the fifth year of our reign.'

As I said before, these things took place in Essex, where the king was staying. And now I must return to writing about what happened at St Albans, so that happily future generations may learn to avoid the crimes of the townspeople there, since 'Happy is he made cautious by another's peril.'[1]

The proceedings at St Albans conducted by the knight Walter Atley[2]

It was while the king was staying for some time in Essex that he learned from information given him by many people of the wrongs and losses that the townspeople of St Albans had not so much brought about but personally inflicted on the monastery. So he decided to visit the town in person, accompanied by the whole of his very large force, in order to see that their crimes received just punishment. But the knight Sir Walter Atley, as he came from that district, opposed the king's plan with all his might. He was afraid of damage being done to the whole area if such a large army turned up. So he convinced the king and his council that he would make a good peace between the townsmen and the abbot of the monastery of St Albans, if they should decide to entrust the business to him. They believed his words and gave him the job.[3] His associates were Edward Benstead, Geoffrey Stukley[4] and some others whose names I do not remember.

It was on the Friday, the eve of the feast of the apostles Peter and Paul [i.e. 27 June, the feast being on 28 June] that the townsmen, in order that they should have a share of the troubles which they themselves had cruelly inflicted on others on that day of the week, as I have described earlier, learned that Sir Walter with a band of soldiers would be arriving the next day. In anguish at what they had done with their own hands, and burdened by bad consciences, they began to feel regret and fear, and at this point many of them were just about to run away, if the wicked stubbornness of William Grindcobbe had not prevented it. I have already described his great influence among the townsmen, and he now strengthened traitors in their disloyalty by saying, 'Be sensible! We have resources, and as long as we are not without money, we shall not be without help. We are in alliance with the surrounding towns, who will come to our aid, if we need them. So in the morning let us ride out like men, to meet this knight outside the town, and let us ask him, before he comes near St Albans, whether he is coming as a man of peace. If he is not, we will beat him and drive him from our town.'

This foolish speech pleased its foolish audience, and next morning they rode out of the town just as he had said. To begin with Sir Walter had no idea why they had come out to meet him. But they met him with apparent kindness, exchanged greetings with him, and gave him an honourable escort into the town after their fashion. Sir Walter had with him fifty spearmen and a great number of bowmen gathered from all sides, who perhaps would have led the resistance to Sir Walter if some danger had befallen him, seeing that some of them were from the district and in

---

[1]   Salimbene, *Cronica*, MGHSS xxxii (Hanover, 1905), p. 418.

[2]   The account of Sir Walter Atley's dealings at St Albans are reproduced verbatim in Walsingham's *Gesta abbatum*, ed. Riley, iii. 335–50. Atley held the manor of Albury, and was a man of some influence amongst the Hertfordshire gentry. He represented the county many times in the parliaments of the 1370s and '80s and also sat three times as a knight of the shire of Essex. His concern to circumvent royal justice and to conduct his own inquisition appears to have reflected a general anxiety amongst the county gentry that the repression of the rebels might prove so severe as to be counter-productive. See Saul, *Richard II*, pp. 78–9 and n.

[3]   In fact the king did come to St Albans a fortnight after these events (13–20 July, see below pp. 162–7) to oversee the trial that resulted from these investigations. His presence is corroborated by the Westminster chronicler who makes no mention of Atley (*WC*, p. 15). See also Saul, *Richard II*, pp. 78–9, 469.

[4]   For Benstead and Stukeley see also *Gesta abbatum*, ed. Riley, iii. 335, 513. Benstead was still involved in the affairs of the abbey in 1401.

alliance with the townsmen. Soon after his arrival in the town on the feast of the apostles Peter and Paul [28 June], he got a proclamation made that both all the townsmen, and those who had been summoned to appear before him from the neighbouring towns, should assemble in Derfold field at three o'clock to hear the wishes and commands of the king. They all met at the time and place appointed, and Sir Walter, surrounded by a large force of armed men, went out together with them. He positioned himself in the middle of his armed men at the edge of Derfold wood, arranged all the people standing in front of him like a rainbow and made this speech to them.

The speech of the knight to the townsmen

'Lords and friends assembled here at my summons, I have thought it fitting, before I make any accusations, to explain to you the reason for my coming. You know how seriously the king's majesty has been insulted by disturbers of the peace, so that even now the king is in Essex, exercising with a heavy hand the strictest of justice upon the whole county and its inhabitants, and increasing considerably the weight of their yoke. He heard about the disturbances and damage and crimes that had happened in this town and monastery, and, being the monastery's patron and advocate, he was saddened more than you could believe. In his wish to take vengeance upon the criminals, he decided to come here in person, accompanied by his present army. And if he had come here with the army which he is maintaining in Essex, there is no doubt that all our fruit crops and every blade of corn must have been destroyed. For the army with him is so big that for a radius of five miles around it no hay, no corn, no fruit crops growing or harvested are left untouched, but all are consumed and trampled upon.

'So I felt sorrowful at the losses that my homeland was about to suffer, and out of my sympathy for my neighbours took steps to prevent them, by working hard to weaken the king's determination on this issue and to prevent his arrival. Indeed, because I hoped to do some good to my town at this point, I willingly took upon my own shoulders a heavy burden on behalf of its inhabitants, for in response to my urgent prayers the king, though with some reluctance, entrusted to me the power of bringing justice to this town on his behalf. And as colleagues in this commission he gave me not unknown strangers, but your neighbours and friends. So do the sensible thing, hand over the main troublemakers at once. Make sure you make amends to the abbot. I think you will find him a very reasonable man, well known for his pious and just behaviour. Do this, and you will recover the king's goodwill and bring back peace.'

When he had finished, many applauded and willingly promised to do as he suggested. Sir Walter called up a jury of twelve of the townsmen and charged them, in accordance with their oath, to return the next day and to name those whom they knew to be guilty parties in this affair. Then for that day he sent away the crowd and returned to his lodging.

On the next day, because he had decided to arrest without disturbance the criminals whom he thought would be brought to justice by his jury of twelve, he called the twelve into his room to learn whom they would be indicting. But on their arrival they replied that they could indict no one and wished to accuse no one, as all the rebels were good men and loyal to the king, and none of them had a reputation for being anything else. When he heard this, Sir Walter realised that the twelve were heading in the direction of preferring to stain their consciences with perjury rather than accuse any of their neighbours, and so he kept quiet. He would outwit guile with guile.

He heard Mass, and then advised them to return the charters that they had extorted from the monastery, saying that they would derive no small advantage from such an action. For the time being they promised that they would give them back after three o'clock. But when at this time they returned to the abbot's lodging, where Sir Walter had taken his dinner, they put forward new excuses, indicating that they were unable to return the charters on account of their fear of the people, and especially because they were not sure who was looking after the charters. Not surprisingly Sir Walter was angry, and swore that they should not leave his presence until the charters had been given back. (Because of this those false liars later said that they had been unjustly imprisoned in the abbot's lodging.) But the abbot did not want men, whom he knew had a tendency to tell lies, to have any opportunity or material for falsehoods, and so he interceded for them with Sir Walter, saying that he had such confidence in their probity that there was no need of any other mediator between themselves besides them and him. Sir Walter's fears were allayed by these words and he dismissed the rebels.

The knight's next action was to order the whole crowd to assemble at Barnet Wood. But there he did little or nothing, out of fear of the townsmen who had collected there about three hundred bowmen from the towns roundabout, especially from Barnet and Berkhamsted, all of whom would probably have attacked Sir Walter if he had tried to execute public justice in that place. Indeed Sir Walter's own men might have left him and sided with the rebels. So for the time being he decided to do nothing else openly, except to advise them to make amends to the abbot and return the charters. But in secret he called up the bailiffs and constables and ordered them in the king's name to wait for the dispersal of the crowd that had flocked to St Albans and then to work immediately for the capture of William Grindcobbe, William Cadington and John the Barber (the men who had removed the millstones from the parlour floor, as I have described above) and various others. All these, he said, had been so openly accused of such manifest crimes that there was no alternative for the honour of the town and the safety of the townsmen but to lock them up for the time being. He also told them to bring the rebels, after their arrest, to him at Hertford at nine o'clock the following morning.

He then quickly mounted his horse and hurried to Hertford with all his men. After his departure the bailiffs, though unwillingly, were persuaded to arrest the leaders through the courage and strict sense of duty shown by Richard Perrers, John Chival, Thomas Eydon and William Eccleshall, who were esquires in the abbot's service at that time.[1] That same night the three leaders were arrested and put in the prison at the gate of the monastery.

The arrested men are taken to prison

The next day the leaders were taken to Hertford as the knight had ordered, escorted by the leading citizens and powerful men of the town of St Albans and by all the esquires and servants of the abbot, properly armed. For Sir Walter had instructed them all to come to support him, as he was intending to execute justice according to the laws on that day.

After this exodus, the whole of St Albans began to riot. The air was full of boastful threats, mixed with empty oaths. If any of their neighbours, they cried, happened to get put to death, a hundred people would be killed for this one man. Another consequence was that on the same day groups of townsmen began to gather for meetings and plotting, not in the town but in the fields and woods and other places outside the town. As a result there was a general belief that the rebels would set fire to the abbey on that day, as there was no one there to defend it, or would beset and besiege it like enemies. So the abbot and his monks in their great panic sent for some of the nobles of the district to protect the place, should the need arise. And when the abbot learned where his esquires had gone and that they intended to stay there until the execution of the prisoners, he at once instructed them by letter to set everything else aside and return to him at top speed in order to forestall the new perils that had unexpectedly arisen. When this message arrived, the esquires were actually standing before the judge, accusing the prisoners with great persistence and demanding that sentence be passed on them according to the laws of the land. They had already seen other such prisoners suffer the death penalty, so that they hoped for the same for their enemies.

So when the esquires had looked at the abbot's letter, they were extremely annoyed at being made to return before seeing the business through to the end. If they had stayed, they would certainly have seen the prisoners executed that day. So, when they had informed Sir Walter of their abbot's request, they returned as fast as they could, being ignorant of the reasons for the sudden recall.

After their departure, the townsmen of St Albans who were in Hertford pressed for the pris-

---

[1]   Perrers was sheriff of Hertfordshire. For him and the other three see also *Gesta abbatum*, ed. Riley, ii. 218, 221, 411; iii. 339, 353.

oners to be set free. Although two of them were kept in custody, the third one, William Grindcobbe, was set free for them. Three of his neighbours bailed him out for three hundred pounds, each one individually binding himself for the whole sum, and promised to return him to prison the following Saturday (it was then the Monday in the octave of St John the Baptist [24 June, the octave being from 24 June–1 July]) unless an agreement was made with the abbot by that date. They went back home with him, feeling pleased with themselves for getting their friend released on bail, but with a nagging fear that he might run away. If this were to happen, they realised that they would be put to death themselves. Meanwhile they discussed the freeing of William with their neighbours, pointing out that there were only two possibilities: either they made amends to the abbot by giving back the charters, or William, on his return to prison, would lose his head. And perhaps more of his associates would lose theirs too.

When they entered the room where William was and were delaying their answer, Grindcobbe, his heart long hardened to evil, spoke as follows. 'Fellow citizens, grudging liberty has at long last set you free from the oppression of centuries. Only stand firm, while you have the chance, and do not have any anxiety about my punishment. If it is my lot to die, I shall die in the cause of gaining our liberty and think myself happy to be able to end my life in such martyrdom. Act today, as you would have been forced to act yesterday, if I had been beheaded at Hertford. In fact nothing could have stopped me seeing the end of my life, but for the timely recall of his men by the abbot. Their accusations were numerous and they had a judge who favoured them and who was out to get my blood.'

In short, the townsmen hardened their hearts and swore they would not yet give up the liberties they had recovered. Indeed they considered themselves unlucky and foolish, in that, while supported by such a crowd, they did not bravely cut off the head of the knight who had acted so arrogantly towards their borough and its people and stick it on the pillory to the terror of judges and false justices everywhere. William Grindcobbe, however, did late in the day regret his own folly, when he could not, even when he wanted to, recall his neighbours from their folly, to such a height of arrogance had they been raised.

But when Saturday came, William was taken back to prison by those who had stood bail for him, just so that those rebels who had caused such uproar on a Saturday should have their troubles renewed on a Saturday. In fact he was kept in prison in Hertford until the time when he was brought back to St Albans to undergo his trial on the arrival of the king, as I shall describe later.

Meanwhile throughout all that week up to the Friday the excited townsmen kept up their threats and their plots. But on that day they were sent some very disturbing news by William Grindcobbe of the arrival of the earl of Warwick [Thomas Beauchamp] and Sir Thomas Percy, who had been sent with a thousand armed men to support the abbot and bring the rebels to justice. For William himself had a brother, who had gone to the king's court at Chelmsford to intercede for him. This brother had heard the news there, and had taken the trouble to pass it on to William, who had told his followers.

Then once more the disloyal townsmen, who had been so elated and high handed, were attacked by pangs of sorrow and sadness, and by quakings of dread. They began to renew negotiations for the return of the abbot's charters and for entering upon new agreements to bring about peace. So on the next day, which was the Saturday in the Octave of the apostles Peter and Paul [i.e. 29 June–6 July], they turned up at the hour of compline[1] to hand back both the charters and a book containing the old suits between the abbey and townspeople, which they had stolen on the day of their madness. But the abbot did not consider the hour a suitable one for discussion with them on such a high matter. So he sent to them brother William Killingworth, prior of Wymondham,[2] to accept the book but to put off the acceptance of the charters and the two hundred pounds which they had offered as restitution money until early next morning.

It so happened that the earl of Warwick [Thomas Beauchamp], who had been entrusted with

---

1   The final office of the day before the monastic community retires to bed.
2   Wymondham Priory, Norfolk, was a dependency of St Albans Abbey: *MRH*, p. 81.

upholding the cause of the monastery, was now told by messengers that a serious rebellion had broken out in parts of his own lands. So he had to hurry home with all speed, forgetting all about his responsibilities elsewhere. He sent on some of his knights to make his excuses to the abbot and to encourage him not to lose heart because of the delay in his arrival. Then he departed on his journey. But when next day the townsmen discovered for certain that the earl was not coming, their fears dissolved into laughter and scorn and they said excitedly to each other, 'What were we afraid of? Why were we scared by lying words? Surely we didn't think that an army would be brought here at the prayers of the abbot? What fools we were! We were stupid to believe the news and we acted stupidly. We must never offer money again and never give back the charters. And even if the charters are to be given back, why should we be the first to set a timid example which will be ruinous to others? This disgrace must never befall our name. In the meantime the abbot can salt the meat he has killed so it doesn't go bad. He can sell the ale he has brewed so it doesn't go sour and the loaves he has baked so they don't go hard or mouldy or get nibbled by mice.'

They daily attacked the abbot and the servants of the abbey with such words as these, until some of the abbot's esquires zealously informed the king of all this aggravation. The king was very annoyed too when he heard the story, and swore that he would go to St Albans in person to put a stop to such outrageous behaviour. The townsmen in the meantime, so it seems, had no thoughts at all of restoring peace. When asked why they were not returning the charters, they replied that the delay was because of their fear of the men of Barnet, Watford and the other towns, who had threatened to kill them and burn St Albans, if they took it upon themselves to attempt this first. But, as the event showed, they were telling lies. For the men of Barnet and the other neighbouring towns, before they in their turn humbly handed back the charters, threw themselves on the abbot's mercy and declared that they were ready to fight the men of St Albans in single combats, or ten against ten or all against all, simply because on this matter they had been so mendaciously slandered. But enough of this. I will now return to what I was saying earlier.

While this was happening, the sad news reached St Albans that the king was intending to visit the town and to exercise judgement there in person. This dismayed the abbot, as he feared the destruction of the countryside by the king's vast army. It also dismayed the townspeople, but for a different reason. They were afraid of undergoing the due punishment for their crimes. The abbot had a deep love for his people, and as he wanted in his great kindness to take precautions for others, he sent messages to his friend, Sir Hugh Segrave, the king's steward, in London and to other important friends and acquaintances at court, asking and beseeching them to prevent the king's arrival by any means possible. But neither the monk dispatched on this mission nor the abbot's friends were able to achieve anything at all. So the monk returned, his task unaccomplished, and reported to the abbot that the king was completely unwilling to change his mind and would definitely be arriving within two days.

This news upset the abbot more than you could believe. He was worried not so much for himself as for the poor people of St Albans and the surrounding district, as he knew the king's arrival would cause them the greatest distress.[1] And yet these same people later on asserted in a lying fabrication that the abbot had given the king a thousand pounds to hurry and destroy them. In inventing such lies to slander someone who, whether they liked it or not, was their lord and spiritual father, these true sons of iniquity behaved just like the devil, that father of all lies and acts of ingratitude. They were a crowd of liars, an untrustworthy tribe, a deceitful people, men of fibs and fraud, next-door neighbours who were always jealous and never grateful for kindnesses received.

When it was reported that the king was definitely on his way, the townsmen, thinking that they did not deserve to be heard themselves because of their crimes, paid a large sum to a certain lawyer called Sir William Crozier[2] to plead and intercede for them, in case the abbot might be

---

[1]   This is somewhat disingenuous. There is no doubt that Abbot de la Mare's principal concern was that the involvement of the king threatened a curtailment of the privileges currently enjoyed by the abbot and convent.
[2]   Sir William Croiser had served as a JP in Surrey: *CPR, 1377–81*, pp. 40, 360, 474, 514.

induced to pardon them out of respect for their mediator. And it was not so difficult for Sir William to persuade the abbot to pardon his suppliants, provided that they repaired the damage done to the church during the recent riots. So with Sir William as mediator, the townsmen, in their fear of the king's arrival, agreed with the abbot that after three o'clock on the day of that arrival they would bring back all the stones for hand-mills which they had lifted from the entrance floor of the outer parlour, rebuild at their own expense the house which they had knocked down, with the abbot giving them the timber which remained from that house, and pay to the abbot or his successors two hundred pounds of genuine silver and sound money before the next feast of St Michael [29 September] for the loss, damage and expense which they had caused him. Several of the leading citizens bound themselves, with their seals attached to the document, to pay this sum under pain of a twofold penalty. They further agreed that the abbot would make no complaint to the king about the wrongs they had committed, but would take pains to get pardon and forgiveness for them if the king should happen to bring accusations against them for their actions during the riots. The abbot in his turn promised that he would make no complaint about them, if they kept their side of the bargain. He declared his willingness to intercede for them with the king to the best of his ability and as far as his prayers might be heard, but made it clear in public that he was not willing to promise them a pardon. This could come only from the king's grace, and he did not know if he could command it. The leading citizens and commons alike accepted these words from the abbot's mouth, and asserted that the goodwill of the abbot was enough for them. As for the things which belonged to the king's honour, they would make the best agreement they could about these with the king. So for the time being the meeting broke up and everyone went away.

About the time of vespers the six stolen millstones were brought back and with the help of the townsmen set down at the place from which the others had been removed. In their fear the rebels humbly begged for pardon for the charters and the bonds that they extracted from the monks, and gave back the charters. Several of them bound themselves with oaths to make reparation according to the number of their crimes. And these things happened on the very day on which the king was to arrive.

When vespers was over, the abbot and monks went in solemn procession to the west door of the monastery to meet the king.[1] He was greeted with the full honours of a peal of bells and the chants of reverence that were his due. About a thousand archers and armed men came with the king, among them the knight Sir Robert Tresilian,[2] a justiciar of the greatest experience, and a man of great courage and the wisdom of a serpent. Sitting next day on his seat of justice at the Moot hall, he gave orders for William Grindcobbe, William Cadington and John the Barber to be summoned from Hertford, these being the men who in a frenzied rage had broken up the floor of the parlour, taken away the millstones and smashed them into pieces. So when the prisoners arrived at St Albans, Sir Robert ordered them to be kept in custody until the Monday. On this Monday the jurors, who on the first day of the sessions had been charged with producing the criminal disturbers of the king's peace, were to give their verdict on the case laid before them. The first day of the sessions described above was a Saturday. It was also the first of the days of the Dog star, which were to be an ill-starred period for the people of St Albans.

John Ball, priest[3]

Also on this day Sir Robert sentenced the priest, John Ball, to be drawn, hanged, beheaded, disembowelled and quartered, to use the common expression. He had been taken prisoner at Coventry

---

1   Richard and his retinue arrived at St Albans on 12 July.
2   For Tresilian see p. 154 above.
3   One of the ever-expanding band of unbeneficed clergy, John Ball appears to have begun his career as a chantry priest at York, as attested by the letter that Walsingham transcribes here, and his unorthodox opinions had attracted the attention of the ecclesiastical authorities as early as 1366 when he was prohibited from preaching in Essex. By the beginning of 1381 he had been imprisoned in the gaol at Maidstone from where in early June he was released by the Kentish men on their way to London. His precise movements in the days that

and brought to St Albans the previous day into the presence of the king. Having stated his case and confessed his most shameful crimes, he was found guilty of treason on an enormous scale. His death was put off until the following Monday at the intervention of William [Courtenay], bishop of London, who in concern for the salvation of his soul, had obtained for him this space for repentance. For twenty years and more he had continually preached up and down the land those things which he knew would please the people, attacking both ecclesiastics and secular lords, and seeking to gain the goodwill of the people more than merit in the eyes of God. He even taught the people that tithes should not be paid to a curate, unless the person paying the tithe was richer than the vicar or rector who received it. Also that tithes and offerings should be taken away from a curate, if it was found that his subject or parishioner was a man of better life than his priest. He also taught that no one was fit for the kingdom of God unless he had been born in wedlock. He also taught the perverse doctrines and opinions and crazy heresies of the perfidious John Wyclif, and still more things which it would take too long to enumerate.[1]

Because of all this the bishops, in whose parishes he had dared to say such things, stopped him from preaching in their churches in the future, and so he took his sermons out into the squares and marketplaces and even the fields. He was never short of hearers from among the common people, whom he always took good care should be attracted to his preaching by his attacks on prelates and his pleasing words. In the end, when, even after excommunication, he did not stop preaching, he was put in prison where he prophesied that he would be set free by twenty thousand friends. This afterwards came true during the troubles in the kingdom which I have described, when the commons unbarred all the prisons and forced the prisoners to depart. Freed in this way, John followed along with them, spurring them on to commit further crimes and declaring that they were completely right to do all these things. So that he might infect still more people with the poison of his preaching, at Blackheath, where two hundred thousand of the commons had assembled together, he began a sermon with these words

> When Adam delve, and Eve span,
> Who was then a gentleman?

Proceeding from this beginning and using the words of the saying which he had taken for his text, he tried to introduce and to prove the argument that in the beginning all men had been created equal by nature, and that servitude had been brought in by the unjust oppression of wicked men contrary to the will of God. Further, that if God had wanted to create slaves, he would have established right at the beginning of the world who was to be a master, and who a slave. And so they should realise that a time had now been given to them by God, in which they could, if they wished, put off the yoke of long endured slavery and enjoy the liberty which they had long desired. His advice therefore was that they should behave sensibly, and, showing the love of a good father for his family, who in tilling his fields roots out or cuts back the harmful weeds which can damage his crops, they themselves likewise at the present time should hurry to do the same thing, first by killing the senior lords of the kingdom, secondly by murdering the lawyers, justiciars and jurors of the land, and finally by uprooting from the soil of England all those whom they knew would do harm to the commons in the future. Thus in the end they would secure peace for themselves and security for the future, if, having done away with the important people, there was equal freedom and the same nobility for all of them, together with honours and powers in which all shared alike.

Having heard this sermon and several other similar ravings, the common people supported him with such enthusiasm that they shouted out that he should be archbishop and the chancellor

followed are uncertain but both the letter and Walsingham's account would suggest he remained in the vanguard of the rebellion until the death of Tyler when he appears to have fled into the Midlands. Writing from Leicester, Knighton also reports that Ball was taken at Coventry: *Knighton*, pp. 240–1. For discussion of Ball's biography see also Aston, 'Corpus Christi and Corpus Regni', 22–3; B. Bird and D. Stephenson, 'Who was John Ball?', *Essex Archaeology and History*, Third Series, 8 (1976), 287–8.
1   Walsingham, was not alone in regarding Ball as an early disciple of, and proselytiser for, Wyclif. Knighton cast him as a John the Baptist figure to Wyclif's diabolical messiah: *Knighton*, pp. 276–7.

of the kingdom; he was the only man worthy of the position of archbishop, for the archbishop, who was then still alive, had been a traitor to the commons and the kingdom and should be executed, wherever in England he could be found.

John Ball had also sent to the rebel leaders in Essex a letter, full of riddles, to encourage them to carry through what they had begun. The letter was later found in the sleeve of a man being hanged for his share in the revolt. It went as follows.

The letter sent by John Ball to the Essex commons[1]

John Schep, once priest of St Mary's in York and now in Colchester, sends greetings to John Nameless, John Miller and John Carter, and tells them to beware of the guile in the borough, and to stand together in God's name. He urges Piers Plowman to go to his work and to chastise well Hobb the robber, and to take with them John Trueman and all his fellows and no more.

> John the Miller hath ground small, small, small.
> The king's son of heaven shall pay for all.
> Beware or there be woe.
> Know your friend from your foe.
> Have enough and then say 'Ho!'
> And do well and better and flee sin,
> And seek peace and hold therein.
> And so bid John Trueman and all his fellows.[2]

John Ball confessed that he had written this letter and sent it to the people of Essex. And for this and many other crimes which he had committed and confessed, as I have said, he was drawn, hung and beheaded at St Albans on 15 July in the presence of the king. His body was cut in four and sent to four cities of the kingdom.

The assizes convened at St Albans

On 15 July the justiciar, Robert Tresilian, convened at St Albans the jury that he had charged three days previously with indicting and producing the malefactors and disturbers of the king's peace. The jurors from the town assembled, and said that they knew no such disturber, nor could they justly indict anybody, since they were all loyal subjects of the king and always had been. As the justiciar was a man of intelligence and deep insight, he could see where this response was tending, and so told them to come back again with their minds focused on the message given them from the king when they had come to meet him as suppliants and had asked for his pity and pardon. For it had told them that they would receive mercy and forgiveness, if they handed over the instigators and authors of the revolt in the land. Otherwise, according to the words of the king, he predicted that they would undergo the same punishment as would be given to the malefactors, if they were caught.

So the jurors returned and the justiciar at once followed them to the place where they were about to discuss the matter, and, taking from his sleeve a roll containing the names and crimes of most of the rebels, said to them, 'In here are the crimes of your fellows, witnessed to by good men and true. Almost everybody knows about them. So do you think you can pull the wool over our eyes by your silence? What you are thinking of will never happen, since we have to hand the names and deeds of the criminals, whom you wish to display to us as just. So take the sensible course! Think about saving your own lives! While you are making these completely futile efforts for your fellows, you may be stirring up danger for yourselves.'

---

1   A number of letters attributed to the ringleaders of the revolt circulated during these days and, in various forms, fell into the hands of the chroniclers. Those attributed to Ball were also noticed by Henry Knighton (*Knighton*, pp. 222–5) who also transcribed three others under the names of 'Jack Miller', 'Jack Carter', and 'Jack Trueman'; Walsingham also appears to have been aware of these since the order to 'chastise Hobb the Robber' is a reference to one of them. See also R. F. Green, 'John Ball's Letters: Literary History and Historical Literature', *Chaucer's England: Literature in Context*, ed. B. Hanawalt (Minneapolis, 1992), pp. 176–200; S. Justice, *Writing and Rebellion: England in 1381* (Berkeley and London, 1994).
2   Walsingham transcribes the text in its original Middle English.

The townsmen were struck with panic and thought it safer to indict their neighbours as guilty than to heap up on their own heads the evils pointed out by Sir Robert. They informed against very many of the rebels, from the surrounding district as well as from the town.

Then the justiciar summoned separately a second jury, showed them the names and the indictments written down against these persons by the first jury, and asked them what they would have wanted to say about these people, if they had been charged with this duty. The men of the second jury, seeing that everything written down by the first jury was true, replied that they would have acted in the same way, if they had been given the responsibility. So Sir Robert kept on this jury so that they could give their verdict on the accused. In giving it, it would be impossible for them to say anything different from what they had said when questioned by the justiciar; they would either have to condemn, whether they wanted to or not, men whom they had previously admitted they were willing to indict for the crimes at issue, or blush for shame at being shown to be liars. By this trick the justiciar lured them into telling the truth, although they would have preferred to lie. None the less he charged yet a third jury to give its verdict on the matter. When it saw the statements of the first jury, it too made the same statements as the first jury had given in writing. And so there was no one who was not condemned by the mouths of thirty-six men. But, as I have said, the second jury was permanently kept on to give the verdict, after the first and third juries had made their indictments.

The execution of the malefactors

Then William Grindcobbe, William Cadington, John the Barber and some other ringleaders were condemned to death for disturbing the king's peace. They were drawn and hanged, some fifteen of them in all. Of the leading citizens of St Albans, Richard Wallingford, John Garleck, William Berewick and Thomas Putor were put in prison when their neighbours informed against them in the king's court, as were several other less important people. Also about eighty people from the surrounding area were sent to prison, but were later pardoned by the king and set free.[1]

The abbot and monks of St Albans are accused of causing the commotion and disturbance

Meanwhile the townsmen, just so that nobody at all should be unaware of their wickedness, of their own accord and without being charged, ordered or compelled to do so, accused the abbot and his monks of being responsible for the initial disturbance. They thought up this trick and told such lies, even though the abbot had more than once interceded for them with the king and made appeals for their life and safety, and on this account had frequently gone in fear of the king's anger, since a proclamation had been made that nobody was allowed to pour forth prayers for another. The townsmen's argument was that the abbot had ordered and compelled them to go and join the crowd that had gathered at London, at a time when they themselves had given little or no thought to such matters. So they claimed that it was the abbot and his monks and servants who had been the initial originators and authors of the first disturbance which later happened in the town, and also that it was he who had sent them to help the enemies of the king and his kingdom.

When the justiciar saw and heard this, he was completely appalled at the enormity of the wickedness of the townsmen, which they made no attempt to conceal, and he cursed them, saying, 'You perfidious people, you must speak out what you believe in your hearts. Did the abbot do this as a traitor to his king and kingdom, or for the better reason of forestalling danger and avoiding the losses for you and for him which the arrival of a rampaging army would bring? You must say if the abbot desired ruin for himself and for you. Was it his intention that you should return with all these forces and inflict ruin upon him and your neighbours? You must swear it on your oath, whether the abbot was responsible for these evils which we have just enumerated.'

---

[1] The handful of executions and larger number of more lenient punishments is consistent with the response to the rebellion throughout the south-eastern counties and may be indicative of the distaste amongst the county gentry – such as Sir Walter Atley – for a policy of severe repression.

The rebels were confounded by their own cunning and for some time they stayed silent, not knowing what answer to make. So the justiciar pressed them more urgently to say what they thought. In the end, overcome by shame and forced to speak the truth, they asserted that the abbot was completely loyal to both king and kingdom and that in all his actions his intention had been for the better. Then, in the presence of many, the justiciar cursed their disloyalty and rebuked them most severely. He gave orders that they should immediately tear up and destroy the accusation with their own hands. This the townsmen did, although with a bad grace.

Seeing that these wicked desires of theirs had come to naught, they cast about for other schemes by which they could cause the abbot trouble. They had been generously entertaining knights and esquires of the king's household as their guests. By means of fictitious accusations they now compelled these courtiers to believe that the abbot was a hypocrite, who with his usual specious sanctity outside the monastery was deceiving and deluding many of the lords and magnates of the land. Being thus bolstered by their support, he now had no fears about playing the unchecked tyrant and oppressing his subjects unjustly. They also claimed that the abbot by underhand tricks had wickedly seized the ancestral rights and liberties of the townsmen of St Albans and had destroyed and suppressed their freedom to such an extent that no one was allowed to set up a hand-mill in his own house, but that all of them, just like bondsmen, were compelled to grind their corn at the abbot's mills. They also said that he had bribed the king with a huge sum of gold to come to St Albans and, as actually happened, order the hanging of their fellow citizens.

And when the townsmen ran out of words, they persuaded the courtiers with gifts, to induce them in some way or other to speak ill of the abbot, that is if they were short of actual crimes to lay at his door. And where the husbands could do nothing, their wives took a hand in the persuasion, getting on very close terms with the courtiers, while they were staying with them. The result was that the smears against the abbot were so widespread that almost all the friends of the monastery were dismayed, even though there was a public proclamation that those men who presumed to make a false accusation against the abbot would be hanged and their wives burned to death. And this was the return that the townsmen made to the abbot, hastening to give back evil for good and hate for love and abusing him instead of showing him affection.

When the king had now been at St Albans for eight days,[1] his council which was with him could realise and see that the hearts of the bondsmen and the servants of the monastery would not be true to their masters, that is the abbot and his monks, in the future, unless careful precautions were taken. So on the king's order they decided to pass a measure, signed with the great seal of the king, as a remedy against future troubles of this king. The fact that the king's chancery was then meeting in the chapter house made it easier for the abbot to get what he wanted.

A commission of enquiry, so that all tenants at St Albans should render their customary services to the abbot

'Richard, by the grace of God, king of England and France and lord of Ireland, sends greetings to his beloved John Lodewyk, John West Wycombe, John Kenting, Richard Perrers, Walter Graunford, Richard Giffard, Thomas Eydon, and William Eccleshall. We strictly order and command each and every one of you, that, immediately you have read this letter, without making any excuses, you should have it publicly proclaimed on our behalf wherever you think it expedient and necessary in all the towns and places in the counties of Hertfordshire and Buckinghamshire, both those inside and outside the liberties, that each and every one of the tenants of our beloved in Christ, the abbot of St Albans, free men as well as bondsmen, should without any arguments or mutterings and without making any kind of resistance or difficulty carry out the customary works and tasks of bondage, which they themselves owe to the abbot and which of old they were accustomed to do before the recent outbreak of troubles in the different

---

1   This would date the king's commission to 20 July but the date clause of the document as Walsingham transcribes it is in fact 15 July.

counties of our kingdom of England. Further you should on our behalf give strict orders that the same tenants or bondsmen or any others should not during these rebellious times withdraw more than usual from doing the customary works and tasks of bondage mentioned above. Nor should they make any excuses to the abbot for delaying to do them, nor are they to demand, claim or clamour for any freedoms or privileges other than those they possessed before the present troubles, under the loyalty and allegiance which they owe to us, and under pain of forfeit of all things which can be forfeited by them to us in the future. And all those, whom you find disobedient and rebellious after this proclamation with its injunctions, you are to arrest and capture and lodge in our prisons, to stay there until we have thought what further orders we should give for their punishment. As you love us and our honour and the well-being of the laws of our kingdom, make sure you carry out our commands to the letter. Witnessed by me, in the town of St Albans, on the fifteenth day of July, in the fifth year of our reign.'

The men of the county of Hertford do fealty to the king

After lunch on the day of St Margaret the Virgin [20 July] the king, who was about to move on to Berkhamsted castle, in the great court of St Albans abbey received an oath of loyalty from all the men of the county of Hertfordshire between the ages of fifteen and sixty, who had been summoned to appear before him. They all at the same time pledged their allegiance, and swore that they would be faithful to their king in the future, never again rebelling to disturb the peace of the land, but dying rather than following disturbers of the kingdom. They would do their best to arrest such disturbers of the peace and take them to prison, while loyally carrying out their customary tasks and services. And if any of their own number were instigators and leaders of rebellion, they would straightaway arrest them and take them before the king.

After taking this oath, they were sent away to their homes, and the king hurried off to Berkhamsted. He stayed there a few days and then moved on to the town of Easthamsted to hunt. While there he was told that the bodies of the rebels hanged at St Albans had been taken down and carried far away from the gallows. The king was very surprised at this piece of effrontery and extremely upset by the insult aimed at him by this action, and at once sent a writ to the bailiffs of St Albans, which went as follows.

The bodies of the traitors, at the order of the king, are suspended from the gallows by means of iron chains

'Richard, by the grace of God, king of England and France and lord of Ireland, sends greetings to the bailiffs of the town of St Albans. It had been adjudged that the bodies of various traitors and criminals, for their crimes committed during the present troubles against us and their allegiance to us, should be hanged and that they should stay hanging as long as their bodies should last. And now we have been infallibly informed that certain malefactors, casting away their fear of our royal majesty, after the traitors and criminals had been hung according to the judgement, have taken down and carried away the bodies from the gallows where they were hanging, in contempt and disdain of us and contrary to the judgement. We are extremely upset and justly annoyed. So we strictly order and command you, under the loyalty and allegiance to us by which you are bound that, as soon as you have read this charge, you are to get iron chains made and the bodies of the victims, wherever found, brought back to the same gallows, and there hung by means of these same chains for as long as they shall last. They are to hang there, according to the terms of the previous judgement. You are to carry this out in every detail, under pain of forfeit of all things that you can forfeit to us. Witnessed by me at Easthamsted, on the third day of August, in the fifth year of our reign.'

The townsmen, compelled by the king's command, hang their citizens for a second time

This proclamation made the people of St Albans, who had been in revolt for a long time in their struggle for liberty, the slaves of a detestable and loathsome servitude. And as they had no one willing to carry out the task for them, they were compelled to re-hang their fellow citizens in iron chains with their own hands. The corpses were now oozing with pus and pullulating with worms and their decaying, fetid flesh gave forth a most noisome stench. That men who had unjustly usurped the name of citizen should be given this task and duty had a certain justice about it, for they could be called, as in fact they were, hangmen, incurring by this action everlasting disgrace. It was no accident that men who preferred to hold back the truth and perjure themselves rather than betray their fellow traitors should be compelled to hang up those same traitors. Even their dogs gained what their masters did not deserve. For the dogs were given freedom when their masters removed the chains by which they had been tied up, while the chains themselves were then used for hanging men, with the masters of these very dogs performing the hanging and by this action, as I have said, remaining in the most abject slavery. And it was of course right that perjurers and slanderers hated by God should be shown by the judgement of God to be worse than their dogs, seeing that their dogs were set free, while their masters themselves were still bound to perform the tasks of the most demeaning servitude. These things indeed took place at St Albans around the time of the feast of the finding of the bones of Alban the martyr, a fact that showed that he had been offended by the sins of the rebels, who had fallen headlong into manifold misfortunes in consequence.

A truce for two years between the English and the Scots

John [of Gaunt], duke of Lancaster, had gone to northern parts a little before the time of the disturbances I have described to keep the annual March Day between the English and the Scots according to custom. When he heard about the peasants' revolt and what country riff-raff had done to their lords and other men of the same class during the period of superiority granted to them, he was greatly alarmed. And thinking ahead for the future, he judged it useful to make a speedy peace with the Scottish people, for once such tearful news reached their ears, it would not only bring them unhoped-for jubilation but also make them bold enough to refuse peace conditions and invade our land.[1]

And by God's will it happened that a truce was concluded as a result of the pressure applied by the duke before the Scots learned of the revolt. In the truce the Scots were given back certain tracts of land which they had not enjoyed for several years previously, but the exceptional nature of the concession was excused by the exceptional nature of the recent revolt, which had been able to cause justified terror and alarm in even the stoutest breast. So the Scots confirmed with an oath that they would faithfully keep a truce for two years. The details were put down on paper and the Scots ratified them under the signatures of the amanuenses. But when they heard from their spies how, during the disturbances I have described, the rebels had lorded it over the king, seized the Tower of London and beheaded the chancellor and treasurer of the land, together with the other various happenings of those days, they then at first began to feel aggrieved that they had so quickly agreed to peace terms, and wished that they had joined in these mighty disturbances and filled the land with slaughter and pillage.

But because it seemed to them shameful to be marked down as perjurers so speedily, they began to reassure the duke and to urge him to accept the free gift of twenty thousand Scottish warriors, so that with their help and assistance he might hurry to England to exact vengeance on the commons for the injuries done to the lords of England and receive compensation for the dishonourable losses inflicted so shamefully on him personally.[2] But the duke flatly refused their

---

1   Gaunt had been dispatched north in May under commission from the king's council to negotiate a new peace with the Scots. The March Day began on 11 June but in any event the threat to his property and person posed by the peasants' revolt persuaded him to remain in the border country for his own safety. He was escorted across the border by William, earl of Douglas, and Archibald Douglas, lord of Galloway, and lodged at Holyrood where he was supported with provisions and 'royal gifts': *Scotichronicon*, vii. 391.

2   Walsingham is suspicious of the motives of the Scots, but their offer to support Gaunt in the suppression of the rebels – which he reports alone amongst the authorities – is a reflection of their regard for Gaunt following the conclusion of a favourable treaty. This is confirmed by the generosity they showed to the duke during his subsequent sojourn in Scotland.

offer. He said that if they were to try this, they would certainly find a bitter enough war waiting for them before they got as far as York, even if they took with them the flower of the Scottish nation. He said he knew of the numbers, bravery, and indeed the bravado of the English, who feared nothing less than war. The Scots, he declared, would soon become a laughing stock to such men, even if their numbers were twice as great.

On the other hand the duke saw the uncertain loyalty of many whom he had thought to have found loyal, for example [Henry Percy] the [first] earl of Northumberland and many other knights who had command of castles in those parts, and indeed the knights who ate at his table, not to mention almost his whole household. Faced with the terror caused by the revolt, they had wasted away to such an extent that barely any were still at his side, for they had heard that the king, in his fear, had given the body of their lord, the duke, to the commons when they asked for it. And so the duke asked the Scots, if they loved him as they claimed, to give him a safe conduct into their lands and to allow him to stay with them as long as he liked, on the understanding that he could send to England whichever of his own men he liked and receive them or any others who came to him peacefully from England, and even to allow himself the freedom to return to England, whenever he wanted to do so. The Scots generously granted all his requests. They welcomed him with full honours when he arrived, and gave him hospitality for a long time.[1]

Dispute between the duke of Lancaster and the earl of Northumberland

From such beginnings a serious quarrel arose between the duke and the earl of Northumberland [Henry Percy], which alarmed the whole of England, as I shall describe later. For when the earl heard of this horrifying and unbelievable reconciliation [with the Scots], he was either afraid to obey the duke openly or, as some say, he despised him. As his fellow Northumbrians followed his example, the duke was very frightened, though he later put down this behaviour to the ingratitude of the earl as well as his disobedience. And since it is written [Isaiah 28: 19] 'Only troubles give understanding to the hearing', it was then that the duke himself first turned to religion and in private and public confessions began to find fault with his former life and to look for the causes of the troubles which had befallen him in his own sins. At one moment he would blame himself for the deaths both of the nobles and of the other men who had been laid low by impious hands at that time, and at another shuddered at his relationship with that Katherine Swynford, or rather renounced it.[1] His tears and sobs seemed to show him producing the fruits that belonged to such repentance. Anyway it is believed that by these lies he soothed the Lord's anger.

And now that peace had returned to that part of the world and the rebels had either been put down or gone into hiding, the duke began to think of returning to London. But in order to show the king and the kingdom before his actual return that he had humbled himself completely, he sent messengers to inform the king of his flight and the reasons for it, though he personally preferred to call it 'his move to Scotland'. His messengers were also to say that, if it was an agreeable offer and required by the situation, he was willing to return to crush the rebels with a vast army of Scots or, if this was displeasing, with the men of his own household who now, as peace

---

[1] Both the *Anonimalle* author (*AC*, pp. 152–3) and Knighton (*Knighton*, pp. 231–7) provide some of the details that are missing here: when news of the of the unrest reached him, Gaunt sought admission to Northumberland's castle at Bamburgh but he was turned away before he reached it by the earl's envoy – named by the *Anonimalle* author as Sir John Hotham – who declared that the earl would not receive the duke 'until he knew whether or not he had the king's good will' (*Knighton*, p. 235). Gaunt was forced into the humiliation of seeking a safe-conduct from the Scots. He crossed the border on 22 June and at Edinburgh received the hospitality of the earls of Douglas and Dunbar. According to Knighton, the duchess of Lancaster suffered similar treatment as she travelled north to escape the rebellion, being refused entry to Pontefract castle (*Knighton*, pp. 230–1).

[2] Katherine Swynford, daughter of the Hainaulter Sir Payn de Roet and wife of Sir Hugh Swynford had been Gaunt's mistress since the early 1370s. Knighton also suggests that Gaunt's enforced exile projected him into a period of soul-searching and that in particular he was moved to renounce his relationship with Katherine: *Knighton*, pp. 237–8. See also Goodman, *John of Gaunt*, pp. 362–4.

dawned, had emerged from their hiding places and were reassembling around him and who were strong enough to deal with all the peasants of the area.

But if his arrival was not welcome even on these terms, or if his return at the head of a crowd of followers made him suspect to the king or his council, the king with the help of his council should decide the identities and numbers of those people that would meet with approval. He personally was ready to come to the king, having dismissed the others, even if the king should decide that he could only have three people with him, a knight, an esquire and a valet. If not even these terms were pleasing to the king, and he himself was so hated by the nobles and the commons that they thought his return would throw the kingdom into confusion or weaken the peace that existed, he was ready, should the king order it, to leave the land as an exile and not to see England again until the king had made the peace and his kingdom secure.

But the king and his nobles had pity on him in his affliction and sent back word that he should dismiss the Scottish nation but return confidently with all his own household. If these numbers were inadequate, he should enrol a certain number of men from each town he passed though to escort him safely to the next town, until finally he came to the king. And it happened just as the king had instructed. The duke came to the king, his master, and received an honourable welcome.[1]

After a few days the duke lodged a complaint against the earl of Northumberland, accusing him of having been at the time of the widespread revolt, as I described above, not only disobedient but also disloyal and ungrateful. The earl was summoned to Berkhamsted to answer this, where almost all the earls of the whole land had gathered together to take part in a council.[2] Here the duke accused him on still more counts, and the earl with the characteristic impatience of his people, ignored the king's prohibition and began to hurl insulting remarks at the duke, though the duke, when ordered to be quiet, very humbly fell silent at the first word of the command. As a result of his disobedience the earl was at once arrested on the charge of having done damage to the king's majesty, but the earls of Warwick [Thomas Beauchamp] and Suffolk [William Ufford] stood bail for him, on condition that he should come to the next parliament and show himself there. He was then dismissed and the council broke up.

A parliament at London

At the time of the feast of All Saints [1 November], the barons and commons of the kingdom assembled for a parliament in London.[3] The duke came to this parliament with such a large following of armed men that it was not easy to count them. The earl also gathered together no less a crowd from northern parts, and came all the way to London.[4] The duke, however, because he was not sure of the loyalty of the people of London towards him owing to their long lasting hatred of him, did not think it safe to lodge in London. But the earl with his men came to the city in great confidence. He was at once warmly welcomed by the citizens who came out on their horses to meet him. They had sent him precious gifts in advance, and now both offered hospitality for his people and provided pastures, which they owned all round the city, for the herds which he had brought with him to supply the needs of such a vast entourage. They also promised their faithful help, if he should need it, so that the earl's strength then greatly increased through the support of so many Londoners, and his party now seemed to be much stronger than the party of the duke.[5]

---

1   Knighton's account of Gaunt's return is different in some particulars. He suggests that the king and Gaunt's brothers tempted him out of his temporary exile with 'letter upon letter' of reassurance, and the king also ordered Northumberland to offer assistance to him on the journey south (*Knighton*, pp. 236–7). See also Goodman, *John of Gaunt*, pp. 87–9.

2   The Council was summoned on 26 July to convene on 4 August: *WC*, pp. 18–19 and n.

3   As the Westminster chronicler recorded, parliament opened on Monday 4 November: *WC*, p. 21; *RP*, iii. 98.

4   The Westminster chronicler reports that Gaunt came to parliament with a force of 500 and that the city authorities placed armed guards on their gates to prevent any further members of his retinue from entering the city: *WC*, pp. 20–1.

5   The Westminster chronicler, who was well placed to observe such dynamics, does not mention the partisanship of the city; doubtless Walsingham was expressing his own preference here as much as any other's.

Meanwhile there was the pitiful spectacle for men's eyes of a kingdom, which once had enjoyed a deeper peace than that of any kingdom, now in turn being tossed on all sides by the waves of faction, by the revolt of the people on this side, and on that side by warring factions among the nobles. Indeed armed men from the two parties of the duke and the earl for several days assembled at Westminster contrary to the customs of the land, providing in their own persons an unprecedented sight for the inhabitants, but by these actions arousing great dread in the hearts of the wiser sort. During all this time the disturbers of the peace were hoping that a fire would be lit which would blaze abroad through the city, and that the passions of the nobles would pass freely into actions. The fickle crowd did not care which of the two nobles it followed to battle, provided that, as with the previous peasants' revolt, it could give them the opportunity of unrestrained roaming around and material for avenging the beheadings, drawings and hangings of their confederates as traitors carried out by the king and his loyalists.

But all the clergy and the majority of the people, whose hearts had been touched by God, were in the meantime deeply afraid and apprehensive on account of the evils from this quarrel which would swamp the whole British world, if the nobles were preparing to express openly the hatred for each other which they had in their hearts. So priests in their public and private prayers asked that God, whose nature is goodness, should allow the breeze of peace to blow between the parties. At last, when for a long time the parliament had been postponed with nothing achieved on account of this quarrel, at the intervention of the nobles of the land the king took the matter of their mutual complaints into his own hands, to prevent all the business of the kingdom suffering not only hindrance but also irreparable damage from this quarrel of two nobles. So in this way, through a merciful God, the hearts of the faithful were set free from fear.

Parliament is dissolved. The sister of the king of Bohemia is welcomed with all honours

This parliament then proceeded to deal with matters concerning the kingdom and the king. But it stayed in the same place for a long time without achieving anything. None of its discussions resulted in actions, even though the long stay was extremely expensive.[1] And just when it was thought some action would have resulted, news came of the arrival at Calais of the new queen [Anna], the sister of Wenceslas [Wenzel IV, b. 1361, emperor from 1378–1400, king, 1378–1419], king of Bohemia, son of the *quondam* king of Bohemia and emperor [Charles IV, b. 1316, emperor from 1355–78], who himself also expected to be crowned emperor and named himself as emperor in all his letters.

The king had chosen this woman to be his wife and had bought her at great expense and after much negotiation, even though the daughter of Barnabò [Visconti], duke of Milan, had been offered to him together with an enormous sum of gold.[2] So, as I have said, when news was brought of the arrival of the future queen, parliament was dissolved, to be resumed after the royal wedding and the feast of Christmas. And also every single man strove with all his might to do honour to such an important wedding with suitable gifts and with services which would win him the king's favour. So the king sent men to meet so important a maid and she was brought with all the glory of the world right across to the port of Dover, escorted by many nobles both of her own country and from this land of England.[3]

And on that day there occurred an omen that all thought miraculous and which, in the opinion of many people, showed the favour of God and presaged future happiness for the land. For just when the princess, disembarking from the ship, had set foot on the ground and every-

---

[1]   The main business of this parliament was to consider the crown's request for a subsidy. It was adjourned on 13 December to allow for the preparations for the king's marriage.
[2]   The sums involved in the transaction were indeed great. The king had agreed to pay £4,500 for Anne and to make a loan of 80,000 florins (£12,000) to Wenzel (reported by Knighton as £10,000: *Knighton*, pp. 240–3); the greater part of both sums had been paid by the close of January 1382. The Westminster chronicler was outraged that such large sums had been used to purchase 'this tiny scrap of humanity' (*WC*, pp. 24–5).
[3]   Anna embarked from Calais on 18 December and was met at Dover by John of Gaunt who escorted her to Leeds castle where she observed the Christmas festivities.

body else had safely left the ship, there suddenly followed a disturbance of the sea greater than any that had been seen for a long time, and which so tossed about even the ships which were anchored in the harbour that they were suddenly driven into collision with each other, and the ship, in which a moment ago the princess had been sitting, came apart and was dreadfully smashed into many pieces.[1]

Some people interpreted the incident differently, and thought it was a forecast of the princess bringing trouble to the land or of some other disaster happening to it. Subsequent events will show why it was a dark, perplexing omen of doubtful meaning.

[1382]

The duke of Brittany dismisses the English after being threatened by the Bretons[2]

Round about this time in 1382, the fifth year of the reign of King Richard II, the Bretons of Brittany, who were angry that the English were treated with such honour by their lord, [John IV] the duke of Brittany, revolted and gathered together against their lord, arrogantly ordering him to dismiss all the English from his employ and to enjoy the services of just themselves, his Bretons; otherwise all the Bretons would kill the English and also stop serving the duke. The duke found himself in a tight spot, and, calling together the English in his household, gave them the sad news of the danger threatening them and commanded all of them, though reluctantly, to leave his land with all possible speed. The English were worried and frightened at the news and in the greatest hurry made preparations to leave in one piece, before possibly some worse things could happen to them owing to the wickedness of the Bretons.

The Lord [Olivier] de Clisson heard of the sudden withdrawal of the English. He himself had been reconciled with the duke, and when he learned from his careful enquiries the reason for the departure of the English, he was extremely angry with those responsible for it. He summoned both the knights and the esquires and also the others whom he knew had been at fault in this matter and asked them on whose authority they had presumed to act in such a way as to send away from the duke, their master, men who were absolutely faithful to their lord and who more than other nations knew how to properly serve and please their masters, by showing him all reverence and providing for his good. 'None of you,' he said, 'knows how to treat his master with such honour as the English do or to love him with such affection or to venerate him with such respect and civility, and yet you, being full of envy, have got them dismissed, a shameful happening to spite your lord. So you must allow those whom you have sent away to your master's distress to return to comfort him, and permit them to serve him in peace. Or, as God is my witness, we will get the most arrogant of you hung and strangled.' After saying this, he sent envoys to recall the household that had been dismissed, so that they might enjoy again the duties that they had performed before. But it was in vain, for by now most of them had sailed across the channel to England and only a few were left, who had remained behind there after their comrades through lack of a ship or a wind. These were recalled and restored again to the court of the duke, their master.

The royal marriage

After the feast of Epiphany [6 January] all the nobles of the kingdom came to London to attend the marriage of the king and to pay their respects, just as had always been done by all noblemen from of old. The emperor's daughter [Anna of Bohemia] was blessed at Westminster as bride of the king, and crowned queen by the archbishop of Canterbury with glory and honour.[3]

---

1 This story is not reported by the other authorities. The Westminster chronicler was more sanguine, repeating the couplet current in the capital: 'worthy to enjoy manna, to Englishmen is given the noble Anna': *WC*, p. 25.

2 Walsingham is the only English authority to report this purge of Breton administration and supporting evidence is scant even amongst the Breton sources. True or not, it does underline the shift in both Breton attitudes and ducal policy in 1382. See also Jones, *Ducal Brittany*, p. 96 and n.

3 In fact the marriage took place a fortnight after Epiphany on 20 January; the new queen was crowned two days later on St Vincent's Day. The Westminster chronicler observes that Archbishop Courtenay conducted

To add to the magnificence of these great celebrations, tournaments were also held for several days, in which the English publicly demonstrated their manliness and the countrymen of the queen their competence, acquiring in the process, though not without injuries to persons on both sides, praise and knightly approval for their deeds.

The parliament recently dissolved resumes

Once the marriage celebrations had been completed, the parliament, which I have said was dissolved for the reasons given, was resumed. Several motions were put forward and passed, for example that allowing foreigners to sell their goods freely in their own person without hindrance from English merchants; that forbidding the use of fur and gold ornament on belts etc. by commoners of the lower class; that about fixing a price on wine so that a jar did not cost more than six marks. And there were many other items which were passed in this same parliament. But what good is achieved by statutes of parliament when subsequently they are not put into effect in any way? For the king with his privy council was accustomed to change or annul all the measures passed in parliaments held previously, even though they had been passed not only by the whole commons of the land but also by the nobles themselves.

There was also passed in this parliament a statute to deal with future revolts by the common people. It said that wherever loyal subjects saw peasants or commoners in groups of six or seven hatching suspicious plots, they had the power to seize them and keep them in custody without waiting for help from anywhere else, that is from a royal writ.

The sudden death of the earl of Suffolk

William Ufford, earl of Suffolk, had been chosen by the knights of the counties to speak on matters of state on their behalf, and in this present parliament, on the day and hour when he had performed this duty which he had undertaken, and had begun to ascend the steps leading to the room to which all the nobility of the kingdom had withdrawn, he suddenly collapsed and there and then breathed his last in the arms of his fellows, although it was only a little previously, indeed a moment ago, that he had entered the court at Westminster in merry mood and not feeling at all ill. It was not only all the nobles of the kingdom but also the middle classes and even the poor who felt great consternation at his sudden death, because throughout his life he had shown himself a loveable person to all men.[1]

After his death the parliament was brought to an end, though not before the merchants of England, in order to help the king, had again granted him for the four years following the custom duties on wool, commonly called the 'maltote'. And also in this parliament, at the request of the nobles and commons, the knight Richard Scrope was appointed chancellor, as being a man of notable learning and impartial regard for justice, who had no equal in the kingdom for wealth. The knight Sir Hugh Segrave was appointed treasurer in his place.[2]

About the same time the earl of March, Lord Edmund Mortimer, died in Ireland. He had brought almost the whole of that land to a state of peace and had governed it nobly and wisely.[3]

---

this ceremony before he had received the papal pallium (*WC*, pp. 24–25); his right to play any part in both marriage and coronation had been disputed by Bishop Robert Braybroke of London, who had been closely involved in the marriage negotiations and now claimed the right to preside over both ceremonies. In the event Braybroke officiated at the marriage but gave way to Courtenay for the coronation: Saul, *Richard II*, p. 89.

[1]   According to the Westminster chronicler, Ufford collapsed in the doorway of St Stephen's chapel: *WC*, pp. 22–3. For his involvement in the peasants' revolt see above, p. 145.

[2]   Scrope was a veteran of royal administration and had emerged as a favourite of the commons in the Good Parliament of 1376. See above p. 96: Saul, *Richard II*, p. 81. Segrave had served as acting chancellor at the height of the peasants' revolt. See above, p. 141 and n.

[3]   Edmund Mortimer, 3rd earl of March, had been a royal councillor in the early years of Richard's reign. He had title to the earldom of Ulster and other lands in Ireland. He had served as lieutenant in Ireland in 1373 and had been reappointed in 1378. He died in December from pneumonia contracted after crossing a river in County Cork. See also A. Tuck, *Richard II and the English Nobility* (London, 1973), pp. 21–3.

During these days Master William Courtenay, bishop of London, was elevated to the archbishopric of Canterbury, and Master Robert Braybroke was made bishop of London.[1]

Charles is crowned king of Naples by the pope[2]

About this time Charles [III of Durazzo] the Peaceful, whom I have mentioned briefly above, was crowned king of the 'land of labour', that is Naples, by the pope [Urban VI]. He entered his kingdom with a strong force to take possession of his territory and, meeting no resistance, arrived peacefully at Naples, the mother city of his realm, where he was welcomed with fitting honours by the citizens. Now the pope, in a sermon addressed to the people of Charles the Peaceful, had said, 'You, dearest son, have been given a not inappropriate surname, for you will set out in peace, in peace will you enter and pass through the land, and you will rejoice in a succession obtained by peace.' And so that events might correspond with the prophecy of the pope, he received in peace and without any tumult or losses in war those cities of that land called Gaeta, Capua, Benevento, Aversa and several others whose names I do not have.

And that great whore who presided over many waters and was called 'the queen of Naples' [Giovanna, queen of Naples] fled from the face of the dread Charles and his army into a castle of that city called Castel Nuovo. Charles immediately engaged in a siege of this castle and the siege was protracted for forty-two days.[3] So on the forty-second day of the siege, he made a fierce assault on the castle. And when he and his men were drenched in sweat in their efforts to throw the occupants into confusion and seize the castle by force, there suddenly came up in the rear of Charles and his army, Otto of Brunswick, the queen's husband, together with Marco de Monte Ferrando and a vast force of armed men. They had been let into the city by the intervention of traitors in order to make an attack on Charles and bring help to the queen.

There was at that time in Charles's army a knight called Jomitus, who was in fact himself the leader of that army, a man of great foresight in military matters and prompt in action. When he suddenly realised the trickery of the traitors and the imminent danger, he stationed part of the army on the walls to stop the defenders from breaking out of the castle, while the other part of the army was to join issue with Otto. At once Otto was bravely confronted by Charles and Jomitus. There was fierce fighting until the enemy troops were scattered and defeated, with very many killed and several taken prisoner. Marco de Monte Ferrando met his end during this battle, and Otto of Brunswick received a fatal wound and was captured. They at once showed Otto to the queen, and threatened that they would put him on a catapult and hurl him to the queen within the castle, unless she speedily showed a wish to surrender the fortress. But, with night coming on, they did not carry out their threat.

So the queen, having spent that night in discussion with her followers, the next day gave up herself and the castle [on 26 August], in which boundless riches were found. She was taken pris-

---

[1]   Courtenay was translated to Canterbury on 9 September 1381. Braybroke was provided to the see of London on the same day but was not consecrated until January 1382.

[2]   The kingdom of Naples, positioned to the south of the papal state, had always been pivotal to the balance of power in the Italian peninsula, but after the schism had begun in 1378 it became absolutely imperative that one or other of the rival parties secured its support or at least succeeded in neutralising it. The reigning monarch, Queen Giovanna (b.1326, queen of Naples from 1343), had declared for Avignon and Clement VII but she was childless and from the beginning of the 1380s both papal parties began to promote claimants of their own. Urban VI chose to support Charles III of Durazzo, a distant kinsman of Giovanna who shared her own tenuous connection with the original Angevin line. Charles had been held in the custody of King Lewis of Hungary, who had executed his father for his complicity in the murder of Lewis's brother, the first consort of Queen Giovanna of Naples. Urban now secured the support of Lewis, and, with the aid of Hungarian troops, Charles of Durazzo made his way to Italy. He entered Rome in November 1380 and prepared for an advance on Naples. In the event he did not embark until June 1381, but met little resistance and entered Naples on 16 July; Giovanna's forces held out for a further month but finally surrendered on 26 August. Charles hoped for Giovanna's recognition as her heir but she proved obdurate and she was imprisoned and subsequently murdered in May 1382. For further background see S. Fodale, *La politica napoletana di Urbano VI* (Rome, 1973).

[3]   In fact the siege continued from 12 July–20 August.

oner and kept in custody until Charles with the pope's council should discuss what to do with her person. Also taken prisoner with the queen from this castle were a count, who was her chancellor, a count, who was her chamberlain, and many others whom it would take too long to name individually. In this way peace was brought about for Charles the Peaceful and a kingdom came into being before his eyes.

Some say that the queen, after her capture, entered a Franciscan religious order of nuns called the 'Poor Clares'. Her friends on both sides suggested it, the pope was willing and Charles gave permission for it. Whether she is likely to win merit from such great perfection is known only to God, to whom every heart lies open.[1]

The seven propositions of Master John Wyclif

That enemy of the Christian faith, John Wyclif, heretic of accursed memory, was keen to lead astray both the more important and the less important of the people of our country with his wicked theories, and during all that period worked hard to spread abroad his damnable views, both on his own and using his followers, and using both the written and the spoken word.[2] And because he did not feel satisfied just to preach his abominable sermons to the common people, he wrote a summary of the new doctrines he had contrived to the lords and nobles who had gathered in London for the parliament held on the feast of St John before the Latin Gate [6 May],[3] hoping by these means that he could win them over as well and bring them into error by these words. I shall set down the nature of his teaching, as written in his summary. This indeed was what he wrote.

The seven propositions of Master John Wyclif, to be put into effect by the lords of England for the safety of their land

1. The king and his subjects are not to give obedience to any bishop or prelate except in as far as it is also in obedience to Jesus Christ and in accordance with a belief in scripture. It is clear that otherwise he would be obeying the Antichrist before Christ. For all obedience which is not of Christ is of the Antichrist. As it says in the second chapter of Luke, 'Whoever is not with me. . . .' [correctly, Matthew 12:30].

2. No money shall be sent from England to the Roman Curia or to Avignon or anywhere else abroad, unless it is proved from holy scripture that this money is owing. It is clear that otherwise such money would be the plunder of a ravening wolf. For Christ says to Matthew [7:20] that by their fruits you shall know them.

3. No cardinal or anyone else is to have revenues from any church or prebend in England unless he either is officially resident in it or unless he is lawfully engaged in a cause which has been reasonably approved by the lords of the land. It is clear that otherwise he would not be entering in through Christ but would be coming in through some other way as a disciple of the Antichrist, and, like a robber, would be following the example of the world to prey upon our realm through its poor subjects without making any equivalent monetary recompense.

4. Both king and kingdom are bound to destroy traitors to the kingdom, and to defend the people from savage enemies.

5. The commons of the land are not to be burdened with uncustomary taxes until all the revenue with which the clergy are endowed has been used up. It is clear that all such endowments are the goods of the poor and are in charity to be used for their wants, with the clergy living in the perfection of poverty.

---

[1]   Walsingham's remark would suggest that he was writing before news reached him of Giovanna's death on 12 May 1382.

[2]   The extent to which Wyclif and his followers were working to 'spread their damnable views' in this period is attested by the evidence of Wyclif's disciples and their preaching, gathered at Leicester by Henry Knighton: *Knighton*, pp. 277–325.

[3]   Parliament opened the next day, 7 May: *RP*, iii. 122. Wyclif presented a petition demanding the disendowment of the church. Walsingham is the only contemporary authority to make any reference to this or to provide any evidence of the substance of the petition itself.

6. If any bishop or curate with an endowment in England notoriously falls into contempt of God, the king shall not just be allowed but actually obliged to confiscate his temporalities. It is clear that otherwise he would be putting the kingdom of Christ second to that of the king, his temporal lord, and considering contempt for his king a greater sin than contempt of Christ.

7. The king is to use no bishop or curate in his secular service. It is clear that both king and cleric would be betraying our Lord Jesus Christ.

Other propositions of John Wyclif

The king shall put no one in prison because his excommunication has been delayed, until it is shown that the delay is illegal according to the law of God. It is clear that often many are excommunicated unwisely, when according to the law of God and the church they ought to be enduring excommunication for ever. To authorise the imprisonment of a man on account of the fact that he is doing what he ought would be the work of a daylight devil. On the other hand things which are not felt are not cured, yet they cause the state still more trouble, because being not felt they are made light of and so grow with the greatest vigour.

And, so that he might put his hearers in still more danger, he wrote and published at this time other conclusions also, anathematised by the whole church. They are as follows:

The substance of the bread remains after the consecration, and it is the substance of the bread after the consecration which is the body of Christ.

God with his absolute power cannot bring it about at the sacrament of the altar that accidental properties exist without a substance.

It will not be possible to prove any heresy of falsity in the whole teaching of John Wyclif.

God must obey the devil.

The pope is under more obligation than the emperor, rather than the other way around.

All monks of the order of St Benedict who are unwilling to win a livelihood from the work of their hands are not only apostates from the order of St Benedict but also, still more truly, from the discipleship of Christ.

No one is a secular lord or bishop or prelate while he is in mortal sin.

If the orders of the friars were founded by Christ and of a sure origin, they would not seek confirmation from the pope.

Subjects are not obliged to obey any human laws not based on holy scripture.

These were the accursed ravings that John put forward at this time. But to add to the pile of things already damning him, he also sent out apostate followers holding a very low view of the Catholic faith in order that they should preach as dogma other most dangerous doctrines which not surprisingly caused a buzzing in the ears of all the faithful who heard them. Among these followers was a man with the outward look and clothing of a hermit for he came indeed dressed in sheepskins, but inside he was a ravening wolf.[1] This emissary of John's publicly preached at Leicester on Palm Sunday the following abominable doctrines.

The Conclusions of John Wyclif[2]

1. Men who give up listening to the word of God and the preaching of the gospel because of excommunications imposed by men are by that excommunicated, and will be considered traitors

[1] This was William Swinderby, an unbeneficed priest of Leicester, who, according to Henry Knighton, who gives a more detailed account of his activities (*Knighton*, pp. 306–25) 'was popularly known as William the hermit because he had long followed the life of a hermit . . . [although] where he came from or what his origins were no one knew' (*Knighton*, pp. 306–7). Knighton also attests that Swinderby had been supported by the patronage of both John of Gaunt and the abbot and convent of St Mary's Abbey, Leicester before he fell in with a whole sect of Leicester Lollards, apparently in 1381. See also Hudson, *Premature Reformation*, pp. 74–6, 153–4.
[2] With the exception of the second, concerning excommunication, these conclusions are different from those errors listed in Swinderby's 'recantation' as recorded by Knighton (*Knighton*, pp. 318–21).

N[icholas] Hertford [Hereford] and a certain canon of Leicester, disciples and followers of John Wyclif

There were at this time several other followers and disciples of these wicked doctrines, who preached the same heresies and others still more outrageous, not in any old town or city but in the university of Oxford itself, on the eves of festivals, since Master Robert Rigg, the chancellor of the university at the time, was a supporter and a follower of this sect.[1] Other notable adherents were Master Nicholas Hereford,[2] a most ardent follower of John Wyclif, a certain canon of Leicester,[3] and others who had not entered the sheepfold of the schools through the door but by other means, namely the power of the magnates, and against the wishes of their brothers and their own abbot.

All these and several other of their followers openly preached their, as it were, Sodomite heresies without any concealment. Nor was it sufficient for them just to keep to themselves their disagreement with the Catholic faith or with other mistaken articles of Catholic doctrine, but they also by their preachings led Christ's faithful people away from the path into their own wicked forests. For example, that canon of Leicester [Philip Repingdon], to show how imperfectly he had learned the rule of monastic life from the teachings of the saints, declared in a sermon that the only monastic order he had praise for was his own, simply because it was closer and nearer to life in the world than the other orders. It was already closer in its rituals, and his wish was that it should now copy the world in its dress as well. The only point, he claimed, which stopped it reaching perfection was that its members wore clothes which were unlike those of the world. He argued that the life of the monks and other religious people was less than perfect, because it was hedged about with so many rules.[4]

The archbishop and his fellow bishops take up the fight against the conclusions of Wyclif

The archbishop of Canterbury, Master William Courtenay, was woken by this outcry. Since he was a man who was believed to be full of the spirit of God, he did not suffer such wickedness to be allowed a free rein. As soon as he was consecrated archbishop to the service of Christ, the son of God, he wished to show that what had been missing so far was not the righteousness of Phinehas [Psalms 106: 30] but an opportunity for reining in the wild and uncontrolled spirits of the heretics. So he summoned his brother suffragans, discussed with them the evils of the times, told them of the misery that was abroad, and complained about the sons of perdition who, although brought up in the bosom of mother church, were now trying to tear their mother to pieces. At last, after a discussion in which he heard the views of various people on the matter, he made up his mind either to crush such outrages and restore the rule of right or to put his head on the block in the cause of God. So first he summoned some of his fellow bishops who had not gone after Baal and several professors of holy scripture, and decided to exterminate the various kinds of leprosy with which his erring sheep had been infected, and, carefully examining these weak doctrines, to distinguish between leprosy and leprosy.[5] And so ulcers of terrifying awfulness were brought into

1   For Rigg's role see Hudson, *Premature Reformation*, pp. 70, 72; J. I. Catto, 'Wyclif and Wyclifism at Oxford, 1356–1430' in *A History of the University of Oxford II Late Medieval Oxford*, ed. J. I. Catto and T. A. R. Evans (Oxford, 1992), pp. 175–261 at 214–17.
2   Nicholas Hereford, a fellow of the Queen's College, had completed his doctorate in theology in 1382 and had used the occasion of his Ascension day (15 May) sermon at St Frideswide's to publicise views sympathetic to Wyclifism: Emden, *BRUO*, ii. 913–15; Hudson, *Premature Reformation*, pp. 70–5, 176–8.
3   Philip Repingdon was a canon of Leicester Abbey; according to his fellow-canon, Henry Knighton, he had preached Wyclifite doctrines in the churches of Leicester: *Knighton*, pp. 282–5 and n. See also Emden, *BRUO*, iii. 1565–7; Hudson, *Premature Reformation*, pp. 43–4, 70–3.
4   Knighton records opinions expressed by Repingdon in his preaching (*Knighton*, pp. 283–5) but makes no mention of his views on the monastic life. Of course, as a fellow Augustinian, Knighton was likely to share Repingdon's view of the priority of that order that was so offensive to the Benedictine Walsingham.
5   Courtenay summoned a council to examine the teachings of Wyclif and his disciples that convened at the London convent of the Dominican friars (i.e. Blackfriars) on 19 May 1382. He acted in response to the peti-

the light of day, needing to be dealt with by the hands of the shepherd whose service would be to consume them with the fires of anathematisation. I shall display these ulcers singly, one by one, showing how they deserved to be condemned.

The doctrines of John Wyclif condemned by the archbishop, etc.[1]

1. That the substance of the material bread and wine remains the same after the consecration in the sacrament of the altar.
2. That the accidental qualities do not remain without their substance after the consecration in the same sacrament.
3. That Christ is not in the sacrament of the altar as his identical self, truly and really there in his own physical presence.
4. That if a bishop or priest is living in mortal sin, he neither ordains, consecrates nor baptises.
5. If a man is properly repentant, all external confession is for him superfluous and pointless.
6. His persistent denial that it is not established in the gospels that Christ ordained the mass.
7. That God has to obey the devil.
8. That if the pope is known to be a bad man and therefore a limb of Satan, he no longer possesses the power over Christ's faithful given him by any man, except perhaps by Caesar.
9. That after Urban VI no one is to be appointed pope, but men should live under their own laws after the fashion of the Greeks.
10. His assertion that it is contrary to holy scripture that churchmen should have temporal possessions.

Having condemned these graver faults, the archbishop logically descended to the lesser ones, aiming to uproot, destroy, scatter and eliminate all the scandals which the son of perdition had sown in the kingdom of God. Some of these I list here below.

1. No prelate should excommunicate anybody, unless he first knows that the man has been excommunicated by God.
2. Also that if he does excommunicate without this knowledge, this makes him a heretic or an excommunicated person.
3. A prelate who excommunicates a cleric who has appealed to the king and the council of the king, is by that very act a traitor to God, the king and the kingdom.
4. Those who stop the preaching or the hearing of the word of God or the preaching of the gospel by means of the excommunication of men, are themselves excommunicated and on the day of judgement will be considered traitors to God.
5. His assertion that any deacon or priest can preach the word of God, without authority of the apostolic see or a Catholic bishop, or other things about which there is sufficient agreement.
6. That temporal lords can decide to take away temporal goods from churchmen who are habitual sinners, and that the people can decide to reform such sinners.
7. That tithes are 'pure' alms, and that parishioners can retain them because of the sins of their curates and give them to others as they please.
8. That, other things being equal, particular prayers offered for one person by priests or monks have no more efficacy for the person than general prayers which include him.

tion that Wyclif had presented to parliament, but there is no doubt that he was also anxious to respond to the signs – such as the preaching of Swinderby, Hereford and Repingdon – of growing support for Wyclif in the provinces. Courtenay summoned delegates of unimpeachable orthodoxy, including Walsingham's fellow monk of St Albans, Nicholas Radcliffe an Oxford doctor of theology. There were seventeen doctors of theology and sixteen doctors of law, as well many other bachelors of theology. For the council in general and Radcliffe in particular see *Fasciculi zizaniorum*, ed. Shirley, pp. 286–91 at 287; Hudson, *Premature Reformation*, pp. 67–73, 93, 95, 98.

1   Once again Walsingham differs somewhat from the other documentary records: the Fasciculi lists twenty-four conclusions condemned by Courtenay: *Fasciculi zizaniorum*, ed. Shirley, pp. 275–82. According to Knighton, the delegates at Blackfriars first pronounced their conclusions on 21 May and then, on Whitsun weekend (30 May), they made solemn procession through the city to St Paul's where a sermon was preached by one of their number expounding the errors: *Knighton*, pp. 260–4.

and frequented no less openly and peacefully than they were in the three or four days before the conflict. When they had sorted out Bruges in their own fashion, the people of Ghent returned home in triumph with many spoils. They then sent men to pursue and besiege those who had fled for refuge to the protection of Oudenaarde and who had the presumption to hold the town against them. Indeed gathered in Oudenaarde were the most noble and powerful knights and esquires of the whole of Flanders, who believed that they would be safe there, both because of the strength of its defences and because that fortified city was adjacent to the provinces of France, from where they believed help could easily be brought to them. And so having established siege works, they besieged the city for the whole of the summer. The count of Flanders [Louis II, of Mäele], who was encamped at St Omer, frequently inflicted much damage on the besiegers, in his efforts to come to the help of the besieged.

A parliament at London

Around the time of the feast of St John before the Latin Gate [6 May] a summons went out to all the magnates of the kingdom and those who were usually invited to a parliament in London, even though a parliament had been held in the Lent preceding it, as I have described. In this parliament, after a petition from the knights of the shires, John Straw [John Wrawe], priest, the leader of the revolt at Bury and Mildenhall, was sentenced to drawing and hanging, although many had thought that he would have bought his way out of it.[1]

A pseudo-physician is placed on a horse and receives a reward for his lies[2]

In London at this time an impostor, claiming to be a physician and astrologer, got a proclamation made throughout the city that no one should dare to leave his bedroom on the eve of the feast of the ascension of Our Lord until he had recited the Lord's Prayer five times and broken his fast by eating, on account of a plague-filled darkness which would descend that day. He had also asked, perhaps trusting in the foolishness of the citizens, that he himself in the meantime be kept unharmed, and punished if his prophecy did not come true. For he had prophesied sudden death for all who did not follow his advice. And very many did believe him and, following his instructions, did not go out to hear Mass that day, and refused to leave the house until they had broken their fast on that day.

But when on the following day his lies could not be concealed, he was seized and put on a horse. The horse's tail was put into his hands as a rein, and two jars, commonly called 'jordans', were tied round his neck together with a touchstone as a sign that he had deserved it by his lies. And in this way he was led through the whole city for all the physicians and surgeons to see, receiving as a reward the mockery that he deserved.

The English snatch from pirates a ship called the *Falcon*[3]

About this time our sailors, together with some men from Rye, and some from the surrounding countryside, left harbour to sweep the seas and clear them of pirate raids. To their surprise they suddenly caught sight of some enemy ships, amongst which they detected one ship which had once belonged to Sir Thomas Latimer[4] and had been called the *Falcon*, on account of the emblem of the falcon which had been painted on it, to enable it to be recognised. Some time ago this ship had been captured by a superior enemy force and taken off by them. So when our men saw that, to the disgrace of the English, the ship had been enlarged and that its former emblem had been replaced as an insult to us, they all committed themselves to the peril of an encounter, and made

---

[1]   None of the other authorities expresses such doubts. For the Westminster chronicler the main business of this parliament was to discuss a subsidy that was granted only 'after a great deal of wrangling': *WC,* pp. 28–9. The session opened on 6 October: *RP,* iii. 134.

[2]   This episode is not reported by the other authorities.

[3]   This episode is not reported by the other authorities.

[4]   Latimer was a household knight of the king's mother, Countess Joan of Kent. He was also one of those identified by Henry Knighton as a supporter of Wyclif: *Knighton,* pp. 294–5.

up their minds, if they were unable to recover it after a victory, to meet their deaths. They sent envoys to urge the enemy sailors on the vessel to give it back peacefully, but when the envoys met with nothing but laughter, they got ready for a general conflict. After a lengthy encounter our men prevailed and the ship was returned, together with the three hundred men who had just been killed in it and in the six other vessels captured with it. Our men also returned home with a praiseworthy victory and bringing with them merchant vessels richly laden with cargoes of wine, wax and goods of various kinds, a windfall for the inhabitants.

The duke of Anjou is crowned king of Naples[1]

The duke of Anjou [Louis], who had been crowned king of Naples by the antipope [Clement VII] at Avignon, about this time set out for Naples, with a large retinue of princes of France and accompanied by the count of Savoy. His purpose was to depose King Charles [of Durazzo], whom, as I said above, had been crowned king of Naples by the pope, and who, after defeating Queen Giovanna, had seized the kingdom by right of conquest. The duke is said to have taken with him three thousand armed men and a thousand crossbowmen, not counting the forces of the count of Savoy [Amadeus VI, 1343–83], whose number, to use the common expression, amounted to six hundred lances. He also had thirty seaworthy galleys, strongly armed and ready to fight a sea battle. He also sent before his face into Italy three imposing envoys, who were to announce his imminent arrival to the peoples living in Lombardy and Tuscany. He also made clear the reason for his arrival, namely that he was coming to support and help Queen Gioranna, whom Charles had deposed, and to recover for her the kingdom of Naples. This message indeed was carried abroad by those envoys to all the lords and peoples of Italy.[2]

Disturbances caused by Londoners

At this time the citizens of London began to exceed their usual bounds of behaviour and to set a pernicious example to other cities. Supported by the authority of the arrogant mayor of that year, John of Northampton,[3] they usurped episcopal rights by inflicting many degrading punishments on those caught in acts of fornication or adultery. Indeed women taken in adultery were first shut up and incarcerated in the prison which they call 'The Tun.' Finally, with their locks shorn like the thieves whom we call 'approvers,' they were brought out for public inspection and, preceded by trumpeters and pipers, were marched around for all the people of London to see, so that their persons might be more widely known. Nor did the citizens any the less spare the men who had sinned. Upon these too they inflicted many shameful punishments. For they had been encouraged to do this by John Wyclif and his followers as a way of reproving prelates, as the citizens also claimed that they both detested the negligence shown by priests in this matter and abhorred their greed. Priests, they said, in their eagerness for money, had foregone the penalties laid down by the law in return for cash, and so permitted those guilty of fornication and incest to live happily in their sins. They added that their especial fear was that, if such sins committed in London were not brought to light, the whole city would be destroyed on the day that God took his revenge. And so they wanted to clean the town of such stains, lest perchance their lot should be the plague or the sword or indeed the earth opening up to swallow them. Their mayor was a tough, clever fellow, whom wealth had made haughty and arrogant. He was able neither to listen to those below him

---

1   Having failed to come to the aid of Giovanna, who had recognised him as her heir, Louis only embarked for Naples almost a year after Charles of Durazzo had seized power, and several weeks after Giovanna herself had been murdered. See also above, pp. 173–4 and n.

2   Louis of Anjou's invasion was also supported by Bernabò Visconti, duke of Milan. Walsingham is the only English authority to report the invasion in detail but there is no doubt that the Angevin force was superior to that of Charles of Durazzo. However, Charles conducted an effective campaign of attrition and with the onset of winter and their supply lines interrupted, the French forces were severely weakened. Amadeus VI, count of Savoy, died of dysentery in March 1383. For another account see Froissart, *Chroniques*, xi. 184–5.

3   John Comberton of Northampton (d.1397), a draper, was elected mayor in October 1381 and held the office for exactly two years. He appears to have enjoyed the patronage of John of Gaunt and the two shared anti-clerical – if not actually Wyclifite – sympathies. See also Barron, *London*, pp. 24, 31, 148–9, 277–8, 333–4.

nor to change his mind because of the allegations or advice of those above him. On the contrary, he strove with grim resolution to bring to some sort of conclusion the schemes that his own brain had concocted. It was clear that he had the agreement of the whole community for his new projects, since

> Always with their leader
> Changes the fickle crowd[1]

and it hurried to follow the mayor in such schemes all the more eagerly, because he was attempting things which had been seldom heard or seen.[2]

It so chanced that their spiritual head, the bishop of London [Robert Braybroke, 1381–1404], did not dare to proceed against them: the unruliness of the crowd and the evil of the times made him afraid for his life. Indeed the irreverent mob even dared to interrupt the archbishop himself, when he was presiding at the trial in London of a master of arts called John Aston,[3] a very close follower of John Wyclif, against whom an action had been brought. The mob broke down the doors of the room in which the bishop, together with a crowd of professors of theology and law, was hearing the case.

Nor did they stop there. Next in that year the mayor, with the help and support of the common people, contrived to reduce all the fishmongers of London to such misery that all foreign fishmongers were better off than those who by inheritance or purchase were citizens of the town.[4] Indeed any foreign fishmonger was allowed to sell his fish in his own person inside the town, when citizen fishmongers had lost the right to do this, and would incur the great forfeiture of having their persons inescapably thrust into prison if they tried to break this rule. In short the mayor reduced citizen fishmongers to such straits that they were driven to admit openly that the craft which they had previously practised was not a craft, did not count as a craft, and was not to be named among the other crafts of the city. So the mayor brought it about that those who previously had stood among the highest in London were barely permitted to stand among the lowest.

On the other hand, the mayor restored to their former status those who had been previously banished and forbidden to take any further part in the counsels and discussions of the city, and London itself and its whole community was now made subject to the schemes and dictates of these reinstated men. For in their keenness to see how they could best please the people and make their mayor more acceptable to them, they now stopped all foreign fishmongers from passing through London to take their goods to the surrounding country. Instead they all had to remain in London and sell their fish to its people at a price fixed according to the wishes of the mayor. So the common people, seeing this improvement in the market, praised the mayor to the skies, and now had conceived such hate for the fishmongers who were their fellow citizens that they were ready to banish them, if that was necessary and what the mayor wanted. But in all these matters they gave not a thought to the surrounding countryside, which, while the town was enjoying an abundance, was suffering extreme shortage, since they allowed no fishmonger to take his goods there.[5] For

---

[1]   Claudian, *Panegyricus de quarto consulatu Honorii Augusti*, 302.

[2]   It is surprising that the other authorities make no mention of these anti-clerical displays in the city. The *Historia vitae et regni Ricardi secundi* records Northampton's challenges to the city's customs (*HVRS*, p. 80) but makes no reference to ecclesiastical controversies.

[3]   Aston was a theologian trained at Oxford and had been a fellow of Merton College, Oxford, from 1365 until at least 1371. Like William Swinderby he was an early disciple of Wyclif and is reported by Knighton as well as Walsingham as a popular preacher active in the years before 1382. He was summoned to the council at Blackfriars where he was examined and where he made formal recantation of his heretical opinions. Walsingham must have known him personally because after his submission at Blackfriars he was placed in custody at St Albans Abbey where he received instruction from the monastic theologian Nicholas Radcliffe. See Emden, *BRUO*, i. 67; Hudson, *Premature Reformation*, pp. 77–8.

[4]   Northampton had made himself the champion of the lesser merchants and tradesmen in the city and provided a focus for their bitter resentment of the monopoly enjoyed by the powerful fishmongers. Walsingham refers here to a statute Northampton secured in the 1382 parliament that would allow the entry of foreign fishmongers to trade in the city.

[5]   The monastic community at St Albans provisioned in London and so Walsingham's criticism here is heartfelt.

while Londoners bought their sea fish cheaply, such fish were not just expensive for those outside the city, but practically unobtainable, as passage of trade had been blocked. As a result the mayor won the favour of Londoners but incurred the curses and the hatred of all the surrounding countryside. This was how matters stood in London at this time.

An earthquake

This summer in England, where such things are rarely seen or heard, there was a big earthquake. It happened on 21 May at three o' clock in the afternoon and alarmed the hearts of many mortals. The earth tremors were particularly strong in Kent, so much so that some churches were destroyed and levelled to the ground.[1] Another earthquake followed on 24 May early in the morning before sunrise, but it was not so bad as the first one.

The cardinals are frightened by the Romans

The citizens of Rome at this time were in a disturbed, rebellious state and began an insurrection against the pope and the cardinals. They struck so much terror into the cardinals that almost all of them fled Rome or sought retreats and hiding places where they could be safe from the face of the fury of the cruel and unruly crowd.[2] But the pope [Urban VI], deriving strength from the justice of his case and expecting help from on high, was not frightened by the armed mob or their terrifying yells or the frantic running hither and thither of the populace, but picked up a cross in his hands and confidently went out to meet them, addressing them in these words. 'What is it, my sons? What are you trying to do? Are you striving to overthrow your friends? What sin has the college of my brothers committed against you? Why has your anger flamed up against those who love you? Or indeed, if it is me you seek, why are you hesitating to cut off my head? Look! My head is in your hands. If you wish it, and if this is the work you have afoot, cut if off, so that peace may return.'

But when the Romans saw the steadfastness of the pope, they were as if struck by a beam and all at once fell to the ground, weeping and begging mercy for their sins and humbly seeking his fatherly blessing. The pope raised his hand and willingly gave them his blessing, admonishing each of them to return peacefully to his home and for the future to refrain from such tumult and sedition. No small miracle took place, for they obeyed their father's strictures, laid aside their evil rage and returned home.

The pope confirms John Timworth as abbot of [Bury] St Edmund's; but not without money

About this time the pope, after delaying for more than two years confirmation of the election of John Timworth at Bury St Edmunds, at last transferred Edmund Broomfield, to whom he had awarded that abbey, to the abbacy of a monastery in Gascony, persuaded to do so by gifts of money and frequent letters from English noblemen. But this could only happen if the king agreed to free Edmund from the lengthy imprisonment that he had been enduring.[3] In fact the pope did not simply confirm for John Timworth the election that had made him abbot, but awarded him the abbacy only on condition that he paid the Roman Curia the sum owing for the double interregnum after both John Brinkley and Edmund Broomfield.[4] And so the last sin seemed worse than the first.

But the brothers of the monastery, who had been without the comfort of a father for so long, agreed to this condition, not considering that they had driven out this same Edmund when he

---

1   The Westminster chronicler reports that the quake occurred the hour after noon and that afterwards a ring could be seen around the sun: *WC*, pp. 26–7.
2   At the outbreak of the schism, Urban VI had created a new college largely of Italian cardinals.
3   Broomfield was not released from captivity in Windsor castle until 8 June 1385, three years after this papal intervention. For his appointment in Gascony see above, p. 96 and n.
4   It had been the death of Abbot Brinkley in 1379 that had projected the Bury monks into this lengthy dispute. To exploit the situation seemed mercenary even for the pro-papal Walsingham.

had previously been given to them as abbot by the provision of the pope, and forgetting how much they had spent to further their own scheme, when they had been afraid that the election they had held by themselves would be held invalid. But the king and his council were not happy with the condition attaching to the pope's appointment, partly because they believed that, if it was agreed to, any elections held in the future would involve the same risk, and partly because it seemed shameful for them to be budged from the position which, at the dictate of conscience, they had defended with zealous stubbornness for so long. And so among the monks it seemed that love of justice and desire for the right was having a short sleep, while being wide awake among the non-religious laity.

In December of this year a comet appeared in the west for more than a fortnight.

Richard Scrope, knight, is deprived of the chancellorship[1]

During these days the knight Sir Richard Scrope, whom I have mentioned earlier as being elected chancellor of England by the commons of the land and the assent of the lords, was deposed from the chancellorship, in which his sensible administration had won him praise. The reason for his deposition was his steady resistance to the wishes of the king, who wanted to impoverish himself in order to promote outsiders. For after the death of Edmund Mortimer, earl of March [in 1381], and of other lords who had recently passed away, ambitious men, both knights and esquires and serving men of a lesser degree, had gone to the king and asked him to grant them certain lands and estates of the dead men, at the time at which, according to the custom of the country, the king should have been keeping possession of them in his own hands. The king, being just a boy, granted them their requests on the spot, and sent them to the chancellor, whom he ordered to hand over to them the charters, signed with the great seal, exactly according to wish and whim.

But the chancellor, in his ardent desire for the welfare of the kingdom and what was advantageous for the king, openly refused what had been asked: the king, he said, was so loaded with debts of many kinds that he needed to keep such windfalls in his own hands, so that he could use them to pay in part the debts which he owed to his creditors. They themselves, he continued, who knew what debts the king had incurred, were not being loyal to him in thinking of their own enrichment before the good of the king, when they asked for such benefits and put private gain before the needs of the state. And so they should stop making requests of this kind and be content with previous gifts from the king, which were quite enough for them. They could be absolutely clear that he himself would not sign or seal any confirmatory charters for such grants from a king, who had not yet left behind his boyhood years, and who might at some time in the future not thank him for such charters.

Richard Scrope gives the seal to the king: the bishop of London becomes chancellor

So those who had come to make these petitions to the chancellor went away empty-handed. They reported to the king the obstinacy of the chancellor, and said that he had been willing to do nothing which the king had commanded, but rather had treated the king's mandate with contempt. The king, they said, ought speedily to rein in such unbridled disobedience with due severity, or it would soon happen that his subjects would put little value on the honour owed to their king and consequently his commands would have no force.

And so the king, having only the wisdom of a small boy, paid more attention to the untrue fabrications of his informants than to the trustworthy arguments of his chancellor, and in his rage sent envoys to demand the seal of the chancellor and bring it back to himself. And after the king had repeatedly sent envoys of increasing importance to ask him to send back the seal, the chancellor at last replied to the envoys, 'I am ready to give back the seal, only not to you but to him

---

[1] Scrope's dismissal from the chancellorship barely registered with other contemporary chroniclers, but Walsingham was probably correct to present it as a crisis not only for the breakdown in the relationship between the king and his councillors but also because of the long delay in appointing a successor, when the administration remained directed only by the king's own hand: see Saul, *Richard II*, pp. 111–12. Walsingham also stands apart from the other authorities in his fulsome praise for Scrope.

who put it into my keeping. There will be no go-between to take it from me to him. I myself shall put it back into the hands of him who entrusted it to me with his own hands and not with those of another.' And so the chancellor went to the king and indeed handed back the seal, renewing his promise to remain as loyal to the king as he had been in the past, but refusing to hold further office under the king. And so the king took back the seal, and did as he pleased for many days, until master Robert Braybroke, bishop of London, took over the office of chancellor.[1]

Not only the magnates of the realm but also the commons themselves were highly indignant when they heard that the king, contrary to the custom of the country, had rashly deposed a chancellor who had been elected by all the nobles of the land together with the support of all the people. But nobody dared to say anything openly on the subject, because of the malice of those at the side of the king and the irrational youthfulness of the king himself. And so the true welfare of the king and his realm was damaged by the foolishness of the king and the malice of those who lived with him.[2]

A conspiracy among the men of Norfolk[3]

Around the feast of the blessed archangel Michael [29 September], some demon-driven men in Norfolk, who had not been deterred by the perils of others or scared by the deaths or tortures that others had suffered, formed a conspiracy. They brought wickedness into their lives by making the firm decision, if fortune favoured them, to ambush the bishop of Norwich [Henry Despenser] and all the nobles of the county and kill them unexpectedly. And to gain extra support for their enterprise, they decided to go in secret to [Horsham] St Faith on a market day and either to force all who had gathered there to swear allegiance to their cause or to kill them on the spot. And when all this had been done, they planned by stealth to seize the [Benedictine] abbey of St Benet's Holme, as they thought this would be a strong post of defence, if any danger was lying in wait for rebels like themselves. But the whole conspiracy was quashed before it could be put into effect, as one of the conspirators betrayed the plans of the others. And so it happened that the conspirators to their surprise were taken prisoner, and at Norwich suffered the penalty which their wickedness deserved, when their heads were cut off.

A parliament, visited by envoys from Flanders

About this time the magnates of the realm were summoned to a parliament according to custom, together with those who usually had an interest in being present.[4] There appeared before this parliament some nobles from Flanders, sent by their fellow citizens to place themselves and their land under the dominion of the king of England, now that their natural master, the count of Flanders [Louis II, of Maële], had abdicated. And since that legation seemed to lack the necessary authority, they were sent back home to bring with them to England men of greater fame and reputation from each of the towns of Flanders, who could be reasonably understood to have the authority to engage in such discussions and to make a firm agreement on the matter. I shall describe at the appropriate place and time the arrival of this embassy, the requests they made, and the answers which they received.[5]

Also in that parliament the mayor of London [John of Northampton], with the support of a

---

1   Scrope surrendered the seal on 11 July 1382 and Bishop Braybroke was appointed on 9 September, although he did not receive the seal for almost a fortnight (20 September): *CCR, 1381–85*, pp. 214–15.
2   Walsingham blames Richard's intimacy with his own household knights for this episode, a suspicion that was to intensify in the months before the appellant crisis. See below, pp. 242–3.
3   This episode is not reported by the other authorities.
4   Parliament opened on 6 October 1382: *RP*, iii. 134.
5   The envoys from Bruges, Ghent and Ypres arrived while parliament was still in session. Led by William Coudenberghe, their mission was to secure repayment of the loan of 20,000 crowns that Jacques van Artvelde was alleged to have granted Edward III at the siege of Tournai in 1340. As the Westminster chronicler attests, they made many other demands (*WC*, pp. 30–1), including the transfer of the wool staple from Calais to Bruges, an impertinent request that, Froissart reports, had the lords of parliament falling about with laughter after their departure: *Chroniques*, xi. 32–3.

great part of the commons, accused the fishmongers before the king and his council of tricks and deceptions, which he claimed they had practised in the selling of their fish. And so they gained a ruling that in the future no fishmonger or any other seller of goods such as wine and meat or any apothecary should be elected mayor of London. In this way the mayor made daily efforts to ensure that fishmongers should nevermore have the opportunity of aspiring to their former status, now that the honour of this important post had been taken away from them.

The mayor also forced Sir John Philipot to resign from his aldermanship. He considered that Sir John was the dominant force in the city and saw that he was the friend of those of whom the mayor himself was envious. And so he did not want Sir John to play any future part in the secret discussions and counsels of the city, even though he was a man who had outstripped all others in his labours for the liberties and honour of the city of London.[1] Instead he brought back to those discussions and counsels other men, who, as I said above, had at one time been found to be disloyal and exiled because of this.

'Censure disturbs the doves, the crows have pardon given.'[2]

A papal bull sent to the bishop of Norwich and his companions who were volunteering to set out for France to destroy the anti-pope

A short time before this the bishop of Norwich, Henry Despenser, had received bulls sent to him from the pope, which instructed him to bless with the sign of the cross all those willing to set out with him to France for the destruction of the antipope called Clement, and to ordain a holy war against all Clement's followers.[3] As these bulls bestowed great power upon him, the bishop had them read out in parliament and had copies widely circulated and ordered them to be fixed to the doors of churches and the gateways of monasteries so that everybody might see them. He also publicised in the same way the bull sent him by the pope that made clear the rights of the pope and the injuries done him by the followers of the antipope.[4] I shall insert here the gist of this bull, rather than a word for word transcript.

The gist of this bull[5]

The bull of the pope, in which he complains about the sons whom the Roman church had raised to high positions, but who, in their turn, tried like serpents to bite their mother. In consequence of this, the pope [Urban VI], on the advice of his brothers, has decided to take measures against them, their followers and supporters, who have formed confederacies and conspiracies against him and plotted schemes of various kinds, and dared to set schism and division in the Church of God and to seize the town of Agnani, the Castel Sant' Angelo in Rome and other forts, lands and places belonging to the pope. They have also organised the arrival of a vast force of armed tribes called the Bretons and the Gascons, in order to take possession by violence of the city of Rome

---

[1]   The monopoly of the fishmongers had long been political as much as commercial. Philipot, who had been a popular public spokesman for the city's commercial interests throughout the 1370s, was a natural target in Northampton's campaign. See also above, pp. 34–6.

[2]   Juvenal, *Satires,* ii. 63.

[3]   By 1382 there was a growing conviction within government that the time was right to reopen the war in France. Bishop Despenser proposed to exploit the situation in Flanders, where the citizens were in revolt and the Count Louis of Mäele had been forced into exile (see above, pp. 180–2). Not only would English intervention strike at Burundian interests, it might also provide them with a bridgehead into the kingdom of France itself. Such an intervention might easily be justified in the context of the papal schism since Count Louis, like his French allies, was a supporter of the Avignon anti-pope, Clement VII. Despenser had prior experience of such campaigns having participated in Urban V's crusade again Bernabò V of Milan in Lombardy. On this occasion, Urban's bulls did not empower Despenser to fight in Flanders but only to preach crusade within England. Nonetheless, as Walsingham and the other authorities all report, this was the interpretation the bishop placed on the papal documents.

[4]   Three bulls were published by Urban VI: *Dudum cum vinea Dei* (23 March 1381), *Dudum cum filii Belial* (25 March 1381) and *Dignum censemus* (15 May 1382). They were published in England on 17 September 1382.

[5]   Walsingham is the only contemporary commentator to summarise the bulls.

and other lands in his province of Campania. And in these places these soldiers committed murder, sacrilege, sack and pillage and other criminal acts of destruction and damage.

The pope urged them to return to their senses, using as envoys Peter, bishop of Portus, two other cardinals and many men of honour and probity, and even repeatedly sending them letters of his own. But they themselves, despite this, had disdained to obey his warnings, even though they were the very people who, together with the others concerned, had once chosen him in this city as their pope, enthroned him with the due, customary solemnities faithfully observed and publicly set his crown upon him. Indeed over many days they had treated him as their pope and high pontiff in celebrations of the mass and public and private consistories, in consultations held and decisions taken concerning the condition of the Roman church and the state, in receiving from him the sacraments of the church and in asking him for ecclesiastical positions and bene-fices both for themselves and for others.

And yet they had produced various defamatory pamphlets, sent to the various prelates and princes of the world, in which they asserted that he was not the true pope, and had dared to say many other outrageous things about him. And finally together with some others, whom by their suggestions they had won over to the support of their wicked scheme, they met together in the house of that son of iniquity, Honoratus of Gaeta, once count of Fondi. And it was there, with the help and support of Honoratus himself, that John [correctly Gérard],[1] with the title of St Clement but commonly called the cardinal priest of the Greater Monastery, and Peter, formerly a cardinal deacon with the title of St Eustace,[2] had the temerity to choose and establish as antipope Robert, once of the basilica of the twelve apostles and commonly called the Genevan. And in an act of sacrilegious daring they presumed to name Robert as pope and still presume to do so, while Robert himself showed rashness and daring in not blushing to name himself pope.

Further, another son of iniquity, Peter, once archbishop of Arles and chamberlain of this same pope, spurred on by the devil, secretly, as it were, withdrew without permission from the city where he was with the pope, taking with him from the chamber very many jewels and other precious things of great value belonging to the pope and the Roman church. He made for the aforesaid town of Agnani, and there with the criminals I have already mentioned he arranged and formed various conspiracies and confederacies, and it was on his advice and with his help and support that hordes of mercenaries were brought to Agnani. The adherents and supporters of Robert, who believe in him and are not afraid to call him pope and to have him so called, are both all those I have mentioned and also those sons of wickedness, James once patriarch of Constanti-nople[3] and Nicholas Brancaccio,[4] once archbishop of Cosenza; and these former bishops, Peter of Orvieto, William of Urbino, Peter of Montefiascone, John of Geneva and Francis of Gaeta;[5] also Bertrand Rasun once priest of the apostolic chamber, Matellus of Cashel, once rector of the church of St Mary Pedisgripta near Naples, and also those sons of iniquity, the aforesaid Honoratus, Antony once count of Caserta, Francis de Vico once prefect of the city, and the knights Jean de Malestroit, Nicholas Spinelli of Giovinazzo otherwise called the Neapolitan, Sylvestre Budes, Bernard de la Salle and Peter de la Sagra and the esquire Guilhonet de la Salle.

They all assert the false and fabricated untruths that our pope himself is not the pope nor the Roman pontiff; and Francis de Vico has dared to seize Viterbo, the pope's city, while Jean de Malestroit, Sylvestre Budes, Peter de la Sagra and Guilhonet with their accomplices have dared to seize the town of Agnani and other lands of the pope and to provide support for the occupying troops, thus committing the damning sins of heresy, schism, treachery and apostasy. When these

---

1   Gérard du Puy (d.1389) abbot of Marmoutier was cardinal priest of St Clement from 1375. Walsingham erroneously gives his name as John.
2   Pierre Flandrin (d.1381) was cardinal deacon of St Eustace from 1371.
3   Giacomo d'Itro (d.1393).
4   Niccolò Branccaccio (d.1412).
5   Peter, bishop of Orvieto (1364–79); William, bishop of Urbino (1373–9) and Otranto (1379–93); Peter, bishop of Montefiascone (1369–79); Jean de Murolio d'Estaing, bishop of Geneva (1378–85); François de Concieu, bishop of Grenoble (1380–8).

monstrous crimes were so notorious that no shilly-shallying could conceal them, for still greater certainty on these matters the pope commissioned both separately and together two priests and cardinals, John of the church of St Sabina and William of the church of St Eusebius, to keep him informed about the charges. They duly did so, and brought back to the pope in the consistory the news that the charges were of monstrous crimes which were plain to see and which everybody had been talking about and still were.

At last the pope was no longer able, without grave offence to Christ and a guilty conscience, to tolerate all these outrageous excesses, and after discussion with his brothers thought it right to rise up against these wicked men as the champion of the Almighty and to exercise justice by proceeding against them. So with the guilty being justly summoned for this purpose and after the other due legal solemnities had been observed, the court decreed and declared that as a result of the definitive judgement of the pope the former cardinals Robert, John, Gerald and Peter and James the former patriarch and Peter formerly of Arelate etc. had been and still were schismatics and conspirators and blasphemers against the pope and were to be punished as heretics and guilty of the crime of treachery; they were all equally under sentence of excommunication and anathema, their crimes being such that they had incurred a sentence and a penalty which had been inflicted on them as the verdict both of the law and of mankind etc.

The court also declared that Robert etc. had been and still were deposed from office, and had been and still were debarred and disqualified from all ecclesiastical benefices of any kind. They were also disqualified from holding them in the future. The court also declared that the patriarch, archbishops and bishops were deposed from all their pontifical offices etc.; also that the pope deposed Honoratus etc. from all his dignities and honours, and took away from him the rank of knight and his belt of knighthood. It also declared that the goods and fixtures, also the legal rights and powers of jurisdiction both of those who had once been cardinals and all others named above had been and were confiscated, and that their persons had been and were accursed and outlawed, and it outlawed them so that they could be taken prisoner by Christ's faithful. Once captured, they were to be straightaway sent to the pope, if this could be done without them escaping and any danger of them getting away: otherwise, they were to be put in close custody and kept under careful watch until the pope himself should give further instructions on the matter.

Further, he put under sentence of excommunication their adherents and supporters and any who sheltered or defended them, the absolution from this excommunication being reserved for the pope alone except at the point of death. He also decreed that any who knowingly presumed to give a church burial to any of the schismatics would lie under sentence of excommunication, from which they could not be absolved, except at the point of death, unless they first disinterred the bodies with their own hands and threw them far away from burial in a church. He next banned all Christ's faithful etc. from knowingly receiving any of the schismatics in their homes, or from taking it upon themselves to carry or send to those places where the schismatics or one of them was living or staying corn, wine, meat, bread, wood or other foods for their use, or from allowing such things to be brought or sent, if this could be stopped. The pope also forbade anyone to hinder in any way the process of Robert etc. being captured, imprisoned and sent on to him, and he also commanded that all people should give help towards their capture.

Those who disobeyed all this, or who knowingly named or considered as pope that Robert who calls himself pope Clement, or who believed or preached that he was pope, would incur sentence of excommunication, if an individual person, or sentence of interdict, if a community or a university, and their cities and lands were to cease trading with other cities, places and lands. And the cities themselves were to know that they would be cut off from papal authority, and that no one could be absolved from a sentence of excommunication of this kind by anybody other than the Roman pope except at the point of death, nor could an interdict of this kind be rescinded by anyone except this same Roman pope. He also disqualified all those who had received any benefits from the said Robert.

He then gave the bishop of Norwich the power of publishing all the foregoing, either by himself or by means of others, and of proceeding against those condemned in the bull.

Moreover the pope granted that indulgence which was usually granted to those setting out to the help of the Holy Land to all those, if penitent and confessing their sins, who would fight in their own persons or with another's against anti-pope Robert and his followers and who would labour in this fight for one year, beginning from the day on which the bishop of Norwich considered the arrangement had begun, either unbrokenly for a year or in instalments, following the banner of the church, whether they were priests or laymen. He also granted the same indulgence to those who would at least send money to the troops according to their abilities and means and who would supply the bishop or his deputy with sufficient wages to enable him to send suitable mercenaries to France, who would stay there and fight for the appointed time.

Privileges granted by the pope to the bishop of Norwich for the execution of the above[1]

Privileges granted to Henry, bishop of Norwich, by the most holy father and lord in Christ, Urban VI, by divine providence pope.

First, that the bishop is able with a strong hand to set up courts against the antipope and his adherents, supporters and counsellors, wherever they are.

Also, that he has the power of making public proceedings against the antipope and his adherents and whatever others were excommunicated by the pope of Rome in his attacks on the anti-papists, both collectively and as individuals.

Also, that he has the power of making legal investigation, summarily and openly, concerning the schismatics, both collectively and individually, and of imprisoning them and of confiscating their goods, both movable and fixed.

Also, that he has the power of depriving lay schismatics of any secular offices, and of conferring them on other suitable people.

Also, that he has the power of deposing any clerical schismatics in the party of the antipope, of declaring that they have been deposed, and of conferring on other suitable persons their benefices, both with or without cure of souls, dignities both major and minor, and offices.

Also, that he has this power in the case of exempt people, lay and clerical, secular and living under a rule, even if they are brothers of the mendicant order, or preachers, or members of other houses or from the hospital of St John of Jerusalem, or that of Blessed Mary of the Teutons or belonging to any other order whatsoever.

Also, that he has the power of granting to any secular, beneficed priests, with or without the cure of souls and also to those having dignities both major and minor or offices, and also to those living under a rule whether exempt or not exempt, the dispensation that individuals from among them will be able to be absent with him from these very benefices, dignities etc. under the banner of Christ, without obtaining permission from their prelates themselves, and while receiving full payment of the revenues from their benefices, just as much as if they were resident in person.

Also all travelling abroad with him at their own cost and expense, or even at the expense of another, are granted full remission of their sins and as many privileges as are granted to those travelling to the help of the Holy Land.

Also, those who in the judgement of the lord bishop or his deputy shall supply from their own goods and resources sufficient wages for suitable soldiers, even though they themselves take no part in carrying out the business in person, will have the same remission of sins and same indulgences as mentioned above, just as if they had been personally present with the bishop.

Also, all who for the overthrow of the schismatics shall supply the bishop with appropriate aid from their possessions are sharers in this remission.

Also, if it happens that a man dies on the journey which he has begun following the banner of Christ, or if it happens that the business itself is completed with a suitable termination before the end of the year, he shall receive in full this very grace, and will be a sharer in the indulgence and remission mentioned above.

---

[1] Walsingham reproduced much of the documentation relating to Despenser's crusade but not the ordinances governing its funding, preserved uniquely by Henry Knighton: *Knighton*, pp. 330–2.

Also, the bishop has the power of excommunicating, suspending from office, and of passing an interdict on any rebellious persons or those who prevent him from exercising the power entrusted to him, whatever their standing, station, rank, pre-eminence, order, position or condition, or even if the effulgence emanating from their position is that of a king, queen, emperor or of any other power-holder, ecclesiastical or secular.

Also, he has the power of making forcible use of any monks, even the teachers of the order of mendicants, if it shall seem to him expedient in the execution of his orders to dispatch or send them overseas.

Mandate of the bishop of Norwich to clerics and rectors for the publication of the above mentioned bull[1]

'Henry, by divine permission bishop of Norwich, nuncio of the apostolic see, sends greetings in the Lord to our beloved in Christ, namely each and every one of the rectors, vicars and parochial chaplains established in the city and diocese of York. We have already with our apostolic authority exhorted you all individually in the Lord and strictly ordered and commanded you, at the times and in the places which are most suitable, to make known to your parishioners the crusade entrusted to us and its importance, and the fact that it enables its supporters, assistants and helpers, according to our discretion or that of our deputies, to have granted to them full remission for their sins and as many indulgences as have been customarily granted to those marching to the help of the Holy Land, and, more than this, that they are promised the further blessing of eternal salvation, as is more fully described in the apostolic letter which has been lawfully published throughout the whole of England.

'But because, according to the evidence of trusty witnesses, we learn that our exhortation and mandate have succeeded in producing no effect or just a modest one, especially, so we believe, because of the neglect of you curates, who have thus diminished the Catholic faith and endangered those souls who through your advice and exhortation could easily have obtained the aforesaid privileges and everlasting grace, we, in our concern for the salvation and well-being of souls and being under the test of the divine judgement, command and order each and every one of you, as we have often done before, to ensure that, as far as in you lies, there may be no parishioner of yours who in the future is unaware of the precious gift of a spiritual and unusual grace of this kind or of your power to bestow it.

'We also command you to get the names of your individual parishioners put on a list together with the sums and donations of those paying them, marking the sums against their names, and we also command you to deal sensibly and persuasively with the confessions of those who from day to day put off payment to those occasions when it shall be more expedient for them to do so, both the rich and the poor, like the poor, little widow in the parable [Mark 12: 41–3; Luke 21: 1–3], and both the healthy and especially the sick, so that they may give a helping hand to this holy expedition for the destruction and extermination of modern day heretics. For they will be able to share in the prized reward of the indulgences available for this force, while you because of this reward will have a very large part of the burden of your care for them lifted from your shoulders.

'Also we give the command that opponents of this holy expedition, or those who, in rebelling against our mandate or, more accurately, the apostolic mandate, are supporters of this modern day schism, should be peremptorily summoned by you or by one of you to appear in person before us or our commissioners in the cathedral church of St Paul in London before a fixed date, determined by you or one of you, in order that they may explain and show why they should not within the strictly fixed term be subject to the punishments pronounced in words of thunder against those who do such things, and in order that they may further receive and carry out what justice shall recommend. Also you, or one of you, are to inform us or our commissioners sensibly and discreetly of the names of those making a contribution to this expedition and the amounts, and of the dates of your summons and its manner and form.

---

[1]   It was a measure of the man that Despenser issued the mandate without waiting for official authorisation.

'All these various individual matters we lay upon the conscience of each one of you, strictly ordering you by virtue of the obedience by which you are bound to the apostolic see, that you make known our present letter to your parishioners, and that, keeping a copy for yourselves, you quickly send it on to the next curate in the diocese. As a testimony to this matter we have sealed this present letter with the seal of the cross which we are using on this expedition. Given in our house at Charing, next to Westminster on the ninth day of February 1382 and in the thirteenth year of our consecration.'

Form of the absolution

'By the apostolic authority given to me on this matter, we absolve you, A. de B., from all your sins, confessed by your mouth and for which you have felt contrition in your heart, and from the sins which you would have wished to confess if they had come into your mind, and we grant you full remission of your sins, and we promise you the additional blessing of eternal salvation, which is the recompense of the just, and we bestow upon you all the privileges granted to those setting out to the help of the Holy Land, and we give you a share of the help afforded by the prayers and benefits of the holy, universal synod and the holy, Catholic church.'

The raising of the siege of the town of Oudenaarde; the great confusion of the Flemish

Scarcely had the parliament ended when gloomy news arrived from Flanders of the raising of the siege of the town of Oudenaarde and the death of Philippe van Artevelde and the great confusion of the Flemish in the war between the Bretons and the French.

For the king of France [Charles VI] had invaded Flanders with all the troops of his own country and all those he was able to summon to help from outside countries.[1] Without delay the people of Ghent went out to meet them, putting their hopes in help from the cities and towns of Flanders that were allied to them. But this turned out to be a cause of great disaster. For when it came to a battle, and the French had now begun to get the best of it, a huge crowd turned up from Bruges and the countryside around it, apparently bringing help to the men of Ghent, when all the time it was bent on betraying them. The Ghent soldiers, not fearing any trickery, immediately began fighting bravely, but their own fellow countrymen from Bruges attacked their rear, so bringing help to the enemy. So with the French cutting them down in front, and the men of Bruges doing so in the rear, the Ghent troops were afflicted with sudden panic and lost heart for the fight. The result was that they were easily defeated, with twenty-five thousand of their soldiers and those of their allies killed in the fighting.

The French expel the townsmen of Bruges from their homes

So while this campaign brought encouragement to the French, it took away from the people of Ghent any hope of further resistance, until they should be strong enough, backed up by yet more fresh help, to take vengeance for their injuries on the French or on their fellow countrymen. So the men of Ghent, compelled to flee, sought their own town. But soon the injustice of their defaulting allies met a just retribution.

For the citizens of Bruges and their other accomplices, who had wickedly betrayed those they should have helped, suddenly found themselves in a serious and desperate situation. For the

---

1   Charles VI had entered Flanders in October with what the Westminster chronicler describes as an 'enormous' army (*WC*, pp. 30–1) under the command of the constable, Olivier de Clisson. According to Froissart an advanced guard of around 2,000 men moved ahead of the main force: Count Louis contributed a further 4000 men: Froissart, *Chroniques*, xi. 1–30. The Franco-Flemish force swiftly seized the advantage as the rebel leader Artvelde remained engaged in the siege of Oudenaarde. Aware of the size of the Franco-Flemish army, Artvelde sought assistance from the English, but the ambassadors sent to treat with the representatives of the rebels were unable to go beyond Calais because of the advancing French. The eastern towns, including Gravelines and Poperinghe, fell quickly and Ypres also capitulated before the Franco-Flemish force engaged the rebel army on 27 November at Roosebeke, where Philippe van Artevelde was killed. Froissart reports that there were many deaths on both sides, but that as many as 20,000 of the rebel forces were killed: *Chroniques*, xi. 32–3, 38–41, 52–55; FCBuchon, ii. 243–52.

French, owing no loyalty or thanks to them for their help, invaded Bruges and all the other towns of the country. They expelled the traitors from their homes, stole all their valuables which they sent back to the provinces of France, and made these traitors serfs of the French king, the result being that the condition of the defeated men of Ghent was far better than that of their treacherous conquerors from Bruges. At least the people of Ghent still had their own town and their freedom, while the men of Bruges had nothing left at all, neither town nor liberty nor possessions.[1] They had had strong hopes that, if they deserted their allies and helped the French, after the victory the French would refrain from ransacking their possessions. But the result was far different from their hopes. For the French unexpectedly garrisoned with soldiers all the towns and places of those who had brought them that wicked help, and these troops, encamped among them, inflicted a dreadful servitude on their very allies.

The English too experienced heavy losses from this disaster. For, although in previous conflicts between the towns of Ghent and Bruges the English merchants had remained unharmed and suffered no damage to their property, now under these changed circumstances of the French being in control, they found that, while all other foreign merchants enjoyed immunity from attack, they alone had their goods seized and confiscated for the uses of the king of France [Charles VI], with their apprentices who showed any resistance being murdered.

So when this news got back to England, the envoys, whom I have mentioned, suddenly became afraid to return and they put off taking back an answer until the king's council should have provided a more suitable time both for their response and for the giving of help to them.

The cruelty of the French king against the Parisians who resist him

This was the situation in Flanders when the French king [Charles VI], proud and haughty because of the victory I have described, returned to Paris. But there in his own country he met with opposition.[2] The people of Paris were busily shutting the gates, fortifying the walls against him and taking up arms. So the king gathered a huge crowd of besiegers and decided to break into the city by force. But when he saw the vast numbers of his enemies inside, he changed his plan and tricked them by speaking to them words of peace. They believed him and allowed him to enter and all his army of soldiers with him. But having entered the city by trickery, he immediately gave the lie to his words, broke his agreement with them and ordered the leading men of the city to be shamefully arrested. Some of them were hanged, and some beheaded. He also had the right arms of those who had borne weapons against him cut off and the amputated arms themselves hung round their necks as a mark of everlasting disgrace. He then had all the gates of the city destroyed except the St Antony Gate, in which the king himself has his special house. Indeed he removed all weapons and equipment of war from the city so that its inhabitants might not have even the smallest opportunity of revolting in the future. He also imposed a new, heavy tribute upon them, which was to be collected by force, if they were not willing to pay it voluntarily. These were the events in Paris.

The earl of Cambridge returns from Portugal

Edmund [of Langley], earl of Cambridge, uncle of the king, and the troops sent with him to Portugal, as described earlier, now came back home to England, though after encountering cruel

---

[1] Ghent's admiral, Frans Acherman now appealed to the English for assistance. See also Froissart, *Chroniques*, xi. 180–1.

[2] From the time the Flemish revolt began in 1380, there were attempts to foment parallel uprisings in the provinces of France. There were disturbances in a number of towns – notably Rouen – and latterly a rebellion in Paris itself in March 1382, when the citizens rejected a new tax on merchandise levied by the city's governors; the disturbance came to be known as the revolt of the Maillotins as the rebels wielded leaded mallets. To forestall the disturbance, the burgesses, led by one Jean de Marès, dropped the levy, but on the king's return the decision was reversed, de Marès executed, and the privileges of the city's merchants suspended. Charles entered the city on 11 January, accompanied, according to Froissart, by a force of 12,000 men. Froissart also reports that the Parisians were compelled to pay 40,000 francs in reparation for the insurrection: *Chroniques*, xi. 76–80; ii. 280–84.

fortune at sea and some loss of goods. As I said, they had been sent to bring help to the king of Portugal against the Bastard of Spain [i.e. Enrique of Trastamara],[1] who called himself king and had done much damage to the king of Portugal, and who would well-nigh have wiped him out altogether, if help had not arrived from England before this could happen.[2] Our army stayed in Portuguese lands for a year, making several raids upon Spain and capturing some fortifications.[3] The Spanish then decided to take to the field of battle against the king of Portugal and the English army. The Portuguese king with our troops went out to meet the enemy just as keenly, determined to fight if fortune allowed and expecting to achieve a victory.[4]

The Spaniards were frightened of the determination of the king and the fighting abilities of our men and sought to treat with the king of Portugal, but on condition that neither the earl of Cambridge nor any Englishman was to be present at their councils. The king himself agreed to their request and went to the meeting. As both Spaniards and Portuguese keenly desired peace, they quickly arrived at an agreement pleasing to them both. The Spanish and the king of Portugal made the concessions wanted by the other party and, with the rights of both sides secured, a peace was secretly concluded, which contained the condition that the king of Portugal should empty the kingdom of his English. And to stop the English claiming that they did not have a fleet, the Spanish king gave them a fleet of his own ships, and the king of Portugal provided the money and the other items which seemed necessary for the sailors. The Spanish, to be sure, were frightened of the boldness of the English, and by now these same English had become burdensome to the Portuguese: they had engaged them to keep them safe against the enemy, but now these English were oppressing them with a more humiliating slavery, not only ransacking their property but assaulting their wives and daughters in a most despicable fashion. And so their hosts had begun to hate them.

When the king of Portugal returned from the conference, he announced to his own army and our men together that they should lay down their arms and return home, and he told everybody that he had made peace again with Spain. So our men had to obey his commands willy-nilly, and in great bitterness of mind they left the field on which they had not been allowed to do battle with the Spanish. So from that day on the English were not so much prepared for a return home as forced into one, until all Portugal was empty of them.[5]

So, as I have said, the earl returned home with his men and taking back with him his wife [Isabella], once the younger daughter of Pedro [the Cruel], king of Castile, and his son [Edward], to whom she had given birth several years before he left England. During his long delay in Portugal, the daughter of the king of Portugal had been given in marriage to his son with all due ceremony. But because he was apprehensive of the dubious loyalty of the men of that country, he was unwilling to leave his son behind, although the king of Portugal asked for this. Neither was the king willing to send his daughter to England with the earl. So this was how things stood in Portugal at this time.

---

1   For Enrique of Trastamara and the conflict over the crown of Castile, see above, p. 63 and n.
2   For the English intervention in Portugal see above, pp. 119–20.
3   Walsingham here embroiders on a year in which very little was achieved; the effectiveness of the earl of Cambridge's force was undermined by the shortage of money, men and even mounts and although they had advanced to the Castilian border by the winter of 1381 there had been no decisive engagement.
4   In July the Castilians advanced on the border town of Elvas and the Anglo-Portuguese forces prepared to engage them near Badajoz.
5   The rapprochment between the Castilians and Portuguese, and the betrayal of the latter's English allies, had been negotiated before, and not after the armies gathered at Badajoz. Cambridge's son Edward (later duke of Albermarle, d.1415) had been betrothed to Fernando's daughter Beatriz Portuguese but now this was dissolved in favour of Castilian match. Walsingham suggests the Portuguese punished Cambridge for the ill-discipline of his troops, but Cambridge is believed to have taken special pains to ensure their respectful behaviour on campaign: see Saul: *Richard II*, p. 98.

[John of Northampton] and his envious accomplices.[1] Now in this present parliament by letters patent of the king these rights were restored to them, except that they were not to keep their former right of holding their own courts. Crimes committed by them would be punished in the public courts according to the decision of the mayor, as was the custom with the other occupations.

But the mayor of the city had still not swallowed the old envy which he had against them. Although they showed him the king's charter concerning their restored liberties and said that it had been decreed as a result of the wishes of the king and of the whole parliament together that they should enjoy these liberties, the mayor was unwilling to grant their claims or accept the charter in any way. He remained as evil as ever and persecuted them fiercely. And so that he might be able to do this more freely, he gave vast sums of gold to his supporters and members of the king's council and thus won them over to his side. But when the fishmongers saw that they were achieving nothing with all this opposition, they decided to remain quiet for the time being. So this was the situation concerning the fishmongers.

The people of Ghent seize by force of arms the tribute collected for the use of the king of France[2]

At about this time the citizens of Bruges and Ypres and all the inhabitants of the western parts of Flanders, who had been made tribute payers to the king of France [Charles VI], were arranging to send men to take the tribute which they had collected for the king of France according to the conditions laid down. To safeguard their journey, they employed armed men to escort the tribute carriers and bring them help if any enemy happened to turn up. The people of Ghent learnt about all this from their spies, and made preparations to rob the envoys of the tribute or certainly to die in the attempt, if things went contrary to their wishes. They placed squads of their troops in hiding along the route, and so took by surprise the enemy bands of French and Flemish who were carrying the money. And as their numbers were superior to the French, they defeated them without difficulty. They deprived the French and those who had come with them of both their lives and the tribute money, and returned to Ghent with the spoils, having suffered no great losses themselves.

The count of Savoy is struck down like Antiochus, and dies

The count of Savoy [Amadeus VI] had set out with the duke of Anjou [Louis] and twenty-eight knights against the pope and Charles [of Durazzo] the Peaceful.[3] After spending a long but ruinous time in those parts, about Easter time he recognised that the hand of God had been sent against him.[4] He had refused to obey God and worship the common father of the world in his own country, and now, after renouncing the peace he had long enjoyed, he decided to persecute God in distant lands as well. But like Antiochus[5] he was pitifully struck down by the just judgement of God and died in a foreign land, although, before he died, he testified that it is right to be subordinate to God and his true vicar, and that he, as a son, had committed a heinous sin in persecuting his father.

And so he gave his own son and heir the salutary advice not to follow his father's example and attack pope Urban [VI], but to strive to make amends with speedy satisfaction for any attempts he might have made against pope Urban, and to devote himself to the unity of the church. However both the count's sorrow and his repentance were increased by the terrible deaths of the soldiers he

[1] See above, pp. 183–5, 188.
[2] This episode is not reported by the other authorities.
[3] For the circumstances surrounding this campaign see above, pp. 173–4, 183.
[4] Amadeus VI died on 1 March 1383. Easter was celebrated on 22 March.
[5] Antiochus IV Epiphanes, Seleucid ruler of Palestine (175–163 BC), whose invasion of Egypt was repelled by the Romans and whose assault on the temple at Jerusalem provoked the revolt of the Maccabees. He died on campaign in the east and Seleucid power in the region never recovered. See also 1 Maccabees 10–64 and for his death 2 Maccabees, 9. 4–29.

had brought with them, for they all except eight died of dysentery before him. Such was the end that carried off the count and almost all his knights. They left behind for the duke of Anjou [Louis I] a warning to repent, which would have been clear enough if he had been in a state of grace, but his haughty mind, although it saw all these happenings, refused to humble itself. His heart had indeed been hardened against the Lord and against his Christ.

The bishop of Norwich and his men hurry to the sea

About the time of the feast of the Trinity, which this year happened in the middle of the month of May [17 May], the crusading bishop of Norwich with some of the army which he had gathered together set off for the sea and quickly arrived in Kent. There he turned aside to the manor of the abbot of St Augustine's [Abbey, Canterbury] called Northbourne, intending to wait there for a favourable wind. But while he was still extending his stay there, he received a letter from the king, ordering him to return to London to speak to the king and to learn his will. But the bishop was afraid that if he returned to the king, he would receive the command to stay in England, so that, to the accompaniment of some laughter, all his efforts and preparations would be wasted. In these circumstances he chose to take his chance with the small forces that he had to hand sooner than stay behind and become a byword among his rivals. And so he got a message taken to the king, saying that he was already prepared and ready for departure, and that it was not expedient that he should be held up at this stage by any conference, which might be perhaps of little or no importance. The need was rather for him to hurry on the journey that he had undertaken for the honour both of God and the king.

He quickly called together the men he had with him, helped by Sir John Philipot, knight and merchant of London, who was in charge of the shipping, and crossed with them to Calais,[1] bearing in mind the advice of that poet who gave these instructions, 'Avoid delay, it always spoils the plan.'[2] So he waited at Calais for a few days until the army which was designed to make up his front line should arrive. As soon as it joined him, he immediately left Calais, raising on high the banner of the Holy Cross, and boldly approached the town of Gravelines, which was surrounded by strong walls and defended by soldiers brought from France and Brittany.[3] The bishop chose not to besiege it, but to make an assault on it while the English still seemed at the summit of their strength. And the townspeople got ready just as vigorously to defend themselves. They hastened keenly to the walls and threw down in succession upon the English lead, iron, quicklime, stones and anything else needed for the defence.[4] But our men had the banner of the Holy Cross before their eyes. They directed their gaze equally on the cause of their crusade and their own absolution, considering that on this field victory was glory but death a gain. So with contempt and disregard for dangers and wounds and despising death, they assaulted the walls and engaged in hand-to-hand combat with the enemy. Both sides inflicted and suffered repulses, wounds and casualties, until on both sides many men lay dead.

Meanwhile the Bretons and the French who were in the town aroused the citizens to a braver resistance and a fiercer fighting by declaring that other Frenchmen were on their way, who would devour the present weak, feeble, beggarly forces of the English in the mouth of the sword as fire devours stubble. But on our side the bishop and Sir Hugh Calveley of blessed memory increased the bravery of our men by their intruction and persuasion, showing them that they were fighting for God and his whole church, which they had undertaken to protect, and declaring that all those, whose lot it was to depart this life on this field, would become martyrs. And so with words of exhortation they asked and adjured them to lay aside all fear and to attack the enemies of the

---

1   Despenser embarked from Sandwich on 16 May and landed at Calais the following day.
2   Lucan, *De bello civili*, i. 281.
3   The crusaders advanced on Gravelines on Tuesday 19 May. See also Froissart, *Chroniques*, xi. 95–99; FCBuchon, ii. 266–71 at 268–9, 272–4.
4   The *Historia vitae et regni Ricardi secundi* recorded that at Gravelines the Bishop 'fortiter oppugnauit' (*HVRS*, p. 77) and the Westminster chronicler also reported his 'spirited assault on the town' but only Walsingham offered an extended, if embroidered account.

was discovered that some of the bishop's monks killed sixteen men in that very battle and all could see that their superiority in courage over their fellows matched the length of time in which they had grown old in the peace of the cloister. About such men the poet once said:

> Give rest, a rested field will well return
> What then is trusted to it.[1]

In the same way those men of God, suddenly translated from rest to the toil of battle, produced a noble harvest from their peace and ease.

But among all and before all it was our archers who on that day deserved praise and glory. For they sent such a rain of flying arrows upon the enemy that at the end of it no more armed warriors were still on their feet than if the very arrows had been piercing bare bodies. Such was the density of the flying arrows that the sky grew dark as if from a black cloud, and such was the frequency with which they were loosed that the enemy dared not lift up their faces. Anybody who tried to look up would in a moment be lamenting a lost eye or a pierced head caused by an arrow. Many, who put their mail-clad hands over their faces, suddenly had both hands fixed together by the arrival of an arrow. Corselets and breastplates could not stop bodies and breasts being pierced and wounded, or helmets help heads from being transfixed. Gloves were no use when hands holding spears or poles were fixed to these very weapons. In short, so different were the fortunes of the combatants that on one side you would have seen men ready to kill, on the other cattle ready to die.[2]

When the French and the Bretons who were present, to the number of one thousand nine hundred, saw the great slaughter of the Flemish, they were struck with the deepest dread. Of course they had put the Flemish in the front line in the battle for two reasons. Firstly, because their loyalty was suspect, and so they exposed them to the first dangers to stop them running away when the need to do so came over them. Secondly, so that, if it happened that the English won, they themselves might have a greater chance of escaping. But, as I have said, when the French saw the great destruction of the Flemish, they were petrified and struck with terror. They turned tail and ran off, and immediately all the rest of the army followed their example. The English, seeing this, quickly hurried to pursue the foe. And when they caught up with those fleeing before their face or to their right or left, they cut them down, and the slain fell in huge numbers. And so that nobody should doubt that this victory had been sent by God, during the hour of the battle there were frightening flashes of lighting and awesome thunderclaps, which helped the English but contributed to the destruction of the enemy. For both during the battle and the flight afterwards, the enemy were blinded by the constant lightning that attacked their eyes, and so were overthrown and slain, whereas the English were encouraged and exhilarated by the storm, seeing in it the helping hand of God. Indeed they could justifiably consider that this passage of Claudian applied to any one of them:

> The north wind from the mountains helping you,
> With cold storms overwhelmed the foe, and turned
> The spears into the throwers' faces, checking
> Their weapons with its blast. Deep loved by God
> Are you, for whom Aeolus from his caves
> Sends forth armed storms, for whom the heavens fight,
> For whom the winds come at your trumpet call.[3]

On the battleground and in the pursuit twelve thousand of the enemy were killed, while on our side only seven men fell, so that it would be clear to all ages that this victory had been sent from heaven.[4]

---

[1]   Ovid, *Ars amatoria*, ii. 351.
[2]   For all this florid imagery, the fierce nature of this battle appears to be corroborated by other sources; the Westminster chronicler claims 'the whole field echoed with the screams of the fallen and cavalry pressed the pursuit of their fleeing enemies' (*WC*, p. 41).
[3]   Claudian, *De tertio consolatu Honorii Augusti*, 93–8.
[4]   Even by Walsingham's standards this is shameless hyperbole. The Westminster chronicler claims that the

The battle took place on 25 May, the day on which holy church celebrates blessed Urban, pope and martyr. And so all things were working together so that no one should doubt that the expedition was pleasing to God.[1] After the battle the bishop and his men withdrew to Dunkirk.

What the king of France did after this battle

When the bishop's enemies heard the news of this victory and of his run of successes in France, their faces fell and they were very frightened. So the French king [Charles VI] and all his nobles took counsel and decided to summon all their friends and acquaintances who lived nearby to bring help against this dangerous foe. While this was happening, the king waited for their arrival in the valley of Soissons and gave help to his French troops there, for it was a region which could contain many people, being fertile and with abundant foodstuffs of all kinds. Down in this valley the king was joined by seven dukes and their armies, ten counts, some of them bound in allegiance to him and some of them coming at his prayer, many other lords and men of great name and power, and also by knights, esquires, servants, citizens and common people, the whole number being more than one hundred thousand.

But the bishop was not dismayed at the amassing of all these troops, and decided in the meantime to gain control of his surrounding area while also waiting for the arrival of those of his troops who had not yet crossed the sea. For he had engaged many men experienced in war and with an aptitude for fighting, if they had chosen to remain loyal to him. One of these was William Beauchamp, brother of the earl of Warwick, Lord Thomas Beauchamp. William had received five hundred marks from the bishop, just for his own presence on the campaign. But because he had not been paid the whole of the agreed sum before crossing the sea, he kept the money he had received but stayed at home, so that the whole people uttered direful curses against his name. Sir Thomas Trivet had also been engaged by the bishop. But he had not yet got together the men who were to set out with him, nor had he yet made his own preparations, but was lying there by the sea waiting for something or other to happen, just like a woman lying in childbed. So the citizens of London and some of the bishop's friends threatened him with death unless he set sail fairly speedily, all of them proclaiming that treachery was the reason for his delay. Thomas was roused by these barbs to cross the Channel, and he quickly joined the bishop, although his arrival brought no benefit to the bishop, as will become clear later.[2]

So the bishop set out from Dunkirk, intending, as I have said, to get control of the area. His appearance immediately threw the whole neighbourhood into confusion. Remembering his actions at Gravelines and his later ones at Dunkirk, the people decided to surrender without resistance rather than to lose their towns and lives by resisting. So he gained without a battle the towns of Nieuport, Bourbourg, Bergues, Poperinghe and many others nearby.[3]

The reinforcement of the crusaders

When the glad news was brought to England by some who had taken part in the capture of the towns of Gravelines and Dunkirk, and who had brought home with them from the booty horses, mares, cattle and quantities of furniture as a proof of the truth of their news, the whole country was in a moment put in a passion for joining the expedition, enticed by hope of booty. Without further thought many apprentices from London and several servants took up white hoods, with

English killed 10,000 of their enemies (*WC*, p. 41) but Knighton, who may have consulted independent sources gives the more modest figure of 3,000 (*Knighton*, pp. 326–7).

1   The coincidence of the feast day and the name of the pope who had sponsored the crusade was a good omen for Walsingham who still supported the offensives of the Roman pope.

2   Walsingham is the only commentator to report in detail on Trivet's delay. He and his troops were quartered in the town of Bourbourg which had surrendered to the English on 20 May shortly after Gravelines was taken.

3   Here Walsingham telescopes the sequence of events. Bourbourg fell shortly after the crusaders arrived but according to the *Historia vitae regni Ricardi* second (*HVRS*, p. 78). Nieuport and five other towns were not taken until after the victory over the French on 25 May. Poperinghe was one of the crusaders' last successes on 6 June.

food, while our men quarrelled and mistrusted each other and were short of bread and water. The result was that a deadly plague broke out in our camp, with several men each day dying of dysentery. So some of our soldiers secretly left the camp every day, made for the sea and on their arrival in England reported what they had seen or heard concerning these traitor knights. So when the bishop saw his numbers diminishing daily, he put pressure on his knights, who were now not his subjects but his masters, to make trial of their forces against the town before his army had been whittled away by death or departure.

The attack on the town of Ypres[2]

At last and with a bad grace the knights agreed to do what the bishop asked, and on the eve of the feast of St Laurence [9 August] moved against the defences of the town. But the townsmen, when they saw the attack, met it with all their might and by using stones, spears, arrows, Greek fire and the engines called 'guns' drove back our men on all sides. Now the bishop had had a very lightweight bridge made to give an easy ascent to the ramparts. But when the townsmen saw that this object had been constructed to do them much harm, they fired a huge stone from one of their guns, which hit the bridge, easily smashed it in pieces, and at the same time inflicted a cruel death on some of our knights who were standing on it. Similar losses happened elsewhere, so that our men were forced to retreat and give up the assault. All who had survived were taken away, and the English withdrew from the place of danger to their lodgings with individual hosts. In a few days the siege was lifted, and the men of Ghent departed sadly, cursing the treacherous English, with some justification, for if there had been as much co-operation among the English generals as there was among those of Ghent, the town of Ypres would not still today be uncaptured.

When they raised the siege, they set fire to all that would burn, to stop these things being a comfort or a help to the enemy. But willy-nilly they left behind there what they could not burn, break up or carry away, namely the great guns, which were worth a huge amount. Very many of the English did not know the time of the departure, and so, when forced to leave suddenly, left behind them all the valuables which they had acquired with so much peril and toil. Such was the end and result of the siege of the town of Ypres.[3]

The English knights oppose the bishop who wants to enter Picardy

After the lifting of the siege the bishop was informed by scouts that the king of France [Charles VI] had arrived at the city of Amiens with his army. He spoke to his knights, Sir Thomas Trivet, Sir William Elmham and the others, and said that he wanted to invade Picardy and to try the fortunes of war in one day's battle against the French king. Although he put forward many arguments that should have been able to arouse them to set out, he achieved nothing. Indeed he received wounding insults from them, for they declared that he was a hot headed man who had no idea of the strength of the French forces which could field a hundred men against each one of their own. It would not be safe, they continued, nor sensible to put God to the test in a battle where there would be no hope of success but a certainty of destruction, unless it had happened that they suddenly got themselves into such a tight corner that there was no way out except by fighting. When he heard this, the bishop said goodbye to these officers, and himself entered Picardy with just a few of his men. The knights indeed hurried to the town of Bourbourg, which they decided to fortify and garrison against the French, should they happen to arrive there.[3]

So when the bishop approached a part of the French army, he displayed himself and his men in open field with banners unfurled. But when nobody dared to give him battle, as the whole of

---

[1]   Walsingham is the only authority to describe this attack in any detail.
[2]   Knighton also describes the siege engines, guns, and 'carts laden with his utensils and other supplies' left behind by the retreating crusaders (*Knighton*, p. 327). They departed on 9 September, returning to their billets at Bourbourg (Trivet, Elmham and Farringdon) and Gravelines (Despenser).
[3]   The Westminster chronicler is outspoken on the betrayal of the bishop by these knights, describing them as 'men who should sooner strive to preserve this world's ephemeral riches than to lay up for themselves that good name which outshines and surpasses all fortune's favours' (*WC*, pp. 46–7).

the French army had not yet assembled, the bishop turned round his standards and marched with all haste to his town of Gravelines, accompanied by Sir Hugh Calveley, who in all trouble spots had always been his inseparable companion and loyal ally.

The bishop returns to Gravelines and the knights to Bourbourg

The king of France was now joined by his armies. He was not a little elated by the departure of our men, and when he learnt that some of them had entered the town of Bourbourg, he turned aside his whole army to that place, swearing that he would ransom none of those who were there at any price or for any prayer, but would either burn all of them in flames together with the town or certainly capture them and slay them in the mouth of the sword.[1] But the duke of Brittany opposed these plans, arguing that it would not turn out as the king believed. For he knew that the persons who were there were all powerful men with a knowledge of war, and that there was no possibility of defeating them without heavy French losses. 'You are not about to fight,' he said, 'against the Flemish, but against the English, who are men with the stoutest of hearts, and who prefer to die than be beaten.' But the king flared up at these words of the duke and said in reply, 'You are one of them, and that is why you are praising them.' The duke quickly said, 'Do not think that I said those words out of fear or favour for them, for you will see me and my men in the vanguard when we make our assault against them.' Indeed he had with him about ten thousand of the choicest troops, whom he had assembled from all his dominions. And so with banners raised he approached the walls.

In the town were the knights Lord Beaumont,[2] Thomas Trivet, William Elmham and William Farringdon and many other brave men. They stationed defenders on the walls and took up their positions, ready for the imminent battle against the Bretons. A terrific fight followed, watched by the king of France and all the French, and in every clash the Bretons came off the worse. For our soldiers had forged iron hooks with which they either speared the attackers and hauled them into the town or at least stung them into retreat and made them fall into ditches full of mud. And so several were yanked over the walls into the town and falling in a heap immediately had their brains dashed out like cattle. And many of those driven back from the walls drowned in the mud of the ditches. Also the standard of the duke of Brittany was forcibly wrenched from the hands of its bearer and hurried off into the town together with many standards of the other leaders. So fear of death forced the Bretons to give up the fight and to withdraw from the walls in shame.[3]

Then the French, also sure that they would prevail, tried to approach the walls, but the dangers they encountered showed them that the Bretons had not retreated without good reason. As soon as they drew near, they were driven back by red-hot darts. For when, in their wish to lay hands on them and draw them towards themselves, many put their hands on one dart, they all received the same pitiful reward of having their hands badly burnt. And so they were immediately put out of action, and when they let go of the darts, they were either dragged into the town or thrown into the ditch. More than five hundred French were killed in that battle, while our men suffered almost no losses, except that a third of the houses with great supplies of food were burnt to the ground by the Greek fire which had been shot into the town.

Night coming on brought the battle to an end. The French withdrew to their tents with the loss of the standards of the king and several of their lords. In the very dead of night the duke of Brittany came to the French king to ask him for his thoughts about the English, and whether he was still planning to make further attacks against them. The king replied that they were devils not men, so fiendishly clever had been the weapons they had devised to deal with Christians. Even so he said that he would not cease from the fight until he had taken them all prisoner by force. To

---

[1]   Charles VI raised the oriflamme at St Denis on 2 August and on 15 August his troops were mustered at Arras. They arrived at Bourbourg in the second week of September. For a summary account of the campaign see R. Vaughan, *Philip the Bold. The Foundations of the Burgundian State* (London, 1962), pp. 30–1.

[2]   John, 4th baron Beaumont (1361–96).

[3]   Walsingham is the only authority to claim the English scored early successes against the Breton vanguard; the Westminster chronicler dwells on the defeat and humiliation of the crusaders: *WC*, pp. 46–7.

Nor were they a small trained army of brave soldiers of the common people, but a large, feeble, inexperienced force of the rich and wealthy. How incredible that our knights did not cross the seas to fight the men they had long desired to meet and had often searched for. They were either kept at home by treachery or held back by stupidity.[1] It is so awful. The land that once bore and gave birth to men who were respected by all who dwelt nearby and feared by those who lived far off, now spews forth weaklings who are laughed at by our enemies and a subject for gossip among our people. For seldom or never is one of our knights found to be a man who devotes himself to his country, or labours for the good of its citizens. They all of them are hunting down their own profits and rummaging for their own gain. But I do not want to scandalise my readers by such talk, so I shall not write any more on these matters but return to my narrative.

So the bishop left France and returned to England. As soon as he landed, he made his way to the duke of Lancaster [John of Gaunt], who was still encamped in the same spot. The duke rebuked the bishop, 'looking for the knot in the bulrush',[2] and quickly sent him away. But he kept Sir Hugh Calveley with him some time longer, and showed him the honour due to his valued military service in the past. So this was the end of the expedition and the bishop's war.[3]

The Scots invade England

The Scots seized the opportunity of numbers of troops being absent with the bishop at this time and invaded Northumberland.[4] It is their custom to do this, when they think they have numerical superiority. They inflicted losses upon the inhabitants, plundering everywhere and taking people prisoner from their homes and hauling them back to Scotland. They also dared to assault with a large force the castle called Wark, which is on the river Tweed. After capturing and looting it, they burnt it to the ground, as nobody opposed their attack or was willing to make a stand against this outrage on account of the fear felt for certain nobles, who at that time were thought by the common people to favour the Scots more than the English. And so the knights and esquires who were in charge of the castles and fortresses in that area came to the king and gave them back into his hands, saying that the Scots had grown enormously powerful and that the English in those parts were too few to resist them unless the king himself gave a helping hand. These knights received a comforting reply, as I shall describe in the chapter I intend to write about the next parliament.

Of the pope and the Romans[5]

About the same time, the pope [Urban VI] began to lose faith in the loyalty of the Romans, and pretending that he wanted to breathe purer air, was in the habit of leaving Rome for a nearby castle. Sometimes he would return at nightfall but occasionally he would spend the night there and return to Rome the next day or the day after. But in order to remove all suspicion from the

---

[1]   The Westminster chronicler suggests the age of the king and the costs of any such campaign were what dissuaded the council from further action: *WC*, pp. 48–9.

[2]   Plautus, *Manaechmi*, 2. 1. See also *St Albans Chronicle*, ed. Taylor *et al.*, p. 706 n.

[3]   Despenser was immediately impeached by the chancellor, now Michael de la Pole.

[4]   The Westminster chronicler dates these incursions to November 1383; the Scots had broken a truce that was to expire in February 1384. The government responded in December and January with the appointment of Henry Percy, earl of Northumberland, and John Neville of Raby as wardens of the marches towards Scotland and Lords Clifford, Fitzwalter and Scrope as wardens of the west march. The *Historia vitae et regni Ricardi secundi* also reports the burning of Wark: *HVRS*, p. 79. The *Scotichronicon* records that the truce was first broken by Lord Archibald Douglas of Galloway when he captured Lochmaben castle: *Scotichronicon*, pp. 394–5.

[5]   Here Walsingham offers a somewhat garbled summary of Urban VI's movements in the twelve months following Charles of Durazzo's success at Naples in August 1382. Fearing that Charles would be unable to halt the Angevin advance on the kingdom, Urban determined to join him in Naples. Under the pretext of escaping the plague, he left Rome in April 1383 and progressed from Tivoli to Valmontone to San Germano and reaching Aversa by the summer. Here he was met by Charles who surprised Urban by his unwillingness to be manipulated; nonetheless, after three days the two agreed to return to Naples together and they entered the city on 9 November, but the balance of power between them had shifted in Charles's favour.

hearts of the Romans, he said that he was intending to build a strong castle near to the place he was visiting, as it was a lovely spot and would give him a retreat if some necessity forced him to leave Rome. The Romans were pleased at this, and without suspecting the truth or asking any questions, freely gave him permission to go to the place whenever and as often as he liked. They did this especially because they saw that the pope had hired great numbers of masons and carpenters and had had large quantities of stone and timber taken to the spot.

So now the pope was sure that no one had any wish to pry into his visits, he secretly summoned a powerful lord of the area, and arranged with him that he should come on a certain day with a troop of soldiers to escort the pope to his birthplace of Naples, as he thought that he would find more loyalty among his fellow-countrymen than among the Romans, should he happen to have need of it. And this was done.

But when the Romans heard that the pope had suddenly vanished, they got on their high horse and sent envoys commanding him to return. Otherwise, they declared, they were intending to depose him and elect as pope one of the cardinals who had remained in Rome, or indeed recall his enemy, the antipope, and enthrone him. But their threats caused the pope little concern, and he decided to stay on in Naples, although many misfortunes were to befall him there, as I shall relate more fully in later chapters, when the place and the time require it.

Enemy ships captured[1]

During the days which the bishop of Norwich [Henry Despenser] and his crusaders were spending besieging the town of Ypres, the enemy fitted out five warships, of the sort we call 'sloops', to block and hinder any ships crossing the seas either to the bishop or to Aquitaine, for crusaders had been sent to Aquitaine as well, with a large contingent of knights and esquires and commanded by Sir Britrigald de la Bret and some other men experienced in war chosen from the English. These five ships put to sea and did much damage, but the men of Portsmouth and Dartmouth were not putting up with this, and armed their own warships to oppose the French attacks. They sailed to meet them, and suddenly engaged them in a very bloody conflict. But with the help of heaven our men ran out winners and killed all but nine of the men in the French ships. They captured the vessels with all their contents and by this glorious victory brought back to their country both booty and peace.

About the same time an English squadron, which was watching the watery paths of the sea, took as prizes by the rights of war eight large ships, packed with stores of cargo including especially wine. Indeed it is said that there were one thousand five hundred casks of good wine aboard them. And so the English were greatly heartened by these successes, small though they were.

How the men of Ghent gained the town of Oudenaarde

The crusaders had now returned to England from Flanders. The French were still protecting the town of Oudenaarde, which had been besieged by the men of Ghent in the previous year from the feast of the finding of the Holy Cross [3 May] right up to Christmas, when, as I have related above, the men of Ghent were defeated by the king of France [Charles VI], and Philip van Artevelde was killed, together with twenty-five thousand Flemings.[2] But these Frenchmen now began to exercise a cruel dominion over the citizens of this town, depriving them of all freedom, and not only seizing their property but also forcibly taking away their wives and raping them just as they wished. The townsmen of Oudenaarde were extremely distressed at all this, and not surprisingly, when they realised that there was no hope of controlling the French and they observed their crimes increasing day by day, they sent envoys in secret to Ghent, who were to report to the citizens the injuries which they had suffered in Oudenaarde and to ask them for help. They also promised that they would let the men of Ghent into Oudenaarde on any night they wished, so that they could thus gain possession of the town, and take proper revenge for the wrongs and losses they had so often received themselves from the French.

---

1   Walsingham is the only English commentator to record these episodes.
2   See above, p. 193 and n.

On hearing this the men of Ghent speedily got ready for the journey and arrived at Oudenaarde by night.[1] Those inside and those outside the town exchanged signals, and the men of Ghent were admitted. The townsmen joined forces with them, and as they knew very well where the French were lodged, they suddenly burst into the houses where the French were sleeping and in sudden assaults upon them killed all the French in the town – and that was a very great number – so that not one of them was left alive. And so the men of Ghent gained possession of the town, and also inflicted great slaughter on the Flemings who had betrayed the citizens of Oudenaarde. The English merchants there partly recovered the losses which they had formerly suffered at Bruges, since they bought cheaply the goods found in the town by the men of Ghent, these including not only furniture but also houses and the various places in the town. Next, the men of Ghent sent envoys to the king of England, saying that they had gained possession of the town and would like to give it to him, if he was willing to send a garrison and reinforcements there from England. Otherwise they would raze it to the ground. The king indeed thanked them, but replied that he did not want to send men there as there were pressing dangers overshadowing his own kingdom from many quarters. He courteously welcomed the envoys, as was fitting, and sent them back to Ghent. This was the end of those French who had committed many wrongs in the town of Oudenaarde.

Nor must I pass over in silence the fact that a vast treasure belonging to the count of Flanders [Louis II, of Maële] was found there,[2] a find which not surprisingly would encourage the men of Ghent to continue the war, but force the count into a state of despair.

A parliament at London

Around the time of the feast of All Saints [1 November] a parliament was held in London.[3] It granted to the king a half fifteenth tax from the laity, and, a little later, a half tenth tax from the clergy.[4] The northern lords asked for a part of this money, seeing that they had been commissioned in this parliament to guard their lands against invasion by the Scots. But William Wykeham, bishop of Winchester, replied that they had been made rich lords instead of paupers precisely so that they might be able more easily to keep off the Scots and so that the king and the southern lords might be less troubled by such demands, especially when every year they were having to dispatch armies elsewhere and annoy the people by enlisting them for these other wars. Also it was not difficult for those on the spot to drive back the Scots, seeing that they had been made lords and magnates, while their fathers and grandfathers before them had been able to resist the Scottish enemy and often to triumph over them just by their own courage and boldness, without being rich lords like they were.

Despite the bishop of Winchester, commissions were granted to the northern lords for gathering together a goodly army, and for resisting the Scots and giving them loss for loss, whenever it happened that the Scots invaded or entered those parts with hostile intent. These commissions were granted especially because it had been agreed on the last occasion of the March Day meeting between the duke of Lancaster and the Scots that for the future advantage of both parties, neither the Scots nor the English should be put to all the usual trouble and expense, but that each year named men on both sides should be sent to the parliament of both kingdoms who were to report publicly on any wrongs sustained and to accept what compensation was judged by the lords to cover the matter. But because the Scots had failed to come to this parliament as agreed, and in the meantime had also dared to make more raids on the north and had even hired mercenaries from France to harm the English, it was decided by parliament that the English should break their word

---

[1]   The Westminster chronicler records that the Ghentois, under the command of Frans Acherman, began their assault on Oudenaarde after abandoning the abortive siege of Ypres: *WC*, pp. 46–7. See also Froissart, *Chroniques*, xi. 180–1; FCBuchon, ii. 284–6.

[2]   The Westminster chronicler reports that they found 'untold treasure and wine galore': *WC*, pp. 46–7.

[3]   The session began on 26 October: *RP*, iii. 149.

[4]   According to the Westminster chronicler the grant was made conditional on the crown pursuing peace negotiations with both the French and the Scots.

just as the Scottish had done, and that a chosen force of a thousand spearmen and two thousand archers should be sent from England to Scotland under the command of Thomas of Woodstock [earl of Buckingham] to check the Scottish attempts.[1]

As soon as they heard this, the Scots were very frightened and at the end of the parliament suppliants from them arrived, who were even willing to discuss terms for a peace or a truce.[2] But the English had had so much experience of Scottish bad faith, that they were unwilling to hold discussions with them or to come to terms, but insulted them and ordered them to go back home, telling them to defend their own lives as they well knew how to do, and to look after their own rights. After the Scottish envoys had left, the northern lords took up the task of protecting the northern frontier, until the earl of Buckingham, Thomas of Woodstock, should be ready to march there with a greater force.

In this parliament the king took the temporalities of the bishop of Norwich into his own hands, on the grounds that the bishop had disobeyed his command, when, as I have related, the king had recalled him by writ when he was making ready to cross the Channel, but the bishop had refused to return to London.[3] Also the knights in the bishop's forces in Flanders were put into prison, because they had themselves disobeyed the bishop, and, what is worse, had been disloyal to him. But they were at once released by friends who ransomed them with gold. Such was the end and the results of this present parliament.[4]

The conclusion of the year

Thus ended a year of good harvests of grain and fruit. But there was a lot of suspicion that the fruits of the various trees such as apples, pears etc. were infected because of the various unhealthy mists and noisome vapours in the atmosphere. And indeed many men this year through eating these fruits died of a virus or suffered serious illness and weakness. It was a sad year for the English, as so many men had died both in Flanders and at home. It was a black year for the Flemings, as their land and its people had been devastated both in civil wars and by foreigners. For the French it was a year both frightening and burdensome. Never before had they feared any English leader as much as they did the awesome bishop. And they had shouldered the burden of the conscription of the vast army assembled by the king of France [Charles VI] and of the money which all of them had poured out for this campaign.

[1384]

A truce between the kingdoms

In 1384, the seventh year of the reign of King Richard II, the king spent Christmas at his manor at Eltham. Queen Anna was with him. John of Gaunt, duke of Lancaster, had set out for France before Christmas to discuss peace between England and France, and after Christmas had ended he returned to England, bringing with him a truce valid until the feast of St John Baptist [24 June]. At this time he was to return to France for further discussions and, if possible, sign a peace treaty between the two kings.[5] Both kingdoms clearly perceived from the profit they made the advan-

---

1   The planned expedition did not embark for Scotland until 1385. See below, pp. 227, 229.
2   Interestingly, the *Scotichronicon* makes no mention of the embassy to England. Indeed in this narrative it is the English who were fearful of the Scots, exclaiming 'if we allow the Scots to rage amongst us in this way, they will remove from us our place and race': *Scotichronicon*, vii. 396–7.
3   Writs for the seizure of the temporalities of Norwich were not issued until on 6 February 1384, three months after this parliament was over.
4   Sir William Elmham, Sir Henry Ferriers, Sir Robert Fitzralph and Sir Thomas Trivet were all arrested but Trivet begged for mercy and was spared the Tower. See also *RP*, iii. 158; *WC*, pp. 50–2.
5   Even before the full extent of the English humiliation in Flanders became known, the council was convinced of the need to renew the peace negotiations. On 8 September, Gaunt was commissioned by Chancellor de la Pole to lead an embassy that was to include the king's half-brother, John Holland, Sir Thomas Percy and Sir William Beauchamp. They embarked for Calais in November and remained there until the end of January. Walsingham misrepresents the terms of the truce; a temporary peace was agreed at Leulingham on 26 January

tages brought to them both by the truce. For during the ensuing Lent, French merchants, particularly Norman ones, filled England with all the essential goods of wine, fruits of different kinds, spices and fish. There was such an abundance of goods that the English marvelled at their cheapness, especially in those parts of the land that were reachable by the Normans. And the French and the Normans were happy because they received prompt payment in silver and gold for their goods from the English. In fact they made far more out of this trading than they would have done for a similar small amount of business in their own country. So the dearest wish of the inhabitants of both lands, and particularly of the commons, was for peace.[1]

The Londoners argue over their mayors

During the night of the feast of the Purification of the Blessed Virgin [2 February] in the same year, huge lightning flashes were seen and thunderclaps heard which greatly terrified men's hearts. And not long afterwards the mayor of London of the previous year, John of Northampton or otherwise called John Comberton, who, following the etymology of his name, had filled the city of London with quarrels, now attempted new schemes of disorder, supported by all those who took pleasure in plunder.[2] With his crowd of supporters he not once but several times, to the terror of the peace-loving masses, dared to cause trouble by making an attack on the legally elected mayor of the city. And when the mayor for that year, a knight called Sir Nicholas Brembre,[3] attempted to check these attacks, the cronies of John Comberton were seized with such madness that a tailor among their number, who was seen in their estimation as a possible mayor, publicly asked for the help of the commons and aroused them to follow John Comberton. But as a punishment for this, on the advice of Sir Robert Knolles, he was dragged from his house and beheaded, as instigator of the revolt and disturber of the king's peace. This execution put a stop to the crowd disturbances for the time being and quietened down the mutinous people, who, so it was said, had conspired at that time to kill the elected mayor and many nobles.[4]

The duke of Lancaster sets out for Scotland

Just before Lent, John, duke of Lancaster, and his brother Thomas of Woodstock, earl of Buckingham, departed for Scotland with an army of knights, esquires and archers that could scarcely be counted, in order to punish the disloyal Scots for their treachery.[5] Having stayed in the north of England until they had consumed the food supplies of the natives and inflicted more losses upon them than had previously been inflicted by the Scots themselves, they at length, around Easter time,[6] invaded the land of the Scots, where the duke showed such restraint towards the inhabitants that he allowed the citizens of Edinburgh to take out of the city whatever goods they liked and to carry them beyond the Firth of Forth.[7] During this time he instructed his

---

that was subsequently extended until 1 October 1385 when negotiations were set to resume. See also Saul, *Richard II*, p. 135.

1 Walsingham's observations as to the benefits of this peace are not found in other sources.

2 Northampton had ended his two-year term as mayor in October 1383. See also Barron, *London*, pp. 148–9, 334.

3 Brembre, a grocer, was elected mayor on 13 October 1383. The Westminster chronicler reports that there were some at the election who called for Northampton, and Brembre prevailed by a narrow margin and 'not having universal support' (*WC*, pp. 62–3 and n).

4 The *Historia vitae et regni Ricardi secundi* describes this man as only 'uno de fautoribus dicti Johannis' (*HVRS*, p. 80) although he confirms the involvement of Sir Robert Knolles, but the Westminster chronicler explains that he was a cordwainer (*WC*, pp. 64–5).

5 Easter fell on 10 April 1384, thus if Walsingham's dating is correct this expedition departed at the end of February. The *Scotichronicon* records that Gaunt entered Scotland in Holy Week (3–10 April): *Scotichronicon*, vii. 396–7. There had been extensive incursions into Cumbria and Northumbria in the preceding winter months; Knighton reports fierce assaults on both Carlisle and Penrith: *Knighton*, pp. 332–5.

6 The Westminster chronicler says the army crossed the border on Palm Sunday (3 April) (*WC*, pp. 66–7), but Knighton places it a week later on Easter Monday (*Knighton*, p. 335).

7 According to the Westminster chronicler the duke's restraint extended to the protection of Melrose Abbey which his men proposed to raze to the ground. The chronicler also reports that it was Gaunt's decision to

soldiers that on pain of death they were not to dare to move towards Edinburgh. So for three whole days our men stayed encamped only some three miles distant from the city, when they could have advanced on the city and attacked the Scots as they were carrying away their property or even seized these very goods under the rights of war. But it was only when the Scots had removed everything they wanted from the city and saved their own skins by flight that the duke gave the signal for the army to move towards Edinburgh.

On their arrival they found nothing except empty houses, from the roofs of which even all the straw had been lifted down and taken away in case of fire. On the night of Easter indeed the duke made his army spend the night under arms in the marshes for fear of the enemy. And as it began to snow and the cold became unendurable, he is said to have lost more than five hundred horses due to the cold, to say nothing of the men who lost their lives. The Scots for their part showed sense all the time and after leaving their city lay hidden in forests or beyond the Firth of Forth. They had no wish to attack our men, as they knew from experience that our men in such a place and at such a time would die of cold and hunger without the Scots needing to draw their swords and fight. And this is what happened. For many of the English died of natural causes, while many others were taken prisoner or killed during Scottish raids on their ranks.

So to win a reputation for good leadership the duke and his brother put a ban on those wishing to roam in search of fodder. And when some did go off, the brothers mounted their swiftest horses and followed them, and, showing them no more mercy than if they had been enemy, they struck, wounded, pierced and killed them with very sharp lances, causing more losses among the English than among the enemy. In the end the English did little damage to the enemy apart from the burning of a few towns. They returned home amid the curses of all the northerners in Northumbria.[1] The lords themselves treated the whole matter with high disdain, but the troops were hungry, harassed and in dire straits. After their departure the Scots immediately invaded the northern parts, driving away booty and inflicting more damage on the inhabitants by the burning of houses than our men had previously inflicted on the Scots. Indeed the result of this expedition was that the kingdom itself suffered greater losses from money squandered, men killed and property lost than it is known to have suffered from previous expeditions made over a number of years.

A parliament at Salisbury

At the end of Eastertide, that is the fifteen or few more days after Easter, at the king's summons the nobles met at Salisbury to attend a parliament.[2] In an unlucky hour there hurried to this parliament a Carmelite friar, a bachelor in theology and of Irish birth.[3] For he had composed and written out a document, in which were described several completely wicked schemes, which, so he asserted, had been thought up by the duke of Lancaster [John of Gaunt]. The nub of the matter was that the duke had planned to suddenly kill the king and seize the kingdom. The document indicated the time, the place and other things which could act as proof for this accusation. The friar obtained an audience with the king, and, as he handed him the document, he swore on the sacrament of the body of Christ which he himself that day had celebrated that no word in the document he had written was untrue, and advised the king not to listen to the duke's excuses. 'With his subtle words,' said the friar, 'he will put off judgement for this day, and if he gets just a mile away from here, he will draw together a crowd of citizens, and the further he is given the

---

allow the Scots time to escape Edinburgh before they entered the city and under his authority that the city was not burned. The story is corroborated by the *Scotichronicon*, which also records that Gaunt 'on account of the courtesy previously shown to him by the Scots . . . imposed as little harm on them as he could': WC, p. 67; *Scotichronicon*, vii. 396–9.

[1]   The expedition remained in Scotland for little more than a fortnight. When they returned across the border around 23 April, the earl of Northumberland was charged with the wardenship of the Scottish marches.

[2]   Parliament sat from 29 April until 27 May: RP, iii. 166.

[3]   John Latimer or Latemer. Although a graduate he does not appear in Emden's *Biographical Register* for Oxford.

The duke of Lancaster departs for France to treat for a truce

About the beginning of the month of August, the duke of Lancaster set out for the kingdoms of France to discuss with the French the possibilities of peace or a truce.[1] Such discussions had always been harmful to the English and the promises made had never borne fruit. So the duke stayed there for a long time with his vast retinue of nobles. It was thought that he would bring back good news for his country, but he returned with a warning that there would be war from the beginning of the summer of the following year, as he only had a truce which lasted up to 1 May.[2] It is said that before he returned to England he had spent 50,000 marks of silver.

The trial and judgement of John of Northampton, formerly mayor of London

At the same, while the duke was still abroad, many of the nobles of the kingdom were summoned by the king to Reading to put a stop to the seditious activities of John of Northampton, lately mayor of London, who had been plotting crimes of immense consequence.[3] But he was found guilty of these at Reading, the evidence being provided by a clerk of his own household, who brought into the light of day the very many schemes which John had thought up to do harm to the king and the whole city of London. And when the sentence was about to be passed in the presence of the king, the villain cried aloud and asserted that such sentence should not be passed in the absence of his master, the duke. At these words both nobles and commons began to suspect the duke of treachery. But, following the process of the law, the judge pronounced these words. 'John,' he said, 'you must refute the crimes of which you are accused by fighting a duel, or according to the laws of the land you must submit to drawing, hanging and quartering.' As John stood there dumb, unwilling to speak one word, it was decreed that he should be put in prison for life and his goods confiscated for the king's use, and that during his lifetime he should not approach within a hundred miles of London.[4]

So he was sent to the castle of Tintagel, which is in Cornwall, while the servants of the king, just like harpies, got their fingers on his possessions. This was the end of the process of law carried out against him at this time.

A miracle that occurred at the feast of Oswin, king and saint

Around this time, well on 20 August, the feast of the passion of St Oswin, king and martyr, a miracle happened at Newcastle-upon-Tyne, of a sort unseen and unheard of in our day. Two sailors were trying on this day to cut a piece of timber to mend their boat. When one of them struck the piece of timber with his axe, he was amazed to see blood spurting copiously from the wood, as though it were an animal. He was greatly awestruck at such an unprecedented happening, and for a long time was uncertain what to do. But in the end he remembered it was St Oswin's day, and realising that he had impaired its sanctity, he vowed that he would never again do manual work on that day. But when his companion, who had scoffed at the miracle, heard this

---

[1]   Gaunt was given a commission to conduct another embassy on 27 May 1384, to be accompanied by his brother, Thomas, earl of Buckingham, Sir John Holland, Sir Thomas Percy as well as several clerks and churchmen. They embarked between 11 and 30 June and negotiations opened at Calais at the beginning of July. See also Saul, *Richard II*, p. 137.

[2]   Since the January negotiations the position of the French had been transformed by the succession of Philip of Burgundy to the Flemish inheritance and they were now unwilling to make any significant concessions. The embassy could secure nothing more than an extension of the truce.

[3]   For Northampton's activities see above, pp. 183–5, 188.

[4]   A council was summoned at Reading for 17 August; Mayor Brembre and the aldermen of the city were also in attendance to witness Northampton's trial. The clerk whose evidence condemned him was Thomas Usk, who had served as Northampton's secretary, according to the Westminster chronicler. The Westminster monk corroborates the exchange between the king and Northampton concerning the presence of Gaunt, but he suggests that it was the intercession of the queen that saved Northampton from the gallows. With two other supporters, Northampton was returned for trial before the chancellor, Michael de la Pole, and then finally conveyed to prison at Tintagel, his associates being dispatched to Corfe Castle and Nottingham Castle, the intention being to keep them as far from the capital as possible. See the *WC*, pp. 91–7.

vow, he swore that on that very day he would cut the timber into shape and put it in its required position. But he also, when he struck the wood, saw blood gushing forth abundantly from the part he had struck. Still unmoved he turned the wood over and began to cut away at another part of it. But there also the same miracle occurred, and blood came forth, as if from an ox or a cow. He turned the wood over on all four sides. But blood flowed out, whichever side he struck. The sight of this converted the sailor who had up to now impiously poured scorn upon the sign, and there and then he vowed that on that day he would never do any manual work. This miracle was seen by many people, upon whom the burden of proof rests, and it is a great testimony to the holiness and exceptional nature of the martyr.[1]

A solar eclipse

On 16 August in the same year, late in the evening and throughout the following night, horrific thunderclaps were heard in England and terrifying lighting flashes seen, all of which dreadfully scared mortal men. And the next day in the afternoon there was an eclipse of the sun lasting about an hour and a conjunction at the same time. Many people saw them.[2]

At a parliament at London, a duel at the same and the condemnation of the earl of Northumberland

In the same year about the time of the feast of St Martin [11 November] a parliament was held in London,[3] in which, as had now been the case for many a year, nothing worth recording took place except that a document was produced for the extortion of taxes from the clergy and the common people for the financing of the useless wars of the king.[4] Also, that a duel was fought in the lists between an English esquire called John Walsh and a native of Navarre [Martlet de Villencuve] who had accused John of treachery to his king and his kingdom. In fact John was not a traitor but was hated by the man from Navarre, because, when under-captain at Cherbourg, he had used force on the man's wife. The Navarrian publicly admitted this, when later on he had been beaten in the duel and was on the point of death. And so the king, who had taken his seat to watch the duel together with the princes of his realm, adjudged that the Navarrian be drawn and hanged, although the queen and several others offered up earnest prayers on his behalf.[5]

The parliament had not yet ended when news arrived from the north about the capture by the Scots of Berwick castle, the custody of which belonged by ancestral right to the earl of Northumberland, Henry Percy. For the Scots had cunningly gained entrance to the castle by bribing the person who was then guarding the castle as a substitute.[6] The duke of Lancaster [John of Gaunt] was very pleased when he heard the news, because, so men said, he now had to hand the means of harming the earl. So the result was that through, it was said, the intervention of the duke, the earl was put on trial by the nobles present at the parliament for the loss of a royal castle and received a sentence of condemnation from the king which was published abroad to his

---

1   The monks of St Albans Abbey had a special devotion to St Oswin, the patronal saint of their northern-most dependent priory at Tynemouth, Northumbria, and stories of the saint's intercession were circulated throughout the St Albans network.
2   The eclipse is not recorded by the other authorities.
3   Parliament opened on 12 November: *RP*, iii. 184.
4   No other authority attests to the presentation of a document in the commons, but there is no doubt that Chancellor de la Pole impressed on the assembly the need to secure the defence of the kingdom and its inter-ests in Flanders, France and Spain. The authorities differ as to the response of the commons, but it appears, as the Westminster chronicler suggests, that the half-subsidy granted at Salisbury was confirmed and another half-subsidy promised on condition that the king did embark on a new campaign in France in the coming months: *WC*, p. 103. See also *RP*, iii. 182, 185; Saul, *Richard II*, p. 138.
5   Although it also reported by the Westminster chronicler, Knighton offers the best account of this curious episode, providing the name and origins of both parties: Walsh is said to be a Grimsby man. Knighton adds that Walsh was knighted after his victory: *Knighton*, p. 335.
6   The *Scotichronicon* records that the castle was captured by night 'in the month of September', an obvious error for December: *Scotichronicon*, vii. 402–3.

discredit.[1] But the king soon mitigated the severity of this verdict, although by doing this he displeased the duke of Lancaster. All this took place on 14 December in the same parliament, even though the earl himself, when summoned by royal writ to attend the parliament, had preferred to stay at home to look after his estates. This dispute between the duke and the earl sparked off the later hatred and anger between them.

The earl of Northumberland captures Berwick castle

The earl of Northumberland [Henry Percy], with this sentence passed on him but restored to life and his possessions by the mercy of the king, found no causes for delay, but made all preparations of war to besiege the castle and capture the men in it. He assembled a large force, collected the equipment necessary for taking the castle by storm and with all speed surrounded and besieged the castle. At length, after some little delay, besiegers and besieged agreed that the besieged should leave the castle, enjoying the possession of their lives and their moveable goods, and that in return for handing over the castle they should receive from the earl 2,000 marks of English money.[2] In this way the earl recovered the castle from the hands of the Scots, having received a lesson to look after his castles more carefully in the future.

A note on Pope Urban [VI]

The duke of Anjou [Louis I (1356–84)] had suffered a long exile, living far away from his homeland.[3] He had poured out indescribable sums of money, had lost by death his noble followers, and now, his hopes frustrated, he fell sick, took to his bed and perished in the same way as his followers, dying with great bitterness of mind in a foreign land. It had happened that the man who had not been content with his position as duke while aspiring to a king's dignity had lost the honour of his dukedom, and had died and ended his life not only courting the favour of others but excommunicated from the church as well. The remnants of his army turned brigand and thief, and filled the land of Sicily [i.e. Naples] and the other regions round about it with their murders and their robberies. These were the achievements and successes of that whole expedition assembled by the duke of Anjou when he was planning to conquer the kingdom of Sicily and attempting to overthrow Pope Urban [VI].

So ended that year, a peaceful one for the French, but with losses for the English from Scottish raids. The grain harvest was good, but the fruit crop was neither a complete failure nor a bumper one. In this land indeed it had been a turbulent year of disturbances, brought about by the violent passions of the Londoners in their wish to restore John Comberton [i.e. John of Northampton] to his former position, and by the covert hatred that had sprung up between two lords, as will become clear in my narrative of the following year.

[1385]

In 1385, the eighth year of the reign of King Richard II, the king spent Christmas with Queen Anna, whom he rarely if ever allowed to be away from his side. The Bohemians, the queen's compatriots, were also present. They were enjoying the delights of England, and, forgetful of their own country, they refused to go back home, but with no sense of shame stayed on as guests who gave no pleasure.

---

1   Northumberland had been appointed keeper of Berwick castle, an office that carried with it the sum of £100 according to the *Historia vitae et regni Ricardi secundi* (*HVRS*, p. 85) or 500 marks, according to the Westminster chronicler: *WC*, pp. 104–5. The Scots had taken advantage of Northumberland's absence at the Westminster parliament.
2   The *Historia vitae et regni Ricardi secundi* gives the figure as £1000: *HVRS*, p. 85.
3   Walsingham refers here to Duke Louis' campaign against Charles of Durazzo and his invasion of the kingdom of Naples in 1382–83. Following Urban's proclamation of a crusade against Louis in January 1384 Charles had abandoned his defensive policy and advanced on the Angevin enemy, although he remained reluctant to be drawn into a pitched battle. An uneasy stalemate ensued and in the summer plague passed through the lines of both protagonists. Louis himself died in September 1384 and, as Walsingham reports here, the remains of his army disbanded. Froissart also reports his death 'without money or men': *Chroniques*, xi. 184–5; FCBuchon, ii. 302–3.

The death of John Wyclif

On the very feast day of St Thomas, archbishop and martyr [29 December], John Wyclif, so it was said, had prepared to deliver a sermon, in which he intended to spew out invective and blasphemy against the saint.[1] But all of a sudden that creature of the devil, enemy of the church, disturber of the people, idol of the heretics, model for hypocrites, fomenter of schism, disseminator of hatred and fabricator of lies was struck by the judgement of God, and he felt a paralysis attack all his limbs together. That mouth indeed, which had spoken such enormities against God, his saints and holy church, was pitifully twisted aside from its proper place and provided a grisly spectacle for those who saw it. His tongue was rendered dumb and denied him the opportunity of confessing or bearing witness to his sins. His shaking head clearly showed that the curse, which God had sent like a bolt of lightning upon Cain, had been sent upon him as well. And so that no one should doubt that he had been assigned to fellowship with Cain, according to those who were present at his deathbed the dying man by external signs showed his despair. Such indeed was the conclusion of all his wickedness.

Lord Bourchier and his successes at Ghent

During these days Lord Edward [i.e. John] Bourchier was sent to Ghent with an armed force to take command of the people as their governor.[2] They indeed had earnestly requested this of the king, and with the testimony of an oath had promised that they would be loyal to Sir Edward [i.e. John]. And even if I were to be silent about it, his enemies, the French themselves, would testify to the good sense he showed in commanding the men of Ghent and his restraint in conducting the war. For no sooner had he arrived than with him as leader the men of Ghent defeated three thousand of the French. Some of these they put to flight, some they took captive, most of them they killed, and besides the other booty they came away with four hundred horses of the enemy.

The French were so violently angry that they viciously mutilated all the prisoners that they were holding in their possession by gouging out their eyes, lopping off their hands and doing other bits of irreparable damage to them, and then they sent them back home to rouse the passions of the citizens. When the men of Ghent saw them, they were so angry that they wanted to inflict the same punishments upon the knights and esquires, whom, as I said, they had taken alive from the French side. But Lord Edward [i.e. John] Bourchier put a stop to these attempts by pointing out that such a thing should not happen to men who had been captured under the laws of war and who had entrusted themselves to the good faith of the men of Ghent so that their lives might be saved. However, he added that would give his full permission for any Frenchmen they could capture by force in the future to be mutilated in the same way, and sent back to France to give their countrymen the same kind of greeting. And a short while later this actually happened, as the two sides met in battle and under the leadership of Lord [i.e. John] Edward the men of Ghent were victorious.[3]

---

[1]   The Westminster chronicler reports that Wyclif fell ill on St Stephen's day (26 December) (*WC*, pp. 106–7), but the *Historia vitae et regni Ricardi secundi* supports Walsingham (*HVRS*, p. 86). The *Vita* also gives the date of his death as 31 December (*HVRS*, p. 87).

[2]   The succession of Philip of Burgundy to the county of Flanders, and the failure of Despenser's crusade, threatened English commercial interests centred on the three cloth towns of Bruges, Ghent and Ypres and the council continued to explore the possibility of concerted action with the Ghentois. The appointment of an English governor for Ghent was at the suggestion of the Ghentois themselves, but the divisions in the council over the merits of this policy were reflected in the choice of a minor magnate, John, 2nd Baron Bourchier. Walsingham's reference to 'Edward' is a mistake. See Saul, *Richard II*, p. 139.

[3]   This skirmish is not reported by the other contemporary chroniclers.

The dispute between the pope and the king of Sicily [i.e. Charles of Durazzo, of Naples] and the degradation of six cardinals

Just about this time, the whole of Sicily [i.e. Naples] and the whole Roman Curia were shaken to their foundations by a great disturbance such as had never been previously experienced or endured. I shall describe the reason for this below.

The pope [Urban VI], as I said earlier, had succumbed to the charms of his homeland and deceived the Romans by his sudden withdrawal to it. But on his approaching Naples, he had been seized unawares in his litter by Charles [of Durazzo], king of Jerusalem and Sicily, who by many was also called king of Naples.[1] For eight days Charles kept the pope with him in a private place and guarded him with such close secrecy that even the papal retinue did not know where their master had gone. Afterwards the pope called this detainment his 'imprisonment'. It was for this reason that a great quarrel sprang up between the pope and the king, and that there was an increase in their mutual hatred. But the queen of Naples was greatly saddened by such a disagreement and used all her strength to make peace again and renew the friendship between them. And her commendable persistence did restore peace between the two, despite the difficulties involved, and the king bound himself by oath never to wrong the pope in word or deed.

On the pope's side, the cardinals and the Romans on the pope's behalf bound themselves to pay a hundred thousand florins to the king if the pope did not keep the conditions of the peace agreed between them, one condition of the agreement being that the pope would provide help to protect the city of Naples. When the agreement had been signed, the pope made the sign of the cross over the king with his hands and strengthened him to make war on the enemies of the church and to take the field against them. And so the king departed and took the field against these adversaries for eight months. But immediately after the king's departure, the pope transferred himself and his whole court to the town called Nocera and thus broke the agreements and pact entered upon by them. So the queen of Naples gave orders to cities and castles, towns and villages, and men of every rank not to dare on pain of death to bring food supplies to the pope and the members of his Curia and she completely forbade all commerce with them from all regions.

Discord then arose not only between the pope and the Sicilians [i.e. Neapolitans], but also between the pope and the Romans on account of the pacts that he had made and sent to them under his own bulls sealed with a lead seal. For he had assured these same Romans under oath and had pledged his word that he would return to Rome and live among them. But not a single one of all his promises did he keep. So the Romans regarded him as a liar and publicly stated that this was so.

A dispute between the pope and some of his college

In the same year on 11 January a serious disagreement broke out between the pope and some of the college of cardinals, who on that very day according to custom had entered the papal palace after being summoned by the pope. They went into the consistory quite ignorant of what the

---

1   Walsingham here describes the final breakdown of the alliance between Urban and Charles of Durazzo. Like his earlier accounts of the schismatic popes, here he conflates the events of many months into a series of short dramas. The events described in the following passages took place between 1383 and 1385. Walsingham rightly traces the beginning of the dispute to the meeting between Pope Urban and Charles at Aversa in 1383 when Urban was held in custody in the castle for three days and the city gates were closed to his retainers before the differences between them were resolved and they progressed together into Naples. When Charles advanced with his army against the Angevin invasion the following spring, Urban removed himself to the castle of Nocera in an attempt to reassert his authority over and independence from the king. Charles's response was to undermine him through his cardinals and with his encouragement six of them conspired at Nocera to have Urban placed under the authority of an ecclesiastical council. The conspiracy was discovered, however, and Urban retained sufficient control to seize and imprison the six cardinals. Convinced of Charles's complicity in the plot, Urban placed the city of Naples under interdict. See S. Fodale, *La politica napoletana di Urbano VI* (Rome, 1973), pp. 112–19.

pope had in mind, for in the meeting he unexpectedly charged and accused in conclave six of them with conspiring to kill him.[1] He declared that they had planned to fix upon him thirty articles of heresy and to have given proof that he had been made rotten by the wickedness of heresy. The cardinals were astonished, and at once one after another swore that they had planned no such things. None the less the pope, without going through any process of law, had them arrested, put in prison and later examined under torture. These were the names of the cardinals.

The names of the degraded cardinals

The cardinal of Venice,[2] the cardinal of England[3] and the cardinal of Genoa.[4] All these were respected men of religion, held in high regard among the people and professors of holy scripture. The names of the other three were cardinal Sangro, the cardinal of Corfu and the cardinal of Taranto.[5] These were powerful men of noble birth, and two of them were doctors of law.[6] So after they had been tortured in this way, it is said that they confessed their crime, whether conscience-stricken or in a wish to escape the pain of the punishment. But the cardinal of England confessed to nothing, except that he admitted having said that the pope was excessively arrogant.[7]

On the next Sunday [15 January] the pope had the members of his Curia and the laity from the town and surrounding villages compelled to come to his castle. Once they were inside, he ordered the gates to be shut so that no one could leave until he had finished preaching. So he climbed up a very high tower above the second gate, and with the people sitting outside on the ground in great cold and hunger he began to preach a sermon, which lasted almost until vespers. In his sermon he gave many reasons for his actions, including the fact that the six cardinals had confessed to devising the articles of heresy and that they had plotted his death in such a manner that the king indeed with his retinue would have suddenly taken him prisoner and deposed him from office and certainly killed him. He also said that all this had been shown him by divine revelation. It would take too long and be too boring to include the tales that he told, for example the story that the cardinal of Reiti,[8] whom he had once made cardinal but long since deposed, was the originator and author of the crimes against him. He had also long ago excommunicated him. This cardinal of Reiti was considered a man of wisdom and judgement in the eyes of the people and was an exceptionally learned doctor of law, and although the pope had deposed him, he was still very highly regarded in the council and among the councillors of King Charles [of Durazzo]. The pope also mentioned in his sermon all his services to the king and the cardinals, how he had raised them up from the dust of the earth, and all the favours he had shown to the king and the queen and to the cardinals.

After he had finished his sermon, together with his cardinals who had not been deposed the pope held up a cross, lit candles and then passed sentence of excommunication on King Charles and his queen, the antipope and the anticardinals, the abbot of Monte Cassino who had once been

---

1   This was Pope Urban's response on discovering the conspiracy against him. Walsingham was well-informed about this episode, probably because of the presence of an English cardinal – Adam Easton – amongst the accused. Easton was a Benedictine monk of Norwich Priory and a distinguished university graduate and his experiences must have been reported in the same circles in which Walsingham himself moved.
2   Luigi Donati (d. 1386).
3   Adam Easton, a Benedictine monk of Norwich Cathedral Priory and cardinal priest of St Cecilia. For his career see Emden, *BRUO*, i. 620–1; M. Harvey, *The English in Rome, 1362–1420. Portrait of an Expatriate Community* (Cambridge, 1999), pp. 188–212.
4   Bartolomeo de Cucurno (d. 1386).
5   These were Gentilis de Sangro, Joannes de Aurelia and Marinus de Judice.
6   The author of the *Historia vitae et regni Ricardi secundi* makes the same distinction between three learned and three noble cardinals and may have been following Walsingham directly: *HVRS*, p. 87.
7   According to the papal secretary, Dietrich of Niem, the six prisoners were tortured with pulleys. Adam Easton's experiences were sufficient for him to vow to promote the canonisation of Brigit of Sweden should he survive: Harvey, *English in Rome*, p. 201.
8   Bartolomeo Mezzavacca, abbot of Monte Cassino. He was deprived of his cardinalate in 1383 but restored in 1389 by Boniface IX.

many as three hundred thousand. The king rejoiced, as he was genuinely able to do, in the numbers and power of the mighty army under his control, and took delight in both the rich, imposing equipment of his men and in the courage that he saw in them.[1]

But at York a cloud was suddenly brought over the joy of the king and all his troops by the violent act of Sir John Holland, the king's brother.[2] For he murdered Sir Ralph Stafford while he was going through the streets on his way to the queen. Sir Ralph was a member of the king's household, and the queen felt a very great affection for him. He was no less very dear to the king himself, as he had grown up with him and been his companion from their early years.[3] So the king was angry and decided to punish Sir John, not wishing so much to take revenge for his own grief as for the loss sustained by the earl of Stafford, the young man's father. So he had the goods of John Holland confiscated so that nobody should be able to entertain any doubt about his sincere wish to exact punishment for the death of the young man. By this action the king won for himself the love of the earls of Stafford and of Warwick, of [Ralph] Lord Basset, and of all those who had been kinsmen or relations to the young man. Sir John himself, realising that his fortune had now changed, fled to Beverley, so that he might enjoy the sanctuary of that place.

The cause of the death of the king's mother

When Lady Joan [of Kent], the mother both of the king and of Sir John Holland, heard of the murder committed by her son and the king's oath that his brother should submit to the rigour of the law, she at once sent envoys to approach the king, carrying a mother's prayers which they were to offer to her son for his brother. They were to plead with the king that he should not drench with tears his mother's face at such a little request, but that he should take pity on both his brother and his mother, and that his brother should receive more mercy just because he was his brother. But when the envoys returned to Wallingford, and the mother of the sons saw that she had gained no favour from the king on this matter, she was indeed overcome by the greatest grief. She took to her bed and after four or five days bade farewell to this world. Her body, wrapped in waxed linen cloths and put in a coffin of lead was kept at Wallingford until the king's return from Scotland and the time when she should receive a proper burial at Stamford in the chapel of the Friars Minor.[4]

Thunder, lightning and earthquakes

In this year on the seventh day after the translation of St Thomas, archbishop of Canterbury and martyr [3 July],[5] beginning about six o'clock in the evening, thunderclaps were heard and flashes of lightning seen continuously for an hour. These phenomena terrified the hearts of many, and in many places some were killed by lightning and others were irreparably injured.

On the fourth day after the storm there was an earthquake at about nine o'clock in the evening, which perhaps foretold the pointless disturbances about to be caused by the two kings of

---

[1]   Richard responded to the invasion with a summons of the feudal levy – the last occasion that such a summons was issued in the Middle Ages – but opposition in the council prevented the levy being raised. But the writ of summons itself appears to have affected recruitment to the royal army and the number of troops that mustered at Newcastle by the end of July was greater than ever before in the fourteenth century, perhaps as many as 14,000, including all of the country's major magnates. See Saul, *Richard II*, p. 144.

[2]   This incident following occurred as the magnates made their way north for the Scottish expedition. According to the Westminster chronicler, two of Holland's esquires had quarrelled with two of the earl of Stafford's grooms and the latter had murdered the former and fled into sanctuary. Holland made his way to the King to protest at the murder and the escape of the grooms when he came upon the earl's son, Ralph, fell into an argument with him over the matter and in the ensuing struggle killed him (*WC*, pp. 122–3). The murder took place on 5 May, at Bishopsthorpe near York, according to Knighton who also says it was the second day after the King had arrived in the north (*Knighton*, pp. 338–39).

[3]   The Westminster chronicler comments that the king 'had loved the lad all the more tenderly for having been a contemporary and comrade in the heyday of his own youth': *WC*, p. 123. In the autumn parliament Holland was appealed for felony, but failed to appear at the King's Bench on 27 November, nor did he send any proxy: *WC*, pp. 144–5.

[4]   Countess Joan died on 8 August 1385 but was not buried at Stamford until January 1386.

[5]   i.e. 10 July.

England and France, who had already assembled armies of unprecedented size, one for an expedition to Scotland to keep the enemy out of his kingdom, and the other for an expedition to England to add this land to his realms.[1]

The English king rides through the whole land of Scotland, burning different places

In the month of August the king of England with a powerful force invaded the kingdom of Scotland.[2] The Scots and the French, seeing that they were inferior to such an army, left the roads and made for the woods, hurrying as fast as they could to places to hide. They did quite often steal out of these lairs and make surprise attacks on our men who did not know the country and were unaware of ambushes, so that some were killed and some taken prisoner. But the English army, the finest and bravest and biggest that had ever been seen, rode through a land lacking inhabitants, devoid of cattle and empty of food supplies. For the Scots and the French, knowing in advance that our men were coming, had driven away all the people, removed the cattle and carried off the food supplies. The land had been made so desolate that our men said as the truth that they had not seen a single bird there, apart from screech owls. They did however come across abundant crops of the finest, green corn. These they either used as fodder for their horses or trampled down under the feet of these same horses. But as the enemy had slunk away from any engagements, nothing worthy of mention was accomplished by our men other than the burning of the abbey of Melrose and the town of Edinburgh with its surrounding villages, which places they happened to pass en route.[3]

The dispute between the king and the duke of Lancaster and the return from Scotland

When our army arrived at Edinburgh [11 August], they were so short of supplies that many began to fall ill, and some were in danger of dying from famine. So the king took counsel concerning the best course of action. The duke of Lancaster [John of Gaunt], the greatest magnate after the king, began to speak as follows. 'My lord king,' he said, 'you have been given a welcome opportunity for praising God and for multiple rejoicing. Firstly, the enemy, who were so confident in their power that they thought to destroy your kingdom, have been so scared by your appearance that they do not dare to come out and fight but have shamefully run away. Secondly, you have with you an impressive number of lords and nobles and a large force of soldiers, such as have never been seen before in these lands, and they are all ready to fight on your behalf. Thirdly, as I truly think, you are accompanied by the favour of God. For up to now the settled summer weather and the calm breezes have so smiled upon our prayers that no contrary wind or harmful storms have stopped us from being able to ride by day or to sleep under the stars by night. We all know that our enemies have fled for refuge across the Firth of Forth, so my advice is that we should cross the Firth of Forth ourselves, especially now that the crossing is easy for us, and destroy their lands with fire and sword, so that the enemy are forced either into battle or at least into shameful flight.'

At these words the king's anger blazed forth, just as if he had found the duke's speech to be evidence of treachery. 'As for you,' he said, 'wherever you have gone with an army you have lost men of mine, taking them into dangerous places through bad leadership and lack of judgement, killing them with hunger and thirst for lack of money, always thinking about your own purse, and never about mine. And now, typically, you are pressing me to cross the Firth of Forth, so that I

---

1   This adverse weather and the attendant portents are not recorded by other authorities, although the Westminster chronicler concurs that it was a hot summer despite there being no shortage of rain: WC, p. 121.
2   The Westminster chronicler reports that the army crossed the border on 6 August, which corresponds with its known arrival at Edinburgh on 11 August; further corroboration can be found in the *Scotichronicon* which reports the arrival of the English 'around St Laurence's day' (10 August): *Scotichronicon*, vii. 406–7. Froissart claimed that the English forces numbered 100,000: *Chroniques*, xi. 258; FCBuchon, ii. 334–5.
3   In fact the English pillaged and burned the abbeys of Dryburgh, Holyrood, Newbattle and Melrose as punishment for their recognition of the Avignon Pope Clement VII. Of the English authorities, the Westminster chronicler gives the most detailed account of their depredations, but the *Scotichronicon* is more emotive: '[Richard] burnt to ashes with consuming flames churches devoted to God and monastic sanctuaries': WC, pp. 128–9, *Scotichronicon*, vii. 406–7.

who was a warrior figure, noted for his loyalty and endowed with good sense, and urged him to oppose these evil schemes. He was master of the Hospitallers, since he was superior to everybody else in piety as well as in power, and his resources were such that he could supply things both old and new for the defence of the kingdom.[2] So, urged on by the citizens, he went with a strong force to the castle where the queen was spending some time with her lover. And indeed he pretended he had come on a peaceful mission, and got the queen to meet him and to receive him with considerable honour as being the brother of the dead king, master of the Hospital and the most famous man in the kingdom.

At their first meeting he began to accuse the queen of breaking her word towards [Edmund of Langley] the earl of Cambridge, and of her wicked ruling of the kingdom, which, so it was said, had brought the kingdom to the point of collapse. When the knight heard this, who, as I have said, had violated the queen, he showed none of the reverence due to such a great personage, but insolently replied that such a one as he had no qualifications for matters of government, but should continue to be a man of religion and devote his time to piety rather than to politics. This response showed the master of Hospitallers that the knight was in no way without responsibility for what had happened and he at once drew out his dagger, rushed at the traitor and killed him on the spot. He gave orders for the queen to be seized and kept under a guard befitting her royal status in the castle, and for the body of the murdered knight to be given burial. When this was done, the whole district went over to his side.[3]

And when later he had fought two successful battles against the king of Spain, he was chosen king with the support of the whole people. But he refused the honour, saying that as he was bound to the religious life by the vows made at his profession, he neither could nor should have the crown of the kingdom placed on his head. But as the people persistently pressed and forced him to accept, he at last said that he was willing to obey their wishes on the condition that he agreed to govern the kingdom only until the arrival of the true heir, [Edward of Langley] the son of the earl of Cambridge, to whom, as I have said, the daughter of his brother, the king of Portugal, had been originally betrothed.

And in this way indeed the king's brother received the respect of the kingdom. He had a deep love for the English and vigorously promoted the welfare of those of them in his kingdom because of their remarkable probity. He did not doubt that it was owing to the English that he had always had the upper hand in all his battles.

The king of Castile, however, was well aware who had helped the king of Portugal [Fernando I] to triumph, and he tried to bribe the English with gold, having learned that their natures were inclined towards greed. He sent some bribes and promised others, if they were willing to betray the king and his people. And indeed there were two esquires through whose courage, good sense and judgement the Portuguese had always previously won the day and the Spaniards had been put to flight, but these two (what a tale of woe!) were won over by their accursed greed for gold[3] and came to an agreement with the king of Castile, putting money before loyalty to their country, and bribes before truth. But their envoys were brought to the king of Portugal by an Englishman whose conscience had not been corrupted and at once proved guilty. The esquires themselves were arrested and sent to prison, to the great shame of their whole people and as a scandal for our nation. This was what happened in Portugal, that place across the seas.[4]

---

[1]   João, the illegitmate son of Pedro I of Portugal, and thus brother to Fernando I, was grand master of the military order of Aviz, hence Walsingham's description of him as a 'warrior figure'; he had supported Cambridge in his inconclusive campaigning while the English army was still in Portugal: Russell, *English Intervention in Spain and Portugal*, pp. 323–4.

[2]   Following the news of the Castilian advance, on 6 December João of Aviz entered the royal palace, confronted Donor Leonor and Andeiro and murdered the count. Walsingham exaggerates the speed with which João assumed control; his first thought was to flee Portugal for England and it was only a deputation of Lisbon citizens that persuaded him otherwise: *English Intervention in Spain and Portugal*, pp. 360–1.

[3]   Virgil, *Aeneid*, iii. 57.

[4]   The subversion of Juan I is not reported by other English authorities. In the same period João I made

Deeds of the pope

About the same time Pope Urban VI, who had been given nothing sweet to taste for a long time, whether because of his own wickedness or that of his enemies is unclear, realised that hostilities had begun again between him and Charles [of Durazzo], king of Sicily [i.e. Naples]. Indeed the pope endured at his hands the insulting and shameful losses inflicted by a siege until he had been brought to the very verge of despair. But at last, owing to the goodness of the Genoese who know how to do everything for a consideration, he was rescued, led away to freedom and in fact taken all the way to Genoa.[1] He was not allowed to travel across the seas from this city until he had paid an uncountable sum of gold for his rescue to the Genoese, who clearly had been bent on his rescue more for love of money than love of God.

The bishop-elect of St Andrews is captured

During these days the bishop elect of St Andrews in Scotland,[2] who was sailing with many knights and esquires towards Lyon to have his appointment confirmed by the antipope [Clement VII], was taken prisoner. He only had the one cog-boat, in which he and his men were seated, but he almost defeated seven of our barges, such was the strength of the armed villains in his own ship. At length he was taken prisoner by the two sons of William Rushby senior, the esquire of the earl of Northumberland, and presented to this same earl. But a little later as sadness overcame him, he put death before life and entered upon the way of all flesh.

A parliament in London and its proceedings

Around the time of the feast of St Martin [11 November] a parliament was held in London, at which the laity granted the king a fifteenth and a half tax, but on condition that the clergy paid him a tenth and a half tax.[3] This condition was stubbornly opposed by the archbishop of Canterbury, Lord William Courtenay, who said that this would be completely wrong, especially since the church should be autonomous and free of any taxation by the laity. Indeed he said that he would sooner put his head on the block to ensure this rather than allow the holy English church to enter upon such enslavement. This reply so angered the ranks of the commons that the knights of the shires together with some nobles of the land furiously pleaded that churchmen should be deprived of their temporalities: they argued that the clergy had grown so arrogant that it in fact would be an act of pious charity to take away the temporalities which raised ecclesiastics so high and so force them to adopt a more humble outlook.[4]

These arguments were vociferously stated, and were also written down and handed to the king in the form of writs. And the madness of the knights on this issue was so great that they actually believed that what they were asking for could be put into effect. You could have seen respected knights, filled with glee, discussing these matters among themselves and, just as if the temporalities of the whole church had now been assigned to them for their misuse, you could have seen them preening themselves, with one of them promising himself a certain sum from this monastery, and another a sum from another monastery. Indeed I myself heard with my own ears one of

formal diplomatic approaches to England that did prove successful: Russell, *English Intervention in Spain and Portugal*, pp. 401–2.

1   The siege at the castle of Nocera continued for almost six months and Urban and his forces were pressed to the point of famine. On 5 July his supporters succeeded in breaking through the cordon of besiegers and brought fresh supplies to the pope and his men; on 7 July they made their escape, Urban taking with him even the six cardinals who had been the cause of the siege. His retreat was protracted but he finally succeeded in taking a ship for Genoa at the end of August and arrived there on 23 September. The Westminster chronicler comments on how he 'established himself with his cardinals in fairly favourable conditions': *WC*, p. 141.

2   This was Stephen Pay (d.1386) who had been elected earlier in 1385.

3   This parliament opened on 12 November: *WC*, p. 141; *RP*, iii. 203.

4   Courtenay's opposition to the conditions of the subsidy and the anti-clerical response of the commons is not reported by the other contemporary chroniclers, even the monastic authors of the *Historia vitae et regni Ricardi secundi* and the Westminster chronicle.

these knights swearing a solemn oath that he was intending to take for himself an annual income of a thousand marks from the temporalities of the monastery of St Albans.[1]

But the king did not give the nod to this madness. He listened to the unruly ravings of the knights on the one side, and the just replies of their opponents on the other, and commanded that their writs should be torn up and that petitions that were out of order should cease. He said that during his time as king he would preserve the Anglican church in the same state and condition as he had found it when he became king or make it still better. For this action he was accounted worthy of a generous reward by the churchmen, and his response won the greatest praise from the good members of the laity. Then the archbishop, having discussed the matter with the clergy, went to the king and said that he and the clergy of the land had unanimously and spontaneously voted for the king's uses the tax of one tenth. The king was so pleased at this grant and received the offer so gratefully that he openly declared that he preferred this present offer, freely made, to taxes on other occasions, which the church had been forced to pay, even though they had been of four times the value. And so for the time being the insatiable greed of the enemies of the church was frustrated.

A new position, not known to the English before, was created in this parliament; the earl of Oxford, Lord Robert de Vere, was given the title and position of marquis of Dublin in Ireland. The other earls were not pleased at this, because they saw that he had obtained through the king's gift a higher position than their own, and they were especially annoyed that he seemed no better than the others either in wisdom or generalship.[2]

Also new dukes were created, although the king had during the Scottish campaign given them these titles on the field of battle: Lord Thomas of Woodstock, earl of Buckingham, received the title of duke and was called duke of Gloucester and Lord Edmund Langley, earl of Cambridge, was called duke of York. The king gave them moneys from the treasury matching the honour of these names, so that they should not seem to have received such an important title for no gain.[3]

Sir Michael de la Pole, who was chancellor of the realm, was made earl of Suffolk in the same parliament. He was given a thousand marks annually from the royal purse. He was a man more fitted for commerce than the conflict of war. He had grown old among financiers in peace, not among soldiers in battle.[4]

The restoration of temporalities to the bishop of Norwich

Another happening in this parliament was that as a result of the concern and intervention of Thomas Arundel, bishop of Ely, the king restored to [Henry Despenser] the bishop of Norwich his temporalities, which, as I have described above, he had kept in his own possession for many years.[5] The chancellor urged him not to make this restoration. Indeed, when the bishop of Ely made his request to the king concerning the matter, the chancellor's venomous, indignant reply to the bishop of Ely was, 'What is it you are asking for, my lord bishop? Does it seem to you such a light matter for the king to give back his temporalities to the bishop of Norwich, seeing that they provide him annually with more than a thousand pounds? The king does not need counsellors

---

[1]   Walsingham's outrage notwithstanding, this sum represented an undervaluation of St Albans Abbey.

[2]   The new creation was made on 1 December. The *Historia vitae et regni Ricardi secundi* follows Walsingham in recording the indignation of the earls but the independent Westminster chronicler does not refer to any magnate opposition to the promotion: *WC*, p. 145. See also *RP*, iii. 203.

[3]   As Walsingham records the new titles were conferred on the Scottish campaign. The *Historia vitae et regni Ricardi secundi* claims that lands and rents to the value of £1000 marks were granted to the two dukes: *HVRS*, p. 92.

[4]   Walsingham refers to the fact that de la Pole had served as chancellor in a period when the government had struggled to conserve its resources and eschewed costly campaigning. He must also have in mind the mercantile origins of the de la Pole family.

[5]   Despenser had been impeached in the parliament of October 1383 and his temporalities seized. His service with the king in the Scottish campaign in the summer of 1385 had served to rehabilitate him: Saul, *Richard II*, p. 106.

like you. He does not need friends of your ilk, who desire to penalise him with the loss of so great a sum.'

The bishop of Ely replied to him, 'What do you mean, Sir Michael? I am not asking the king for his own money, but for that which belongs to another, which he is keeping under an unjust claim, persuaded by the wicked advice of you and your like, and which never, in my judgement, will do him any real benefit. If you are so worried and concerned about losses incurred by the king, why did you accept so avidly from him an annual income of a thousand marks, when he made you earl of Suffolk?' When the chancellor heard this, he was stopped in his tracks as if struck by a javelin, and did not dare to oppose this restoration any longer.[1] And this was the end of the present parliament.

So passed this year. It was a reasonably calm year in which the harvest was fairly good. It was a very unlucky year for the French with heavy expenditure, losses, deaths, and the capture of prisoners and the town of Damme. For the English it was a moderately happy year, but for the Scots it had been expensive, full of alarms and ruinous.

[1386]

In 1386, the ninth year of the reign of King Richard II, the king kept Christmas at Eltham with Queen Anna. While he was there, he was visited by the king of Armenia [Leo VI, 1373 93].[2] The pretext for his visit was the renewing of peace between the kings of England and of France, but only the king of Armenia knew the gains achieved by his visit. For besides the countless gifts that he received from king and nobles of the land, the king also gave him a document which granted him £1000 annually for the rest of his life. For, so he claimed, he had been driven out of his kingdom by the Tartars, and for this reason he extracted many gifts from the kings of Christendom, so much so that his flight to foreign lands brought him more blessings than did his rule over his own people in his own kingdom.

The death of [king] Charles of Naples

About the same time came the death of Charles [of Durazzo] the Peaceful, king of Sicily, who, to tell the truth, had inflicted many losses upon the pope.[3] But he had departed this life under excommunication from the pope and had left Naples. For the time being the pope was satisfied with that type of punishment, as other kinds were not then available. But there is no doubt that the pope would have been willing to punish Charles in a severer and more material fashion, if he had not been totally lacking power in his secular arm. Men say that Charles himself was treacherously murdered by a certain knight while sitting at table, on the very day and at the very hour at which he had planned to kill the pope.

---

[1] Walsingham is the only chronicler to identify Bishop Arundel as influential in the restoration of Despenser.
[2] Leo VI arrived in England shortly before Christmas. He presented himself as a potential mediator in the Anglo-French conflict in the hope that in return the two kingdoms might support him in a crusade against the Ottoman Turks who had occupied Armenia since 1375. His visit was the culmination of several months of diplomatic activity during which Richard's councillors, determined on reopening the war, had done their best to prevaricate. Walsingham is the only authority to record the grant of £1000. The Westminster chronicler reports that the king remained in England until early February and returning via Calais was robbed of many of his treasurers by thieves: WC, pp. 158–9.
[3] Walsingham again offers a confused and conflated account of the closing months of Charles's life. He had abandoned Naples for Hungary where he had been offered the crown in the face of growing dissatisfaction at the regency of Elizabeth, widow of King Lewis and custodian of the crown in the name of her daughter Mary, Lewis's heir. Charles was welcomed to Hungary but Elizabeth and her councillors conspired to murder him. He died on 27 February 1386 at Vissegrad, Hungary. It was alleged that as the Hungarian officials attempted to crown Lewis's daughter, Charles snatched the crown and placed it on his own head and that the Hungarians attacked him, fatally wounding him. The knight that struck him was Nicholas Gara. See also Froissart, *Chroniques*, xi. 221–3.

After they had spent a long time there, which was fruitless for themselves and their countrymen, they were ordered to go back home and to be ready to return, whenever the king should decide to recall them. Several of them through lack of supplies were compelled to sell their horses or their weapons on their return, while some turned to looting and raiding to get provisions.[1] The parliament had not yet come to an end. The commons had gone back home, but the nobles stayed on in London, waiting for news of the arrival of the French, who were said to be coming every day.

So that the lord king should not seem to have done too little in this situation, he appointed Lord Robert de Vere duke of Ireland.[2] Sir Robert had formerly been earl of Oxford, but recently in the last parliament he had been made marquis of Dublin [1 December 1385].[3] And in the future the king intended to promote him from duke to king of Ireland, if fortune favoured this scheme. According to rumour, his closeness to Lord Robert and his deep love and affection for him was not without some taint of an obscene relationship, and Lord Robert's fellow nobles and barons spoke in whispers of their indignation that so mediocre a man should aim at so high an office, seeing that he had no nobility of birth or endowment of other virtues which might rank him above the others.[4]

Accusations in parliament against Michael de la Pole

During all this time the parliament continued to sit, with every day fresh rumours about the arrival of the French, so that many members felt great alarm, when they saw the barons disagreeing over many matters, and some of the sensible sort thought that, particularly if there was a lack of unity among the lords, the cost to the kingdom would be great, when so many perils for it were being plotted by the enemy. In fact the king was at odds not only with the knights of the parliament but also with almost all the lords, because they supported the same people, namely those who were making many false accusations against Michael de la Pole, and vehemently demanding that he be brought to trial. For they had laid at his door many acts of deceit and some of treachery in his dealings with the king, and he was by no means able to refute these charges. So that when he stood there to make his reply, and could not deny the charges, the king blushed for shame at him, and, shaking his head, said, 'Alas, alas, Michael, see what you have done.'[5]

Of the many charges brought against him the most heinous was that in his greedy desire for other people's money he had persuaded the king to grant him the fees from all the pardoners in the land, whose practice it is to travel around carrying indulgences and to collect the money for the needs of the fraternity of St Antony. His intention was to give the king twenty marks from these revenues, although it is thought that he raised seventy marks each year by these means. When these and many other misdeeds had been proved against him as matters that he could not

---

were to lodge no more than thirty leagues from London but not to approach the city any closer than ten leagues (*Knighton*, pp. 350–1).

1   The dispersal of this force is not recorded by Knighton.

2   It is unclear whether Walsingham intended this reference to the King's absence from parliament and from Westminster as a criticism. It was the case that Richard was preoccupied with preparing for De Vere's proposed expedition to Ireland and had passed the summer months in Bristol.

3   See above, p. 236.

4   In spite of Walsingham's smear, de Vere was regarded by contemporaries as something of a womaniser who abandoned his wife after an affair with Agnes Lancerona, lady-in-waiting to the queen: Saul, *Richard II*, p. 121.

5   The proceedings of this parliament, known as the 'Wonderful Parliament' are not well documented and the best account is given by Henry Knighton who appears to have worked from a narrative account apparently compiled by an eyewitness. De la Pole made a poor start to the session by revealing the parlous state of royal finances and admitting that the king hoped for a massive subsidy of four fifteenths. The response of the commons was to call for the chancellor's dismissal and they added that they had business with him that could not be dealt with whilst he remained in office; in other words, they intended to impeach him. See also J. S. Roskell, *The Impeachment of Michael de la Pole, Earl of Suffolk, in 1386* (Manchester, 1984).

deny, he was deposed from his office of chancellor, fined a sum of money which of course he had to pay to the king, and in addition adjudged by parliament to be worthy of death.[1]

His reply to the king was that he personally did not need taxes from the king's subjects, seeing that he could properly make provision for himself from the great sums that came in from those who lawfully were debtors of the king. This whole attack on the chancellor, which should have greatly pleased the king, in fact made him exceedingly displeased, such was his trust in a man who could not be trusted and the protection that he gave to a rascal. And it happened not long afterwards that the king, out of his affection for Lord Michael, annulled the whole sentence of parliament against him, and treated him as a greater friend than ever before, not only in private but also in public.

This went so far that at a banquet the following Christmas the king made Lord Michael sit at the royal table, not wearing just the garments usually worn by the lords, but clad in the robes which from antiquity onwards have been the prerogative of kings alone. And to stop the carrying out of the sentence against him, the king chose to use treachery and to eliminate Lord Michael's accusers together with the duke of Gloucester [Thomas of Woodstock], who was seen to be the chief influence of those working for the good of the kingdom.[2] And so the king and his household made a plot that some of the knights of parliament, who had most opposed even the king's request for financial help or had been enemies of Michael, together with the duke of Gloucester should be invited to supper at the house of a citizen of London and there suddenly murdered. The king judged that only by their death would he gain the power of exercising his will.[3] But this highly wicked scheme was not put into effect, for the duke of Gloucester was warned beforehand about the whole plan, and he warned the others to take care, bidding them to be content with suppers at home, and not to get entangled in suppers with others. Men say that Sir Nicholas Brembre, the mayor of London of the previous year, had assented to this plot, but that the intended crime was given up due to the laudable integrity of Richard Exton,[4] the current mayor, who, when the king asked him to support this dark deed, openly declared that he would never agree to the killing of such innocent people. This remark was repeated publicly by all those living in the same district as the mayor, with the result that everywhere there was an increase of hatred for the dastardly plotters and of affection for the duke and the knights, who themselves did not cease from saying those things which were true and for the good of the kingdom but opposed the king's request for aid with grater determination, and indeed that verse from [the apocryphal] book of Susanna which says, 'It is better for us to fall into the hands of men than to disobey the law of our God,'[5] often impressed itself on the minds of the duke and the knights. In the end

---

1   The commons levelled a series of charges against de la Pole of which this is only one. He was accused of failing to fulfil the responsibilities of chancellor, of having suppressed the report commissioned in the previous parliament for considering the better government of the realm and that the previous subsidies granted under his supervision had not been properly collected and that it was his failings that had led to the collapse of the alliance with Ghent and the surrender of the city to the French. He was also accused of diverting various revenues due to the crown into his own hands, including the income from St Anthony's hospital, the only English property belonging to the Augustinian order of St Antoine de Vienne which had been seized by the crown at the outbreak of the schism, and of purchasing lands and other properties which should have passed to the crown. Richard had no choice but to depose him, but the decision was not made as rapidly as Walsingham suggests here. At first Richard refused and it was only after a delegation, led by Bishop Thomas Arundel and the king's uncle, Thomas, duke of Gloucester, had warned him of the danger of his own deposition, that Richard authorised de la Pole's dismissal. He appointed Bishop Arundel as chancellor in his stead and allowed de la Pole to be arrested and committed for trial. He was held in custody at Corfe castle. See also Saul, *Richard II*, pp. 158–61.
2   The king's favour to the deposed chancellor was also reported by the Westminster chronicler: *WC*, p. 179.
3   Knighton reports rumours that passed through the commons before the close of parliament that the king planned to murder the knights of the shire that had brought the case against chancellor de la Pole: *Knighton*, pp. 354–5.
4   Correctly, Nicholas Exton, a grocer who had served as sheriff (1384–5) before his term as mayor: Barron, *London*, pp. 17, 31, 334–5.
5   *Susanna*, 1: 23.

through the wickedness of the powerful a tax was granted, but just a half of one tenth and a half of one fifteenth, and this tax was to be spent not as the king willed but as the nobles judged to be for the good of the kingdom.[1] In fact the money went to the earl of Arundel, who was just about to set out across the seas.

At the king's insistence provision was made for the duke of Ireland, namely that the heirs of Charles de Blois,[2] who once had claim to the dukedom of Brittany, should sell it to the French for thirty thousand marks, so that, helped by this money, the duke of Ireland [Robert de Vere] might make a strong attempt to recover the dominions which the king had given to him in Ireland, on this condition: that he should cross the sea to Ireland before the next Easter.[3] Indeed such was the keenness of both nobles and commons for his departure, that they preferred that the kingdom should be deprived of such a sum rather than that they should have among them the presence of one who was seducing the infatuated king.

A safe conduct is refused to the king of Armenia

About the same time the king of Armenia [Leo VI], who had long enjoyed the generosity of the king of England and his nobles, sent for a safe conduct, on the grounds that he was making his journey out of his desire for renewing the peace between the kingdoms of England and France, although for a long time one of these kingdoms had been making thorough preparations for invading the other. But in fact he desired gifts rather than peace, and was more in love with money and the gold of the kingdom than with the people or its king. And although the king was kind to him, the nobles judged that he was a trickster, and told the king that they were unwilling to have dealings with him. And so his visit was blocked, his second attempt having been no more successful than his first attempt.[4]

The arrival of the king of France is miraculously prevented

Meanwhile the king of France [Charles VI] with an unheard-of mass of dukes, counts and other nobles was still in Flanders, ready indeed to sack the kingdom of England, if only God had not blocked his attempts. For during the whole time that passed between 1 August right down to the eve of the feast of All Saints [1 November], never even for a few hours did a breeze blow which was favourable for him. But then on the eve itself a breeze of some strength did get up, and, judging it to be favourable to him, he launched his ships after their long period in port and with the force of the wind left the harbour of Sluys. But when all the ships had got under way and were now in deep water, in fact about twenty miles from the port, there was a miracle. A contrary wind began blowing in their faces and drove them all back home, and not only drove them home but also drove them into collisions with each other so that some of them were wrecked in the very entrance to the port of Sluys. The occurrence of this wind freed England from fear and caused the king of France to sail back home.

The French king's fleet numbered 1,200 ships, and his force consisted of 15 dukes, 26 counts, 3,600 knights and 100,000 soldiers.[5]

---

[1] Following the departure of de la Pole, the Wonderful Parliament continued its assault on Richard by demanding the appointment of a new continual council to implement a policy of retrenchment in the royal finances; the much reduced subsidy was a part of this policy. A new expedition in the English Channel to be led by Richard, earl of Arundel, was planned in the winter months for embarkation in the spring.

[2] Charles of Blois (d.1364) was the son of Margaret, sister of Philip VI of France. He claimed the dukedom of Brittany by the right of his wife, Jeanne of Dreux, niece of the childless Jean II of Dreux, duke of Brittany. With French support Charles gained control of the duchy after the death of Duke Jean in 1341. He captured his rival Jean de Montfort in 1343. Montfort died the following year and Charles retained control of the duchy until he was defeated and killed by Montfort's son, supported by the English, at Auray, in September 1364.

[3] The ransom of Jean de Blois was granted to de Vere on 23 March providing the income for 500 men-at-arms and 1,000 archers to serve for two years: Saul, *Richard II*, p. 155.

[4] Leo VI's aim of mediating a peace between England and France was without hope following the invasion threat and the council's plans for a new campaign.

[5] The number of troops is perhaps three times more than there were, but the number of ships may be close

Trial of Michael de la Pole

Parliament was still in session, and although the king was angry at the accusations made against Michael de la Pole and the other men whom he unwisely loved, he was compelled after many attempts at evasion to select jurors and judges with full power to listen to and pass judgement on the case against Michael and the others whom the knights of parliament had accused.[1] The judges chosen were Thomas [of Woodstock], duke of Gloucester, and Richard, earl of Arundel. They quickly carried out the task assigned to them, as the king had gone elsewhere, being unwilling to be present at these trials, even though the verdicts might be to his liking, and in the end, so it is said, they convicted Michael of many crimes and deceitful actions, judged him worthy of death, and decided that his property should pass to the royal treasury.[2] But he was let out on bail, as certain rich men bound themselves to a large sum of money on his behalf.[3] But, as I have said, as soon as parliament was over, the king took him back and had him to live in the same house as himself, together with the duke of Ireland [Robert de Vere] and Alexander Neville, the archbishop of York, men who at that time were working as hard as they could day and night to set the king against the lords and to annul the decrees of parliament.

So the hatred felt by the king for his loyal, proper lords increased daily, as long as these others whispered in his ear that he would be a shadow king without substance and with no legal rights remaining, if the lords were to rejoice in the power they had received. The king believed his cronies, and so henceforth treated all his lords as objects of suspicion, although despite this Michael de la Pole was removed from the chancellorship, and his place there taken by Thomas Arundel, bishop of Ely, a man who put justice before riches and fairness before pure gold. Also John Fordham, bishop of Durham, was removed from the office of treasurer, although he had worked hard and involved himself in expense in his love for this position, and installed in his place was friar John Gilbert of the order of preachers, bishop of Hereford, a man whose tongue was stronger than his loyalty. Such was the end of this parliament.[4]

The conclusion of the year

Thus ended a year rich in crops but with a moderate fruit harvest. For the Spanish it was an anxious year of foreboding, owing to the arrival of the duke of Lancaster and his laying claim to their kingdom. It was a ruinous year for the Austrians, as their duke [Leopold III] and nobles were killed by the commons.[5] The French had been faced with heavy expenditure, as they made preparations to invade England. It had been a fearful year for the English as a whole because of the serious rumours, but an especially shameful one for the people of London, such had been their womanly timidity.

[1387]

In 1387, the twelfth year of King Richard II, the king spent Christmas with queen Anna and her Bohemians [at Windsor].

At the beginning of March, according to the decree of parliament, Richard, earl of Arundel, and Lord Thomas Mowbray, earl of Nottingham, got themselves ready to plough the plains of the

---

to reality. Despite Walsingham's report there is no evidence that the fleet even attempted to embark from Sluys. See also Saul, *Richard II*, pp. 152–6, 164.

1   The impeachment of de la Pole began in early November. See also Saul, *Richard II*, p. 193.
2   Knighton records that rents and possessions to the value of £1,000 which de la Pole had secured for himself were to paid to the crown together with £12,000 worth of other fees and payments which he had diverted into his own hands: *Knighton*, pp. 362–3.
3   The other authorities say only that he received the protection of the king.
4   The proceedings of the Wonderful Parliament finally ended on 28 November 1386: *RP*, iii. 215–27.
5   The Swiss cities of Basel, Bern, Lucerne, Zug and Zurich had rebelled against Leopold III's attempts to annex them, and when he led an army of the Swabian nobility against them in 1386 he was ambushed and killed at Sempach on the mountain pass near Lake Lucerne.

sea, with the earl of Arundel being appointed admiral for the immediate term of command.[1] He was a good, very conscientious man, and as he now wished to wipe out the taunts once made against him for refusing to fight when the French were attacking the Sussex coast, he was determined to put all his strength into the attempt.

The earl of Arundel sets out for the sea

When the earl of Arundel was about to depart for the sea and to review his army drawn up on the plain, he was told that the duke of Gloucester [Thomas of Woodstock] and many nobles wanted to inspect the troops he had collected. And so he took the trouble to collect good reputable soldiers, and avoided hiring cobblers and tailors from London and the other towns, as certain generals before him had done, hiring troops cheaply so that the amount of gold in their purses could grow. Those other generals, who had behaved like that, had not been fighting for the good of the kingdom but for their own gain. So it had happened that for a long time England had received little or no benefit from their appointments, as they had no thoughts of testing their strength in an attack on the enemy, but only of remaining inactive for their allotted period, so that they might be able to preserve intact the sums of money entrusted to them.

The earl of Arundel on the other hand, as I have said, spared no expense but chose valiant men whom he knew, so that with them he could achieve some great success for his country. When the duke of Gloucester saw that the soldiers in front of him were fine, hand-picked troops, he urged and persuaded each and every one of them to set sail, and to give up the excuses for delay which many of them had been using, that they had to say goodbye to their friends, or had business to deal with at home. For he guessed, as was in fact the case, that some of them had borrowed weapons for the review to earn praise from the lords as being adequately equipped, but that, if they had a chance of slipping off, they would no doubt return these weapons to their owners and come back to the sea practically weaponless, and so, in all likelihood, less keen to face the foe.[2]

So at a lucky hour they set sail willy-nilly with all the equipment that they had, for it was not long before they encountered the enemy.[3] In fact on the Sunday which was the eve of the Annunciation of our Lady [25 March],[4] a great fleet of Flemish, French and Spanish ships, crammed with soldiers and equipped with various engines of war, was seen sailing far off by a lookout. The announcement of this to the earl, their admiral, immediately filled him and all his men with great joy. But the enemy were not expecting any such meeting, for they had been promised by certain English traitors (our kingdom was rarely free of these) that our fleet would not be in any way ready this side of May. So they had felt completely secure, using the wind as a means of locomotion and protected by the troops on board.

But when they approached our men and veered to the wind as if intending to attack us, our men deliberately pretended to flee, as though they were no match for such a fine fleet. The enemy, indeed, who were more desirous of a safe passage than a fight, began to sail past, but then it happened that our men, getting the wind they had prayed for, made for the enemy, suddenly attacked them and brought on a fierce conflict. In the end victory fell to our side. Eighty ships and many fighting men of different ranks were captured, and several soldiers were also killed. And some ships, which had got away from the struggle, were pursued for two days by the earl of Arundel, who finally captured them and brought them back to our fleet.[5]

---

[1]   Arundel was appointed admiral for the northern and western coasts on 10 December and on 16 December he was retained to serve the king with 2,500 men from 1 March 1387. See also *CPR, 1385–9*, p. 323; Saul, *Richard II*, p. 161.

[2]   Arundel had raised his force over the winter months and by the beginning of March had sixty ships assembled at Sandwich.

[3]   Arundel's fleet sailed on 23 March with the aim of pursuing the French fleet which was reported to have repaired to La Rochelle to provision before returning to Sluys. See also *Knighton*, pp. 388–9; Saul, *Richard II*, p. 168.

[4]   i.e., on 24 March.

[5]   Walsingham is correct in claiming that Arundel encountered the Franco-Flemish fleet the day after he left

The number of ships and casks captured

The number of the larger and smaller ships, all filled with wine, was a hundred and more. The number of casks amounted to more than nineteen thousand.[1] The wine with its casks, apart from that which was set aside for the king's party, was immediately sent to the port of Orwell and other ports of the kingdom. Although the citizens of Middleburgh approached the earl [of Arundel] and begged him to allow them to buy the wine for a hundred shillings a cask, cash down, on the grounds that they were regarded as our friends and needed the wine, the admiral replied to them that it was fairer for the people who had paid for his expedition to the sea, namely the people of England, to enjoy this wine than that others should take it away, no matter what price they paid. 'But, since you are friends,' he said, 'and have come a long way, we will give you twenty casks, so that you are not seen to return home completely empty-handed.'[2]

Indeed the earl behaved so generously in his distribution of the wine to different people in his party that, so the story goes, not even one cask remained for his own use. So the earl was lauded to the skies by the common people for foregoing what he could have made for himself by selling the captured wine to others, and thus putting the general good before private gain. And the commons were particularly pleased because they realised from the event that the money which they had contributed towards the earl's expedition had not been completely wasted.

But the earl wanted to do still greater things for his country. So he reassembled and patched up his fleet, hired fresh recruits to replace those who had been hurt and wounded or killed,[3] and set sail for the castle of Brest, which is regarded as the key to Lower Brittany. The French or the Bretons had already built, or were about to build, two fortifications surrounding Brest, which were larger and far stronger than the ones which the duke of Lancaster [John of Gaunt] had attacked and destroyed while on his journey to Spain.[4] The earl captured one of these, after over-powering the men inside it, and because it seemed that such a strong fortification would neces-sarily be a help to the castle of Brest if our men were manning it, he stationed some of our troops in it. The other fortification had been built at great expense but not yet put in position, and this one the earl set fire to and burnt. And so in a short time the French suffered a double loss in the same place, first at the hands of the soldiers of the duke, and then at those of the earl's recruits.

He also brought in fresh supplies to the castle at Brest, providing all that was necessary for the next year, and he gave clothing and shoes to the garrison. Having put everything in order, he returned to England with the blessing of all the common people.[5]

But those who were with the king, the duke of Ireland [Robert de Vere], the earl of Suffolk

England (24 March). The enemy had as many as 250 ships, but several were Dutch and German vessels, which defected to Arundel in the course of the engagement. They also carried fewer troops, which may have been decisive. Arundel pursued the remnant of the fleet as it made its return to Sluys, where, both Knighton and the Westminster chronicler record, he not only captured or destroyed further enemy ships, but also allowed his men to make a brief landfall and 'played havoc with the surrounding countryside' and 'pillaged, wasted and burned the land' (*WC*, p. 183, *Knighton*, p. 391). When disease began to spread through his troops, however, he made for home, arriving on 14 April: Saul, *Richard II*, p. 168.

1 Both Knighton and the Westminster chronicler give lower figures for the number of ships captured (56 and 50 respectively) in the first engagement, and report that as Arundel pursued the remnant of the fleet he made further seizures (Knighton records another 70 but the Westminster chronicler has only 18). The West-minster chronicler specifies that three of these vessels were carracks with various cargoes, two were Norman bargettes and one a fine Spanish ship. He also notes that several Scottish ships carrying wool were also taken. Both authorities agree that there was an enormous haul of French wine; Knighton estimates 12–13,000 tuns, the Westminster chronicler has the more modest figure of 8,000: *WC*, p. 183, *Knighton*, p. 391; Saul, *Richard II*, pp. 168–9.

2 The Westminster chronicler reports that the wine was sold a 4d per gallon: *WC*, p. 185.

3 According to the Westminster chronicler, Arundel delayed while his men recovered from sickness (*WC*, p. 185).

4 See above, pp. 238–9.

5 The Westminster chronicle reports that Arundel embarked for Brittany on 1 May and advanced as much as ten miles inland in pursuit of the new siege tower (*WC*, p. 185).

[Michael de la Pole], [Sir] Simon Burley and [Sir] Richard Stury were jealous that the earl had acted so well, and they disparaged his achievements before the king, claiming that the earl had done nothing very special, seeing that he had only attacked merchants, whom it would have been more profitable to have kept as friends of our country rather than to have turned them into implacable foes.[1]

Some people are jealous of the deeds of the earl

It is no wonder these favourites were jealous, for several of them were more soldiers of Venus than of Bellona [Goddess of War], more valorous in the bedchamber than on the field of battle, and more likely to defend themselves with their tongues than their spears, for although they slept on when the trumpet sounded for deeds of war, they were always wide awake to make speeches. They were ever in the king's company, but they made no effort to teach him what befitted a great knight. I am not referring just to the use of arms but also to the pursuits which especially befit well-born kings in peacetime such as hunting or falconry or similar things, which increase a king's honour. And it was at their instigation that the king was so angry with those who had fought on this recent expedition. For when the earl of Nottingham [Thomas Mowbray], the earl marshal and contemporary of the king and ever his friend, came to the king with hopes of receiving hearty thanks from him, the king, instead of giving him a friendly look, just stared at the ground. And the duke of Ireland [Robert de Vere] would not look at the two earls or even speak to them, perhaps being envious of their virtuous behaviour, which he himself could not match. The earls themselves indeed, when they saw this, took little notice of it but departed for their estates and a life more peaceful than that around the king.[2]

Henry Percy the younger is sent to the sea

A short time afterwards the members of the king's council advised him that Henry Percy [i.e. Hotspur], son of the earl of Northumberland, should be sent to the sea to repel attacks by the enemy, as there were reports that the enemy were getting ready to make attacks on England on account of the blow which they had recently received from the earl of Arundel. The council neither gave him an adequate force nor provided the proper support, doing this, so it was said, out of envy for the ability of one who had already won a great name for his worth among both English and Scots. But Henry himself was either unaware of their treacherous schemes or made light of them, for he fearlessly undertook the commission laid upon him and bravely and vigorously carried it out, and, having finished the term of his command, returned home safe and sound.[3]

The power given to friar Walter Diss

At this same time there was in England a Carmelite brother called Walter Diss. He had formerly been the confessor of the duke of Lancaster, but when the duke was setting out for Spain, Walter showed no inclination to go with him but had stayed at home for the reason I shall give below.[4]

---

[1]   These were the principal favourites of the king and the target of the appellants. See below, pp. 251, 255–6.

[2]   Walsingham was more outspoken in his criticism of the king's favourites than many other contemporary commentators, although Knighton also described these men as the king's 'seducers' (seductores: *Knighton*, pp. 392–3). His account of the disrespect shown by de Vere to Nottingham is not recorded in the other independent accounts, but it is indicative of an increasing polarisation between the members of the continual council appointed in the Wonderful Parliament and the king's own clique of courtiers. As the Westminster chronicler reports, in the spring of 1387 Richard broke away from the council and embarked on a tour of the provinces, taking in those parts of the country – such as Cheshire and the East Midlands – where he could count on support. See also Saul, *Richard II*, pp. 112–27, 171–2.

[3]   Out of chronological sequence, this appears to refer to the expedition that Percy led to Brest in September 1387, when, as the Westminster chronicler records (*WC*, pp. 196–7) he entered the harbour and destroyed the enemy siege towers 'planted close by'. He restored the castle of Brest to John Roches, the castellan, by 12 October: *CPR, 1385–89*, pp. 358–9.

[4]   Diss, a Carmelite of the Cambridge convent, had served as Gaunt's confessor from 1375–86 and had negotiated the bulls that supported his Spanish campaign: see above, p. 236. For his career see Emden, *BRUC*, p. 188.

For pope Urban VI knew that the kingdom of Spain was great and full of riches, and he thought, though vainly, of all the advantages that would accrue to him if the duke gained possession of the Spanish dominions. So in addition to the privileges that he had given to the duke when he was about to set out for Spain, he now, after his departure, awarded him fresh privileges. These were to be distributed to those asking for them by the said friar Walter Diss, but were only to be acquired at a price.

Among these privileges or powers received by Walter from the pope was one which everybody came running to obtain, and offering huge sums for it. Walter was more inclined to favour those who offered the larger sums, and it was these men that he made papal chaplains according to the manner and lawful practice habitually used in the Roman Curia.[1] He gave this privilege, amongst many others, to an Augustinian brother called Peter Pateshull, who, thinking that he had now been given complete freedom from his religious vows, began first by joining the followers of Wyclif (called by some people the Lollards).[2] Following the doctrines of their master these Lollards had already gained many swarms of followers among the people of London, and had infected several others with their wicked doctrines. So Peter, having submitted himself to their teaching, learnt that he had done well in leaving his private religion and entering public life, as the latter was thought by them to give more holiness and perfection, and to be more distinguished and safer.

In the end Peter, infected by their wickedness and driven on by his own villainy, was compelled to preach and reveal in public the evils of the Augustinian order. So he came to the church of St Christopher in London, followed by about a hundred of the Lollards, and there he vomited forth crimes of such great evil attributed to his former fellow friars, that those who heard him were amazed and horror-struck. Meanwhile some ran off and told the Augustinians what was happening. And at once about twelve of them, who had been stirred to greater anger than the rest, came to the church where the disgraceful Peter was still proclaiming their heinous crimes. When they heard what was being said, they were greatly moved and one of them, showing more zeal for his religion, boldly stood up and contradicted the accusations that the rascal was making. When the Lollards saw this, they sprang to their feet and threw to the ground the Augustinian heckler, wounding and hurting him with kicks and blows. They also threw out the other eleven Augustinians and followed them from the church, wishing to kill them and to burn down their dwellings and saying with angry shouts, 'Let us destroy the murderers, set fire to the sodomites, and hang the traitors to the king and to England.' So uttering these furious shouts, they ran off, intending to set fire to the dwellings of the friars. But they were stopped by the humble words of brother Thomas Ashbourne and his companion, who were both good men and professors of holy scripture.[3] Also the intervention of one of the aldermen of London helped to quell the frenzy of the mob. He calmed them down by his persuasive words, and got them to go back home.

Meanwhile the Lollards still held on to Peter, and as he had been interrupted in his speech on that occasion, they urged him to produce a document in which he put down in writing all that he had said and any other crimes he knew about. He at once acquiesced in their wicked plan and produced a document in which he accused certain of his Augustinians of the murder of various of their brothers. And to give greater credence to his words, he set down the names of the victims and the names of the perpetrators. He also revealed the places in which those murdered had been killed and buried. He also said that they were sodomites, traitors to king and kingdom, and many other things which it would take too long to enumerate, and he fixed the paper on the doors of

---

1   Walsingham was particularly hostile to the privilege of papal chaplaincy that proved popular with members of the religious in England in this period. He regarded it as a threat to the regular discipline of the order as it dispensed the recipient from their vow of stability. He condemned members of his own community who sought it in his continuation of the *Gesta abbatum*, ed. Riley, ii. 204–5.
2   For Peter Pateshull see Emden, *BRUO*, iii. 1434. One William Pateshull an apostate friar was arrested on 18 July 1387: *CPR, 1385–89*, p. 386.
3   Thomas Ashbourne was prior of the London convent of the Augustinian Friars. See also Emden, *BRUO*, i. 54.

people from London whom he knew had feet in both camps, and all the sheriffs and all the justiciars of the land. He summoned these people from London, because they could be swayed like reeds in the wind, and, fickle and never still, they sided now with the lords, now with the king. Many of them had recently confessed their treachery against the king, but had obtained his pardon, with the king hoping that they themselves would pay him some favour in return for the favour that he had shown to them, and would accuse the lords of many crimes, which the king, while in distant parts, had cunningly thought up against them. And he had the sheriffs assembled, so that he might know how many troops they could gather together for the king's business against the barons, and also to ask that they should permit no one to be chosen as knight from town or shire unless he was someone whom the king and his council had chosen.

But to this the sheriffs replied that all the common people were on the side of the lords, so that it was not in their power to assemble an army for this purpose. They made a similar reply about the selection of knights, declaring that the commons wished to retain the customary practices, which meant that knights were chosen by the commons.

So the sheriffs, having given these replies, were dismissed.[1] Next the justiciars were called, that they might decide that the indictments were legal, and that they might put their seals to them. This was then done by [Sir] Robert Tresilian and John Blake,[2] a legal apprentice, whom Robert Tresilian had brought to the king's court to commit this crime. Once these indictments against the lords and many other nobles and barons had been drawn up according to the king's wishes, those who had been summoned for this purpose were dismissed.[3]

The king raises troops

Also the king and the duke of Ireland [Robert de Vere] at once sent out messengers and got all the troops they could assembled, to stand at their side if it came to the day of war against the lords. Many of those approached replied that they had neither the power nor the wish to make a stand against the lords, whom they knew for certain loved the king deeply and whose every scheme and action showed their zeal for his honour. Many simply regarded the king's call as a means of earning money and promised they would be ready whenever the king summoned them.[4]

Meanwhile news of this action reached the lords. The great hatred shown them by the king upset them and made them very sad, as they were not conscious of any fault that they had committed.

---

[1] Richard's questions to the sheriffs and to the delegation of Londoners were the natural extension of the search for supporters that he had conducted during his travels in the preceding months. Neither group gave the king the answer he had hoped for; the Londoners declined to give a direct answer, and predictably, the sheriffs made clear that they would do nothing which would undermine the customs of the commons and its relationship with the magnates. They argued that raising an army was impossible since the commons were sympathetic to Gloucester and the other councillors, and that they could not countenance interference in any election.

[2] Blake had previously been engaged in an inquisition in Wiltshire: *CPR, 1385–9*, p. 165.

[3] Richard conducted two meetings with his judges at Shrewsbury (probably between 1–5 July) and Nottingham (probably between 25–29 August). They were asked to answer ten questions regarding the extent to which the prerogatives of the crown had been encroached in the Wonderful Parliament, in particular whether the statute appointing the continual council and the impeachment of Chancellor de la Pole had been lawful. The questions were drafted by the lawyer John Blake, named here by Walsingham. The judges' answers supported Richard's contention that the royal prerogative had been encroached and declared both the council and the impeachment of de la Pole unlawful. See also Saul, *Richard II*, pp. 173–4; S. B. Chrimes, 'Richard II's Questions to the Judges, 1387', *Law Quarterly Review*, lxxii (1956), 365–90. Walsingham's account is very brief in comparison both to Knighton and the Westminster chronicler who incorporate a text of the ten questions (*WC*, pp. 196–203; *Knighton*, pp. 392–401).

[4] Knighton reports that after his success with the judges the king progressed slowly southwards in September and October, entering London on 10 November when he was given a warm reception by the Londoners; a point corroborated by the Westminster chronicler: *Knighton*, pp. 401–2; *WC*, pp. 206–8. See also Saul, *Richard II*, p. 186.

The duke of Gloucester tries to placate the king

In this situation it was especially the king's uncle, Thomas, duke of Gloucester, who tried to allay the king's hatred and to bring back his mind to thoughts of harmony and peace.[1] In the presence of the bishop of London [Robert Braybroke] and many other nobles of the land he touched a halidom[2] and swore an oath that he never devised any scheme to the king's hurt, but that to the best of his ability he had only promoted and performed those actions which had as their aim the king's honour, advantage and pleasure. The one exception was that he had not looked with joyful countenance upon the duke of Ireland, whom the king loved, and would not be willing so to look upon him in the future, seeing that he had dishonoured a lady who was not only his own kins-woman but also the king's. His firm decision was to avenge her against the duke of Ireland.[3]

The bishop of London speaks to Michael de la Pole

But when the bishop of London reported this to the king, as he had been asked to do, and showed some inclination to believe the duke's oath, Michael de la Pole made an attack on the duke in an attempt to turn the mind of the king against him, since he was afraid that any restoration of harmony between duke and king would be to his own disadvantage. But the bishop of London at once said to him, 'Michael, keep quiet. It is not right for you to open your mouth any more.' 'Why do you say this?', said Michael. 'Because,' said the bishop, 'in the last parliament you were condemned to death, and it is only by the king's grace that you are still alive.' The king flamed up in anger at this, and ordered the bishop to withdraw and return to his church. He hurriedly did so, and reported to the duke what he had seen and heard.

This increased the ill-feeling and displeasure of the duke and his party, while day by day the king and his wicked counsellors developed an overmastering hatred against them, their anger against the duke being stirred up, increased and strengthened by the duke of Ireland [Robert de Vere], Michael de la Pole, [Sir] Robert Tresilian, Alexander Neville, archbishop of York, and many others.

The king sends the earl of Northumberland to arrest the earl of Arundel, but the earl of Arundel escapes

When the duke of Gloucester saw where things were heading, he secretly summoned the earls of Arundel, Warwick and Derby,[4] who would be under the same condemnation as himself if they did not speedily look to their own interests, and revealed his thoughts and told them of the danger which affected all of them alike. At once they assembled their armies and decided to call the king to account for what had just happened and for the favour which he had shown to men who were traitors not only to himself but to the realm and also for the peril which was overhanging the land, unless it was speedily given help.

On the other hand the king on his side was under pressure from the traitors, and considered how he could remove individual lords before they came against him with united forces. And first he sent the earl of Northumberland [Henry Percy] with many others to the castle of Reigate, where the earl of Arundel was staying, to arrest him. But when he saw how angry the earl of Arundel was and how great was the force he had around him, the earl of Northumberland was

---

[1]   The Westminster chronicler claims that Gloucester had been apprised of the king's plans and preparations against the council, and in particular, presumably, of the questions he had put to the judges at Nottingham and Shrewsbury, by the archbishop of Dublin, Robert Wickford: *WC*, pp. 206–7. See also Saul, *Richard II*, pp. 185–6.

[2]   i.e. a sacred object

[3]   Walsingham is the only authority to report Gloucester's oath. If the episode took place at all, it must have occurred by October by which time the duke must have known of the king's plans. See also Saul, *Richard II*, p. 186.

[4]   Henry of Bolingbroke, earl of Derby, and eldest legitimate son of John of Gaunt, was only a junior partner of the three principal appellants and only latterly made an overt display of support for them, when de Vere was pursued towards Radcot Bridge. See below, p. 257

afraid to carry out his orders and withdrew without having done anything. After him several others were sent to arrest the earl by night and bring him before the king, or at least kill him if there was any way they could do this. But a messenger from the duke of Gloucester reached Arundel before they did, and compelled the earl of Arundel to ride throughout the night so that at first light he arrived at Harringay wood after a thirty-mile journey of great difficulty, and there he found the duke of Gloucester and the earl of Warwick gathered together with a very large army.[1]

The king sets out for Canterbury

At this time, so it was said, the king had made preparations for a journey to Canterbury, not just to make his vows to the blessed St Thomas [Becket], but also that he might cross the Channel and sign the promised agreement with the king of France [Charles VI], to whom he had sold Calais together with the castle of Guisnes and all the fortresses which his ancestors had owned in those parts either by ancestral right or by conquest in war.[2]

The nobles gather; the king is alarmed

But the king's departure was suddenly prevented when he learned of the gathering of the lords in Harringay wood. He was nonplussed[3] by this, and called together the members of his household to ask them what such an unexpected massing of forces portended for him.[4] And when he discovered that the lords had met with the idea of bringing him back to a better, more fruitful life and a more helpful style of kingship, the king at once grew pale and asked what he should do in such a crisis. Some declared that the lords should be appeased and that he should make a vow and promise that he would do what they proposed. Others were all for joining the members of the king's household with the people of London and marching out to meet the lords and trying the fortunes of war.[5] The keenest proponent of this second plan was the archbishop of York [Alexander Neville]. But the more sensible counsellors were against his scheme, arguing that no advantage would accrue to the king, even if he won, whereas he would suffer great shame and damage, if he lost.

While this discussion was going on, there arrived on the scene an energetic but half-witted knight called Sir Hugh Lynn.[6] (Because he was a fool who had lost his wits, he was supported by alms from many of the lords). So the king jokingly asked him what he would do against the lords who were said to be assembled in that wood. Hugh very sadly at once replied, 'You must march out and we must attack them and kill every mother's son. And, by the eyes of God, when this has

---

1   Northumberland was dispatched to Reigate in early November. The castle was too well defended and on or before 13 November Arundel was able to leave, accompanied by his retinue, to join Gloucester and Warwick at Hornsea Great Park in the bishop of London's manor of Harringay. Knighton's narrative would suggest that Gloucester and Warwick had assembled by 11 November and that Arundel had reached them next day, when a royal proclamation was issued in the city of London that the earl should not be supplied with any arms or food on pain of death (*Knighton*, pp. 402–3). See also Saul *Richard II*, p. 186.

2   It was the opinion of some of Richard's counsellors that he should seek the support of the king of France to resolve the situation. Knighton corroborates Walsingham's story that it was proposed to surrender to Charles V Calais, Guisnes, Picardy and other territories in France apart from Aquitaine in return for aid, and that instructions to this effect were sent to Sir William Beauchamp, the captain of Calais. Knighton also claims that Beauchamp countermanded the order and redirected the letter intended for the king of France to Thomas, duke of Gloucester: *Knighton*, pp. 404–7. Froissart reports that it was while the king was at Canterbury that Simon Burley secreted the celebrated casket of St Thomas in Dover Castle: *Chroniques*, xiv. 41; FCBuchon, ii. 613. See also Saul, *Richard II*, p. 186.

3   The Westminster chronicler comments: 'rex vero stupefactus'. He adds that the king's first response – on 11 November – was to summon Gloucester and Arundel but that they refused 'on the ground that they had arch-enemies at the king's elbow' (*WC*, pp. 208–10).

4   The king convened an emergency meeting of his council on 14 November to considers his options.

5   Knighton, who may have been working from a source written in support of the appellants, claims that one of Richard's counsellors maintained that Brembre and the Londoners could supply a force of 50,000 in a short time: *Knighton*, pp. 406–7.

6   This scene is not reported by any other authority. Nothing further is known of Lynn himself.

been done, you will have killed all the faithful friends that you have in the kingdom.' This reply may have been put in a foolish manner, but it was very deeply pondered by wise men.

But in the meantime mediators for peace intervened, and the conclusion of the matter was that the lords should meet at Westminster in the presence of the king, to receive his reply about those matters that had caused them concern.[1] The bishop of Ely [Thomas Arundel] and many other reliable authorities declared on oath on behalf of the king that no tricks, deceptions or dangers were being plotted, such as might cause the lords themselves to experience loss of life or limb: and if it happened that the king or those who were with him openly or secretly reneged on this pact, they, the mediators, would forewarn the lords.

But no sooner had the lords made ready to meet in London as arranged than the peace mediators sent secret messages to them, informing them that an ambush had been set for them in a place called the Mews near London, and therefore they were not willing to advise the lords to come to London, unless they did so with a strong force. When the lords heard this, they postponed their visit to London. So that when the appointed hour had passed and they had not turned up, the king asked why the lords were not keeping the agreement. And the bishop of Ely [Thomas Arundel] said to him, 'It is because an ambush is set. In such and such a place there are a thousand armed men or more, contrary to the agreement, and that is why they do not come and they consider that you have broken your word.'

The king indeed flared up at once, and swore that he had not been party to this ambush. He ordered the sheriffs of London to go to the Mews, make a thorough search and put to death any they found gathered there for this purpose. But treachery was not lying hid at the Mews, but at Westminster, thanks to the action of the knights, [Sir] Thomas Trivet and [Sir] Nicholas Brembre, who, on learning that they would be discovered, had secretly removed their armed men from the Mews and sent them back to London. So the king sent a second time to the lords, promising them a safe passage, if they would come. And soon the lords came to Westminster with a strong force.[2]

Negotiations at Westminster between the king and the lords

When the lords arrived there, the king indeed adorned himself with his royal insignia of robe and sceptre and entered the court of Westminster.[3] The chancellor, the bishop of Ely, spoke for the king as follows: 'My lords, when our lord king heard recently that you had assembled in Harringay park contrary to custom, he was not willing to make an attack on you, although he could easily have done so, if he had not been thinking of you and those who were with you. For no one doubts that, if he had amassed an army, he would have had many more men than you and perhaps much human blood would have been spilt. But we all know that our lord king has a particular abhorrence of that. So adopting an attitude of patience and mercy he chose to summon you here peacefully and to ask the reason why you gathered together so many men.'

The lords replied to this that they had assembled for the good of the king and the kingdom, and so that they might tear away from the king the traitors whom he continually kept by his side.[4] And they named the traitors as Robert de Vere duke of Ireland, Alexander Neville archbishop of

---

[1]   In fact before a meeting in the presence of the king was agreed, on 14 November (Knighton gives the date as 15 November: *Knighton*, p. 413) Richard had dispatched a delegation including Archbishop Courtenay, the duke of York, the bishops of Ely and Winchester and other council members to negotiate with the three lords who had moved their encampment from Hornsea Great Park to Waltham. It was here that they made their first appeal of treason against the king's favourites. A meeting in the presence of the king was agreed for the following Sunday, 17 November: *WC*, p. 208; Saul, *Richard II*, p. 187.

[2]   Apparently devised by Sir Thomas Trivet, the plot had been to seize the appellant lords as they passed the Mews at Charing Cross and the archbishop of York's house at York Place. The appellants followed a different route but the meeting was delayed by two hours. According to the Westminster chronicler, the lords arrived with a force of '300 horse': *Knighton*, pp. 412–15; *WC*, pp. 212–13.

[3]   The Westminster chronicler recounts that the appellant lords prostrated themselves three times as they approached the king: *WC*, p. 213. See also Saul, *Richard II*, p. 186.

[4]   According to the Westminster chronicler, Richard, Lord Scrope, one of the delegation that had met them at Waltham, now acted as their spokesman.

York, Michael de la Pole earl of Suffolk, the false justiciar Robert Tresilian, and the false knight of London Nicholas Brembre.[1] And to demonstrate that this allegation was true, they threw down their gauntlets and swore that they were willing to prove it in combat. To this the king replied, 'This will not happen now, but in the next parliament which we appoint for the day after the feast of the Purification of the Blessed Virgin [2 February].[2] Both you and they, on arrival at this parliament, will receive according to the requirements of the law that verdict which universal reason dictates. And now, my lords, this is what I have to say to you. How and why could you have had the audacity to dare to rise in revolt against me in this land? Did you think to have frightened me by this highly presumptuous act of yours? Do I not have soldiers, who, had I wished it, would have herded you together and slaughtered you like cattle? You can be sure that in this matter I have no more regard for all of you than for the lowest scullery boy in my kitchens.'

When he had finished saying this and several other things, he lifted up the duke of Gloucester, who thus far had stayed kneeling, and ordered the rest to rise to their feet. After this he took them in friendly fashion into his chamber, where they sat and drank side by side and heard the king's final word, namely that all of them, as had been said, should meet at the next parliament, at which there would be full justice for both sides.[3] And meanwhile the king took the duke of Ireland [Robert de Vere] and his associates under his protection and likewise the duke of Gloucester and his allies, so that neither party should do harm to the other in the interval, or dare to assemble before the day and time appointed. With these words the council was dismissed. These things happened in the absence of the traitors. They did not dare to appear before the lords, because they knew for certain that if they had done so, they would have paid the penalty there and then, without any regard for the king's majesty.

The duke of Ireland raises a force to eliminate the lords

As the lords went away, they did not judge it yet safe to separate, both on account of the fickleness of the king and the notorious falsity of the traitors. Later this was seen to be a wise move. For with the connivance of the king the duke of Ireland raised a great force in Cheshire and Wales, whose general was Thomas Molyneux, constable of Cheshire, a man both wealthy and bold, for whose nod that whole county of Cheshire waited.[4] But trickery on this scale could not for long be kept secret from the lords. They were forewarned about all these actions and about the fact that the duke of Ireland was hurrying to London with this great army so that he could join up with the citizens of London and form one well-nigh invincible army out of the two forces. So the lords at once armed their own men and encouraged each other not to neglect their own safety now, but to hurry to seize or kill the men who had treacherously plotted to kill them.[5]

---

1   Whilst the resentment towards the other appellees had grown steadily over the previous years, Brembre had only recently emerged as a figure of suspicion. A wealthy merchant and former mayor, he had become the king's strongest and most generous supporter in the city, providing loans to the value of almost £3,000 over the previous five years. He was also present at the questioning of the judges in August.
2   Writs for parliament were issued on 17 December.
3   This hospitable end to the meeting is recorded only by Walsingham. See also Saul, *Richard II*, p. 187.
4   Richard's first response, on 28 November, was to raise troops in London, but as the Westminster chronicler reports, when he met the mayor and aldermen on 1 December they proved reluctant to comply. Letters were then directed under the privy seal to the Cheshire sheriffs to arrange musters at Flint and Pulford; by mid-December a substantial force had been raised. Adam Usk describes it as a 'great crowd of armed Cheshiremen' (*Usk*, p. 11), Henry Knighton and the Westminster chronicler estimate there were as many as 5,000 men (*Knighton*, pp. 418–19; *WC*, p. 221) and Froissart characteristically claims a prodigious 12–15,000 (*Chroniques*, xiv. 75; FCBuchon, ii. 61516), although in reality there not likely to have been more than 4,000. See also Saul, *Richard II*, p. 187.
5   The appellants were informed of the mustering of Cheshire men from the earl of Arundel's garrison at Holt-on-Dee. The Westminster chronicler (*WC*, pp. 218–19) claims that both Arundel and Gloucester were minded to depose Richard, but Warwick persuaded them to pursue their quarrel with de Vere and to muster their own forces outside London to cut off the de Vere's approach to the capital. They left London in early December and having been joined by the earls of Derby and Nottingham at Huntingdon, they marched northwards to Northampton and then westwards to consolidate their control over the Midlands, the Cotswolds and the upper Thames Valley. See also Saul, *Richard II*, pp. 187–8.

The lords march out to meet the duke of Ireland

So they secretly left London to meet the duke of Ireland and sent out detachments to block all the roads by which it was expected he might come.[1] But as the duke of Ireland, seated high on his horse, was riding proudly along with the army which he had collected and believing that no one would dare to oppose him, he suddenly looked sideways and saw the army of the lords not far distant from him and awaiting his arrival in the middle of a valley. When he saw this, he felt fear in his heart, and spoke to his men.[2]

The duke of Ireland speaks to his men

'My friends,' he said, 'as far as I can see, there is much greater strength in the enemy army than in our own, so that I must flee for an hour. Before battle is joined, I shall take myself off and save myself, if I can, since they are only after me, and have nothing against you. So, once I have slipped away, you will easily get clear.' One of his knights said to him, 'You compelled us to leave our homes, you assured us of your loyalty, you forced us on to this march. So we are ready to fight with you, to conquer with you, if that should be our luck, or to die with you like men, if fortune does not favour us.' 'We are not so prepared,' said the duke, 'but you can do as you like.' And at once, setting spurs to his horse, he hurried off in flight. So the many men who had come with him cursed his timidity and prepared to make submission to the lords.[3]

Thomas Molyneux is killed

Thomas Molyneux[4] was there on that occasion, and he made ready to fight, as all the lords had not yet assembled at that place but only one of them had arrived: Henry, son of the duke of Lancaster and earl of Derby [Henry of Bolingbroke]. Thomas fought for some time, but then exhausted and in despair made his way into a river nearby. A knight called Thomas Mortimer[5] was one of many who called to him to come out: if he did not, he would certainly pierce him with arrows in the river. 'If I climb out,' said Thomas Molyneux, 'are you willing to preserve my life?' 'I am not promising this,' replied the knight, 'but either come out or die at once.' 'If I must do this,' said Thomas, 'allow me to come out and fight with you or any one of your force, so that I may die like a man.' But as he climbed out, the knight caught hold of him by the helmet, pulled it off his head, and at once took out his dagger and plunged it into his brain.[6]

Meanwhile the duke of Ireland [Robert de Vere] in his flight reached the river, but when he wanted to cross it at the bridge, he found the bridge destroyed.[7] He went to another bridge, but there he found archers to stop him crossing. So he sheered off and, searching for a ford, forced his horse to enter the river. And in no time at all, once he had become a swimmer instead of a rider,

---

1   Arundel and Warwick appear to have occupied Banbury and Chipping Campden while Derby watched the bridgeheads across the Thames; *WC*, pp. 220–1; Saul, *Richard II*, p. 187.
2   De Vere and his troops came south into the Cotswolds on or around 20 December, when they encountered Arundel's troop near Burford (although the Westminster chronicler says Witney: *WC*, pp. 220–1).
3   The Westminster monk challenges Walsingham's account claiming that on seeing Arundel's forces de Vere was 'roused [with] the fighting spirit' and raised the standard of St George, signifying a state of war (*WC*, pp. 221–3), explaining that it was only after the remaining appellants and their retinues had appeared that his resolve faltered and he fled.
4   Constable of Chester Castle. See also *CPR, 1385–89*, p. 156.
5   Steward to Richard, earl of Arundel.
6   Both Walsingham and the Westminster chronicler agree that Molyneux was killed in the first encounter between de Vere and the appellants, before the decisive battle at Radcot Bridge; Knighton, however, has him meet his death in that second encounter (*Knighton*, pp. 422–3).
7   De Vere and his men reached Radcot Bridge (identified by both Knighton and the Westminster chronicler) where they were met by Henry of Derby's men. Battle was drawn in deep fog which may explain why de Vere was able to escape and also why many of his men drowned in the surrounding marshland. De Vere escaped, apparently disguised as a groom, and after a brief interview with the king, removed himself to Queenborough castle, from where he fled abroad: *WC*, pp. 222–5; *Knighton*, pp. 422–5; Froissart, *Chroniques*, ix. 67–70; FCBuchon, ii. 622–6; *Usk*, p. 27. See also Saul, *Richard II*, p. 188.

he reached the further bank. It was now night, and so the servants of the lords did not pursue the fleeing duke, especially as they did not know the byways of that part of the country. But the duke's horse, with his helmet, gauntlets and breastplate did fall into the hands of the lords. And so for long after it was thought that he had been drowned. The lords also intercepted the duke's carriage and baggage. They found many things in it, particularly letters from the king to the duke, urging him to hurry to come with a great army to the king in London, as the king was ready to do his damnedest and live or die with him. These despatches were a great proof to the lords of the fickleness and unreliability of the king.[1]

The deeds of Michael de la Pole

At this same time Michael de la Pole, in his fear of some future punishment, fled in secret to Calais, escorted by a knight called Sir William atte Hoo.[2] On his arrival there, he changed his clothing, shaved off his beard and, carrying poultry apparently for sale, he came to the gates of the castle of Calais, whose governor was Sir Edmund de la Pole,[3] his own brother. He was recognised by his brother, though with some difficulty because of his ragged clothing and shaven chin, and asked him to shelter and hide him, his story being that he had left England because he was afraid of certain rivals. But Sir Edmund said to him, 'You are my brother, but you must know that I refuse to be found false to the land of England from any claims of kinship. Nor am I willing to let you in without the knowledge or permission of Sir William Beauchamp, the governor of this town, because I believe and guess the truth to be that you have not fled without having done great wrong.'[4]

So he sent a messenger to Sir William Beauchamp to report that his brother, no marvel but a mass of misery, had arrived in Calais, and to beg Sir William to allow him to admit his brother and look after him, until Sir William should decide to send him back to England. This is what happened. For he was finally taken back to the king, who allowed him to go wherever he liked, making light of his own promise to keep him with the others for the next parliament.

Also at this time the archbishop of York and Robert Tresilian made their escape. They were afraid of the lords' anger, which they had deserved.[5]

The lords returned from the battle, which had been at Burford near Bablake. The knights and esquires who had gathered with the duke of Ireland for the battle were given back their weapons and horses and kept with the lords, but the rank and file were deprived of their horses, bows and arrows and sent back home. There was great rejoicing among the common people at this victory over the enemies of the kingdom. But their joy was tempered by the escape of the duke of Ireland, as it was not known what had happened to him.

A messenger of the French king is captured

It happened at this time that a messenger of the French king called Lustratus fell into English hands.[6] He had been carrying letters, in which the king of France [Charles VI] had authorised the

---

[1]   Both Knighton and the Westminster monk record the capture of money and equipment left behind by de Vere and his men but neither record the discovery of any incriminating letters.
[2]   Captain of the castle of Oye: *CPR, 1385–9*, p. 139. His family were tenants of St Albans: *Palmer, England, France and Christendom*, pp. 109–12.
[3]   For de la Pole see *CCR, 1385–9*, pp. 306, 366.
[4]   Walsingham's colourful account, attested by the Westminster chronicler, has long been accepted but it has been suggested that in fact de la Pole had travelled to Calais to raise troops and only fled (via Hull) after Radcot Bridge. He remained in exile and died at Paris in September 1389. Saul suggests he was captured after his first flight but then escaped a second time: Saul, *Richard II*, p. 187 and n.
[5]   Both Tresilian and Neville fled immediately after the meeting between the appellants and Richard at Westminster Hall on 17 November. Tresilian went into hiding and was not recovered until 19 February 1388. Neville fled abroad; he was translated to the see of St Andrews in April 1388 but his appointment was opposed by the Scots who recognised the Avignon pope, Clement VII. Neville remained abroad and died at Louvain in 1397.
[6]   This report is unique to Walsingham and the name of the messenger cannot be corroborated.

king of England, the duke of Ireland and some others to come with a fixed number of men to Boulogne. There the king of France [Charles VI] at the head of an army was waiting for the arrival of King Richard so that he might welcome him with great pomp and receive from him the possession of Calais and all the fortresses that the English king possessed in those parts of France. In return for all these the French king would pay a certain sum, and the king of England would become the liegeman of the king of France in order to keep Gascony.[1]

The lords kept quiet about this capture, and hurried with all speed to London, where the king was about to celebrate Christmas, not at Westminster but in the Tower, because he thought that could be a safe place for him, if anything untoward happened. So the lords collected an army of about forty thousand stout warriors, who went with them all the more willingly because they hoped to sack London, and on the day after Christmas Day [26 December] they arrived at London.[2] They made a show of their might, by drawing themselves up in lines of battle in open fields, where they could be seen from the Tower. And because my history has reached this point, it is time for my summary of the past year.

The year passed as one that had good corn crops and a good fruit harvest, and was reasonably healthy. It was a disturbing year for the English, apart from the casks of wine captured by the earl of Arundel that gladdened the hearts of many. It was a happy year for the Spanish, owing to the departure of the duke of Lancaster who had been laying claim to the kingdom and the piteous deaths of his men. It was a sad and gloomy year for the French, who had lost not only the wine but also their ships and men, and a sad year for the Flemish, as their wine had been lost as well when the French goods were seized.

[1388]

What happened between the king and the citizens of London

In 1388 the king spent Christmas in London in the Tower, as I have said. It was the eleventh year of his reign. The lords with their men had assembled at London, but they were lodged in the suburbs to avoid the tricks of the citizens.[3] At that time the people of London were very afraid. They weighed different dangers against each other. There was the anger of the king if they opened the gates to the lords, but, if they kept them out, there was the wrath of the undisciplined mob who had come with the lords and who were on the spot to break down the walls or gates of the city, if they were even the slightest bit annoyed. And there remained another very serious danger, namely that if the important citizens did not open the gates to the lords, the commons of the city and the poor, always keener on trouble than peace, were ready to admit the lords and their men and to ransack the houses of the rich for valuables.

At last, after much consideration, the mayor of London [Nicholas Exton] went out of the city and promised to the lords, in good faith, lodgings inside the city and all the provisions they needed, if they were willing to accept them. Then he distributed to all in the army wine and beer, and bread and cheese. This action was subsequently of no small advantage to the city.[4]

Meanwhile the king, after hearing and learning of all these happenings, pretended that he felt little concern at the assembled army and that he was not afraid of the lords, and he said to the archbishop of Canterbury and the others who were running to and fro to establish peace, 'Let them be allowed to stay here with their mob, until they have used up all their provisions, and then finally they will go back to their homes empty-handed and in want, and then I will speak of justice to them one by one.'

---

1 For these proposals see above, pp. 218, 226.
2 The size of the appellants' retinue is grossly exaggerated; the Westminster chronicler records that there were 500 men although he also notes that they were 'accoutred for war' (WC, pp. 224–5).
3 According to Henry Knighton they 'presented themselves . . . in a splendid and amazing array', the Westminster chronicler also observed 'their lines were drawn in battle array': *Knighton*, p. 425; WC, pp. 226–7.
4 The principal authorities disagree as to the dating of the appellants' advance on the Tower, but this deputation appears to have approached them on 26 or 27 December and it was on the latter date the appellants and their retinues entered the city: *Saul, Richard II*, p. 188.

When the lords heard this, they were very angry, and swore they would never depart, until they had had conference with the king, face to face. And at once they sent men to guard the Thames, that the king might not slip through their hands and subsequently laugh at them. But then the king, seeing that he was encircled on all sides, began to speak to his envoys and ordered them to announce to the lords that he was willing to treat with them. They demanded that he should come to Westminster the next day, as that was where they wished to make their requests known to him. The king said, 'I am not willing to treat with them at Westminster, but only here in the Tower.' The reply of the lords was that the Tower was suspect, because traps for them could be laid inside and perils prepared. To this the king said, 'Let them send two hundred or as many as they like of their own men to inspect everything beforehand and make a complete examination, so that there can be no secret trickery.' This was done.[1]

Then the duke of Gloucester and his companions entered the Tower.[2] He had an open but brief discussion with the king, and then at the king's request the lords entered his chamber, where in his presence they mentioned his plot against them in which they had been indicted, and showed him the letter which he had sent to the duke of Ireland, asking him to raise an army to destroy the lords. They also showed him the letters they had intercepted from the king of France [Charles VI], in which safe conduct was given to King Richard for his arrival in France and confirmation of other things that would lead to the decrease of the king's honour, the dwindling of his power and the loss of his good reputation.

On seeing the letters the king did not know what to do next, particularly as he realised that he had been spectacularly caught out. Finally the lords, having asked the king's permission, left him alone, in tears and all confused, on condition that he came the next day to Westminster [31 December] to hear their further points and to discuss the essential business of the realm. The king agreed to this condition, and kept the earl of Derby [Henry of Bolingbroke] with him for supper, as a pledge of the love between king and lords.[3] But before the king went to bed, whisperers were at work, telling him that it was not right, safe or honourable for the king to proceed to Westminster, so that the king changed his mind.[4]

But when the lords learned of this, they felt disappointed and bitter and sent back the message that, unless he came quickly in the morning as agreed, they would choose another king to rule over them, who would be willing and see it as his duty to obey the decisions of the lords. Once the king had been pierced by this shaft, he did go back to Westminster the next day [31 December], where, after a little discussion, the lords said that for his own honour and the good of his kingdom

[1]　According to the Westminster chronicler, the day after entering the city (28 December) the appellants demanded the delivery of the appellees into their custody (*WC*, pp. 226–7). The king refused but sent a delegation led by the duke of York and the bishops of Ely and Winchester – the same mediators that had been employed the previous November – to arrange for a meeting three days later on 30 December. It is unclear whether, as Walsingham suggests here, the appellants had demanded the meeting take place at Westminster but they were certainly wary (as Knighton relates, *Knighton*, p. 425) that any such meeting would be an ambush. See also Saul, *Richard II*, pp. 188–90.

[2]　Knighton claims that the five lords came before the king with their arms linked, the Westminster chronicler claims they prostrated themselves: *Knighton*, pp. 426–7.

[3]　Knighton reports that it was the earls of Derby and Nottingham who remained with the king: *Knighton*, p. 427.

[4]　Exactly what transpired in the Tower when the appellants confronted Richard remains unclear. Knighton suggests the exchanges between the appellants and the king were comparatively mild and that Gloucester reassured Richard that their troops were there to oppose only 'the false betrayers of the king and the kingdom' (*Knighton*, pp. 426–7). Like Walsingham, the Westminster chronicler presents a darker scene, in which appellants threatened Richard with deposition (*WC*, pp. 228–9). Whether, as Walsingham suggests here, the appellants' immediate demands included a council meeting to be convened the next day, or whether their main concern remained the surrender of the appellees is unclear but the council meeting did take place on 31 December and in the days that followed proceedings against the appellees began. The Westminster chronicler added that 'there was much else in what they said to [the king] that did not come to public knowledge' and the author of the Whalley Abbey chronicle claimed that Richard was actually deposed by the appellants for three days. There is no contemporary evidence to corroborate this, but Gloucester confessed to having done so in 1397 and it does remain a distinct possibility. See also Saul, *Richard II*, pp. 188–90.

it was essential that he banish from his palace and company traitors, whisperers, toadies, evil slanderers and drones, and that he substitute in their place other men who would be willing and would know how to serve the king with greater honour and loyalty.

When the king agreed to this, although sadly, the lords decided that the men to be banished from court[1] were Alexander Neville archbishop of York, John Fordham, bishop of Durham, and brother Thomas Rushook, of the order of preachers [i.e. Dominicans], who was the king's confessor and the bishop of Chichester. But brother Thomas, conscious of his guilt, took to flight and the archbishop of York looked for a hiding place. The lords also expelled the Lords, [William, Lord] Zouche of Harringworth, [Hugh, Lord] Burnell,[2] and [John, 4th Baron] Beaumont, Aubrey de Vere[3] and the knights Baldwin Bereford,[4] Richard Abberbury,[5] John Worth,[6] Thomas Clifford[7] and John Lovell.[8] These were not altogether banished, but were to appear before the next parliament.

They also banished as being no use at court[9] the Lady Poynings, the wife of Sir John Worth,[10] Lady Mohun[11] and Lady Moleyns.[12] All these were granted bail on condition that they replied to the charges against them at the next parliament. They also arrested the following knights, Simon Burley, William Elmham, John Beauchamp of Holt the king's steward, John Salisbury, Thomas Trivet, James Berners, Nicholas Dagworth, and Nicholas Brembre.[13] They also took captive the following clerks, Richard Clifford,[14] John Lincoln, Richard Medford,[15] Nicholas Slake the dean of the Chapel Royal who said a lot at court, and John Blake, apprentice at law. All of these, both knights and priests, they sent to various prisons, to be kept under close watch until the next parliament, when they would have to stand up and reply to the charges against them.

The parliament at London

Following the feast of the Purification [2 February], a parliament was begun at London, although the king had wanted to avoid altogether holding a parliament at that time. The lords came to it with sufficient troops to check any movements of rebellion that might arise. That parliament lasted right down to the feast of Pentecost, with many men waiting very anxiously to see what would happen.[16]

---

1   On 1 January the appellants seized control of the royal household and began to purge it of suspect courtiers and chamber knights whilst at the same time gathering evidence for the forthcoming trials. Walsingham's list of victims matches that of the Westminster chronicler and is likely to have been derived from official documentation. Some of these dismissals may have taken place before 1 January: Saul, *Richard II*, p. 190.
2   Burnell (c.1347–1420), a Shropshire magnate, perhaps suffered by association with the appellees since his first wife was the daughter of de la Pole: *CPR, 1385–9*, pp. 63–4, 87, 147, 178, 545.
3   De Vere, who had served on the third of Richard's continual councils, subsequently became the 3rd earl of Oxford.
4   Sir Baldwin Bereford held the manor of Watlington, Oxfordshire: *CPR, 1385–9*, p 8.
5   One of Richard's three tutors. See above, p. 34.
6   Steward of the lands of Countess Joan of Kent before her death in 1385: *CPR, 1385–89*, pp. 7, 252, 349.
7   Clifford was one of Richard's most favoured courtiers; a chamber knight by 1382 he was also appointed governor of Carlisle Castle in 1384.
8   A courtier knight holding lands in the East Midlands and Wiltshire: *CPR, 1385–89*, pp. 82, 63, 500, 546.
9   The Westminster chronicler describes how the appellants now rooted out 'the horde of officials ensconced in every department of the royal household' (*WC*, p. 229).
10   Blanche, daughter of John Lord, Mowbray and formerly the wife of Thomas, Lord Poynings.
11   Joan, daughter of Bartholomew Burghersh, Edward III's chamberlain and widow of John, Lord Mohun (d.1375).
12   Margery, the widow of Sir William Moleyns (d.1381).
13   With the exception of Beauchamp and Brembre these were all chamber knights.
14   Clerk of the Chapel Royal: *CPR, 1385–89*, p. 234.
15   Richard's secretary: *CPR, 1385–89*, pp. 100, 140, 145, 179, 340.
16   The parliamentary session did indeed begin on 3 February: *RP*, iii. 228. There was an adjournment for Easter between 22 March and 12 April. Pentecost fell on 17 May in 1388 but Knighton records that session was not over until 4 June: *Knighton*, pp. 430–1.

[Sir] Robert Tresilian is taken prisoner[1]

During this parliament the first man to be taken prisoner was Robert Tresilian. This was unlucky for him, as he was at once dragged to the gallows and hanged.[2] Next the lords sat in judgement on the knight Nicholas Brembre. He was put under the same condemnation, even though he had more people who pleaded for him. The accusation was that he had planned to wipe out the name of London and give the city the new name of Little Troy, and had decided that he himself was to be made and named duke of this newly named city. To put his plan into effect more easily, he had got tablets or rolls inscribed, on which had been written down several thousand names of his subjects whom he feared would resist his scheme and who were to be all suddenly murdered. But, as I said, he was hanged before he could put his schemes into effect.[3]

Other knights hanged

After this John Salisbury and James Berners, both young knights and both traitors, were by judgement of the parliament drawn and hanged. Then John Beauchamp of Holt, the king's steward, after a long career of deceit and trickery and disloyalty both to Lord Edward Windsor [i.e. Edward III] and to his son Lionel, once duke of Clarence, was drawn and hanged by decision of this parliament. Next was hanged the esquire John Blake, who in the council at Nottingham had in an unlucky hour opposed the lords.[4]

The execution of Simon Burley

Finally Simon Burley was beheaded, although the earl of Derby [Henry of Bolingbroke] had done his utmost to save him. On account of this a great quarrel arose between the earl of Derby and duke of Gloucester, but, praise God, it was rapidly brought to an end.[5] Wherever he went, Simon Burley did not show himself as the knight that he actually was, but in all his apparel as a duke or prince. Also he was governor of Dover castle, which, at the king's nod, he had agreed to sell to the French. He had been insufferably proud and arrogant, an oppressor of the poor, a hater of the church, a fornicator and adulterer.[6]

Also condemned to exile in this parliament were the justiciars, [Sir] Robert Bealknap, [Sir] John Holt, [Sir] Roger Fulthorpe and [Sir] William Burgh. Certain sums of money were granted to each of them for daily sustenance to keep them alive.[7] Then an oath was exacted from the king,

---

1   Walsingham offers an uncharacteristically brisk account of this momentous session known as the 'Merciless Parliament'. In contrast, other contemporary chroniclers – Knighton and the Westminster monk – dwell on its proceedings, including transcripts of the articles that condemned the appellees and their associates (see *WC*, pp. 235–345; *Knighton*, pp. 430–505). The appellants proceeded against their five appellees in spite of the fact that the three principals – de Vere, de la Pole and Neville – had escaped. De Vere, de la Pole, Brembre and Tresilian and a number of other chamber knights and counsellors of the king were found guilty and condemned to death. See also Saul, *Richard II*, pp. 191–5.
2   Tresilian was discovered in hiding in one of sacrist's houses at Westminster and executed at Tyburn on 19 February.
3   Brembre was executed on 20 February, the Westminster chronicler noting the contrition he showed at the end: *WC*, p. 315. Froissart reports that he had fled to Wales after Radcot Bridge: *Chroniques*, xiv. 75; FCBuchon, ii. 625. See also Barron, *London*, p. 334; Saul, *Richard II*, pp. 191–3.
4   Berners and Beauchamp were executed on 12 May, the sentence of hanging and drawing being remitted to beheading at the Tower on account of their positions in the king's household. Salisbury, found guilty 'on this side of the sea and beyond it' (*WC*, p. 293) was sentenced to strangulation. Blake was executed on 4 March. For his role see above, p. 250.
5   Burley was executed at Tower Hill on 5 May. Not only Derby, but also Edmund duke of York, Richard and Queen Anna all attempted to intercede on Burley's behalf.
6   The son of a minor Herefordshire gentleman, Burley had made some socially advantageous marriages; there is some suggestion that the last of these was contracted bigamously, which might account for Walsingham's condemnation. See Saul, *Richard II*, pp. 113–14 and n. Not every commentator expressed such antipathy towards the fallen knight. Froissart maintained that he had been a 'bien doulx chevalier': *Chroniques*, xiv. 41.
7   The judges, including Sir John Carey, not named by Walsingham and John Lockton, a serjeant-at-law,

that he should abide by the ruling of the lords. And this same oath was demanded not only of the king but of all the inhabitants of the land.

The expedition of the earl of Arundel[1]

After the feast of Pentecost [17 May], Richard [Fitzalan], earl of Arundel, with a crowd of powerful men, made for the sea and sailing up and down looked everywhere for the enemy. Having at last found their ships, he joined battle and won a victory, sinking, capturing or burning eighty ships. He landed on the Île de Batz and captured and burnt it. He also attacked, captured and looted the isles of Yeu, Ré, Lemustre, Rochelle, Olonne and Oléron – where the laws of the sea are stored. From some of these islands he received ransom money and some he destroyed by fire. He defeated the French or Bretons, who attempted resistance, and put them to flight. When he had completed this expedition most successfully, he returned to England.

The French invade the territory of the duke of Guelders

At the same time the French, taking no notice of the peace, invaded with a large number of armed men the territory of the duke of Guelders [William of Jülian, 1371–1402] to create trouble for him, especially as he was a loyal friend to the English.[2] But the duke with some Englishmen at once came out to meet them, and taught them how dangerous it was to arouse a sleeping dog. For most of them he killed and many he took prisoner, although a few escaped by running away. And in this battle France suffered losses such as she had not suffered since days of old.[3]

At the same time the Flemings themselves went out to meet the French, and inflicted great slaughter upon them. Nor was this slaughter undeserved, for the French had previously troubled and oppressed them with the heavy hand of tyranny and an arrogance that knew no bounds.[4]

In the same year the Scots, who know not how to be quiet, realised that the English were planning no raid against them, and made preparations, so that, when the truce was over, they might all be ready to invade the northern parts of England. And it happened that they entered our kingdom with a large army before the English could make any dispositions against them. And so they advanced without meeting any resistance, looting and killing everywhere, taking many prisoners and burning the towns which were on their route, unless their lords paid a ransom for them.[5] In this high and mighty fashion they got to near Newcastle upon Tyne and pitched camp not far

---

were seized on 1 February and committed to the Tower before the parliamentary session began, perhaps because the appellants had already discovered the records of the deliberations at Nottingham and Shrewsbury. They were tried in parliament on 6 March and initially condemned to death but at the intercession of the king, queen and archbishop of Canterbury they were sentenced to disinheritance and perpetual exile to Ireland, with sums ranging from between £20 and 40 marks for their support: *Knighton*, pp. 502–5; Saul, *Richard II*, pp. 193–4.

1   Richard himself had planned to revive the peace negotiations but with power in the hands of the appellants a new series of campaign was prepared. Arundel's expedition was to be a co-ordinated action with the duke of Brittany and John of Gaunt making incursions into mainland France, but in the event Arundel acted alone. Froissart describes the force of 1,300 archers and men-at-arms as 'tres bel et tres joly': *Chroniques*, xv. 16–18, 39–40; FCBuchon, esp. ii. 702. After the coastal raiding Walsingham describes here, notably at Bréhat and La Rochelle, he returned to England on 3 September.

2   The duke had entered into a formal alliance with the English in June 1387. Froissart gives a detailed account of the relationship between Guelders and the crown of France as an introduction to his report of this episode: *Chroniques*, xiv. 141–80; FCBuchon, ii. 679–88, 709–19.

3   The French withdrew having concluded a peace – the treaty of Körenzig – on 12 October 1388. The Westminster chronicler suggests Charles lost as many as 500 men on his return journey: *WC*, pp. 372–3.

4   Walsingham was not alone in recording a Flemish uprising in the spring of 1388; Henry Knighton describes a terrible slaughter of some 16,000 French and pro-French Flemings at Antwerp, Ghent and Ypres (*Knighton*, p. 453). Whether anything on this scale actually occurred must be doubted.

5   In mid-summer (probably late June) the Scots invaded in a campaign intended as a retaliation for the English invasion of 1385 (see above, pp. 227–8, 229–30). Robert, earl of Fife advanced through Cumberland and Westmorland whilst Archibald Douglas, known as 'the Tyneman' led another force into Northumbria; according to the *Scotichronicon*, at the same time the Tyneman's son William Douglas led an expedition to Ireland to harry the English there: *Scotichronicon*, vii. 412–15.

away. There were in the town at the time Henry Percy the younger and his brother Ralph. Both were knights, both eager for military glory, and both enemies to the Scots, although it was Henry with his energetic personality who caused most fear to the Scots. Henry now took it badly that the Scots were raging unchecked in this fashion, and especially because he had been challenged by them to a battle, he promised them in reply that he assuredly would join battle with them within three days, even if his forces were altogether inferior to their hordes. So, just as he had said, he suddenly came upon them, attacked them while still in their tents, and wrought great slaughter upon them.

The Douglas is killed and Henry Percy captured

When the commander-in-chief of the Scots, William[1] Douglas, himself also an ambitious young man, saw the thing he had a thousand times prayed for, namely Henry Percy inside his camp, he eagerly spurred his horse against him. And there you could have seen a splendid sight, two outstanding young men joining in combat and contending for glory. And although neither lacked courage, yet luck gave the victory to Henry, who with his own hands killed the Scot, who was the leading man of the Scots. But up rode [George] the earl of Dunbar with a huge number of Scots, and took Henry and his brother prisoner, also killing many of the English there. But the Scots themselves also suffered irreparable losses because of the slaughter of their most powerful men at the hands of Henry and the few who followed him into this battle.

In the meantime, while the English lords were arranging their troops to meet the enemy, the Scots who had been humiliated by this disgrace which they had experienced, fled from England with those whom they had taken prisoner, not daring to wait for the arrival of our lords. And so the whole kingdom through the virtue of one man, Henry, captured though he was, had been set completely free from fear and from the Scots.[2]

A parliament at Cambridge

After the feast of the nativity of the blessed Mary [8 September], a parliament was held at Cambridge in which new statutes were enacted.[3] They dealt with wages of workers; beggars; a ban on carrying weapons; a ban on sports except archery; the taking back of the staple from Middleburgh to Calais; a ban on labourers being received into a village not their own without the seal of their hundred; a ban on papal appointees leaving the kingdom to take up their benefices (with or without the cure of souls), unless they had permission to do this from the lips of the king, with failure to do so automatically meaning their exclusion from the king's protection.[4]

---

[1]   Correctly, James, 2nd earl of Douglas and Mar (c.1358–88). Following his death at Otterburn, reported here, he was buried at Melrose Abbey.

[2]   Here Walsingham does his best to provide a positive gloss on the English defeat at the battle of Otterburn, which occurred during the night of 5–6 August 1388. The Westminster chronicler confirms that Percy attempted to make a surprise assault on the Scots' encampment 'at the time of vespers'; the Scotichronicon adds a little local colour, observing that the Scots had disarmed and donned their 'gowns and ankle-length robes and were sitting down to supper' (*Scotichronicon*, vii. 416–19). But Walsingham notwithstanding, the attack was bungled and although the earl of Douglas met his death – according to the *Scotichronicon* having failed to fasten his protective neck armour in the hurry to defend the camp – so too did many of Percy's men (the *Scotichronicon* suggests 1,500) and he himself was captured. Knighton records that there were 1,000 fatalities from both sides and a further 30,000 Scots were put to flight: *Knighton*, pp. 504–7. Froissart also reports sizeable forces on both sides, remarking that such an assembly of Scots had not been seen for sixty years: *Chroniques*, xv. 119–21, 150–2. Sir Matthew Redmayne pursued the remaining Scots back across the border but great damage had already been done to the border communities. Meanwhile, the westward assault of the earl of Fife had not been interrupted and much of the region around Shap and Eden valley had been laid waste: Saul, *Richard II*, p. 198.

[3]   Parliament convened at Barnwell Priory, on 9 September: *RP*, iii. 228.

[4]   The succession of statutes reflected the demands of the commons, determined to assert their own agenda after the appellants had dominated the proceedings of the previous session. The matter of sports and weapons and the problem of beggars point to a growing concern over public order. The return of the staple to Calais had been promised in the Merciless Parliament although it was further delayed until February 1389. Walsingham shows only passing interest in the detail of these measures but Knighton and the Westminster

Many other statutes were enacted there, details of which I omit here, mainly because these same statutes were often enacted in the past but completely disregarded.[1] The parliament finally concluded with a tax being levied to help the king. It was a tenth for the clergy and a fifteenth for the laity.[2]

During this parliament Sir Thomas Trivet was riding on a tall horse alongside the king to the king's residence at Barnwell. He set spurs to his horse too fiercely, so that the horse fell and crushed almost all the insides of its rider, although he did prolong his life until the following day. This time, I suppose, was given to him for repentance, if he wished to use it. There was great jubilation from very many people at his death, partly because of his excessive haughtiness, partly because of the talk that he had been disloyal to the bishop of Norwich [Henry Despenser] on his crusade, but chiefly because in the previous year, he had been on the side of the king against the lords, and had counselled the king to put them to death.[3]

In the same parliament Sir John Holland, the brother of the king on the mother's side, was made earl of Huntingdon. He had recently returned from Spain, where he had fought for the duke of Lancaster.

The abbot of Monte Cassino bars the passage of the pope

During this period, Pope Urban [VI], who had always been fond of change, frequently moved to different places. Finally, when he was intending to transfer himself secretly from Pisa to Naples, the Romans with an army came out to meet him in order to keep him in Rome by force and violence, if he was unwilling to stay there of his own accord. But when they came up with him, they saw that their own army was far inferior to the one accompanying the pope, and so, putting aside any peremptory demands, they greeted him peacefully. The pope asked them why they had come with such a large army, and they immediately claimed that that they had come to do him honour, and, if it seemed good to him, to escort him wherever he wished to go.

The pope himself was alarmed at this, and replied that he had no need of their escort, but that they should return to Rome with his blessing. They, however, outwitting his trick with another, accepted his permission and returned to Rome, but immediately took good care to signify his arrival to the abbot of Monte Cassino [Bartolomeo Mezzavacca]. He was the man who had once been cardinal of Reati, as I have described, but who had been stripped of his office by this pope.[4] The abbot at once collected together a force of soldiers and waited for the arrival of the pope, as the pope had no choice but to pass through his territory. So that when the pope arrived there, the abbot resisted him and barred his passage through. But the pope, who was gripped by an overwhelming love for his native town of Naples, drew up bulls about the restoration of the abbot to the rank of cardinal, to the degree of doctor and to the office of the abbacy of Monte Cassino, all of which he sent to the abbot, asking only that he would allow him to pass through to visit his native land.

But the abbot replied that he did not need the pope's bulls to restore him to offices which he already enjoyed and with which he had been invested by the gift of the pope's predecessor, during whose papacy there had not been a schism in the church so that he had been universally recognised as the Roman Catholic pope. Now, on the other hand, it was doubtful if Urban would

---

monk, working from a version of the official records, went so far as to transcribe the commons' petitions: *WC*, pp. 356–69; *Knighton*, pp. 509–27; Saul, *Richard II*, pp. 199–201.

1   Walsingham omits several important statutes also designed to preserve public order, including that introducing a ban on all liveries adopted since 1327 (1 Edward III) and measures intended to reduce the corruption of juries: Saul, *Richard II*, pp. 200–1.

2   For the governing appellants this was the main purpose of the parliament: much had been hoped for from the sequestered estates and properties of the victims of the Merciless Parliament but these resources were only slowly recovered; a half subsidy had been granted in that parliament but more was needed. See also Saul, *Richard II*, pp. 199–200.

3   The Westminster chronicler, who dates this episode to 6 October, also saw Trivet's sudden demise in moral terms: *WC*, pp. 368–9. For Trivet's earlier history see above, pp. 203–7.

4   See above, pp. 223–4.

continue to be recognised as pope, seeing that his adversary, Clement [VII], was still alive. And so he sent back the messengers and the papal bulls, instructing the messengers to tell the pope that it was his job to return to Rome, the metropolis of the world, and to live there among Romans as the Roman pope, as without doubt it was not convenient that his subjects should be seeking him in such a remote spot and travelling all the way to the Mediterranean, if they wished to enjoy his blessings. So the pope willy-nilly returned to Rome, where he was received with great honour by the people.[1]

Episcopal promotions

In the same year the pope promoted Lord Thomas Arundel, bishop of Ely, to the archbishopric of York, with Alexander Neville, traitor and tale-bearer, being promoted to the archbishopric of St Andrews in Scotland, although he was not likely to take up the post, as the Scots at that time were schismatic. He made John Fordham of Durham bishop of Ely, Master Walter Skirlaw of Bath [and Wells] bishop of Durham, Master Ralph Ergom of Salisbury bishop of Bath, and he conferred the bishopric of Salisbury on John Waltham, a priest of the privy seal.[2]

The end of the year

So ended a year of abundant grain and fruit harvests. A gloomy year for traitors; a happy one for loyal subjects; a ruinous year for the French because of the vessels they had lost during the invasion of the earl of Arundel; a quiet year for the Spanish as they negotiated for peace; an unpropitious year of varying fortunes for the Scots, although during that period they had taken Henry Percy prisoner; a hateful and horrible year for the pope, because he had not achieved his wishes.

[1389]

Discussions about a truce

In 1389, the twelfth year of the reign of King Richard II, the king spent Christmas with Anna [of Bohemia] his queen at [Eltham].

During this year envoys were sent on behalf of the king of England to ask for a peace or at least a truce from the king of France [Charles VI].[3] They were Master Walter Skirlaw, bishop of Durham, and the knights John Clanvow and Nicholas Dagworth. After spending a long time at Calais and speeding across the Channel now this way and now that to announce conditions of the truce or to receive them, in the end they received as their final answer the verdict that the French would not agree to a truce, unless the Spaniards and the Scots enjoyed a similar respite under the conditions of the truce. So for a long time the peace negotiations were broken off, since our men declared that the Scots were liegemen of the king of England and had made massive infringe-

---

[1]   Urban entered Rome in September 1388. The Westminster chronicler presents a different version of events, suggesting that Abbot Tartaret sought to protect Urban by advising him not to travel through the region: *WC*, pp. 345–7.

[2]   John Fordham (d.1415), bishop of Durham since 1381, was translated to Ely on 3 April, Walter Skirlaw (d.1406), bishop of Bath and Wells since 1386, was translated to Durham on the same day. Ralph Ergom (d.1400), bishop of Salisbury since 1375, was translated to Bath also on 3 April and John Waltham was presented to Salisbury on the same day.

[3]   In the first half of 1388 the appellants were anxious to reopen the war, but the poor state of royal finances soon made the renewal of the peace a necessity. After his damaging defeat in Guelders, Philip of Burgundy also showed a new commitment to peace. The negotiations began in December 1388 – the Westminster chronicler reports the envoys' departure on 5 December – but made little progress for six months or more, as Burgundy remained preoccupied with his campaign in the Low Countries, and latterly, as Walsingham reports here, when the English envoys proved reluctant to accept the inclusion of the Scots and Castilians in the truce. This added a delay of two months, but a truce, which did incorporate the Scots and Spanish, was finally agreed and ratified at Leulingham on 18 June 1389. Walsingham omits the name of several envoys supplied by the Westminster chronicler, including John Sheppey, Richard Ronhale and Sir John Devereux: *Knighton*, p. 531; *WC*, pp. 374–7; Froissart, *Chroniques*, xv. 221–36; FCBuchon, ii. 760–1. See also Saul, *Richard II*, p. 205; Palmer, *England, France and Christendom*, pp. 138–9, 142.

ments of the peace of their king, and so as breakers of the laws ought to be punished as the king and nobles of England thought fit. Nor was it right that the king should make such a concession to law-breaking subjects as to come to such an agreement with them without having punished them. So on this occasion the truce was postponed. But the Scots meanwhile took such little notice of our blustering threats that they invaded Northumberland, inflicting great slaughter on the men, taking several away as prisoners, and carrying off huge amounts of plunder to their land.

At the time Thomas Mowbray, earl of Buckingham[1] and marshal, was sent with an armed force to combat the villainies of the Scots. But because he was unequal in numbers to their great forces, he achieved nothing. Indeed he took with him not more than five hundred spearmen to oppose thirty thousand of the enemy.[2]

The death of the abbot of [Bury] St Edmunds

During these days occurred the death of John Timworth, once abbot of Bury St Edmunds. He was succeeded through election by a monk of the abbey called William Cratfield. William journeyed to Rome where his appointment was confirmed by the pope, though first he was asked for a promise that his house would pay a fixed annual pension to Edmund Broomfield. The promise was not given or the pension paid. Indeed it was through the ambitions of Edmund, as I have said, that this monastery sustained various losses.[3]

The death of the bishop of Rochester

At the same time Thomas Brinton, the bishop of Rochester, departed this life.[4] When the pope learned of his death, he immediately awarded the bishopric to friar John[5] Bottlesham of the order of preachers, who was bishop of Llandaff. And then he made Edmund Broomfield bishop of Llandaff. And so, because of the benefice which had been awarded to him, the abbey of Bury St Edmunds was released from the pension asked for by the pope. Now the monks of Rochester had unanimously chosen Master John Barnet as bishop. But the pope was keen to bestow favour on two other persons, on John [i.e. William] Bottlesham, because he had stayed at his side during the attacks made on him when he was being besieged at Lucera, and on Edmund Broomfield, because he had sustained loss and imprisonment in the cause of the pope when the pope had appointed him to the abbacy of Bury St Edmunds. And so the pope cancelled the election of John Barnet, so that he might be freer to make provision for those two, Edmund and John [i.e. William] Bottlesham.[6]

The king claims by hereditary right the free ordering of the kingdom

In the same year the king was persuaded by the counsel of certain sycophants to summon a meeting of the nobles and the many powerful men of the realm. All of a sudden he stole into the

---

1   Correctly, Nottingham.
2   Mowbray was appointed warden of the east march on 8 March, following the appointment of the earl of Northumberland, Roger Clifford, John Lord Roos and Ralph Lord Neville as wardens of the western march. Nottingham was promised a sum of £12,000 to raise a force of 400 men-at-arms and 800 archers, and according to the Westminster chronicler, he was to be allowed to raise 600 spearmen and 2,000 archers in Northumbria. When the anticipated Scots invasion came on 29 June, Mowbray's force was no match for a massive Scots army that the Westminster monk, like Walsingham, estimates to have been 30,000 strong. Parts of Northumbria were devastated, including Tynemouth, where St Albans maintained a dependent priory: WC, pp. 396–7.
3   Abbot Timworth died on 16 January 1389. Cratfield was elected on 28 January and the election received royal assent on 1 February; the temporalities were restored on 8 October. For Edmund Broomfield see above, pp. 93–5.
4   Brinton, who had been a monk of Rochester before he was elected bishop, was a distinguished scholar, preacher and opponent of Wyclif. See also Emden, *BRUO*, i. 268–9. Walsingham's support for the monks' preferred candidate was not simply a case of monastic solidarity; Barnet had St Albans connections and was understood to have been a pupil of the abbey's almonry school.
5   Correctly, William. He held the see of Rochester until his death in 1400.
6   For Broomfield, see above, pp. 92–6, 102–3, 143, 185–6 and n.

council chamber, where the lords were awaiting his arrival, and, sitting down, he asked them how many years old he was. They replied that he had now lived for twenty years. 'Therefore,' he said, 'I am of the right age to govern my house and household, and also my kingdom. It seems unfair to me that the conditions of my life should be worse than those of the meanest of my subjects. Why, any heir in my kingdom, if he is past twenty when his father dies, is permitted to handle his own affairs freely. So why am I denied that which is allowed by law to all others of inferior rank?'

The barons were astonished at these remarks, and answered that he should not be deprived of any of his legal rights, but should have the ruling of his kingdom owed to him by law. And at this the king said, 'Well then! You know that I have long been ruled by guardians, and that I was not allowed to do even the smallest thing without their approval. So now for the future I am dismissing these guardians from my council, and, as an heir of lawful age, shall invite on to the council whomever I wish, and I shall handle my own affairs myself. And this being so my first command is that the chancellor should hand back to me the seal.'[1]

When the archbishop of York [Thomas Arundel] had handed back the seal, the king tucked it into his robe and suddenly got up and went out. After a little while he returned, sat down and handed the seal to the bishop of Winchester, William [of] Wykeham, thus making him chancellor, even though he was extremely reluctant to take the office.[2] The king also removed the old proctors and created very many new ones, making use of his own judgement and power in all matters pertaining to himself. He also removed the duke of Gloucester, the earl of Warwick and many other men of power from the council, and put in their place other men who were pleasing in his eyes. At the same time the king made five new justiciars.

The king is led astray and grows angry with the duke of Gloucester without reason

Meanwhile certain malicious men got round the king and made him so witless that he believed that his uncle, the duke of Gloucester, had collected armies to attack him. In the end, after the duke had been summoned, and the rumour discovered to be false, the king blushed in his confusion. There were present on that occasion some of those who had sown this lie. The duke wanted to speak out against them and to reveal their treachery publicly, but the king protested his love and asked him not to proceed further in this matter. The duke assented to this request the more easily, as he knew well that his innocence had now been shown to the king. But after the duke had returned to his own home, suspicion grew on all sides, as the whisperers intervened and did their bit.[3]

A truce is made

About the feast of the nativity of John the Baptist [24 June], a three year truce was made between the kingdoms of England and France.[4] The knight John Clanvow and the clerk Richard Ronhale[5] received the oath in France from the king of France [Charles VI]; and, as you might expect, a little later, about the feast of St Laurence [10 August], [Waleran] the count of St Pol, husband of Matilda de Courtenay, the sister of the king of England, came to England with other nobles[6] to receive the oath for the faithful observance of the truce from the king of England. The count was welcomed with full honours.

[1]   Richard announced his assumption of direct rule at a council meeting at Westminster on 3 May. It was the culmination of the personal and political recovery which had taken place over the previous months. With the removal of his former favourites, his character appeared to have moderated and his standing had undoubtedly improved. The conciliar reshuffle occurred on 4 May. See Saul, *Richard II*, p. 203.
[2]   Given his great age, Wykeham's reluctance was understandable.
[3]   There is no corroboration for this clash between the king and Gloucester, but its resolution is indicative of the new conciliatory mood that is said to have characterised Richard in this period.
[4]   This was the truce of Leulingham, concluded on 18 June, which secured a three-year peace beginning on 15 August. In April 1392 it was extended to September 1393 and in April 1393 to September 1394. See Palmer, *England, France and Christendom*, pp. 138–9, 142; Saul, *Richard II*, p. 205 and p. 266 above.
[5]   A royal clerk and former warden of the King's Hall, Cambridge: Emden, *BRUC*, pp. 487–8.
[6]   Amongst them were Jean d'Estouteville and Yves Derain.

Messengers are sent to the Scots

At this point some of the envoys who had come from France were sent to Scotland, to give the Scots the choice of being included in the treaty between the kings under certain conditions, or of being excluded completely from the protection of the king of France.[1] The Scottish noblemen replied that they themselves would willingly accept the truce and its conditions, but that they were well aware that it would be a hard matter to persuade the common people of this, since they were already prepared yet again to invade England with a still larger force and had hopes of a great deal of loot from such an attack, especially as in the past there had been no one who dared to resist a smaller force. And to show their obedience to the king of France [Charles VI], they asked that the envoys should go with them, so that at one and the same time they might see the preparations for battle which the Scots had made, and hear the reply which the commons would want to make to the envoys.

When the French envoys arrived at the Scottish army, they found the Scots arranged in good order by squadrons, properly armed with gleaming weapons, and prepared as it were for the onset of battle. As soon as the indisciplined crowd learned the reason for the arrival of the French envoys, they boldy proclaimed that they did not want to abandon all their preparations and to waste all that money which they had collected for the invasion of England, especially as they had mortgaged for this purpose homes, income, estates and furniture and had made themselves paupers in a multitude of ways. Even after hearing this the envoys did not give up, but using now threats and terror and now promises and wheedling words they so handled the Scottish commons that they laid aside their arms and agreed to the peace. A great help towards quietening the minds of the mob was the assertion of the Scottish nobles, who swore as one man that they would not provide the leadership for the commons against England, but that if they were completely set on carrying on with what they had begun, they should do it themselves at their own risk and choose their leaders from out of their own number.

And so it came to pass that the wicked Scots accepted the peace, and agreed to the treaty, though not without reproaches from the English.

A miracle at Ely[1]

During these days at Ely the blessed Etheldreda, perpetual virgin and queen, appeared in a vision to a young man. She told him to beware of the dangers which were overhanging him, and told him about the gravest dangers which would befall the kingdom, unless a merciful God was placated by the pious prayers of the faithful and thus stayed his hand from punishment. So she advised the young man to go to the prior and the monks and to take to them her commands that they should pray to the Lord for the salvation of the people, and beg him to avert his angry wrath from the people of England. The blessed virgin promised that she would also offer her own prayers to the Lord on this matter. But as the young man hesitated, lacking the boldness to carry our her orders, she gave him a sign, saying, 'You, who are now known to be healthy and well, will become bent double and lame and completely useless until the day of the festival commemorating my burial. On this day, when you are carried to my shrine, you will regain your full health.'

So the young man revealed all that he had seen, and the punishment of his lameness persuaded many to believe his words. What stopped people believing that the occurrence was a

---

1   The French envoys, Pierre Fresnel, Hennart de Campbernart and an unidentified third, arrived in London on 1 July on route for Scotland. Walsingham is the only contemporary chronicler to report their visit in any detail. The *Scotichronicon* records that Richard sent two envoys of his own, Sir Nicholas Dagworth and another unidentified knight who attended King Robert II at Dunfermline. This account challenges Walsingham claiming that the Scots willingly accepted the truce (*Scotichronicon*, vii. 444–5). It was during this time that the Scots released Henry Percy, earl of Northumberland who had been captured at Otterburn (See above, p. 264).

2   It was natural for Walsingham to record miracles from Ely and Cambridge. St Albans Abbey recruited monks from Cambridgeshire and its links to the church of Ely were of long-standing.

fake and the invention of human cunning was the fact that his flesh wasted away, his shanks were so thin that they were just skin clinging to bones, and his legs were so bent double that his ankles were inseparably joined to his buttocks. Many people, attracted by the news of the event, rushed up and prodded with their knives the shins or feet of the young man. But his wasted flesh and his dead skin felt nothing. They tried to pull away the bent up shins from his behind, but had absolutely no success. So they decided to wait for the appointed day, on which the story would be shown to be false or completely true.

When the feast day of that glorious virgin and queen [23 June] dawned, the young man was carried into the church. At first he began to sleep, but he was soon roused from his slumber and started up. The people heard his sinews creak. Next his limbs straightened themselves out and then he began to jump up and down and, before many onlookers, to circle around the shrine of the holy virgin. And because the young man had previously, at the orders of the holy virgin Etheldreda, made many prophecies in secret about many matters, revealing them under the seal of the confessional to his parish priest, which were found all to have been true, men had an unshakeable belief in all that he foretold of the future.

For he prophesied that many dangers were imminent. These included a summer of extreme heat which would melt the lead on the churches, unless God gave a helping hand. We did indeed experience a heat, but we would have undergone one still more intolerable, so we believe, if the prayers of the faithful had not prevented it. For during this period the heat from the sky did melt the lead on the churches. At the town of Maunfield in Sussex, the collegiate church of the archbishop of Canterbury, went up in flames, as did almost the whole town, and in Essex some manors and some ships with their crews were destroyed by bolts of lightning in various places.

Another miracle at Ely

This vision and miracle was confirmed by another vision which soon followed, manifested this time to a crippled woman of eighty. More than once she saw the blessed queen and virgin Etheldreda standing by her side and telling her that the same, or still more, dangers were on their way, unless the Omnipotent was placated by sincere prayers. The blessed virgin added that she herself had joined the people in offering up prayers to the Lord that he would remove the evil which he proposed to send upon the land as punishment for its sins. And she advised the old woman on her behalf to tell the prior and the monks and the people to continue their processions, redouble their intercessions, and to pray without ceasing that God would remove the sword which hung over their heads. 'Let them know for certain,' said the saint, 'that it is I with my persistent prayers who have averted the various disasters that have been threatening them.' The glorious lady told the old woman to speak out all of this in public, and on the feast of St Mary Magdalene [22 July] to get herself carried to the shrine of Etheldreda, where in the presence of the people she would find a cure for her crippled state and for her weakness. For the past three years she had suffered so horribly from arthritis in her legs that she had continually lain motionless in one place, except when from time to time she had been carried from one place to another by the kindness of her sympathetic neighbours.

So on Mary Magdalene's feast day [22 July] the old woman was carried on a litter to the shrine of the blessed Etheldreda, where, sinking into sleep, she saw the glorious virgin coming towards her. The virgin came up, took hold of her legs and stretched them out into their proper length. Several of the people who were sitting nearby heard the sinews of her shins creak. And the old woman immediately rose to her feet, cured of her former long-lasting arthritic weakness. Three times she walked around the shrine, piously kissing it and giving thanks to God and to the glorious lady Etheldreda.

A miracle concerning Christ's body which took place at Cambridge

About the same time at Cambridge, on the feast of the commemoration of St [Peter and St] Paul [30 June], there also occurred there the feast of the dedication of St Mary. To increase the honour paid to this festival, the body of our Lord was carried in procession around the parish on the shoulders of two priests. The bier was not heavy but so light that the whole contrivance could could have been carried without any trouble by a seven year old boy. Well the two priests went on their way at the head of the procession, carrying the body of our Lord through the town, until they came to the house of the Augustinian friars, which is situated just by the marketplace. And there suddenly the bier, which was resting equally on the shoulders of both men, began to rise up and as if possessed by some unseen strength to try to leave their shoulders. And then it became so heavy that the priests could scarcely carry such a great weight, nor could they remove the ends of the bier from their shoulders and put it down on the ground again. So they were struggling and sweating and panting and asked the laity to help them in this massive undertaking. Some of the people did run up and put their hands under the bier, but by a miracle to them it seemed weightless. The priests' struggle lasted as long as they were processing before the house of the Augustinian friars, but as soon as they had left the place all behind, the bier suddenly again rested lightly and levelly on their shoulders. But then some poor fool began dancing or rather capering with extravagant movements of his body in front of the Host. But a truly horrible punishment was his grisly lot. For while he was fooling about he suddenly collapsed and after a little while breathed his last.

These miracles have been explained and interpreted by many people in many different ways. I forebear to give my judgement of them, preferring to leave the decision to others rather than to pass a rash verdict on things which I did not see. I only venture to add this, that there immediately followed a great and terrible plague at Cambridge, as a result of which, so it was said, men who were perfectly well were struck down and died in madness without the last sacrament or being in their right minds.

The battle of the gnats

At this time in the royal manor at East Sheen, such a host of gnats suddenly gathered that they seemed to darken the whole sky. At once they began fighting and the battle was so fiercely contested that two thirds of that innumerable multitude fell to the ground dead. The remaining third, having finished the war and gained the victory, flew away, no man knows where. The numbers of the dead were so many that they could be swept up in a heap, and there were several bucketfuls of them. I leave others to tell us the meaning of all this.[1]

The frenzy of the friars[2]

About the same time the Preaching Friars [i.e. Dominicans] in France took up again their old opinion about the conception of the blessed Mary, and preached that she had been conceived in original sin. They reached such a pitch of frenzied arrogance that they refused to obey the bishops who ordered them to keep silent on this matter. Finally they even refused to obey the king and the nobles, when they commanded this. As a result they were put outside the royal protection and stopped from travelling about the country in their usual way, for fear that they might perhaps lead the common people astray into the same heresy and seduce the innocent. They were also ordered to stay inside their own buildings, to keep themselves alive within their lands by the labour of their own hands and not to dare to leave them for anywhere else, on pain of death. They were also ordered not to admit or receive anyone into their order in the future, on the same pain of death. But they themselves were to bring things to such a close that after those friars then living there would be no one to carry on their order.

---

[1] This incident is also reported by Henry Knighton (*Knighton*, pp. 530–1) and the Westminster chronicler (*WC*, pp. 400–1), who claimed the number of dead was so great it could be measured in pecks (a peck being two gallons). Knighton's editor, G. H. Martin, observes that this was 'a swarm of chironomids, in which the sexes differ markedly in size and colour'.

[2] This refers to the maculists, a Dominican sect that opposed the doctrine of the Immaculate Conception. See also W. A. Hinnebusch, *The History of the Dominican Order* (New York, 1973), ii. 171–90.

When he first arrived at Spanish parts with a strong enough army but insufficient supplies, his Englishmen began to die, first of hunger, then of dysentery, until ninety famous knights of his army had perished miserably. So the remainder, under the pressure of necessity, deserted the duke on the field of battle and deserted to the French army, which was there helping the king of Castile [Juan I], having first obtained a safe conduct from the French army. The French sympathised with them in their woes, treated them with great humanity and restored them to health from their own supplies. For it is the custom of both the English and French nations to help each other as brothers in foreign parts, however hostile to each other in their own lands, and to show in turn an unbreakable loyalty to each other.

The king of Portugal [João I] indeed, who was then present with four thousand soldiers, said to the duke when he saw the English thus deserting, 'Just look at your English, deserting you and going over to the enemy! As soon as they have been refuelled, I've no doubt they will be the deadliest of foes to both you and me. I will go and join battle with them, and leave none of them alive.' But the duke said to him, 'My lord king, never let that happen. I know that they have done this, only because they have been overcome by necessity and not out of treachery.' And immediately the duke, who was seated on his horse, bent his head and shed most bitter tears over the horse, pouring out silent prayers to omnipotent God and remembering in his heart how previously in his times of felicity and great wealth he had neither paid attention to God as he should have done nor worshipped him as would have been right. So heaving great sighs he silently prayed for mercy, promising for the future to take steps to amend his life, and to keep the picture of God continually before the eyes of his heart. And he, who once picked up the sobs of Mary the sinner, from that day on continually made everything prosperous and happy for the duke, contrary to his expectation.

For his enemy, the king of Castile, not terrified by the strength of men's forces but driven by the fear of nobody but God alone, began to discuss with the duke the conditions for making a peace between them, even though he himself was safely lodged among his own people while he saw and knew about the sufferings of our troops. The discussions ended in it being arranged that the king of Castile should receive the daughter of the duke [Catalina] as a wife for his son [Enrique], and that their descendants should enjoy the kingdom of Spain. And if they had no children, the Spanish inheritance would pass to the son of the duke of York [Edward of Langley], who was the brother of the duke of Lancaster and who had married the younger daughter of Pedro [the Cruel], the former king of Castile. And if it should happen that the duke of York's son died without legitimate offspring, the right to the kingdom should pass to offspring procreated by the duke of Lancaster and Constanza, the daughter of the same Pedro.

Having made this agreement, the duke received for the time being an incredibly large sum from the king of Castile, and as security for the payment of the remaining money was given the sons of noblemen as hostages. For the future indeed, for every year of the duke's life, the king of Castile agreed to pay him £10,000, and the same amount to his wife, Lady Constanza, and so that this money should be paid without fail, four towns were assigned to the Lady Constanza.

A council at Reading

At that time the king of England summoned the nobles to a council at Reading.[1] The duke of Lancaster had a particular reason for hurrying to the council with all speed, for he saw that the king was refusing to look fairly upon some of the nobles, and he feared that quarrels were about to arise which he could nip in the bud by his arrival. Nor indeed were his efforts in vain, for he graciously brought peace to the heart of the king and the minds of the nobles. As a result the council was dissolved, and all returned peacefully home.

So ended a year of moderate corn crops but of very abundant fruit harvests. It was a year of grief for the men of Northumberland because of the troubles inflicted upon them by the Scots; a reasonably happy one for other parts of the kingdom because of the renewal of miracles; a very

---

1   The council convened on 9 December 1389.

harmonious one for the kingdoms of England and France because of the truce that was made; but for many Englishmen it was a year of great dread because of the plague which struck different parts of the kingdom.

[1390]

The death of the earl of Pembroke, wounded at a tournament

In 1390, the thirteenth year of King Richard II, the king kept Christmas at his manor of Woodstock with Anna his queen. The duke of Lancaster was at Hertford castle for Christmas.

During this time John Hastings, earl of Pembroke, in his wish to try his skill at a tournament, was struck in the groin by his opponent knight, John of St John.[1] His entrails were shattered at the blow and he died immediately. His death caused indescribable grief, not only among the nobles but also among all the common people. For he had been generous and kind to everybody, and humble and good above all the young lords of his age in the kingdom. A remarkable thing had befallen his ancestors. From Aymer de Valence, earl of Pembroke, who had been one of the assessors and judges concerned with the death of Thomas of Lancaster, right down to that John Hastings, no earl of Pembroke ever saw his father, nor did the father enjoy the sight of his son.[2]

Also in this year St Thomas of Lancaster was canonised as a saint.[3]

A parliament at London

On the Monday after the feast of St Hilary [13 January] a parliament was held at London,[4] in which the commons persistently demanded that the badges carried by nobles and their households should be abolished, since already those men in the shires who had obtained such badges had become tyrants, malefactors and the maintainers of malefactors.[5] But after much heated argument, with the nobles being unwilling to give up their badges, it was at least agreed that no one should wear their badges unless they were of their personal household and received a certain sum annually from the purses of the magnates.[6]

In the same parliament some fresh insurgents from Kent were captured, drawn and hanged.[7]

It was also decided in the same parliament that in future no one should sail overseas to obtain papal appointments in a church or churches. Any one who broke this rule should be taken prisoner, if he could be caught, as a rebel against the king, and put in prison.[8] It was also decided that no secret killer (whom the English call murderers) should in future obtain a charter of the king's favour. If any duke should dare to appeal on behalf of such a man, the king would fine him £100, while an earl would be fined 100 marks, an archbishop £100 and a bishop 100 marks.[9]

In this parliament it was also granted to the king that he should receive forty shillings[10] from each sack of wool sold, and that of this forty shillings ten should be assigned to the present uses of

---

1 Hastings (b. 1373) was the 14th earl of Pembroke although only the third Hastings to bear the title. The Westminster chronicler reports that St John did as was customary and directed the point of his lance to the ground but Pembroke was caught by the other end as he passed: *WC*, pp. 408–9.

2 Amyer de Valence, 11th earl of Pembroke, died in 1324. His successor in the earldom, Laurence Hastings, died in 1348 when his son was a year old. This son, John Hastings I, died in 1375 when his son was only two years old.

3 Thomas, 2nd earl of Lancaster (c.1278–1322) led the baronial opposition to Edward II and the Despensers. After his execution at Pontefract a popular cult grew up although he was never canonised.

4 Parliament sat from 17 January until 2 March: *RP*, iii. 277.

5 This was in accordance with the statute passed in the Cambridge parliament of 1388. See above, pp. 264–5.

6 For the 'multas altercationes' on this issue see also *HVRS*, p. 131.

7 This may be the same group of insurgents described by the Westminster chronicler as having been arrested at Croydon 'whose intention was to rise against the clergy and their lay neighbours' (*WC*, p. 410–11).

8 This also was a reiteration of the petition presented at the Cambridge parliament of 1388. The terms represented a renewal of Edward III's statute of provisors of 1352. Walsingham offers no comment on this enactment but the Westminster monks regarded it as 'detestable': *WC*, pp. 412–13.

9 The author of the *Historia vitae et regni Ricardi secundi* records higher figures for these fines, 1000 marks for both an archbishop and an earl: *HVRS*, p. 131.

10 The author of the *Historiae vitae* records 50 shillings: *HVRS*, p. 131.

the king and thirty kept for the future in the hands of treasurers appointed by parliament, and not to be used unless there seemed to be pressure from the necessities of war. Likewise the king was to have sixpence from each pound, four pence to be set aside for uses indicated by the said treasurers, and two pence to be used and spent now according to the wishes of the king.

This year saw the death of Dom Laurence, once a monk at Battle, afterwards confessor of the pope, and finally bishop of St Asaph. Alexander Bache was chosen in his place, and he at once by virtue of a statute of parliament asked to be consecrated by the archbishop of Canterbury.[1]

A new duke of Aquitaine

In the same year at this parliament John, duke of Lancaster, was made duke of Aquitaine, with sceptre and cap given him by the hand of the king.[2]

At that time the son and heir of the duke of York [Edward of Langley] was made earl of Rutland.[3]

On 5 March a great, awesome, damaging gale sprang up in England harming everybody as it tore off roofs, flattened houses, dashed animals to the ground and uprooted trees. [4]

In this year a mighty pestilence raged in this land, affecting especially the young men and the boys, who died in all the towns and villages in incredibly huge numbers. This epidemic was immediately followed by such a dearth of corn that in some places a measure of corn was sold for twenty-three pence.[5]

At the same time Dom Adam [Easton], the English cardinal, who had been shamefully deposed and deprived of his office by Pope Urban, was honourably restored to his position by Boniface.[6] Men say that when Urban was plotting his tyrannical schemes, he was especially afraid of Adam more than of any of the others because of his deep learning and intelligence, and for that reason had quite unjustly had him arrested, tortured and shamefully put in prison, just so that he should not be a stumbling block for any of his schemes. But at his death Pope Urban was very sorry for what he had done. He publicly did penance for it and declared that Adam had been guilty of no crime.

A declaration concerning indulgences

It was also at Adam's request that Pope Boniface declared that bulls of plenary indulgence, granted to people in extremis, were only valid for those who obtained them by a confession which immediately preceded death. Up until the last gasp they would gain nothing from these bulls, although they might often in various perils have made their confession and got better.

The deeds of Henry, earl of Derby

At the same time Henry [of Bolingbroke], earl of Derby, set out for Prussia.[7] With the help of the marshal of this country and a certain king called Witold he completely defeated the army of the king of Lithuania.[8] Four dukes were taken prisoner, three were killed, and more than three

---

1   Bishop Laurence Child had died in December 1389. Dominican Alexander Bache was consecrated on 8 May. He was also Richard's confessor.
2   Gaunt received his new title on 2 March. See also *HVRS*, p. 131; *RP*, iii. 263.
3   On 25 February; *RP*, iii. 264.
4   This is not reported by other authorities.
5   Knighton, who describes this in detail (*Knighton*, pp. 538–9), blames the statute which prohibited the sale of English wool outside the kingdom. This caused much of the crop to be left unsold which in turn led to shortage of money for food, which left the 1390 harvest of wheat itself unsold. He cites low rates for wheat at Leicester 16s 8d per quarter, and London, 10s per quarter.
6   Easton and two other cardinals were restored on 18 December 1389. For the events surrounding their deposition in 1385 see above, pp. 223–4.
7   Derby departed in early May; the Westminster chronicler gives 4 May although he does not appear to have passed through Calais until 13 May; Knighton wrongly records 25 July: *WC*, pp. 432–3; *Knighton*, pp. 536–7. He joined the Teutonic knights in a *reyse*, a crusading campaign against the pagans of Lithuania. He returned the following spring.
8   Walsingham's account of the political situation in Lithuania is confused although he correctly identifies

hundred of the more powerful men in this army were all slain. The king of Lithuania whose name was Skirgiello had fled for refuge to the castle of the town of Vilnius, but this town was also captured by the great abilities of the earl. For it was men from his own household who were the first to scale the town wall and to place his standard on its top, while the rest of the army were still drowsing or unaware of what was happening. Four thousand ordinary people were captured or killed, and among the others killed there was the brother of the king of Poland, our enemy. For five weeks the earl laid siege to the town's castle, but then the masters of Prussia and of Livonia were unwilling to stay there any longer because of weaknesses affecting their armies. Eight Lithuanians became Christians and the master of Livonia took three thousand prisoners with him to his land.

So passed that year, one whose spring had promised much only to deceive, for there was no abundance of either fruits or grain crops, with the result that the following year was more difficult than usual. It was a hateful year not only for the Romans and the Roman Curia, but also for the great numbers of English who followed the Curia around to get papal appointments and benefices. In fact it was a year which aroused suspicions in the breasts of English who were prelates and monks, as they now feared the pope's condemnation or even an interdict on their kingdom, because of the statute passed in the last parliament against the Roman church, even though at that time the prelates themselves had left the parliament, protesting that for their part they did not agree with those who were wishing to propose this statute.

[1391]

The arrival of an envoy from the king of France

In 1391, the fourteenth year of the reign of King Richard II, the king spent Christmas with Queen Anna [of Bohemia].

The king of France [Charles VI]'s chamberlain, who had been sent by his king and the French nobles, arrived in England, bearing the peace which had been so long wished for and desired.[1] After his return, some of our men were sent to France, to establish more certainly the truth of the matter. They were welcomed with honour by the king of France, and sent home with great gifts. The French indeed declared that they knew very well that they were not enough to conquer the kingdom of England, and that the English were no way strong enough to subjugate France, and that both countries were being impoverished time after time by useless expeditions. So they said that they wished to give up the war altogether, and not to attempt any longer that which all knew was completely impossible. They said they were willing to put aside the various ruinous quarrels, and in every way to look for peace and seek peace and keep the peace, unless the English were to be responsible for such overwhelming advantages not being enjoyed. To make the peace more stable, with firmer conditions after discussions of more propriety, the king of France asked our king both through his own envoys and through ours for a personal meeting, to take place near Calais.[2]

Although many people were suspicious of all discussions with the French, the king of England decided to go to Calais. And because it was right that his appearance there should be an impressive one worthy of honour, he sent round all the abbeys of his land for noble horses, such as it was fitting for a king to sit upon. And in case the giving of horses should seem too small a gift for their king, he also asked the same abbeys to lend him great sums of money, as the monks would not want to think that it was they who had impeded peace negotiations by refusing the king's requests. Leaving aside the other abbeys, from the monastery at St Albans he received a horse worth

---

the key figures. The Grand Duchy of Lithuania had joined with the kingdom of Poland in the union of Krewo of 1386 and Grand Prince Jogaila of Lithuania (c.1350–1434) had become king of Poland as Wladislaus II, at the same time converting to Christianity. His cousin Vytautas or Witold had been in exile with the Teutonic knights but now returned to exercise power as Grand Duke himself.

1   Peace negotiations had resumed after Gaunt's creation as duke of Aquitaine in March 1390.

2   On 14 February 1391 Richard's envoys Sir Thomas Percy and Sir Lewis Clifford agreed with the duke of Bourbon, the French envoy, on a meeting between the kings to take place on 24 June 1392.

twenty-four marks, and he also asked the abbot for a loan of five hundred marks. Because it had proved impossible to pay such a sum at that time, John duke of Lancaster, out of his affection for St Albans, promised the treasurers that he was willing to produce such a sum for the king, on condition that they then left the abbot of St Albans [Thomas de la Mare] in peace. For only a little while before the abbot had loaned the king £5,000, and this had emboldened the king to make his request. Nor was the king any more sparing of the towns and boroughs of the land. He asked each one to make its individual contribution towards this business, and he received their monies, although very many of them grumbled about it.

The recall of the English from the Roman Curia

During these days with the consent of the king and the king's council a proclamation was made in London that all those who were at the Roman Curia having received benefices should return to England before the feast of St Nicholas [6 December], under the penalty of losing all their benefices, and that those in Rome who had not yet received benefices should return by the same time, under penalty of forfeit.[1] When the English in faraway Rome heard this mighty thunderbolt, they deserted the Curia in fear of its striking them and fled back to their native soil. The pope, too, was disturbed by this great crash of thunder and speedily sent as envoy a certain abbot [Nicholas, abbot of the Benedictine abbey of Nonantola] who was to explore the reasons for all these things, including the statute of parliament which had been recently passed about provisors contrary to the practice of the Roman church.[2]

On his arrival the abbot greeted the king in the name of the pope, and commended the devotion of the king and his predecessors towards the Roman church, in that they had always taken the side of the true popes. Then he introduced the point that the pope had been surprised when he had read the king's letter informing him that such far reaching statutes had been passed, and that, as their good shepherd and in his desire for the salvation of their souls, he had frequently begged and beseeched promulgators of such statutes to remove them from the book as harming ecclesiastical liberty.

The abbot also said that the pope did not intend to diminish the power of the English crown, or to take away from its king the power of enacting statutes which were not against ecclesiastical liberty: on the contrary, he was prepared to preserve the honours of the king to the best of his ability, as he recognised that he was under a deep obligation to the king on this point. The papal nuncio [Damian de Cataneis] also said that the pope, although waiting for quite a long time, had not heard of any obedience to his commands. All the same, without starting anything new or embarking on any legal processes, he merely reminded them of what the laws state against those who pass statutes against ecclesiastical freedom; and under strong presssure from several people he had proclaimed that such statutes were null and void, as far as they infringed ecclesiastical liberty.

And so the pope, not seeing any change of heart on the part of the promulgators of the statutes, had sent to England his nuncio, although this had caused him great distress of mind as he knew that such a move amounted to a blackening of the king's fame, and through this nuncio he now begged, asked and required that the king should get these statutes annulled, and that in particular he should get removed from the chapter-book the statutes, 'Wherefore it impedes', and 'You must make provision', and others like these. The pope also offered that, if the promulgators of the statutes wished to make any complaint by sending ambassadors to him, he would promptly

---

[1]   The recall of English clerks at the Curia was ordered on 3 May 1391: *CCR, 1389–92*, p. 341. See also Harvey, *English in Rome*, p. 40. It was the culmination of a deterioration in Anglo-Papal relations which had continued for much of the decade.

[2]   Abbot Nicholas arrived in England in mid-June and met Richard on 24 June at Sheen (*WC*, pp. 458–9). He brought correspondence referring to the earlier embassy of the nuncio Damian de Cataneis, in which the statute of provisors had also been discussed. Richard held firm and for his part Boniface IX declared the statute to be invalid and proceeded to provide his own candidates to English benefices until the confirmation of the statute in the next session of parliament established a permanent block on papal interference.

do what was pleasing to king and kingdom, as far as he could do this with divine approval. And if the promulgators did not remove their statutes etc., he was not able to pass over such things without endangering the honour of the church and the safety of souls.

Also the pope informed the king through this nuncio that the king of France [Charles VI] and the antipope [Clement VII] had entered on a double-pronged agreement, namely that the king with the help of the powerful dukes [Philip] of Burgundy and [Louis of] Touraine should get the antipope established on the seat of Peter, while the antipope promised to crown the king of France emperor, to do great things for the duke of Burgundy and to invest the duke of Touraine with all church lands in Italian parts. He further promised to crown another man king of Tuscany and Lombardy and to establish the duke of Anjou in the kingdom of Sicily.[1]

In this situation the pope asked and urged King Richard to show himself the defender of the faith and of holy mother church. The pope also outlined the dangers if the king of France [Charles VI] and the antipope prevailed, namely that French popes had tried to diminish the rights of the kingdom of England, and that if the French got possession of the Holy Roman empire, they would as a result get possession of the whole world and so finally England. The pope therefore advised the king of England that he should see to it and make suitable provision for remedying this situation. The pope also pointed out that the French were negotiating with the English in order that, once they had entered upon a peace agreement, they might be able to make the above usurpations more freely and in the end, by breaking the peace pact, cunningly grab possession of England.

And so the pope urged King Richard, that since the French were schismatics, there should be no communication with them for any other reason except for bringing them back into the faith and their obedience due to the pope. Also, if there were further discussions with the French about peace, the pope asked and urged that there should be no agreement unless a clause, hedged about with penalties, were established by which the king of France would not send his peoples into Italy or permit his subjects to go there for the reason mentioned above or in any way interfere with the doings of the Roman church, the Roman empire or Italy, and that he would not support the antipope in Italy, under pain of the relevant penalties; otherwise the peace would be understood to be broken.

The pope also desired that the king of England should send ambassadors to the emperor, asking that, for the honour of the church and his imperial position, he should agree with the king of England on the above matters. Also, as it was being said that peoples were ready to invade Italy, as mentioned above, the pope asked and urged the king of England to provide help for him to make his defence and resist the French, together with the others who were willing to come to his help.

The above paragraphs show the fame of our king at that time and the respect in which he was held, if the pope was hoping that it was his help particularly which could provide him with protection and defence.

As a son of obedience our king listened to the nuncio's points, considered them sensibly, and decided to do as the pope asked and to provide help, on the various matters where help was most needed and could be lawfully provided. So he told the papal nuncio to wait for the next parliament, when, after all had been consulted, a reply would be given to the pope's individual points. And the nuncio was quite willing to wait, because he had previously experienced English generosity.

---

[1]   A tripartite treaty between the dukes of Burgundy and Touraine and Giangaleazzo Visconti of Milan, the latter's father-in-law stated that the dukes would recognise Visconti's claims to the lordship of Lombardy if Clement VII should crown an emperor. See also Palmer, *England, France and Christendom*, p. 193; Vaughan, *Philip the Bold*, p. 55.

The duke of Gloucester travels to foreign parts but meets with ill luck

At the same time the duke of Gloucester, Thomas of Woodstock, to the sorrow of many set off on a journey to Prussia.[1] Neither the lamentations of the people of London nor the general sadness of the people had been able to stop him from being absolutely determined to make this journey. The point was that the whole population, both townspeople and countrymen, were afraid that in his absence some new calamity would crop up. As long as he was present, they had no such fears, since it was indeed the duke of Gloucester who gave the whole people feelings of optimism and reassurance.

But as soon as the duke passed the frontiers of his own land, he was immediately harassed by ill fortune, driven hither and thither by turbulent storms and brought to such extremity that he even despaired of his life. Finally, after sailing past Denmark, Norway and the wilds of Scotland, all the time fearing death, he arrived in Northumberland, and took himself to the castle at Tynemouth, as a refuge well known to him of old. He spent several days there recovering, and then resumed his journey, making for his own manor of Pleshey [Essex] and bringing as he did so great joy to the whole kingdom both by his escape and by his arrival.[2]

Mortality

In the summer of this year on 9 July the sun was seen glowing red through a barrier of thick, evil-smelling clouds. From midday right up until sunset it seemed to provide almost no light. And for almost six weeks afterwards there was a superabundance of clouds. Some of them indeed lasted all day and night and never disappeared.

At that time the deaths in Norfolk and many other counties increased to such a number that this plague seemed just as bad as the big plagues preceding it. For example, if I leave out other cities and towns, at York alone within a short time eleven thousand corpses were carried out for burial.[3]

In the same year Lord Henry Percy, earl of Northumberland, was recalled from Calais and made keeper of the march of Scotland, and Sir Robert Mowbray[4] was made governor [i.e. Captain] of Calais.

A parliament at London

During these same days, in fact on the Friday following the feast of All Souls [2 November], a parliament was begun in London.[5] There was a discussion about the pope's request concerning the statute lately passed against papal appointees. Although the king and the duke of Lancaster were seen to defer to the pope's wishes, the knights in parliament refused point blank to allow people to go to Rome and obtain benefices there with impunity, as previously. But so that they should seem to be paying some honour to the pope or king, they did agree that it should be allowed to such people by the king's grace to obtain these benefices up to the next parliament.[6]

This parliament granted half tenth and half fifteenth taxes to the king. This money was to be used for discussions concerning peace with the French, and the duke of Lancaster [John of

---

[1] Gloucester was given the king's licence on 16 September 1391 to embark for Prussia, on commission to treat with the grand master of the Teutonic Order.

[2] The Westminster chronicler also gives an account of Gloucester's 'storm-tossed' journey, and the losses of vessels and precious treasures he suffered. He adds that he made a safe landing at Bamburgh shortly before Christmas (*WC*, pp. 482–5). Walsingham was bound to favour Tynemouth as the landing place, given its connection to St Albans.

[3] The Westminster chronicler, who observes that the plague was preceded by terrible thunderstorms and that its effects were worst in the northern and western counties, reports 12,000 deaths at York: *WC*, pp. 476–7.

[4] Correctly, Thomas Mowbray, earl of Nottingham. See also *CPR, 1388–92*, p. 460.

[5] Parliament began on 3 November and continued until 2 December: *RP*, iii. 284.

[6] The papal nuncio arrived seeking a repeal of the Edwardian statute of provisors that Richard had renewed (see above, p. 277). The appeal was rejected by council and commons but it was agreed that clergy should continue to travel to Rome in fulfilment of a vow or for other personal reasons.

Gaunt] was to be in charge of these discussions. The king himself was also granted conditionally a full tenth tax and a whole fifteenth tax, if during the year itself he should undertake an expedition against the Scots. This was the end and outcome of this parliament.[1]

The end of the year

So ended that year, which had been a very hard and difficult one for the poor and the moderately well off on account of the price of corn now continuing high for two years, so that when the season for nuts, apples and other such fruits came around several poor people caught dysentery from eating them and died. And the mortality happening from the famine would have been still greater if the excellent mayor of London [Nicholas Exton] had not taken the trouble to help the people. Over a long period he carefully provided that corn should always be imported from overseas countries to London, otherwise there is no doubt that the country would not have provided enough for the capital or the capital for the country. But when the season of autumn came

> The smiling land pours gifts of different fruits,
> As spring's rich promise finds fulfilment good[2]

and the price of corn began to fall.

In many places, as I have said, the present year was noted for its plagues. For England and France it was a quiet year with no war. But it was a hateful, detestable year for the Roman Curia because of the recall of the English[3] and the obduracy of the statute makers.

[1392]

In 1392, the fifteenth year of King Richard's reign, the king kept Christmas in splendid style at Langley near St Albans. With him were Anna [of Bohemia] his queen, four bishops, as many earls, the duke of York [Edmund of Langley], many lords and fifteen ladies.[4]

On Christmas Day itself a dolphin arrived from the sea and sported in the Thames at London, getting as far as London Bridge.[5] Perhaps it was an omen of the storms which were soon to follow within a week. When the citizens saw it, they chased after it, caught it though with difficulty and brought it back to London. Many were astounded on seeing the size of its body, which was quite ten feet long.

Dolphins are sea creatures who will follow men's voices.[6] They enjoy the playing of pipes, and often arrive in shoals for the music. Their headlong dives as they play in the waves signify the approach of storms. They are the fastest and most agile creatures of the sea. Often in their jumps they leap over the sails of ships. After mating, the females go off and give birth. The gestation period is ten months. Birth takes place on a summer's day. They feed their newly produced young with their teats and pick them up in their mouths. They take care of their sick. They live for thirty years, as has been proved by the experiment of cutting off their tails. They have their mouths where other animals do, but they alone move their tongues in their bellies, contrary to the nature of sea creatures. The fins on their back are pointed and grow stiff when they get angry. When their passion dies down, the fins retract into certain coverings. Men say that they do not breathe when in the water but take in vital breath only in the air above. The cry, which serves them for a voice, is

---

1   Walsingham does not report the most important financial measure of this session, as attested by the Westminster chronicle, that the staple would be retuned to Calais by the following Easter: *WC*, p. 478.

2   Venantius Fortunatus, *PL*, vii. 285.

3   The traffic was not all one-way: the Westminster chronicler records that Abbot William Colchester journeyed to Rome in December 1391: *WC*, p. 485.

4   The Westminster chronicler reports the arrival at this time of a delegation from Aquitaine requesting that Richard assume direct rule of the duchy rather than it remaining in the hands of John of Gaunt: *WC*, p. 485.

5   Walsingham is the only chronicler to report this phenomenon.

6   The following digression on dolphins is derived from Pliny's *Natural History* although it may be that Walsingham was working from a medieval encyclopaedia such as Vincent of Beauvais' *Speculum naturale*. For Walsingham's use of classical sources see above, pp. 9–10, 18.

like a human cry. They have a particular name and, when they hear it, they follow the callers. This proper name for them is Simones. They hear men's voices more quickly when the wind is in the north, but when the south wind blows, their hearing is blocked.

In the days of the emperor Augustus a boy began by luring a dolphin with bits of bread. The dolphin got so used to it that it would come to the boy's hand to be fed. And soon the boy grew so bold that he would get on the dolphin's back and be given rides over wide sweeps of water. This happened over a long time for very many years, until it had been seen so often that it ceased to be miraculous. But as soon as the boy died, before the eyes of many the dolphin died too. It was sad and missed the boy.

At Hippo in Africa a dolphin was fed by the citizens. It would allow itself to be stroked and often gave rides to many people who got on its back. At Iassus, a city of Babylon, a dolphin became friends with a boy. After their usual play, the dolphin followed the boy back to the shore too eagerly. It was carried on to the sand, stuck fast there and died. Another boy rider on a dolphin's back was killed by a huge wave. The dolphin brought the boy back to land, and, as if confessing its guilt, punished its repentance by death, for it refused to return to the deep water any more. I have taken the trouble to insert here these details about the nature of the dolphin, to amuse the ignorant without boring the knowledgeable.

How the duke of Lancaster crossed the Channel and was splendidly received by the king of France

In this year John [of Gaunt], duke of Lancaster, crossed the Channel to France for a meeting with the French king, to discuss that final peace which the king of France [Charles VI] so greatly desired.[1] He was sent on this mission by the king of England and the whole council of the land. The preparations made by the French king for his arrival were no less than those which he had made for the arrival of the greatest emperors. For he welcomed Duke John and the bishop of Durham [Walter Skirlaw] at his own expense with almost one thousand horses and entertained them all the way from Calais to Amiens. None of the servants of duke or bishop had to worry about providing any food, as the attendants and stewards of the French king brought straight to the hands of the servants of duke and prelate all the things that seemed necessary.

When the duke came into his presence, the king honoured him beyond belief and boasted triumphantly of his good fortune in enjoying a meeting with a duke of such wisdom, honour and power. At the order of the king, the duke was met on that occasion at Amiens by the dukes, counts and barons of France to discuss peace terms and settle the matter: the king thought that the outcome of the negotiations would be made happier by the presence of so many negotiators. The duke finally returned to England at the end of the discussions bringing back a truce for one year, during which time all the nobles of England could gather together and discuss whether it was better to give their assent to this final peace than to engage in the doubtful business of war.[2]

So King Richard summoned to meet him at Stamford not only the lords of the realm but also the men from each town who were accustomed to attend parliament, so that they might discuss what was to be done about so important a matter.[3] But such an assembly achieved nothing on this

---

[1]　According to the Westminster chronicler (*WC*, p. 487), Gaunt embarked on 25 February, although it may have been as much as a fortnight later because he did not arrive at Calais until 11 March.

[2]　Richard might have hoped for more from these negotiations than an extension of the truce. But the price of a permanent peace as presented by the French ambassadors was wholly unacceptable: the king was to surrender his claim not only on Normandy but to the French crown itself and Aquitaine was to be granted to Jean, duke of Berry, to be held directly by him during his lifetime. Gaunt may have been honoured at Amiens as Walsingham describes, but the treaty he agreed there on 8 April guaranteed nothing more than the suspension of hostilities for twelve months from the forthcoming Michaelmas (29 September). The Westminster chronicler's assessment of the talks was less sanguine and more accurate than Walsingham's, recording that the delegation returned 'empty-handed' (*WC*, p. 487). See also Palmer, *England, France and Christendom*, pp. 143–5.

[3]　The great council at Stamford was convened on 25 May 1392, one of several such assemblies summoned by Richard in 1391–2. The Westminster chronicler described it as 'as great as any parliament' (*WC*, pp. 488–92

occasion, other than the acceptance of the truce which was to last for a whole year, and which both the English and French kings swore a corporal oath to observe without breach. The marshal of France came over to receive our king's oath, and some of our knights were dispatched to France to claim the same oath from their king. This they succeeded in doing.

The arrival of the duke of Guelders

The duke of Guelders came to England at this time.[1] He was a relative of the king of England, a very famous soldier, honoured by the English and dreaded by the French. In his own land he had energetically crushed the French whenever they arrogantly invaded. He gave our king the spirited and forceful advice not to make peace with French or Scots unless it befitted his royal majesty, and the duke promised that he was ready to come to the help of the king with the flower of his knights, whether it was to cross to France or to invade Scotland. In return he was showered with honours, praises and gifts by the king and treated with equal respect by the dukes of Gloucester and Lancaster and the nobles of the realm. Finally he was allowed to return to his own country as all men's favourite.

The arrival of the count of Ostrevantz

Around the same time, though not in the same year, the count of Ostrevantz came to our land as a friend and a mediator of peace between nations. Loaded with various gifts he soon departed.[2]

In this year the king of Mauretania invaded the lands of the great Khan and wrought great slaughter there.[3] Not long afterwards he invaded the lands of the king of Hungary,[4] but there he met the obstacle of a trained force of knights and was repelled in lively fashion by the king with all his troops.

A new feast day in honour of Mary and Elizabeth

During these days the pope, Boniface IX, decreed the celebration in the church of a new feast day for the salutation of the blessed Mary to her kinswoman Elizabeth.[5] He devised a suitable service and readings, full of mystery and packed with indulgences, to awaken devotion. For to those attending divine office whether on the eve, the day itself or during the octave of the feast he granted the same indulgences as those granted for the feast of Corpus Christi by Urban IV [1261–64]. He wished this day to be celebrated on 25 June, the day after the feast of the nativity of John the Baptist, because during those days St Mary was staying with Elizabeth and ministered to her.

at 488–9). The meeting must have been over by 22 June when another council convened at Nottingham. Walsingham should have been well informed about its proceedings since his St Albans colleague, Simon Southerey, was one of the delegates.

1   William I of Jülich, duke of Guelders (1372–1402). Richard's government had been cultivating friendship with Guelders and other peripheral rulers of the Low Countries for several years. After protracted negotiations an alliance with Guelders against France and the Burgundian interest had been agreed in 1386, and as Philip of Burgundy's power continued to grow at the beginning of the 1390s, the government sought to reinforce the relationship. The Westminster chronicler describes his reception at court '[he was] feasted sumptuously and plied with lavish entertainments . . . and paid very flattering attention': WC, pp. 434–5; the *Historia vitae et regni Ricardi secundi* echoes '. . . quem rex magnifice honoravit': HVRS, p. 131. Duke William was present at the Stamford council.

2   William VI, count of Ostrevantz, heir of Albert, duke of Holland, Zeeland and Hainault. He came at the personal invitation of Richard, the council regarding Ostrevantz, like Guelders, as a possible ally to counterbalance the influence of Philip of Burgundy in the Low Countries. Ostrevantz was invested with the order of the garter and remained in the country for jousting at Smithfield at Michaelmas (29 September).

3   This appears to refer to Timur's (Tamerlane, 1336–1405) conquest of the Khanate of Kipchak, which culminated in the sacking in 1395 of the capital at Sarai Berke.

4   Sigismund, the younger son of Emperor Charles IV, had been king of Hungary since 1386, claiming the crown by right of his bride, Maria, daughter of Lewis the Great of Hungary. The greatest threat to his kingdom in this period, and his principal preoccupation, was the expansion not of the Mongols but the Turks under Bayezid Bey.

5   Urban VI had instituted the feast of the visitation on 8 April 1389; Boniface IX ratified it in the same year.

The crimes of the people of London and the anger of the king

About the same time the king sent envoys to the citizens of London, asking for a loan of £1,000.[1] Showing no shame, the citizens put up an unseemly resistance and with one voice declared that they could not provide the money asked for. They even beat up, whipped and almost killed a Lombard who was willing to lend the sum to the king. The king was very angry when he heard about it, and called together almost all the leading nobles of the kingdom to tell them of the impudence of the citizens of London and to complain about their arrogance.

As the nobles were all enemies of the people for one reason or another, they advised the king to check the citizens' hotheadedness without delay and to crush their pride. The people of London at that time surpassed all other nations for pride, arrogance and greed. They had little belief in God and the traditions of their ancestors. They supported the Lollards, slandered the monks, refused to pay tithes and impoverished the common people. Their superciliousness reached such heights that, contrary to all human thought and to God and to justice, they even dared to draw up laws by which to vex, harass and fatigue people arriving from the surrounding districts and towns. I pass over their inhumanity, I keep quiet and am silent about their greed and disloyalty, and I ignore the malice with which they indiscriminately treated visitors. If I wanted to describe all their crimes of this period, I shudder at the volume that would result.[2]

The people of London submit themselves to the king's mercy

So they were accused of crimes against the king and of notoriously infringing his majesty. They were also accused of attacks against visitors from the provinces, that had been to the detriment of the king, the lords and the people of the land. If they refused to make amends, accusers from the country were at hand who would be willing under oath to give proof of their wicked deeds. So the citizens of London suddenly found themselves surrounded by troubles, caught as it were between the hammer and the anvil, and as there was no place for excuses, they decided to submit themselves to the king's mercy, rather than to be exposed to the verdict or the judgement of a jury.

Arrest of the mayor and sheriffs

At the king's bidding the mayor of London and the sheriffs were arrested together with some of the leading citizens, but the rest were allowed to return home.[3] The mayor was sent to Windsor castle and the others distributed between various other castles. They were to be kept under close custody until the king and his council should decide what to do with them. And it was then decreed that Londoners should not elect or have a mayor in future,[4] but that from now on the king should provide from among his own knights someone to govern the city who would be called keeper of the city, though we also commonly call him warden, and there would be a succession of such wardens. The privileges of the citizens were revoked, liberties annulled and laws

---

[1]   Richard faced renewed financial problems at the beginning of the 1390s after a comparatively buoyant period since the Merciless Parliament, and after several peaceful years in city politics – following the storm surrounding John of Northampton (see above, pp. 214, 218) – his excessive demands provoked a fresh quarrel. He first attempted to draw on the city's resources by compelling those who met the financial qualifications for knighthood to take up the privilege with all the attendant fees. When the city authorities refused to enforce this, Richard responded with his demand for a loan. See also Barron, *London*, p. 24.
[2]   Previously sympathetic towards the Londoners' independence (see above, pp. 34–6, 65–6), Walsingham was now sharply critical of their stand against the King, perhaps largely because now he suspected them of supporting Lollardy.
[3]   Richard's retaliation was made at Stamford where he had consulted his council before acting. On 29 May the mayor, John Hende, a draper, and his sheriffs, John Shadworth, a mercer, and Henry Vanner, a vintner, were arrested together with the aldermen and twenty-four citizens. Hende was imprisoned at Windsor, as Walsingham reports, Shadworth at Odiham (Kent) and Vanner at Wallingford. They were brought before the king at the council at Nottingham on 25 June where they were convicted of failing to act on the king's writ and of maladministration in their capacity as city officers. See also *HVRS*, p. 133; *WC*, pp. 498–501; Barron, *London*, pp. 334–5.
[4]   Before the 'keeper of the city' was appointed, William Standon, a grocer, deputised as mayor.

abrogated, both the laws which they had drawn up and the ones which they had enjoyed from ancient times.

So, having got rid of the name of mayor, the king appointed as the first warden of the city a knight called Edward Dallingridge.[1] He was to govern the citizens and to give equal attention to justice for all of them. But he was soon dismissed by the king, as he had been found guilty of swearing an oath to the citizens that he would defend their customary rights or at least, to the best of his ability, stealthily reintroduce them. There were those who said that he had done this deliberately, with a view to the advantage of the king rather than the interests of the citizens, so that, when the king found out, he was sad that he had treated a well-meaning knight so badly. Even so he appointed another knight called Baldwin Raddington in his place.[2] He was a far-seeing, sensible person, and knew how to comfort the citizens when they were unhappy and to lift up their minds to hopes of good things. For they were almost wasting away in sadness and sorrow.

The Londoners are called to Windsor

But in the meantime, because of the intercession of many but especially because of pressure exerted by the duke of Gloucester, the king calmed down and gradually relented of his harsh decision. He brought before his mind's eye the various honours that he had received from the people of London and the magnificent gifts they had given him. So he decided to deal with them more gently and to rouse in them hope of some forgiveness. So he sent them instructions to come to Windsor castle, so that before him and his council they could make plain the privileges, liberties and rights of their city, both new and old.[3] He would then decide which should be preserved in the city and which should be completely abolished.

After their demonstration, some rights were ratified, some allowed to continue and some cancelled.[4] But on that occasion they did not recover the person or position of mayor or the full forgiveness of the king. That would not happen until they had made restitution to the king for the losses and injuries they had previously inflicted upon the king and upon his people. Indeed at this meeting the king and his lords agreed that the king would not accept any restitution offered, or make any sort of agreement with the people without the lords' consent.

When indeed the king had first blazed out in anger for the reasons noted above, he considered collecting an army, forcibly attacking the city and wiping out the citizens from under heaven. But some words from the duke of Lancaster had changed this plan. The duke advocated summoning them to Windsor, as we have seen, and rebuking them, but only if they remained obstinate should they then according to the king's plan be attacked and taken away from the land of the living. The king indeed, in this levy at Windsor, had collected together all the lords temporal of the realm, almost all the bishops, and an army of such a size that the citizens of London could legitimately feel terrified. The cost of all this was immense, and it was certain that the Londoners would pay it. They for their part were well aware that the end of the matter would be an outlay of gold and silver by them. So of their own free will they handed themselves and their property over to the king, offering to lend him £10,000. But they were sent back home, still not certain of what they

---

1   Dallingridge, a knight of the shire for Sussex, who held the manor of Bodiam and built the castle there after the French attacks on Rye and Winchelsea had intensified invasion fears, was a chamber knight and a member of the council. He was appointed keeper of London on 25 June, with Gilbert Mayfield and Thomas Newton serving as his sheriffs.

2   Raddington was another household knight and controller of the wardrobe. He replaced Dallingridge in July.

3   According to the Westminster chronicler, the former mayor, sheriffs, twenty-four aldermen and 400 other citizens all came to Windsor; although Shadworth was at first reluctant, in the event each one of them made a formal submission to the king (*WC*, pp. 498–501). See also Barron, *London*, pp. 502–3.

4   According to the Westminster chronicler three of the city's privileges were now rescinded as punishment, namely the liberty to bequeath city rents or properties for the endowment of chantries or fraternities without royal licence, the protection of jurors who returned false verdicts, and the right of a villein to invoke any franchise in his defence against his lord's claim upon his person (*WC*, pp. 506–7).

would have to pay until the king's council should have decided upon the form their restitution was to take and the sum to be paid.[1]

The king goes to London

So the citizens returned to London and the nobles who had been with the king and the rest of the people went back to their own homes. But the king, hearing that the citizens of London were in low spirits and had settled into a deep gloom, said to his councillors, 'I shall go to London and comfort the people; no longer shall I allow them to despair of my favour.' As soon as this decision became known, all the citizens were filled with incredible happiness. One and all they decided to meet him together and to spend as much on presents and gifts as they had done at his coronation. And so on his arrival at London, the king was greeted with the sort of splendid procession and the variety of different offerings that would have been fitting for a king holding a triumph to receive. Horses with their trappings, gold and silver tablets, clothes of gold and silk, golden basins and ewers, gold coins, jewels and necklaces were all given to him, a splendid collection of such richness and beauty that its total price and value could not be easily reckoned.[2]

So in this way, of their former customs and liberties the citizens recovered at least those that could be of profit to themselves without being a loss to others. They were also permitted to elect their own mayor, as before. Indeed they believed that by their gifts they had escaped the fine and that they would be left alone in the future. But they were completely mistaken, for they were forced later on to pay the king £10,000, which caused much mental anguish when it was collected from the community. But the nobles of the realm, who had been present at the king's council, showed great displeasure among themselves when they heard that the king had pardoned the people of London contrary to what they had decided, and criticised his fickleness and lack of resolution. But nobody openly rebuked the king on the matter, and the outcome for the crowd of citizens was such as was perhaps forecast long ago by the dolphin that played in the Thames on Christmas day in the previous year.[3]

The duke of Gloucester is recalled when about to set out for Ireland

At this time the duke of Gloucester, long ago appointed by the king as duke of Ireland, had received the wages money for going there with an army, but just when he was all set and ready to depart, he was suddenly recalled for no reason, to the great loss of both England and Ireland.[4] For when they heard the news that he was coming, almost all the chieftains of Ireland had decided to

---

[1]   The Westminster chronicler reports that the king demanded a payment of £40,000 in jewels to be made over the next ten years (*WC*, p. 503). Hende and his sheriffs were to pay fines of £3,000 and the city as a whole was to pay a fine of £100,000.

[2]   Richard made his entrance into the city in August. Walsingham's description of the pageant, which was comparable to that mounted for the king's coronation celebrations, is disappointingly brief. The Westminster chronicler reports that the whole community of the city came out to greet the returning king; there were representatives from every craft guild and, by the chronicler's reckoning, no fewer than 22,000 horsemen and an 'uncountable number' on foot. As Richard made his way westward through Cheapside he was presented with four tableaux, in which London was allegorised as the new Jerusalem with the king as Christ at the second coming. As they passed, Richard and Queen Anna were censed from two gold thuribles and were showered with golden coins. They were also presented with costly gifts, including a golden table valued at 100 marks. Their procession led them to Westminster Abbey where they paid their devotions to the shrine of St Edward.

[3]   See above, pp. 283–4.

[4]   Walsingham's report here is confused. The council had contemplated creating Gloucester duke of Ireland during the winter of 1388–89, but had abandoned the idea in favour of returning Sir John Stanley, the former lieutenant, to the lordship. Stanley was dispatched in July 1389, but his administration attracted criticism both in Dublin and at Westminster and he was dismissed on 11 September 1391. Gloucester replaced him in early October, and was to hold the office for five years, with 32,000 marks paid for the first three years. An expedition was planned for the spring for which preparations were still being made in May 1392, but in July Gloucester was suddenly removed from office. Given the unsatisfactory conclusion to the peace negotiations at Amiens, it may be that Richard now planned to deploy his uncle elsewhere. See Saul, *Richard II*, pp. 275–6.

submit to him.[1] But the opinion of the spiteful prevailed with the king and unfortunately the chance was lost.

Illness of the king of France and death of the earl of Oxford

In this year the king of France [Charles VI], so it was said, was bewitched, lost his wits and went mad, just when he was planning an apparently less than just expedition against the duke of Brittany.[2] His affliction lasted as long as the heat of summer, but his sufferings lessened when winter came on so that the king seemed restored to his senses.[3] But he never recovered completely and ever after he would lose his senses at the season of the illness's first attack.

In the same year Robert de Vere died at Louvain in anguish of mind and pitiable poverty. Once earl of Oxford, he had climbed by many steps to the title of duke of Ireland.[4] As a young man indeed he would have been suitable for all posts requiring integrity – if discipline had not been missing in his boyhood.

[1393]

In 1393 a parliament was held at Winchester after Christmas at which the king was granted a half tenth tax from the clergy and a half fifteenth tax from the commons for the expenses of the dukes of Lancaster and Gloucester, who were about to set out for France to discuss a peace treaty between the countries.[5]

[How the king of France was saved from the treachery prepared for him][6]

At this time the king of France [Charles VI] was dancing in his hall with four of the knights of his household. He had dressed up as a forester, wearing a tight garment smeared with resin and pitch so that the linen material fixed to the garment might stick more closely and give a clearer impression. During this dance, if help had not been at hand, the king would have suddenly been burnt to a cinder, thanks to the scheming of his brother, the duke, who had been aspiring to the kingdom since the king's illness. The king was leading the dance with his friends when the man appointed for the attempt, holding a torch downwards, set alight the linen, that is the unburnt material which was covering their bodies. The fire spread right through to the skin-tight clothes, and as they had been sewed tightly to the body, when the flames got to the pitch and resin on them, nothing could stop the flames burning right up to the body. A lady-in-waiting, who saw the great danger the king was in, rushed up and pulled him out of the dance. But although the king was saved in this way, no means could be found of saving his four friends before they expired with charred skins and flesh.

---

1   Stanley had led a campaign against the Ulster chieftains and it was for his mishandling of it that he was dismissed. Walsingham's confidence that Gloucester could swiftly resolve the continuing tensions was surely misplaced.
2   Charles VI was with his army at Le Mans and was well enough to lead his troops out of the town on 5 August. According to the French chroniclers, as the column was passing through open country, the sound of a collision of lances of two mounted pages caused the king to panic and he began to strike out at those surrounding him, killing five men before he could be restrained. Philip, duke of Burgundy, now assumed control and the campaign was cancelled: FCBuchon, iii. 160–1.
3   When Charles's envoy, Hanart de Campbernart was dispatched to England on 13 September he was instructed to inform King Richard that Charles was fully recovered.
4   de Vere had been convicted in his absence at the Merciless Parliament of September 1388 (see above, pp. 261–3), and his estates and titles declared forfeit. He died on 22 November. His body was returned to England in November 1395 and reburied at Earl's Colne in the presence of the king (see below, p. 295).
5   Parliament met from 20 January to 11 February: *RP*, iii. 300–8. In fact three half-subsidies were granted to two of which the commons attached conditions, that one should be spent on an expedition either to Ireland or Scotland and one should support an unspecified expedition which the king would lead in person.
6   This episode, known as the 'bal des ardents', occurred at the Hotel de St Pol in January 1393, when the convalescent Charles was in the care of the queen and Louis, duke of Orléans. Four courtiers, le comte de Joigny, le batard de Foix, Amery de Poitiers and a Norman, died in the fire and as Walsingham suggests Charles was saved only by the action of one of the attendant ladies, apparently the duchess of Berry: FCBuchon, iii. 176–9.

[Events of 1393]

In this year the king's bench and chancery were moved from London to York, either, so the story goes, to spite the people of London or to show favour to the people of York, as the archbishop of York was chancellor and wanted to advance his own city. But this change did not last long. With the same facility with which they had been taken to York, the king's bench and chancery were brought back to London.

Also in this year[1] Aubrey de Vere was made earl of Oxford,[2] and in the same year on the feast of St Peter in Cathedra [22 February] there occurred the sudden death of the knight, Sir John Devereux, constable of Dover and steward of the king.[3] He was succeeded as steward by Sir Thomas Percy, formerly the king's sub-chamberlain, and as constable of Dover by Lord Thomas [correctly, John] Beaumont. The replacement as sub-chamberlain was Lord William Scrope, than whom it would be difficult to find in the whole human race a more wicked or cruel man.[4]

At this time William Scrope bought the island of Eubonia with its crown from Lord William Montagu, earl of Salisbury. For the ruler of this island is called king and even has the right to be crowned with a gold crown. This island, situated between England and Ireland, is popularly known as the Isle of Man.

In this year the dukes of Lancaster and Gloucester crossed to France to finalise the truce I have mentioned above or to make a final peace between the kingdoms.[5] But such a conclusion could not yet be made because the king of France [Charles VI] was ill again. At the same time Sir Henry Percy, the younger [i.e. Hotspur], was appointed a warden of Bordeaux.

In September much damage was done by thunder and flashes of lightning in many parts of the kingdom but especially in Cambridgeshire, where houses and crops in and around Lolworth were burnt to a cinder. And soon afterwards in October floodwater burst in and filled the whole of the church at Bury St Edmunds and destroyed house walls at Newmarket, so that the men and women there were well nigh in danger of drowning. In September in the same year there were many deaths from an attack of the plague in Essex.

In this year the control of the town of Cherbourg was restored to its former ruler, the king of Navarre.[6] It had been mortgaged to the king of England for a fixed number of years for 22,000 marks received on loan from the English king.

In the same year Sir John Roos[7] died at the city of Paphos in Cyprus while returning from the Holy Land. He had been affected by the unpleasant atmosphere of the air in that country.

---

[1]   The appointments recorded here were all confirmed in the Winchester parliament held from 20 January to 11 February: *RP*, iii. 300.
[2]   Aubrey de Vere (1338x1340–1400), third son of the 7th earl of Oxford and uncle of the disgraced Robert.
[3]   Devereux had served on the continual council at the start of Richard's reign and had subsequently been steward of the king's household. The Westminster chronicler corroborates the date of his death.
[4]   William Scrope was the son and heir of Sir Richard Scrope, chancellor in the early years of Richard's reign. He had served as seneschal of Aquitaine for a decade, returning in the 1390s to emerge as the rising star of the post-Appellant court. Walsingham's colleague, the *Annales* author, described him as both 'prudent and rich': *Trokelowe*, ed. Riley, p. 157.
[5]   This embassy had been arranged at the conclusion of the negotiations at Amiens the previous year. Gaunt, Gloucester and their other English delegates departed at the beginning of March. The French were in a more conciliatory mood than a year before and were now willing to accept an English Calais and much of Aquitaine as it had been constituted under the treaty of Bretigny, providing that the English accepted French sovereignty over the duchy and agreed to liege homage, which the English delegates now proved willing to accept. A provisional treaty was agreed on 16 June in which certain unresolved issues, such as the ransom owing from King John II and the English tenure of La Rochelle, were held back for final negotiation between the two kings themselves to take place in September. The recurrence of Charles's insanity, however, forced the postponement of these talks until the following spring.
[6]   Charles III, king of Navarre (1387–1425) received Cherbourg in January. See Jones, *Ducal Brittany*, p. 137.
[7]   John, Lord Roos was a Yorkshire knight: *CPR, 1391–6*, pp. 67, 76, 93, 188. See also above, p. 267 n.

[Murad [i.e.Bayezid] besieges Constantinople]

In 1394 Murad of Turkey laid siege to the city of Constantinople but was repelled by the valour of the besieged.[1]

In the octave of St Hilary [20 January] a parliament was held in London, in which a subsidy was sought for the king who wanted to set out for Ireland.[2] The clergy granted him a full tenth tax if he made the journey, and half that only if he did not have the labour of it.

[The duke of Lancaster and the earl of Arundel fall out]

At the time of this parliament a serious dispute arose between the duke of Lancaster and the earl of Arundel. The duke accused the earl of establishing himself with an army, around the time of the feast of the Exaltation of the Holy Cross [14 September] in his castle of Holt in the district of Chester. It was just the time when that district had risen in rebellion against the duke of Lancaster, with Nicholas Clifton and his accomplices thought to be helping the rebels as their leaders. The earl completely denied this charge and gave very good evidence in his defence. So for the time being a great storm abated.[3]

[A four years truce and deaths of famous people, including Queen Anna]

During the feast of [the nativity of] St John the Baptist [24 June] the duke of Lancaster came back from France, having gone there for negotiations in May. He brought back a four year truce, in which the Scots also were due to be included, if they were willing to be subject to the king of England, as they were accustomed to be by law.[4]

While the duke was in France, his wife, Lady Constanza, died in England.[5] She was the daughter of Lord Pedro, once king of Castile, and an exceptionally innocent and pious lady. And so that her funeral should not be the only cause for tears at that time, there also occurred the death of the countess of Derby, the wife of Lord Henry [of Bolingbroke], earl of Derby, the son of the duke of Lancaster.[6]

---

1   In fact it was Bayezid Bey (1389–1402, d. 1403), Murad I's (1362–89) successor in the Sultanate who began a blockade of Constantinople as part of his progressive assault on the borders of Europe. The blockade continued until 1402 when the Turks were defeated at the battle of Ankara (28 July).
2   The parliament met at Westminster and sat from 29 January until 6 March. Walsingham gives a different report of its proceedings to that made by the Westminster chronicler, who records only the discussion of the peace negotiations: *RP*, iii. 309.
3   There is no evidence to corroborate the claim that Gaunt and Arundel were in dispute, but the spring and early summer had been marked by tensions serious enough to force the recall of Gaunt and Gloucester from the continuing peace negotiations. In Cheshire there appeared to be the beginnings of a rebellion, led by county knights alarmed at the drift of recent diplomacy, which looked set to bring about a permanent peace – thus depriving professional soldiers, for which Cheshire was a common recruiting ground, of long-standing, lucrative employment – and armed with suspicions of a (wholly spurious) plot by leading magnates to deprive Cheshire of its palatine status. Two veteran Cheshire knights, Sir Thomas Talbot and Sir Nicholas Clifton, published manifestos outlining these grievances. In April, John Holland, earl of Huntingdon and Sir John Stanley were sent to quell the disturbance and on 6 May Gaunt, as palatine lord, and Gloucester, as justice of Chester, were also summoned. See Saul, *Richard II*, pp. 219–21.
4   The negotiations suspended the previous year resumed at the end of March at Leulingham, where they had been conducted five years before. It was still anticipated that the discussions would conclude with a meeting between the two monarchs, but this was soon forgotten. To observers, these negotiations appear to have achieved nothing; no final agreement over territories or sovereignty, which had seemed a distinct possibility in 1393, was made before the negotiations broke up in late May or early June. It has been conjectured that a secret treaty was signed but given the evident rapprochement between the two sides it is surprising that if agreement had been reached it was not made public. Gaunt returned with nothing more than a renewal of the truce of 1389, this time extended for four years, until 1398. See also Palmer, *England, France and Christendom*, pp. 149–50.
5   Constanza of Castile died on 24 March 1394. She was buried at St Mary's Abbey, Leicester.
6   Mary de Bohun, daughter of Humphrey de Bohun, earl of Hereford, Essex and Northamptonshire (d.1373) died giving birth to her daughter Philippa (see below, p. 339) on or around the 4 July.

Queen Anna [of Bohemia] also died and was buried at Westminster [Abbey].[1] Her funeral was famous because of its expense, but equally infamous because of the king's polluting the place with the blood of the earl of Arundel at the beginning of the funeral service.[2]

In the same year died Lady Isabel, the duchess of York, half sister of the duchess of Lancaster. She was a pampered and voluptuous lady, but men said that she was very sorrowful and repentant at the end. At the king's order she was buried at his manor of [King's] Langley with the Friars [i.e. Dominicans].[3]

Also in this year died Sir John Hawkwood. He was the most famous soldier in the whole world and his deeds need a history of their own.[4]

[The king crosses to Ireland]

During August it was proclaimed throughout England that all the Irish, on pain of death should return to their own country by the feast of the nativity of the blessed Mary [8 September], to wait there for the arrival of the king.[5] For it was said that so many Irish had come to England in the hope of making their fortune that their own land was almost completely devoid of men. In consequence the true Irishmen who were anti-English had devastated the part of the island that was subject to the English king without meeting any resistance. For when that illustrious king, Edward III, put his bench with judges and the exchequer in Ireland, he received from there £30,000 annually for the royal coffers. But lately, because of the absence of men and the unchecked power of the enemy, no revenues had come from Ireland, but year-by-year the king had paid from his own purse 30,000 marks to his own disgrace and the heavy losses of his treasure chest.[6]

During the feast of the nativity of the blessed Mary [8 September], the king of England crossed to Ireland, accompanied by the duke of Gloucester and the earls of March [Roger Mortimer], Nottingham [Thomas Mowbray] and Rutland [Edward of Langley].[7] The Irish were really terrified by this great force and did not dare to attack it in open battle, although their secret raids often wearied the king's army. But the English prevailed, and several of the Irish chieftains were compelled to submit to the king, who kept some of them with him so that they could not hatch new plots. The king indeed stayed on in Ireland until after Easter [17 April].[8]

During this time there arrived a deputation for the king from England, consisting of the archbishop of York, the bishop of London and other envoys sent by the clergy. They asked the king that he should regard it as his duty to return home as quickly as possible to give his help to the church and its faith, as it was now enduring unbelievable suffering at the hands of the Lollards

---

1   Queen Anna died on 7 June but was not buried until 3 August.

2   Richard struck Arundel apparently after the earl had insulted the memory of the queen. The incident is also reported by Walsingham's St Albans colleague, the *Annales* author: Trokelowe, ed. Riley, p. 169. The author of the *Historia vitae et regni Ricardi secundi* reports that in his grief Richard also demolished the palace at Sheen where Anna had died: *HVRS*, p. 134 and n.

3   Isabel of Castile died on 23 December 1397.

4   Sir John Hawkwood died at Florence on 16/17 March 1494.

5   Walsingham's chronology is incorrect: according to the Westminster chronicler the proclamation was published in London on 20 June, and the writ itself is dated four days previously (*WC*, pp. 520–1); Irishmen were required to return by 15 August, which is in fact the feast of the Assumption.

6   Walsingham was right that rebellion was the most pressing problem facing Richard in Ireland, but his impulse to lead an expedition in person stemmed as much from a desire to assert his authority as it did from the need to restore stability and thus the regular flow of money into the royal coffers.

7   In fact it was not until 1 October that Richard made the crossing from Milford Haven to Waterford. He was accompanied by an army of about 7–8000 men, the core of which was formed around his own household knights. Walsingham's colleague the *Annales* author also gives the date as 8 September, while the *Historia vitae et regni Ricardi secundi* gives 21 September: Trokelowe, ed. Riley, p. 172; *HVRS*, p. 134.

8   Richard mounted a naval blockade and at the same time sent raiding parties against the rebels. After two months of this activity, Art MacMurrough, the 'king of Leinster' made a formal submission to the king and he was soon followed by other chieftains, including the O'Neills. Richard remained in Ireland long after Easter, returning only on 1 May 1395.

and their supporters.[1] For the one concern of the Lollards was working out how to make off with the possessions of the whole church and, what was worse, how to destroy the whole of canon law. On hearing this, the king, fired with the holy spirit, returned with all speed to England, thinking it more necessary to aid the faith in this crisis than to battle for temporal kingdoms.

[1395]

Parliaments at Dublin and London

In 1395 the king kept Christmas in the city of Dublin, capital of Ireland. After Christmas he held a parliament there, attended both by his liegemen and those who had recently submitted to him.[2]

At the same time after the octave of Epiphany [13 January] a parliament was held in London.[3] It was summoned by the protector of the kingdom of England, Lord Edmund [of Langley] the king's uncle, the duke of York. The duke of Gloucester was sent from Ireland to attend it. Before all its members he explained that the king had used up all the stock of money from his treasury in Ireland and now needed more. His mission was so successful that the clergy granted a tenth tax and the commons a fifteenth tax, though not without first protesting that they were led to make this grant not by any strict law but by their affection for their king.[4]

[The king deals with the nobles supporting the Lollards]

At that time the Lollards and their supporters were so emboldened to practise any and every villainy, that they publicly fixed on the doors of St Paul's church in London and of Westminster abbey horrific accusations against the clergy and hitherto unheard-of doctrines by which they sought to destroy both churchmen and the sacraments of the church. People said the Lollards were encouraged by massive support from some of the nobles and knights of England, the chief of these being [Sir] Richard Stury, [Sir] Lewis Clifford, [Sir] Thomas Latimer and [Sir] John Montagu, who were inciting and encouraging the heretics to attack especially the monks, if the chance was given them.[5]

So when the king, as I have said, discovered the wicked plans of the Lollards, he hurried to England so that the sight of him might dissipate such evil. After a happy voyage, he made a fierce attack on some of the nobles, with terrible threats of the consequences if in the future they helped the Lollards or encouraged them in any way. Furthermore, he received from Richard Stury his sworn oath that he would never again hold Lollard views. After he had sworn, the king added, 'And I swear to you that, if you ever break your oath, you will die the most shameful of deaths.' When the rest heard this fearsome rebuke, they drew in their horns and lay low for the time being.

At that time in the French town of Laon an image of the crucified Christ with bloody stigmata

---

1 Thomas Arundel, archbishop of York, and Robert Braybroke, bishop of London, led the deputation to Dublin. Walsingham places their visit before the end of the year, but in fact it was in February 1395. As the chronicler suggests, the prelates may have been responding to renewed Lollard activity, and in particular the circulation of manifestos at Westminster, but in his capacity as chancellor, Arundel may also have had in mind the rumours of imminent French invasions and Scots activity across the border.
2 In a letter to Edmund, duke of York, Richard said that he had summoned a parliament for 1 December 1394, but he also refers to a parliament summoned for 19 April 1395. It may be that both assemblies did take place.
3 In fact the parliamentary session began on 27 January: *RP*, iii. 329.
4 As Walsingham suggests, the commons was probably persuaded by the success of the Irish campaign, but also by the perceived threat from France and Scotland. Royal finances were in a poor state; the expenditure of the wardrobe had doubled between 1390 and 1394 from £8,000 to £16,000.
5 Walsingham had already expressed his suspicions about Stury, Clifford, Latimer and Montagu (see above, p. 248). There is no evidence of their involvement in the circulation of the manifestos that appeared in London and at Westminster at this time, but it is possible that they continued to express sympathy for the Wyclifite cause. Walsingham is the only authority for the suggestion that Richard now tackled Stury over his orthodoxy, although it is a plausible action for a king whose own orthodoxy was beyond question. See also Saul, *Richard II*, pp. 297–8, 302–3.

was seen above the bell tower of the cathedral church. For almost an hour it was clearly seen by bishop, priests and people.[1]

[The misfortunes of Murad [correctly, Bayezid]]

In this year the barbarian Murad with three hundred and fifty thousand pagans fought against the prior of St John of Rhodes [of the order of Knights' Hospitallers] and other Christians. But through the goodness of God he was beaten and a hundred thousand of his army killed. And because fortune had not been on his side in the land battle, he decided to try his luck at sea. But the Lord of land and sea nullified his attempts and for the second time compelled him to flee in great confusion. Also the city of Constantinople, which, as I said earlier, was being besieged by a vast host of Murad's soldiers, was set free by the emperor of Constantinople, who came to its help with a small number of Christians. By a miracle five hundred thousand pagans were killed.[2]

In that year England experienced heavy losses from the pirates of the queen of Denmark.[3] These pirates despoiled sailors and mercenary soldiers, particularly the men of Norfolk who dared to gather together a force to meet them in battle. But the Danes won. Many of the men of Norfolk were killed and several were kept under guard until a heavy ransom was paid. Also they lost £20,000 which they had been carrying for their trading activities.[4]

[A papal bull permitting a levy on church goods]

In the same year William [Courtenay], archbishop of Canterbury, with no concern for the depression of his church and its burden of unceasingly paying taxes to the king each year, and thinking more of his own advantage rather than of the disadvantage to the community, obtained a favourable papal bull by which he could levy throughout his whole province four pence in the pound an all ecclesiastical goods, both exempt and non exempt. He put forward no genuine or legal reason for this action. The archbishop of York [Thomas Arundel] and the bishop of London [Robert Braybroke] were appointed as the executors of the bull. Many clergy, through fear of the censure of such eminent persons, preferred to go on paying the money than run the risk of a lawsuit where the result was uncertain and the loss of money possible. Some appealed to the apostolic see, just as if they were under oppression, and attempted to defend their position and somehow to remove the subsidy as being unlawful. The clergy of Lincoln were particularly up in arms on this matter. But the death of the archbishop, which followed soon afterwards, put a stop to these upheavals.

[Deaths of famous people including Robert de Vere]

In this year died John Waltham, bishop of Salisbury and treasurer of the kingdom. The king had been so pleased with him that on his orders John even earned a burial among the kings at Westminster, although many grumbled about this.[5] He was succeeded as treasurer by Sir Roger Walden, previously king's secretary and treasurer at Calais, and as bishop by Sir John Mitford, bishop of Chichester.[6] The archbishop of Dublin was translated to Chichester: Dublin was a more important ecclesiastical post but less wealthy in temporal goods.[7]

The deaths also occurred of William, bishop of Exeter, succeeded at the king's request by

---

[1]   It was natural for Walsingham to juxtapose a story of the power of images with an account of the Lollards who were openly opposed to the veneration of images.

[2]   Bayezid Bey continued his advance on the eastern fringes of Christendom throughout this period, although a skirmish with the prior of St John of Rhodes was no widely reported in the west. Walsingham's optimism as to the situation at Constantinople was unfounded and Bayezid's blockade held until 1402.

[3]   Margaret, queen of Denmark (1353–1412), who ruled Denmark from 1376 and Norway from 1380. Latterly she ruled Denmark conjointly with he great-nephew, Erik of Pomerania.

[4]   This episode is recorded only by Walsingham and his colleague the *Annales* author. See *Trokelowe*, ed. Riley, p. 186.

[5]   Bishop Waltham died on 17 September 1395.

[6]   Correctly, Richard Mitford, who was translated to Salisbury on 25 October 1395.

[7]   Robert Waldby, archbishop of Dublin, was translated to Chichester on 3 November 1395.

Master Edmund Stafford, keeper of the privy seal,[1] and of Sir Henry Wakefield, bishop of Worcester.[2] Through the prayers of the king and with the permission of the pope, Henry was succeeded by a Cistercian monk called Robert Tideman, who was also the king's physician. The lawful election to this bishopric of Master John Green was made null and void.[3]

In November of this year the body of Robert de Vere was brought back from Louvain. A favourite of the king, he had been appointed duke of Ireland by him. He would have been happy if he had not aspired to high office, for it was his exalted position which brought him unhappiness. The king ordered a solemn funeral at [Earl's] Colne priory in Essex, and enhanced the importance of the funeral service by being present at it himself. He took care to open the cypress wood coffin, in which the body lay after being embalmed. He looked long at the face and touched it with his finger, publicly showing to Robert, when dead, the affection which he had shown him previously, when alive. The king was accompanied by the countess of Oxford, the mother of the deceased, the archbishop of Canterbury, [William Courtenay] very many bishops, abbots and priors and other churchmen. But few nobles attended the funeral. They had not yet swallowed the hate that they had conceived against Robert.[4]

[1396]

[The duke of Lancaster is recalled from Aquitaine]

In 1396 the duke of Lancaster, upon whom the king had bestowed the duchy of Aquitaine, and who by now had spent an unimaginable amount of treasury money on successfully winning the goodwill of its people, was suddenly recalled at the king's command.[4] Nevertheless he obeyed the summons, returned to England and went to Langley, where the king was keeping Christmas that year. He was received by the king with honour, as was fitting, but not, so some said, with love. With the king's permission he withdrew from the court and hurried to Lincoln, where Katherine Swynford was staying at that time. He married her after the octave of the Epiphany [13 January], to the amazement of all at such a miraculous happening, for she had a very small fortune. Such was the magnitude of his error.[6]

---

1 Correctly, Thomas Brantingham, bishop of Exeter, died on 23 December 1394. Stafford, son of Sir Richard Stafford a household knight of Edward the Black Prince and a younger son of the 1st earl of Stafford, had been in royal service for more than a decade. He was consecrated bishop on 20 June 1395.

2 Bishop Wakefield died on 11 March 1395; his successor, Robert Tideman, was translated from Llandaff and provided to the see on 12 June 1395. He died in 1401.

3 Green was the candidate elected by the prior and monks of the Benedictine cathedral chapter; such candidates were often overruled in favour of royal or papal candidates. Green, a former fellow of Merton College, Oxford, had been elected to the see in May 1395 and his election had initially received royal assent but this was withdrawn when the pope provided Tideman. See also Emden, *BRUO*, i. 815. Walsingham here perhaps betrays a degree of anti-Cistercian prejudice.

4 Walsingham is the only contemporary authority to describe Richard's behaviour at de Vere's reburial in detail: it is indicative of his enduring attachment to his early favourite. See also Saul, *Richard II*, p. 461.

5 Since Gaunt had been created duke of Aquitaine in March 1390 there had been growing tension in Gascony as the Gascon estates feared his appointment could lead to the permanent alienation of the territory from the crown and the end of the privileges they enjoyed in this capacity; these fears intensified as a Lancastrian Gascony emerged as an important condition of the continuing Anglo-French peace negotiations. On 6 April 1394, the Gascons formally renounced their allegiance to Gaunt and in the months that followed alliances were formed between the leading Gascon magnates in preparation for what seemed certain to become a military confrontation. After the conclusion of the Leulingham peace conference in June, Gaunt raised a modest force (about 1500 men) and embarked for Gascony in November. His actions on arrival are not well documented and although he threatened the Gascon estates with force, he appears to have sought a negotiated settlement although it was only after significant concessions were granted to the estates and the city of Bordeaux in March 1395 that a resolution was finally reached. Gaunt remained in France until December 1395. See also Goodman, *John of Gaunt*, pp. 199–200; Saul, *Richard II*, pp. 209–15; Vale, *English Gascony*, pp. 27–9, 32–3.

6 Walsingham notwithstanding, Gaunt's marriage to Katherine Swynford was unsurprising. The daughter of Sir Paen de Roet, a knight in the service of Queen Philippa of Hainault, Katherine had been the duke's mistress since the early 1370s. Gaunt married now to legitimise their four children. See also *Trokelowe*, ed. Riley, p. 188; Froissart, *Chroniques*, xv. 279–307; Goodman, *John of Gaunt*, pp. 363–4.

[A letter and bulls from the pope]

In this year the pope [Boniface IX] wrote to the king of England and begged him to help the leaders of the church in the cause of God, himself and his kingdom against the Lollards, whom he declared to be traitors not only to the church but also to the king himself. He asked him most urgently to condemn those whom the church leaders had declared to be heretics.

At that time he also published bulls to recall to their houses those religious who had received chaplaincies from the pope himself or someone else or the papal legate. These bulls were welcomed as a most pleasing gift by the mendicant orders and especially by the Friars Minor, who speedily tried to seize and get hold of and bring back home their brothers who had been separated from them by the exemption bestowed by a chaplaincy.[1]

[Peace made between the kings of England and France]

At that time the kings of England and France met together in accordance with the agreement previously signed between them.[2] The place appointed for their conference was just outside Calais, where the tents of both kings were set up in splendid fashion. Before the discussion, they provided the following corporal oath in the presence of all as a pledge of their loyalty to a genuine peace:

'We, Charles, king of France, swear in a king's words on the gospels on behalf of ourselves, all our subjects, friends, relations and well-wishers that neither we nor any of them will cause or allow to happen any kind of loss, interference, trouble, disturbance or check to our son, the king of England, or to any of his subjects, friends, relations or well-wishers, either during the time of our conference or for eight days beforehand or seven days afterwards. And if by any chance any person on our side exhibits any insolent or litigious behaviour – which God forbid! – we promise in a king's words according to the pledge just given that we shall cause this behaviour to be duly amended and altered without delay. And we further swear as part of the pledge just given that if any individual or group of any class or condition wishes to oppose the pledge we have given, we shall help our son to the best of our ability to resist the malice of such evil people and to protect our son and his people as best we and our people know how. As above we swear and promise to hold to all this and to carry it out without deceit or malicious intent.'

On 26 October the king of England rode from Calais to his castle at Guisnes accompanied by [Jean] the duke of Berry, who had had been sent to receive the oath of our king. The next day the kings met on equal terms.[3] The king of England was escorted by French lords – the four dukes of

---

[1]   Walsingham had been an outspoken critic of papal chaplaincies although his contention that the privilege was sought in particular by Franciscans is disingenuous since several of his own St Albans colleagues also held them.

[2]   This was the meeting of the monarchs that had been deferred for more than two years. It was the culmination of months of diplomatic activity which had continued, at regular intervals, since the spring of 1395. Richard had embarked on these negotiations in a less conciliatory mood than in 1392–94, initially instructing his ambassadors to seek a settlement that included the cession of Aquitaine without homage and the full reparation for the ransom of King John II, the sticking point in almost all previous negotiations. His ambassadors also now aimed to negotiate a marriage between the widowed king and Charles VI's daughter Isabel (b.1389). The demands for a peace settlement on Richard's terms were rapidly rejected and the French pressured instead for an extended truce. In contrast, the marriage negotiations proceeded smoothly. Finally on 9 March 1396 a twenty-eight year truce was sealed at Paris and on the same day the terms of the marriage settlement were settled. Both were to be underpinned by the meeting of the monarchs which was to be followed by the marriage ceremony itself. The meeting-place was Ardres near Calais. As Walsingham reports here, Richard arrived on 26 October. See also Palmer, *England, France and Christendom*, pp. 166–79 at 171–4; Saul, *Richard II*, pp. 226–8.

[3]   The meeting was extremely formal, with almost every step of the monarchs choreographed with studied ceremonial. They met at 3p.m. A post was raised at the centre of the tent and as each king entered he advanced towards it. They greeted one another with a kiss as their retinues knelt behind them. Richard was dressed in a red gown embroidered with his personal badge of the white hart, whilst as a mark of respect Charles was dressed in a gown bearing the badge of Anna of Bohemia. The following day they met again for the peace negotiations that continued for four hours. See also Saul, *Richard II*, pp. 229–34.

Berry, Burgundy, Orléans[1] and Bourbon,[2] the count of Sancerre,[3] the viscount de Melun,[4] the bishop of Valence[5] and Lord de Boissay.[6]

To match this, we on our side sent to escort the French king the two dukes of Lancaster and Gloucester and the earls of Derby [Henry of Bolingbroke], Rutland [Edward of Langley] and Northumberland [Henry Percy]. The two kings conferred and mutually agreed that a chapel, to be called the Chapel of Peace and Our Lady, should be built on the spot at their joint expense as an everlasting memorial.

[The daughter of the king of France is given in marriage to the king of England]

On the Sunday, the feast day of St Simon and St Jude [28 October], the kings conferred concerning certain points in their treaty. Afterwards they swore on the gospels to keep the agreement. Then the king of England asked the king of France [Charles VI] to dine with him next day. On Monday the French king came to the tent of the English king, bringing with him at that hour the princess. He gave her in marriage to our king, who took her by the hand and kissed her, thanking her father, the king of France, for such an honourable and welcome gift. He also declared that he received her on the conditions made between them, the object being that through this marriage both kings might be able to live in peace and tranquillity and arrive at the good end and conclusion of a perpetual peace made between their kingdoms, and that no more Christian blood should be spilt, a thing which was very likely to happen, if such a marriage uniting the peoples did not take place at that time.

The princess was entrusted to the duchesses of Lancaster and Gloucester, to the countesses of Huntingdon [Elizabeth] and Stafford [Anne] and to other noble ladies then present. They escorted her to Calais with a great troop of men and horses. The princess had with her twelve carriages full of ladies and maidservants.

After this the kings met to dine in the tent of the English king. The French king sat on the right side of the hall. He was served after the fashion of the kings of his country, that is by all the waiters of the first course together on a big dish, and in the same way for the second course. Then the king of England was served after the fashion of his country. After dinner the kings exchanged kisses and got on their horses. The English king escorted the French king to his road home and finally, after clasping hands, they rode away from each other. The French king rode to Ardres, while the English king turned towards Calais, where he married the daughter of the French king, a little girl of eight or nine years.[7]

The equipment of the kings was imposing and much money was spent on gifts and other expenses. For besides the presents that the king of England gave to the king of France [Charles VI] and the other nobles of his kingdom, which exceeded ten thousand marks, he is also said to have spent more than three hundred thousand marks on that occasion.[8] He and his wife soon afterwards returned safe to England,[9] but his tents and a great part of the furnishings of his encampment were lost in a great storm.[10]

---

[1] Louis, duke of Orléans (1372–1407), brother of Charles VI.
[2] Louis II, 3rd duke of Bourbon (1337–1410).
[3] Jean III, count of Sancerre.
[4] Guillaume de Melun, count of Tancarville.
[5] Jean de Poitiers, bishop of Valence from 1390.
[6] Robert, sire de Boissay.
[7] The marriage took place on 30 October; it was solemnized in the presence of Archbishop Arundel on 4 November.
[8] Richard had presented Charles with a cup worth 700 marks and a collar of pearls and a gilt ewer worth 5,000 marks; the duke of Orléans had been given a hanaper and ewer worth £200 and the duke of Berry a buckle worth 500 marks.
[9] The author of the *Historia vitae et regni Ricardi secundi* gives a unique account of the entry of the new queen into London and the citizens hurrying to meet her: *HVRS*, p. 136 and n.
[10] The French tents suffered the greatest damage; the English had pitched theirs at the foot of a slope and were protected from the worst of the weather. See also Saul, *Richard II*, p. 230.

[Obituary of the year]

In this year Master William Courtenay, archbishop of Canterbury, said farewell to the world, and at the request of the Chapter General was succeeded by Thomas Arundel, brother of the earl of Arundel and chancellor of the kingdom.[1] He soon gave up the post of chancellor, entrusting that burden with the agreement of the king to Master Edmund Stafford. In the same year died the father and mirror of the whole monastic order, Thomas, abbot of the monastery of St Albans.[2]

[1397]

[Parliament in London]

In the year of grace 1397 a parliament was held in London after Christmas,[3] in which the duke of Lancaster had a child legitimised whom he had conceived with Katherine Swynford. The same parliament decided that justiciars should not have assessors. Also Thomas[4] Beaufort, son of the duke of Lancaster and of Katherine, was created earl of Somerset (Beaufort was the name decided upon by the duke for the sons borne to him by Katherine).

At that time the clergy granted the king a half tenth tax, to be paid at the two term-days of that very year.

[The king recalls the justiciars from Ireland; a rumour he has been elected emperor]

In this year Richard, king of England, contrary to the oath that he had sworn, recalled from Ireland the justiciars, whom his nobles, with the king's consent, had formerly decided to exile there because of their marked shortcomings.

At that time rumours that were in fact unfounded spread abroad that the king of England had been elected emperor.[5] He was so elated by this, so men said, that from then on he began to have higher thoughts than before, to impoverish the commons and to borrow large sums of money from anybody he could, so much so that there was no prelate, no town, no famously rich citizen in the whole kingdom who was able to escape loaning money to the king.

[The king imprisons the duke of Gloucester and the earls of Warwick and Arundel]

In this year the kingdom of England seemed about to enjoy a period of unbroken peace, on account of the recent royal wedding and the riches that it had brought with it, the thirty years peace that had been arranged, and the presence of so many lords, more in number and quality than could be shown by any foreign state. But suddenly everything was upset by the deviousness of the king.[6] Without warning he arrested by force of arms at Pleshey in Essex his uncle, the duke of Gloucester, who had been fearing no such thing, and had him taken all the way to Calais and put under prison guard.[7] He also had the earl of Warwick arrested on the very day on which he

---

[1]   Courtenay died on 31 July 1396. Arundel was provided on 25 September.
[2]   Abbot Thomas de la Mare died on 21 September 1396, at the age of eighty-seven. He had held the abbacy since 1349 and steered the monastic community from its lowest ebb at the Black Death to a position of pre-eminence. He had also served as co-president of the English Benedictines' General Chapter. Walsingham described him elsewhere as the 'patriarch of English monks'. See Clark, *Monastic Renaissance*, p. 15.
[3]   The parliamentary session began on 22 January: *RP*, iii. 337.
[4]   Correctly, John.
[5]   The rumours were indeed unfounded. Richard had not been elected emperor, but German envoys had arrived in England hoping to persuade Richard to seek the title. Walsingham and other commentators considered that it was this suggestion that elevated Richard's self-esteem and led him to tyrannise his people: Saul, *Richard II*, p. 270.
[6]   The arrests Walsingham describes in the following passage took place on 10 January 1397. There was apparently no warning that the three appellants were about to be seized which would explain the ease with which it was accomplished. Saul, *Richard II*, pp. 373–4.
[7]   Richard is alleged to have warned Gloucester that he would show him as much mercy as he himself had shown to Sir Simon Burley nine years before. See above, p. 262.

had invited him to dinner and had him immediately thrown into prison,[1] although on this same day the king had given the earl the friendliest of glances and promised that he would be a good master to him and his close friend. He also deceived with persuasive flatteries the earl of Arundel, who meekly gave himself up, even though he was strong enough to have saved himself and set free his friends, the duke of Gloucester and earl of Warwick. The king sent him to the Isle of Wight to be kept in prison in the same way.[2]

The king was afraid that the arrest of these nobles would cause a public outcry, so he had it proclaimed throughout the kingdom that the reason for their arrest was not any old crimes of theirs but recent transgressions against the king, of which a public account would be given in a future parliament.[3] But as was shown by the outcome, this proclamation was a lie.

What the king was afraid of is not known. But at this same time he did fear that the bishops or other prelates would hold processions or intercessions for the cause of the rebels or even for the rescue of such important nobles. Shortly afterwards at Nottingham he caused the lords I have named indicted for treachery, and he suborned as their appellants at a future parliament Edward earl of Rutland, Thomas Mowbray earl marshal [of York], Thomas Holland earl of Kent, John Holland earl of Huntingdon, Thomas [i.e. John] Beaufort earl of Somerset, John Montagu earl of Salisbury, Lord Thomas Despenser and William Scrope chamberlain of the king.[4] After this, he had it proclaimed through the whole kingdom that the lords arrested were traitors and were being kept in prison because of their treachery.

Meanwhile in fear of his life the king summoned several malefactors from the county of Chester to protect his person, and to keep watch in turn over him night and day.[5]

[The trial of the lords begins]

During the octave of the nativity of the blessed Mary [15 September], a parliament was held in London.[6] All the nobles of the kingdom with their retainers attended this parliament in arms, persuaded to come to London by their fear of the king.[7] The main speakers at this parliament were some very covetous, ambitious and cowardly knights,[8] namely [Sir] John Bushy,[9] [Sir] William Bagot and [Sir] Henry Green.[10] They persistently shouted out their demands that above

---

1   Warwick was indeed seized at a banquet in the city of London.
2   Arundel surrendered himself at Reigate after his brother, Archbishop Arundel, persuaded him that he had no reason to fear for his life.
3   The proclamation was made on 15 July: it argued that the arrests were due to 'the great number of extortions, oppressions and grievances committed against the king and his people' and 'other offences' (unspecified) to be made clear, as Walsingham reports, in the next parliament. The author of the contemporary account, the *Traison et Mort*, maintains that the three appellants had formed a conspiracy against Richard, and some traces of such a plot appear to have been revealed in the interrogation of the three before their trial. See also Saul, *Richard II*, p. 375.
4   These magnates, a roll-call of Richard's strongest supporters, were rewarded for their role as appellants with new titles and estates. See below, p. 302.
5   In fact the king arranged for 4,000 marks to be distributed to the Cheshire men who had fought for de Vere at Radcot bridge in 1397.
6   In fact parliament opened on Monday 17 September, the feast of St Lambert: *RP*, iii. 347. It was to be Richard's last parliament. It has often been suggested that this parliament was packed with Ricardian loyalists. It is unlikely that this level of interference in the nomination of representatives was possible at this time, but it is true that many of those who had been present at the January parliament now absented themselves. See also Saul, *Richard II*, pp. 375–81.
7   The author of the *Historia vitae et regni Ricardi secundi* reports that there gathered into the chamber such a multitude of men as had not been seen for many years: *HVRS*, p. 138. The king himself attended with a guard of 300 Cheshire archers.
8   Them session was opened by Bishop Edmund Stafford of Exeter preaching on the text 'There will be one king for all', Ezekiel, xxxvii. 22: *HVRS*, p. 138; *RP*, iii. 347.
9   Bushy, a long serving retainer of the king, acted as speaker of the commons. The author of the *Historia vitae et regni Ricardi secundi* described him as 'vir utique magne discrecionis et eloquens valde' (*HVRS*, p. 139) but the *Annales* author echoes Walsingham's assessment: *Trokelowe*, ed. Riley, p. 209.
10   Green was grandson of Sir Henry Green, chief justice under Edward III.

all the charters of pardon should be revoked and annulled, and when the bishops were asked about this, they found no difficulty in deciding that charters such as these could be rescinded. They did not see that the rescinding of this grace was extremely prejudicial to the king's person, since mercy is the confirmation of the throne of the king and he who takes from the king his acts of mercy takes from him the foundation of his royal throne. So when the lords temporal saw the clergy giving their assent, they too voted that these charters should be annulled, though more through fear of the king than logical reasoning. The churchmen also demanded the right to set up a lay proctor to act for them. As they themselves could not be present at a judgement of blood, their proctor could consent to the death penalty, should this be necessary.[1]

[The archbishop of Canterbury is banished]

The next day [20 September], on the command and advice of the king, the archbishop of Canterbury [Thomas Arundel] stayed away from the parliament.[2] He believed that the king was his close friend, and indeed that king had sworn him an oath that no measures would be taken which were prejudicial to him, but in his absence the archbishop was sentenced to exile, contrary to all justice. There was a rider to the sentence that said he should not stay in the kingdom more than six weeks, counting from the next day. After he had been condemned in this way, the king sent a messenger in secret to the Roman Curia about the archbishop's translation, and also took measures for having Roger Walden, then treasurer of the kingdom, appointed archbishop in his place.[3] But two years later, because he had presumed to climb into his father's bed while his father was still alive, he was deposed by the authority of this same pope.[4]

[The earl of Arundel is condemned to death]

On St Matthew's day [21 September] judgement was passed on Richard [Fitzalan], earl of Arundel. He alleged and claimed the support of the charters and his pardon from the king, but this defence did him no good. He was condemned to be hanged, drawn, disembowelled, beheaded and quartered and his innards were to be burned. But the sentence passed was modified by the king's grace: the earl was to undergo execution only and was let off the additional penalties. But the earl kept a steady countenance throughout the proceedings, when he stood to make his defence,[5] when he suffered the sad sentence of the king, when he passed from the place of judgement to the place of execution, and finally when on bended knee he waited for the blow of the sword. The colour in his face stayed the same all the time and he grew no paler than if he had been

---

1   From the beginning there could have no doubt in the commons that the king would use parliament to undo the work of the Merciless Parliament ten years before, although Adam Usk reports that on the opening day Richard declared that any person guilty of undermining the king's regality was permitted to sue for pardon before 13 January, excepting only fifty named persons who would now be committed to trial (*Usk*, pp. 20–1). As the way was made clear for a 'judgement of blood' as Walsingham terms it, Gaunt was told to stay away from the assembly. See also Saul, *Richard II*, pp. 375–81.

2   After the opening session, led by Bushy, the commons moved to revoke the pardon granted to the three appellants after the events of 1387. Bushy declared that since Arundel's pardon had been secured through the agency of his brother the archbishop, then he too was guilty by association. Arundel rose and attempted to respond, but Richard gestured at him to remain silent. Richard was said to have signalled to him 'tomorrow' as if to suggest that further discussion would be deferred. But perhaps advisedly Arundel did not appear the next day and in his absence he was deposed and exiled. He had attempted to enter the session but was prevented apparently by Bishop Thomas Merke of Carlisle, acting for the king. The author of the *Historia vitae et regni Ricardi secundi* gives a detailed account of the treatment of Arundel: *HVRS*, pp. 139–41; Saul, *Richard II*, pp. 377–8.

3   Walden was provided to Canterbury on 8 November 1397.

4   In other words, by accepting provision to the see when the consecrated archbishop was still living, Walden had acted uncanonically.

5   Both the author of the *Historia vitae et regni Ricardi secundi* and Walsingham's colleague the *Annales* author record the exchanges between Arundel and his judges, which included Gaunt sitting in his capacity as high steward: *HVRS*, pp. 142–4; *Trokelowe*, ed. Riley, pp. 214–15.

asked out to dinner.[1] Before and after him in the procession went the wild roughs from Chester, armed with axes, swords, bows and arrows, and he was led and pushed to the goal of death by the earl Marshal [Thomas Mowbray] and the earl of Kent [Thomas Holland] (one his son in law and the other his daughter's son)[2] and by the earl of Huntingdon [John Holland], brother of the king.

And then, looking at his kinsmen and relations, the earl marshal and the earl of Kent, he urged them to finish the business of his execution and said to them 'Yes, you especially should have been absent and stayed away from this business. The time is soon coming when as many people will marvel at your misfortunes as now they marvel at my downfall.' Then he pardoned the executioner and asked him not to torture him any longer but to cut off his head with one stroke. He tested with his fingers the edge of the sword for his execution and said, 'It seems sharp enough. Do quickly what you have to do.' The executioner cut off his head with one blow. His body with the head was buried at the Austin Friars [i.e. Augustinian Friars] in London.[3]

[The ghost of the earl of Arundel disturbs the king]

After the earl's death, various visions disturbed the king's rest. As soon as he had fallen asleep, the earl's ghost flitted before his eyes and threatened him with indescribable terrors, as if he was saying with the poet Ovid

> I come, a ghost, still mindful of your deeds,
> A bony form in pursuit of your face[4]

The king was alarmed by these appearances that woke him in terror in the middle of the night, and he cursed the day on which he got to know the earl of Arundel. His mental turmoil grew still worse when he heard that that the common people were regarding the earl as a martyr and making pilgrimages to his body. So on the tenth day after the burial the king sent some dukes and earls at four o'clock in the morning to get the earl's body dug up and see if the head had been joined back to the body, as the people said it had. When the body was dug up, the nobles found the story was untrue and reported all this to the king. But he was not satisfied with this experiment and ordered the Augustinian friars to take down the signs which had been set up around the body and to hide his burial place at once under the floor.[5]

[The trial of the earl of Warwick]

After the death of the earl of Arundel the earl of Warwick [Thomas Beauchamp] was arraigned to stand trial before parliament. But he lacked the firmness that was part of the earl of Arundel's character. When asked what he wished to say about the ridings made with the duke of Gloucester and the earl of Arundel against the king, his fear of death and the sentence passed against the earl of Arundel soon made him tearfully confess that those ridings showed him to be a traitor.[6] So sentence of death was passed against him. But this was soon modified by the king, who in his

---

[1] The execution took place at Tower Hill. Walsingham's description of the earl's behaviour brings to mind Horace's description of Regulus, *Odes*, III. 5. 50–5.
[2] Holland was his daughter Alice's son. The author of the *Historia vitae* confirms the crowd that followed Arundel to his execution: *HVRS*, pp. 143–4.
[3] It was a small measure of the king's mercy that Arundel was spared the customary punishment of his head being publicly displayed. Saul, *Richard II*, p. 377 and n.
[4] Ovid, *Ibis*, ll. 145–6.
[5] Walsingham is the only authority to report this story, but he reflects a sense of injustice that was widespread at least amongst contemporary commentators. His colleague the *Annales* author claimed that his remains were venerated and miracles were recorded at his tomb (*Trokelowe*, ed., Riley, p. 218–19). Adam Usk opined, 'Would that I might be deemed worthy to accompany his soul for I have no doubt that he has been admitted to the fellowship of the saints.' He also attested to the fact that his remains were 'venerated . . . and people continually make offerings there' (*Usk*, p. 31).
[6] Warwick was tried on 28 September, a week after Arundel's death. Adam Usk reports that Warwick broke down 'like a wretched old woman' (*Usk*, pp. 34–5). The author of the *Historia vitae et regni Ricardi secundi* confirms his 'crying and wailing' before the king: *HVRS*, p. 145; Saul, *Richard II*, pp. 378–9.

mercy pardoned him and gave him his life. He was soon sent to the Isle of Man, which belonged to Sir William Scrope and there he passed the rest of his life in prison custody.[1]

[The murder of the duke of Gloucester]

Meanwhile, because it did not seem safe to the king that the duke of Gloucester should take his stand in public to answer the charges against him because of the support of the people, who had a deep affection for him, he ordered the earl marshal to kill him in secret, and the earl marshal dispatched his ministers of iniquity and had him suffocated. Quilts and bed-clothes stuffed with feathers were thrown over his face.[2] So died that best of men, son of a king and uncle of a king, on whom depended the hopes and comfort of the people of the whole kingdom. Afterwards the king cleverly had that parliament postponed until after Christmas. It was restarted or rather continued in Shrewsbury on the Welsh border.[3]

[1398]

[Constitutional changes and appointments]

In 1398, which was the twenty-first year of the reign of King Richard, at the parliament which was continued at Shrewsbury after Christmas, the king cleverly got all the estates of the realm to agree to the concession being made that the powers of parliament should remain in the hands of some seven or eight named people, who after the dissolution of parliament should be allowed to determine certain matters which had been brought before this parliament but had only received minimal attention during it.[4] The persons thus appointed later used this concession to move on to other things affecting that parliament in general. Although this concession was at the king's wish, it lowered the prestige of parliament and was a disadvantage to the whole kingdom and a pernicious precedent. To give some seeming colour of authority to the change, the king got alterations and deletions made in the rolls of parliament in preparation for putting the concession into effect.

The king then assumed the name of the prince of Chester. He made the earl of Derby [Henry of Bolingbroke] duke of Hereford, the earl marshal [Thomas Mowbray, earl of Nottingham] duke of Norfolk, the earl of Rutland [Edward of York] duke of Albemarle, the earl of Kent [Thomas Holland] duke of Surrey, the earl of Huntingdon [John Holland] duke of Exeter, the countess of Norfolk the duchess of Norfolk, the earl of Somerset [John Beaufort] the marquis there,[5] [Thomas] Lord Despenser, the earl of Gloucester, [Ralph] Lord Neville, earl of Westmoreland, Lord William Scrope, earl of Wiltshire, Lord Thomas Percy steward of the king and earl of Worcester.[6] Then the king changed his arms by adding to his shield the arms of St Edward, king and confessor.

---

1   Warwick was sentenced to exile 'outside the kingdom'; he was held in the castle on Man. According to Adam Usk he was granted 500 marks for the term of his life but the sum was never paid and he was deprived of everything even down to his shoe straps (*Usk*, pp. 34–5).
2   Gloucester had been committed to the custody of Thomas Mowbray, earl of Nottingham at Calais, where Mowbray was captain. Mowbray was ordered to produce the duke for trial on 21 September but three days later he reported that the prisoner was dead. Rumours of the duke's death had circulated since August, but one of the king's justices, Sir William Rickhill had interviewed him at Calais on 8 September in an attempt to extract a confession. The account of his murder only emerged after Richard's deposition, when John Hall, Mowbray's valet admitted to having smothered the duke.
3   Parliament was adjourned to meet again on 27 January.
4   Parliament resumed for only four days, being adjourned again on 31 January. As Walsingham describes, a parliamentary committee was appointed to transact outstanding business.
5   Beaufort was created marquis of Dorset.
6   Walsingham's chronology is incorrect here: these promotions were effected on 29 September, the final day of the parliamentary session at Westminster in 1397. The beneficiaries became known as the *duketti* because they were not equal to the dignity of a dukedom as they owed the promotion purely to the personal favour the king.

At this time the king bestowed a great part of the lands of the duke of Gloucester and the earls of Arundel and Warwick on his newly created dukes and earls.[1]

[Decisions of a parliament held at Shrewsbury]

In this parliament continued at Shrewsbury, with the consent of his lords the king exiled Sir John Cobham to Guernsey.[2] He also condemned Sir Reginald Cobham, as being one of the men appointed by the lords to advise and look after the king in the eleventh year of his reign, and the parliament held in that eleventh year was annulled. And in order that the decrees and judgements made in that parliament at Shrewsbury should be strong, firm and lasting, the king obtained a papal letter in which grave censure was laid down for any who presumed to contravene these statutes in any way. The king had the letter read out at St Paul's cross in London and in other famous places in the kingdom

[The king banishes the duke of Hereford and the duke of Norfolk]

About the present time, the duke of Hereford [i.e. Henry of Bolingboke] accused the duke of Norfolk [Thomas Mowbray] of speaking certain words that brought disgrace upon the king.[3] Consequently a duel was arranged for them at Coventry. When at length they entered the lists in pride and splendour, the king took matters into his own hands and had it proclaimed that the duke of Hereford had done his duty honourably. But immediately afterwards, for no legitimate reason he got the duke of Hereford banished for ten years at his command, although this was contrary to justice, the laws of knighthood and the customs of the kingdom. He also condemned the duke of Norfolk to perpetual banishment. He added the pitiless decree that nobody on pain of heavy punishment should ask or presume to beg the king to show favour towards the two dukes. All this happened a year to the day after the duke of Norfolk had got the duke of Gloucester suffocated.

[The pope interferes in the affairs of the church]

In this year the pope translated John [Buckingham], bishop of Lincoln, to the bishopric of Chester,[4] which was then vacant, and then gave the bishopric of Lincoln to Henry Beaufort, one of the sons of John, duke of Lancaster, and Katherine Swynford, out of his respect and love for the duke of Lancaster. But the veteran bishop of Lincoln was unwilling to accept this translation, and in his scorn of it took himself to Canterbury where he finished his life among the monks of Christchurch. The king's confessor, a monk from the order of Preachers [i.e. Dominicans], was translated from the bishopric of Llandaff to the bishopric of Chester.[5]

---

1 Kent was given Warwick castle and other Beauchamp estates, Huntingdon was given Arundel's Sussex estates, Thomas Percy received Arundel's estates in the Welsh marches and Rutland was granted the northern estates of the duke of Gloucester. The duke of York was also given Gloucester's Norfolk estates.

2 Cobham, aged eighty, had been one of the twelve commissioners of the realm during the appellants ascendancy. According to other accounts he was exiled to Jersey (see *Usk*, pp. 38–9).

3 The 'certain words' that passed between Hereford and Norfolk that provoked the wrath of the king remain somewhat confused, but it appears that Norfolk warned Hereford that after the deaths of the three appellants his own life was also in danger and that Surrey, Somerset, Gloucester and Wiltshire were now conspiring, with the support of the king, to seize the Lancastrian inheritance. Walsingham's colleague, the *Annales*, author is equally vague about the issue, but the author of the *Historia vitae et regni Ricardi secundi* reports an account of the dealings between them: *Trokelowe*, ed. Riley, pp. 225–6; *HVRS*, p. 149. Hereford relayed the story to his father, John of Gaunt, and Norfolk, as the source of the rumour fearing reprisals, made an abortive attempt on the life of the duke. After this he was seized and imprisoned and both he and Hereford were examined before Richard on 23 February, and again by a parliamentary committee on 19 March, after which it was decided that the two should undergo trial-by-battle at Coventry on 16 September. Such a rare occurrence was richly anticipated but Richard intervened at the eleventh hour and passed a sentence of exile on both, Hereford for ten years and given his guilt over the murder of Gloucester, Norfolk for life. Saul, *Richard II*, pp. 395–401. Shakespeare dramatised the episode: *Richard II*, Act 1, Scene 3.

4 Buckingham was compelled to resign between March and July 1398. He was not translated to 'Chester', i.e. Coventry and Lichfield, although that see was vacant. He died on 10 March 1399.

5 John Burghill was translated from Llandaff on 2 July 1398. He held Coventry and Lichfield until his death

At that time the king summoned the clergy to establish if the pope was permitted to make such arbitrary translations, just because he wished to. Instead of a direct reply, the clergy handed an appeal to the king, that he should think it proper to write to the pope and ask him to refrain from such translations for the good of the whole church in England. When the king heard this answer, he appeared to be offended by the liberties taken by the pope and swore that if the clergy continued to oppose the pope on this matter, he himself would lift up his hand to help them.

At that time a papal nuncio called Peter de Bosco, bishop of Aix, arrived in England to advise the king to allow his subjects to receive appointments from the hand of the pope and to revoke the statute published against such provisors and the writ beginning 'And so the impediment', and many similar writs. The nuncio had little success in his mission but, to make up for this, the king packed his purse with gifts of jewels of great worth and value.

During this year they found at Rome the treasure of Helena,[1] mother of the emperor Constantine, at the foot of a wall which had fallen down. The treasure itself consisted of gold coins which carried the picture of the empress with her name written in a circle. They were worth one precious stone and twenty shillings in our currency. The pope later got the Capitol and the Castel Sant' Angelo rebuilt with this treasure.

In this year in almost all the districts of England the old laurels withered but revived again later, although many had thought they would not.

[1399]

[The division of a stream presages a division in the kingdom]

In 1399, the twenty-second year of King Richard II, on the day of the circumcision of our Lord a very deep stream, which ran between the villages of Selston and Harewood near Bedford, suddenly stopped and divided into two, in such a way that its original bed stayed dry for three miles, providing a dry path for anyone who wanted it.[2] This miracle seemed to many to foretell a division of property and a rebellion from the king, things which actually happened in this year.

[The king prepares to avenge the death of the earl of March]

At this time Roger [Mortimer] earl of March was slain by the Irish in Ireland, while putting too much trust in his own valour.[3] Having learned of his death, the king decided to avenge his death in person and to subdue the Irish, paying no heed to the vast amount of hatred which had piled up for him from his own subjects and to the bitter feelings which the common people had against him. And so throughout the whole time of Lent [16 February–30 March] and then continuously up to the moment of his departure he made the greatest of preparations, extorting sums of money, demanding horses and chariots, seizing provisions for his expedition, and paying nothing for them. So he became an object of hate and loathing for his subjects.

---

in 1414. Walsingham regarded these promotions as indicative of papal interference, but there is no doubt that both candidates also represented the king's interest.

1   Flavia Iulia Helena (c.248–c.329), according to legend an innkeeper's daughter, the first consort of Constantius Chlorus, emperor of the western Roman empire (305–6), mother of Constantine the Great (272–337). She converted to Christianity under the influence of her son and undertook a pilgrimage to the Holy Land where she is said to have founded churches. She was widely revered as a saint.

2   A portent with a local flavour: the abbey of St Albans was a prominent Bedfordshire landowner and many of the monks were recruited from there.

3   Walsingham's chronology and commentary here is not wholly reliable: Mortimer was killed but the circumstances which led to Richard's second expedition to Ireland were rather different. Roger Mortimer, 4th earl of March, had been reappointed lieutenant of Ireland in April 1398, but he been in office barely three months when Richard dismissed him, apparently anxious about his loyalty. Thomas, duke of Surrey, was appointed in his place on 26 July. He made the crossing to Ireland in September and was sworn in on 7 October. His role was to prepare the way for a new royal expedition which was certainly being planned by the winter of 1398. On 1 February Richard wrote to several monasteries for horses to be used on the expedition and on 7 February writs were issued for the arrest of shipping. Richard made the crossing to Waterford on 1 June. See also Saul, *Richard II*, pp. 288–9.

[The pope asks for funds for the emperor of Constantinople against the Turks]

At the same time the bishop of Chalcedon came to England. He carried threatening letters from the pope, which asked that faithful Christians of England should make contributions from their wealth to the emperor of Constantinople, who was sore beset by the Tartars and their leader named Murad [correctly, Bayezid]. And so that the English should be made the more ready to contribute to this cause, the pope granted full remission of sins to benefactors who were truly contrite and repentant, and involved in bitter sentence of censure all who hindered those wishing to make a contribution for this purpose. The pope pointed out that although the emperor was a schismatic he was at least a Christian, and if he himself was overthrown by the infidels, destruction was imminent for the whole of Christianity. He had in mind the line of the poet, 'A fire next door involves your house as well.'[1]

At this time occurred the death of John [of Gaunt], duke of Lancaster. His body was buried in the church of St Paul's in London.[2]

[The king sentences the duke of Hereford to perpetual exile]

After the duke's death, the king decreed perpetual exile for his son, duke Henry, whom he had previously banished for ten years, revoking his public letters patent which he had formerly granted to Henry, and which stated that in Henry's absence caused by his banishment attorney-generals could take steps to obtain for him the freedom to take up any inheritance or succession which came his way at that time, and that Henry himself could postpone his homage in return for paying a reasonable fine.[3] After this change of heart, everybody saw more clearly that the king had no sincere love for the duke of Hereford, and that he had not banished him just for the quarrels which could have arisen between his household and that of the duke of Norfolk, as he had pretended, but also because it was a good opportunity of seizing the duke's property, as many had said.

About the present time there died that noble woman, Lady Margaret duchess of Norfolk.[4] Her body was buried in the church of the Friars minor [i.e. Franciscans] in London.

[The king tyrannically extorts money and oaths from his subjects[5]]

Meanwhile the king acquired, by borrowing, huge sums of money from very many lords, both temporal and spiritual, and from other people in the land. He promised faithfully in letters patent

---

1   Horace, *Epistles*, 1. 18. 24.

2   Gaunt died on 3 February 1399 at Leicester castle. It has been suggested that he was inconsolable in his last months, depressed by the exile of his son and the prospect that Richard would seize the Lancastrian inheritance as soon as he died. Given his evident fascination for Gaunt, and his early hostility towards him, Walsingham's cursory obituary is surprising, although other contemporary chroniclers were equally brief, perhaps because they were now preoccupied with the gathering storm surrounding King Richard. Gaunt died remaining loyal to the king and made generous personal bequests to him in his will, but Richard's attitude appears to have been a good deal cooler and according to Froissart he wrote to inform Charles VI of his uncle's death 'with a sort of joy': FCBuchon, iii. 332. Under the terms of his will, Gaunt's body lay unburied and unembalmed for forty days after his death and the funeral does not appear to have taken place until 16 March (Passion Sunday). The funeral cortège passed through St Albans on its way to London, where Walsingham must surely have witnessed it. See Goodman, *John of Gaunt*, pp. 166–8; Saul, *Richard II*, p. 403.

3   Just as Gaunt had feared, the writ of perpetual banishment was issued on 18 March 1399.

4   Margaret was the daughter of Thomas of Brotherton, earl of Norfolk and fifth son of Edward I. As sole heir of her father she had been styled countess of Norfolk but was created duchess on 29 September 1392. She died on 24 March 1399.

5   Despite its position in the chronicle, Walsingham's account here describes Richard's actions in the three years up to 1399. He began to exact 'forced loans' in the summer of 1397, sending out letters under the privy seal demanding loans of specific sums of money but with the name of the lender left blank so those in a position to pay might be identified. Charters were also demanded from individuals in which both their person and property was pledged to the king. It was in the aftermath of the 1397 parliament that Richard also began to compel sheriffs and other provincial officials to take new, more stringent oaths, which, amongst other conditions, enjoined them to uphold the acts of the Westminster/Shrewsbury parliament. See also *HVRS*, p. 150;

that he would repay those sums of money thus borrowed by a fixed date, but he never did subsequently return the moneys to his creditors.

In the same year he extorted by means of fear of death larger sums of money from seventeen counties of the kingdom. He placed this impost on them because they had sided with the duke of Gloucester against him, and with the earls of Arundel and Warwick etc., so that he was ready to ride against them as against public enemies. And so he received from these seventeen counties a fresh pledge of loyalty, backed up by an oath. Once this was done, he sent certain bishops with other respected men to these counties to persuade the lords spiritual and temporal and the men of moderate standing of these counties to submit to the king and to acknowledge that they themselves had been traitors by means of letters signed with their own seals. On this occasion the clergy, the common people and the temporal lords of these counties were forced to grant to the king insupportable sums of money to regain his goodwill.

And wishing, so men said, to trample on and oppress the people of his land, he sent letters patent to all the counties of England, and through terror induced every one of his subjects, temporal and spiritual, to generally provide him with oaths unheard of before which could very likely cause the final destruction of his people, and he compelled his subjects to confirm the oaths themselves by letters with the seals attached. He also forced these same subjects to affix their seals to blank sheets of paper so that whenever he wished to make attacks on them, he might have the means to attack them individually or in a body.

He also caused the sheriffs throughout the whole land to swear new, unheard of oaths that they would obey all the king's commands sent them under the great seal and the privy seal and even in letters sent under his own seal. Further, supposing these sheriffs could discover that any of their subordinates, of whatever rank, were saying or uttering, publicly or in secret, anything malicious which could result in dishonour or scandal against the person of the king, they were to imprison such subordinates, until they received some further instruction from the king. And so it happened that very many of the king's subjects were maliciously accused and charged with having said something publicly or in secret which could result in censure, scandal or dishonour for the king. They were arrested, put in prison and brought before the constable and marshal of England in the court of the knights. Nor would they be let off unless they defended and justified themselves by submitting their bodies to single combat, despite the fact that their accusers and appellants were strong, healthy young men while those thus accused were for the most part weak and feeble old men with mutilated bodies. And so there was a general fear of the likelihood of great destruction both of the kingdom and also of all the individual people in its population.

[The king departs for Ireland]

During the feast of Pentecost [18 May] the king left his kingdom, which as I have said was in a very troubled state, and sailed to Ireland with his men from Chester and with certain magnates of the land, namely the dukes of Albemarle [Edward of Langley] and Exeter [John Holland] and also many others.[1] He also took with him boys of noble birth, the sons of the dukes of Gloucester and Hereford, whose relatives he especially feared.[2] He also took with him many bishops and the abbot of Westminster [William Colchester], so that whenever he wished to hold a parliament with the assent of the eight people, as he had previously decided, the bishops would be at hand to give their own confirmation to what had been decided. He also, on his departure to Ireland, took away with him, without the consent of the estates of the land, the sacred relics in the treasuries, and also the jewels and riches of the land which of old had been stored in the vaults of the

C. M. Barron, 'The Tyranny of Richard II', *Bulletin of the Institute of Historical Research* 41 (1968), 1–18; Saul, *Richard II*, pp. 366–7, 388–91.

[1] In fact Richard crossed to Waterford on 1 June 1399. Edmund, duke of York, again remained in England as regent: Saul, *Richard II*, pp. 289–90.

[2] Among these boys was Henry of Monmouth, the future Henry V. His presence with the king on this final expedition was to have a profound affect on him and his attitude to Richard after his deposition. See below, p. 394 and n.

kingdom for the honour of its kings.[1] And when he came to Ireland, at first indeed he seemed to prosper and to hold the whip hand over his enemies.[2] But even so there was little rejoicing among his own people. They always thought the worse of him, and feared being tyrannised over by him still more heavily.

[The duke of Lancaster sails for England]

Meanwhile Henry [of Bolingbroke], once duke of Hereford but now by paternal right duke of Lancaster, who had endured his banishment with a heavy heart, but his exile and disinheritance with a much heavier one, could now see that the king was being unjust to all his subjects for the reasons stated, and so he seized the opportunity of the king's absence and decided to return to England to seek his inheritance.[3] He brought with him to England Lord Thomas Arundel, once archbishop of Canterbury, and the son and heir of the earl of Arundel, who had long since been his supporters, and set sail with a modest following, in fact consisting of no more than fifteen lances, to use the common expression, although he could have had with him a much stronger force, so great was his trust in the justice of his cause and the support of the English people. Even so he was not willing to sail straight for England and make a landing, nor to appear suddenly, but instead he showed himself to his countrymen now in one part of the kingdom, now in another, to see if men were preparing to resist him along the coast.[4]

The duke of Lancaster lands at Ravenspur and pursues the king's counsellors to Bristol

Lord Edmund [of Langley], duke of York and uncle of the king, to whom the governorship of the land had been entrusted in the absence of the king, heard that the duke of Lancaster was now at sea and ready to enter the kingdom. So he summoned the chancellor of the kingdom Lord Edmund Stafford, the bishop of Chichester, the treasurer William Scrope earl of Wiltshire, and the following knights of the king's council, John Bushy, William Bagot, Henry Green and John Russell, and asked them what should be done about this business. They replied that he should take himself from London to St Albans, and wait there for a force that would be able to resist the approach of the duke of Lancaster.[5] But the outcome showed the emptiness of this idea of theirs. For the people who came to St Albans from many quarters said vehemently that they were not willing to harm the duke of Lancaster, as they knew that he had been treated badly. Then indeed those wicked counsellors, John Bushy, William Bagot, Henry Green together with the treasurer William Scrope, when they realised that the people were now wanting to side with the duke of Lancaster, abandoned the governor of the land and the chancellor and hurriedly fled to Bristol castle.

And the duke of Lancaster, during the feast of the Translation of St Martin, landed near the place where once was the town of Ravenspur. No one tried to stop him. He was joined by the earl

---

1   Walsingham is the only authority for this, but it can be corroborated. A ruby ring valued at 1,000 marks was recovered from the custody of the abbot and convent of Westminster in 1399 apparently because Richard planned to take it with him to Ireland: Saul, *Richard II*, p. 289 and n. 61.
2   Surrey scored an early success against Art MacMurrough in which more than 150 Irish rebels were killed, but thereafter there were few engagements and little significant success.
3   Henry had been at Paris and appears to have prepared to return to England almost as soon as he received the news of his disinheritance. Archbishop Arundel and his nephew joined him from their own exile in Germany and the party made for Boulogne, apparently giving out that the duke was preparing for a pilgrimage, although his true intentions were difficult to conceal.
4   It seems Henry was determined to land where Richard's defences were weakest; an advance guard under John Pelham landed at Pevensey and took the castle, but Henry sailed northwards and landed at Ravenspur at the mouth of the Humber at the end of June: Richard, still in Ireland, received news of his landing more than a week later, on 10 July. See also Saul, *Richard II*, p. 408.
5   On 28 June, apparently unaware that Henry was about to land, York issued writs to the county sheriffs to raise forces to muster at Ware, Hertfordshire, for the defence of Richard's realm. Resistance was still envisaged on 4 July when York wrote to Richard to inform him that Lancaster had made landfall. On or around 20 July York began to lead his own force towards the west with a view to meeting Richard moving east but he was intercepted by Lancaster at Berkeley, near Gloucester, and on 27 July he made his submission to him.

of Northumberland, Lord Henry Percy and by Sir Henry Percy [i.e. Hotspur] his son, by the earl of Westmorland, Sir Ralph Neville and by other lords who feared the tyranny of the king, most of them very greatly.[1] In a short time there was assembled an army of about six thousand soldiers, who all with one accord decided first to pursue the evil counsellors of the king.[2] They quickly came to Bristol and set siege to the castle where the counsellors were prepared to resist them. And there at last the treasurer William Scrope, John Bushy and Henry Green were taken prisoner and immediately on the following day amid the shouting of the commons were beheaded. William Bagot was the only one of them who escaped, by sailing to Ireland. For he had not gone with his accomplices to Bristol, but had fled to Chester, intending to hide there.[3]

The king surrenders to the duke of Lancaster

When king Richard heard in Ireland of the duke's landing, he at once took steps to shut the sons of the dukes of Gloucester and Lancaster in Trim castle, a noted stronghold in Ireland, and sped with all haste to his ships, accompanied by the dukes of Albemarle [Edward of Langley], Exeter [John Holland] and Surrey [Thomas Holland], the bishops of London [Robert Braybroke], Lincoln [Henry Beaufort] and Carlisle [Thomas Merke], and many others, in order that he might meet the duke with his army, before Henry had collected helpers.[4]

But when he reached England and learned of the forces the duke had amassed, he lost heart for fighting, being certain that the people assembled to fight him would sooner want to die than to yield, out of their hate and fear of him. So he sent away his household, telling them through his steward Lord Thomas Percy to keep themselves for better times. Then the king himself, seeking the side roads, for many days went now here, now there, but always with the duke and his army in pursuit.[5] In the end, when there was no hope of fleeing further, he took up his position in Conway castle, and asked to have a meeting with Lord Thomas Arundel, whom he had deposed from the archbishopric of Canterbury, and with the earl of Northumberland. He informed them that he was willing to give up his kingdom, if he was given a livelihood suitable to his position and the sure promise of safety of life for eight persons whom he wished to name.[6]

---

1   Henry was joined by the Percies at Doncaster on or around 16 July. Contemporary commentators regarded the defection of the Percies as decisive in Richard's eventual deposition. The *Scotichronicon* called the deposition 'the conspiracy of the three Henries', i.e. Henry of Lancaster and Henry Percy, father and son: *Scotichronicon*, viii. 20–1. The exact terms of their submission to the duke would be disputed for almost a decade after the event and became the root cause of the Percies' eventual rebellion. See below, pp. 326–9, 359–60.

2   Walsingham's estimate is excessive but the exact size of Henry's force is difficult to determine: it has been suggested that at Ravenspur he had no more than sixty followers: Saul, *Richard II*, p. 408.

3   Henry entered Bristol on 28 July. Bushy, Green and Bagot were executed the following day: Bagot did not escape as Walsingham suggests here, although other authorities (eg. the *Scotichronicon*) report the same story and it was reiterated even in Shakespeare's *Richard II*: Act 2 Scene 2, Act 3 Scene 1, Act 4 Scene 1.

4   Contrary to Walsingham's account, Richard did not hurry to return and it was almost a fortnight after he received news of Lancaster's return (24 July) that he himself landed in mid-Wales, having sent an advanced guard under Salisbury a week before. See also Saul, *Richard II*, p. 411.

5   At first Richard planned to advance south and west into the marches to meet Lancaster head on, but as the strength and success of his enemy became clear he decided instead to escape northwards where Salisbury was already established. According to the account of the Dieulacres chronicler, Richard fled from his own camp accompanied by only fifteen followers, amongst whom were probably Exeter, Surrey, Gloucester, and the bishops of Carlisle, Lincoln and St David's. In this account, Richard did not dismiss his household, as Walsingham suggests, but they dispersed in bitterness once the betrayal had been discovered. Meanwhile, Richard moved northwards, reaching Conway in early August. Henry followed him north and entered Chester on 9 August: See also Saul, *Richard II*, pp. 411–12.

6   In common with all other pro-Lancastrian accounts, Walsingham maintains that Richard willingly resigned the crown. Other accounts suggest a more complex chain of events. Richard sent Exeter and Surrey to Henry at Chester to negotiate with him but the two were immediately arrested. Henry then dispatched his own envoy, Henry Percy, earl of Northumberland to approach Richard at Conway and begin talks. Northumberland reached Conway on 12 August: Walsingham claims that Archbishop Arundel accompanied him but there is no evidence to support this; Northumberland may have been alone. It appears that the terms Henry offered through his envoy were modest, at least at this stage, that a parliament be summoned in which

When these concessions had been granted and confirmed, he came to Flint castle. There he had a brief meeting with the duke of Lancaster, but straightaway that night they mounted their horses and came to Chester castle, attended by the very numerous army following the duke. And on the twentieth day of the month of August and the forty-seventh day after the arrival of the duke in England the king gave himself up to the duke. The treasure of the king, his horses and other valuables and all the equipment of his house came into the hands of the duke, and the supporters of the king throughout Wales and Northumberland, both magnates, lords and lesser men were all despoiled of their wealth. Then the king was led to London, to be kept in the Tower until the next parliament was held.

King Richard resigns the crown

Meanwhile writs were sent in the name of King Richard to the persons in the land who had a legal obligation to attend parliament, bidding them assemble in London at Westminster on the day after the feast of St Michael [29 September]. And on the feast day of St Michael itself in the Tower of London the following people assembled:[1] the archbishop of Canterbury, Thomas Arundel, the archbishop of York, Richard Scrope, and John [Trefnant], the bishop of Hereford;[2] also Henry, duke of Lancaster, Henry [Percy], earl of Northumberland, Ralph [Neville], earl of Westmorland, Lord Hugh Burnell, Lord Thomas Berkeley,[3] the abbot of Westminster [William Colchester], the prior of Canterbury [Thomas Chillenden], and the Lords Roos,[4] Willoughby,[5] Abergavenny,[6] [Sir William] Thirning, and J. Makeham, justiciars; T. Stoke and John Burbage, doctors of the laws; T[homas] Erpingham[7] and T[homas] Grey,[8] knights; William Ferriby and Dionysius Lopham, public notaries. To all these the king clearly read out with seeming gladness and a cheerful countenance the form of his deposition. He absolved his subjects from their oaths of loyalty and homage, released them from all other oaths of any kind, renounced and quit his royal powers and took an oath. And as he said such things, he held up the document as he read it and signed it with his own hand. All this is described more fully in the actual form of resignation. And he at once added that he wished the duke of Lancaster to succeed him in the kingdom; but that as this was not in his own power, he appointed as proctors for that occasion the archbishop of York and the bishop of Hereford, so that they might declare and publish to all estates of the kingdom this cession and renunciation which he had made.

On the following day [30 September] in the great court at Westminster, the king's chair then being empty and without anyone presiding, the proctors of king Richard, namely the archbishop of York [Richard Scope] and the bishop of Hereford [John Trefnant], there publicly read out the

his own claim to the Lancastrian inheritance be confirmed and in which the *duketti* be tried for treason. Richard held his position for three days but on 15 August announced his agreement and surrendered himself into Henry's custody. There is no evidence that, as Walsingham claims here, Richard resigned the crown at Conway, although he must have known that such a resignation would soon be demanded of him: Saul, *Richard II*, pp. 412–13, 418–19, 421–3.

1   It was now that Richard was compelled to resign the crown. In Lancastrian interests, Walsingham again suggests that it was a smoother, swifter process than was the reality. The delegation visited Richard twice on 28 and 29 September and each time failed to secure an unconditional resignation from him. It was only after Henry approached him in person on the evening of 29th September that he finally capitulated: Saul, *Richard II*, pp. 421–3.
2   Bishop from 1389 until his death in 1404.
3   Thomas, lord Berkeley (1353–1417).
4   William, lord Roos (c.1369–1414).
5   William, 5th baron Willoughby (d.1409).
6   William Beauchamp, lord (A)bergavenny (d.1411).
7   Thomas Erpingham (1355–1428) a veteran of the French war, appointed constable of Dover Castle in 1399. He assisted King Henry in putting down the rebellion of 1400.
8   Sir Thomas Grey of Heaton, Northumberland (d. 1415) a loyal supporter of Henry IV who subsequently conspired against his son. His brother John (d. 1421) served with distinction in Henry V's Normandy campaign. See also below, pp. 423, 427.

lants should grant liveries or badges, or keep a retinue of men apart from the domestic officials in their houses and the outside officials to look after their guest houses, lands and possessions and the other domestic officials, as would be reasonable and suitable for persons of such status.

'And further the lords temporal, with the assent of the king, judge and decree that those said lords, the duke of Albemarle and the others, or any single one of them, are to be under the penalty of treachery and held and imprisoned as traitors, if they ever support Richard, who was king and has been deposed, by bringing him counsel, help or comfort contrary to the deposition, judgement, ordinance or declaration touching the person of the said Richard made in the present parliament. And also, because there has been and still is great clamour and uproar among the commons, because the servants of the said lords oppressed and harmed the common people and extorted huge sums from them for the sake of maintaining their forces, the lords in this present parliament, with the assent of the king, judge and decree that proclamations etc. should be made, stating that if any one wishes to complain about the accused lords or about any person from their households, who is still with them or was with them at those times, that is complaints about the extortions and about the injuries and injustices inflicted upon them by these men, he is to come forward and register his complaint and he is to then receive compensation.'

After this judgement had been given against the lords, there arose a very great murmuring among the common people against the king and the archbishop of Canterbury, the earl of Northumberland and the other members of the king's council, because they had preserved the lives of men, whom the people regarded as the greatest of criminals and most deserving of death.

Envoys sent abroad. An invasion by the Scots

So that the king might show to all the lands that encircled England by what right and title and with what support be had received the crown of the realm, he sent as ambassadors to the Roman Curia the bishop of Hereford Master John Trefnant,[1] the knight John Cheyne[2] and the esquire John Cheyne. To France he sent the bishop of Durham, Master Walter Skirlaw, and the earl of Worcester, Lord Thomas Percy. To Spain he sent the bishop of St Asaph, Master John Trevor,[3] and the knight Sir William Parr.[4] To Germany he sent the bishop of Bangor,[5] with others whose names I do not know.

During the time of the parliament the Scots seized the opportunity provided by the absence of the northern lords and by a great pestilence which was then sweeping through the north of England to invade those parts. They captured and held for a time the castle of Wark which had been assigned to the care of the knight Sir Thomas Grey [of Heaton], who was then present in the parliament to look after the interests of his people. In the end the Scots despoiled and totally destroyed the castle, and did much other damage in the land.[6]

Deaths of Thomas Mowbray and the duchess of Gloucester

Thomas Mowbray, once duke of Norfolk, died in the land of his exile.[7] His death would have been deservedly mourned by the whole kingdom, if he had refused to give any consent to the murder of the duke of Gloucester.

---

[1]   Trefnant held the see from 1389 until his death in 1404.
[2]   Cheyne (d.1414) passed much of his career in diplomatic service.
[3]   Trevor held the see from 1394 until 1404 when he was deprived for his support for Glyn Dŵr. He died after 1410.
[4]   Parr (c.1350–1404) a Lancashire knight in the service of John of Gaunt.
[5]   Perhaps Richard Young who had been translated to the see in December 1398 but did not receive the temporalities until 1400.
[6]   Warkworth was one of a chain of Percy castles. Walsingham is the only authority to record this attack; the *Scotichronicon* reports only that the Scots settlements on the borders were constantly harried by the English in the months after Richard's deposition: *Scotichronicon*, viii. 32–3.
[7]   i.e. Ireland. Mowbray died of plague in Venice on 22 September 1399.

There also died in this year the lady duchess of Gloucester [Eleanor].[1] She, after a very unlucky omen, had lost her son and heir called Humphrey. He was taken from her by the pestilence, after his return from Spain.[2]

Flagellants in Italy[3]

During this time in Rome statues of the crucified Christ and the blessed virgin Mary sweated a bloody liquid. At the same time throughout almost the whole of Italy noblemen and commoners, affected by a novel form of worship, dressed themselves in clothes of linen with red crosses embroidered on them. Carrying crosses in their hands and bearing banners and with a statue of the Crucified carried before them, they went on procession. Day and night they halted at stations for worship, where they bared their bodies right down to the navel and flagellated themselves, all the while singing holy songs in Italian and in Latin, but their favourite which they sang with especial devotion was

> Sadly stood his mother
> Weeping at the cross
> On which hung her son

and time after time they cried aloud in their own tongue for pity and peace. There were 40,000 in one company, 20,000 in another and also in another 10,000. As soon as one company had finished its devotions at Rome, another would then take its place and do exactly the same as the first one. And during the time of their journeying they did not sleep on beds, they abstained from meat and milk dishes, and generally fasted on the sabbath.

[1400]

In 1400 the earls of Kent [Thomas Holland], Salisbury [John Montagu] and Huntingdon [John Holland], showing no gratitude to the king for his help in saving their lives contrary to the wishes of all the commons and many of the nobles of the realm,[4] met together for criminal purposes and in meetings held in different places conspired and planned to make a sudden attack on the king in Windsor castle under the pretence of playing Christmas games and cruelly kill the king together with his sons.[5] Then, seeking out King Richard, they would restore him to his kingdom and through such wicked deeds recover the titles and possessions of their dukedoms, of which they had been deprived. But the king luckily got wind of the plots which they had concocted, withdrew from Windsor and hurriedly returned to London.[6]

---

1   Eleanor, duchess of Gloucester died on 3 October 1399.
2   Humphrey (b.c.1381), son of Thomas of Woodstock, duke of Gloucester and Eleanor, had been imprisoned at Trim Castle in Ireland by Richard II. He was released in August 1399 under the authority of Bolingbroke but died before his return to England. The source of Walsingham's story of the plague in Spain is unclear.
3   The flagellants were one of a number of popular penitential movements that emerged briefly in Europe in the second half of the fourteenth century. Followers were to be found in both urban and rural areas and were notorious for their public spectacles of self-flagellation, often accompanied by vernacular hymn singing. Here Walsingham refers to the processions of the Bianchi that were seen in several Italian towns in 1399; the Bianchi were flagellants who wore distinctive white clothing.
4   Henry had not only saved their lives but also gone some way towards rehabilitating them: both Edward, earl of Rutland (formerly duke of Albermarle), and John, earl of Huntingdon, had been appointed to the king's council and Rutland had also been appointed justiciar of the New Forest. John Montagu, earl of Salisbury had been appointed chamberlain on 9 November 1399, barely a week after facing judgement in parliament. See also Wylie, *Henry IV*, i. 95–9.
5   The conspiracy was formed in mid-December 1399. The instigator may have been Bishop Merke, and on 17 December he met with the former dukes at a house in which he was lodging belonging to William Colchester, abbot of Westminster. Probably their plans for despatching Henry and his family were not well formed, although Usk confirms Walsingham's suggestions as to Windsor and the Christmas celebrations: *Usk*, pp. 88–9.
6   Henry was forewarned after Rutland, whose commitment to the conspiracy had wavered, had confided in

But the earls of Kent and Salisbury thought that the king was unaware of their conspiracy, and on the Sunday after the feast of the circumcision of our Lord [1 January], that is in the octave of the holy innocents [4 January], they entered Windsor as dusk fell that night to do their deed and arrived at the castle with an armed force of about four hundred men.[1] But when they discovered that the king had been forewarned of their attempt, they were very alarmed and making for the side roads they rode as quickly as possible to Sonning, a manor near Reading, where the queen [Isabella of Valois] of King Richard was then staying. The earl of Kent, accompanied by the earl of Salisbury, entered the house, and, pretending to be sad in the presence of the household of the queen who now met him, he lifted his right hand to his forehead, crossed himself and said, 'Blessings be upon you. What can have happened to cause Henry, duke of Lancaster, to flee from my face as he has done? He was always making great boasts about his energy and his military prowess.' And immediately he added, 'My lords and friends, I must tell you that Henry of Lancaster with his sons and friends was chased by me and has fled to the Tower of London. And it is my intention to go to Richard, who was, is and will be our true king, for he has now escaped from prison and lies at Pontefract with a hundred thousand soldiers to defend him.'

To make his words believed, he contemptuously took the collars, which were the devices of King Henry, from the necks of some there whom he saw bearing such devices, and said that they were not to wear such devices in the future.[2] He also took from the arms of the ladies-in-waiting the devices of the crescent moon[3] and threw them on to the ground. So having gladdened the queen though with a fabrication, the earl withdrew, making first for Wallingford and then Abingdon, and all along the way he urged the people to take up arms and join Richard, their king.

At last he arrived at Cirencester in the dead of night. The men of the town were suspicious of such a large force, and thinking that their tales were false, as indeed they were, they blocked all the entrances and exits at the house where the conspirators were staying, and when they tried to slip away unobserved in the middle of the night, the townsmen, armed with bows and arrows, would not allow them to depart. The two earls could see the danger they were faced with, and themselves hurriedly took up arms, thinking that it would be an easy matter to defeat the townsmen. So a battle was fought up and down the town from the middle of the night until nine o'clock in the morning. In the end the earls' men, tired out, surrendered to the citizens of Cirencester, earnestly beseeching the townsmen that they be saved from death until they had talked with the king. And this would have happened had not a priest in the retinue of the two earls set fire to some of the houses of the town, his intention being to give his lords the chance to escape, while the townspeople were busy with putting out the fire. But his plan failed, for the citizens left their houses, despite the danger of them being burnt down, and rushed with still greater fury to take their vengeance on the earls for the damage done by the fire. So they took the earls from the abbey and beheaded them just when dusk was falling.[4]

The earl of Salisbury, who all his life had been a supporter of the Lollards, and had belittled, despised and laughed at images, canon law and the sacraments, died, so it was said, without the sacrament of confession.[5]

his father, the duke of York. Henry had returned to London by the evening of 4 January: Wylie, *Henry IV*, i. 94, 98; Saul, *Richard II*, p. 425.

[1]   Adam Usk, the only other contemporary authority to give a detailed account, has nothing of this abortive assault on Windsor, reporting only that on hearing the plot had been discovered, Kent and Salisbury made directly for Cheshire by way of the Cotswolds: *Usk*, pp. 88–9.

[2]   The 'SS' collar which was the badge of Lancastrian allegiance. See *Gothic: Art for England, 1400–1547*, ed. R. Marks and P. Williamson (London, 2003), 71a.

[3]   The device of the crescent moon was the badge of the Percies.

[4]   This was 8 January 1400.

[5]   Writing fifteen years before, Walsingham had named the earl as one of six courtiers who had shown strong support for the teachings of Wyclif. See above p. 250.

[The fates of the other conspirators]

The earl of Huntingdon, Lord John Holland, was not with the other two earls at Windsor castle, but waited in London to see how the plot would turn out. When he learned that it had not gone as they had hoped, he tried to escape in a boat, but he was driven back by the force of a contrary wind. So he mounted a horse and rode to Essex with a knight called John Schevele [i.e. Thomas Shelley]. From there he tried to flee across the sea, but as often as he tried to set sail, he was driven back by the force of the winds, until, in complete despair of help from Neptune, he gave up this plan. Finally turning back to the land, he went to the house of a friend of his, and it was while he was sitting at dinner there with the knight mentioned above that he was taken prisoner by the common people of that place and led first to the town of Chelmsford and then to the fortress at Pleshey, so that he might be guarded there in a more secure place. But as the commons of the region gathered before Pleshey, Sir John was brought out at sunset on the feast of St Maurus [15 January] and beheaded on the spot where their lord, the duke of Gloucester, had once been arrested by King Richard. Before his execution, he miserably confessed his multiple sins against his God and his king, for he had known of the plans of the earls, but had taken no steps to warn the king.[1]

At the same time Sir Thomas Despenser, the so-called 'earl of Gloucester', had planned to flee abroad, but he was suddenly captured and taken to Bristol, where he was beheaded at the wishes of the commons.[2] Several other people in this conspiracy were taken prisoner and punished by death, some at Oxford, some in London. The clerks, John Maude[3] and William Ferriby,[4] were condemned to death in London, and finished their lives by being drawn, hanged and beheaded. The knights, Bernard Brocas[5] and John Schevele [Thomas Shelley], received the same manner of death. The bishop of Carlisle [Thomas Merke] was accused of a share in the conspiracy and condemned, but he was allowed to live by the mercy of the king.[6]

[The death and funeral of King Richard once king of England]

When Richard, once king of England, heard of these unhappy events, his mind became disturbed and he killed himself by voluntary fasting, so the rumour went.[7] He met his end in Pontefract

---

1   Walsingham's account of Huntingdon's escape is second only in its detail to his St Albans colleague the *Annales* author (*Trokelowe*, ed. Riley, p. 326). His only substantial error is in the name of Huntingdon's companion, whom Usk correctly identifies as Thomas Shelley, a Buckinghamshire knight who had long been one of the earl's retainers (*Usk*, pp. 88–9). Huntingdon was captured at Shoeburyness and taken to the castle at Pleshey then in the custody of the countess of Hereford, who, as sister of the appellant earl of Arundel and the mother-in-law of his co-appellant Gloucester, did not hesitate to pass her prisoner into the hands of the Essex commons. As Walsingham observes, Pleshey had once been the home of Gloucester in whose murder Huntingdon was implicated. See also Wylie, *Henry IV*, i. 103–4.
2   Walsingham is misinformed. Despenser had kept the rendezvous with his co-conspirators at Cirencester and had escaped the mob that killed them. He fled to Bristol where he too was lynched.
3   Correctly, Richard Maudeleyn. See *Usk*, pp. 88–9. With William Ferriby, he had been a clerk in the household of Richard II.
4   See note above.
5   Sir Bernard Brocas was a former life-retainer of Richard II.
6   The trials and executions at Oxford took place between 11 and 13 January, those at London between 4 and 5 February. Usk adds that Archbishop Arundel published a sermon to the people of London declaring the king's victory over the rebels: *Usk*, pp. 92–3.
7   Adam Usk claimed that when told that 'those in whom he had placed his hopes of restoration were now dead, his suffering deepened and he pined away', although he adds that he was also starved of food by his gaoler, Sir Thomas Swynford (*Usk*, pp. 90–1); the author of the *Historia vitae et regni Ricardi secundi* supports this story (*HVRS*, p. 166). There is no doubt that the rising of the former dukes had made Richard's death a political imperative for Henry IV and the matter appears to have been given tacit approval at a council meeting on 8 February when it was declared that were Richard to die his body should be publicly displayed, but the claim in some contemporary accounts that he was hacked to death by a group of knights is probably unfounded, and the suggestion of starvation and even a loss of hope – seems more likely; Wylie, *Henry IV*, i. 91–118; Saul, *Richard II*, pp. 425–6. In Shakespeare's *Richard II* his death was more dramatic: Act 5, Scenes 4–5.

castle on the feast of St Valentine [14 February]. After the office for the dead and after a celebration of a Mass on the next day, his body was shown in all the towns that lie between Pontefract and London, where it was arranged for it to spend the night.[1] And after a funeral service in the church of St Paul's in London, in the presence of the king and the citizens of London, the order was given for the body to be taken quickly to Langley and buried in the church of the preaching friars. And there the last office was performed by the bishop of Chester,[2] the abbot of St Albans[3] and the abbot of Waltham,[4] without the presence of magnates or a crowd of the people. Nor was there any one to invite the officials to a meal after their labour.

[The war with Scotland]

In the summer of the same year there was an epidemic which killed many people.[5] During this time the men of Lynn captured some Scottish ships, whose admiral, Sir Robert Logan, had made an agreement,[6] to destroy the English fleet, and especially those boats that fished off Aberdeen. At the same time our men ravaged some of the Orkney islands. Soon even the king gathered an army and set off for Scotland. But the Scots retreated before him and gave him no opportunity for a battle, so the king laid waste the country and went back home.[7]

[Owain Glyn Dŵr rebels against King Henry]

Meanwhile the Welsh, led by a certain Owain Glyn Dŵr, seized the opportunity of the king's absence and started a rebellion. This Owain had originally been a law apprentice at Westminster and then an esquire of the present king.[8] But a dispute arose between him and Sir Reginald Grey of Ruthin[9] over lands which Owain claimed belonged to him by hereditary right, and when Owain saw that Sir Reginald paid no attention to his reasonable claims, he began by leading a force against him, destroying his possessions by fire and putting to the sword in an exceptionally cruel and barbaric manner several members of his household.[10] And so the king decided to attack

---

1   Walsingham's colleague, the *Annales* author, records the presence of Richard's body at St Albans: *Trokelowe*, ed. Riley, p. 331.
2   Correctly, Coventry and Lichfield. John Burghill was bishop from 1398–1414.
3   John Moot, abbot of St Albans from 1396 until his death in 1401.
4   William Harleton, abbot of the Augustinian abbey at Waltham from 1400 until his death in 1420.
5   Usk also reports this 'terrible plague' that 'carried off many souls, especially amongst the children': *Usk*, pp. 98–9.
6   Sir Robert Logan of Restalrig, later captured at the battle of Homildon (Humbleton) Hill: *Scotichronicon*, viii. 49.
7   Henry planned an expedition into Scotland in the spring in retaliation for the attacks of the previous autumn, and thus to enforce upon Robert III the terms of the 1396 treaty which bound the Scots to maintain peace with England as long as it was observed also by France. There is evidence that Henry also intended to reassert the English claim to overlordship of Scotland and to demand an act of homage from Robert. In March, he received the unexpected support of George, earl Dunbar, who crossed the border to join with the earl of Northumberland on the English side of the march. Henry himself led his troops into Scotland on 17 August. He marched to Edinburgh and besieged the castle held by Archibald, earl of Douglas, and the duke of Rothsay. He commanded Robert III to pay homage on 23 August but when Robert failed to present himself he was forced to return, crossing the border again on 29 August, less than a fortnight after the expedition began. The *Scotichronicon* reports that disputes between Rothsay and the other magnates prevented the Scots from confronting the English army in the field. It also challenges Walsingham's assertion that the English army laid waste to the border country, commending Henry for his merciful moderation: *Scotichronicon*, viii. 34–7.
8   Owain Glyn Dŵr (b.c.1350), who claimed descent from the Welsh princes of Powys, held substantial lands in Berwyn, Corwen, Iscoed, Gwynionydd and Llangollen. He married the daughter of Sir David Hamner, a judge in the King's Bench, and himself trained in law in one of the London inns of court. He served with Richard II in the Scottish Campaign of 1385. For a full account of him and the revolt see R. R. Davies, *The Revolt of Owain Glyn Dŵr* (Oxford, 1995), pp. 129–52.
9   Reginald, 3rd baron Grey of Ruthin (c.1362–1440), had served Richard II as governor of Ireland in 1398 but became a member of Henry IV's council as early as 1401.
10   The origins of the dispute are obscure; it may have been a disagreement over boundaries but it may be that Grey had delayed in issuing the king's summons for service in Scotland deliberately to misrepresent him

Owain as a disturber of the peace of the land, and entered Wales with an army. But the Welsh with their leader occupied the mountains of Snowdonia and at once put themselves beyond the reach of the threatened punishment.[1] The king set fire to the area and killed some men whom chance then put in the way of their unscabbarded swords, before returning home with horses and other animals as booty.[2]

This year saw the death of Master Ralph Ergom, the bishop of Bath. Master Henry Bowet was chosen bishop in his place at the prompting of the king.[3]

At the same time the emperor of Constantinople visited England to ask for help against the Turks.[4] The king with an imposing retinue, met him at Blackheath on the feast of St Thomas [29 December], gave so great a hero an appropriate welcome and escorted him to London. He entertained him there right royally for many days, paying the expenses of the emperor's stay, and by grand presents showing respect for a person of such eminence.

The pope translated the bishop of Carlisle [Thomas Merke] to another bishopric, from which he received neither profits nor revenues.[5] Master William Strickland succeeded him as bishop of Carlisle.

[1401]

[A Statute against the Lollards and the defeat of Balsak]

In 1401 a parliament was held in London after Epiphany [6 January], in which a statute was issued about the Lollards, stating that wherever they were found promulgating their wicked doctrines they were to be seized and handed over to the bishop of the diocese. If they stubbornly persisted in defending their opinions, they were to lose their position[6] and be handed over to secular juris-diction.[7] This law was put into practice with a false priest, who was burnt at Smithfield before a large crowd.[8]

as a traitor to the new regime. Glyn Dŵr, supported by his son, brother and brother-in-law, led a force against Grey on 16 September, burned Ruthin two days later and then went on to attack other English settlements at Denbigh, Rhuddlan, Flint, Hawarden and Holt. In the course of the insurrection Glyn Dŵr was proclaimed 'Prince of Wales'. News of the rebellion reached Henry IV at Northampton on 19 September and Hugh, Lord Burnel, captain of Bridgenorth, was dispatched to quell the unrest, defeating and dispersing Glyn Dŵr's men near Welshpool on 24 September. See also Davies, *Revolt*, p. 102.
1   Henry arrived at Shrewsbury on 26 September and toured north Wales, returning to the same border town on 15 October. According to Adam Usk the rebels dispersed and Glyn Dŵr himself took to the moun-tains with only seven companions: *Usk*, pp. 100–1.
2   Henry took his troops as far as Beaumaris where he engaged Rhys the Black of Erddreiniog and returned to Shrewsbury by way of Bangor. Walsingham is the only authority to refer to this unspecified action. See also Davies, *Revolt*, p. 103.
3   Ralph Ergom had been bishop since 1388; he died on 10 April 1400. Henry Bowet was a committed servant of the Lancastrian cause who had joined Henry in exile in 1399. He was translated to York in 1407. See below, p. 351.
4   Emperor Manuel Palaiologos II (1391–1425) followed the example of his father John V and toured Western Europe between 1400 and 1403 in search of support for another crusade against the Turks after the disaster of Nicopolis in 1396. He arrived in England on 11 December and was met by Henry at Blackheath on 21 December, as Usk reports: *Usk*, p. 119.
5   Merke was condemned to death but since the pope failed to issue a formal deprivation the sentence was commuted. On 28 November 1400 Boniface IX translated him to the titular see of Salmas in Asia Minor. He received a conditional pardon from the crown in June 1401 and was presented to the prebend of Masham in Yorkshire and also served as assistant bishop in the diocese of Salisbury. Strickland was presented to the see on 6 December 1399 and consecrated on 15 August 1400. See also Wylie, *Henry IV*, ii. 70.
6   i.e. their benefit of clergy which protected them from capital punishment.
7   Parliament met from 20 January until 10 March, *RP*, iii. 454. The statute concerning Lollardy was *De heretico comburendo*. It was promulgated at the petition of the clergy, who were meeting in convocation at the same time as this parliament, and it empowered bishops to arrest anyone suspected of unlicensed preaching; they were to proceed against them within three months and if they proved implacable they were to be surren-dered to the officers of the crown to be executed. See also Wylie, *Henry IV*, i. 186, 189; Hudson, *Premature Ref-ormation*, pp. 41, 115, 118.
8   This was William Sawtry, who had been arrested and examined in convocation (on 23 February) before

The king of Letto slew in battle Balsak the son of the famous Bazajet, nicknamed 'the marvel', and destroyed Jerusalem and the country round about. And because he had defeated him unexpectedly through the grace of God, he converted to the Christian faith with sixty thousand men of his religion.[1] The emperor of Constantinople [Marvel II] was greatly pleased when he heard this news and he left England, honoured by the king with precious gifts.[2]

On 8 April in this year came the death of Sir Thomas Beauchamp, earl of Warwick, who had experienced cruel misfortune in the reign of King Richard.[3]

In the same year master John[4] Bottlesham paid his debt to nature. He had been a brother of the order of Preachers [Dominicans] and had been made bishop of Bethlehem[5] and then of Rochester [1389–1400] by Pope Urban [VI].[6] He was succeeded by another John Bottlesham, a priest of the household of the lord of Canterbury.[7]

During this present period of stable peace between the kingdoms, Isabella, once queen of England, when all necessary preparations for her departure had been made, went back to her father and her country of France. She was not yet twelve years old.[8]

At this time Owain Glyn Dŵr with his Welshmen inflicted heavy damage on the English.[9]

The king was about to go to bed one night, when, under the protection of God, he escaped from a deadly peril. For by the contrivance of a traitor there had been placed under his bedclothes a three-pronged piece of iron. The three prongs were long, thin and rounded with very sharp points sticking out from them at intervals. It was such a cunning device that once the king had lain down and pressed down on the bedcovering with the weight of his body, he could have been wounded by these prongs or perhaps killed. But, by the will of God, the king luckily felt the deadly instrument and avoided the danger.[10]

[1402]

[The defeat of Sir Reginald Grey by Owain Glyn Dŵr]

In the March of 1402 a comet was seen. It was first observed shooting out its flames in between the Great Bear and the Maiden, that is, in the Circinus. Finally it transferred its flaming hair to the north of England. Perhaps it foretold the human blood that would later be spilt in the regions of Wales and Northumberland.[11]

De heretico comburendo was passed, but in anticipation of its terms, Henry IV order him to be surrendered to the city authorities in London to be burned. See also *Fasciculi zizanniorum*, ed. Shirley, pp. 408–11.

1   This is a garbled report of Timur's first campaign in Asia Minor, news of which reached England in 1401; Adam Usk includes a similar note in his chronicle: *Usk*, pp. 130–1 and n. There was no attack on Jerusalem at this time.

2   Manuel II departed at the end of February after a two-month stay in England.

3   See above, pp. 301–2.

4   Correctly, William. He died in February 1400.

5   A titular see.

6   Bottlesham had served as bishop of Llandaff from 1386–89 before being translated to Rochester.

7   John Bottlesham was Archbishop Arundel's chancellor.

8   Following an agreement negotiated at Leulingham, Isabella returned to France on 28 July accompanied by Thomas Percy, earl of Worcester, and was surrendered to her family on 31 July. She was given an escort of 500 men and the cost of the expedition was £8,242, 10d. According to Usk, she left London 'dressed in black and scowling with deep hatred at King Henry': *Usk*, pp. 132–3.

9   Adam Usk, who provides a more detailed description of the Glyn Dŵr rebellion, reports that 'all this summer [Glyn Dŵr] severely devastated West and North Wales, taking refuge in the mountains and woodlands before emerging either to pillage or slaughter' and that in the autumn he 'continually assailed with fire and sword' the English settlements in Cardigan and Powys (*Usk*, pp. 134–5, 144–5). There was heavy damage on both sides, but Usk observes that it was the English who utterly destroyed Welshpool and the abbey of Strata Florida. See also Davies, *Revolt*, pp. 104–6.

10   Of the contemporary chroniclers, only Walsingham and his colleague the *Annales* author (*Trokelowe*, ed. Riley, p. 339) report this incident.

11   The comet was reported by many contemporary chroniclers, including the *Annales* author and the continuator of the *Eulogium historiarum*: *Trokelowe*, ed. Riley, p. 338; *Eulogium historiarum*, ed. F. C.

At that time Owain Glyn Dŵr laid waste the lands of Sir Reginald Grey. Sir Reginald met him in battle, thinking that it would be an easy matter to defeat Owain, but contrary to his expectation the dice of Mars came down the other way and he was taken prisoner and very many of his men killed. This disaster raised the Welsh to new heights of pride and increased their arrogance.[1]

[Plots against the King][2]

During the feast of Pentecost [14 May] certain people conspired to kill the king. They declared that King Richard was alive and that he would speedily come out of hiding and suitably reward those who had stayed faithful to him. Fear of this conspiracy vanished in part when a priest was captured at Ware [Hertfordshire] who had written a list of the names of the many people who had planned this disturbance or supported it. For just out of his own head he had written down the names of very many people who had had absolutely no part in this plot, as later became clear from the priest's own confession. For when he was asked if he knew certain persons standing before him whose names were on the list, he replied that he did not. And when he was asked why he had put them on the list, he said it was because he thought they wanted to make an attempt on the king's life if they could find accomplices, seeing that they had once received riches and promotion from King Richard. On this occasion the very many people who had been suspected were set free and the priest was drawn and hanged.

Soon afterwards, the former prior of Launde,[3] who had been deprived of his benefice and position because of maladministration during his time as prior, suffered a similar fate. This was not because he had been caught doing some treacherous action, but because he confessed that he had been privy to the evil plan but had kept completely quiet about it. This man, whose name was Walter Baldock, had once been a canon at Dunstable [Priory].[4] But at an unlucky hour he had left the cloister, gone to the court of King Richard, and had stayed there for a very long time enjoying good fortune until finally he had been appointed prior of Launde through the gift of the king.

At this time some Friars Minor [i.e. Franciscans] who under a very unlucky star had been thinking thoughts of treason were taken prisoner before they were able to proceed with their plot. One of them was asked what he would wish to do if King Richard was still alive and was there before him, and he stoutly replied that he would want to fight for him even to the death against any opponent whatever. So sentence was passed against him, and he was drawn and hanged wearing the habit of his order.[5] But his brothers, who could not endure such a disgrace, obtained permission to give the body of the dead man the last rites that were its due.

Also hanged at this time was the knight called Roger Clarendon, who was said to have been a bastard son of the noble Prince Edward, son of King Edward III.[6] His squire and valet were hanged together with him. When accused of treachery, they had been unable to clear themselves.

At Danbury in Essex at the hour of vespers on the feast of Corpus Christi [2 June] there was an appearance of the devil in the likeness of one of the Friars Minor. His entry into the church and his outrageous ravings struck indescribable terror into the parishioners. And at the same hour

---

Hingeston, 3 vols., Rolls Series, 9 (1858–63), iii. 389. Adam Usk saw it while travelling between Germany and Italy and he, given his circumstances, preferred to see it as a portent of the imminent death of the duke of Milan: *Usk*, pp. 154–7.

1 Grey was defeated and captured in April 1402. Glyn Dŵr demanded a ransom of between 6–10,000 marks that was not paid until the end of the year. See Davies, *Revolt*, p. 107.

2 These conspiracies are reported by all of the contemporary authorities, although characteristically Walsingham gives an extended and somewhat embroidered coverage. Walsingham presents them as if they were independent plots, but Baldock, Clarendon and the friars appear to have been partners in crime. This is the implication of Usk's report (*Usk*, pp. 174–5). Usk records eleven friars involved in the rebellion although the continuation of the *Eulogium*, which is the total number Walsingham mentions here: *Eulogium*, ed. Hingeston, iii. 389. See also his St Albans colleague in the *Annales, Trokelowe*, ed. Riley, pp. 339–40.

3 The Augustinian priory of Launde, Leicestershire.

4 From Walsingham's point of view he had local connections and was perhaps known to the community at St Albans.

5 Reputedly this was the first English Franciscan to be executed for treason.

6 Sir Roger Clarendon was the illegitimate son of Edward the Black Prince. See Wylie, *Henry IV*, i. 270.

there was a violent storm with dreadful thunder and flashes of lightning and shining globes of light, and the roof of the whole church was smashed and the middle of the chancel destroyed and scattered.

Some days later eight Friars Minor were taken prisoner and shamefully brought before a public court. After examination there, they were found guilty of conspiring against the king and were drawn, hanged and beheaded in London.

At that time Owain Glyn Dŵr and his band of Welshmen, bent on their usual raids, roused to arms almost the whole militia of the county of Herefordshire. And when the men of the county had assembled, [Sir] Edmund Mortimer offered himself as their leader. But when it came to the battle, through treachery Edmund was taken prisoner and the others defeated, with more than a thousand of our own men being killed. And then was perpetrated a crime never heard of before. For after the battle the Welsh women cut off the genitalia of the dead, put the member of each dead man in his mouth, and hung his testicles from his chin. They also cut off their noses and stuck them up their arses. Nor did they allow the bodies of the dead to be commended to God with the last rites of burial until a huge sum of money had been paid.[1]

[A daughter of King Henry marries the son of the emperor]

In this year the king sent his daughter with an imposing retinue to Cologne. There she was met by the son of the emperor, with an escort befitting the fame of such a high position and enabling him to meet so splendid a maid on equal terms. He was but a lad, but he took the girl to wife according to the custom of the region.[2]

[An English army is driven from Wales by the arts of magic]

About the feast of the assumption of St Mary [15 August] the king of England assembled his armies and set off for Wales in pursuit of Owain Glyn Dŵr.[3] But all this din of weapons did him no good, for the Welshman withdrew into his favourite hiding places. In fact, so it was thought, Owain with his arts of magic almost destroyed the king and the army he was leading, for it was believed that with devilish skill the Welshman aroused storms of rain and snow and hail. Indeed on the eve of the nativity of St Mary [8 September] the king had pitched his tents in a pleasant spot, and was looking forward to a good night's sleep with no alarms, when suddenly at the very start of the night the winds blew and there were such heavy storms of rain that they knocked over the king's tent and by their mighty force dislodged the king's spear so that it stuck in his armour. And that would have been the last night of the king, if he had not gone to bed wearing his armour. Nor could the English, experienced campaigners though they were, remember ever having been

[1] Following the defeat and capture of Grey, Glyn Dŵr struck a greater blow against Henry IV in his defeat and capture of Edmund Mortimer (b. c.1376), youngest son of Edmund, 3rd earl of March, and a claimant to the English throne. Mortimer was seized at Bryn Glas or Pilleth, near Knighton, on the Welsh border with Herefordshire on 22 June. The English forces suffered heavy losses; Usk estimated 8,000 dead in total although he does not corroborate Walsingham's claims as to the disfiguring of the bodies (*Usk*, pp. 158–9). Walsingham was probably wrong to suggest that Mortimer willingly capitulated to Glyn Dŵr; it was the fact that the Welsh archers within Mortimer's forces turned their weapons on their English colleagues that was decisive. It was only after Henry IV made no attempt to free Mortimer that he sided with Glyn Dŵr and married his daughter, Catherine, in December 1402. See also Davies, *Revolt*, p. 107.
[2] Walsingham's chronology is incorrect here: Blanche (d.1406), the elder daughter of Henry IV, was escorted to Germany on 27 April 1401 to conclude a marriage with Louis, Count Palatine of Bavaria and the Rhineland, son of Rupert III, the recently elected king of the Romans. The marriage was at Heidelberg on 6 July. See also Wylie, *Henry IV*, i. 202, 252–6. Walsingham's comment 'so splendid a maid on equal terms' requires reading 'nec impar erat' and not 'nec par erat' as printed in *Historia Anglicana*, ed. Riley, ii. 250.
[3] After his successes in the spring, Glyn Dŵr had driven southwards threatening the marches and South Wales; Adam Usk reports that abortive assaults were made on the castles of Carleon, Newport and Usk. Henry's response was to lead substantial forces across the border, advancing in three divisions simultaneously from Chester, Shrewsbury and Hereford. But he was unable to engage Glyn Dŵr who disappeared into the mountains as Walsingham suggests here. His return 'bootless . . . and weather beaten' recalls Shakespeare, *Henry IV*, part 1, Act 3, Scene 1. See also *Usk*, pp. 160–3; Davies, *Revolt*, p. 108.

so harassed and so exposed to danger on any expedition. There were many of them, if it is right to believe this, who said that these misfortunes had been contrived against the king by the arts of the Friars Minor [Franciscans], who were said to favour the Welsh side. But men who had taken vows to observe so holy a rule should not be suspected of such intimate hobnobbing with evil spirits or of putting on their glorious record a stain that could never afterwards be wiped out. Anyway the king, a victim of circumstances, went back to England after burning and looting the countryside.[1]

[The English archers defeat the Scots at the battle of Homildon Hill]

At this time the Scots, driven by their usual arrogance, carried out a very hostile invasion of England.[2] They of course thought that all the lords from north of the Humber were detained in Wales obeying the king's orders. But the earl of Northumberland, Henry Percy, and his son Henry [Hotspur], and [George] the earl of Dunbar, who long since had left the Scots and pledged his loyalty to the king of England,[3] suddenly opposed the Scots with an army of soldiers and a band of archers, when the Scots, after looting and burning the land, were wanting to go back home. This sudden blocking of their route home meant that the Scots were forced to halt and choose ground for battle.

So they chose a hill near the town of Wooler called Homildon hill,[4] and took up position on it with their armed men and archers. When our men saw this, they left the road on which they had blocked the Scottish retreat, and climbed up a hill opposite the enemy. And straightaway our archers, who were positioned in the valley, shot arrows into the Scottish ranks so that they might somehow provoke them to come down from their hill. And the Scottish archers opposite were shooting arrows into our ranks with all their might, but when they felt the density of the rain-storm of arrows from our side, they ran away. The [Archibald, 4th] Earl Douglas,[5] the Scottish general, saw his men running away and not wishing to be seen to be a coward himself, as he was their commander-in-chief, he picked up his spear and with a crowd of his own men bravely made his way down the hill, having great confidence in his own armour and that of his men which they had now been working on and improving for three years, and tried to make an attack on the English archers.

But when they saw him coming, our archers, though retreating, courageously shot such a powerful, dense storm of arrows that they went right in through the armour of the enemy, pene-trating helmets, going through swords, splitting spears in two and easily piercing defensive equip-ment of any kind. The Earl Douglas himself was pierced with five wounds, receiving no protection from his expensive armour. The remaining Scottish infantry who had not yet come down from the hill, turned tail and made their escape from the flying arrows. But their flight did them no good, for our archers pursued them and forced them to surrender out of fear of the death-bringing darts. The Earl Douglas was also taken prisoner, as were many of those who had run away, though many of them were drowned in the fast flowing river Tweed, as they did not know the crossing places. The number of those drowned was said to be five hundred. In this battle no blow was inflicted on the enemy by any lord, knight or esquire. God omnipotent miraculously

---

1   Not for the first time Walsingham worked anti-mendicant polemic into his narrative. Usk reports that Henry seized 'an enormous booty in animals': *Usk*, pp. 162–3.
2   This was the culmination of raids that had disturbed the borders since 1399. According to the *Scotichronicon*, the Scottish magnates mounted a campaign in June 1402 'to attack the English in warlike raids'. They advanced into Northumbria but were repelled by the combined forces of Henry Percy, earl of Northumberland and George, earl Dunbar at the battle of Nisbet Moor on 22 June. Then Archibald, earl Douglas, and Albany's son Murdach sought revenge and launched a second raid in late summer which pil-laged and plundered as far as Newcastle before they began their return. Percy, in pursuit, succeeded in over-taking them at Milfield forcing them into a pitched battle at Homildon (Humbleton) Hill on 14 September. The Scots army was devastated by Percy's archers and many of the Scots magnates were killed or captured: *Scotichronicon*, viii. 42–5 (Nisbet), 44–9 (Humbleton). See also Wylie, *Henry IV*, i. 258–305.
3   See above, p. 318 and n.
4   Correctly, Humbleton, Northumbria.
5   Son of Archibald 'the Grim', 3rd earl of Douglas, he lived c.1369–1424.

gave the whole victory to the English archers alone, with the noblemen and the armed knights reduced to the status of non-participating spectators.

On that day the flower of Scottish knighthood was taken into captivity, for besides Earl Douglas, Murdoch earl of Fife,[1] the eldest son of the duke of Albany [Robert Stewart] and the heir apparent to the Scottish throne, was taken prisoner, and a similar fate befell the earls of Moray,[2] Angus[3] and Orkney,[4] and the barons Montgomery,[5] Erskine[6] and Graham,[7] together with many other knights, numbering about eighty, and leaving out the esquires and valets, whose numbers I do not know.[8] In this battle Baron Gordon and Baron John Swinton were killed. They had betrayed both kingdoms in turn.[9] The battle was fought on the day of the raising of the Holy Cross [i.e. 14 September].

[Sir Lewis Clifford informs against the Lollards]

At that time the Lollards taught accursed doctrines, doing it secretly for fear of the laws. The doctrines were as follows.

1. The seven sacraments are nothing but dead letters, and have no validity in the form in which they are used by the church.
2. Chastity and the priesthood are not states approved by God. The best state is that of marriage, and this has been ordained by God. And so if all virgins, priests and monks wish to be saved, it is altogether necessary that they are married, or wishing and planning to get married. Otherwise they are murderers and destroy the holy seed, from which could spring the second Trinity, and thus limit the number both of the saved and the damned.
3. If a man and a woman come together, and both wish to be married, the wish itself is sufficient to make it a marriage, without any extra obedience being made to the church. And so, according to the Lollards, more people are married than we think.
4. The church is nothing but the synagogue of Satan. So the Lollards refuse to go there to worship the lord or to receive any sacrament, and especially the sacrament of the altar. Because, so they assert, it is nothing but a mouthful of dead bread, and a the tower or pinnacle of the Antichrist.
5. If a boy is now born to them, he is not to be baptised by the hands of the priests in church, because that boy is a second Trinity, unspotted by sin, and worse off if he comes into their hands.
6. We do not keep a sanctified or holy day, as there is no one Lord's day, but on each day we have the same freedom to work, eat and drink.
7. There is no purgatory after this life, and it is not necessary to do any more repentance for any sin, even the vilest. The only thing necessary is for the sinner to depart from his sin and repent in his heart, because, according to them, everything depends on faith. As Christ said to Mary Magdalene, 'Your faith has made you whole.'

It was the knight, Sir Lewis Clifford, a long-term follower of the Lollards, who revealed these doctrines to the archbishop of Canterbury [Thomas Arundel].[10] They had long been cloaked in

---

[1]   Murdoch Murdach (d.1425), son of Robert Stewart, 1st duke of Albany and known by the title earl of Fife until the death of his father in 1420. Governor of Scotland from 1420–24.
[2]   Thomas Dunbar, earl of Moray.
[3]   George Douglas, 1st earl of Angus (b. c.1380) contracted plague and died while still in captivity.
[4]   Henry Sinclair, 2nd earl of Orkney (d.1418).
[5]   John Montgomery of that Ilk, Lord of Ardrossan.
[6]   Sir Robert, 1st Lord Erskine of Alloa.
[7]   Sir Patrick Graham of Kincardine.
[8]   The *Scotichronicon* names another twenty captives: *Scotichronicon*, viii. 48–9. A number of the prisoners were presented to the parliament that met in October 1402, with the notable exception of the earl of Douglas, whom Northumberland refused to surrender to Henry.
[9]   Walsingham's allegation as to the treachery of Sir Adam Gordon and Sir John Swinton of that Ilk is unfounded. The *Scotichronicon* reports that the brave Swinton had 'contended intrepidly with a thousand Englishmen'. This source also records the names of a further five knights who fell in the battle: *Scotichronicon*, viii. 46–7. See also Wylie, *Henry IV*, i. 292.
[10]   Writing fifteen years earlier (see above, p. 250) Walsingham had identified Clifford as one of six promi-

terminological wrappings, but were now laid bare. Sir Lewis informed against them to show that he had not associated with impious men out of some ingrained wickedness of his, but out of the simplicity and ignorance of his heart. He also gave to the archbishop the names of those who were preaching these heresies.

[Ely gains full remission for benefactors during Trinity week]

At this time the people of Ely wanted to be equal with the people of Norwich, who had obtained indulgences from the apostolic see for the feast of Trinity [21 May], and with the people of Bury St Edmunds, who had obtained them for the feast of St Edmund [20 November]. And they did obtain a full remission for those truly contrite and confessing sinners who came to Ely on pilgrimage and made some benefaction to the church there during the feast of Trinity, starting from the first vespers of Trinity and continuing until the last vespers of the Thursday in Trinity week [25 May].

At this time came the death of [Sir] Edmund Mortimer.[1] He was the young man whom I said before was taken prisoner by Owain Glyn Dŵr. Either through the boredom of his awful captivity or through fear of death or for some other unknown reason, he had changed sides and declared his allegiance to Owain and enmity to the king of England by marrying Owain's daughter, although it was a very humble marriage and below the level of his high birth.[2]

As for Owain, the beginning of his birth, so the story goes, had been accompanied by dreadful omens. For on the night in which he was brought into the light, all the horses in his father's stable were found to be standing sunk in deep pools of blood right up to their shins. Many people at the time gave the omen a sinister interpretation.[3]

A parliament held in London, which started the day after the feast of St Michael [29 September] lasted for seven weeks. Its final measure was the granting of a tenth and a half tax from the clergy, a tenth tax from the townsmen and a fifteenth from the commons of the kingdom.[4]

[1403]

[King Henry marries the widow of John, duke of Brittany]

In 1403 after the feast of the purification a new queen came to England. She came from smaller Brittany to greater Britain, from a dukedom to a kingdom, from a fierce tribe to a peace-loving people, and I hope her coming was a good omen. She had formerly been married to the noble John [IV] de Montfort, duke of Brittany, to whom she had borne children of both sexes. But to Henry, king of England, whom she now married, she bore no children at all. She was magnificently crowned in London at Westminster on 26 January.[5]

---

nent courtiers who showed strong support for Wyclifism and Lollardy. See also Hudson, *Premature Reformation*, pp. 291–2.

1   Walsingham's chronology is incorrect here; Mortimer died at Harlech in 1409. For his marriage to Glyn Dŵr's daughter see above, p. 322 and n. The *Annales* author reproduces this passage verbatim but omits the reference to Mortimer's death: *Trokelowe*, ed. Riley, p. 349. See also Davies, *Revolt*, pp. 108, 179–80.

2   See above, p. 322 and n.

3   These portents are repeated by the *Annales* but not by any independent authority.

4   Parliament opened on 2 October barely a week after Henry returned from Wales: *RP*, iii. 485. In addition to their subsidy, the commons also granted the king the revenue from the wool and tunnage and poundage. It was to be the last time Henry secured such grants without the opposition of the commons.

5   The new queen was Joan of Navarre, sister of King Charles III of Navarre, and in her own right, duchess and titular regent of Brittany, the widow of Jean IV, one time ally of the English. Duke Jean had died in November 1399; Henry had visited him while still in exile earlier in the year, although contemporary reports that Brittany had colluded in the deposition were unfounded (Jones, *Ducal Brittany*, pp. 141–2). After negotiations concluded the previous year, she arrived at Falmouth on 19 January accompanied by Bishop Henry Beaufort. The negotiations for the match had been kept secret and the marriage surprised Henry's subjects. He hoped it would increase his influence on the French mainland and perhaps even pass him control of Brittany, but he was unpopular with the Bretons who raided the south-west coast of England only shortly after. See below, p. 330.

In the following summer near the towns of Bedford and Biggleswade, there were frequently seen both early in the morning and at midday monstrous shapes emerging from the woods. They were in various colours, in the likeness of warriors, and they were seen to clash in battle and initiate the fiercest of contests. And even though they could be seen from afar, when you approached they could not be found at all. So this phantasmal apparition of death time and again tricked the majority of people, who had a desire to come close to it.[1]

[Rebellion against the king by Henry Percy the younger and his uncle, the earl of Worcester]

At the same time Henry Percy, the younger, to whom fortune up to that point had always been kind, and in whom were placed the hopes of the whole people, suddenly showed himself an enemy to the king. And to the general astonishment he was joined by Sir Thomas Percy, earl of Worcester, his uncle. Sir Thomas abruptly left the house of Prince Henry [of Monmouth], the king's eldest son, who had been put in his special care by the king, and took himself off to his nephew, increasing his forces and his determination to rebel. To give some excuse for their conspiracy, they wrote letters to all the provincial magnates, saying that the plan which they had adopted was not contrary to the allegiance and pledge of loyalty which they had given to the king, since they had gathered an army for no other reason than the safety of their persons and the better government of the country. For, so they claimed, the rents and taxes granted to the king for the safe care of the kingdom were being converted to improper uses and spent to no purpose. They further complained that owing to the vicious lies of their rivals the king had been so hostile to them that they did not dare to come into his presence in person, until the prelates and barons of the realm had made supplication to the king on their behalf, that they might be permitted face to face before the king to declare their innocence and to be legally vindicated by their equals. Many magnates therefore, on reading these letters, praised the quick perception of the rebels and lauded the loyalty that they showed towards their country.[2]

[The king answers their complaints]

But when the king heard of their disloyalty, he was greatly disturbed and considered by what means he might satisfy the commons and undo the lies which the rebels had fabricated. So he wrote to the persons to whom the conspirators had written, saying that he was completely at a loss as to how the earl of Northumberland [Henry Percy] and Henry his son had collected the material for such complaints, or rather such manifest slander, seeing that they had received a very great part of the sums granted to them by the clergy or the commons of England for the protection of the Scottish marches, as he could clearly show. He also wrote that he had understood that the earl of Northumberland and his son and the earl of Worcester [Thomas Percy] had declared to many that they did not dare because of the accusations of their rivals to come into the presence of the king, without the previous intervention of prelates and nobles, and therefore they were begging

---

[1]   These apparitions are reported by the *Annales* author (*Trokelowe*, ed. Riley, p. 360) but not by other authorities.

[2]   In the spring of 1402 Sir Henry Percy, 'Hotspur', was in Northumbria with his father and both were apparently waiting to join the king in a campaign against the Scots. But at the beginning of July Hotspur began to march south and at Chester issued a proclamation – in effect a manifesto for revolt – in which he claimed that Richard was still alive and condemned 'Henry of Lancaster' for breaking the oath that Percy alleged he had made in his presence at Doncaster in 1399, that he came to restore order to the kingdom but not to usurp the throne, and that he had compounded his crime by misappropriating the tax revenue that had been raised to pay for the recent campaigns against the Scots and the Welsh, by undermining the church with unwarranted demands for clerical subsidies, and by interfering with the independence of the sheriffs in an attempt to 'pack' parliament. Percy's claim that had Henry had pledged not to seize the throne was almost certainly unfounded, but there was some substance to his complaints about the recent subsidies and there is no doubt that Percy and his father had not been paid fully for their part in the defence of the Scottish march. As Walsingham relates, Hotspur's uncle, Thomas, earl of Worcester, now broke from the company of Prince Henry at Shrewsbury to join his nephew.

them to intervene, so that of the king's grace they might be able to come before him to defend themselves and declare their innocence. The king, therefore, had written to the earl of Northumberland etc., under the royal seal, saying that they could come before him without harm and retire in safety without experiencing danger or trickery.[1]

[Henry Percy joins Glyn Dŵr at Shrewsbury and gives out that King Richard is still alive]

But the conspirators, now that they had taken the reins off their boldness, took no notice of the gentle answer of the king but hardened themselves to rebel and hurried to Shrewsbury. They placed their hopes, so it was thought, in the help of Owain Glyn Dŵr and [Sir] Edmund Mortimer and other men of Cheshire and Wales.[2] But when the king saw the obstinate wickedness of the younger Henry, for his father had not left the boundaries of his own land, he decided that he should speedily give battle to the son and his uncle, Lord Thomas Percy, before they had collected a stronger army. Indeed they and their accomplices had got it published throughout the land that King Richard was alive and with their army and that it was in his name and for his cause that they had taken up arms against the king. And if men wished to see Richard without delay, they were to come equipped with arms and in their camp at Chester they would without fail see their king. Although this announcement was a lie, it roused varying emotions in the minds of many, and caused the majority to waver, so that they did not know which side it was safer to support. And indeed many felt affection for King Richard, especially those who once had been members of his household and had been awarded fiefs and other gifts by him.

King Henry carefully noted all this, and as he was a brave and bold fighter, he gathered as many troops as he could. He was especially urged to do this by the earl of Dunbar [George], a Scot, who advised him to avoid all reasons for delay and reminded him of the lines of Lucan:

> Avoid delay, it always hinders plans.
> The foe now fears, his strength not yet amassed.[3]

The king did as the Scot advised him, and unexpectedly came to the place where the rebels were exhibiting their madness.[4] But Henry Percy, suddenly seeing the king's banners, as he was now pressing on with the attempt to take the town of Shrewsbury, at once ceased from his attack on the townsmen and said to his men, 'We must instead give up what we have begun, and turn our weapons against those who come against us. You see for certain the royal standard, and we do not have the time to look for a hiding place, even if we wanted to. So be of good courage. Stand your ground, as this day will either advance us all, if we win, or free us from high hopes of rule, if we lose. For it is fairer to fall in war for our country than to be put to death after the battle by the sentence of our enemy.'

[The lying answer of Lord Thomas Percy brings on the battle of Shrewsbury]

Those who followed Henry Percy, about fourteen thousand of the finest men, at once acceded to his wish and promised that they would stand side by side with Henry until their last breath. Now

---

1   Henry learned of the conspiracy as he marched north to join Northumberland in the Scottish campaign, probably from George, Earl Dunbar, on 12 or 13 July. He diverted from Derby to Burton on Trent from where he sent letters to the council to raise troops against the rebels. There is no evidence to corroborate Walsingham's claim that he also sent letters to each of the Percies, although he was willing to negotiate terms with them even at the point of battle, as reported below. See also Wylie, *Henry IV*, i. 351–8.
2   Hotspur reached Shrewsbury on or around 18 July. His aim was to capture Prince Henry who was protected by only a small number of troops. How far his plans had developed beyond this point remains unclear. There appears to have been some communication with the Welsh rebels since Glyn Dŵr, who was campaigning in the south between Dryslwyn and Carmarthen, was expected to join them in the subsequent confrontation with the king. Percy's support for Mortimer reflected family ties, his wife being Mortimer's sister. See also Davies, *Revolt*, p. 112.
3   Lucan, *De bello ciuili*, i. 20.
4   Henry reached Shrewsbury by the 20 July, more rapidly than Hotspur had anticipated and rather than waiting until the following Monday to attack the rebels, he began his assault on the rebel encampment the next day, Saturday 21 July. Usk also reports that Henry acted on the advice of Dunbar: *Usk*, pp. 169–71.

they had previously taken up for themselves the better position, and the king with his men took up his position opposite them. And while the soldiers on both sides were awaiting the signal for battle, the abbot of Shrewsbury [Thomas Westbury, 1399–1426] and a clerk of the royal seal acted as envoys for the king, and offered Henry Percy peace and pardon, if he would give up his attempt. Henry was persuaded by their words to abate his rage, and he sent his uncle, Sir Thomas Percy, to accompany the envoys on their return to the king, and to give him the reasons for this great rebellion and to ask that he should right these wrongs in word and deed. And the story is that although the king made every reasonable concession and humbled himself more than was fitting for a royal person, this same Sir Thomas Percy, when he returned to his nephew, brought back the opposite answer to the one given by the king, thus embittering the young man's mind and driving him into battle even against his will.[1]

So Henry Percy's archers began the battle, and there was no place on the ground for their arrows, for they all lodged in bodies, and the men on the king's side fell like the leaves that fall in the cold weather after frost.[2] But the king's archers did their job as well and sent a dense shower of shafts into the ranks of the enemy. So on both sides men fell in great numbers, just as the apples fall in autumn, when shaken by the south wind, and many thousands fled from the place of the battle at the same time, as they thought the king had been killed by arrows. Indeed Henry Percy, the enemy commander, and earl Douglas [Archibald] the Scot, the bravest soldiers any one has ever seen, took no thought for the arrows shot by the king's side or the ranks of armed men packed close together, and roused their strength and turned their weapons against nobody but the person of the king.[3] Thinking that he was worth ten thousand of his men, they looked for him, mowing down those who stood in their way and searching for him with death-dealing spears and swords. But when [George] the earl of Dunbar saw their purpose, he led the king away from his station, a deed which on that occasion saved the king as the royal standard bearer was laid low by the raging rebels, the standard thrown to the ground and all those around it killed. Among these fell [Edmund] the earl of Stafford[4] and Sir Walter Blount, a knight of the king.[5] And the prince, the king's eldest son, whose first taste of fighting this was, was wounded in the face when hit by an arrow.[6]

Meanwhile Sir Henry Percy was at the head of his men in the battle, and without thought of danger, penetrating the enemy ranks, when he was unexpectedly killed and fell, it is not certain by whose hand. When this was realised, the rebels defending him fled, at least those who were given the chance to do so. But the earl of Douglas was captured in this battle, which made it twice in one year. Fighting against the English, he always met with bad luck. For in the first battle he was wounded in the head and lost an eye, and in the second he was wounded in the genitals and lost his smaller ball, and came under the yoke of a second captivity. Also taken prisoner was Sir Thomas Percy, earl of Worcester, the instigator of the whole rebellion, so it was said, and the cause

---

[1]   Walsingham and the *Annales* author are the only authorities to allege that Worcester misrepresented the terms Henry offered to Hotspur but the suggestion supports the contemporary view that Thomas Percy was the primary mover in the rebellion. See also *Trokelowe*, ed. Riley, pp. 366–7. Shakespeare also suggested that Percy had a powerful influence on his nephew: Henry IV, part 1, Act 4, Scene 3.
[2]   Perhaps derived from Virgil, *Aeneid*, vi. 309–10.
[3]   The *Scotichronicon* reports that Archibald Douglas 'wreaked so much slaughter that besides the others he killed with his great mace three men disguised as kings in the hope that each was the real King Henry' although he himself 'lost one testicle . . . just as earlier at Humbleton he lost one eye': *Scotichronicon*, viii. 59.
[4]   Edmund, 5th earl of Stafford (b.1378), third son of Hugh, 1st earl, and son-in-law of Thomas, duke of Gloucester (d. 1397), had served as Lieutenant for the borders of South Wales. See Wylie, *Henry IV*, i. 360, 362–3.
[5]   Blount, brother of Sir John, was an experienced campaigner who had served with both the Black Prince and Gaunt in their Iberian campaigns. He had also been one of Gaunt's executors. See Goodman, *John of Gaunt*, pp. 134–6, 210; Wylie, *Henry IV*, i. 90; iii. 302.
[6]   At first the rebels appear to have had the upper hand; in addition to Blount and Stafford, Henry also lost eight or nine other knights including several of those who – in the customary fashion – were dressed as decoys for him.

of the disaster of that day, together with Sir Richard Vernon,[1] and Baron Kinderton[2] and many others. On the king's side fell ten knights, many esquires, several servants and about three thousand were seriously wounded. On the rebel side most of the knights and esquires of Cheshire fell, in number about two hundred, not counting servants and foot soldiers, whose numbers I do no know.[3] The battle was fought on the eve of the feast of St Mary Magdalene [22 July], and it was thought that no fiercer battle had ever been fought.

On the following Monday, for the battle had been fought on the sabbath, the earl of Worcester, Baron Kinderton [Sir Richard Venables] and Sir Richard Vernon were beheaded at Shrewsbury by sentence of the court.

[The earl of Northumberland, although not present at the battle, is placed in custody by the king]

Also on the next Monday following, the earl of Northumberland [Henry Percy] with a strong force and outstretched arm of war was hurrying to his son or, as was thought, towards the king to renew peace talks, when he was stopped in his march by the earl of Westmorland [Ralph Neville] and [Sir] Robert Waterton. For they had gathered a large force and suddenly decided to bar his way. As the earl of Northumberland realised that neither of them was his friend, he turned his horses round and returned to his own castle of Warkworth.[4]

At that time envoys sent to France returned with a truce and respite from war, which were to last until the first day of March, and they were thought to have achieved something worthwhile at such a troublesome time.[5]

After matters had been settled at Shrewsbury, the king proceeded to York and, staying there for a time, he ordered the earl of Northumberland by letter to meet him there. The earl dismissed his army and came at the king's bidding on the day after the feast of St Laurence [10 August] with a small retinue. But he was not given the usual friendly welcome. He was rather in the position of a suppliant asking for the king's favour. The king did grant him his life and the necessary things to keep him alive, but decided to place him in safekeeping.[6]

[Lack of means prevents the king from invading Wales]

When the king returned from the north, he decided to go to Wales to check the arrogance of the Welsh, who had inflicted many losses on his country after his withdrawal from Wales.[7] But want of means held him back, for he lacked the money to hire an army.[8] The knights and esquires that he had around him at that time were more followers of Venus than Mars and of Laverna[9] rather than Pallas Athene.[10] They proposed that the bishops, who by chance were meeting in London at

1   Sir Richard Vernon, a Shropshire knight, JP and constable of Beaumaris Castle.
2   Sir Richard Venables of Kinderton, Cheshire: *CPR, 1401–5*, p. 293; *CPR, 1405–8*, p. 327.
3   Walsingham's modest figures for the number of dead and wounded are more accurate than the 16,000 estimated by Usk (*Usk*, pp. 168–71). In fact as many as 3,000 were killed and a similar number wounded. As Usk reports, Henry founded a chantry on the site in 1409. See also Wylie, *Henry IV*, i. 360–3.
4   Northumberland was marching south to support his brother and son when he heard that Neville and Waterton were in pursuit. He retreated northwards but gained entry to Newcastle only when he had detached himself from his troops. When news of his son's death reached him he turned towards Warkworth. Here, as Walsingham describes below, he received the king's summons to present himself at York.
5   A renewal of the truce was agreed on 27 June 1403.
6   Northumberland's castles at Alnwick, Berwick, Cockermouth, Prudhoe, Langley and Warkworth were placed in the custody of royal officers and his estates were put in charge of the steward of the royal household and the treasurer of the duchy of Lancaster. Northumberland himself was kept under guard.
7   According to Usk, in the aftermath of the Percy rebellion Glyn Dŵr had 'emerged with his manikins from the caves and the woods and marched with a great host right across Wales'; attacks as far south as Abergavenny and Cardiff were reported: *Usk*, pp. 172–3. See also Davies, *Revolt*, pp. 112–13.
8   The crown's finances could not support a full-scale expedition but nonetheless Henry embarked from Hereford on 11 September and led his troops through the Usk valley. Fund raising efforts continued but a muster at Shrewsbury planned for October was finally abandoned. See also Wylie, *Henry IV*, i. 365.
9   Goddess of thieves.
10 Pallas Athene, the patron goddess of Athens, was most commonly represented as a war goddess.

that time, should be despoiled of their horses and money and sent home on foot, in order that this abundance of theirs should alleviate the needs of the king's household. But thankfully there was one bishop present, who, speaking for all of them, is said to have replied very sharply that the wicked knights were not going to despoil any of the bishops unless they first paid for their rash daring with hard blows and won spoils from combat. The king in the meantime behaved with reasonable moderation and somehow won the goodwill of the prelates, so that the archbishop of Canterbury, at a meeting of his clergy, won with the consent of the prelates a tax of one tenth for the king.[1]

[The French attack Plymouth and the Isle of Wight]

The Amorican[2] Bretons, led by [Guillaume] the lord of Castel attacked the town of Plymouth with impunity and burnt it.[3] Immediately a western fleet, under the command of the esquire William Wilford,[4] captured in the region of Brittany forty ships laden with iron, oil, soap and about a thousand casks of wine from Rupella.[5] Returning, this same William and his men burnt forty ships, and, landing at Penmarch, burnt the towns and manors over a distance of six miles. He also consumed with avenging flames the town of St Mathias, and a three mile area surrounding it. A few days before Christmas, French sailors, closely followed by a crowd of marines, landed in the Isle of Wight, and boasted that they would spend Christmas there, even if the king of England was unwilling. But when a thousand French had landed in the island and were driving flocks and herds before them so that they might return to the sea with substantial booty, they were suddenly met by a force of English auxiliaries and were forced to give up their booty and shamefully hurry back to their ships, suffering some losses on the way. And so it happened that those who previously had forcibly demanded from the islanders sums of money for their property, were hardly able to escape from an intervention by its people.

[1404]

In 1404 at a parliament held in London after the octave of Epiphany [13 January][6] the earl of Northumberland was completely restored, both himself and his heirs, to his former dignities and possessions, both moveable and immovable.[7]

In this parliament the king was granted a novel tax that was a particularly vexatious burden on the people. I would have inserted details of it at this point, had not the bestowers themselves and the authors of this tax preferred that later generations should forever remain in ignorance of it. In fact it was granted only under the condition that it should not be dragged up later as a precedent, or copies of it be kept in the royal treasury or the exchequer but that its documents and records and remembrances of it should be burnt immediately its period had finished. Furthermore, no writs or complaints were to be issued against the collectors and officials concerned with the more efficient collection of this tax.[8]

---

[1]   In fact Archbishop Arundel secured a grant of 1½ tenths from convocation when it convened in September. It was the Archbishop's skilful management, and not the king, which 'won them over'. See also Wylie, *Henry IV*, i. 469–86.
[2]   In the later part of the chronicle, Walsingham employed the archaic names for Brittany, Normandy and the kingdom of France.
[3]   On 10 August 1403.
[4]   William Wilford (d.1413) was a wealthy merchant of Exeter and had held the mayoralty seven times between 1400 and 1411. In the latter year he also represented the city in parliament. He was the skipper of the *Mary of Exmouth*: Wylie, *Henry IV*, iv. 23 and n.
[5]   Wilford captured the ships at Belle Île and went on to attack Brest as well as the towns mentioned here by Walsingham. No other authority reports these episodes.
[6]   Parliament opened on 14 January: *RP*, iii. 522.
[7]   Barely six months after his surrender and the seizure of his estates, the restoration of Northumberland had come at the request of the commons.
[8]   It was a measure of the commons' reluctance to consent to the crown's continued demands for money that a new levy was devised in place of the usual subsidy; 20s was to be raised from each knight's fee and 1s from each pound's worth of land, goods and other sources of income. The monies were to be administered by

[The French at the Isle of Wight and Dartmouth]

About this time the French appeared before the Isle of Wight with a large fleet, and sent some of their number to demand of the islanders tribute or a special subsidy in the name of King Richard and Queen Isabella.[1] The people replied that king Richard was dead, and that the queen who had once been his wife had been peacefully sent back to her parents and her country without any conditions of tribute. And so their final answer was that they would not give a subsidy, but that, if what the French wanted was a fight, their terms were that the French could land without anyone stopping them, that after landing they would be given a period of six hours for refreshment, and that once that time was up they would infallibly get their fight. Once the French heard this they sailed away without doing anything.[2]

About the same time [Guillaume] the lord of Castel of Brittany, a pawn in the hands of destiny, with his crowd of French and Bretons had the intolerable arrogance to make a landing at Dartmouth, just as he had done previously at Plymouth. But this time it did not go according to his hopes. For he was killed by opponents for whom he had the utmost contempt, namely the peasants, and the men who landed after him were also immediately overwhelmed by the peasants, and at once taken prisoner or killed. Even the Dartmouth women should not be deprived of praise for this achievement, for they too laid low the enemy, inflicting dire damage with the missiles from their slings. And so several Frenchmen were killed or captured by women, and several by peasants. Indeed many of the Frenchmen were killed by the peasants because the French did not know their language. In fact the French were offering huge sums for their ransom, but the rough rustics, understanding their words differently, thought that they were uttering threats, when in fact they were pleading and begging for their lives. Anyway on that day three lords and twenty named knights were taken prisoner, as God on that day brought low the pride of the haughty and gave the victory to the country people. The peasants took their captives all the way to the presence of the king, and asked for some reward for their catch. The king willingly came to an agreement with them, and allowed them to go back home with their purses stuffed with gold, while he kept the prisoners at his court, to be ransomed in the future at a heavier cost.

In the month of April the clergy granted the king a tenth tax, on condition that no provisor should in the future take goods or carriages away from churchmen against their wishes. But, although the money was paid, no notice was taken of the condition from the beginning.

On 11 March in the current year miracles were witnessed around the body of St John, once prior of the canons at Bridlington, and on the order of the pope his body was translated by the hands of those honourable men, the archbishop of York and the bishops of Durham [Walter Skirlaw, 1388–1406] and Carlisle [William Strickland, 1399–1419].[3]

[Ravages committed by Glyn Dŵr]

Throughout all the time of this present summer Owain Glyn Dŵr and his Welshmen looted, burnt and ravaged the lands adjoining Wales, and now by trickery, now by ambush and now by

---

four treasurers for war appointed by the commons, a clear demonstration of the commons' mistrust of the officers of the royal household. As Walsingham reports here, the commons insisted that the mechanics of the levy were not to be recorded to ensure that no precedent was established. Usk described this tax as 'even harsher than . . . usual': *Usk*, pp. 176–7. It was not levied until after the October parliament at Coventry: see below, pp. 340–1.

1   The demand was for the expenses of former Queen Isabella to be paid.

2   Walsingham is the only authority to describe this and the assault on Dartmouth in any detail. The people of Dartmouth were experienced in direction action of this sort: in 1401 they attacked tax-collectors and drove them into the sea: *Usk*, pp. 130–1.

3   John Thweng of Bridlington (c.1320–79), prior of the Augustinian community at Bridlington, gained a considerable reputation as a monastic reformer and mystic and was canonised by Pope Boniface IX in 1401. The archbishop of York, Richard Scrope, had been one of those who had supported Thweng's canonisation: Hughes, *Pastors and Visionaries*, p. 99. At St Albans the monks of Walsingham's generation appear to have had a special devotion to his cult: see Clark, *Monastic Renaissance*, p. 138.

open warfare they took many prisoners, killed great numbers of Englishmen, and, of the castles that they took, some they levelled to the ground, while others they preserved whole to serve as strong-points.[1] John Trevor, the bishop of St Asaph, saw Glyn Dŵr succeeding with all his attempts, and changed into a bad man and fled to join Owain.[2]

At the same time the Flemings and the Bretons captured some of our ships, which were laden with merchandise, and killed the sailors with the sword or by hanging them.

[The countess of Oxford, helped by [William] Serle, spreads a report that King Richard is alive]

At the same time the old former countess of Oxford, the mother of Robert de Vere, duke of Ireland, whose exile and death at Louvain I have described,[3] got a report spread by herself and the members of her household through all the quarters of Essex that King Richard was alive, and would soon come and claim his former honours. She had quantities of silver and gold hinds made, the badges which King Richard had customarily given to his knights, esquires and friends,[4] so that, when these had been distributed as a sign of the king, the knights and other powerful men of Essex might be the more easily persuaded to carry out her wishes. For she was pressing very many people to think that King Richard was alive, and also there were daily reports from Scotland that King Richard was established there and only waiting for a suitable time when, with the strong arms of the French and the Scots, he might be able to recover his kingdom.

This mistaken belief was strengthened by the fabrications of a man called [William] Serle, a former chamberlain of King Richard.[5] He had deceitfully forged a private seal with the name of King Richard, and had sent letters to many people in the kingdom who had once belonged to the king's household, which at the same time brought comfort and a threat, for they contained the information that Richard was safe, and that before long they would see him prosper. It was because of this ploy that many believed the words and writings of the lady countess herself, and the belief spread so far that her lies were even believed by some of the abbots of monasteries in Essex. On the grounds that they had been seen to side with the countess, these abbots were later by the king's order held and kept in prison and the countess herself, after the confiscation of all her property, was kept in close confinement. And a priest who had deceitfully dropped all these lies into the ears of many was rewarded with drawing and hanging. For he had personally taken the trouble to go around the country in his efforts to get prominent people to believe that King Richard was not only alive but would soon reveal himself to everybody. He would even add that he had lately in such and such a place spoken to the king who had been wearing such and such apparel.

[Serle is taken prisoner by Sir William Clifford and hanged]

On the feast of [the nativity of] St John the Baptist [24 June] the earl of Northumberland [Henry Percy] at the summons of the king came to Pontefract bringing with him his nephews and grand-

---

1   Glyn Dŵr captured Aberystwyth and Harlech and his hold over the north was sufficient for him to summon his own parliament. The English marches were now under severe threat and in June the sheriffs of Herefordshire petitioned Henry IV for assistance, while Prince Henry wrote from Worcester pleading for money to expand his meagre forces. See also Davies, *Revolt*, p. 117.

2   Trevor had been bishop of St Asaph since 1395. On his defection he was deprived of the see, which remained in the king's hands until Robert Lancaster, Cistercian abbot of Valle Crucis, was presented in 1411. Trevor was presented to the see of St Andrews in 1408 and died in 1410 whilst in Rome. Usk alleges that he undertook embassies to the French on Glyn Dŵr's behalf: *Usk*, pp. 218–19.

3   Maud, countess of Oxford, was imprisoned for her part in the conspiracy: Wylie, *Henry IV*, i. 426, ii. 46. See also above, pp. 257, 295.

4   The white hart was Richard II's personal badge. See also Saul, *Richard II*, plates 8–9.

5   Sir William Serle had been an esquire of Richard II's chamber and was alleged to have carried out the murder of Thomas, duke of Gloucester, at Calais in 1397. At Richard's deposition he had escaped into Scotland but continued to circulate the rumour of former king's survival. In 1404 he surrendered to the custody of William Clifford who delivered him to Henry IV in June.

sons. This action softened the hearts of many who thought that he had counselled the young men to revolt. The knight, Sir William Clifford,[1] arrived together with the earl, bringing with him that [William] Serle, who was hated by the whole kingdom and whom I have mentioned above. Sir William had taken the precaution of arresting him as a prisoner a little while before, and by this deed deserved to be excused by the king for his holding on to Berwick castle beyond the appointed time. By doing so he had become guilty of treason against the king's majesty.

At the sight of Serle, men of all ages in the king's palace were burning to ask questions and discover or hear by what means and methods and with what accomplices Serle had strangled that famous son of a king and uncle of a king, the duke of Gloucester [Thomas of Woodstock].[2] Serle indeed could now see that it was all up with him, and his only confession was that he deserved a thousand deaths for this crime. He so softened the hearts of many with this confession and his repentance that they promised of their own accord to pay priests to say holy prayers every day for his soul.

When he was asked why he had wished to delude many people into thinking that Richard was alive, he replied that he had done this out of hatred for King Henry and to alienate the hearts of his subjects from him. He said that he could have been happier in the court of the king of France than in the Scottish king's court, if he had had the luck to stay there. But just when he was doing well in the French king's palace, the news had come that king Richard was alive, and he had taken himself off to Scotland, to see if the news was true. When on his arrival in Scotland he discovered not the king he was seeking but an impostor, he none the less affirmed that this impostor was unmistakably king Richard, preserved from his enemies by a divine miracle, just so that he could make mock of both the Scots and the English. But when he later realised that his deceitful fabrication had been exploded and found himself in want of cash, he had gone to Sir William Clifford at Berwick, thinking that Sir William would allay his worries by helping him with the money that would enable him to return to France. But he was disappointed of his hopes here. For Sir William kept him prisoner, employing the very cunning trick of gaining the favour of the king in exchange for this act of service. So sentence was finally passed on Serle, and he was drawn in one of the chief towns between Pontefract and London, beginning his merited punishment in the royal town of Pontefract itself.[3]

[At a parliament at Coventry the knights make a proposal to confiscate the property of the church]

At that time the king, being in need of money, so it was said, summoned the magnates of the kingdom to a parliament to be held at Coventry, around the time of the feast of St Faith the Virgin [6 October], forgetting that in the Lent of that very year a parliament had been held in London, which, so it seemed to many, had dragged on uselessly for twelve weeks.[4] So the king sent writs to the sheriffs, enjoining them to avoid completely choosing knights for their counties who were doctors of the law of the land or apprentices-at-law, and to send to this parliament only such men as were known to be ignorant of all the ways of the law.[5] And this was done.

So when they met together for this purpose, and it was explained on behalf of the king that he

---

1   Clifford was a Northumbrian knight, loyal to the Percy earl of Northumberland and son-in-law of Thomas, Lord Bardolf, who joined them in rebellion against Henry IV in 1408: Wylie, *Henry IV*, i. 397–8, ii. 175. See also below, pp. 359–60.
2   For Gloucester's murder see above, p. 302.
3   Serle suffered an horrific fate: he was dragged by horses through four towns before being hanged, drawn, disembowelled and finally beheaded. See also *Usk*, pp. 176–7.
4   By late summer it was clear that the crown was effectively bankrupt: in August Henry had instructed sheriffs and other royal officers to cease paying annuities and other dues. See Wylie, *Henry IV*, i. 469–79; Kirby, *Henry IV*, p. 173. Parliament convened on 6 October and the session continued until 12 November: *RP*, ii. 546.
5   Lawyers were barred on the basis that they were likely to serve their own or their client's interests rather than the king's. It may have been for this reason that the assembly at Coventry became known as the 'Unlearned Parliament', although the nickname also owes something to the members' attitude towards the

was under pressure from lack of money, seeing that the Scots and the Welsh were harassing him from nearby and the Bretons, Flemish and French from afar, these selected parliamentary knights could find no other remedy for aiding the king than the confiscation of the patrimony of Christ throughout the whole kingdom, in fact the complete removal from the church of its temporal goods. And then there arose a mighty quarrel between the clergy and the laity, with the king's knights declaring that they had often gone on campaign for the king and with the king against rebels and enemies, and had not only emptied their pockets in so doing but had also exposed their very bodies to many perils and toils, while the clergy in the meantime were sitting around idly at home and doing nothing to help to the king.[1]

The archbishop stoutly resists this proposal

The archbishop of Canterbury [Thomas Arundel] said in reply to this that the clergy had always contributed as much to the king as the laity, since they had more often given a tenth tax to the king than the laity had given a fifteenth, and furthermore, the clergy's vassals had followed the king to war and danger in just as great numbers as the vassals of lay estates. And over and above all this, the clergy were day and night offering masses and prayers for the king and for the welfare of his household.

And when the speaker of the knights in reply to this made a public demonstration by his gestures and his words that he did not care a fig for the prayers of the church, the archbishop of Canterbury said, 'I now see clearly where the fortunes of our land are tending, when the very prayers by which the Divinity is customarily appeased are ruled out as being of little worth. Assuredly that kingdom was never stable for long, in which no prayers and devotions were heard. But you who despise the religion of the clergy need not think that you will ransack the possessions of the church with impunity, since, if the archbishop of Canterbury lives, any seizure of his property will lead to your ruin.' Now the knight acting as speaker was Sir John Cheyne,[2] who, it was said had apostatised and had left and deserted the service and the fortunes of Christ for the fortunes of Mars. For, so men said, he had once been ordained a deacon, although his licence had not included any permission to renounce his diaconate.

The archbishop could see that the king was wavering during this debate, and rose to his feet. Then on bended knee before the king he asked him to be true to his original declaration that to the best of his ability he would preserve the lawful rights of all men, and to his voluntarily given oath that he would honour, support and maintain the church and her ministers, while being aware of the danger and shame that would follow if he broke his oath. He asked the king to allow the church to enjoy the rights and privileges which she had enjoyed in the reigns of his ancestors, and finally he said that the king should go in fear of offending that King through whom kings rule and of the censure incurred by all who loot church property, it being well known that all such were inextricably bound to sentence of excommunication.

After this speech from [the archbishop of] Canterbury, the king told him to sit down again, and asserted that it was his intention to leave the church in as good a state as he had found it or preferably a better one. The archbishop then spoke these words to the knights. 'You and your fellows have advised our present lord and king and his predecessors to confiscate the property of the monastic houses which the French and the Normans owned in England, telling them that by

---

church. Analysis of its composition has shown that there was no significant difference between the representatives here and at earlier assemblies: *RP,* iii. 545; Wylie, *Henry IV,* i. 469–79; Kirby, *Henry IV,* p. 174.

1   The conspicuous anticlericalism of both commons and lords at this parliament was remarked in a number of contemporary accounts; it was even alleged that they had not shown reverence to the host as they passed through the streets of Coventry. See Wylie, *Henry IV,* i. 469–79; Kirby, *Henry IV,* p. 174.

2   Cheyne was not speaker, but the error is to be found in every one of the contemporary chronicles. Of course, given the apparently anticlerical character of the assembly it was fitting for Walsingham to claim that Cheyne was speaker since he was one of the knights suspected as a conspicuous follower of the Lollards. The speaker was in fact Sir William Sturmy of Wolfhall, Wiltshire. See also *RP,* iii. 546; Wylie, *Henry IV,* i. 51, 476 and n; iv. 143 and n.

this means great store of riches could be piled up, to the value of many thousand pounds of gold. But despite this it is well known that the king is not half a mark richer today, for you knights by force or by begging have taken this wealth from his hands and appropriated these goods as your own. We can infer from this that you are not seeking our temporalities for the good of the king but for your own greed. Because there is no doubt that if the king, which God forbid, assented to your criminal request, he would not be a penny richer in the coming year. And be sure that I will offer this neck of mine to the sword before the church is stripped of the smallest of her rights.'

[Some temporal lords support the archbishop and the proposal is defeated]

The knights and the metropolitan bishops were stunned by the stubbornness of this statement and fell silent. The archbishop indeed, gazing all around the assembly just like Argus, realised that the knights were going to persist in their demand for the temporalities of the church, but he won over to his side some of the temporal lords who stoutly declared that they would never be willing for holy church to be despoiled of her temporalities. And they explained that they were showing this favour to the archbishop and his prelates in return for the favour which the church had previously shown them, at the time when the knights had demanded that all lands held by the lords from the crown, whether from the gift of the present king or of his predecessors, Kings Edward [III] and Richard [II], should be given back to help the king. For the archbishop of Canterbury and the prelates had very firmly resisted this demand. The result of all this was that no further mention was made about seizing the temporalities of the church.[1]

But even those very knights who had ruthlessly persisted in their mistaken request begged the archbishop of Canterbury to pardon them, as they confessed their wickedness and guilt, and thanked him that his courage in this crisis had allowed the church to breathe again. And they quoted the lines of the heathen poet who said

> Under a fierce ruler and in bad times
> You dared to be good.[2]

In addition to the many grants made to the king in this parliament the laity granted two taxes of a fifteenth, on condition that all the money went to the Lord Furnivall[3] for use in the wars of the king. Parliament also recalled royal patents previously given to various persons for their annual upkeep by Kings Edward [III] and Richard [II]. The knights in parliament agreed to this, although it did not redound to the king's credit. The clergy granted to the king a tenth and a half tax, despite the fact that only a half of the last tenth tax previously granted on the feast of St Martin [11 November] had been paid.[4]

At that time on the land of the archbishop of Canterbury and other people in Kent there was suddenly such an inundation of flood waters, as the dykes burst that its like had never been seen there before. The waters drowned immense numbers of very valuable animals. Nor was it only England that wept for such losses, for, so it was said, Zeeland, Flanders and Holland also sustained losses that year from the numberless floods of sea water.[5]

At this time Lord William Wykeham, bishop of Winchester, being now very old, ceased to live

---

[1]   Although the subject resurfaced in 1410. See below, pp. 376–8.
[2]   Martial, *Epigrams*, xii. 6.
[3]   Thomas Neville, Lord Furnivall, brother of Ralph, earl of Westmorland: Wylie, *Henry IV*, i. 479, iii. 111, iv. 256–8.
[4]   The commons finally acceded to a grant on 12 November after more than a month of debate; the first tenth was to be paid at Christmas and the second in two halves between June and November in the following year; a grant of the custom duty of wool and of tunnage and poundage was also agreed. The monies were to be paid to two new war treasurers, Thomas, Lord Furnivall, and Sir John Pelham, who were to replace the four officers appointed in the previous parliament. The new tax first discussed in the previous parliament was also now levied. Given the disposition of the commons the grant was a generous one but it was bound by a number of conditions, not least that the king submit to a commission of enquiry to establish the extent of crown lands as at 40 Edward III and what subsequently had been alienated. See *RP*, iii. 546; Wylie, *Henry IV*, i. 469–79; Kirby, *Henry IV*, pp. 175–6.
[5]   This is not reported by the other authorities.

in this world. Thanks to his energy and expenditure English clerks every day increase and grow in number. For he founded at Winchester a college for fledgling grammar school pupils, and at Oxford he founded a house for priests studying the more rarefied branches of knowledge. In both places a hundred persons are maintained by moneys provided by him.[1]

On 1 October came the death at Rome of Pope Boniface IX. He was succeeded by the Bishop of Bononia, who was called Pope Innocent VII, and also known as Cosmo Gentili. In all respects he was a man worthy of such an important a title and position.[2]

[1405]

In 1405, around the feast of St Valentine [14 February], the sons of the earl of March[3] were stolen and abducted, but were soon afterwards recovered from Windsor castle. The blacksmith who had made the keys by which entrance to the boys was obtained was punished by having his hands and his head cut off.

While [Constance] Lady Despenser,[4] the widow of Sir Thomas Despenser [former earl of Gloucester] lately executed at Bristol, was fleeing, so the story goes, to Owain Glyn Dŵr with her eight-year-old daughter, she was taken captive and robbed of all her treasures. She was taken back to the king by the king's men and endured the inconvenience of a quite close confinement.[5]

After the feast of the Purification [of the Virgin, 2 February] the king summoned the barons of the realm to London and discussed with them the government of the kingdom and the financial help that they ought to give him. But on that occasion the barons paid minimal heed to the king's wishes.

In the Lent following this feast the king had the clergy and barons of the land summoned to St Albans for the same business. But the barons resisted the king's wishes, so that he achieved nothing. And on the eve of Palm Sunday [12 April] everybody went home, all as it were agreeing to disagree with the king.[6]

[The archbishop of York and the earl marshal rebel against the king][7]

During these days the earl marshal, Thomas Mowbray, with an armed force, marched to join the archbishop of York, Master Richard Scrope. It is in doubt whether he went of his own accord or

---

1   William Wykeham died on 27 September 1404. He had occupied the see for thirty-eight years. He had founded Winchester College and New College, Oxford in 1379. Walsingham exaggerated the size of the foundation at both colleges; the statutes for the Oxford college made provision for a fellowship of seventy but there is no evidence that this number had been reached by 1404. In comparison to other Oxford foundations, and in particular to the monastic colleges that Walsingham knew best, this was an enormous number.
2   According to Adam Usk, Boniface's death was followed by rioting in Rome between Ghelphs and Ghibellines and he suggests that it was for this reason that a candidate unconnected with either party was elected on 17 October, Cosmato di Megliorato. See *Usk*, pp. 182–3. The nuncii of Benedict XIII then in Rome also pressured the cardinals to postpone the election. See Harvey, *Solutions to the Schism*, p. 131.
3   Edmund (b.1391) and Roger Mortimer (b.1393), sons of Roger Mortimer, 4th earl of March (d.1398). Henry IV had held them at Windsor since the start of his reign. After the attempted abduction they were placed in the custody of Richard, lord Grey of Codnor.
4   Sister of Edmund, duke of York.
5   Walsingham's version of this story is somewhat garbled, but Lady Despenser had herself stolen the Mortimer boys away from Windsor castle although her brother, the duke of York and Thomas Mowbray, the earl marshal, were also implicated in the plot. York was imprisoned in the tower and his titles and estates seized, only to be restored to the following year; the exact fate of his sister is unrecorded. See also Wylie, *Henry IV*, ii. 42–50.
6   In spite of the provisions made in the previous parliament, the financial position of the crown had not improved. As Walsingham reports, neither of these councils provided a solution.
7   Richard Scrope (b. c.1350), younger son of Lord Scrope of Masham, had been translated to York by Richard II in March 1398; he had previously held the see of Lichfield (1386–98). He supported Henry IV in 1399 and assisted at his coronation but he came to sympathise with the Percy cause when Hotspur was killed at Shrewsbury in 1403. The conspiracy was planned in the spring of 1405 and although Northumberland may have been the instigator, Scrope appears to have played a leading role. He himself may have drafted the mani-

whether he was asked by the archbishop to come. And at the same time Lord Thomas Bardolf [1] approached the earl of Northumberland [Henry Percy] with the plan that they should cause trouble to the king, as afterwards became clear. But the archbishop and the earl marshal did not keep their designs hidden for long, but soon brought their intentions out into the open. For the citizens of York, with many people from elsewhere, put their trust, so it was said, in reinforcements from the earl of Northumberland and Lord Thomas Bardolf, and summoned people to arms in great numbers, asking them to join forces with themselves for the good of the kingdom and the safety of the commons. And so that people should be made readier to undertake this business, they fixed notices, written in English, on the doors of the monasteries and the churches of the city, which would cause people to be willing to take up arms. And indeed, once the notices had been read and the holy plan understood, knights, esquires and the commons from city and countryside thronged in very great numbers around the archbishop, who was commended to everybody by his weight of years, the holiness of his life up to that point, his unrivalled knowledge of letters and his consistently friendly personality.

The earl of Westmorland [Ralph Neville] and John,[2] the son of the king, were at that time near at hand, as, having heard rumours of the uprising, they had assembled troops and hurried to meet the crowd of people led by the archbishop, before it multiplied and became impossible to be defeated easily.[3] But their efforts were in vain, for the army of the archbishop was much stronger than their own people. So the earl sent envoys to ask the reason for such a massing together of troops, and why they were in arms against the king's peace.

The archbishop answered that he was not doing anything against the king's peace, but rather that all his actions were aimed to preserve that peace and tranquillity, and that he was in arms and hedged around by troops only because of his fear of the king, as he could have no safe access to the king unless a crowd of the king's yes-men agreed to the conference. Furthermore, added the archbishop, his manifesto was for the good of the king and the kingdom, and perhaps they would be willing to look through it. And he showed them the document in which the various points were set out. When the earl of Westmorland had read the document, he openly praised the holy and pious intentions of the archbishop, and pledged his word that he and his men were willing to discuss the archbishop's manifesto. And so he asked the archbishop to meet him half way attended by a few men, that he might discuss the matter with them, and he himself would also come to the meeting with just a few men, so that there would be equal numbers on both sides.

The archbishop joyfully believed the words of the earl, and persuaded the earl marshal, unwilling though he was, to go with him to the spot appointed for the meeting. They arrived at the place with equal numbers on both sides, and the charter containing the various points was read right through. And immediately the earl of Westmorland and his followers gave their assent and support to the document.

And then the earl himself, who was cleverer than the rest of them, said, 'Well now. This is the

---

festo that was circulated in York and its environs in May, and as Walsingham suggests here, he may have been influential in persuading the nineteen-year-old Mowbray to join them. The conspirators' manifesto reiterated the complaints made by Hotspur two years before, claiming that Henry had disregarded his oath made in 1399 not to depose Richard and that he had broken his pledge to remove the burden of taxation, placing undue pressures in particular upon the clerical estate. The text was transcribed and translated from English to Latin by Walsingham's colleague, the *Annales* author (*Trokelowe*, ed. Riley, pp. 403–5). Having issued the manifesto, Scrope raised a force from amongst the citizens of York and mustered them at Shipton Moor north west of the city. As Walsingham relates here, support was dispatched from the Percy estates at Cleveland, Northallerton and Topcliffe, whilst, according to the *Annales* author, William Lord Clifford also raised an army from his estates at Brougham and Appleby. See also Wylie, *Henry IV*, ii. 211–12, 224–36.

1   Thomas (1369–1408), 5th baron Bardolf, lord of Wormgay.
2   Henry IV's second son, John of Lancaster, the future duke of Bedford. For his subsequent career, see below, pp. 415, 426–7, 434, 444.
3   Westmorland had been moving southwards in an attempt to intercept the troops raised by Clifford and Northumberland who were heading southwards for their rendezvous with Scrope. He arrived at Shipton Moor on 27 May and the negotiations with Scrope and Mowbray continued for three days before he was able to manipulate them into a surrender, as Walsingham recounts here.

desired outcome of the enterprise you have undertaken. Your men have been sweating away under arms for a long time now. Let one of you go and tell your people to go back home and lay down their arms and give their usual attention to their usual occupations. And let us, meanwhile, as a sign of our agreement, drink together in the sight of the people on both sides.' And without delay they shook hands, and a knight of the archbishop's party was sent to announce the peace to their people, and to bid each man to lay down his arms and go back home, as the two parties now thought as one. And the archbishop's men, seeing the signs of peace and the lords drinking together, and being tired out by their unaccustomed soldiering, gladly turned their horses for home. And so what happened was that, as the archbishop's men went away, by prior arrangement the number of the earl of Westmorland's men gradually began to increase. Nor did the archbishop realise that he had been tricked until he was arrested at the hands of the earl, and many others with him. They were all promised indemnity, but none of them received it, for the archbishop and the earl marshal were later beheaded, when the king came to York on the day after Pentecost.[1] And as a result that prophecy of the madman at Bridlington was able to come true, for in very obscure language it had foretold the present deed, in these lines:

> They'll discuss peace,
> But underwritten with fraud.
> No money will save
> That priest from the grave.[2]

After the archbishop had been beheaded, since he had endured death very bravely, he finished up in the popular opinion as a glorious martyr. Indeed it was even claimed that miracles had taken place both in the open space where he was beheaded and at the place of his burial. And at once the common people began a vigorous worship of the ashes of the now defunct archbishop, whom they had previously loved when he was alive.[3] This lasted until they were forbidden to do so by some of the king's men, and so became afraid to make further visits to the archbishop's tomb. As for the body of Lord Thomas Mowbray, earl marshal, this by permission of the king was buried in the cathedral church, as many wept for his downfall. But his head was fixed on a pole, which for a long time was placed on the city walls, exposed to the heat and the rain.[4] When the king finally gave permission for the head to be buried with the body, men say that no decay or wastage or deep discoloration was found in it, but that it still displayed the handsome qualities of the living man.

After this the king at his pleasure imposed fines on the citizens of York who had taken sides with the archbishop, and then, at the head of an army of thirty-seven thousand men and with all the equipment of war, marched in pursuit of the earl of Northumberland and Lord Thomas Bardolf. But the earl moved to Berwick when he learned of the king's intention.[5]

At this time envoys came to England from [Eric VII] the king of Denmark, Norway and

---

[1]   As soon as Westmorland had persuaded them to send their supporters away on 29 May, Scrope and Mowbray were arrested. They were taken to Pontefract where Henry himself arrived on 6 June. With the king they returned to York and after a summary trial, at which the chief justice Sir William Gascoigne refused to preside on principle, they were executed. Scrope was spared the ignominy of his head being displayed at one of the city's gates and his remains were taken directly to the minster for burial. According to Adam Usk, for their part in the rising, the citizens of York were compelled to prostrate themselves to beg the king's pardon (*Usk*, pp. 202–3).

[2]   Walsingham's reference here is to a popular collection of prophecies, *The Prophecies of Saint John of Bridlington*, which first appeared in the reign of Richard II but remained popular during the Lancastrian period, so popular that a commentary also circulated. See also A. G. Rigg, *Anglo-Latin Literature, 1066–1422* (Cambridge, 1993), pp. 265–8; Sharpe, *Latin writers*, p. 220.

[3]   The *Annales* author confirms the enduring popularity of Scrope, reporting a number of miracles attributed to his relics: *Trokelowe*, ed. Riley, pp. 409–10.

[4]   At Bootham Bar.

[5]   After the executions, Henry did head north although Walsingham surely exaggerates the size of his army. He subdued the Percy castle at Prudhoe and Warkworth and reached Berwick on 6 July. He succeeded in taking it six days later; Alnwick was also surrendered to him on 14 July. Northumberland and Bardolf, however, fled across the border into Scotland: *Scotichronicon*, viii. 65–6.

Sweden to ask for the hand of the king's daughter in marriage to their lord.[1] The chief envoy was the bishop of Soluca. He had discussions with the writer of this history about the life of St Alban. For this martyr of ours is widely celebrated in Denmark, so the bishop knew all about him and shared his knowledge with me.[2]

[The king captures Berwick castle but meets with misfortune in Wales]

Meanwhile the king set his face against the earl of Northumberland and came to Berwick. But the earl and Sir Thomas Bardolf with him fled from the face of their formidable foe to Scotland, where they took oaths of loyalty to Sir David Fleming, the Scot.[3] But when the king discovered that the earl had fled, he instructed the garrison of the castle to hand it over to him. And when they in precise language refused to do this, he brought a huge gun up against it, which, with one firing, demolished part of one of the towers and so frightened the garrison that they preferred voluntarily to expose themselves to the king's swords rather than to wait for a second firing. So the castle was returned to the king. Some of the garrison were beheaded, some imprisoned. And once the king had regained Berwick and settled it to his liking, Alnwick castle and the other castles of the earl were delivered up into his hands without any opposition.[4]

Elated by these successes, the king at once returned to Wales. But there on the other hand nothing went well for him, and whatever he tried was dogged by ill luck. So he withdrew without having achieved anything, and on the return journey he lost, so it was said, about fifty chariots, carts and wagons together with a great deal of treasure and his crowns, when he met with unexpected floods.[5]

So he came to Worcester, summoned the archbishop [of Canterbury, Thomas Arundel] and the other bishops, told them of the misfortunes which had befallen him and asked for their help. The archbishop replied that he would discuss the matter with the clergy.[6]

[French forces arrive to help Owain Glyn Dŵr]

In the meantime the French came to the help of the Welshman, Owain Glyn Dŵr, and put into Milford Haven with one hundred and forty ships, having previously lost through lack of fresh water almost all their horses. Lord Thomas Berkeley[7] and Henry Pay burnt fifteen of their ships while they were in harbour. Then the French laid siege to the town of Carmarthen and captured it, having first allowed its defenders to keep all their movable goods, and giving them permission to go wherever they liked. About the same time fourteen other ships were captured by Lord Thomas

---

1   The kingdoms of Denmark and Norway had been combined with Sweden under the federal union of Kalmar in 1397. The marriage between King Eric VII and Philippa, second daughter of Henry IV, was first proposed in 1402 to be one half of a reciprocal match in which Henry, prince of Wales, would also marry King Eric's sister, Katherine. This second match was abandoned but negotiations for the first continued until the marriage finally took place in 1406. Wylie, *Henry IV*, ii. 308, 425, 434, 436–7.

2   Walsingham was fascinated by the history of St Alban and copied a number of the earlier, twelfth- and thirteenth-century lives into his own compilations. He may also have been the author of the only later medieval Latin life to have been composed at St Albans, the *Tractatus*. The cult of Alban was popular both in Germany and Scandinavia and Walsingham must have been delighted by this opportunity to compare traditions with the Danish envoy. See also Clark, 'St Albans Monks and the Cult of St Alban', pp. 218–30.

3   Sir David Fleming of Biggar and Cumbernauld, councillor of Robert III.

4   Berwick surrendered on 12 July after almost a week. Alnwick was subdued two days later. Walsingham is the only authority to report these actions in detail.

5   Henry had returned to the Welsh border by 23 August; the *Scotichronicon* claims that he had assembled a force of 140,000 men-at-arms but the figure is grossly exaggerated: *Scotichronicon*, viii. 95. Walsingham and his St Albans colleague, the *Annales* author, are the main authorities for the failure of this new campaign, due in part to the poor weather conditions as Walsingham reports, but also to the fact that Glyn Dŵr, once again, could not be drawn into a pitched battle. Henry had returned to Worcester by mid-September. See also Davies, *Revolt*, pp. 119–20.

6   Henry now asked for an advance of the tenths that had been granted in the previous parliament and convocation to be paid by 26 September, an unrealistically short period of time: Wylie, *Henry IV*, ii. 120.

7   Berkeley, admiral of the south and west, was one of the experienced captains who had supported Henry IV in his seizure of power in 1399: Wylie, *Henry IV*, i. 377, 389, 432.

Berkeley, Sir Thomas Swinburne[1] and Henry Pay while they were sailing towards Wales to help Owain. The steward of France and eight other captains were taken prisoner from aboard these ships.[2]

The town of Royston [Hertfordshire] was burnt down on the day of the translation of the blessed Martin [4 July].[3]

In London on the day after the feast of St Katherine [25 November] the earl of Arundel married the bastard daughter of the king of Portugal.[4] It was a very splendid ceremony, and the king and queen of England were present.

On the feast of the conception of St Mary [8 December] a herald's voice proclaimed the king's daughter [Philippa] as queen of Denmark, Norway and Sweden, in the presence of the envoys who had come to ask for her as wife for their king.

[1406]

In 1406 Roger Walden paid his debt to nature. He had lived through varying fortunes and had experienced over a short time how fortune is:

> Unsure, inconstant, ever changing,
> Shifting and moving, never still.
> You think you have it, but it's gone.
> Her joys are lies, her face a fraud.[6]

Certainly fortune lifted Roger from poverty to the treasurership of the kingdom and soon to the archbishopric of Canterbury,[7] and it was as archbishop of Canterbury that the world knew him, even though Thomas Arundel was still alive. He was immediately deposed, and remained without office for a long time, until he was finally again elevated to the venerable throne of London. But he was not permitted to enjoy this office for even one year.

At this time the lord pope publicly excommunicated the killers of Richard Scrope, once archbishop of York.[7]

At that time a parliament began which lasted for almost a year without being of use.[8] For a

---

1   Swinburne was an experienced captain and from 1406, the mayor of Bordeaux: *CPR, 1405–8*, p. 60.

2   The French landed at Milford Haven around 7 August and attacked Haverfordwest and Tenby before joining with Glyn Dŵr's forces and also taking Carmarthen. From there they advanced within three miles of Worcester, where the king was waiting. Berkeley, Pay and Swinburne were experienced captains; Pay of Poole, Dorset, a privateer, had been prominent in the counter-attacks against French pirates off the Devon coast two years before. See Davies, *Revolt*, p. 117; Wylie, *Henry IV*, i. 380–1, 443–4; iii. 302.

3   For the burning of Royston, which had happened also in 1324, see *VCH Herts.*, iii. 259.

4   Thomas Fitzalan (1381–1415), 5th earl of Arundel, married Béatriz, illegitimate daughter of King João I of Portugal. The marriage was brokered by Henry's sister, Philippa, João's queen, with the intention of cementing the bond between England and Portugal. Arundel complained that his losses in the Welsh rebellion were such that he was unable to provide for such a distinguished bride, but Henry himself stood as guarantor. The wedding took place at Lambeth on 26 November: Russell, *English Intervention*, pp. 545–6.

5   The origin of this verse is obscure.

6   Walden died on 6 January 1406. His social origins were in marked contrast to those of his rival, the blue-blood Thomas Arundel; the son of a butcher, Adam Usk described Walden as 'better versed in the ways of the world than in church affairs or learning'; the *Annales* author was more outspoken, 'totally inadequate and illiterate': *Trokelowe*, ed. Riley, p. 213. He was reputed to have once been married and to have served as a soldier. He had been treasurer of Calais from 1387–92, the king's secretary from 1393–95 and treasurer of England from 1395–98. After the deprivation of Thomas Arundel, Richard II had appointed him archbishop of Canterbury (10 November 1397), but in his turn he was deprived by Henry IV in October 1399. He was provided to the see of London in 1404.

7   The papal condemnation was delivered by two papal envoys. Archbishop Arundel chose not to publish it: Wylie, *Henry IV*, ii. 346. For Scrope's execution see above, p. 338 and n.

8   Parliament was summoned in the early spring, first to Coventry, then to Gloucester, to be convenient for a campaign in Wales, and then to Westminster where it finally opened on 2 March. This first session was adjourned on 3 April, resumed on 25 April and adjourned again on 19 June. A third and final session began on 15 October and continued until the end of December. As Walsingham relates, the commons were in obdu-

long time the knights in the parliament put off granting a subsidy to the king, and then when finally their resistance was broken and they did grant the tax that had been asked for, it was only to the harm of the community. For because of the delay before the grant, the expenses of the knights were almost equal to the subsidy that had been asked for.[1] Also the clergy granted a new tax to the king, which was to be levied from stipendiary priests and the mendicant friars and other monks who celebrated an annual festival. Each of these was to give half a mark to the king. This would act as a relief to the clergy, who had previously always carried the whole burden for them.[2]

[The son of the Scottish king is delivered to King Henry]

About the same time, on the advice of David Fleming, the earl of Northumberland [Henry Percy] and Thomas [Lord] Bardolf fled to Wales.[3] For David had revealed to them the plots of those Scots who had conspired to hand them over to King Henry in exchange for certain prisoners.[4] As a result of this David was killed by the Scots, and the Scots became embroiled in such a bitter civil war that, as the strife intensified, they were forced to ask for a three years truce. When this truce had been arranged to cover events on land, the Scots sent by sea the son and heir of their king [Robert III, 1390–1406] to France, that he might grow up into a strong youth there and learn the courtesy and the language of the French. But he and a bishop and the earl of Orkney, to whom his father had entrusted him, had the bad luck to be captured by some sailors from Cley in Norfolk, who took them to England and handed them over to the king. The king was relaxed enough to make a joke about it, and said, 'Of course, if the Scots had been our friends, they would have sent the young man to me for his education, as I know the French language.' The young man and the earl of Orkney [Henry Sinclair] were sent to the Tower of London, but the bishop managed to slip away and escape.[5]

[French ships captured. The king's daughter taken to Denmark as bride of the Danish king]

While the French at this period were hurrying to help Owain Glyn Dŵr with thirty-eight ships, eight of them, packed with armed men, were captured, although the remainder sailed off in fear towards Wales.[6] And soon afterwards fifteen ships carrying wine and wax, were captured by our merchants, who had been assigned the guardianship of the seas.

The pope bestowed the archbishopric of York upon Robert Hallum, the chancellor of Oxford, who was at the Roman Curia at that time. This angered the king of England, who opposed the appointment.[7]

---

rate mood. They reiterated their demand, first made in 1401, for their petitions to be answered before any subsidy was provided. They also insisted on their own nomination of members of the council and promulgated new articles for the councillors to follow. Furthermore they demanded an audit of the novel land tax that had been introduced in the parliaments two years before and impertinently suggested that the council stand surety for any part of the subsidy revenue that was misspent. See also *RP*, iii. 567–603; Wylie, *Henry IV*, ii. 78, 408, 411, 461.

1   That is to say the expenses of those sitting in parliament.
2   Walsingham was the only authority to record this innovation.
3   Sir David Fleming of Biggar and Cumbernauld was a councillor of King Robert III. He was involved in the unsuccessful attempt to smuggle Robert's son James out of Scotland in February 1406 and for his part in the attempt was assassinated by James Douglas, 'the Gross', 1st earl of Avondale.
4   The two fugitives departed Scotland for Wales in the spring of 1406.
5   The young Scottish heir (son of Robert III) was James, the future James I of Scotland. He was smuggled out of the country with the assistance of Sir David Fleming, accompanied by Sir Henry Sinclair, earl of Orkney. They waited for a month on the Bass Rock before they boarded the Prussian merchant ship *Maryenknyght* but the vessel was intercepted off Flamborough Head by pirates of Great Yarmouth under the command of one Hugh atte Fenn. The *Scotichronicon* dates the capture to 30 March (viii. 60–1): James was imprisoned in the Tower of London where he remained for the next eighteen years.
6   The French ships departed from Brest on 22 July and finally arrived on the coast of Wales in early August. The force numbered 2,500 men: Davies, *Revolt*, pp. 193–4.
7   Hallum was an Oxford scholar who supported the conciliar solution to the schism. For his career see Emden, *BRUO*, ii. 854–5. The king preferred Thomas Langley, his chancellor and a loyal Lancastrian servant,

During this summer the king and the queen took the young, virgin daughter of the king by his first wife [Philippa of Lancaster] to the town of Lynn [King's Lynn, Norfolk], that from there she might cross the seas to Denmark to marry the king of Denmark. She was escorted by various nobles, amongst whom were the bishop of Bath [and Wells, Henry Bowet] and Lord Richard [of Conisbrough, later earl of Cambridge], the son of the duke of York [Edmund of Langley]. When these nobles returned to England after completing their escort duty, they brought back with them little or nothing that was of any good for their country.

The bishop of Norwich dies

About the end of autumn Lord Henry Despenser, bishop of Norwich, entered upon the path of his fathers. He was a man who in his day had fulfilled the office of a knight, but did not neglect his pontifical duties. The monks of Norwich elected as bishop in his place their fellow monk and prior, Alexander.[1]

A tournament

At that time the Scots challenged the English to a series of combats or duels, and at London, in the presence of the king, the earl of Kent [Edmund Holland] fought against the earl of Mar[2] and Sir John Cornwall[3] and Sir [Henry] Beaumont[4] and certain other Englishmen who had been challenged fought against other Scots. The English gave the Scots such a beating that the result brought dismay to the challengers, fame and honour to our men and praise to God.[5]

The Duke of York is restored

While the parliament of this year was still continuing,[6] the duke of York [Edward], who was thought by many to have died in prison before this, was restored to his former rank.

The earl of Kent [Edmund Holland] married the daughter of a lord of Milan.[7]

A mad sermon preached at the [St Paul's] Cross in London, the reply to it and the premature action of [Sir] R[obert] Waterton

Also about the same time a certain William Taylor, master of arts of the university of Oxford, preached in London a sycophantic sermon to curry favour with the lords temporal, setting forth the heretical opinions or conclusions of the former John Wyclif, which had been devised by Wyclif to attack property owning clergy.[8] Taylor declared that men of religion ought not to hold worldly possessions and that those which they did hold could in certain cases be rightly taken away from them by the lords temporal. And there were several other crazy ideas that this wastrel belched forth on that day.

On the next day a true catholic, master Thomas Alkerton, professor of the holy scriptures, preached a sermon in the same place.[9] He destroyed by clear reasoning all the arguments of the

---

and had already suffered the disappointment of Langley being overlooked for the see of London to which the pope had provided the Ricardian Roger Walden. With the execution of Scrope still a recent memory, Henry was compelled to be conciliatory.

1   Despenser died on 23 August 1406. His successor was Alexander Tottington, elected on 14 September. For Despenser's martial prowess see above, pp. 145–6, 199–210.

2   Alexander Stewart, earl of Mar.

3   Sir John Cornwall (d. 1443) or Greencornwall was constable of Queenborough. He was married to Henry IV's sister Elizabeth of Lancaster: Wylie, *Henry IV*, i. 105; ii. 280 and n. He served with Clarence in 1412 and Henry V in Normandy. He was later raised to the peerage as Lord Fanhope.

4   Henry, Lord Beaumont (d.1413), a chamber knight and councillor of Henry IV: Wylie, *Henry IV*, ii. 411, iii. 282, iv. 247.

5   The tournament took place at London on 15 September 1406. It was not recorded by the *Scotichronicon*.

6   The parliamentary session continued from 1 March until 22 December: *RP*, iii. 567–603.

7   Edmund Holland (b.1383), earl of Kent, married Lucia Visconti, daughter of Bernabò Visconti, duke of Milan: Wylie, *Henry IV*, ii. 40.

8   Taylor was a scholar of St Edmund Hall, Oxford and an acolyte of its Principal, Peter Payne a notorious Wyclifite. For Taylor's career see Emden, *BRUO*, iii. 1852–53.

9   For Alkerton see Emden, *BRUO*, i. 70.

former preacher and showed that all plunderers of ecclesiastical property without exception were bound by the chains of anathema. [Sir] Robert Waterton was standing listening to this sermon, as he had to many others, in order to pick up a few crumbs of truth, and as soon as the sermon was over he told his servant on his behalf to offer the preacher his curry-comb (this article is a comb for rubbing down a horse), on the grounds that he too had been currying favour, only with the prelates of the church. His servant did what his master had commanded in the sight of all, and offered the comb to the preacher as he was coming down the steps of the pulpit.[1]

Thomas was extremely upset. He reported the matter to the archbishop [of Canterbury, Thomas Arundel] and the archbishop reported it to his king. The king wanted to make an amusing story out of it, but the archbishop said, 'By St James, that is not the way to take it. Waterton must atone in person for the disgrace he inflicted on our preacher.' Seeing that Canterbury was upset, the king asked him to do what was necessary on condition that he tempered his punishment with some consideration for the offender. So the archbishop compelled a very reluctant Waterton to ask for forgiveness publicly in parliament and to swear and abide by an oath that he would obey the commands of the church. As the king had asked for special treatment for Waterton, this was sufficient public shame, and so he also enjoined upon himself to do private penance, and so he gave instructions to his servant that on certain days he was to go at the head of a procession all naked, with the curry-comb in one hand and a candle in the other.

A quarrelsome end to parliament, with only the grant of a tax

As the end of the present year and Christmas approached, the king increased the urgency of his requests for the grant of a subsidy from the commons.[2] Although the knights in parliament were sick of the king continuing to expect such a grant every year, they were compelled to make some concession to him, just so that they could revisit their homes and families at this festive season. And so on the fourth day before Christmas [i.e. 22 December], when by their shilly-shallying against the king they had now extended the discussion to the evening and the darkness of the night, they did make a grant to him of a fifteenth tax, on the two conditions that it was not spent on anything except the clear good of the kingdom, and that certain lords there present were willing to sign and seal their willingness to go bail that the first condition should be carried out; and that if it were not, these lords were to bind themselves to pay back to the knights out of their own pockets the fifteenth tax previously paid. The lords flatly refused to do this, and the king was furiously angry with everybody, and told the two sides that, if they were bent upon treating him with such contempt, they should seek a battlefield on the morrow to find out who ought to prevail. So the knights, in fear that force would be used against them, seeing that the lords were not willing to put themselves under an obligation for the king or to swear an oath, climbed down although unwillingly and for their part obeyed the wishes of the king and granted him a fifteenth tax. When this had been done, each man returned to his own home.

Pope Innocent VII dies[3]

During this time, on the feast of St Leonard [6 November] Pope Innocent VII ceased to see the light of this world and was taken up to the light eternal, as men thought.[4] His funeral service was

---

[1]   Waterton (c.1360–1425) had been in the service of Henry IV since the beginning of the 1390s, originally as one of his squires. Walsingham regarded his action as evidence that anticlericalism was still endemic amongst the household knights despite the recent change in regime. Archbishop Arundel's anger was understandable given the renewed anxiety over the spread of Lollardy. See also Wylie, *Henry IV*, ii. 47, 111, 114, 231, 261; iv. 177, 184.

[2]   Parliament convened from 1 March until 22 December: *RP*, iii. 604. See above, p. 340.

[3]   In the earliest recension of the chronicle Walsingham offered the following account of the succession of Gregory XII:

The apostolic see was vacant because of the death of Pope Innocent VII, and on the feast of St Clement [23 November] in this year there was a meeting of the seven Roman cardinals to consider the bad name which the Christian religion had acquired from the pestilential schism, which, to their great sorrow, had now lasted for such a long time. They made a vow to our Lord and his mother Mary and the apostles St Peter and St Paul,

Footnote 4 on page 344

carried out by the recently appointed archbishop of York [Henry Bowet]. The cardinals then met and elected as supreme pontiff a man who had been a cardinal in Venice and a patriarch at Constantinople. He was an old man, who had seen eighty years.[1] Their reason for choosing a man of such advanced age was that he would be less concerned to stop making efforts to make the divided church one again, if circumstances demanded this, seeing that he knew that he would die soon and would receive the greatest of rewards from God for such efforts. The cardinals also demanded an oath that he would cease his efforts, if the antipope did such a thing before they crowned him pope. And he was crowned on the feast of St Andrew [30 November].[2]

A copy of the Instrument drawn up in conclave concerning catholic unity[3]

'In the name of the holy and undivided trinity, amen. On Tuesday 23 November 1406, the feast of St Clement, as the apostolic see was vacant owing to the death of Pope Innocent VII of happy memory, there met and gathered together as a college for holding the due election of a high pontiff the following reverend fathers and masters in Christ: the bishops were Angelo,[4] bishop of Ostia and Florence, Enrico,[5] bishop of Tusculum and Naples, Antonio,[6] bishop of Palestrina and Aquileia; the priests were Angelo[7] of the church of St Pudentiana of Lodi, Conrado[8] of the church of St Chrysogono of Mileto, Giordano de Orsini,[9] cardinal of St Martin on the hills, Giovanni,[10]

and they swore an oath to the whole heavenly court, and they solemnly promised, each one binding himself in turn to the other and then conversely, that if any one of themselves was chosen for the summit of the high apostleship, he would actually renounce his right to the papacy. Further, whoever happened for the time being to be antipope, should similarly renounce and relinquish his position. And then the anti-cardinals should be willing in the same way to meet together and come to an agreement with the sacred college of the seven lord cardinals. From this union of the two colleges and for its benefit there would follow the properly canonical election of one Roman pontiff. Further the anti-cardinals should promise that they would take great care to bring it about that if any of the lord cardinals not present or from outside the college was chosen by them to be pope, he too should bind himself by the same oath. Finally that none of the people mentioned should seek or obtain any absolution from his promise, vow and oath. And that the above measures should have greater validity, each of the cardinals of the college signed the document in his own hand.

4   Innocent VII (Cosmato Gentilis Migliorati of Sulmona) took the papal throne in October 1404 but the position of the papacy in Rome was so weak and the threat from the supporters of Ladislas of Naples so strong, that even his coronation was postponed for almost a month. With virtually no sure support outside the Vatican itself, Innocent's position in Rome soon became untenable and he was forced to flee in August 1405. The Romans' growing disillusionment with Ladislas led Innocent to return in March 1406 and he was able to consolidate his position with the surrender of the Castel Sant'Angelo into his custody in May. He made some diplomatic gestures towards the Avignon party, but died on 6 November before these could be taken any further forward.

1   The candidate was Angelo Correr or Corrario, a Venetian and cardinal of St Mark, who had served as a legate under Boniface IX and was raised to the cardinalate by Innocent VII, whose favourite he became. According to contemporary accounts he was now extremely frail and appeared to be little more than skin and bones. Correr was elected on 23 November after the cardinals had been in conclave for five days.

2   In fact he was crowned on 5 December.

3   Walsingham stands apart from his English contemporaries for the number of documents he transcribed relating to Gregory XII, Benedict XIII and the preparations for the council of Pisa. The oath, for which this instrument provided formal record, bound the new pope, Gregory XII, to work for a resolution of the schism and when required, to resign. His willingness to fulfil it weakened after the conclave was over. See also Harvey, *Solutions to the Schism*, pp. 187–8, id., 'England and the Council of Pisa: Some New Information', *Annuarium Historiae Conciliorum*, 2 (1970), 263–83.

4   Angelo Accaciaioli, (d.1408) bishop of Florence, created cardinal in 1384 by Urban VI.

5   Enrico Minutoli (d. before June 1412), archbishop of Naples, created cardinal in 1389 by Boniface IX.

6   Antonio Gaetani (d.1411), bishop of Palestrina and patriarch of Aquileia, created cardinal in 1402 by Boniface IX.

7   Angelo d'Anna de Sommariva (d.1428), bishop of Ostia, created cardinal in 1384 by Urban VI.

8   Conrado Carraciolo, (d.1411) bishop of Mileto, created cardinal by Innocent VII in 1405.

9   Giordano Orsini (d.1438) created cardinal of St Martino di Monti by Innocent VII in 1405 and later granted the title of St Lorenzo in Damaso.

10   Giovanni Migliorati (d.1410), nephew of Innocent VII, whom he had succeeded as archbishop of Ravenna in 1400 and by whom he was created cardinal in 1405.

cardinal of the Holy Cross in Jerusalem and the archbishop of Ravenna, Antonio,[1] priest of the church of St Praxedis and bishop of Todi; the so-called deacon cardinals of the holy Roman church were Rainaldo Brancaccio[2] of St Vitus in the Meat Market, Landolfo[3] of the church of St Nicholas in the Tullianum prison and archbishop of Bari, Oddone Colonna[4] of the church of St George of the golden sail, Pietro[5] of St Angelo, and Jean[6] of the church of St Cosmas and St Damianus.

'In the presence of myself, Barontus de Pistorio, and the other notaries and witnesses written below, they considered the disgrace and damage to religion and the serious troubles and perils of the faithful which had so far emerged and which must be thought likely to emerge, unless they were met with a healthier remedy and with the support at the time of the divine mercy, through which things are done. For they noted that since the beginning of the deadly and damnable schism, which sadly had lasted for so long and was still going on, to the grievous splitting of the Christian faith, none of their other pious provisions for the removal of this schism had produced any effect.

'And so they were turning to stronger remedies and choosing, not that which the justice of the law was urging them to do for their part, even though that justice was abundant and supported by abundant truth, but that which from the evil of the times was *de facto* if not *de iure* expedient for the integration and unity of Christians. And raising on high from their watchtower the consideration that it would be extremely dangerous, when the wickedness of the times was taken into account, if there was any delay in the election of the high pontiff to be, they had met together as a body of individuals and as individuals in a body, in which to their certain knowledge there was unity and concord and no disagreements. And they made a vow to God, and to Christ's mother the glorious virgin and to the holy apostles Peter and Paul and to the whole heavenly court, and they solemnly promised, each one binding himself in turn to the others and then conversely, that if any one of themselves was chosen for the summit of the high apostleship, he would actually renounce his right to the papacy, clearly, freely and simply, for the integration and unity of Christian people.

Further, whoever happened for the time being to be antipope, should similarly renounce and relinquish or give up his pretensions to his rights to the papacy. The idea then was that the anti-cardinals should be willing in fact so to meet together and come to an agreement with the same lord cardinals of the sacred college that from this sacred college and the anti-cardinals themselves there would follow the properly canonical election of one Roman pontiff. Further, the anti-cardinals should promise that they would take great care to bring it about to the best of their ability, without resorting to any tricks, fraud or spiteful interpretations, that if any of the lords not present or from outside the college was chosen by them to be pope, he too should bind himself by the same oath. And in a month, counting from the day of his enthronement, the pope should by extensive apostolic letters show to the emperor of the Romans, the antipope and his pseudo-college, the king of France and all other famous kings, to princes, prelates, universities and communities throughout Christendom, all the preceding points as they had been seen by the said lords of the college, and he should also offer to fulfil all these demands and to be ready to relinquish his position in the way described and to carry out all other reasonable measures by which the said schism might be ended and followed by the wholeness of union in the Christian church.

1   Antonio Calvo (d.1411) created cardinal priest of St Praxedis by Innocent VII in 1405.
2   Rainaldo II Brancaccio (d.1427), cardinal priest of St Vitus and St Modestus and archbishop of Taranto from 1412–17.
3   Landolfo Maramaldo (d.1415), cardinal priest of St Nicholas and archbishop of Bari.
4   Oddone Colonna (1368–1431), created cardinal deacon of St Giorgio in Velabro in 1402
5   Pietro Stefaneschi (d.1417), papal protonotary, created cardinal deacon of St Angelo in 1404 by Innocent VII.
6   Jean Gilles (d. 1408), provost of Liège and legate in the diocese of Cologne, Rheims and Trier, created cardinal deacon of St Cosimus and St Damian in 1405 by Innocent VII.

Also in addition to all the things said on the foregoing points, within three months counting from the day of the said enthronement he is to appoint his own eminent envoys for those announcements which are decided upon by the council of the lords of the sacred college, and he is effectually to instruct his envoys that together with the council of these same lords appropriate places are to be chosen by both parties, and he is to give them full power to agree upon a suitably appropriate place, and he is also similarly to promise, as was said above, that while discussions about a union of this kind are in progress, he will not create or appoint any cardinal except for the reason of making the numbers of his sacred college equal with those of the pseudo-college of anti-cardinals, unless it happens that due to the failings of the opposition party the accomplishment of the aforesaid union does not follow within a year counting from the end of the three months mentioned above. In that case he is allowed to elect and create cardinals, as will seem to him to be suitable for the state of holy mother church. Also he is to make known to the antipope and his pseudo-college this point about not creating cardinals unless in a form that fits the method outlined above, so that they themselves may act likewise.

And he is to mediate all the above points which have been begun and which are to be begun, to follow them up and bring them to a due conclusion, to the best of his ability, leaving out none of the necessary, useful or in any way opportune items that may arise. Rather, immediately after his election and before it is made public, he is to confirm and show his approval in a genuine fashion of the above points, both as a whole and one by one, and to make afresh a second promise concerning all of them and in all these ways in the presence of the lords of the college and witnesses and notaries, and he is to sign the documents with his own hand, just as was mentioned above concerning the cardinals. Similarly he is to make an effectual ratification, approval, vow and promise of this course of action in the first public or general consistory suitable for this that he holds after his ordination at a customary and convenient time.

Moreover the lord cardinals have vowed, sworn and together promised that within a month of the day of the said enthronement they will, as a college, make known the election which has been made, just as he who has been elected is also bound to do, and will also to the best of their ability mediate, follow up and bring to an end what has been begun, leaving out none of the necessary, useful or opportune items of any kind that may arise. All together and one by one they promised, as said above, that they would attend to, observe, do, carry out and effectually complete with a sound, pure and sincere faith and putting on one side all trickery and fraud all these things both in their entirety and one by one. And to this effect they all of them swore a corporal oath, touching with their hand the holy gospels, in the presence of those placed face to face before them to listen, that they would observe, complete and carry out all the points mentioned above. Also that none of them would seek or obtain by their own efforts or those of other people absolution from the above mentioned promise, vow, obligation, taking and observation of the oath and all things mentioned above in their entirety and singly. Further, none of them would make any use of absolutions which had been obtained or were being obtained and would in no way accept one if granted, or make it possible for another to be absolved by making the grant of absolution himself or even make an allowance with this other person on some matter, but be willing to remain bound under the said obligation for ever.

Nevertheless, for the greater certainty and sureness of the foregoing points, each of the lord cardinals of the college is to be required to sign with his own hand the documents in their entirety and singly as they are completed one by one, and each of the lord cardinals of the college himself is to be allowed to have one or more copies of these documents according to the decision of his will.

Drawn up in the aforementioned chapel by the venerable and careful Francisco de Duce, priest of the apostolic chamber, Jacopo de Calvis and Pietro de Sacco, canons of the basilica of the prince of the apostles of the city, Johannellus Caraczulus, writer of the apostolic letters, Nicolo Blasi, canon of Narni, Antonello Suracha and Johanellus Caraczulus, writers of the holy penitentiary court; Lorenzo Turinache, canon of St Mary across the Tiber, Nicolo Leoni, canon of St Cosmas and St Damianus of the city, Giovanni Pantaminori, canon of the churches at Lodi of St

Cross, Andreas de Cavaleriis of Sicily, Gabotto de Ratasolis of Florence, Luisinus squire of Lord Gorbasio de Mormillis of Naples; the witnesses especially asked and summoned for this purpose, namely Paolo Pietro Francini of Rome, priest, Martino Georgi, priest of the diocese of Verona, Francisco Paulicio, priest of Perusia, Pieter Surmut, priest of Utrecht, Salvatore Belli and Pietro Blanchi, a Roman citizen.

And I, Barontus de Pistorio, writer and epitomist of the apostolic letters, by apostolic authority public notary, because I was present together with the witnesses and notaries mentioned and named above at the foregoing actions in their entirety and singly, while, as I have described, they were being performed and carried out by the aforementioned venerable lord cardinals, for that reason I have drawn up this present public document, published it as authentic, put it into this form for public reading and signed it with my usual and customary seal and signature, just as I was asked and required to do as a reliable testimony to all the proceedings in their entirety and singly.

And I, Stephanus Georgi de Parco, priest of the said sacred college and public notary by apostolic and imperial authority, was summoned with the other notaries and was present in person at the events mentioned in their entirety and singly and I have drawn up and transmitted a record of them, signed by my own hand. And I Gerlacus etc. And I Clement etc. And I Francisco etc. And I Johanellus etc. And I Angelo, bishop of Ostia and cardinal of Florence, I Enrico, bishop of Tusculum and cardinal of Naples, I Antonio, bishop of Palestrina and cardinal of Aquileia, as described above, have vowed and sworn, and in testimony of this have signed the document with my own hand.

I Angelo [d'Anna de Sommarira, bishop of Ostia], cardinal priest of St Pudentiana at Lodi.
I Conrado [Carraciolo], bishop of Mileto and cardinal priest of St Chrysogono.
I Angelo [Corrario, i.e. Gregory XII], bishop of Constantinople and cardinal priest of St Mark.
I Giordano de Orsini, cardinal priest of St Martin in the hills.
I Giovanni [Migliorate], archbishop of Ravenna and cardinal priest of the Holy Cross in Jerusalem.
I Antonio [Carlo], bishop of Todi and cardinal priest of St Praxedis.
As described above etc.
I Rainaldo Brancaccio [archbishop of Tarante], cardinal deacon of St Vitus in Macellum.
I Landolfo [Maramaldo], archbishop of Bari and cardinal deacon of St Nicholas in the Tullianum prison.
I Oddone Colonna, cardinal deacon of St George of the golden sail.
I Pietro [Stefaneschi], cardinal deacon of St Angelo
I Jean [Gilles], cardinal deacon of St Cosmas and St Damianus.
As described above, I have vowed, promised and sworn etc.'

[The election of pope Gregory XII]

In 1406 on the thirtieth day of the month mentioned above the said lord cardinals with unanimous agreement elected as high pontiff, Lord Angelo, archbishop of Constantinople and cardinal presbyter of St Mark. He took the name of Gregory XII. And on the same day immediately after his election he made the same vow, oath and promise, as described above, in the presence of the said lord cardinals and the witnesses and notaries named above, and he signed in his own hand the single document, of which each lord cardinal has one copy, and which said, 'I, Gregory, chosen as Roman pontiff today this last day of November in the year 1406, swear, vow, and promise and confirm all the points previously agreed and mentioned'. And he was crowned on the day of St Andrew the apostle [30 November], being a man of about eighty years.

[Four ships from Lynn lost off Bordeaux]

During the feast of St Martin [11 November] some English ships were sailing towards Bordeaux, when four ships of Lynn, making trial of waters previously unfrequented and unvisited by our wine merchants and proceeding without proper caution, suddenly fell into the Charybdis which is said to be in the Spanish sea, and in the sight of their fellows were sucked down to the bottom. For the sea there is said to be full of whirlpools that suck down ships in hidden abysses. For three times a day the sea draws down the waves and three times a day it vomits the waters forth. And so the sea takes in the waters to vomit them forth, and vomits them forth to take them in. This gives us the line in Ovid, 'The dire Charybdis spouts the waters drunk'.[1] The remaining ships learned from the perils encountered by the first ships. They sailed away from such a dangerous sea and came safely to Bordeaux, though with reduced numbers.[2]

As Christmas approached, more urgent demands were made for the king to be provided with financial assistance. And so in the end he was granted a fifteenth tax from the commons.

[1407]

In 1407, the eighth year of the reign of king Henry IV, the king kept Christmas at Eltham. At this time the archbishop of Canterbury [Thomas Arundel], under pressure from the prayers of many, took up the office of chancellor, though this was against the wishes of those in love with the honour of this position.[3]

The arrogance of [Louis] the duke of Orléans and his troubles at Bourg[4]

These days saw the lifting of the sieges of the towns of Bourg and Blois in Gascony, which were being undertaken by the duke of Orléans. He had arrived there in proud arrogance the previous year with a vast host of fifty thousand men to lay siege to these towns. But during the eight successive weeks of his siege of these towns, not a single day dawned without bringing for him ice, snow or rain or hail mixed with winds and lightning, which drove to death both men and beasts. The result was that in this period he lost six thousand men, who died of various illnesses but especially of dysentery. And their leader who at his arrival had ambitions far above his station and had ordered a cloth of gold to be carried over his head by four knights, now ingloriously went back home, pleased that the heavens had now stopped raining.

Nor must I fail to mention that during the whole time of the siege disasters were always happening to the duke, while the besieged suffered very few, even though the duke was extremely well equipped with siege-engines and guns and other weapons. So because the duke was annoyed that he had been wasting his time there, he dispatched thirty warships, which he had brought over the sea with him for the siege of Bourg, it being situated on the river Garonne, in order that they might burn in flames the English ships which were then at anchor with their cargo of wine in the harbour of Bordeaux and about to return immediately to their homeland. But the English learnt that danger was approaching, unloaded the wine and replaced it with armed men. Then with twenty ships they spiritedly made an attack on the thirty ships of the enemy. After a fiercely fought fight with varying fortunes our men finally captured some of the enemy ships and in them one hundred and twenty men of the type commonly known as 'surcoats', and they deliberately sent one large ship, which they had fired, down the Garonne so that it might blaze away before the eyes of the proud duke. When he saw it, the duke cursed God and shortly afterwards lifted the siege, being in very great fear of the arrival of the king of England, who, it was said, was ready to help the townsmen and would be arriving very soon.[5]

1 Ovid, *Remedia amoris*, l. 740.
2 Walsingham is the only authority to report this episode.
3 Arundel was appointed chancellor on 30 January 1407.
4 The English-fortified Gascon towns had been under assault from French forces for much of 1406. On 31 October they besieged Bourg, the last stronghold before Bordeaux, the capital of the English territories. After almost three inconclusive months, a counter-attack mounted by the citizens of Bordeaux forced the French into retreat on 23 December. Walsingham is the only authority to report these actions in any detail. See Wylie, *Henry IV*, iii. 78–84; Vale, *English Gascony*, p. 53.
5 Such fears were unfounded. The Gascons had made repeated demands for aid from the mother-country since the closing months of 1405 but Henry IV's penury and personal infirmity prevented any rapid response.

A major expedition of the western fleet

About the same time Henry Pay[1] and various others from the Cinque Ports armed fifteen ships to clear the sea of pirates and bring relief to our wine merchants who were about to return home from Bordeaux. And when they reached the area of the shore of Brittany, they caught sight of one hundred and twenty ships at anchor off the coast with cargoes of iron, salt, oil and wine from La Rochelle. They attacked them and captured them with no trouble, except that they burnt some and sank some that seemed too difficult to take home. But the others, ninety-five of them, they did take back to England, singing glad songs of triumph as they did so. The reason this expedition was so successful was that the French had heard that our king was on his way to Gascony. So when they saw our ships from far off, they thought the king of England had arrived. So, not giving a thought to their cargoes, they scurried to save their own heads and in the greatest haste crossed the waves in small boats to the solid ground, leaving just a few men on board their ships who were no defence.

A council at London

At that time the king held a great council at London that lasted from Easter [27 March] for almost nine complete weeks. We have not been allowed to know what happened there, except perhaps that the king immediately demanded moneys both from the clergy and the laity, to what end God knows.[2]

The bishop of Salisbury dies

About this time came the death of Richard Mitford, bishop of Salisbury.[3] At the same time notices were fixed up in many places in London and on the doors of St Paul's saying that king Richard was alive, and that he would soon be coming in majesty and glory to take up his kingdom again. But the person who had rashly dared to invent such a foolish lie was soon captured and punished, and the fact that it was a lie qualified the joy that many people had felt.

A pestilence

This summer as a result of an infection in the air a pestilence greater than any that had been seen in this land for several years attacked the bodies of men so violently that I could quote the poet, 'The warm winds from the south breathed blasts of death, and plague ruled 'mid the mighty city's walls'.[4] For within a short time thirty thousand people of both sexes died in London. And then also 'with greater loss it reached the wretched folk' of the towns of the countryside, so that many homes, which a little while ago had been places of large, happy families, were now completely emptied of inhabitants.

Portents

In the Isle of Ely portents were seen which seemed to be of armies fighting one another, one clad in white armour, one in red.

---

1   For Pay, a privateer see above, p. 340.
2   The great council opened a new phase in Henry's government, as Archbishop Arundel presided as the king's newly appointed chancellor and, for the first time, Henry, Prince of Wales, was also closely involved. As in previous months, the main purpose of this meeting was to consider the means of raising further funds; the continuing truce with Scotland was also discussed as was the legitimation (excluding the royal succession) of Henry's half-brothers, the Beauforts. See also Wylie, *Henry IV*, ii. 296, 378; iii. 304, 314, 323, 331.
3   Mitford died in late April or early May 1407. His successor was Nicholas Bubwith, who was translated from the see of London in June.
4   Ovid, *Metamorphoses*, vii., ll. 532, 553.

[Agreement between Pope Gregory and the antipope. The letter of Pope Gregory]

At that time the pope at Rome and the antipope came to agreement by letter. The documents were as follows:[1]

'To Peter de Luna, whom some call Pope Benedict XIII during this unhappy schism, Gregory sends a plan etc. for bringing about peace and union. As the truth says, he who humbles himself will be exalted, and he who exalts himself will be humbled [Luke, xiv. 11]. So obediently following this most salutary precept, as far as is allowed us from on high, we have decided to set aside all disagreement and to speak to you kindly in our letter and to press you to reunite the church, or rather to invite you to take part in a council, which we have taken on ourselves to summon on behalf of Christians.

'You can see the shame suffered by the Christian religion and the great evils, dangers, and disadvantages which for the last thirty years have happened to the people of God owing to this pestilential and wicked schism, and which will go on happening daily, unless something is done about it. It seems certain that those who were the cause of all these troubles in the first place have not given up the strict justice of their case or been persuaded, perhaps, by considerations of fairness. Nevertheless they do not doubt that the Christian religion has suffered grave harm. So if the same thing continues to happen now, it is difficult to see how a remedy can be found to stop the church remaining in these straits to which it has become accustomed. You know how you yourself and your conscience stand on this matter. But we shall most openly declare our mind and our intention. It is not our plan to waste time in any way, but just as our legal rights are stronger, more certain and firmer, so do we think it more laudable to abandon them for the sake of peace and the reunification of Christians. For one should not argue always from a position of strict legality. Often strictness itself yields to goodwill and circumstance. For if that famous woman [1 Kings, 3: 16–28] was willing to give up her rights and to deprive herself of her own son, to avoid seeing the cutting in half of the one boy, how much more does it seem that we should piously give up our rights, if we cannot achieve the desired unity by going down the paths of strict justice owing to malice.

'So let us both arise, and eagerly embrace one plan for unity and so bring salvation to our church that has now been afflicted by this disease for so long! To this we urge you; to this we invite you. We are ready to offer to give up and renounce our most undoubted right to the papacy, and we shall put this into effect, if ever you renounce and give up your alleged right to the papacy or depart from it, or if any successor to you renounces and gives up his alleged right to the papacy or departs from it. This we shall do, on condition that those who are acting as cardinals in your arrangements are willing so to meet and come to an actual agreement with our venerable brother cardinals of the holy Roman church that there follows the canonical election of one Roman pontiff.

'And so that this plan may be more quickly put into effect, we shall speedily send to you our envoys, so that they may arrange with you a convenient and suitable place for the completion of this matter. Also while discussions about this union are in progress, we shall not appoint or create any cardinal, except perhaps for the reason of making equal the number of our brothers with the number of those who are acting as cardinals with you, so that we can proceed to the solemn and canonical election of one Roman pontiff with the numbers thus equal on both sides. And apart from this need to make numbers equal, as I have said, we have decided to appoint no other cardinal, unless it happens, through your failings or those of your party, that the accomplishment of the aforesaid union has not followed within a year and three months, counting from the day of our enthronement. But we have said this about not creating cardinals while discussions on this

---

[1]   As noted above (p. 344) these documents were not widely quoted by the English authorities. Gregory XII opened the correspondence barely a month after his election. See also Harvey, Solutions to the Schism, p. 187. Gregory's letter is known by its incipit 'Quis se humiliat'. See *Sacrorum conciliorum nova et amplissima collectio*, ed. J. D. Mansi (53 vols., Graz, 1960–2, reprinting earlier edition), xxvi. 1013–14.

matter are in progress, thus intending to give it a place in our thinking, provided that you also are willing to abide by the same condition. As for this offer and declaration that we will not appoint cardinals, and our previous offer of renouncing the papacy in the manner described above, that we might be put under a stricter obligation to make them, before our election we swore, vowed and promised that we would effectively make them, putting ourselves under the same obligation as all our other aforementioned individual brothers in the event of any of us being chosen for the height of the apostolate, and now again after our election we have made the very same oath, vow, promise and ratification to show a firmer determination. And nobody should be surprised that the seal affixed to the present document is without the impression of our name, for the use of the seal completed with such an impression of our name is not considered to be proper before the ceremony of our coronation. Given at Rome at St Peter's on 11 December 1406, the tenth day after our election.'[1]

The reply of the antipope[2]

'Benedict, bishop and servant of the servants of God, sends wishes and plans equally for peace and union to all those who as cardinals give support in this wicked schism to Angelo Corrario, who calls himself Gregory [XII]. Recently, in fact on the fifteenth day of this month of January, we received a letter from you and the said Angelo, which contained vows, oaths, promises, ideas and schemes of yours for a discussion on the unity of the holy church of God. Such a discussion has been frequently tried for by us in the past by many ways and means, but sadly it has not so far actually happened, although we and all the faithful are awaiting this end. Having understood the tenor of your letter, and having gained from its various individual points much material, which it not unworthily supplied to us, for joy and exultation in the Lord, we give thanks to Him from whose streams the charisma of all men's graces are derived, and who has thought it right to illuminate your hearts in this way with the splendour of his gift, that, as the indications of your promise bear witness, you have decided to join with us in a longing for pursuing and obtaining union. For our hearts have always aspired to this, this is the object of our desires, for this we are ready and offer ourselves, so that there may follow the union in the church of God which is longed for by all the faithful. And so that our plan and intentions may be clearer and better known to the said Angelo, to you and to all the faithful, we have sent the following letter in reply to Angelo, after previous discussions with our venerable brother cardinals of the holy Roman church.'

'Benedict, bishop and servant of the servants of God, sends wishes and plans equally for true peace and union to Angelo called Corrario, whom some people who support him in this wicked schism call Gregory. We received your letter from the hands of a lay brother of the order of the preaching brothers on the fifteenth day of this month of January. Part of it contained a summary of ideas concerning a discussion about the union of the holy church of God. In the past we have tried with frequent repetitions for such a discussion, but it has never been brought to fruition as sins have driven it away. Now having seen the tenor of your letter, we give thanks to Him, who of his ineffable mercy when the fullness of time came put on the covering of our humility and at his birth's beginning had already begun to join together different walls, and who now has granted us, who seek peace and union with our whole hearts, at the beginning of our elevation to the height of the supreme apostolate to find a man of such a kind, as your letter bears witness, that he has the sincere intention of making the agreement with us that we have longed for and do still long for,

---

[1]   This message of unity was exactly what the cardinal electors had expected from Gregory. His letter was received warmly in Paris where support for the antipope Benedict was waning fast, and at first even Benedict himself appeared to welcome it and preparations were made for a meeting of the two pontiffs at Savona.
[2]   Benedict's positive response to the proposal was made only a matter of weeks after his receipt of Gregory's letter. At this stage the auspices for at least a meeting, if not a solution to the schism, were good. See also *Sacrorum conciliorum . . . collectio*, ed. Mansi, xxvi. 1014–16.

judging by this salutary proposal of his, which is acceptable to God, meet for the saving of souls, necessary for the world, useful and the object of our most fervent prayers.

'For, as we have no doubt you are aware, we and our party have often in the past laboured and sweated to persuade your immediate two predecessors in the office, which you have taken up, to pluck out by the roots this deadly evil from the midst of Christendom and to drive it far away from the bounds of the church militant. For we sadly are well aware of the damage which this accursed quarrel has caused to Christian people over a long period. For those who started these troubles are those who have continued and promoted the schism by time after time neglecting justice and suppressing truth, as seems certain particularly to those who know the truth of the matter and have considered fairly the attempts made to deal with the current problem. But it pains us to say that these labours of ours were brought to nothing by the evil actions of your aforesaid predecessors. We got opened up for them the paths of justice and of reason as well, and we showed ourselves ready to receive and follow up similar openings from them, but from them came no answer of co-operation or any helpful word.

'But happy are you if the lord has reserved you for this co-operation, and if, as you make every effort to take advantage of the opportunity for it, and as you show yourselves to be like us in our efforts to attain unity, you omit no part of the things you have pledged yourself to do. For we with pious pleadings invite you to such co-operation. You will find us ready, and we have the keenest desire to see it happen. It is something which our hearts have always aspired to and still do aspire, something which has been the subject of our prayers and longings, in order that, with the Lord directing us with his knowledge and enabling us with his power, we may humbly serve him and bring about the desired union in the church of God.

'But what we cannot pass over in silence (in fact it causes us awe-struck surprise and amazement) is your seeming to intimate, if your letter is any guide, that you are unable to arrive at the desired union along the paths of justice, because it is we who seem in some measure to be painted as the ones who have refused to enter or somehow blocked the roads of discussion, truth and justice. But never think this of us! For, as God is our witness, on this matter we have never refused or blocked the way of justice, discussion and truth, but, to speak truly, we offered it, we desired it and still do desire it. With due thoughtfulness we sought and pursued this means with your predecessors, as you yourself can witness since, as we saw, you were sometimes present with them yourself, and we pursued it with those other people who were concerned in the matter. It is not we who have failed or do fail now or ever will fail to see how important to us is justice and truth in this matter, as can be perfectly clearly seen from the aforesaid offers which we made to your predecessors, since we are completely certain of our rights through our knowledge of the facts and the evidence of the law itself.

'And so in order that you may be sure of our past and present intentions concerning the uprooting of this lamentable schism and the achieving of unity, we are making clear to you in the contents of this present letter our offer to bring about the speedier and more efficient carrying out of the longed for discussions on unity. This offer is that we, together with the college of our venerable brothers, are ready to meet in person in a place judged safe, proper and suitable by the cardinals of the holy Roman church with you and with anyone who may succeed you and with the college of yourself or of your successor, or with you or your successor on your own after the withdrawal of the said people who on your side are acting or in the future shall act as cardinals. We are willing to do this so that with the help of the lord we may discuss the unity of the church and bring it into being. So at this meeting, once we have decided and agreed upon those things which shall seem appropriate and necessary to arrange for a sure and swift union, we are prepared, for the sake of the peace and salvation of souls and for the restored unity of Christians, in person freely and simply to give up and renounce our most just right to the papacy, provided that you at the same time in the same way will renounce and give up your alleged right to the papacy or withdraw from it, or provided that whoever is your successor will in the same way renounce and give up his alleged right to the papacy or withdraw from it. And all this, of course, depends on you or your successor and those who on your side are acting or shall act as cardinals, as said above, all being willing actually to come to a meeting and to come to an agreement with us and our vener-able brothers, so that there may then follow from this the canonical election of a single Roman pontiff and the union of the holy church of God.

'As for those envoys whom you declare you intend speedily to send to our presence, we shall be pleased and glad to see them and to listen to their words. We shall look after them kindly and we have already sent them a safe conduct by means of the aforesaid lay brother. As for your further point about abstaining from creating cardinals except in certain cases, we are willing to abide by it and intend to do so.

'So hurry, don't delay, but come with speed to meet us. Bearing in mind the shortness of our human span, do not procrastinate and put off this immense good any longer, but quickly embrace the road to salvation and peace, so that finally at the last judgement we, together with the count-less hosts of those who will follow us in this eagerly awaited union and whom we shall lead into our lord's sheepfold in his presence, may, as we hope for his mercy, be led by the good shepherd who laid down his life for his sheep into the delectable dwelling places. Amen. Given at Marseilles at the church of the holy Victor on 31 January in the twelfth year of our papacy.'

'And so by the bowels of mercy of Jesus Christ we beseech and urge you to stand firm by this offer that you have made. May the words proceeding from your lips not have been spoken in vain! Help to bring it about. May you be willing to carry out your share of the bargain, omitting none of the conditions to which you have pledged yourself, so that our eagerly awaited discussions of union may not suffer the harm of further delay, but, in the presence of God whose cause is the subject of them, be speedily and successfully brought to the desired end.[1] For as you know, for our part we wish and desire to resume all possible efforts that may lead to the hastening of unity, since after eternal salvation there is nothing in this life that we want more. Given at Marseilles at the church of Saint Victor, 31 January, in the twelfth year of our papacy.'

A letter sent to the king of France

'Gregory etc. to his dearest son in Christ, Charles [VI] illustrious king of France, sends greetings and his apostolic benediction. My dearest son, even before we became pope, our heart felt a deep inward affection for you and your famous kingdom, such were the glorious services to God of your predecessors and such the extent of the Christian fame of your kingdom, and now, inspired by the Highest one, we believe that, if your holy mother church cannot win over you and your kingdom in any other way, we should finally come to the resignation of our own right for the salvation of your great country and the reunion of Christian people, a resignation to which we have pledged ourself, in the manner you will see described in this letter. So do you and your kingdom lift your eyes to God, in whom you will see us bound to declare the truth to all men.

'Indeed the truth is this. Our predecessor, Pope Innocent VII [1404–6] of happy memory, was taken from the mortality of this world on 7 November. His funeral was solemnly celebrated as custom demands, and then our venerable brothers, the cardinals of the holy Roman church, of whose number we then were, called upon the grace of the holy spirit and entered conclave in the apostolic palace at St Peter's to elect a new Roman pontiff. After many discussions lasting several days, in the end they unanimously turned their gaze on us, then the cardinal presbyter of the church of St Mark, and as one man chose me as Roman pontiff. We indeed in our weakness shud-dered at the prospect of shouldering such a vast burden, but in the power of him who miracu-lously brings our hopes to fruition we put our shoulders underneath it, trusting not in our own goodness but in the extreme kindness of the God whose cause, of course, we would be upholding.

'So once we had taken on the responsibilities of this pastoral office, not for our own sake but for the honour of God and the advantage and good of the people, before everything else we

---

1   The phrase 'discussions of union' was the key to the whole letter. As the masters of the university of Paris emphasised on seeing Benedict's letter, the antipope had committed himself to nothing more than discussion; this letter was not an acceptance of the need for his resignation. But his response was receptive enough for the agents of both popes to prepare the ground for a conference between them, and after negotiations at Mar-seilles, it was agreed that the two should meet at Savona by 1 November at the latest.

turned our minds to ways in which we could end this ruinous, deadly schism which had spread its effects throughout Christendom for so many decades and bring back the renewal of unity. On this matter we are hoping for such grace to be given us from on high that we have already persuaded ourselves in a brief space of time to bring our desires into effect, and, so that everybody may know what we have in mind, we have decided not to rely on our right, completely valid though that is, but to renounce all the powers with their consequences both of legal right and practice which can reasonably be said to be ours but which have the effect of hindering that unity of Christendom which we all long for and of plunging holy church into calamity after calamity. But the more valid, assured and certain our rights, and the more they admit of not the slightest question, the more praiseworthy, in our opinion, is our laying them down for the peace of Christendom. For we should not always stand on our rights. Often we should consider the useful thing to do in the circumstances.

'And so we have put aside all contention and already written to our adversary, kindly inviting him to peace and union, and offering ourselves as ready to give up our rights and renounce the papacy. This is to be brought into actual effect by us as soon as our adversary himself or any successor to him does the same thing, that is to say renounces or gives up his alleged rights to the papacy, provided that those who are acting as our adversary's cardinals should be willing so to meet and come to terms with our brother cardinals that the result consequent upon their meeting is the canonical election of one Roman pontiff. Also we offer all other reasonable ways in which the schism may be removed and followed by an integrated union.

'So that we might bind ourselves still more firmly to this offer, before our election we swore, vowed and promised with our previously mentioned brothers, one by one, that we were all bound by the same chain to make good this offer, in case one of us was elected to the lofty height of the chief apostolate, and that after this election we would a second time swear, vow, promise and ratify this offer to make for greater certainty. We also are about to speedily dispatch our envoys to arrange with those same opponents of ours a suitable and convenient place for making this union. So by the glorious blood of our lord Jesus Christ we beg and beseech you to rise up without delay and to play your part, making every effort and every attempt that you can that such a holy, health giving and long awaited scheme, and one which is pleasing and acceptable to all Christian people, should be put into effect and practice.

'This is the tenor of the letter that we wrote to the said adversary. We ordered it to be signed at this point. As follows, Gregory etc. Peter de Luna etc. See the preceding letter etc. Given etc.[1]

[The capture of Oye][2]

During these days the French captured and destroyed the town of Oye, and seized and carried off the goods that they found there. This angered the mercenaries at Calais, who in their desire to pay back the French captured the castle of Poil in their turn. They took away with them the huge quantities of furnishings that they found there and returned to Calais.

On Sunday, the eve of the feast of St James [25 July], the daughter of the Comte de Vertus, Lord of Milan,[3] a wise and beautiful lady with great ambitions, married the earl of Kent [Edmund Holland] in the presence of the king.

Pope Gregory's meeting with the antipope is delayed

Some time after the middle of the month of June, Pope Gregory had completed his preparations for his journey to Savona for the meeting between himself and the antipope to bring about unity

---

[1]   Charles VI proved receptive to Gregory's plea for peace and on 7 January forbade the payment of annates to Benedict XIII and agreed in principle to withdraw from him the right to collate to all benefices in France unless a General Council should decide otherwise.

[2]   Oye was one of the seigniories of Calais ceded to the English under the terms of the treaty of Bretigny. It was part of the defensive cordon of English fortifications in the Pay-de-Calais.

[3]   Walsingham is confused here: the Comte de Vertus was Gian Galeazzo Visconti, the nephew of the duke of Milan. It was the duke's daughter, Lucia, who married Edmund Holland, earl of Kent. See above, p. 342 and n.

in the holy church of God.[1] But the king [Ladislas] of Naples suddenly arrived in Rome and took up a position with his army in front of the door of the church of St Laurence. The pope was thrown into confusion by his unexpected arrival and fled for refuge with his cardinals into the Castel Sant' Angelo.[2] There he summoned that famous nobleman, Paolo Orsini, and gave orders for Paolo in person to give help with a strong force, if, by chance, omnipotent God thought it right to smash the might of the haughty king through Paolo's help.[3]

The king indeed, relying on the help of the men of Colonna and especially on that of Nicolo and his kinsmen, dared to use them to break down the castle wall, though, so men thought, this did not happen without the connivance of certain Roman traitors within the castle. But when the king and his forces secretly went in to the castle by night across the broken-down wall, he was suddenly met by Paolo Orsini supported by his army. A battle was fought in which Orsini killed or captured seven thousand men, first having captured Nicolo and his brother and the nephew of both of them and eight noblemen, whom in Italy they call counts. When in the morning the unlucky king [i.e. Ladislas] heard what had happened inside the city (for the king himself had stayed at the gates), he was filled with sorrow. He fled in the depths of despair and marched back ingloriously to Naples. This happening postponed for the time being the public business affecting the whole of Christendom, namely the union of the holy church of God.[4]

The death of Sir Robert Knolles

On the feast of the assumption of the blessed Virgin [15 August] occurred the death of Sir Robert Knolles, that unconquered soldier. The kingdom of France experienced his deadly might in war over very many years, the dukedom of Brittany feared it, and the people of Spain quaked at it. Besides the praise won by his deeds of war, he built a most handsome bridge across the river Medway near Rochester, was a benefactor of the house of the Carmelite brothers in London, founded a chantry chapel at Pontefract and brought to completion many other laudable projects, which could even have emptied the treasuries of kings.[5]

[Ecclesiastical appointments]

In the same year Guy Mone, bishop of St David's, felt the eclipse of the light of this life, having, while he lived, been the cause of great evils.[6]

About the same time master Henry Bowet at the king's instance was translated from the bishopric of Bath to the archbishopric of York, and Nicholas Bubwith was translated from London to Bath. Master Robert Hallum, whom the pope had appointed to the archbishopric of York, was enthroned as bishop of Salisbury, which was vacant through the death of master Henry Chichele.[7]

---

1   See above, pp. 351–3.
2   Ladislas of Naples was alarmed that a resolution to the schism was near at hand and feared that any new pontiff elected at the forthcoming conference at Savona would fall under French influence and favour the Angevin claim to the crown of Naples. With the support of the Colonna, the Roman magnate family forced into submission after the return of Innocent VII, Ladislas led his troops into Rome on the night of 17 June. Walsingham was unusually well informed as to the obstacles that now stood in the way of the meeting at Savona: Harvey, *Solutions to the Schism*, p. 187.
3   Paolo Orsino was Gregory's general. He advanced on Rome from Castle Valcha and drove Ladislas and his supporters from the city, killing also many of the magnates and citizens who had rallied to his cause.
4   Gregory was now reluctant to attend the conference at Savona and when he met Benedict XIII's ambassadors at Rome on 8 July he made his excuses, highlighting not only the threat from Ladislas but also his transport problems. He asked for another venue to be found.
5   For Knolles's exploits see above, pp. 48, 61, 68, 107, 130. For his death see Wylie, *Henry IV*, iii. 238 n.
6   Mone, a former favourite of Richard II, to whom he owed his bishopric, died on 31 August 1407. He was succeeded by Henry Chichele, who was consecrated in June 1408.
7   Henry Bowet was provided to the see in October 1407. On Salisbury, however, Walsingham or his copyist is in error. The see fell vacant twice in 1407, first following the death of Richard Mitford, which Walsingham reported in an earlier passage (see above, p. 349) and secondly when Mitford's successor, Nicholas Bubwith, was translated to Bath. It was as his successor that Hallum was presented to the see. For the tensions between Henry IV and the Roman pope over episcopal appointments see Harvey, *Solutions to the Schism*, p. 162, and above, p. 340.

Then master Richard Clifford was translated from the bishopric of Worcester to the see of London, and Thomas Peverell of the Carmelite order from the bishopric of Llandaff to the cathedral of Worcester.[1]

[The prince of Wales captures Aberystwyth castle and makes a truce with the Welsh]

In this summer Henry, prince of Wales,[2] laid siege to the castle of Aberystwyth and reduced the besieged to such straits that they humbly begged for a truce, as is shown by the documents drawn up concerning this matter:[3]

This indenture was drawn up before the castle of Aberystwyth, near the new town built at Lampader, on 2 September in the eighth year of the reign of the illustrious King Henry IV, between his serene highness Prince Henry, by the grace of God the firstborn son of the king of England and of France, prince of Wales, duke of Aquitaine and Lancaster and Cornwall, earl of Chester and deputy for that illustrious and pre-eminent king of England and of France on the one side, and on the other side Rees ap Gruffydd ap Llewelyn ap Ieuan[4] (otherwise Rees ap Llewelyn Cadagan),[5] Redderuch ap Thomas, Heire Ewyn, Master Louis Mone, Ieuan ap Gruffydd, Rees David ap Gruffydd ap Ieuan, Gruffydd ap David ap Ieuan ap Madoc, Meredith ap Rees ap Roderagh, and Owain ap Gruffydd ap Ieuan Blont.[6]

This indenture testifies that the aforesaid Rees and his followers, on the precious blood of our lord which they received (and each one of them received it) ministered to them by the hands of the venerable Master Richard Courtenay, chancellor of the university of Oxford, in the presence of the following noblemen, Edward, duke of York, Richard [Beauchamp] earl of Warwick, John, Lord Furnivall,[7] Thomas, Lord Carew,[8] John, Lord Audley,[9] and the knights [Sir] William Bourchier,[10] [Sir] Francis Court,[11] William Harrington,[12] Thomas Gunstalle, [Sir] Roger Leche,[13] John St John,[14] John Oldcastle,[15] John Greindor,[16] John Blount,[17] Richard Kighley,[18] [Sir]

---

[1] Clifford, who had been bishop of Worcester since 1401, was translated to London on 22 June 1407. Peverell, who had been bishop of Llandaff since 1398, was translated to Worcester on 4 July 1407.
[2] Henry of Monmouth (b.1387), created prince of Wales, duke of Cornwall and earl of Chester on 15 October 1399.
[3] Glyn Dŵr's supporters had held Aberystwyth since 1403. Walsingham gives an unduly sanguine impression of Prince Henry's position. The siege had continued for more than a month, during which time Henry had seen a number of his troops desert him. The terms of the truce, which were agreed on 12 September, were negotiated by the clerk, Richard Courtenay. See also *CPR, 1405–8*, pp. 361–2. Davies, *Revolt*, pp. 124–5.
[4] Also known as Rhys Ddu or Rees the Black.
[5] Cadagan and ap Llewelyn ap Ieuan were separate individuals.
[6] For those listed here see also *CCR, 1402–5*, p. 252.
[7] John Talbot (b.1384), later earl of Shrewsbury: Wylie, *Henry IV*, iii. 112, 265.
[8] Thomas, Lord Carew: Wylie, *Henry IV*, i. 346–7, iii. 111.
[9] John, Lord Audeley, had been given custody of Brecon Castle in 1404: *CPR, 1401–5*, pp. 311, 370.
[10] Sir William Bourchier (c. 1374–1420), began his military career in the service of Thomas, duke of Gloucester and became constable in 1415.
[11] Sir Francis Court, lord of Pembroke, was knighted at Henry IV's coronation: Wylie, *Henry IV*, ii. 309, iv. 37 and n.
[12] Sir William Harrington (d.1440), a Lincolnshire knight, who subsequently served as the king's banner-bearer at Agincourt.
[13] Sir Roger Leche of Chatsworth represented Derbyshire in parliament: Wylie, *Henry IV*, iii. 222, 230, 418, 481.
[14] For Sir John St John see above, p. 277 and *CCR, 1401–5*, pp. 204, 207.
[15] It is worth noting the presence of the heretic and future traitor in the company of the young prince. For his later career see below, pp. 390–5, 405–6, 425–8.
[16] Sir John Greindor was sheriff of Glamorgan and constable of Chepstow, Monmouth and Radnor: Wylie, *Henry IV*, iii. 33.
[17] Sir John Blount was constable of Newcastle-under-Lyme and Tutbury: Wylie, *Henry IV*, iii. 302.
[18] Perhaps to be identified with the Gilbert or John Knightly who served in Clarence's campaign of 1412, see below, pp. 388.

Humphrey Stafford[1] and William Newport[2] and in the presence of very many other trustworthy witnesses, swore an oath (and each of them swore a corporal oath) that, if the illustrious princes Henry by the grace of God king of England and of France and lord of Ireland and Henry by the same grace prince of Wales, or either of them, or the deputy of them or of either of them, whether appointed or to be appointed, or those appointed or to be appointed by the deputy should be in or near the town of Aberystwyth, otherwise called the new town of Lampader, on 24 October next at sunrise and should continue to stay in the town or nearby right up to the next following feast of All Saints [1 November] with such and so great a number of soldiers, because Owen ap Gruff' de Glendord [i.e. Glyn Dŵr] or his deputy or deputies, appointed or to be appointed, did not by force of war or by relieving the besieged drive away in flight the aforesaid illustrious princes Henry or Henry or the deputy of the one or of the both of them, in such a way that the English are compelled just by Owain's attack, both met and made, to leave Aberystwyth between the aforesaid dates of 24 October and the feast of All Saints next following, which happens to fall on 1 November, then the aforesaid Rees and each and every one of his allies should be prevented by virtue of the oath which they had taken from any delaying tactics or any further discussion, and, avoiding all kinds of trickery and deceit, should give up the castle of Aberystwyth into the peaceful possession of the illustrious princes Henry and Henry or the one of them, or the deputy or deputies of one of them, without any hindrance or argument of any kind whatsoever.

Moreover the aforesaid Rees ap Gruffydd ap Llywelyn ap Ieuan and his allies named above swore an oath and were bound by it that, from the date of the present indentures, absolutely no one at all of those who are staying or will be staying in the castle right up to the time of its surrender and who have the freedom to go out and come back in, no matter what their status, position or condition, (except only for those who for the greater security of the castle should happen to be driven out of it by the orders and command of the said Rees), shall not leave the castle so as to go to the relief or the help of the said Owen or his men or his supporters against the illustrious princes Henry and Henry, or any of their men or any of the men of the deputy or deputies of them or either of them, or against any liege or lieges of them or either of them, and especially not against those who have ceased to be rebels and have entrusted themselves to the grace of King Henry and the prince, his son.

Moreover it has been agreed under oath that the dwellings and houses inside the town, whether old and repaired or built afresh during the time of the siege of Aberystwyth castle shall not be destroyed or harmed in any way by the illustrious Henry, prince of Wales, or by the said Rees or by any other party or parties to the oath.

Moreover if any ships are forced by storms at sea or any other contingency to put into the harbour or adjacent shore of the town and the castle, neither the goods contained in them nor their men are to be harmed or damaged by the said Rees and his allies, or by any one of them.

Moreover the said Rees and his allies and the allies individually have sworn that they will keep, look after and eventually hand over the castle in as good a state (or even better) as it was on the day of the making of the present treaty, and that from the date of the present treaty right up to the said feast of All Saints no person or persons of any kind, status, nationality or condition whatsoever is to be in charge of the castle apart from the said Rees, his allies or any one of them, in fact those who swore on our lord's body and then received the sacrament to confirm the oath, and whose names are listed above.

Moreover it has been agreed under oath that the said Rees and his allies, or any one of them, at the time of the surrender of the same castle, shall freely hand over all the cannons or instruments of war, called 'guns' in English, bows, arrows, siege-engines and other machines of war, which have been inside the castle from the time that it was occupied by Rees or his allies, and also the contents that have been part of the castle from of old.

---

1   Sir Humphrey Stafford of Abbotsbury: Wylie. *Henry IV*, ii. 285 and n.
2   For William Newport, 'chivalier', one-time constable of Beaumaris, see *CCR, 1405–9*, p. 394; *CCR, 1409–13*, p. 407; *CPR, 1416–22*, p. 46.

And for the greater security of all the above promises, the said Rees and his allies in the matter of hostages have, without compulsion or force being applied, freely handed over to us the following persons, who likewise were not compelled or forced to be hostages, Richard ap Gruffydd abbot of Strata Florida, a pious man and one honoured for his services to Christ, and Iankyn ap Rees ap David, Meredith ap Owen Gruffydd, Thomas ap Roderich ap Ieuan Blount, esquires of the country of Cardigan. And on the other side, the illustrious Prince Henry, prince of Wales etc., because of his reverence for God and all the saints, and especially for his patron John of Bridlington, for the saving of human blood, whose spilling he feels so strongly about, and because he was humbly asked and pressed to do so by Richard abbot of Strata Florida, Rees ap Gruffydd ap Llywelyn ap Ieuan and all the Welsh nobles inside the castle, of his abundant grace has granted to every one of all those people, who at the time of the surrender of the same castle shall become the liege or lieges of the illustrious Prince Henry king of England and of France, special grace and pardon for their lives and bodies, their estates and revenues.

Also the same illustrious prince of his special grace has granted to the same Rees and to his allies named above who are inside the castle, that from the date of the present treaty up to the feast of All Saints, Rees or his allies or any one of them shall freely be able without any let, hindrance or impediment to transport, send away and dispose of all their moveable goods which are inside the castle from the time of the date of the present treaty, by sea as well as by land, and that the said illustrious prince and all his allies are not in any way, as far as in them lies, to impede these goods, or to seize, steal or sell them. And he has also granted that, as far as in him lies, as said above, the servants of these men or anyone of them shall be allowed to come and go freely by sea as well as by land. And if any of the goods belonging to the said Rees or to one of his allies are violently snatched from them inside the aforementioned period by any of the subjects or lieges of the illustrious prince, the same illustrious prince will get the extreme wrong of such seizure duly punished, as is only proper.

And if the said Owain, his deputy or deputies, should by force of arms or by virtue of war or of relieving the castle compel or force into flight the said illustrious princes Henry and Henry, or one of them, or the deputy or deputies of them both or of the one of them, whether appointed or to be appointed, from 24 October down to the next following feast of All Saints, then as a result the aforesaid hostages would without delay or trickery be freely handed back to Rees, his deputy or deputies together with their servants and their goods both moveable and immovable.

Moreover this same illustrious Prince Henry etc. finally is willing and concedes that, from the date of the present treaty up to the next following feast of All Saints, there shall not be by him any attack on the castle, nor will he attempt to gain possession of it during the said period by any kind of underhand means or tricks.

As a sure testimony to the reliability of each and every one of the preceding articles, the said illustrious Prince Henry, prince of Wales, and the above named Rees and all his allies, affixed their seals one by one to these indentures in the month and year and at the place cited above.

[Owain Glyn Dŵr recovers Aberystwyth castle]

But as soon as the prince withdrew, the agreement and the promises lost all value. For Owain Glyn Dŵr immediately by trickery wrenched the castle from the hands of the people mentioned above, drove out, not without the taint of treachery, those who had made this treaty, and brought in others to garrison the castle in their place. And the last mishap was worse than the first.[1]

In November of this year a parliament was held in London, whose decrees I pass over because there was almost no record of measures taken there, except for a financial levy on the whole kingdom.[2]

---

[1]   There was no trickery, as Walsingham suggests. Prince Henry had gambled that Glyn Dŵr could not relieve the castle by the deadline of 1 November, but, with very little time to spare, Glyn Dŵr did just that. See also Davies, *Revolt*, pp. 124–5.
[2]   The parliament was summoned to meet on 20 October at Gloucester, which may account for the lack of

[1408]

A bitter winter

In 1408, the ninth year of the reign of king Henry IV, the winter was extremely severe because of heavy snowfalls, which lasted throughout the months of December, January, February and March. As a result almost all the thrushes and blackbirds died of hunger and cold. They were so cold that when men picked them up they remained motionless and frozen.

The madness of the earl of Northumberland

At that time, while the king was holding an important council in London with the magnates of the kingdom, the earl of Northumberland [Henry Percy] and Lord Thomas Bardolf, who had long ago left the kingdom as they could not endure the successes of the king, returned to England at an unlucky hour for themselves.[1] For they had such a conception of the hatred of the people for the king and such a presumption of the support of the people for themselves, that they thought all common folk would desert their king and come to the support of themselves.[2] Followed by the bishop of Bangor [Lewis alias Llewelyn Bifort] and his household,[3] whose members took a delight in the novelty of change, they came to a place called Reidswire and rode through the whole of Tynedale until they got to Durham and Darlington, where they spent the night on the feast of St Valentine [14 February]. The next day they carried on with the journey which they had begun, and spent the night in the town of Northallerton. When they reached the town of Thirsk, they had it proclaimed in public that they had come for the comfort of the English people and to help them against unjust oppression, which they knew they had suffered from for a long time now. Their advice was that all those who had loved liberty in any way should follow them. So large numbers of people rose up in rebellion, imagining that everything was happening just as they wished.[4] They followed their leaders all the way to Grimbald bridge near Knaresborough where their passage was blocked by the sheriff of York, Sir Thomas Rokeby,[5] helped by Alexander Lounde,[6] Peter de la Hay,[7] Robert Ellis and others whom the sheriff had been able to collect together at such a critical juncture. But when the traitor lords saw that their crossing of the bridge was blocked, they turned around, circled the estate of de la Hay and went on to Wetherby that night. The sheriff with the followers whom I have described stayed in their rear in the town of Knaresborough.

The next day, which was a Sunday, the earl moved to Tadcaster, followed by a crowd. The sheriff followed him to past the town of Tadcaster, where he set watches of guards all round the town so that the traitors could not get away without some sort of a fight. The rebel lords weighed up the situation and vowed that they would stay where they were and try their luck on the field of battle. So between one and two o'clock in the afternoon the earl with his men rode as far as Bramham Moor near Hazelwood, where he picked his own spot for a battle. No less keenly did the sheriff himself choose a position for his knights, unfurling the banner of St George with a pennon with his arms on waving out behind it. On the other side the earl unfurled his pennon with his arms on it, and fought a very hard fight with the sheriff, in which, as he preferred to die for his cause rather than be taken prisoner, he was cut down and fell. He was immediately despoiled and

information available to Walsingham. The king arrived on that day but the majority of members were delayed by a further four days. Although the parlous state of royal finances remained the principal issues, the commons did agree a grant of 1½ 15ths and 10ths. See also *RP*, iii. 608; Wylie, *Henry IV*, iii. 114–21.
1   For the earlier flight of Bardolf and Northumberland see above, p. 338.
2   Certainly it was a deliberate decision to attack in winter – one of the worst in recent years, as Walsingham reports – when Henry would have least expected it.
3   Bifort had been provided to the see of Bangor in 1405 by Pope Boniface IX with the support of Glyn Dŵr.
4   The size of the rebel force is difficult to pinpoint, but there is no doubt that the advance southwards was made possible by the number of local figures who supported them. See also Wylie, *Henry IV*, iii. 153–6.
5   For Rokeby a Yorkshire knight, *CCR, 1405–9*, p. 281. See Wylie, *Henry IV*, iii. 154–5.
6   Lounde had served as commissioner of array in 1403.
7   De la Hay had served as a JP in the East Riding of Yorkshire.

A sermon of the cardinal in the presence of the king

During the feast of All Saints [1 November], a cardinal of Bordeaux,[1] a man mighty in deed and word, arrived in England. He had been sent by the college of his fellow cardinals to inform the king and the clergy of the realm of the fickleness of Pope Gregory, having already given this information to the king and people of France, in order that these two kings, who were regarded as the leading kings of the world, should lend a helping hand in persuading Gregory to keep the oath he had taken, so that through their authority there could be brought about the splendour of unity in the church.[2] The French king had willingly agreed to make the effort, and he had sent high ranking envoys to Gregory with letters which were full of fruitful suggestions and persuasive ideas, even if they had been written to an inflexible recipient.

So when the cardinal arrived at London, the king gave orders that the mayor of the city and those citizens who were knights should meet the cardinal in solemn procession and welcome him with all reverence. And this they did. Indeed the archbishop of Canterbury together with the bishops who were then in London met him at the door of St Paul's, took him up in a solemn procession and then led him to the guest rooms which had been prepared for him in the house of the preaching friars. Not many days later the king and his lords came to Westminster, together with a huge crowd of many noblemen and priests including the archbishop of Canterbury. The king took his seat on his royal throne. The cardinal was solemnly brought into the king's presence, and, after they had exchanged greetings, the cardinal on the king's order took his seat on a chair set ready for him next to the king in order that he might explain the reasons for his coming to England.

The text of the sermon

The cardinal began by taking as his text, 'My word is for you, o king.' Then he gave his subheadings (1) words of committal (2) narrative and explanation of the events (3) an exhortation and plea that the advice should be carried out. Finally, as usual, there would be a conclusion.

'Your most serene highness, the sacred college of my lord cardinals entrusts to your majesty the badly torn condition of the Roman church and their own persons, unhesitatingly confident that they will find not only the justice which is due to all, but also grace and help from your devotion to them.'

And shortly after this, 'I now come to a narrative of the events which affect the subject of the unity of the church.[3] While Urban, Boniface and Innocent presided over the Roman church, and various others and then Peter de Luna presided over the other side, different discussions were held concerning the unity of the church. But no one was ready for union, and so men of experience concluded that that notorious schism would never be removed unless by some middle way, which would cause neither side to think that they had lost. And so on the death of Pope Innocent, it was that middle way which was chosen by the cardinals who were then responsible for electing his successor. For, as soon as they had gathered in conclave, they decided to put themselves under an

---

[1] Franciscus Uguccione, cardinal archbishop of Bordeaux, who arrived in England in the autumn of 1408 and delivered his speech to the king and his court on 28 or 29 October. His purpose was to provide justification for the actions of his fellow cardinals and in doing so to secure English support for the forthcoming council. His narrative account of the affair was intended to demonstrate the bad faith of Gregory XII, who, the cardinal claimed, was determined to resist all efforts to persuade him to step down. His speech had the desired effect and by 12 November Henry's government had made public England's support for the council at Pisa. The influence of the sermon on the change of English policy is reflected in the fact that Henry IV's Proctor at Pisa quoted directly from Uguccione's text. Harvey, *Solutions to the Schism*, pp. 143–5; id., 'England and the Council of Pisa', 280.

[2] Uguccione had come to England as representative of the cardinals already assembled at Pisa to secure English support for the proposed council.

[3] The archbishop's narrative rehearses some of the events, such as the death of Innocent VII and the election of Gregory XII, and the proposal for a conference at Savona, that Walsingham has already described, but he also reports on the failure of the Savona conference and its immediate consequences.

obligation and actually did so. The form of this obligation is contained in the very many public documents, which the individual cardinals signed with their own hands. Among them was the one who was elected pope, and this was Pope Gregory, who is now at the centre of the dispute. Once the person of this Gregory had been elected and enthroned, he himself ratified and approved this same obligation in the form that had been decided in the conclave, and he also made his promise and swore his oath a second time.

'And because it seemed sensible that a definite place should be chosen in which both sides with their colleges could meet for discussion, for this reason ambassadors were appointed and sent on behalf of Gregory to Peter de Luna, who calls himself Benedict. They met him in the city of Marseilles, came quite easily to an agreement about the words and the external form of the agreement, and unanimously chose Savona as the place, a choice that was approved by the Lord Gregory.

'And it is said that, despite all this, the same Peter de Luna sent his secretary in one galley in very great haste to Pope Gregory, in order to make a bargain with him. And as the time fixed for their meeting in the city of Savona drew near, the said Peter de Luna arrived with his college. But when the said Pope Gregory had now got as far as Siena, he sent his envoys to Savona to make excuses and apologies for why Pope Gregory had not come to Savona and was not intending to come. And because the excuses made did not seem legally valid, there arose a strong presumption that Pope Gregory had been wrong to change his mind, and a strong justification of Peter de Luna as being in the right.[1]

'So having renewed discussions about the place, and not being able to agree on the one, same place, they agreed on two places which were side by side, so that Peter de Luna should come to the place called Portovenere, which was in fealty to the Genoese or the French, and that Pope Gregory should come to the place called Pietra Santa, in the dominions of the city of Lucca, and in fealty to Pope Gregory himself. And Peter de Luna's side showed public documents concerning this meeting, and Peter de Luna accepted that way forward offered him by the envoys of Pope Gregory.[2]

'After this a dispute broke out because the pope said that he was not obliged to go to Pietra Santa, unless he had the higher position, which the lord of Lucca was unwilling to surrender to him. Many days passed in discussions concerning this meeting, with Luna's envoys saying that their master had made a promise without conditions and with the pope saying that he would only attend on certain conditions. And here out of the goodness of my heart I pass over certain matters that tell against Lord Gregory. After this with great difficulty he promised [Peter de Luna] that he would meet him at the city of Lucca and he actually arrived at Lucca.[3] But having settled there, he strongly recommended the city of Pisa as a place where both parties could meet and offered Pisa to Luna by word of mouth and by letter, but [Peter de] Luna did not accept this suggestion.

Another day the antipope's envoys returned to Lucca and said in public to Gregory in reply to a question from his secretary that they would agree to the place called Avenza, and that they would ensure that their master whom they called Benedict would come there, notwithstanding the fact that this place of Avenza was in fealty to Gregory and also under the temporal rule of the lord of Lucca, who himself is in obedience to the pope and effectively his vassal. But Gregory declined the offer, even though the place had been chosen as favourable to him, and said that

---

[1]   Gregory had left Rome on 9 August and had reached Siena by the beginning of September. He was still there on 1 November, the date at which the conference at Savona had been set to begin. Benedict XIII, however, had reached Savona and now made the most of his moral victory.

[2]   Porto Venere was in Genoese territory but, as Walsingham reports, it was occupied by the French with Marshal Bouccicault as governor; Petra Santa was the furthest extreme of the Luccese. Both popes were reluctant to move beyond the region where their personal safety might be (more or less guaranteed). Leonardo Bruni reported wrily, 'One pope like a land animal refused to approach the shore, the other, like a water-beast refused to leave the sea.'

[3]   Gregory XII arrived at Lucca in January 1408. He proposed a meeting at Pisa in a letter to Benedict XIII on April 1.

Corrario, which was only two miles distant from Avenza, would be much more suitable than Avenza for receiving the pope and his college. So I said to him, "Holy father, if you refuse so suitable a place which is in fealty to you, while your opponent accepts a place less suitable to himself as it is in fealty to you, your opponent is totally justified, and the whole burden of responsibility remains with you." [1]

'After this the pope could see that all the lord cardinals were of one mind for unity, and so he determined to create new cardinals who would follow his will without question. So he entered the consistory, surrounded, unusually, by armed men, made his way up to his seat and abruptly said, "My wish is the welfare of the church." And, having made the sign of the cross, he then took out a paper that contained the names of those he wanted to make cardinals. Then the cardinals cried out, saying, "Holy father, what is it you are wishing to do? Do you wish to throw the church into confusion? Are you willing to break your oaths?" And on that occasion he did not proceed any further with that matter.

'But then he took out another paper and said with a fierce expression on his face, "Well, I am certainly going to do something." And having read out the paper, he gave his orders to the cardinals, firstly that on pain of dismissal from the chapter of cardinals and all its benefits they were not to leave the city of Lucca; secondly that in future they were not to meet or assemble as a body on their own; thirdly that they were not to speak in person or through intermediaries with the envoys of the antipope or of the French, without his express permission coming from his own lips. The cardinal from Mileto[2] replied to him by saying, "Holy father, you can save a lot of time by adding just one further order, namely that there shall be no more talk about union."

'And next he broke his oath, and on his own with his attendants he himself appointed cardinals. When the old cardinals saw Gregory's great resistance and unwillingness to accept Luna's offer and realised that they could not influence him any more, they withdrew on 12 May to the city of Pisa, so that there they might be able to pursue the subject of union, as they were bound to do by the form of the vow and the oath which they had taken. They chose Pisa, as they had noticed that Pope Gregory had selected it above all other places and had offered it to his opponents by word of mouth and by letter. Also, if Gregory sought still more securities, these could be provided by the city of Florence, which had dominion over the said city of Pisa.

'After this, as the cardinals were leaving the consistory, they were told that for the whole day and night in which they were in the consistory master carpenters had been making various devices to keep them imprisoned, and, so the story went, if the lord of Lucca[3] had not opposed the plan, Gregory had been intending to detain under arrest all or some of the cardinals and then do still worse to them. Also that morning the lord of Lucca in armour had taken up his position with his people in the courtyard of the palace of the pope, and had not departed until all the cardinals had returned to the places where they were staying. Indeed the cardinal from Liège[4] tried to escape from Pisa, and Gregory had him pursued by an armed band which had been instructed to kill him unless he returned of his own free will, but when the lord of Lucca learnt of this, he sent a

---

[1] It was not only Gregory's policy that changed after the initial proposal of Pisa, as Walsingham suggests here; Benedict XIII also embarked on a policy that would subvert the hopes for a conference. With Ladislas of Naples now taking advantage of Gregory's prolonged absence and advancing on Rome, Benedict XIII attempted to precede him and take the city for the Avignon cause. His efforts came too late to prevent Ladislas' triumphant entry into the city in April, but they were conspicuous enough to give Gregory the justification to withdraw his support for the Pisa conferences. With the encouragement of Ladislas, he now sought to stifle the cardinals who still supported the proposals and as Walsingham recounts in the passages following, he undertook to create four new cardinals on 9 May 1408. The supplanted cardinals refused to recognise the new creations and before the end of May they had left Lucca and assembled at Pisa, where they issued summons for a general council in Gregory's name. On 19 September Gregory created a further nine new cardinals.

[2] Conrado Caracciolo, archbishop of Nicosia and Bishop of Mileto, created cardinal priest of San Crisogono in 1405.

[3] Paolo Guingi, Lord of Lucca.

[4] Jean Gilles, chancellor of the university of Paris and provost of Liège, created cardinal of SS Cosmas and Damian in 1405.

strong force of his own people which terrified the papal troops, and so the cardinal from Liège got away thanks to the lord of Lucca. So on all these matters and many others the cardinals made an appeal, to Gregory himself, if it so happened that he was presiding over them in sober fashion, or to Lord Jesus Christ, who is the head of the church, or to Gregory's successor, who has the job of correcting and undoing all the mistakes.

'Now because there are some people who maintain that Gregory does wish to come to union by the method of his resignation from the papacy to which he swore, such people can assemble the contrary view from his deeds. For deeds outweigh words. "Believe in the works" [John, 10.38], as it says in the gospel. For very often, while I myself and other people were present, Gregory stated that the method of resignation, which everybody had judged to be fair and equal, was pernicious and diabolical.

'If you wish to know more clearly the reasons inducing the cardinals to withdraw from Lucca, I will tell you. I put before all other reasons the obligation taken under vow and oath by each cardinal then present at the conclave that he would pursue the goal of unity by the method of resignation and all other reasonable means, and that he would not fail to do everything that was necessary, useful and appropriate for this end. You can see this in the original document. I also put before other reasons the fact that vows and oaths are matters of natural law from God, as is very well known, for scripture says, "Make your vow and keep it," and "Fulfil to God your vows" [Psalms, 25:12]. So vows and oaths must be kept for God, whom it is more important to obey than men. I argue then that the cardinals were not able to attend to or carry out that which they were bound by divine law to do, because of the opposition of the pope, as I described above. So they were morally compelled to flee, as in fact they did, from Lucca to another city in which they would be more likely to be able to keep their vows and oaths, on the authority of Christ who says in the gospel, "If you etc." And Pisa is such a city, as you will discover if you attend carefully to the events which followed and which I shall deal with below.[1]

'Also the pope, by swearing and vowing to resign the papacy, consequently also swears that he does not retain the papacy but casts it away. And so the more he clings to the papacy, the more he forswears himself and fosters schism. So then this conclusion emerges: whoever obeys the pope, by doing so supports his holding of the papacy, and so indirectly shares in his perjury and supports the schism. Such a conclusion is shown to be valid by the common laws that state that a participant in a criminal activity commits the same crime as its originator. So think of the nature of the penalty that awaits such perjurers.

'Also the university of Bologna, which is the leading university in the world on the subject of canon or civil law, reaches a similar conclusion, namely that, since the Lord Gregory is facing those particular charges which are deservedly brought against him, any person ought and is able to leave him, as one who is a notorious fomenter of schism from of old. To understand this point, one needs to know the explanation they give of the difference between schism and heresy, namely that although in the beginning there may be a difference between them as there is between disposition and habit, nevertheless later, when they have grown old, heresy and schism are the same thing. This explanation is to be found in the twenty-fourth quarto, the second chapter, beginning "Let us not bring."[2] Perhaps this reasoning will be said to tell against the party of the antipope, in that they are schismatics and therefore by continuing to be so are implicated in heresy. To which we can reply that, although all this may be so, nevertheless ever since Pope Gregory took the oath described above and then is able to remove the schism but does not do so, it can be said that he is the fomenter of the schism, as is clear from the twenty-third quarto "Who is able"[3] and the eighty-third section "The mistake."[4] Also this material is collected more fully in the chapter

---

1   There is no doubt that, as Walsingham suggests, these cardinals did support the possibility of union that the Pisa conference presented, but it is also likely that pragmatically they recognised that Gregory's position was soon to become untenable.

2   Gratian, *Decretum*, ii. 24. 1. 21.

3   ibid., ii. 23. 3. 8.

4   ibid., i. 83. 3.

"Concerning the sentence of excommunication."[1] These then are the reasons that moved and had the power to move the cardinals to withdraw from their Lord Gregory.'

The meeting of both colleges

'Once the cardinals were in Pisa, they met with the college of Peter de Luna at a place called Livorno in the diocese of Pisa. In Luna's college, although only six cardinals were present, they had the power to make an agreement on behalf of the three absent cardinals, namely the lord bishop of Viviers[2] and the Spanish bishop[3] and duke of Bar,[4] who is of the royal family of France on his mother's side.[5]

'You can see very clearly in the letters that they sent throughout the world the decisions and resolutions which they took to renew unity in the church, once they had gathered together in this joint meeting. Amongst other things they bound themselves to stay together in the same place and not leave it unless all the members or a majority wished to do, and also faithfully and carefully to pursue the issue of unity right up to the death. And because that issue affects the whole of Christendom, they thought that a meeting of the general council was necessary. For the place of this meeting they chose the city of Pisa as being more suitable and fitting, since delegates could come to it by sea and land, and could stay in safety in a place where also there were large supplies of food. They also noted that Pope Gregory was accustomed to recommend this very place above all other places, and had offered it to his opponents by word of mouth and by letter. Also if Gregory sought further security, it could be provided for him by the city of Florence which rules over the city of Pisa. Also Lord Peter de Luna would be able to attend as he would have the reliable securities that he had asked for.[6]

'But it is then said that the college of cardinals cannot convene the general council, as the right to do this belongs to the pope, and confirmation of this point can be found in section fourteen which deals with this matter.[7] I merely make this simple assertion that the pope has the power to convene a general council and a bishop the power to convene a synod, but that ecclesiastics lower than the pope cannot convene a general council. And so they had to take this ruling into account. But here we must note that if we wish to make a judgement according to the letter of the law, we must consider not only the words of the law as the Jews do, but also the reason and intention behind the law itself. For if the law lacks reason, it is not a law and so must be rooted out (see section 1 d. 'custom'),[8] and if the case in question is not found in the written law, reason itself has the force of law. For law and reason are interchangeable. For law is everything which is based on reason, as is said in the section 'custom' which I have mentioned.

'Now to their decision. The canons state that it is the pope who convenes a general council and not his inferior. The intention behind these canons is to support the unity of the church and it was to give that support that the canons were published, by stopping the pope's subjects from convening a general council in order to make accusations or for other schemes and thus destroy the unity of the church, as happened at the time of the schism. Now that intention is still to be

---

1   Gregory, *Decretales*, v. 39. 47.
2   Jean de Bronhiaco, bishop of Viviers and cardinal priest of St Anastasia since 1385.
3   Pedro Fernandez de Frias, bishop of Osma and cardinal priest of St Praxedis since 1394.
4   Louis de Bar, bishop of Langres and Verdun and cardinal priest of the twelve apostles since 1409.
5   The colleges of pope and antipope issued their own summons to a general council and then as a united college issued an invitation to Europe's clergy between 2 and 5 July 1408. The council was to convene on 25 March 1409. Gregory's cardinals had already called upon his entire obedience to reject him and await the election of a common pope.
6   Archbishop Franciscus may have held out to his English audience the possibility that both popes might attend the council, but by the summer of 1408 it was certain that they would not. French support for Benedict XIII was fast evaporating and despite his best efforts to threaten Charles VI and the French clergy with excommunication the French formally withdrew their obedience on 22 May. Benedict was forced to flee into the relative safety of his own lands at Perpignan from where he summoned his own council to meet on 1 November. Gregory XII was also now in retreat and from Lucca he made his way to Siena and then Rimini.
7   Gratian, *Decretum*, i. 17. 1.
8   ibid., i. 1. 5.

found in the present case. For the cardinals did not convene a council to disturb the unity of the church, but to renew it. They moved the argument from a peace-loving pope sure of his papacy to a pope whose position was a matter of dispute even if we regard him as pope, and where there is a great dissimilarity instead of a similarity, the argument does not cover both cases. Also, the case of the present schism is not found in the chronicles or the law books. So, because there was no way of removing the schism already laid down, able men through some chain of reasoning had to discover a way of removing the schism, and no sane, intelligent man will be able to find a better and more useful method than that the universal church should meet together and that those who are in dispute should be told to attend as a duty laid upon them, and that, whether those in dispute attend it or not, the meeting should take steps to see that the unity of the church is renewed.

'And if it is claimed that the pope is doing this, the reply is that it is very common knowledge that the pope is not willing to do this, since he himself made the remark that he did not want any schismatic in his council; and he himself regards as schismatics all those who do not follow and obey him, and so such a gathering would be useless for bringing about union but would rather have the effect of giving colour to the error of its ways and so prolonging the schism.

'For the genuine integration of a united church we need a council of those obedient to both popes meeting in the same place. I do not know why we insist that Pope Gregory should summon this council, when it is impossible for him to do this, seeing that men of a different party or obedience would not answer his summons. And if the antipope similarly summoned a council, so that one summoned a council in the east, and the other in the west, no union could come from such two councils. The more likely result would be a perpetuation of the schism. And so our reason shows us very clearly that the proposal of those two colleges, which requires both obediences to come to one place at the same time, is a scrupulously fair and just proposal. For in the church militant there is no other office higher than the college of cardinals, through whose counsel even the pope himself is indubitably bound to conduct all his difficult matters of business. If anyone wishes for full information about the powers of cardinals, he should look at what Hostiensis [Henry of Segusio, Cardinal Bishop of Ostia] has written in the chapter 'Since from him etc.'[1] The four patriarchs, concerning whose privileges some laws speak, are in Greece and are schismatics and therefore etc.

'Also, in my judgement, this doubt is eliminated by both the reason for and the form of the previously described obligation, entered into in the conclave by the pope, concerning and on the subject of the discussions for union. For the reason for the obligation was the general good which can result from the union of the church, and the form of it was communal and collegiate, as can be seen by looking at it, although the obligation under oath is an individual matter only, simply because a college does not have a soul. And so they can be bound over for perjury as individuals, but it is as a college that they bind themselves to the action. Then just as in those matters which come before the college, the minority is bound to follow the majority, so much more strongly is one single man bound to follow it. And Pope Gregory comes into this category, who, after the renewal of his obligation and of his approval which he had given, remained under obligation as one of the college.

'I now come to the third part of my sermon, the appeal. Benevolent prince, both the sacred college and I myself, with my fervent zeal for your honour and salvation, appeal to you by the bowels of mercy of our god to awake your devotion to our cause, and we ask you not only to give your permission but to ensure that the prelates of your kingdom attend the said council at the stated time, in order that by the help and counsel of your devoted self and your priests the peace we long for may follow etc.'

'When the sermon came to an end, the king gave orders for all kindness to be shown to the cardinal. He also promised him all the help and support that he could provide, and invited him to stay on until after the end of the winter, offering him and his retinue generous sums of money to

---

1 Gregory, *Decretales*, v. 38. 14.

persuade him to remain in England. The cardinal thanked the king but refused the sums offered, saying that he wished to provide for his livelihood out of his own pocket.

[A letter from the French clergy to the archbishop of Canterbury]

After a few days the clergy of the kingdom of France sent the following letter to the archbishop of Canterbury [Thomas Arundel]:[1]

'To the most reverend father in Christ, archbishop of Canterbury, primate of all England, natural legate of the apostolic see, salvation and the truth of the spirit in the bond of peace from the patriarch of Alexandria,[2] archbishops, bishops, abbots, representative masters of the universities and chapters, and other high-ranking chosen men now gathered together in a council of the French church at Paris.

'We ask you as a shepherd who cares for his sheep to consider how the livid wound caused by the blow of this deadly schism has been swelling now for thirty years unbandaged and uncured by medicine. Just as Jerome on Arrius[3] tells how in Alexandria one church was the spark that destroyed almost the whole world, because its flame was not speedily extinguished, we also in our day have seen the same thing happen in the church of God. For after the promptings of the one who has a thousand ways of doing harm and who from the day of his downfall has been trying to divide a united church, damage the mutual love of its members and infect with the poison of jealously the sweet honey of good works, and because God has allowed it to happen, we see that in the church of God every head is drooping and every heart is in sorrow, so much so that unless God stops it happening, there will be no health in it from the sole of its foot to the top of its head. No, as Isaiah foretold,[4] strangers will devour its regions before our eyes and it will be as desolate as though laid waste by an enemy.

'But he who prayed for Peter that his faith should not fail and who had already foretold that false prophets and false Christs would arise and mislead many and that his faithful in the world would be subject to many pressures and who is said to have added for the comfort of all his followers that the gates of hell could not prevail against them, he has now looked down from heaven with a more merciful eye on his famous bride being tempest-tossed by successive waves of tribulation, and, clearing the sky of clouds, is now beginning again to open the eyes of the princes of the church and to awaken them from their overlong sleep of sloth and torpor, so that, roused to action, they are at least seeking that which they neglected in their long years of slothful slumber. For now at least the eyes of those who are helpers in the government of the church of the successors of Peter, which had been covered with the clouds of error, are clear with the light of fraternal illumination, and, just as in the time of the apostles, not only Peter but the elders of the church are said to have called a council, those helpers are now calling us to a general council. At this council the two contenders for the papacy will be participants, not judges, because, in all legal systems there is said to be a prohibition against any one passing judgement in his own case, and we know for certain that you have been fully informed about all this by the most reverend father, the lord cardinal from Bordeaux.

'We indeed have now seen with gladness that the face of the sky, which the south wind had made an angry mass of clouds for so many years, has been in part returned to tranquil conditions by a wind from the north, that the storm of schismatic tempest has died away and that a kinder breeze is allowing a safer harbour for the ship of Peter. So we, with a light hand on the tiller, have travelled over the sea and with Christ as our leader sight land and have decided to put in to the

---

[1] Walsingham was again unusual among English authorities in recording this correspondence. The letter from the French clergy gathered at the council of Paris was dated 27 October. As Walsingham reports, it was brought to England by the envoy Robert L'Ermite. See also *Concilia magnae Britanniae et Hiberniae*, ed. D. Wilkins (4 vols., London, 1737), iii. 291–3. For the proceedings of the council of Paris and the response of Archbishop Arundel see *Sacrorum conciliorum . . . collectio*, ed. Mansi, xxvi. 1029–48.

[2] Simon de Cramaud, bishop of Poitiers 1385–89 and Patriarch of Alexandria from 1391–1409.

[3] Jerome, Commentary on Galatians, v. 9 (*PL*, xxvi. 403).

[4] Isaiah 1:7.

harbour of Pisa on an appointed day, so that, as one fair army of soldiers of Christ, we may crush the angry ferocity of oppressive persecution with our firm united approach, canonically breaking the chains put on us by those two men who are so damnably contending for the primacy among us and throwing from our shoulders the yoke which they have imposed. And then God will speedily give us calm weather and after as it were the darkness of night we shall look upon the bright daylight, and after the winter with its ice and snow has passed away, we shall find a serene season of gold taking its place.

'And because not all those invited were able to come to the appointed place at that time agreed upon, but have been prevented from doing so for good reasons, we have decided to send from each province an archbishop, bishops, abbots, doctors and masters of universities and chapters as chosen men in very great numbers with the power to act with sufficient authority for all the others. So, good father, in the account given in this letter we have brought these matters to your fraternal attention, and, knowing your personal qualities, we strongly and rightly implore you to be present at this holy council, so that, if you consent, the news of the presence of your wisdom may be brought with healthy effect to the notice of others. We earnestly ask you that for God's sake you will be willing to do this good work in his service, because we ought to live like brothers in unity, as it is good and pleasant to do. For a man of your charity knows that you read in canon law that both you and we are required to have eyes only for God and the salvation of his people, and that, setting aside all lukewarmness, we should provide the counsel and the help for establishing an harmonious peace between us. The church of God should not suffer the losses of disunity through the quarrels of its leaders, but we are obliged earnestly to preserve the peace that we preach to one and all. And, if the annals of the church are referred to, it is significant that we read that our predecessors have so far always preserved it.

'May God almighty, who makes his people to live in unity in his house, bring it about that you and we, France and England, both together as one, work together with one mind for seeking and attaining the peace of the church. Amen.' This letter was signed as follows: 'Your brothers in Christ, the one whom we read said to his faithful, "All you are my brothers," the patriarch of Alexandria [Simon de Cranaud], the archbishops of Bourges,[1] Tours,[2] Toulouse,[3] Sens,[4] Besançon[5] and Vienne,[6] bishops, abbots, doctors and masters and others called to the council of the church now assembled in Paris.'

[Robert the hermit [i.e. Robert L'Ermite] brings the letter to England]

The taking of this letter to the archbishop of Canterbury [Thomas Arundel] and a copy of it to the university of Oxford[7] was entrusted to a French hermit called Robert, who because of his opinion of the schism was regarded as a great friend by the present king of France [Charles VI] and by Richard, the former king of England. Robert's instructions were that, once he had accomplished his task in England, he was to set out for Scotland and find the duke of Albany,[8] who was then governing the kingdom in the absence of the heir, and the prelates of the Scottish kingdom, and give the duke a letter from the king of France and the lord cardinals and also to tell them by word of mouth the following.

Firstly that the king of France asks the duke of Albany [Robert Stewart] how he wishes to think of this dreadful blow so damnably inflicted on the church by two priests on account of their evil ambitions and contrary to the vows and oaths which they had made to God and the church,

---

1   Pierre Aymery, archbishop of Bourges, 1390–1409.
2   Amelius du Breuil, archbishop of Tours 1395–1414.
3   Pierre Rabati, archbishop of Toulouse 1401–08.
4   Jean de Montaigu, archbishop of Sens 1407–15.
5   Theobald de Rougemont, archbishop de Besançon 1405–19.
6   Jean de Nantes, archbishop of Vienne 1405–23.
7   For the letter directed to Oxford see *Concilia*, ed. Wilkins, iii. 291–3.
8   Robert Stewart (d. 1420) duke of Albany, brother of Robert III, ruled Scotland as regent after the death of his brother (1406) and during the captivity of his nephew.

because the law affecting himself will be split in two and destroyed, unless God averts this catastrophe.

Also the king of France says that the kings and princes of Scotland are bound by the danger to their souls if they refuse strictly to force and constrain the actual schismatics into the way of peace.

Also that the king of France and his royal lords, after consideration of the preceding points, and the views of the universities of Paris, Bologna, Orléans, Montpellier and Toulouse, who ought to be given complete credence on such matters, have solemnly declared that no prince or catholic prelate can obey one or other of the two contenders without being punished for supporting the schism or heresy. And the same conclusion has been reached by the archbishops, the bishops, the abbots and the chapters of the kingdom of France. Also all the lord cardinals in the other obedience, who number fifteen or sixteen, and many kings, princes and communities have reached the same conclusion.

Also that the king of France, to avoid punishment for supporting the schism, has followed the counsel of the authorities named above and intends to obey neither contender for the papacy until peace is established in the church of God.

Also the French king urges his brothers, the duke and the prelates of the Scottish kingdom, to be willing themselves to adopt the same conclusion out of reverence for God and for the good of the peace of the church, and so the lord cardinals ask them to send reliable representatives to a general council to be held in the city of Pisa on 25 March next. For in a council of the French church it was solemnly agreed that the king and the church should send to this council bishops, abbots, doctors and masters up to the number of two hundred persons.

Also, if they agree to send representatives to the council, the aforesaid representatives of the king and kingdom of France will receive and honour like brothers the envoys of the king and kingdom of Scotland, so that, just as through the grace of God their kings and kingdoms have been in political unity, so also they will be one heart and one mind spiritually.[1]

Robert was also given the task of collecting brief replies and confirmatory letters on all these matters, after the presentation of the letter of the lord cardinals to the duke and the prelates of the kingdom.

The archbishop of Canterbury [Thomas Arundel] was indescribably happy to receive this letter from the clergy of France begging him to come in person to the general council. He could rightly rejoice that his standing with the French clergy was so high that this venerable assembly badly wanted his assistance on a matter that would benefit the whole of Christendom. Immediately he counted up the days of his journey, his stay at Pisa and his return, all of which would need adequate financing. He chose the people he would take with him. Indeed his keenness to make the journey in the service of God was so great that, paying no regard to the weakness of his own old age, he there and then approached the king about his relinquishing the burden of the chancellorship. He asked the king's permission to travel. He badgered him in season and out of season until the king nodded 'Yes' to his wishes. But the council of the land was more sensible. It considered that the king's own ill health was now more or less constant. And when it weighed up how much good could result for the kingdom from the presence of such a person as the archbishop, and how much bad from his absence, although the archbishop had already received from the king letters patent giving him permission to travel, the council brought it about that the permission was revoked and the archbishop compelled to stay in England.

[1409]

In 1409, the tenth year of the reign of King Henry IV, the king together with the queen spent Christmas at Eltham. After Epiphany [6 January] the archbishop of Canterbury [Thomas Arundel] called the clergy to a council in London at St Paul's church. After long deliberations

---

[1]   Acts 4: 32.

those chosen to attend the general council were Master Robert Hallum, bishop of Salisbury, master Henry Chichele, bishop of St David's, and Master Thomas Chillenden, prior of Christ Church, Canterbury.

[King Henry's letter to the pope][1]

The king had already sent as envoys to Pope Gregory and the cardinals the knight Sir John Colville and the priest, Master Nicholas Rissheton, with letters to be shown to them.[2] And in the letter addressed to the pope, the king, among other matters, wrote as follows:

'Most blessed father, the apostolic see in its wisdom may have thought it right to notice the widespread perils which have occurred through as it were the whole world because of the schism. And especially it may have noticed the slaughter of Christian people. It is said that the number is more than two hundred thousand persons as a result of the noise of wars arising in different parts of the world. And now, sad to say, of the men fighting on battlefields as a result of the quarrel over the bishopric of Liège between two men, the one with the authority of the true pope, and the other with the authority from the title of antipope, there have already been thirty thousand killed. So, if this has been noticed, the pope should be anxious in spirit and, at the dictates of his good conscience, suffering mentally in sorrow, and should rather leave the office of the apostolic see than endure in the future under a cloak of dissimulation the hateful reproaches for these deaths. He should follow the example of the true mother, who, in the lawsuit judged by King Solomon, preferred to give up her son than have him cut in two. And although, as a result of your extremely surprising recent creation of nine new cardinals[3] contrary to your oath (to use other people's words) it could perhaps be that your intentions do not include putting an end to the schism (especially as the creation of the cardinals must be considered as a true fact), my wish is that the world may never hear your distinguished apostolic see accused by anybody of such inconstancy, that the last sin is considered worse than the first.'

I have given this extract from the letter that the king sent to the pope that it may be clear to everybody with what sober restraint he tried to persuade the pope to fulfil his vow and oath, so that people should not hold the king of England responsible for unity not being restored to the church.

And in a letter addressed to the cardinals, among other things he wrote as follows:

'In our desire to show our past and present zeal for the restoration of peace to the church, with the consent of the estates of our realm we have sent our letter to the high pontiff, with recommendations to be put into effect, according to the contents of the copy sent with this present letter. And so we earnestly beseech your respected assembly that, if it happens that this Gregory is present at this general council at Pisa and gives up the papacy according to the vow and oath which he took when the cardinals took these in turn and assents to your wishes and ours, as we desire and believe to be right, you yourselves will be willing to arrange all things concerning his

---

1   Henry had written to the cardinals on 12 November 1408 declaring his support for the council and on the same day had addressed an accusatory letter to Gregory XII, known by its incipit 'Inscrutabilis'; the letter was not dispatched until about 20 December. Walsingham's summary of it follows here. Delegates to attend the council were selected at the Canterbury and York convocations that were convened in December 1408 and January 1409. Walsingham records only the names of the delegates representing the province of Canterbury; of these Thomas Chillenden was prior of the Benedictine cathedral priory of Christ Church, Canterbury from 1391–1411. Representing York there were Bishop Thomas Langley of Durham, Thomas Spofforth, abbot of St Mary's, York and Richard Gower, abbot of Jervaulx. For Chillenden see Emden, *BRUO*, i. 415–16. For the full list of delegates see Harvey, *Solutions to the Schism*, pp. 151–2.

2   Colville was a chamber knight, Risshton a Lancashire clerk who had previously conducted the negotiations with the Flemings at Calais between 1401–3. For their careers see Wylie, *Henry IV*, iii. 369, 373, 376n, 386; iv. 74; Emden, *BRUO*, iii. 1619–20. The envoys were also accompanied by the abbot of Westminster, William Colchester. The aim of the embassy was to add English voices to the pressure upon Gregory to attend the council at Pisa. They presented themselves to the pope at Rimini on 28 February 1409. Colville delivered a speech and Abbot Colchester a sermon. Gregory insisted on postponing a response until he had apprised himself of the king's letter.

3   On 19 September 1408.

position, as is then most pleasing to God, and that both Gregory himself and we ourselves, who have the affectionate love for his position and its welfare which he deserves, may be obliged to you as a body and as individuals for the bountiful giving of the thanks which we deserve.'

The bishop of Lincoln

On the feast of the purification of the blessed Virgin [2 February] the bishop of Lincoln [Philip Repingdon, 1404–19], having sent an envoy in advance to the abbot of St Albans [William Heyworth, 1401–20] to ask his permission to celebrate a solemn Mass in his monastery and having received this permission, did indeed celebrate the divine office there, the abbot having allowed and given him permission for a High Mass.[1]

Erroneous conclusions

At this time one of the shits to come out of that idol of abomination, John Wyclif, dared to preach a sermon publicly at Oxford that made the following points. That just as the Jewish priests who conspired to kill Christ were guilty of his death, even though they did not put him to death personally with their own hands, in the same way the lords spiritual and land-owning monks, although they have bailiffs and justiciars to condemn people to death, are just as much out of order as their own justiciars and bailiffs. That just as clippers of the king's coinage are excommunicated three times a year, so those who pierce holes in gold coins and put them in the tunics of images would even more reasonably be excommunicated. That just as Rebecca was not a fit bride for Isaac until she had descended from her humpback camel,[2] so the church is not fit to be joined to Christ until it is brought back to its original state of poverty in which Christ left it in the beginning. That, just as Solomon's concubines did not work to gain an inheritance for their own sons but just to accumulate riches,[3] so the monks do not preach the gospel to save souls but to fill their purses, and because they are without the law, they will perish without the law.

The works of John Wyclif condemned at Oxford

On 6 June in the house of the congregation by special order of the lord chancellor sentence was passed by the venerable master John Wells, doctor of decrees,[4] against books published by master J[ohn] Wyclif, perverter of holy scripture.[5] Those present on that occasion were the lord proctors, both those who were lecturers and those who were not, various high-standing nobles, Master Richard Courtenay,[6] Richard Talbot,[7] John de la Zouche,[8] Walter Mitford[9] and a huge crowd of other people. The first book against which sentence was passed was called *The Sermon of Our Lord on the Mount*, the second, *Trialogus*, the third another *Trialogus*, the fourth, *Simony*, the fifth, *The Perfection of the Estates*, the sixth, *Christian Ordination*, the seventh, *The Ranks of the Clergy of the Church*. Also lumped together with these was his third published treatise called *Sophistry*. After a

---

1   This apparently routine request was a sensitive issue at St Albans since the abbey enjoyed the (papal) privilege of exemption from Episcopal jurisdiction and the presence of the bishop in whose diocese the abbey lay might be regarded as an hostile attempt to challenge this privilege.
2   Genesis 24: 10.
3   3 Kings 11.
4   For Wells see Emden, *BRUO*, iii. 2010–11.
5   Congregation was the governing body of Oxford University; the proceedings of this session are recorded in the Junior Proctor's register and dated 25 June 1410. This record also includes a list of some sixty-one erroneous or heretical conclusions that were condemned at this time, not only attributable to Wyclif but also to other teachers. The eighteen conclusions Walsingham reports here, however, are not found in this list, nor do they appear in any other contemporary source. See *St Albans Chronicle*, ed. Galbraith, p. 47.
6   Both a former and future chancellor of the university, Courtenay was also a close associate of Prince Henry. See above, p. 356.
7   Richard Talbot was brother of John, earl of Shrewsbury. He was a member of Archbishop Arundel's anti-Wyclifite committee of 1411 and later archbishop of Dublin: Emden, *BRUO*, iii. 1845.
8   Bishop of Llandaff from August 1408.
9   Walter Mitford, brother of Bishop Mitford of Salisbury, was a member of Archbishop Arundel's anti-Wyclifite committee of 1411 and later dean of Wells cathedral: Emden, *BRUO*, ii. 1252–3.

proper examination had been carried out, these books deservedly brought the sentence of his eternal damnation. Here are conclusions smacking of heresy that have been extracted from the books I mentioned above:

Conclusion 1
The state of the whole, which the pope vows to preserve in this life, is damnable, and if the pope is in any order, he is in the order of demons who serve God more culpably. And this applies not only to his one, single person but to the mass of popes from the time of the gift of the church, and there is a symbolic abomination of desolation, since the pope's heart has been hardened by the wickedness of the devil. For this conclusion see the work of the same master called *The Sermon of Our Lord*, books two and three.

Conclusion 2
Peter and Clement were never popes. See the pamphlet, *Christian Ordination*.

Conclusion 3
The powers which are imagined as belonging to the pope and his other lesser prelates are all fictitious and prompted by the devil, since they imagine that they have the power to excommunicate, which they do not have any more than devils do. For this also see the first book of his *The Sermon of Our Lord,* chapter 44.

Conclusion 4
The twelve officers of the antichrist and his disciples are of course the pope, cardinals, patriarchs, archbishops, bishops, archdeacons, monks, mitre-wearing canons and pseudo friars. See *Trialogus*.

Conclusion 5
The lords temporal can legally take away its temporal property from a church that sins, and on this matter there is no need to wait for a decree from the pope at Rome, who often together with his cardinals is also a simoniac. See the book called *Simony*.

Conclusion 6
There is no greater heretic or antichrist than that priest who teaches that it is legal for priests and deacons to be endowed with temporal possessions by the grace of the law.
See the *Trialogus*.

Conclusion 7
Nobody who is in mortal sin is a true lord of anything. Also see the *Trialogus*.

Conclusion 8
Just as Christ is at the same time God and man, so the consecrated host is at the same time the body of Christ and real bread. It is only the body of Christ as a symbol, and its matter is real bread; or, which amounts to the same thing, it is real bread naturally, the body of Christ symbolically. See the third book of *The Sermon of Our Lord*, chapter 43.

Conclusion 9
Those who feed the people with the Eucharist feed them with everlasting poison, and the opinion of the church on this is manifest heresy. See the second book of the same work.

Conclusion 10
When a faithful communicant asks for bread, meaning the Eucharist as being supernatural bread, the heretics of our times with their fictitious and false beliefs offer him something worse than a stone or a serpent or poison or an accident without substance or some other one thing likewise unheard of or nothing. See the same book.

Conclusion 11
Private confession made to a priest is laughable folly and a practice introduced by the devil. See book 1, chapter 3 of the same work.

Conclusion 12
Just as from the time of Christ right up to the times of Jerome and the other holy doctors more

people have more frequently flown up to their homeland in heaven without making a verbal confession, so ever since Innocent III made such confession mandatory, they have more frequently gone down to Tartarus. See book 3, chapter 3 of the same work.

Conclusion 13

Just as the ceremonies of the old law had to come to an end because of their weight and number when the law of grace appeared, so much the more should the baseless, fictitious traditions of men, which are more in number even than the ceremonies of the old law, be removed by the law of grace at this time. See the above book chapter 6.

Conclusion 14

All religion which is remote from life knows, through being so, the imperfection and sin through which a man is made unfit to serve God freely. See the book called *The Imperfection of the Estates*, also by John Wyclif, chapter 2.

Conclusion 15

Every priest should obey Caesar, precisely because he himself has taught the faith and virtues preached by Christ. And because of this teaching a Catholic should even obey the devil incarnate, while he does not have to obey his priests by copying or doing what they command him to do with their ampler powers of reason. For it is clear that as a result of doing this a man would be ceasing to follow Christ and would be in sin by following the footsteps of the Antichrist. For this conclusion see *The Sermon of Our Lord*, book 3, chapter 5.

Conclusion 16

In the Eucharist the body which is transubstantiated body is not destroyed or spoilt by the force of the change, but in the sacrament itself it remains the one body, being the subject for the accidents of the bread, which I call the mathematical body and the abstract idea behind the perpetual quiddity of the bread. For just as substance is by nature corporeal before it is bread or endowed with the characteristics of some other item, so similarly what formerly was bread remains corporeal when its general essence takes the step of transubstantiation. See the first book of *The Sermon of Our Lord*.

Conclusion 17

From the beginning of the millennium right up to today a heresy of the devil has held sway on the subject of the consecrated host. This can be seen by any reader of the decretal letters of the popes, and the commentators and the parties of the church have stubbornly clung to this heresy ever since the devil introduced it. See the third book of the above work.

Conclusion 18

It is not only God but also the freedom of the will that makes a man sin. For this see the third treatise.

All these publicly preached conclusions and the books containing them, together with other conclusions which were to be preached later, were refuted, damned, abrogated and made null and void by the chancellor of the university of Oxford[1] with the general consent and agreement of the proctors, both those who were lecturers and those not. And the chancellor publicly declared that they had been so refuted, damned, abrogated and made null and void, and also he prohibited any man from in the future affirming, teaching or preaching to anybody these heretical books with their mistaken conclusions, under the penalty of the greater excommunication and being banned from all scholastic appointments. But if it were to happen in opposition to this that any man or men in the university should preach these doctrines, the chancellor with words of canonical warning decreed and pronounced that such a man or men would incur the sentence of the greater excommunication and by their actions would be deprived of all scholastic office and rights of leadership which they had had in the university already or might obtain in the future, and deprived of all honour, status and fame.

---

[1] Chancellor at least until late July 1409 was William Clynt, a former fellow of Merton College: Emden, *BRUO*, i. 448–9. See also Catto, 'Wyclif and Wyclifism', p. 246.

The Death of Queen Margaret of Denmark[1]

The council at Pisa

In 1410, the eleventh year of King Henry IV, the cardinals of both colleges, that of Gregory [XII, 1406–15] and that of Benedict [XIII, 1394–1417], met at Pisa as agreed for effective and final discussions on the reshaping of the church into one.[2] The prelates of almost the whole Latin world met there for this purpose, together with those venerable cardinals chosen to vote on the matter, so that there was a very great number of mitred clergy present. And, having invoked the grace of the holy spirit, they agreed upon one person and chose one man to be head of the whole church, when the other two had abdicated. They called him pope Alexander V, although Gregory and Benedict, who had voluntarily withdrawn from the council, shamelessly growled their displeasure.[3]

This Alexander at the beginning of his period of office granted full remission of all sins to all truly contrite and repentant sinners who were benefactors of the church and priory of the canons of St Bartholemew at Smithfield in London. This could happen on any of the days of Maundy Thursday, Good Friday, Holy Saturday and also the feast of the annunciation to the blessed Mary from the first vespers right up to the second vespers.

In this year Thomas Beaufort was made chancellor of the kingdom, and Henry Scrope [Lord of Masham] treasurer of the kingdom.[4]

The burning of a Lollard

This year a parliament was held in London during the days of Lent,[5] and at this time a mere layman, a tailor of rough appearance, was brought before the archbishop [of Canterbury, Thomas Arundel] on the grounds that he had abandoned Christian teaching and held the opinion that it was not the body of Christ which was handled in church during the sacrament, but that the host is an inanimate object, lower down the scale than a toad or a spider, which are animate creatures.[6] When he was questioned about this, he declared in public that he wished to hold that opinion until the day of his death. And the story spread abroad that while he was facing examination and shamelessly making a strong defence of his disbelief in flowery language, a fearsomely gigantic spider ran over his face, trying to find a way into his mouth, and the heretic was completely

---

1   The heading appears in the manuscript, Oxford, Bodl., Bodley MS 462, the earliest and best source for the revised recension of Walsingham chronicle, but it is followed by a blank space. See *St Albans Chronicle*, ed. Galbraith, p. 47. For Margaret of Denmark who died on 28 October 1412, see Wylie, *Henry IV*, ii. 449 and n, 451.

2   Walsingham's chronology is incorrect here. The council met between March and August 1409. It opened on 25 March in the presence of twenty-two cardinals and almost one hundred archbishops and bishops as well as representatives from the rulers of England, France, Burgundy and the king of the Romans. There followed almost four months of discussions in which the learned opinions of university masters were exchanged; it was not until the twelfth session in 25 May that the two popes were declared contumacious and they were not formally deposed until 5 June. The delegates now proceeded to a new election on 15 June and announced their candidate on 26 June. The preliminary discussions had proved so protracted that any hopes of a general reform were dashed and although the delegates did address the matter in their final session at the end of July the council dispersed on 7 August without having made any notable decision. Given his detailed documentation of the preparations for the council it is surprising that Walsingham reported its proceedings in a single paragraph. See also Harvey, *Solutions to the Schism*, pp. 147–80; *Sacrorum conciliorum . . . collectio*, ed. Mansi, xxvi. 1131–1256; xxvii. 1–502.

3   The new pontiff was the Franciscan Pierre Philarge, archbishop of Milan. Neither Benedict not Gregory accepted the election and thus there were now three candidates contesting for control of the church. Gregory remained at Siena until his death in 1415, Benedict at Valencia, where he lived on until 1417.

4   Beaufort was appointed on 31 January 1410 and Scrope on 6 January: Wylie, *Henry IV*, iii. 301–2.

5   Parliament met from 27 January–9 May: *RP*, iii. 622.

6   This was John Badby, an Evesham tailor. He was examined by Archbishop Arundel on 1 March 1410. For Badby and the politics behind his burning see also Wylie, *Henry IV*, iii. 437–9; P. N. McNiven, *Heresy and Politics in the Reign of Henry IV: The Burning of John Badby* (Woodbridge, 1987).

unable to push it off, although he kept on trying to do so with both hands. In the end, according to the usual version, the spider was swallowed up between the rascal's lips and did not come out again.

As the wretched fellow was in no way willing to give up his opinion, he was handed over to the secular courts.[3] After he had been condemned to burning and shut in the cask at Smithfield, Prince Henry, the king's eldest son, who was then at Smithfield, went up to him and counselled and advised him to abandon his foolishness and submit to Christian teaching. But the worthless rascal ignored the salutary advice of so great a prince and chose rather to be burnt to death than to show reverence to the life-giving sacrament. And so, shut up in his cask, he was attacked by the flames of devouring fire, and bellowed pitiably in this position of extreme peril.

The prince was moved by his pitiful shrieks, and gave orders for the materials of the fire to be dragged away from him and for the heat to be moved far away. When this had been done, he ordered the cask to be lifted off him, while he prepared to renew his words to the criminal. The man was now almost dead, but the prince comforted him and promised that, if he recanted even now, he should keep his life and obtain pardon and receive three pence daily from the royal treasury for the rest of his life. But the unhappy fellow had recovered his spirits after being revived by the colder air and rejected such a handsome offer, his heart no doubt hardened by an evil demon. And so the prince ordered him to be shut back in the cask, with no chance of getting any more favours. And so it happened that this meddler burnt to ashes there at Smithfield, miserably dying in his sin. Men say that on the following night many people who lived near the place of his punishment were terrified by his ghost and suffered discomfort and stress and from gale force winds.

The maliciousness of the parliamentary knights and a very wrong suggestion

In this parliament the parliamentary knights (or, to name them more truly, the 'minions of Pilate') with no thought for the good of the kingdom but with malice in their hearts and no time for anything but this one crime, proposed despoiling the church of God throughout England. Evidence for this is the document that they handed to the king, the gist of which I have decided to insert at this point.[4]

'All the loyal commons, speaking the truth, humbly point out to our excellent lord king and all the magnates present in this parliament that our lord king is able to fund from the temporalities now enjoyed in the land but arrogantly not properly used by bishops, abbots and priors 15 earls, 1,500 knights, 6,200 esquires and a hundred almshouses more than there are now, all properly and reliably maintained from those ecclesiastical lands and holdings.

And on all these lands our lord king will be able to levy more than £20,000 net each year, a fact which has been shown to be true after calculation. Each earl will have an annual income of 3,000 marks from his lands and holdings. And each knight who has in his own possession four ploughlands will have an income of 300 marks. And each esquire from two ploughlands will have 40 marks. And each almshouse will have an annual income of 100 marks for the proper care of the faithful, seeing that the secular servants of the prelates and the clerics have now almost destroyed all the almshouses in the land. And similarly our proposal will help the requirement

---

1   Under the terms of the recent statute *De heretico comburendo*. See above, p. 319.

2   There is no record of this proposal in the rolls of parliament and Walsingham is the only contemporary chronicler to report it in any detail although English versions of the document were preserved in the London chronicle and by Robert Fabyan. The commons' demands were extreme but in the context of the troubled parliaments of Henry's reign perhaps not exactly unexpected. Whether the parliament was indeed packed with Lollards, as Walsingham suggests, is difficult to prove although it is worth noting that this was the first session in which Sir John Oldcastle was summoned as Lord Cobham, a title he had inherited from his wife. It may be that the commons, or an element amongst them, sought to take advantage of the departure of Archbishop Arundel from the chancellorship; he had resigned in December 1409. It is significant that Walsingham locates this episode alongside the burning of John Badby. See also Wylie, *Henry IV*, iii. 307–16; Hudson, *Premature Reformation*, pp. 114–15; M. Aston, 'Caim's Castles: Poverty, Politics and Disendowment' in *The Church, Politics and Patronage in the Fifteenth Century*, ed. R. B. Dobson (Gloucester, 1984), pp. 45–81.

that each town in the kingdom shall look after and support all its poor and mendicant people, who are unable to work for a livelihood because of the statute published at Cambridge.[1] For in cases in which the towns could not support all such people, then the aforementioned almshouses would support poor people of this kind.

To see how this could come about, you may wish to know that the temporalities of bishops, abbots and priors are worth as much as 332,000 marks a year. The temporalities of the archbishop of Canterbury with two abbeys there and at Shrewsbury, Coggeshall and St Osyth are worth 20,000 marks a year. The bishop of Durham and the abbey 20,000 marks.[2] The archbishopric of York and the two abbeys there 20,000 marks.[3] The bishop of Winchester and the two abbeys there 20,000 marks.[4] Clerkenwell[5] and its manors 20,000 marks. And so this first total amounts to 100,000 marks.

The bishop of Lincoln and the abbeys of Ramsey and Peterborough 20,000 marks. The abbeys of Bury St Edmunds and Glastonbury 20,000 marks. The bishop of Ely with the abbeys of Spalding and Lenton[6] 20,000 marks. The bishop of Bath and the abbeys of Westminster, St Albans and Ogbourne[7] 20,000 marks. The bishop of Worcester with the abbeys of Gloucester, Evesham, Abingdon, Eynsham and Reading 20,000 marks. And so the second total amounts to 100,000 marks.

The bishop of Chester with the abbey there of Roucester, and the bishops of London, [Hereford], Salisbury and Exeter 20,000 marks. The abbeys of Rievaulx, Fountains, Jervaulx, Mount Grace, Warden,[8] Vale Royal, Whalley and Sawley 20,000 marks. The abbeys of Leicester, Waltham, Gisbourne, Merton, Cirencester and Osney 20,000 marks. Dover, Battle, Lewes, Coventry, Daventry, and Thorney 20,000 marks. Bristol, Northampton, Thornton, Kenilworth, Hailes, Winchcombe, Pershore, St Frideswide's, Notley and Grimsby 20,000 marks. And so the third total amounts to 100,000 marks.

The bishops of Carlisle, Chichester and Rochester, and the priories of St Mary Overy, St Bartholemew,[9] Sawtry,[10] Huntingdon[11] and Swineshead[12] 10,000 marks. The bishop of Norwich with the abbey[13] and Crowland 10,000 marks. Malmesbury, Bruton, Tewkesbury, Dunstable, Sherborne, Taunton, Byland and Burton [upon Trent] 12,000 marks. And so the fourth total amounts to 32,000 marks.

And in the case where a bishopric, abbey or priory exceeds its usual revenue, the excess is counted for help in insuring that the aforesaid sum of 32,000 marks is kept fully topped up so that any of the persons mentioned above can draw net sums from it, as was described. And there will still be left over £20,000 for the royal treasury. And what is more £100,000 can be levied from the temporalities which have been left destitute and occupied by secular priests: these temporalities will be able to maintain 10,500 priests and clerks, with each clerk getting 40 shillings a year, and 6,2000 esquires as described above. And so in the whole kingdom provision can be made for 15 earls, 1,500 knights and more esquires than there are now to be adequately provided for from these lands and revenues. And further five universities and the 1,500 priests and clerics in them can be adequately provided for from the temporalities of almshouses, if the king and the lords

---

1 The 1388 Statute of Cambridge prohibited the movement of labourers except by licence of letters patent issued by a justice.
2 Correctly, the Benedictine priory of Durham cathedral: *MRH*, p. 64.
3 The Benedictine abbey of St Mary's and priory of Holy Trinity: *MRH*, p. 82.
4 The Benedictine cathedral priory of St Swithun and the abbey of Hyde: *MRH*, pp. 80–1.
5 The Augustinian nunnery of Clerkenwell, London: *MRH*, p. 281.
6 Lenton was a Cluniac priory: *MRH*, p. 100.
7 Obgourne was an alien priory founded by and dependent upon the Norman abbey of Bec: *MRH*, p. 90.
8 Warden, Bedfordshire, was a Cistercian Abbey founded from Rievaulx: *MRH*, p. 127.
9 The Augustinian priory of St Bartholemew in the city of London: *MRH*, p. 165.
10 The Cistercian abbey of Sawtry, Huntingdon: *MRH*, p. 125.
11 The Augustinian priory at Huntingdon: *MRH*, p. 166.
12 The Cistercian abbey at Swineshead, Lincolnshire: *MRH*, p. 126.
13 Correctly, the Benedictine cathedral priory of Norwich: *MRH*, p. 72.

should decide that this money should be spent in this way and for these uses. And there will be £20,000 annually for the king's treasury. And further there can be a hundred more almshouses than there now are, and there can be assigned to each almshouse land worth 100 marks for the maintenance of the poor. And even though all this were to happen, the kingdom would not be burdened by the expense, but this money would all come from the terminated and wasted temporalities of those haughty secular priests. And even if these high and mighty priests lose their temporalities, they still have an annual revenue from their spiritualities, as in their exchequer from these there is the very substantial sum of £100,000 and £40,000 and £734, ten shillings and four pence.

And so far we have not laid a finger on the collegiate foundations, the chantries, the white canons [i.e. secular canons] of the cathedral churches with their temporalities and the churches assigned to them, the Carthusian monks, the monks from France,[1] the glebes, the hospitals for lepers, the hermitages or the crusader monks (i.e. the Hospitallers).

The whole body of faithful Christians, for the honour of God and the good of the kingdom, desire that those worldly priests, bishops, abbots and priors, being the sort of secular masters that they are, should be compelled to live on their spiritualities. As it is, they are not living or fulfilling their duties as faithful priests and curates ought to do. They do not help the body of the faithful out of their lands as trustworthy secular lords should do. Their lives are devoid of the repentance and hard work that should be shown by faithful men of religion according to the profession they once made. At all levels they take for themselves the delights of luxury and ease and spurn toil, making use of the profits which accrue to men of faith. The bad example set by their lives has been so harmful over such a long period that all the commons and the lords of England have been so damagingly infected by a brazenness caught from their crimes that there is scarcely anyone who fears God or the devil.

In England there are 46,822 parish churches. There are 52,000 towns. There are 17 bishoprics. There are 34,215 manors belonging to knights, of which 28,015 are in the hands of the religious communities.[2]

Such were the inventories handed to the king by the knights of Pilate rather than of parliament, striving by their words to do all they could to wreck the Christian religion throughout the kingdom, and to drag the king himself to perjury, in their desire to promote the interests of the Lollard group.

The king and various others care for the church

But the malice of these men was checked by the king himself, that catholic and orthodox prince, who banned them from presuming to disseminate or publish such poisonous inventories in the future.[3] At that time there was only one man in a thousand who opposed this wickedness. He was a powerful statesman and a whole-hearted lover of the church called John Norbury.[4] As soon as he heard the wishes of these wrong-headed men, he went straight to the archbishop of Canterbury [Thomas Arundel] and with tears in his eyes reported the schemes which those pseudo knights had hatched to overthrow the holy church of God and empty the land of all religion. He advised the metropolitan to act like a man, to lift up the cross against the enemies of the cross and to declare a holy war on them, promising that he himself with all his supporters would follow the

---

1   i.e. the diminishing number of communities that remained dependent on Norman abbeys; the number of French-born monks in these houses was very small.

2   The figures are inaccurate. There were fewer than ten thousand parishes, for example and a far smaller number of towns; only 200 boroughs returned MPs. There were 17 bishoprics in England and a further 3 in Wales.

3   The author of the London chronicle suggested Henry prevaricated over the proposal but there is no way he would support it. See also Wylie, *Henry IV*, iii. 307–16.

4   Norbury was a chamber knight of Henry IV who had served as keeper of privy wardrobe, treasurer and overseas as captain of Guisnes. See also Wylie, *Henry IV*, i. 28, 73; iii. 161; iv. 173, 177, 184: *CCR, 1399–1401*, pp. 41, 43, 171; *CCR1402–5*, p. 407; *CPR, 1405–8*, p. 288.

cross and, if necessary, die for the liberties of the church under the cross of Canterbury sooner than see such damage done to God.

But although that detestable gang of Lollard knights saw that they could not make any progress with this wicked scheme or do anything prejudicial to the church itself, they still went on working and pressed very hard for clergy found guilty in the future being handed over not to episcopal jails but to the prisons of the king and the lords temporal. But they failed here as well. They also asked for a change or modification in the statute made concerning the Lollards in which it was laid down that, wherever they were found preaching their heresies, they should be taken prisoner without any writ of the king and put into the nearest royal jail. And they received the reply that they would not be granted what they had asked for in their petition, but rather that the statute concerning this matter would be made stricter still.

The king indeed in the present parliament powerfully pleaded for a decision to be made that he should receive each year as long as he lived, without holding a parliament, a tenth tax from the clergy and a fifteenth from the laity. However he did not get what he asked for. But the parliament was prolonged on these trifling matters from the octave of St Hilary [21 January] almost until the middle of the month of May with great damage to the commons of the kingdom.[1] Finally the end of the matter was that the king was granted a fifteenth tax from the laity, and on top of this the commons were compelled to make a payment almost as heavy for the maintenance of the parliamentary knights. For it did not amount to a small sum when the commons were compelled to make a daily payment of four shillings to each knight or his deputy.[2]

The earl of Surrey dies

At this time Sir Thomas Beaufort, the earl of Surrey, died.[3]

The burning of St Omer and the weapons made to attack Calais

About 9 April the town and abbey [of St Bertin] of St Omer were burnt. Remarkable equipment designed for the destruction of Calais had been stored there by the duke of Burgundy [John the Fearless], consisting of various siege-engines of a sort never seen anywhere before together with cylinders containing poison, which they planned to fire into Calais, so that they might destroy with poison the defenders of the town, whom they had not been able to harm with the sword or by firing stones.[4] With the utmost care they had collected snakes, scorpions, toads and other poisonous creatures and shut them in small containers. The idea was that the flesh of these harmful creatures would decay and liquefy into an ooze, so that, when the duke was besieging Calais, he could fire these cylinders into the town by shooting them from siege-engines. They would be broken open by the force of their landing and choke the inhabitants by their deadly foulness. The poisons would spread and infect the whole city, while even armed men would be victims when they came into contact with their power.

When the citizens of Calais heard reports of this and realised that they were true, they were very afraid and worried what might happen. But, amazingly, in the meantime, a young man, led on by greed for gold or love for the royal town, asked the rulers of Calais what reward he would deserve to receive if he freed Calais from this frightening peril by setting fire to all those terrifying weapons. He received the reply that he would receive as a reward one hundred and forty gold crowns in French money: he would also be famous and dear to all his countrymen in the future.

[1] In fact parliament adjourned for Easter on 15 March, resuming on 7 April.
[2] Payment of the subsidy granted was to spread over the next three years to obviate the need for another session of parliament until that period had elapsed.
[3] Correctly, John Beaufort, 1st earl of Somerset and marquis of Dorset, b. c.1371, the eldest son of John of Gaunt and his mistress Katherine Swynford, who died in April 1410. He had served Henry IV as captain of Calais (1410), lieutenant in South Wales (1403) and deputy constable (1404): *CCR, 1402–5*, pp. 256, 391, 448. 473, 633; *CCR, 1409–13*, pp. 14, 31. See Wylie, *Henry IV*, iii. 303–7.
[4] For John, duke of Burgundy's military preparations in the spring of 1411 see Vaughan, R. Vaughan, *John the Fearless. The Growth of Burgundian Power* (London, 1966), pp. 87–93.

(A French crown is worth forty pence of our money.) Without delay the young man went off to St Omer and made good his promises, for he started a fire in various places which burnt not only the weapons of destruction but also almost the whole town together with its monastery. So on this occasion Calais itself was freed from its great fear.

Pope Alexander V, who had been elected pope in the council held at Pisa, died a few days after his coronation. He was succeeded by Balthazar, archbishop of Bologna,[1] by the election of both colleges of cardinals. He was known as Pope John XXIII.

[1411]

The king of Cracow

In 1411, the twelfth year of the reign of King Henry IV, the enemy of the human race, in his jealousy of the growth of the Christian world, inflicted a heavy loss upon Christians. For the king of Cracow, inspired by a love of Christianity, was baptised in the name of the holy and undivided trinity, and because of this all his friends and acquaintances, who had remained heathen Saracens, withdrew from him and planned to overthrow him or at least defeat him in battle. When the king heard of their plans, as a follower of Christ he asked his Christian neighbours for help against the enemies of his faith. Now his neighbours were the lords and rulers of Prussia, who, before the king became a Christian, were accustomed to invade his lands and carry home from there by right of war substantial booty. But now they should have stopped doing this because of their shared religion. But those Prussian lords paid no attention to this, and when they learned that the king's own people had genuinely decided to attack him, they had no fear of the Lord as an avenger, and, to make the beleaguered king's position still worse, they cruelly and pitilessly declared war on him, even though he had first asked them for help against the Saracens.

And so, caught between the hammer and the anvil, the king did not know where to turn. But at last, emboldened and imbued with courage, so it is believed, from on high, he turned to face the greater danger that threatened him. And although the Prussians were superior in numbers and equipment, the neophyte king called upon the name of Christ, joined battle with the Prussians, and wrought great slaughter among them. So great was his success that he subdued not only his enemy but also all their territory, though in his victory he still had a holy consideration for those he had recently defeated, as he allowed them to enjoy their ancient privileges and to carry on trading as usual.[2]

A plague in Gascony

In this year almost four thousand people died of dysentery in Bordeaux. The pestilence also did such damage in Aquitaine and Gascony that the country had a shortage of grape pickers and treaders.

---

1   Alexander had remained at Pisa for the first months of his pontificate, while Rome remained in the hands of the supporters of Ladislas of Naples. The papal party slowly but steadily recovered control over the city, but it was his cardinal Balthazar Cossa and not Alexander who became the dominant presence in Rome. Alexander remained with the Curia at Bologna where he died on 3 May 1410. It was inevitable that Cossa would succeed him. He was elected on 17 May and consecrated on 25 May 1410.

2   This appears to be a confused account of the battle of Grunwald, which in fact took place on 15 July 1410 between the combined Polish-Lithuanian forces of Jogaila (Wladislaus II) king of Poland and Vytautas Grand Duke of Lithuania and the Teutonic knights under their Grand Master, Ulrich von Jungingen. The need for a crusade in Poland-Lithuania had been removed with the conversion of Jogaila in 1385 but the Teutonic knights continued to threaten the kingdom. Following an uprising in Teutonic Samogitia in 1409, the knights declared war on Poland-Lithuania. The combined armies of Jogaila and Vytautas adopted an offensive strategy, advancing on the knights' own territory. The numbers engaged at Grunwald were enormous by contemporary standards and the casualties were considerable. The defeat of the Teutonic knights effectively ended their influence in the region. See N. Davies, *God's Playground: A History of Poland I. From the Origins to 1795* (Oxford, 1981), pp. 122–3.

At this time two stout hearted, very experienced sailors, the knight John Prendergast[1] and William Long of Rye, saw the disasters that the Flemish and the Normans were inflicting upon our shipping. So they took ships and crews from the Cinque ports and sailed out to sea. They defended our own sailors and captured or drove off the enemy, so that a deep peace was established by land and sea. But some nasty, overbearing people could not endure this, and accused them of theft, looting, and illegal pillage of goods. And perhaps if there had been some truth of which to accuse them, they would not have made up a total tissue of lies against them, as there would have been a substratum of truth. As it was John Prendergast sought asylum at the church of Edward, king and saint, and claimed the sanctuary of Westminster. But he was not able to find a house or a room where he could lay down his head, because of the fear of the king who had forbidden this, but he had to unfold his tent and take his rest in the vestibule of St Paul's, with guards set at his side for fear of the night attacks which were being prepared by those jealous of him. Meanwhile his colleague William Long stayed at sea until the admiral,[2] who at that time was chancellor of the land, had equipped ships, sailed to him in person and intervened with a pledge that guaranteed his safety. In these circumstances William left his ships and followed the admiral all the way to London. But none the less the prayers of various people on his behalf did not stop him being imprisoned in the Tower of London.[3] He was kept there until the parliament that took place on the day after the feast of All Souls [2 November].[4]

The visitation of the archbishop [of Canterbury] at Oxford

The archbishop of Canterbury [Thomas Arundel] tried to make a visitation of the university of Oxford, but he was not allowed in.[5]

War between the dukes of Orléans and Burgundy

War began at that time between two of the most powerful princes of France, the duke of Burgundy [John the Fearless] and [Charles] the duke of Orléans, the son of that duke of Orléans [Louis] who had recently been killed by the party of the duke of Burgundy.[6] Each side had many

---

[1] Prendergast was an experienced campaigner in the channel: Wylie, *Henry IV*, iv. 24: *CCR, 1409–13*, 210.
[2] Thomas Beaufort was admiral of the west and north and held the chancellorship from January 1410 until December 1411. See also *CPR, 1408–13*, p. 92.
[3] Long was imprisoned on 13 June 1411: *CCR, 1409–13*, pp. 157, 210, 375.
[4] Parliament did indeed meet on 3 November 1411: *RP*, iii. 647.
[5] There had been growing anxiety about the activity of Wyclifites at Oxford, but it was not until the committee convened to examine Wyclif's teachings had presented their list of no fewer than 267 erroneous or heretical conclusions to be found in his work that Archbishop Arundel felt confident enough to take action. He presented himself at the door of the university church, St Mary the Virgin on 7 July, but was refused entry. After some delay he was able to enter the church, but the chancellor and masters refused to cooperate with the visitation, citing the bull of exemption granted by Pope Boniface IX (1389–1404). Arundel responded by placing St Mary's church under interdict and summoning the chancellor and masters to appear before him on 9 September. For his part, Chancellor Richard Courtenay appealed to Henry, Prince of Wales, in whose service he had already distinguished himself at the siege of Aberystwyth (see above, p. 356). Henry IV himself was inclined to support his archbishop and sought and secured the revocation of Boniface's bull from John XXIII. The new bull, subjecting the university to archiepiscopal visitation, was published at Oxford in 1412 and as a gesture of reconciliation the chancellor and masters undertook to celebrate a Mass of the Holy Ghost on 31 October on that and every subsequent year of the king's life as well as various funerary commemorations.
[6] This was in effect a civil war, with the principal magnates of France and their retainers contending for control of the incapacitated king, Charles VI, and his fourteen-year-old son Louis (1397–1415), dauphin and duke of Guyenne. The breach between Burgundy and the other magnates had begun with the murder of Orléans but had intensified in the months that followed as Burgundy, in Paris, assumed control not only of the king but also of the person and the household of the dauphin Louis. When Charles VI descended into another bout of madness in the spring of 1410, the magnates brought their conflict into the open: at Gien on 15 April the dukes of Berry, Brittany and Orléans and the counts of Alençon, Armagnac and Clermont entered into a formal alliance, the so-called 'League of Gien' and although diplomatic efforts continued to be made on both sides, and Berry's own commitment to the conflict wavered, the Orléanists now prepared for war. On 14 July the three brothers of the murdered duke presented their grievances in an open letter to Charles VI known as the manifesto of Jargeau. War began in the late summer of 1411, with Orléans making

supporters. The duke [Charles] of Orléans was supported by the kings of Navarre[1] and Aragon,[2] the dukes of Bourbon[3] and Brittany,[4] the men of Gascony and Aquitaine, the counts of Eu[5] and Armagnac and many others. The duke of Burgundy, who had the king of France on his side together with the king's eldest son, called 'the ruler of France,' and many others, could see that the opposition party was stronger and more numerous, and, wishing to strengthen his forces, sent ambassadors to England who were to ask for help from the king of England against the duke of Orléans. The envoys were to hand over many gifts, and promise still more, including the marriage of his daughter to the prince and a substantial sum of gold.[6] The king is said to have given this reply to the duke:

'We advise you not to take the initiative in this matter and join battle with your enemy, seeing that he seems to be justly harassing you because of the death of his father, which, so it is said, was cunningly engineered by you. But as far as you can, consider how to calm down the angry young man and promise him a reasonable satisfaction that takes account of the wishes of both sides. If, after this, he still does not decide to stop attacking you, withdraw to a safer part of your dominions, and there assemble forces sufficient to repel his violent attack. If he brings up his forces to fight after this, you will more justly move to join battle with him. And in these circumstances we will provide the support you ask for.'[7]

So the earl of Arundel [Thomas Fitzalan, 5th earl], the earl of Warwick [Richard Beauchamp], the earl of Kyme,[8] Sir John Oldcastle and various others were sent across with large numbers of armed men and active, experienced archers to help the duke of Burgundy. They were very thankfully received by the duke and quite well looked after. But the English could not stay long in Paris without trying to make some attack on the enemy.[9] At that time the duke of Orléans with his household was lying not far off in a strong position near the town of St Cloud, in which a large part of his army was stationed, midway as it were between himself and his enemies. So the English set out to get supplies to satisfy their needs. But when they decided to attack St Cloud, they found that the bridge had been broken down by the enemy. The enemy had laid long, narrow planks over the gap, so that they could emerge from the city gates and fight off our men and, if necessary, retreat back into it with the help of the planks, depending on how the fight went. Well, there was a battle, and the French were routed, and in their panic-stricken flight they fell into the river owing to the narrowness of the path of planks and were drowned. One thousand, three hundred are said to have been killed there, while the remainder got away into the town and in tears told the duke what had happened. He, thinking of his own safety, hurriedly escaped in a different direction. Our men then went back, looted the town of St Cloud, and returned to Paris, taking many captives with them.

When the French king and his nobles saw the mighty hand that the Lord had laid on the enemy by means of our force, they praised God for this great success and thanked our men. But

---

assaults in Picardy while the Armagnacs laid siege to St Denis. Burgundy, however, retained his hold on Paris and before the end of the year the Orléanists began to make diplomatic overtures towards the English. See also Famiglietti, *Royal Intrigue*, pp. 85–110.

1 Charles III, king of Navarre (1387–1425).
2 Martin I (b.c.1356) had held the throne of Aragon since 1396. He died in 1410 and a two-year interregnum followed.
3 Jean, count of Clermont and duke of Bourbon (d.1434).
4 Jean VI, duke of Brittany (d.1442).
5 Charles d'Artois, count of Eu.
6 John the Fearless opened negotiations with the envoys of Henry IV in July 1411. As Walsingham suggests, the promises of the Burgundians were both generous and tempting to the English. Duke John appeared willing to grant the Flemish towns of Dixmuide, Dunkirk, Gravelines and Sluys to the English in return for military aid in his own conquest of Normandy. He also proposed a marriage between his daughter Anne and Henry, prince of Wales. See also Wylie, *Henry IV*, iii. 285.
7 A force of 800 lances and 2,000 archers was offered.
8 Sir Gilbert Umfraville. For his career see Wylie, *Henry IV*, iv. 57, 63 and below, p. 423.
9 Arundel's army joined Duke John at Arras on 2 October and advanced on Paris, which they entered on 22 October, routing the Armagnac forces that had held the city in a stranglehold.

because our men had brought captives with them who were under accusation of treason, the French immediately sought to punish these captives according to the law. Our men objected to this, as they had saved their lives according to the laws of war with a ransom agreed upon, and they were afraid that they would lose the sums that had been promised. And so they were filled with resentment and while they were trying to save those whom they had taken captive to protect, they killed several of the Parisians. But finally the crowd of citizens and of the people who had flocked together won a victory over the English, and they were compelled, having received from the royal treasury and from the citizens the money which had been agreed upon for the ransom of the captives, to allow the French to enjoy putting their traitors to death. Some of them were beheaded and some of them were forced to die by various tortures according to the customs of the country.

A parliament was held in London on the day after the feast of All Souls [2 November].[1]

[1412]

In 1412, the thirteenth year of the reign of King Henry IV, the king spent Christmas at [ ].[2]

David Gam was betrayed by his friend and captured, and, so the story goes, came into the hands of Owain Glyn Dŵr.[3] Mercenaries from Oye took the fort of Balinghem. John Prendergast sailed the seas with thirty ships, and unexpectedly captured the town of Creil, while market day was going on there. He took as booty from the estate of the count of St Pol twenty thousand animals, and afterwards he himself set fire to the town of Guisnes.

The duke of Orléans, who had thought himself unbeatable, straightaway after the defeat inflicted on him by the English thought of means by which he could entice on to his side the king and nobles and commons of England. Having formed a plan to gain this end, he wrote the following letter of proxy:[3]

'We, Jean, son of the king of France,[4] duke of Berry and Auvergne, count of Poitou, Etampes, Boulogne and Auvergne,[5] Charles, duke of Orléans and Valois, count of Blois and Beaumont, and lord of Coucy;[6] Jean, duke of Bourbon,[7] count of Clermont and La Forez and lord of Beaujeu;[8] and Jean, count of Alençon,[9] [Armagnac][10] and Perche, lord of Filgerie and [La] Guerche [de

---

[1] Parliament met on 3 November. The session continued until 19 December: *RP*, iii. 647.

[2] Here there is a blank space in the manuscript.

[3] David Gam (Dafydd Gan) also known as David ap Llewelyn was a Brecon gentleman whose family ties to the de Bohuns bound him to Henry IV when other kinsmen rallied to the cause of Glyn Dŵr. He fought with distinction at the battle of Pwll Melyn in 1405 and was alleged to have attempted to assassinate the rebel leader. He was one of the handful of distinguished English knights to die at Agincourt. See also Davies, *Revolt*, pp. 206–7, 225–7, and below, p. 412.

[4] Orléanist envoys arrived in England on 1 February 1412 bearing equally enticing promises as their Burgundian counterparts the previous summer, amongst which were confirmation of the English claim to the duchy of Aquitaine and marital alliances between the sons of Henry IV and the daughters of the French princes allied to the Armagnac-Orléans cause. As Walsingham describes in the passages that follow, these offers were well received: Henry and his councillors remained unconvinced by the constancy of Duke John of Burgundy and the prospect of Aquitaine represented a greater prize than the extension of English interests in Flanders. Burgundy was made aware of the negotiations after the arrest of one of the Armagnac ambassadors. See also Wylie, *Henry IV*, iv. 65, 211; Vaughan, *John the Fearless*, p. 94. See also Wylie, *Henry IV*, iv. 65, 211.
  Walsingham's text of the letter itself is badly corrupted; the names of the magnates are in many cases mistranscribed and Bernard, count of Armagnac appears although he was not named in this document.

[5] Jean, duke of Berry (1340–1416) third son of Jean II, and uncle of Charles VI. Walsingham's addition of 'and Auvergne' to his style is an error.

[6] Charles, duke of Orléans (1394–1465); captured at the battle of Agincourt (1415) he remained a prisoner in England until 1440.

[7] Jean, duke of Bourbon (b.1381) who succeeded to the title on the death of his father Louis II in 1410.

[8] Perhaps Charles de Bourbon, son of Duke Jean and Marie de Berry.

[9] Jean, count of Alençon (1388–1415) cousin of Charles VI. His title was raised to the dignity of a dukedom in 1414. He was killed at Agincourt having first killed Edward, duke of York.

[10] In Bodley MS 462 the name of Armagnac was added in error to the title of Alençon. Bernard, count of Armagnac, was not amongst those named in this document

Bretaigne], inform all of you that each of us from our great experience of public affairs has learnt to have full trust in the loyalty, probity, and good sense of the knights Falconet Dacot and Galois d'Acy, our venerable, experienced professors of holy scripture James Mayne and Peter of Versailles, and the pages Hector of Poutbriant and Jean Louvency. For the present business we have made, created and appointed them, and we do so make, create and appoint them, and each of us makes, creates and appoints them, our definite, undoubted, unchangeable messengers and special envoys to discuss, and come to an agreement and conclusion with that most serene prince, Henry, by the grace of God king of England, and his illustrious sons, jointly and with each of them as single individuals, concerning the restitution and handing back of the actual dukedom of Aquitaine together with all its appurtenances and rights, which, so it is claimed, belong by hereditary right to that most serene lord, the king of England, all this to be done by us for the king.

'Also we appoint them to make, agree upon and finalise, with the persons mentioned above and any one of them, any decisions, pacts, bargains and dealings of whatever kind, in ways, manner and format which may be better and more suitable, just as it shall seem expedient to the aforesaid proxies, envoys and delegates of ours or at least to any two of them, concerning and because of both the matters mentioned above and any other matters whatsoever.

Also we appoint them to take oaths affecting our souls and those of each one of us on the holy gospels of God, physically touching the book as they do so, and on holy relics and on any other objects as shall be more pleasing to that serene highness, the king of England, to the effect that each and every point and article finally agreed upon shall be observed in their entirety and singly, and that all demands in their entirety and singly shall be met in actual fact on the part of ourselves and each one of us, with a cessation of any kind of trickery, fraud, quibbling and evasion whatsoever.

'Also we appoint them to receive in our turn from that serene highness, the king of England, and from his illustrious sons and each one of them and from any others, similar oaths concerning the keeping of the agreements made by them on their part. And we grant and concede to our proxies, envoys and legates or at least to two of them full and complete power and an expressly special mandate for dealing with all the individual matters mentioned above and whatever else shall occur more important than the things referred to and mentioned above and which require this extra special mandate, and in general for dealing with the matter, as a whole and in its details, in the way in which we ourselves and any one of us would be able to do, if we were present in person, without any exceptions or reservations whatsoever.

'And we promise that we, as a body and as individuals, will keep our word, pledging and binding ourselves to lose all our present and future property, both moveable and immovable, and suffering the besmirchment of the honour of our name and that of our successors for ever, and the brand and taint for ever which now we are willing to incur, if it should happen, which God forbid, that in the future we or any one of us infringes the agreements made by our envoys or any one of them. To corroborate and bear witness to all these points we have thought it right to append to this present letter the seals of ourselves and of each one of us together with our signatures in our own hands. Given at Bourges etc.'

After the envoys had shown their letter of proxy, they made the offers which are described in the articles below:

The offers made by the lords[1]

Firstly, with a loyalty which can always be relied upon, they offer their bodies to be used in the service of the king of England in all his causes and exploits, knowing that he will not be willing to ask for anything less.

Secondly they offer their sons, daughters, nieces, nephews, and absolutely all their kinsmen in marriage alliances, to be arranged as the king of England shall decide.

---

[1] Walsingham is the only contemporary chronicler to report the terms in detail.

Thirdly they put their fortresses, towns, treasuries and other goods at the disposal of the said king.

Fourthly they offer their friends, that is almost all the nobles of France, clergy of repute and the honest citizens who assist them, as will be shown by what happens.

Fifthly they offer the entire dukedom of Aquitaine on the same terms as it was held by his predecessors,[1] with none of the appurtenances of the said dukedom being excluded from the agreement. In other words they are ready to review the lands that they hold from the lord king, to put back into his hands those that they can, and to come to an agreement about the others to the best of their ability.

The requests of the lords

Firstly they ask that the king of England and his successors shall help these same lords against the duke of Burgundy as far as is legally possible, for the crime which he had committed on the person of the duke of Orléans.

Secondly they ask that the king of England shall help them against the duke of Burgundy and his allies, so that their honour was restored and their enemies' offences punished.[2]

Thirdly they ask that he shall assist them against the duke of Burgundy by restoring all the goods that they had lost through the intervention and at the hands of the duke of Burgundy and his men.

Fourthly they ask him that he should assist against the duke of Burgundy by restoring their losses and by getting reparation for the damage caused to their friends, vassals and subjects.

Fifthly they ask him the he shall help them to secure peace between the kingdoms, as far as he is able etc.

Upon hearing the delivery of their message by the envoys, the king was overjoyed and delighted by the amazing promises made.[3] He vigorously rose to his feet, clapping his hands, and said to the archbishop of Canterbury [Thomas Arundel], who was then chancellor of the kingdom, 'Do you see how omnipotent God arranges things for our advantage? Here now is the acceptable time, this is the day for which we have longed. So let us make use of God's generosity. Let us go to France and with little trouble take possession of the country which is owing to us by law.'[4] And I think the king could have regained it, if the strength of his body had matched the strength of his mind. But the sad truth is that he was victim of an incurable illness, and could no longer walk or ride a horse without pain. But he gave orders for all who owed him military service to assemble, ostensibly to plough the seas with him and to invade France or Gascony and defeat the duke of Burgundy [John the Fearless]. So his subjects were greatly puzzled, trying to work out the reason for this sudden change of plan: for reinforcements which had not only been promised but actually sent to the duke of Burgundy were being recalled, and these same troops together with many others being used to prop up the duke [Charles] of Orléans. The king's counsellors, seeing his illness, dissuaded him from concerning himself personally in this expedition, but persuaded him to give the command of it to his second son, Thomas, duke of Clarence. So the king acted on the advice of his counsellors and entrusted that expedition in its entirety to Lord Thomas.[5]

1   From the time of Edward I (1272–1307).
2   As security for the territorial concessions granted, English forces were to occupy Pontieu, Niort, Lusignan and Chateauneuf on the Charente in Angoûleme.
3   The terms of the Orléanist offer were delivered to Henry on 6 April 1412. See also Wylie, *Henry IV*, iv. 64–87.
4   Walsingham's account of Henry's rapid agreement to the Orléanist offer is accurate; what became known as the treaty of Bourges was guaranteed at Westminster by the Orléanist representatives in the presence of the kings' four sons on 18 May. See also Wylie, *Henry IV*, iv. 64, 72; Vaughan, *John the Fearless*, pp. 94–5.
5   A force of 1,000 men-at-arms and 3,000 archers was mustered under the command of Henry's second son Thomas, newly created duke of Clarence. He was to be accompanied by Henry's half-brother Thomas Beaufort marquis of Dorset, James Butler earl of Ormonde, Richard de Vere earl of Oxford, Thomas Montagu 4th

[An open letter of Prince Henry][1]

Meanwhile Prince Henry was angry with the king's advisers, who, so men said, sowed discord between father and son, and wrote this open letter to almost all parts of the kingdom, seeking to rebut all the lies of his critics in the following words.

'Dearest and sincerely beloved, I am sure you are well aware of the widely publicised news that the serene highness, my most feared father, Henry, famous king of England and of France, has recently decided to go on a journey to lands overseas, to recover his dukedom of Aquitaine and other hereditary lands and rights which belong to his regality and the English crown and which have been part of England from of old. Now at this time his serene highness named me as the one who could expect to accompany him, and he assigned to me a fixed number of troops, whose help I could rely on to serve him personally on the journey.

'But quickly noticing that as a consequence I had been given so feeble a force that I was likely to be cut off from any chance of honourable service to my most feared father and lord or of making proper provision for the safety of my own person, I humbly begged his royal majesty that his highness should consider it right to allow me to hold a conference in a certain place for possession of mine with my kinsmen, relations, friends and other servants. I did this so that there might be an exchange of views between us, and so that he might find ways and means of increasing the number of assistants assigned to me. For then I would be able to please and satisfy my royal father, take measures for my own security and honour, and, helped by an adequate force, be able to further the general good of this kingdom, which is my fervent wish and desire above all else.

'His royal highness kindly granted this request of mine, I had supposed on terms of guaranteed reliability, and with this order and permission from the king that I have mentioned I was proceeding to my city of Coventry to the lands mentioned above to assemble these troops, although I was not hedged about by an armed force or supported by any uprising from the people but was travelling in my usual fashion with a retinue too small to be capable of providing adequate safety. But then some sons of iniquity, nurselings of dissent, schism fomenters, sowers of anger and agents of discord, with their usual behaviour of envying the stable foundation of the king's security and desiring with a serpentine cunning to upset the ordered succession to his throne, who, so I believe, will aim to be died-in-the-wool villains until the end of their days, these villains, God be my witness, struck at my innocence with their evil lips and tongues of trickery. For they, in a sudden flight of the imagination, wickedly suggested to my most revered father and lord, whose happiness is desired beyond every other thing by me and most of the other nobles and princes of this land, that I was affected with a bloody desire for the crown of England, that I was planning an unbelievably horrible crime and would rise up against my own father at the head of a popular outbreak of violence, and that in this way I would seize his sceptre and other royal insignia on the grounds that my father and liege lord was living a life to which he had no proper title and which relied on tyrannical persuasion.

'Also in some parts of the kingdom they tried to separate and snatch away from me the faithful

---

earl of Salisbury and Sir John Cornwall, each of them contributing 200 men-at-arms and several hundred archers. It appears that the command of this army was given to Clarence because his elder brother, Henry, Prince of Wales, had been an advocate of the Burgundian alliance and had been dismissed from the king's council the previous winter. The prince's place in the king's counsels had been undermined still further by the fact that Bishop Henry Beaufort, also an advocate of the Burgundian alliance, had suggested to Henry that he abdicate when it became clear that he was unable to lead any campaign in person. The exclusion of the prince, however, bred rumours of a far deeper rift as Walsingham describes in the passages following. See also *CPR, 1408–13*, p. 373; Wylie, *Henry IV*, ii. 72–87.

[1]   Walsingham is the only contemporary authority to document the dispute between Henry and his eldest son in detail and the only one to give the text of Prince Henry's letter. There is no reason to doubt his explanation as to his absence from Clarence's army, that is that he had sought to raise a larger force at Coventry before joining the expedition. See also Wylie, *Henry IV*, ii. 90–1.

hearts of the people, whose support I hoped was a sure source of strength, by spreading abroad on all sides the repeated rumour that I was planning to make every effort to prevent the expedition arranged to recover the dukedom of Aquitaine, although in fact it was and will be my dearest wish to risk my heart and body in its recovery. Indeed their intention behind these barkings, the end they were aiming at by these mutterings among the people was that the kingdom of England, which up to now had been a kingdom of peace, should in the future be lashed by harmful discord, that civil strife should take the place of peace, that insecurity should follow security and that war should follow peace. And yet, as God himself knows who sees into all our hearts, my affection, love, loyalty and obedience towards that serene highness, my most feared father and lord, the illustrious king of England and of France, is so strong that no humble son could conceive or show greater.

'Another point is that I am actually supplying such help and support for the recovery of the dukedom of Aquitaine and all other inheritances and rights belonging to the crown of England, in whatever way acquired, as I am allowed to supply by the permission given to me that I mentioned above.

'And so to stop those people, whose plan and choice it is to spread such harmful and contagious slanders among the people, from ever rejoicing as time goes by that they have seen in the kingdom of England those many, evil woes for which they thirst, I lay before you the naked truth of the matter in the contents of this present letter, in which is revealed to each and every one of you the unfeigned truth and intention of my inmost heart, so that your assembly may have a complete assurance of their truth. Given under my seal in our city of Coventry 17 June.'

To show still more clearly the truth of the foregoing, during the feast of the apostles Peter and Paul [29 June] he came to the king with a large crowd of friends and a retinue of servants bigger than any that had been seen before during those days. He arrived at the place where the king his father was, and, after waiting for the allotted interval, was warmly welcomed.[1] He made one petition of the king, namely that if his accusers were found guilty, they should be punished not indeed according to their deserts, but, after their lies had been discovered, on the merciful side of justly. The king indeed seemed to assent to his request, but then stated that they ought to wait for the occasion of the next parliament, so that such people as these might be punished by the judgement of their equals.

[An expedition to aid the duke of Orléans]

John Prendergast, who was patrolling the seas with thirty ships, captured casks of wine and foodstuffs, which were of great use to the people if not to the nobles. And amongst other things he made a landing and unexpectedly captured the marketplace of the town of Creil.

Owain Glyn Dŵr, that established villain, took David Gamme prisoner, though by a trick and not in fair fight.[2] In this year a pound of pepper was sold for four pence.

The king with a decree from his council decided to provide help for the duke of Orléans, and about the time of the feast of the assumption of the blessed Virgin sent his second son, Thomas, duke of Clarence, and Edward, duke of York and Sir Thomas Beaufort, earl of Dorset and very many powerful men of with a strong force to support the forces of the duke [Charles] of Orléans against the duke of Burgundy, although those who had already previously crossed the seas with the earl of Arundel to strengthen the Burgundian faction, as described above, had not yet returned to England. This caused many to marvel at the unexpectedness of the king's change of mind, which meant that in a very short space of time the English, as it were, were holding in their hands two opposites.

Anyway the nobles named above set out and, helped by a favouring wind, landed in Neustria

---

[1]   Walsingham is the only authority for Prince Henry's interview with his father, but there is no reason to doubt its authenticity. See also *Henry IV*, part 2, Act 4, Scene 3.

[2]   This was previously reported at the opening of this section.

[i.e. Normandy]. But when [Charles] the duke of Orléans did not meet them at the appointed time they had agreed upon, they burnt his cities, sacked his villages and captured many towns, some of which they destroyed and some of which at an agreed price they refrained from burning. At length, though late in the day, the dukes [Thomas] of Clarence and Orléans met for talks, and there was a discussion about our men ceasing their hostile raids and refraining from looting. When this point was granted, our dukes withdrew to Aquitaine to winter there, while the duke of Orléans returned exultantly to his own lands.[1]

While this was going on, Jean [correctly, Jacques] de Heilly, the marshal of France, with many nobles and men at arms and other troops numbering four thousand soldiers laid siege to a town in Aquitaine, which the Englishman Sir John Blount was holding. Sir John with three hundred auxiliary troops put to flight and routed the whole French army, capturing twelve noblemen and one hundred and twenty others of good birth. His principal prisoner was the above mentioned John de Heilly, marshal of France, whom he sent across to England to Wisbech castle. Afterwards, slackness among the guard allowed the marshal to escape. He returned to France where he joined the duke of Orléans and was present at the battle of Agincourt. He himself was killed in the battle and the duke was taken away as a prisoner.[2]

[1413]

In 1413 King Henry kept Christmas at Eltham, although he had been beset by such a serious illness that it was thought that he might die at any time. But, as it was the will of God, he recovered his strength and celebrated the days of Christmas with as much cheerfulness as he could muster.

After Christmas he summoned the nobles of the realm to a parliament to be held in London on the day after the feast of the purification of the blessed Mary [2 February]. But he did not last out until the end of the parliament, for before that he was carried off by fate on 21 March, after a glorious reign of thirteen and a half years minus five days. He was buried in Church of Christ at Canterbury.[3]

---

[1]   For the campaigning of Clarence and his captains see Vale, *English Gascony*, pp. 62–8.
[2]   For the casualties at Agincourt see below, pp. 412–13 and n.
[3]   In the closing months of 1412, perhaps already anticipating death, Henry had removed himself from public life and moved between his palaces close to London, including Croydon, Merton and Eltham, in the company of his Dominican confessor, John Till. Writs for a parliament were issued on December 1 but although the commons did assemble at Westminster on 3 February the session was never formally opened. In early March Henry suffered a seizure while making an offering at Westminster Abbey; he died a day earlier than Walsingham reports here, on 20 March, in the Jerusalem Chamber at Westminster Abbey. Contemporaries ruefully remarked that the place of his death represented a fulfilment of the prophecy made to Henry at the time of his accession that he had been marked out by providence as the king who would reconquer Jerusalem. See also *Henry IV*, part 2, Act 4, Scene 3. He was buried at Canterbury in Thomas Becket's chapel behind the High Altar: Wylie, *Henry IV*, iv. 100–13.

The Reign of King Henry V

Coronation of the new king

In the same year Henry [of Monmouth], the eldest son of the dead king, was crowned in London at Westminster by the hands of Thomas Arundel, archbishop of Canterbury, on 9 April, Passion Sunday. There was a great fall of snow on this day. Everybody was surprised by the severity of the weather. Some people connected the climatic harshness with the fate that awaited them at the hands of the new king, suggesting that he too would be a man of cold deeds and severe in his management of the kingdom, while others who knew of a gentler side to the king took the unseasonable weather as the best of omens, suggesting that he would cause to fall upon the land snowstorms which would freeze vice and allow the fair fruits of virtue to spring up, so that his subjects would truthfully be able to say of him:

> Winter is now past
> The rains are over and gone [Song of Songs 2: 11]

And indeed as soon as he was invested with the emblems of royalty, he suddenly became a different man. His care now was for self-restraint and goodness and gravity, and there was no kind of virtue which he put on one side and did not desire to practise himself. His conduct and behaviour were an example to all men, clergy and laity alike, and those to whom it was granted to follow in his footsteps accounted themselves happy.[1]

After the Easter feast [23 April] the king held a solemn parliament in London, at which he asked for and received a subsidy, both from the clergy and the laity.[2]

About the present time Thomas, duke of Clarence, the brother of the king, returned from the lands of Gascony. As I have said, he had been sent there to help the duke of Orléans against the duke [John the Fearless] of Burgundy.[3]

During these days a sudden conflagration, starting inside the city, burnt down a great part of Norwich, including the whole house and property of the preaching brothers of the order of St Dominic. Two of the brothers of the order also died in the fire.[4]

On the feast of the Holy Trinity [18 June] a solemn funeral service was held at Canterbury for King Henry IV. King Henry V, his son and heir, was present.

At that time it was decided by a council of clergy [i.e. convocation] meeting in London at St Paul's, under very great pressure from the present king, that in future the feast of St George the martyr [23 April] should be celebrated in the church as a double feast. The archbishop of Canterbury decreed that the same should also be done for the feast of St Dunstan [19 May].[5]

Alexander [Tottington], bishop of Norwich, who had become bishop after a long spell as prior of the monastery, said farewell to the troubles of this world,[6] and the monks elected as his

---

1   The conjunction of the coronation and the winter weather was not observed by the author of the *Gesta Henrici quinti*, who also did not detect a dramatic change in Henry's character but commented only that the new king was 'young in years but old in experience': *Gesta Henrici*, pp. 2–3; Wylie, *Henry V*, i. 1–6.

2   Parliament convened on 14 May: *RP*, iv. 6.

3   Clarence and his captains had been compelled to agree terms with the Orléanists after the latter's repudiation of their treaty with the English. He remained at Bordeaux over the winter but returned at the death of his father in March.

4   For the fire at the Norwich Blackfriars see *VCH Norfolk*, ii. 429.

5   For Henry's policy towards the commemoration of English saints see J. I Catto, 'Religious Change under Henry V' in *Henry V: The Practice of Kingship*, ed. G. L. Harriss (Oxford, 1985), pp. 97–115.

6   In other recensions: 'at an advanced age ceased to breathe'.

successor Master Richard Courtenay, who in birth, behaviour and learning was thought worthy of this position and equal to it.[1]

The ugly presumption of the Lollards

At this time the Lollards, those perverters of the apostolic doctrines of the gospels, pinned on the doors of London churches notices recording the names of one hundred thousand people who were ready to rise against all those who were not followers of their sect. They were relying upon the energy and ability of a certain John Oldcastle, who out of reverence for the marriage that he had contracted with the grand-daughter of that noble man, Sir John Cobham, had been allotted the surname of this lord.[2] Although John Oldcastle was strong and brave and very suited to the deeds of war, he was also a most stubborn enemy of the church. His worth as a knight made him a dear friend of the king, but he was deeply suspect because of his evil heretical opinions.

John Oldcastle is convicted of heresy

At this time the archbishop of Canterbury [Thomas Arundel] held a convocation of clergy at London, especially because of the aforesaid John.[3] It had been discovered that this knight had been and still was the chief harbourer of Lollards and their main supporter, protector and defender. Particularly in the dioceses of London, Rochester[4] and Hereford he had sent out these very Lollards to preach their doctrines, although they absolutely had not been licensed to do so by any directors or bishops in those dioceses, and although such preaching was contrary to the regulations for the provinces set up to deal with them. Sir John had been present in person during their wicked sermons, and had put down any hecklers he found by terrifying threats of what the power of the secular sword would do to them, declaring, amongst other things, that the archbishop of Canterbury and his suffragans did not possess and never had possessed any power to draw up regulations of this kind. Furthermore he disagreed and always had disagreed with the teachings and affirmations of the Roman church about the sacraments of the altar and of repentance, and about pilgrimages and the adoration of images and keys: the dogmas he was teaching were quite different.

Because of all this the whole body of the clergy had asked the archbishop of Canterbury to think it right to proceed against Sir John about and concerning these matters. But the archbishop, out of reverence for the king whose friend Sir John then was, and out of honour for the order of knights, went with all the suffragans present at the council and a great part of the clergy to seek audience with the king who was then at his manor of Kennington, that he might reveal to the king the failings of Sir John. But under pressure from the king who wished to recall Sir John to the right path without disgracing him, the matter was postponed for a long time. But when the king had wasted a lot of time to no purpose in trying to bring him back, he told the archbishop of Canterbury, verbally and in writing, that his labours for Sir John had been in vain.[5]

So the archbishop of Canterbury decided that he would summon him to reply in person to

---

[1]   Courtenay had been a member of Henry's circle since his days in Wales. See above, p. 356. For his career see Emden, *BRUO*, i. 500–2.

[2]   Oldcastle (b. c.1378) was the son of Sir Richard Oldcastle of Almeley, Herefordshire. His early career was spent in the service of Lord Grey of Codnor, in whose retinue he fought on the Scottish campaign of 1400. He served as knight of the shire for Herefordshire in 1404 and sheriff of the county in 1406–7. In 1408 he married Joan, daughter of Sir John de la Pole (d.1380) and heir to the estates of her grandfather, John, Lord Cobham (d.1408).

[3]   Convocation convened in early March, before the death of Henry IV.

[4]   The Cobham estates included Cooling Castle in Kent. Oldcastle was said to support a chaplain there who openly expressed heretical opinions. Oldcastle was also in correspondence with the Bohemian heretic Jan Hus. See also Wylie, *Henry V*, i. 248, 261.

[5]   The young king interviewed Oldcastle in June 1413 when the knight admitted to possessing heretical tracts. The king postponed his punishment for a further two months in the hope of persuading him out of his errors, but after further interviews he finally surrendered him to the custody of Arundel. See also Wylie, *Henry V*, i. 236–57.

these charges face to face by a certain date, and he sent his messenger with a summons for Sir John, who was then at his castle of Cooling. The archbishop instructed his messenger to refuse absolutely to enter the castle unless he was given permission to do so, and that he should get a certain John Butler, a doorkeeper of the king's chamber, to ask Sir John himself to give him permission to enter. So that either Sir John would summon him inside or at least give him the opportunity of a meeting outside so that he could be served with this summons. But even though this proposal was put to Sir John by John Butler on behalf of the king, he received the public reply that Sir John absolutely refused to be summonsed or to tolerate receiving any sort of a summons from him.

On hearing about this, the archbishop of Canterbury decided to summons him by a writ, which was to be publicly fixed to the doors of his neighbouring church of Rochester, which was about three English miles from the aforesaid castle, asking him to appear before him on 11 September to make a reply in person to the charges listed above and other matters concerning his wicked heresy. When the day came, the archbishop seated himself on a platform in the larger chapel within Leeds castle, where he was staying at the time. When he heard and received the news that Sir John was incastellated and entrenched inside his own castle, defending his own views and volubly denouncing the keys of the church and the power of the archbishop, he had him publicly summoned by proclamation of a herald. And when Sir John completely failed to appear, although they waited for a long time, the archbishop punished his stubbornness with the excommunication in writing that he deserved.

And because Sir John was still incastellated and entrenched in defence of his heresy against the keys of the church, the archbishop of Canterbury decided to summons him a second time, if he could be got to receive the summons, or otherwise to do it by writ as formerly, bidding Sir John to appear before him on the next Sabbath after the feast of St Matthew, apostle and evangelist [21 September], and to give a good reason, if he had one, why he should not now be dealt with more severely as a public heretic and schismatic, and as an enemy and opponent of the universal church, and why he should not be pronounced to be so and why the aid of the secular arm should not be solemnly invoked against him. On all these matters, collectively and singly, he was to make his reply in person and receive and undergo his just deserts.

When the term appointed arrived, the archbishop took his seat on the platform in the chapter house of St Paul's in London. With him on the platform were Richard [Clifford], bishop of London, and Henry [Beaufort], bishop of Winchester. Sir Robert Murley, governor of the Tower of London, brought Sir John with him to the hearing, as he had been arrested a little while previously by the king's men and lodged in the Tower. The archbishop read out the charge against him, namely that informants had revealed his heresy in a convocation of the clergy, and that he had been summonsed and then excommunicated because of his stubbornness. The archbishop offered himself as a channel of grace, and promised that he was ready to absolve him. But Sir John refused to ask for the archbishop's absolution, and, turning from that to other matters, said that he would willingly read out before the archbishop the faith to which he held. And he took out of his pocket a document, of which he handed a copy to the archbishop after he had read it.

And after the reading of the document, the archbishop said, 'Well, Sir John! There are many sound beliefs in this document of yours which are very Catholic. But this is the term fixed for you to make an answer concerning other beliefs which smack of deviation and heresy, and which have not been fully explained in the contents of this document. Therefore you have to give an answer and tell us your views on these matters and give us a fuller description of your faith, particularly whether you hold, believe and affirm that in the sacrament of the altar after the consecration has been properly carried out the bread remains ordinary bread, or whether it does not. Also, whether you hold, believe and affirm that in the sacrament of repentance it is essential that a Christian has a priest available and makes confession of his sins to a priest ordained by the church.'

Sir John briefly replied that he did not wish to make any statements on these matters other than those contained in his document. The archbishop felt compassion for him and said, 'Do not forget, Sir John, that if you do not give a clear answer to the points I have raised within the lawful term now given to you, we shall be able to denounce you and declare you a heretic.' But Sir John scorned to give a different answer.

Then the archbishop of Canterbury expounded the doctrines of the holy Roman church, based on the words of the blessed Augustine, Jerome, Ambrose and the other saints, and to which all Catholics were bound to adhere. Sir John replied to this that he was willing to believe and adhere to all the doctrines of holy church and to all those which God wished him to believe and adhere to. But he still absolutely refused to affirm that the pope and his cardinals, or the arch-bishops, bishops and other prelates of the church had any power to decide upon such doctrines. At this the archbishop, still showing him compassion and hoping that he might come to a better view, gave him various items written in English and asked him to give a clear and full answer on these points on the following Monday.

On this Monday, which was 25 September, the knight Sir Robert Murley, governor of the Tower of London, appeared before the archbishop of Canterbury and the other two bishops previously mentioned, augmented on this occasion by Benedict [Nichols], bishop of Bangor,[1] and placed Sir John whom he had brought with him, before the archbishop and all the clergy then gathered together. The archbishop in a kind and gentle voice read out the proceedings of the previous day, and the fact that he had been excommunicated and still was, and then asked and required him to seek and receive in due form the absolution of the church. Sir John refused to do this, and said that he would ask for absolution from God alone. And so the archbishop, as gently and as controlled as before, asked and required him to give a clear reply on and concerning the points in his document which were contrary to the doctrines of the church which had been handed down to him.

The first point was the sacrament of the Eucharist. On this point Sir John replied, amongst other things, that just as Christ while here on this earth was both God and man with his divinity veiled and invisible under his revealed and visible humanity, so in the sacrament of the altar the body of Christ, which we do not see, is veiled under the actual substance of the actual bread which we do see. And he expressly denied any belief in the sacrament of the kind contained in the docu-ment handed to him by the archbishop as being the doctrine of the holy Roman church and its holy doctors, saying that the doctrine of the church was contrary to holy scripture, and amounted to a poison poured into the church after it had been established and not before that. And secondly, as for the sacrament of repentance and confession, he said and asserted that if someone found himself trapped in a serious sin from which he could not see how to escape by his own efforts, it was expedient and good for such a person to go to a holy and wise priest for counsel from him. But it was not necessary for salvation that the man should make confession of this sin of his to his own curate or some other priest, even if one was available, seeing that through contrition alone a sin of this kind could be wiped out and the sinner cleansed.

As for the adoration of the holy cross, he said and asserted that it was only the body of Christ, which hung on the cross that should be adored, because that body alone was and is worthy of worship. When asked what honour should be paid to an image of the cross itself, he replied in clear words that the only honour he would pay to a crucifix was to keep it spotlessly clean and put it under safe and proper guard. As for the power of the keys, the pope, the archbishops and other prelates, he said that our lord the pope is the true Antichrist, that is the head of the church, the archbishops, bishops and other prelates being its limbs, and the monastic brethren its tail, but that no obedience is to be given to pope, archbishops and prelates unless they are imitators of Christ and Peter in their lives, morals and behaviour, and that the pope's successor should be none other than the man who lives the best life and has the purest morals. And then in a loud voice and with his arms outspread Sir John addressed the bystanders and said, 'These judges of mine who wish to condemn me are leading both you and themselves astray, and are taking you down to hell, so you beware of them.'

---

[1]   Benedict Nichols (d.1433), Bishop of Bangor from 1408 until his translation to St David's in December 1418.

When all these words had been thus spoken by Sir John, the archbishop of Canterbury time and time again with tears running down his face spoke to Sir John, urging him with all the arguments he could think of to return to the unity of the church and to believe and hold to the beliefs and tenets of the Roman church. Sir John briefly replied that his faith was none other than the one he had described earlier. So seeing that he could make no progress on any front, the archbishop in great bitterness of spirit proceeded to the pronouncement of the definitive sentence in these words:

> In the name of God, amen. We, Thomas, by divine permission etc. in a case or matter of wicked heresy concerning various articles of belief held by the knight Sir John Oldcastle, otherwise Lord Cobham, after a careful enquiry which took place during the last convocation of our clergy of the Canterbury province held in the church of St Paul's in London, found that this same Sir John was and is a heretic believing in heresies, and is in error concerning his faith in the observances of the holy, universal Roman church and especially concerning his views of the sacraments of the Eucharist and repentance. In this matter, as a son of wickedness and darkness, he has so hardened his heart that he does not listen to the voice of his shepherd, nor is he willing to be persuaded by any advice or brought back to the truth by any enticements. So, now that we have considered his own sins and faults which have been made worse by his own accursed stubbornness, as we do not wish that a wicked man should become more wicked and infect others with his poison, with the advice and consent of the wise and sensible venerable men assisting us, we judge, declare and confirm in this definitive written sentence that the knight Sir John Oldcastle, otherwise Lord Cobham, is convicted of detestable guilt on and concerning this matter, and, in his refusal to return in repentance to the unity of the church, is a heretic and in error concerning the doctrines which the holy, universal Roman church holds, teaches, decides upon and promulgates, and especially the doctrines mentioned above. So now we abandon him, as a heretic, to the secular courts. Nonetheless, as he is a heretic, we excommunicate and declare excommunicated in this document both Sir John himself and all those others, collectively and singly, who, as supporters, receivers and defenders of heretics, henceforth shall receive him in support of their own wrong beliefs, or defend him, or offer him advice, support or help on this matter.

After these proceedings, the archbishop of Canterbury [Thomas Arundel] informed the king of what had happened. Then with a prayer from his living voice he made the strongest possible petition to the king and asked that he should think it right, now that Sir John had been condemned in the courts, to graciously grant him forty days in which to relent. For in their affection for him both king and archbishop desired not his death but his life, and they worked hard to save him.[1] And so it happened that he was taken back to the Tower, where he could come to his senses in the period allowed him to relent, and so deserve the grace he had received from both church and king. But that special concession from king and archbishop became an opportunity for devilment, since within the fixed term he had escaped from captivity, and, collecting his wicked supporters around him, thought of nothing but vengeance.[2] Indeed he sent secret letters to his very many followers, both knights and esquires, urging them to write to their friends and accomplices, so that they too might stir up the Lollards for a united vengeance. And so for all the time which elapsed from his escape up to the feast of the circumcision of our Lord [1 January] or Epiphany [6 January], Lollard envoys were running hither and thither, to induce country dwellers and any others they could by promise of generous wages to be ready by a certain day to be announced to them to stand forth like men and engage in acts of war. Many people in their ignorance asked the cause for which or concerning which they ought to take up arms, and they were told that that did not matter, provided they received handsome payment and could definitely

---

[1] The forty days was a stay of execution in all but name. The author the *Gesta* confirms that Henry was anxious to afford Oldcastle further opportunity to recant, but does not suggest, as Walsingham does here, that Arundel shared his affection for the knight: *Gesta Henrici*, pp. 6–7. See also Wylie, *Henry V,* i. 258.

[2] Oldcastle escaped from the Tower on the night of 19 October, apparently with the assistance of a Warrington Franciscan, a Shropshire scrivener and a London parchment-maker. The *Gesta* author claims that he had been formally released from custody and was awaiting a further examination from Arundel when he made his escape: *Gesta Henrici*, pp. 6–7. See also Wylie, *Henry V,* i. 259–60.

hope that they would be generously rewarded for their brave deeds. But I shall give fuller details about all this later on in the course of my history.

In this year many English people were struck down by a pestilence or epidemic and ceased to live.

Also in this year the body of Richard, once king of England, which had been buried in the church of the preaching brothers [i.e. Dominicans] at [King's] Langley, was lifted from its tomb and taken to London and buried at Westminster [Abbey] as a king should be. This was not without a great expense of money by the present king, who confessed that he owed as much veneration to Richard as to his own father in the flesh.[1]

[1414]

The first year of Henry V

In 1414, the first year of the reign of King Henry V, the young king celebrated Christmas in solemn fashion at Eltham, where the Lollards who had formed a conspiracy, had decided to catch him unawares and either capture or kill the king and his brothers and friends. But omnipotent God was unwilling for an innocent man to run into any danger at the hands of the guilty, and he put his fear into the hearts of certain of the conspirators who warned the king to avoid the danger and to sidestep the plot which had now been formed against him. And so without any great fuss the king quietly transferred himself to his palace near Westminster, where he was in a safer place and surrounded by a greater crowd of people.[2]

But now that their wicked plans were complete, the Lollards began to blab about their schemes and they were keen to make trial of the circumstances which they thought would be favourable to their hopes. In the very stillness of the night they came to the fields called St Giles' fields near London, where it was said that their leader, John Oldcastle, Lord Cobham, was waiting for his supporters. At every path, street and crossroads you could have seen crowds of people flocking together, brought to London from almost every county of England by the extravagant promises of the Lollards, and assembling for the appointed day and hour which were now nigh at hand.[3] When they were asked why they were in such a rush that they were running along panting, they replied that they were hurrying to join Sir John Cobham [i.e. Oldcastle], who had summoned and hired them at his own expense.

But the king, by the will of God, was not unaware of all these happenings, and in the dead of night ordered his men to arm themselves and get ready, and then for the first time told them what he had decided to do. There were several with the king on that occasion who advocated putting off any interference until daylight, when they would be able to determine those who were willing to take their stand with the king against Sir John. And there were others whose counsel was that the king should wait until he had assembled a sizeable army, to avoid attacking the enemy with a small force and coming off the worse – perish the thought! But the king listened to neither party,

1   The reburial of Richard was both a personal act of atonement and a political act to finally dispel any rumour that the deposed king was still alive. The ceremony of re-interment was a grand one, with a procession of bishops, abbots and nobles following the body in a new elm coffin and no less a sum than 100 marks distributed to the poor en route. Henry also made generous provision for the perpetual commemoration of Richard, providing for four large tapers to burn at the tomb, a dirge and requiem mass to be sung, 6s 8d to be given each week to the poor in his memory and the sum of £20 annually on the anniversary of his death. See Saul, *Richard II*, p. 428; Wylie, *Henry V*, i. 209–11.
2   It appears the conspirators had planned to gain entry to the royal palace at Eltham in the guise of mummers on or around the feast of Epiphany (6 January) where they would assassinate the king and his brothers, thus destroying the Lancastrian dynasty at a stroke. As it happened a number of the conspirators were intercepted several days before and having been apprised of the plan, Henry removed himself to the security of Westminster on Monday 8 January. Further conspirators were captured by the mayor of London outside Bishopsgate. See also Wylie, *Henry V*, i. 263–73.
3   The rising drew support from a wide catchment area, from Bristol in the west to Derby in the Midlands. The conspirators hoped to raise as many as 20,000 to be supported by a further 50,000 apprentices and masters from the city of London. See also Wylie, *Henry V*, i. 270–2.

particularly because he had heard that the Lollards planned in the event of their vain schemes being successful to destroy first the monastic houses of Westminster, St Albans and St Paul's and those of all the friars situated in London. And so the king, confronting these evils and entering on the path of danger, a little after midnight advanced into St Giles' fields against the wishes of his advisers. There he halted, intending to wait for what the next day would bring with it when it came. As a result it happened that many from distant parts, in their haste to reach the enemy lines, first mistakenly entered the king's lines and when asked where they were going, replied that they were seeking their leader, Sir John Cobham [i.e. Oldcastle]. And so contrary to their expectations they were taken captive and put in prison.

Finally the news reached the leaders of the rebels that the king with a strong force had occupied the fields next to them and had taken prisoner very many of their own troops.[1] And they were still more disturbed because they saw no one coming out to join them from London, although they had thought that thousands of Londoners would rush to their aid. In fact the king had given orders for the gates of the city to be shut and closely guarded by armed men, so that nobody was able to get out except those whom the guards knew were hurrying to the king's standards. And indeed if the king had not shown this shrewdness, it is said that about fifty thousand servants and apprentices together with some of the citizens who were their masters would have left the city that night to oppose the king.

So when the Lollard ranks heard that the king had now stationed his army in the same fields, they lost heart and sought safety by running away, but the king's men followed in pursuit and killed some, and took some prisoner. But the whereabouts of their leader was a complete mystery, although the king through the voice of his herald had publicly promised a thousand marks from his own purse to any individual who would reveal his hiding place, and the greatest privileges and freedoms to any city or district that would expose him. And what shows that almost the whole country had embraced the Lollard madness was that no one could be found who was willing to reveal his whereabouts, even for such a great reward. Very many of his followers were taken prisoner, who were said to have formed a plot for the wholesale destruction of king, nobles, prelates, property-owning monks, mendicant friars and citizens. Found guilty of this, they were not only sentenced to be drawn and hanged on the gallows, but after this unhappy end were also cremated.[2]

Among them was a certain William Murley from Dunstable. A brewer by trade and quite rich, he had been a close follower of the views of [Sir] John Oldcastle and more than all others of that pernicious sect had troubled the minds of countless orthodox believers. He was at St Giles's fields and when he learned of the king's presence he timidly crept back to Dunstable and looked for a hiding place. According to the story, it had been arranged beforehand that on that day he would receive from the hand of [Sir] John Oldcastle the order of knighthood. Proof of the story was provided by the two warhorses with gold harness which were following him, and by the golden spurs which he had tucked away inside his cloak and which were taken out of it once he had been taken prisoner, something which happened only a very short time after he had run off. So he was drawn, hanged and cremated, thus obtaining his deserved end.[3]

The roll of the precentor of St Albans containing the names of the monks

There was also found up his sleeve a roll belonging to the precentor of St Albans which contained all the names of the monks of the abbey and which he or his companions had secretly stolen.[4] It is

[1] The *Gesta* author reports that a meteor was observed just at the moment that Henry arrived at St Giles's fields: *Gesta Henrici*, pp. 10–11.
[2] Commissions of inquiry were appointed on 10 and 11 January and those condemned were hanged two days later. As Walsingham reports here, the bodies of convicted Lollards were also burned. Others involved in the rising, however, escaped with a royal pardon.
[3] Murley was tried on 12 January and hanged the following day.
[4] As a former precentor of the abbey, Walsingham was bound to be alarmed by this episode. The theft of the roll was the first of several occurrences reported by Walsingham that would suggest that St Albans and its

said that this William had planned to eliminate all of them and to take over their house himself as lord and earl of the county of Hertfordshire, by the gift of his leader John Oldcastle. There were also many others, both priests and laymen, who were taken prisoner, found guilty, condemned and given a similar end. Very many of them were not even willing to repent. And these are men of religion, who for outer show displayed in their looks and words self-restraint, patience, humility, and love, but whose minds and inner selves, as afterwards became clear, were full of bitterness, rancorous bile, disdain, falsity, trickery and deceit and vindictiveness in equal measure. A prophecy had been spoken about the aggression of these people, or, more accurately, about their transgression a long time before they had put off sheep's clothing and put on that of wolves. It went as follows:

> Between the rocky fountain
> And the rugged mountain
> Ruin will fall on English rebels
> Through trickery of traitors

We can see that this came true, because rebels did assemble against the king in between two such places, and they were ruined there by the trickery of their own side, as some of their number reported their plot to the king.[1]

[The horrific end of the king of Naples]

In this year the king of Naples [Ladislas] assaulted a great part of Italy. He laid waste almost all the lands of Tuscany, trampled upon and devastated Rome and overthrew the rights of the Roman church.[2] But after he had performed these many acts of wickedness in the land, God gave him a deserved punishment in return, for in the midst of his high-handed career of lust and adultery he felt in his private parts the presence of death from a poisoned cloth. In fact he was such a slave to sex that there was no class of women whom he passed by and did not make submit to his foul lust. And so it happened that he raped a maid whom he had noticed in Rome. Her parents were livid, but they did not dare to criticise him openly. However their sorrow and anguish of mind dictated a means of revenge, and they gave their daughter a cloth, drenched in poison from some herbs or other, with which, they told the girl, she was to wipe the private parts of the king and herself after sex, so that in this way she might make the king still more deeply grateful. But as soon as she had done this, the girl died from the poison and did not live to see the dawn. The king indeed who was infected with the same poison, realised that his own death was at hand. He hurriedly got himself carried back to Naples, where he turned to words of religion and vowed that he would be a vassal of St Peter and would restore all the plunder he had taken from Rome. But in vain. For as the poison spread through his whole body he was brought to the gate of death, and there was no escape for him, as, cursing God, he met the death that he had deserved.

[The death of the archbishop of Canterbury]

In this year on 20 February there collapsed and died that lofty tower of the English church and its never defeated champion, Sir Thomas Arundel. As primate of all England he had waged the Lord's wars time after time against the Lollards, and it was thought that he would never have been

---

environs harboured an unusually high number of Lollards in this period. The name of the precentor in this period is not recorded.

1   Thomas Elmham records the same prophecy in his *Liber metricus: Memorials of Henry the Fifth, King of England*, ed. C. A. Cole, Rolls Series, 11 (1858), p. 99.

2   Ladislas of Naples had begun his assault in response to the alliance that had been forged between Pope John XXIII and Sigismund of Hungary in January 1414. John XXIII had begun his pontificate in support of Ladislas' enemy, Louis of Anjou, but there had been a brief rapprochement in 1412. This had ended emphatically with Ladislas' occupation of Rome the following year, and the king now sought to extend his influence further north. He had secured the submission of Florence by 22 June but was already stricken by disease and was forced to retreat. He returned to Naples where he died on 6 August. As Walsingham maintains here, it was widely believed that Ladislas' mortal illness was the result of his sexual excesses.

defeated, if only his suffragan bishops had determined to fight with equal devotion.[1] His successor as archbishop of Canterbury was the bishop of St David's, Master Henry Chichele, the king's confessor.[2] Master Stephen Patrington, brother of the order of Carmelites, a man learned in the Trivium and Quadrivium, was made bishop of St Davids.[3]

[The king takes pity on Henry Percy. Envoys from France]

The king took pity on young Henry Percy, who, after the death of his father, killed in battle at Shrewsbury when his son was still a little boy, had been taken to Scotland by his grandfather, Henry Percy, earl of Northumberland. The king gave orders to his kinsmen that he was troubling them for the lad's recall, as he had not only decided to honour him by recalling him from Scotland, but also to raise him to the position of earl of Northumberland.[4]

In that year there came to the parliament held by the king at Leicester[5] envoys from the king of France and from the duke of Burgundy [John the Fearless]. But they did not come for the same purpose. For the duke of Burgundy asked to be strengthened for his war against the duke of Orléans, who was backed by the king of France, and promised, so it was said, more than he was able to provide, or perhaps more than he had intended.[6] So envoys were properly sent by the king of England to both these petitioners, with two bishops, the high-ranking occupants of Durham, Lord Thomas Langley, and of Norwich, Master Richard Courtenay, leading the delegations.[7] And more than once these envoys were sent to France and the French envoys were sent to England, and both sides spent vast amounts of money, while hopes of peace were completely put to sleep.[8]

---

[1]   The sixty-two year old archbishop died on 19 February 1414 after a sudden affliction of the throat had rendered him speechless for several days. It was reported that his last suffering was divine judgement for his assault on popular preaching.

[2]   Chichele (c.1362–1443) was the third son of a merchant, Thomas Chichele. After serving Henry IV as an ambassador, envoy and later proctor to the Roman Curia, he was appointed bishop of St David's by papal provision in October 1407. In this capacity he also became a councillor of Henry, Prince of Wales, in the latter years of the reign and through him had secured a place on the king's council by 1410. For Henry V he was an experienced candidate for the archbishopric and in political terms far less provocative than the other contender, Bishop Henry Beaufort of Winchester. Chichele was translated to Canterbury on 27 April 1414. For Chichele see also Emden, *BRUO*, i. 410–12.

[3]   Patrington (d. 22 September 1417), a Carmelite friar, was an Oxford scholar of some standing, the author of learned commentaries on scripture and (perhaps) classical literature, hence Walsingham's description of him as a man steeped in the liberal arts. He was confessor to Henry V, an office he had also fulfilled for his father, and had assisted Archbishop Arundel in the examination of Oldcastle. Patrington was consecrated bishop of St David's on 9 June 1415 and was translated to the see of Chichester two years later, barely a week before his death. See also Emden, *BRUO*, iii. 1435–6; Wylie, *Henry V*, i. 238.

[4]   Henry Percy (1394–1455) thus became the 2nd earl of Northumberland. For the deaths of his father, 'Hotspur', and grandfather, Northumberland, see above, pp. 328, 359–60.

[5]   The choice of Leicester as the location for this parliament was not coincidental since it was recognised to be a centre of Lollardy. The session opened on 30 April: *RP*, iv. 15.

[6]   Duke John's envoys now renewed the proposals they had made to Henry's father in 1411, that Henry V might make a marriage alliance with the duke's daughter Catherine, whilst Henry would provide a modest force (500 men-at-arms, 200 archers) to assist the duke in his projected conquest of the territories controlled by Orléans and Bourbon.

[7]   For Courtenay and Langley see above, pp. 341, 389 and n.

[8]   The English envoys made their first journey to Paris in April 1414, but returned in May and were dispatched a second time in July, the negotiations continuing into August. Their demands were substantial, in the first instance that the crown and kingdom of France be surrendered to Henry and that he might take the king's daughter Katherine as his bride together with a dowry of two million crowns. Such demands might only be moderated, the envoys explained, in return for the cession of all the territories previously granted to Edward III under the Treaty of Brétigny (1360), including Anjou, Brittany, Flanders, Maine, Normandy, Touraine and an extended Aquitaine, in full sovereignty, together with exemplification for the ransom promised in respect of King John II, captured at the battle of Poitiers (1356). The French were willing to concede some, perhaps all of the territories demanded but were immovable both on the issue of the crown and of King John's ransom and were simply unable to satisfy such an excessive dowry. Despite their frequency, the negotiations were moving towards deadlock. See also Wylie, *Henry V*, i. 417–30.

The foundation of three houses near Sheen[1]

In this year King Henry began the foundation of three religious houses near to his manor commonly known as Sheen.[2] One was for the order of Carthusian monks; another for the monks called the Celestines,[3] (these profess the Rule of St Benedict, which they say they follow to the letter, and, going beyond it, they bind themselves to perpetual seclusion); the third for the Brigittines,[4] who follow the rule of St Augustine, which, with other rites added to it, they now call 'the rule of the Saviour'.[5]

The Brigittines are not allowed to have their own property, not even a penny's worth, or to touch money in any way. In this monastery, according to the rule, there must be sixty sisters, thirteen priests, four deacons and eight lay persons, so that, when all these are counted up, there will be the same number of persons as the sum of the thirteen apostles and seventy-two disciples of Christ. They always wear not linen, but wool. The two communities have one church in common, the nuns using the upper floor next to the roof, and the monks the lower ground floor, and each community is separately enclosed: after their profession they are not allowed to leave the building, unless with the special permission of the pope. The two communities are required by their rule to have sufficient endowments to maintain their members and their servants and to perform the tasks of such a large house, so that, without needing to beg whether the harvest is barren or bountiful, they can have sufficient to live in peace. Afterwards indeed, if the whole world were to offer them possessions and estates, they would not be allowed to receive any of them at all. Before the festival of All Saints [1 November] each year they have to calculate their budget for food and other necessities for the following year, and whatever of their food or money remains over from the current year has to be distributed to the poor on the day after All Saints. If ever indeed it seems that there will not be sufficient food for the following year, then they have to add the exact amount of money or food required from the current year to the following year, but without exceeding this exact amount, if the abbess and the general confessor of the house wish to avoid endangering their souls. And afterwards, whatever is left from the current year, must be given to the poor. The abbess with the agreement of the sisters and the brothers must choose one of the thirteen priests to be the general confessor for the monastery. All the brothers must obey him and do nothing at all which is contrary to his precepts. No man or woman from the world outside nor any monk shall enter the nuns' cloister, apart from doctors or workmen when they are needed, or when a dead nun has to be carried out for burial. These are the customs, which, together with several others, are observed by those who profess this new rule. But for the time being I will leave this subject and hurry on to other matters.

---

[1] Walsingham dwells on the foundation of these houses not only because they reinforced the reputation of Henry V as a defender of the church, but also because his fellow monks of St Albans appear to have been closely involved in their establishment. Abbot William Heyworth acted as an advisor to the king and another monk, Thomas Fishbourne, was appointed as a chaplain to the Brigittines of Syon and subsequently entered the house as one of the brethren. See Wylie, *Henry V,* i. 212–15; Clark, *Monastic Renaissance,* p. 25.

[2] It was at the manor of Sheen that Edward III and Anne of Bohemia had died. After the latter's death Richard II had the buildings demolished.

[3] The reformed order of Benedictines was established by Peter of Moronne, known as 'the Hermit', in the middle years of the thirteenth century and received papal recognition from Urban IV (1261–4); the monks became known as Celestines after Peter was elected Pope in 1294, taking the title Celestine V. The English envoys had spent part of their embassy at Paris securing support from French representatives of the order for a Celestine colony in England.

[4] The order of St Saviour, commonly know as the Brigittines, was first established by Birgitta of Sweden (d.1397) at Vadstena in 1346 and received recognition from Urban V in 1370.

[5] The charter for the foundation of the 'house of Mount Syon of Sheen' was issued on 3 March 1415, the charter for the foundation of the 'house of Jesu of Bethlehem of Sheen' and on 1 April; in the event the Celestine community was never established. The two houses were established on either side of the river bank at Sheen. See also Wylie, *Henry V,* i. 212–15.

[The king decides to stop the trickery of the French]

On their return from France the second time, our envoys there, the bishops of Durham [Thomas Langley] and Norwich [Richard Courtenay], declared that so far the French had been using trickery.[1] The king was annoyed at this and decided to put a stop to their jokes and to punish his mockers in the courts of war, showing them by his deeds and actions how mad they had been to arouse a sleeping dog.

At the convocation which followed a two-tenths tax was granted to the king, to be paid by the feast of the Purification [2 February] next following, and by the same feast in each succeeding year. In the following parliament, a two-fifteenths tax was granted to the king by the laity.[2]

During the feast of Michaelmas [29 September] the king ordered all the prelates and nobles of the kingdom to come to a council at London, that he might discuss with them difficult matters affecting their land.

[Delegates chosen for the council of Constance]

At this time indeed the archbishop of Canterbury [Henry Chichele] was holding a great council of clergy there [i.e. London],[3] at which there was a discussion about the abolition of the privileges enjoyed up to now by those who had been granted exemptions by the popes of Rome. This was the first of the signs given by the new metropolitan to indicate his anger.[4]

Also at this council, representatives for the clergy of England were chosen to attend the general council that was to be held in the German city of Constance. And it happened that the most learned popes and prelates, attended by countless outstanding other priests, flocked to this council, mainly because of the praiseworthy scruples of that devout Christian, the king of the Romans and of Hungary, who, though chosen as emperor of Germany, refused to receive the crown until he knew for certain who was to be appointed pope of the whole of Christendom.[5] To

---

[1]   This was the embassy of July and August 1414. After a warm welcome at Paris by Jean, duke of Berry, on behalf of the king and ascendant Armagnac faction, the discussion soon became strained. The French were prepared to offer a portion of the financial and territorial demands that Henry had made, including a dowry of 600,000 crowns on his marriage to Princess Katherine, and the cession of lands south of the Charente, restoring the old boundaries of English Aquitaine down to the Pyrenees. But they were dismissive of the king's *demande incivile* for the crown and kingdom of France itself. None of this supports Walsingham's suggestion that the French treated Henry and his envoys with scorn. The *Gesta* author reports only that the French council 'could not be induced to accept a peace without immense injury to the crown of England' (*Gesta Henrici*, pp. 14–15) but later chroniclers echo Walsingham's contention that the French openly mocked King Henry. John Streeche, canon of Kenilworth, writing after Henry's death, recorded that the French had suggested sending balls and cushions to appease a young man more suited to a life of leisure (John Streeche, p. 150). It was this story that was embroidered by later writers, becoming the tennis ball gift of Shakespeare's *Henry V*. See also Wylie, *Henry V*, Act 2, Scene 1, i. 417–30.

[2]   When parliament met on November 19, Chancellor Beaufort urged the commons to prepare for war. The fact that they responded with a generous grant reflects their change of mood with the succession of the new king. In spite of this, the speaker, Thomas Chaucer, advised the king to send another embassy to see whether an agreement might be reached at the eleventh hour by peace means. The envoys were sent on 12 March 1415. See also *RP*, iv. 34; Wylie, *Henry V*, i. 432–4.

[3]   Convocation met at London in October 1414: Wylie, *Henry V*, i. 434.

[4]   Walsingham has in mind the privilege of papal chaplaincy, which he regarded as one of the chief abuses to have prospered under the schism, as he commented in an earlier section of the chronicle. He does not record the fact that this convocation also saw the clergy compelled to agree to the curtailment of other privileges enjoyed in England, such as the freedom to levy excessive probate fees, an abuse which had been the subject of several commons' petitions.

[5]   Sigismund (1368–1437), second son of Emperor Charles IV, had been crowned king of Hungary in 1387 as a result of his marriage to Maria, daughter and heir of Lewis the Great, king of Poland and Hungary. Following the deposition of his half-brother Wenzel IV as king of the Romans, Sigismund was elected to the title in 1410 and, to reinforce his claim, re-elected in 1411 when he was also recognised as emperor elect of the Holy Roman Empire. It was Sigismund who had pressured John XXIII into convening a council to seek a resolution to the continuing schism which had been only compounded by the election of a third pope at Pisa in 1409 (see above, p. 375). He issued a summons on 30 October 1413 for the council to meet at the imperial city

pass over other details, the representatives sent to the council from England were the most vener-able bishops of Salisbury [Robert Hallum],[1] Bath [Nicholas Bubwith] and Hereford,[2] and together with these the abbot of Westminster,[3] the prior of the cathedral church of Worcester[4] and several other high-powered individuals famous for their piety and learning. They had the very great honour of having the person of the earl of Warwick [Richard Beauchamp] present as one of their number.

[The council of Constance][5]

So at Constance before these people and the colleges of cardinals of the former Gregory [XII] and of Peter de Luna [i.e. Benedict XIII], which had of their own free will united into one college, and in the presence of other prelates and leading clerics, who had gathered in Constance from the whole of Christendom, Gregory of his own accord renounced the papacy, provided that the same renunciation was made by Peter de Luna, who had taken the name of pope in Aragon, and John, who had taken it in Rome. But although Peter de Luna made his renunciation through proxies, as he was not able to be present himself, our John [XXIII] tried to get out of doing this until, after warnings and persuasion from the emperor, he at last agreed to make his renunciation like the others. Once he had done this, all who were present there were filled with indescribable joy, thinking that an end had now been put to the schism.[6]

[Pope John is imprisoned]

But, sad to say, just when people were hoping they had seen the beginnings of a peaceful solution, the start of a new quarrel made its appearance. For Pope John, pretending he was ill, suddenly left the council by night with the duke [Frederick] of Austria for one of the cities of the duke. But in a letter sent to the emperor he made the excuse that he had left Constance because the air did not agree with him, but that nevertheless he would be ready to return to the council immediately to fulfil and carry out his promises, whenever the emperor thought to summon him. This excuse and promise so pleased the emperor that he wrote to the king of England a whole series of papal letters.

So when, some days later, the emperor and the council decided that he should show his face among them and begged him through envoys to come at once to the council, as he had promised to do, John was not happy about it and flatly refused to obey. Indeed, wearing a disguise, he fled

---

of Constance. John XXIII began to issue individuals bulls of summons in early December. The council was to open on 1 November 1414. The delegates were to meet at Constance on 1 November 1414. Sigismund had also sought the support of Henry V from the very beginning of his reign, writing to him in March 1413 encouraging him to join him in his efforts towards the restoration of a unified Christendom. Henry responded by dispatching envoys to the emperor in July 1414 to discuss a possible tripartite agreement between the empire, England and France in which the warring parties' territorial claims would be settled by a division of Burgundy.

1   Hallum was to die at Constance, on 4 September 1417.
2   Robert Mascall, bishop of Hereford since 1404. He died in December 1416 before the close of the council.
3   William Colchester; elected in 1386 he was now of advanced age and in failing health. He died in 1420.
4   John Malvern, prior from 1395 until his death in 1423.
5   The council opened at 7am. on 5 November 1414 in the presence of John XXIII and the first session began on 16 November. There were twenty-nine cardinals and more than six hundred archbishops, bishops, abbots and university scholars in attendance. It was not until the emperor Sigismund arrived on Christmas Day that the delegates began to discuss the procedure for resolving the continuing schism. See *Magnum oecumenicum Constantiense concilium de universali ecclesiae unione et fide Constantiensis concilii acta et decreta de Benedicto XIII papa de papali sede dejecto aliisque rebus sessione XXVII–XXXVIII*, ed. H. von der Hardt (Frankfurt and Leipzig, 1699–1701), iv. 12–13, 28.
6   The proposal for a tripartite abdication was made on 15 February 1415 and it was immediately clear that John XXIII would prove obdurate. He appeared to give his assent on 1 March but then was reluctant to confirm his abdication in a bull. This was secured at the intervention of Emperor Sigismund on 7 March, but it was now suspected that John would not abide by the agreement: *Constantiensis concilii acta et decreta*, ed. von der Hardt, iv. 41–2.

with the duke of Austria to his own land.[1] So the emperor sent envoys to the duke, commanding him to bring John back and restore him to the council. When the duke [Frederick] of Austria refrained from doing this, the emperor made an armed invasion of his territories, and, having captured or destroyed his defences, he forced the duke to submit, and to bring back the pope in the same disguise in which he had spirited him away as a fugitive.

So he was brought back and displayed to the council, not wearing his robes of religion, but half-naked like a brigand and carrying a bow in his left hand and at his side the short arrows used by the horsemen of those parts who are known as the Malendrini.[2] He was jeered and laughed at by the whole assembly, both clergy and laity, and sent to prison to be kept under close guard. And immediately all his moveable goods became an open invitation to looters, for it is said that he was robbed of £75,000 of gold and silver, which he had transferred to his own use for safe keeping. When news of this reached England, the chest at St Paul's, in which the money collected for his use had been stored, was unlocked, and the money taken out and used for better purposes.

[Sentence of deprivation on the three claimants to the papacy][3]

'In the name of the holy and undivided trinity, father, son and holy spirit, amen. The holy general synod of Constance, properly assembled in the holy spirit, invoking the name of Christ and with its eyes fixed only on God, has looked at the articles drawn up in this case against Pope John XXIII. And after mature deliberation upon them, it pronounces as its decision and declares as its definitive sentence, in these writings which we now publish, that the withdrawal of Pope John XXIII from this city of Constance secretly, by night and at a suspicious time in an unseemly disguise, while the sacred general council was being held, both was and is illegal, a scandal for the church of God and the council, a disturbance and an impediment to the peace and union of the church itself, nourishment for a long lasting schism, and a deviation by pope John from his vow, promise and oath made to God, the church and this holy council.

'And the synod also declares that Pope John both was and is a notorious simoniac, a notorious squanderer of honours, goods and rights not only of the church at Rome but also those belonging to other churches and many other pious people, and a wicked administrator and dispenser of the spiritualities and temporalities of the church, notoriously scandalising the church of God and Christian people by his detestable and dishonest life and behaviour both before his assumption to the papacy and subsequently up to this time, and that he was and is a notorious stumbling block to the church of God and the people of Christ though all these things we have mentioned. Despite warnings prompted by duty and affection and repeated frequently time and time again, he has stubbornly persisted in his evil course, and so notoriously shown himself by this to be incorrigible.

'And so this synod declares that on account of these charges and others, brought and contained in the proceedings of the case against him, he should be removed and deposed from and deprived of the papacy and all spiritual and temporal government as being unworthy, of no use and wicked. And this synod does so remove, depose and deprive him, declaring that Chris-

---

[1] John XXIII fled from Constance on 20 March while many of the delegates were attending a tournament at which Duke Frederick was the main contender. At the conclusion of the jousting, Frederick also left the city and joined John at Schaffhausen: *Constantiensis concilii acta et decreta*, ed. von der Hardt, iv. 41–2.

[2] The delegates at Constance at first attempted to negotiate for John XXIII's return but then transferred their attention to Duke Frederick and when reconciliation was effected between him and Emperor Sigismund, Frederick took John into his own custody. The council was now in a position to proceed against John and he was formally condemned for contumacy on 14 May and deprived of the papal throne on 20 May. Stripped of his title, Balthazar Cossa was imprisoned first at Gottlieben and then at Heidelberg until the council was dispersed.

[3] The sentence of deprivation was passed on 29 May. Walsingham reproduces the text that appears in the collected *acta* of Constance although he omits the closing paragraphs, which make reference to the emperor Sigismund. The fourth paragraph given here 'And so for the good of the union of the church...' is in fact taken from another decree issued together with the deprivation. See *Constantiensis concilii acta et decreta*, ed. von der Hardt, iv. 280–1, 284–5.

tians everywhere, both as a body and individually, of whatever status, position or condition, are freed from obedience, loyalty and any oaths made to him. It also forbids all the faithful of Christ ever in the future to name him as pope, to support him as pope, or to obey him on any matter. And none the less this holy synod out of its certain knowledge and the fullness of its power makes up for each and every deficiency that may have occurred in the preceding sentences or in any part of them.

'And so for the good of the union of the church of God, this holy synod determines, decides and decrees that neither Balthazar Cossa, lately Pope John XXIII, nor Peter de Luna, Benedict XIII, nor Angelus Corrario, Gregory XII, here named with their offices, should ever at any time be re-elected to the papacy. And if the contrary should happen, it is to be by its very nature invalid and illegal. And it also decrees that no one, of whatever position and pre-eminence, even if he is resplendent in the office of emperor, king, cardinal or bishop, is at any time to go against this decree and give obedience or support to these three, or to any one of them, under the penalty of an everlasting curse for being a supporter of this schism. If anyone in the future should presume to go against this decree, the secular arm of the law will be called in as well and stern proceedings taken against him.'

[1415]

[New ambassadors from France]

When the king of England had now found out for certain that the French with their fraudulent tricks and false promises had been engaging in meaningless negotiations with him,[1] he collected ships, chose armed men and archers, prepared machines and ammunition and got ready all the apparatus of war, so that he could attack the enemy more effectively. And he gave orders that all who were to go on the expedition with him be at Southampton in readiness to sail on the feast of [the nativity of] St John the Baptist [24 June].[2]

At this time there came to him new ambassadors from France not seen before, headed by the archbishop of Sens, a verbose and arrogant man but lacking in discipline, as the sequel will show, who behaved with great insolence when he made the closing speech for the embassy in the presence of the king and his nobles.[3] In the end the king rejected the offers and promises of the ambassadors as being neither reasonable nor showing honour to himself, and sent them back to London. When they saw the forces the king had prepared and his immediate readiness to embark,

---

[1]   Henry had responded to the pressure from the previous parliament and dispatched another embassy to France in March 1415. There remained a significant distance between the two parties, but the French now demonstrated a willingness to raise their offers, both of territory (an enlarged Aquitaine), and the dowry for the proposed marriage between Henry and the king's daughter Katherine (now 800,000 crowns, just short of the revised demands by the English). The English envoys were not empowered to accept a compromise agreement and the discussions broke up. It was agreed that Henry would send his secretary to discuss the offer in detail but acting under the king's authority his stipulations were too severe and still no agreement could be concluded. See also Wylie, *Henry V*, i. 452–3.

[2]   Henry's preparations began at the very beginning of the year even before the March embassy had been appointed. Shipmen from Bristol, Hull, Sandwich and Winchelsea were summoned in January. Tents were ordered in February. Writing from Kenilworth, John Streeche reported that artillery and other equipment was being sought by royal agents from the autumn of 1414 onwards (John Streeche, pp. 150–1). On 10 March Henry appealed to the city of London for funds to support his campaign and on 16 April he made arrangement for the government of the country while he was abroad. See Wylie, *Henry V*, i. 157–63, 457–82; C. T. Allmand, *Henry V* (London, 1992), p. 72.

[3]   The French envoys arrived at Dover on 17 June when Henry had already left the capital for Southampton. The delegation was led by the Guillaume Boisratier, archbishop of Bourges (Walsingham is in error with his reference to Jean de Montaigu, the archbishop of Sens), accompanied by Pierre Fresnel, the bishop of Lisieux, Louis of Bourbon, count of Vendôme, the lords of Ivry and Bracquemont and two royal secretaries. See Famiglietti, *Royal Intrigue*, pp. 163, 286 n. 74. Henry met them at Wolvesey castle and the discussion continued from 2–6 July. The archbishop offered an increased dowry of 850,000 crowns for the marriage to Katherine but was now far less compliant as to Henry's territorial demands, claiming that Henry's title to Aquitaine and other lands, and to the crown of France itself, was not clearly, or uniformly established. Henry responded with a reiteration of his claims and stated that he was now compelled to recover his territory by force.

the ambassadors were seriously worried and tried to escape unseen from England so that they could arrive in France before the king, thus enabling the French to have the increased safety of greater precautions. But their plans were foiled, for they were seized and captured and put under guard.

At this time the Scottish earl of Fife[1] was being escorted back to Scotland according to the agreement, so that there could be an exchange of his person for the person of young Henry Percy, whom his grandfather, the former earl of Northumberland, had once taken with him to those parts when he was still a young lad. But a knight of the district called Thomas Talbot[2] ambushed the earl of Fife, took him prisoner and carried him off. But he was recaptured immediately by the praiseworthy action of the upright earl of Westmorland [Ralph Neville], the said Thomas having fled and run away in fright. And so the restitution of each to his own people was held up for several days.

[The treachery of Henry Scrope]

While the king was at Southampton awaiting the arrival of the nobles whose duty it was to cross the channel with him, three powerful men, in whom the king had the greatest trust, conspired to kill him. If I wanted to suppress their names, the notoriousness of their crime would spread them abroad, even if I kept silent. So I shall record that which it pains me to relate, and reveal the names of the murderers.[3] The first and foremost of them was named as Lord Henry Scrope,[4] in whose loyalty and constancy the king had complete confidence. Covering all his actions with an outer cloak of hypocrisy, and 'In his dark heart playing the cunning fox',[5] in everything he did he showed to the world the innocence of a lamb.

> He learnt to feign his loyalty, his threats
> To hide, and screen deceit with winning smile.
> A cruel man, on fire with lust for gold,
> And skilled at spoiling friends' close trust with hate.[6]

He was so highly regarded by the king that discussions on private or public matters were usually brought to an end by his verdicts. For in all his actions he showed such a restrained gravity and sanctity that the king judged that all his pronouncements should be carried out just as if they were oracles fallen from heaven. If an important embassy had to be sent to France, the king thought that Henry Scrope was the man who had the ability to perform this task.[7] But all the while he was actually negotiating with the enemy, as a covert enemy of his own master, the king, and soothing the king with empty guarantees. He also deceived the council with empty promises, bringing back to both king and council delusory reports, a friend to his own side judging by his face, but in his heart a friend of the French.[8] Unaware of this the king had great confidence in him, on many

---

[1]   Murdoch Stewart, earl of Fife and son of Robert Stewart, duke of Albany, who had been held in captivity since the battle of Homildon (Humbleton) Hill. Negotiations for payment of the ransom demanded and his release had prospered in the summer of 1415 but almost immediately after his release he was abducted, apparently by Lollard conspirators who aimed to use Stewart to secure Percy who in turn would be used as the figurehead for an anti-Lancastrian uprising. However, Murdoch was soon recaptured.

[2]   Sir Thomas Talbot of Easington, Craven: *CCR, 1413–19*, pp. 177, 359, 384.

[3]   The *Gesta* author was no less severe in his condemnation, describing the 'brutal madness and mad brutality' of the conspirators (*Gesta Henrici*, pp. 18–19).

[4]   Henry, 3rd Lord Scrope of Masham (b.1376), nephew of Archbishop Richard Scrope who had been executed for fomenting rebellion against Henry IV in 1405. Scrope had spent his early years in the service of Henry IV, joining the escort for Princess Philippa on her journey to Denmark in 1406 and serving as the king's treasurer from 1410–11, while Henry, prince of Wales was predominant in the council. See Wylie, *Henry IV*, ii. 100; iii. 284, 314; Kirby, *Henry IV*, pp. 202, 226, 241, 258; Wylie, *Henry V*, i. 148, 157, 268, 511–43.

[5]   Persius, *Satirae*, v. 117.

[6]   Claudian, *In Rufinum*, ll. 98–101.

[7]   Scrope had not been involved in the principal negotiations at Paris, but had led the negotiations with the envoys of the duke of Burgundy in June 1414 over a possible marriage between the king and one of the duke's daughters.

[8]   There is no hard evidence to support the allegation that Scrope was in league with the French, but

matters entrusting himself to Henry's judgement and giving him many special gifts. There was almost no Englishman, apart from his brothers, who was dearer to the king than that Henry Scrope, as the king had openly proved by the frequent exhibitions of his affection which he showed him.

But he made a wicked return for all these marks of esteem, for, just as his master, the king, was on the point of departing with his fleet prepared and his army collected, Lord Henry suddenly made ready to deprive him of his life by the sword, as he had been unable to do this by poison. In his support of the French he was contriving a double blow for his own country, for not only was he trying to kill its great king but also to ensure that all the equipment prepared for the war was destroyed. He had promised this to the French envoys, so the story goes, in return for a sum of money agreed on for the betrayal, and when the envoys now got back home, they brought their people such certain news from England that their report was that everything was quiet and peaceful and likely to help the French, as the king of England, following the terms of the agreement, had now changed his mind, and had either gone back to London, or at least, and this they thought more likely, had been killed.

Lord Henry was joined in his treason by Richard, earl of Cambridge, brother of [Edward] the duke of York,[1] and by Thomas Grey, a knight from the north.[2] In fact it was the king who had made Richard an earl, enriching him with many goods and so honouring him by sitting next to him in parliament and other public places that he raised him above his other companions because of his birth and family. But no kindness shown, no benefit bestowed was able to prevent the traitors from taking up arms together to kill their great benefactor. So when they had put the finishing touches to their wicked plot, they approached the earl of March [Edmund Mortimer] with winning words and said they had formed a plan by which his own honour would necessarily be immensely increased, if only he would agree to their designs and confirm by taking a corporal oath that he would in no way reveal their plan. When he had done this, they said that they would suddenly kill the king with their swords and at once take the earl himself and elevate him to the throne of England. The young man shuddered with horror when he heard this, but on that occasion did not dare to oppose them or to say anything.[3]

But as soon as he could, when a suitable hour arrived, he went to the king and revealed to him

---

Walsingham here reflects a suspicion common amongst contemporary chroniclers: the author of the *Gesta* claims that Scrope and his co-conspirators were 'tempted by the stench of French promises or bribes' (*Gesta Henrici*, pp. 18–19). There seems to have been genuine surprise that a conspiracy should have been engendered inside Henry's inner circle amongst men who had served him since his days as prince of Wales. See also Wylie, *Henry V*, i. 531–2; Allmand, *Henry V*, pp. 74–8.

1   Richard of Conisbrough, the second son of Edmund Langley, duke of York (d.1404) had been created earl of Cambridge by Henry V in the Leicester parliament of May 1414. He was heir to his brother's duchy, but for the time being lacked the estates to support the dignity of his earldom, a fact that may have bred resentment. He had familial ties to his co-conspirator, Sir Thomas Grey, since his daughter, Isabel, had married Grey's son. He was also connected by marriage to some of the most rebellious spirits in early Lancastrian England; his second marriage to Maud Clifford in 1414 had linked him to the Percies whilst his first marriage had been to Anne, sister of Edmund Mortimer. Mortimer, as a legitimate claimant to the crown, was to be the focal point in the plot.

2   Sir Thomas Grey of Heaton, Northumberland, was probably drawn into the conspiracy because of his familial connections to Richard, earl of Cambridge. He had long been a Lancastrian loyalist, joining Henry IV shortly after he landed at Ravenspur in 1399 and serving in the early years of his reign as captain of Berwick: see Wylie, *Henry IV*, i. 80, 83; ii. 273; Kirby, *Henry IV*, p. 68; Wylie, *Henry V*, i. 517.

3   The 'wicked plot' was as ambitious and unrealistic as the earlier anti-Lancastrian uprisings: just as Henry's army was preparing to embark from Southampton, Mortimer was to withdraw to the New Forest from where he would declare a general uprising; in the ensuing chaos, he would steal away to the Welsh border where he would be joined by Glyn Dŵr, Sir John Oldcastle, the young Henry Percy, and unnumbered Scots supporters, a sufficient force to confront King Henry and his sons and kill them in a pitched battle. Whether Mortimer was to be crowned king, or whether there was to be division of the kingdom between the rebel leaders, as in the earlier Percy rebellion, is unclear. As Walsingham suggests here, it is also possible that the conspirators had reached some covert agreement with the French. See also Wylie, *Henry V*, i. 510–43.

the plot of these wicked men.[1] And so it happened that the traitors were arrested and condemned by the judgement of their peers. The king justly ordered their execution, after he had personally taxed Henry Scrope with ingratitude and asked him what he had received that they wished to kill him, after so many signs of gratitude from the king, which had not only been promised in light words but actually and as a matter of seriousness been carried out and performed.[2] It is said that Henry, seeing that he would inescapably be executed, replied with just this one sentence, 'I have sinned.' When the king heard this reply, he went away weeping and sighing,[3] so that his royal person could have shown the truth of the verses once written about the goodness of Augustus Caesar by the poet

> Our prince is slow to punish, quick to reward,
> And when compelled to toughness, a man of grief.[4]

[A rising of the Lollards]

At the same time, as if by agreement, and as if they knew about the plot, there was a rising of the Lollards.[5] They began to lift up their tails, vomiting blasphemies against the king, making grand claims, and scattering their threats over written documents that they fastened to the doors of the churches and in many other places. The goal and final intention of all these notices was the overthrow of the king, the subversion of the orthodox faith and the destruction of holy church. Against the king indeed, after he had started on his journey overseas, they spat out many insults, urging each other on by saying such things as, 'Now that the prince of priests has departed and our enemy gone away, a favourable time has smiled upon us in which we shall be allowed to avenge our injuries with impunity.' And encouraging each other in this way, they wrote that many thousands had come together in answer to their prayers.

Meanwhile their general and head, [Sir] John Oldcastle, who had been in hiding near Malvern, heard the false report that the king had crossed the sea for Harfleur, and, recovering his boldness in the king's absence, sent arrogant letters to Sir Richard Beauchamp, the lord of Abergavenny,[6] threatening his intention to avenge on Sir Richard's head the wrongs which he had inflicted on him and his followers. But Sir Richard took sensible precautions on hearing this news about the middle of the night, and the same night sent private messengers to Worcester, Pershore and Tewkesbury to ask that all who loved their king and country and had their hearts set on the safety of the state should meet him, armed, at daybreak, at his castle of Hanley. Without delay the prelates of these places with the people in their care obeyed Sir Richard's commands, and meeting him on the plain at the time agreed made up a number of five thousand archers and soldiers. When John Oldcastle learned of this, in his usual fashion he looked for a hiding place.

But the same lord of Abergavenny captured a priest of John Oldcastle and another man called William Fisher who had guarded and guided him ever since he had fled from the Tower of London together with three other of his accomplices and various other followers of John Oldcastle. Sir Richard cross-examined these men until they revealed the place in which John had

---

[1]   Mortimer revealed the plot to the king on 1 August. Perhaps he panicked but possibly he had been peripheral to its planning all along and was only apprised of the part he was to play at the last minute.

[2]   The three conspirators were executed on 2 August 1415.

[3]   Henry may have been grief stricken by the fall of his friend, but his desire to punish him went beyond the scaffold; Scrope was denied his wish to be buried at York Minster and his head was displayed instead at Mickelgate. In contrast to the properties of his co-conspirators, his estates were seized by the crown and redistributed to beneficiaries outside his own family circle: Wylie, *Henry V*, i. 535–6; Allmand, *Henry V*, p. 77.

[4]   Ovid, *Epistulae ex ponto*, 1. ii. 123–4.

[5]   Walsingham is the principal authority for the activities of Oldcastle and his supporters in the summer of 1415 as Henry departed for France. The *Gesta* author corroborates Walsingham's claim that rumours were in circulation of renewed Lollard sedition (*Gesta Henrici*, pp. 20–1) but he does not report any further details. Certainly, Oldcastle had hidden himself in the Welsh marches and it appears that he planned some action to take advantage of the king's absence abroad; as Walsingham describes, Sir Richard Beauchamp came close to capturing him at the same time as taking his two followers named here.

[6]   Richard Beauchamp, lord (A)bergavenny (1397–1422). He died at the siege of Meaux.

hidden his weapons and his money. They were all piled up in a certain house between two walls, which were so constructed that no one unless he was shown could detect the hidden space. And there were found there his banners and a standard on which he had got splendidly painted a chalice and the host in the shape of a loaf of bread, just as if that was the element in the sacrament that was to be worshipped. And there were also seen there a sort of cross of Christ with scourges, and a spear with nails, which he had painted on his banners to deceive the simple-minded, if ever he had the chance to raise the banners in support of a public show of madness. But when John Oldcastle heard of the forces gathered against him, he lowered the horns which he had arrogantly raised, checked his haughty threats, and, so it is said, went back to his former hiding place all the more quickly and timidly because he had heard that Henry Scrope and his fellow-plotters had paid the due penalty for their treason at Southampton.

Soon afterwards came the capture of a dyed-in-the-wool Lollard called William Cleydon. His Lollard beliefs had driven him to such mad behaviour that he even appointed his own son as a priest, and got him to celebrate Mass in his own home,[1] on the day on which his wife, rising from her childbirth bed, had gone to the church for cleansing. After his capture he was examined, lawfully convicted of heresy and burnt at London.

[The king besieges Harfleur]

After his most just punishment of the traitors, as I have described, the king of England [Henry V] embarked, and, cutting a furrow across the sea, landed unopposed very safely in Normandy, at a place called Chef de Caux.[2] He brought with him a fleet of one thousand five hundred vessels, properly equipped for the business of war, so that while he himself and his men were besieging the town of Harfleur on dry land, the fleet would be stationed at sea off the town, cutting off all food from the townsmen, and keeping other comforts from reaching the town. Indeed, having landed on the Wednesday which was the eve of the feast of the assumption of the blessed Mary [15 August], on the Saturday following he encircled the town with siege-works in the place named above, and he honourably continued the siege for five weeks right up to the Sunday before the feast of St Michael [29 September].[3] On this Sunday the town was surrendered to our king in the following way.

On the Tuesday before this Sunday the French lords who were in command at Harfleur, that is de Gaucort,[4] de Estouteville,[5] de Anquetonville[6] and de Clère,[7] could not endure the repeated battering of the walls and their houses inside the town, and the other perils which they had suffered from our king's guns (for the stones that flew through the air from these guns with the huge force of their blow smashed everything that got in their way as they landed, not only killing the bodies which they flattened, but also scattering around whole, bleeding limbs, and the weapons of the besieged yielded one by one to their blows, and not only were the combatants laid flat but also the beautiful buildings of the town)[8] and in their confusion and panic they were

---

1   It was widely suspected that Lollards celebrated Mass for themselves.
2   Henry embarked from Southampton on 7 August and landed at Chef de Caux (now St Adresse) on 14 August, the lengthy crossing reflecting the number of ships involved as much as the sea and weather conditions. It has been estimated that the king had mustered some 2,000 men-at-arms and 6,000 archers who were transported in no fewer than 1,500 ships, sailing from every harbour from Gosport westwards to Southampton. See also Wylie, *Henry V,* ii. 4–6.
3   After landing his troops, Henry marched to Grauville on 17 August and had surrounded Harfleur itself two days later. See also Wylie, *Henry V,* ii. 11–12.
4   Raoul VI, sire de Gaucort. In anticipation of the English invasion, the Armagnac-controlled council had appointed him captain of Harfleur. He was equipped with a force of 300 men-at-arms.
5   Jehannet de Estouteville, sire de Charlesmesnil.
6   Raoul d'Anquetonville.
7   George, Baron Clère, chamberlain to Charles VI.
8   Walsingham exaggerates the ease with which Gaucourt's garrison capitulated. The *Gesta* author (an eye-witness) recalled that the town was well defended with 'high and well built towers' and that each night the inhabitants repaired the damage inflicted during the day. The English forces engaged in a constant bombard-ment – as Walsingham describes vividly – whilst also undermining the foundations of the fortification.

forced to send in the middle of the night a serving-man-at-arms to [Thomas] the duke of Clarence, the brother of the king, to beg him to think it right for the honour of God to go to King Henry and on their behalf humbly plead with him to give them the opportunity of negotiating with whatever persons the king should think ought to be sent to the meeting. When the duke of Clarence had made known the wishes of the townsmen to the king, at his intervention and especially out of reverence for God, the king listened to the townsmen's prayers and sent the earl of Dorset [Thomas Beaufort], Lord Fitzhugh,[1] and Sir Thomas Erpingham[2] to learn the desires of the besieged. And they humbly begged that the king out of charity should cease from the siege from that hour in the middle of the night until the next Sunday after the feast of St Michael [29 September], unless it should happen that the French king or the dauphin, his first-born, should end the siege by an attack made upon our king and restore the people to their former liberty. Otherwise they would be prepared to hand over the town to our king, provided that their lives and all their property were saved.[3]

Having heard this appeal, the king ordered word to be taken back to them that unless they surrendered the town unconditionally the next day, there would be no more discussion of the matter.[4] The French lords still persevered, and put pressure on the king's messengers to urge the king and to beg him on their behalf to think it right to grant them a truce, to last from that hour until 3 o'clock in the afternoon the following Sunday.[5] And they promised that at this hour they would come to the king with twenty-two knights and esquires and with other highly respected men from inside the town, and that they would give all these as hostages until the Sunday mentioned. And further, that the French commanders had guaranteed that they would swear on the body of Christ before all the people that if the French king or his son and heir, the dauphin, did not arrive to set them free before the hour suggested on that Sunday, they would unconditionally surrender to the king of England for him to do with their bodies and goods according to the pleasure of his will, with this proviso that he should allow them to send messengers to the king of France and the dauphin, to tell them of the agreement that had been made.

[Harfleur is surrendered to the English]

When the king had accepted this offer, he gave letters of safe conduct for the French envoys. Their leader was de Anquetonville, who was followed by twelve noblemen. And early on the next day, the Wednesday [18 September], these lords with their twenty-two knights and esquires and leading citizens came out of the town, and were met by a solemn procession from the tent of the English king of seventeen priests of one brotherhood [i.e. of the royal chapel] wearing copes, preceding the body of our Lord, and of many honourable lords, knights and esquires and a very great crowd of people. This procession made its way to the side of the town to receive the oaths of the French princes and their allies. The whole affair was conducted with such pomp that no one there remembered having seen so splendid a procession.[6] But the king himself was not there

---

According to the *Gesta* author it was only after a force led by John Holland, earl of Huntingdon had breached the main barbican that the English victory was assured (*Gesta Henrici*, pp. 36–9, 46–7). See also Wylie, *Henry V*, ii. 51–76; Allmand, *Henry V*, pp. 79–80.

1   Henry, Lord Fitzhugh, chamberlain and treasurer: *CCR, 1413–19*, pp. 346, 368, 435.
2   Sir Thomas Erpingham was steward of the king's household: *CCR, 1413–19*, pp. 275, 346.
3   There is no corroboration for Walsingham's story of the covert appeal to Clarence. It appears that rumours that Henry was about to make an assault on the town had become known to the besieged and this caused an embassy of burgesses to approach the king on 17 September with the offer of their surrender if no assistance was forthcoming five days later (i.e. 22 September). See also Wylie, *Henry V*, ii. 53–5.
4   Walsingham suggests the king was unwilling to negotiate in this way, but the *Gesta* author suggests that he willingly consented to their terms: *Gesta Henrici*, pp. 50–51.
5   The *Gesta* author records the hour as 1p.m.: *Gesta Henrici*, pp. 50–1.
6   According to the *Gesta* author, on Wednesday 18 September indentures of the agreement between the king and the burgesses were drawn up and then the company, led by Bishop Benedict Nicholls of Bangor bearing the Host, processed to the foot of the town walls where oaths were taken on both sides. The French knights – Walsingham records 22 here but the *Gesta* author says 24 – were then surrendered to the English captains as hostages: *Gesta Henrici*, pp. 50–1.

present in person; and in this way omnipotent God gave the king his original wish without any loss of his men.[1] When oaths had been publicly completed and accepted, all the French with their retinue were taken into the king's tent, where they also feasted on that day at the royal table, but without as yet seeing the king. After the meal they were split up and different individuals were entrusted to different lords, that they might be honourably treated until the return of the English ambassadors who had been sent to the French king. These ambassadors faithfully completed their mission and returned on the agreed Sunday [22 September] at the appointed hour, without any help having been given to the besieged by the French king or the dauphin. And so all those within the town unconditionally surrendered to the king's grace.[2]

At the same hour on this Sunday the king's tent was placed on the hill situated in front of the town. And there he took his seat in royal state, surrounded by a handsome circle of his nobles. And the French lords together with the sixty-four who had been hostages right up to that hour entered the tent. Of these some were lords, some knights, some honourable esquires, some leading burgesses of Harfleur, and they humbly surrendered the keys of the town together with their bodies and all their goods to the king.[3] And all the lords with the knights and esquires and nobles who had been sent by the French king to defend the town remained as captives of the king of England. The king appointed Thomas Beaufort, earl of Dorset, as governor of Harfleur, giving him a strong force of archers and armed men to defend the town.[4]

While King Henry was besieging Harfleur, many of his men died of stomach troubles or dysentery. These deaths were caused by the eating of fruit, the cold nights and the fetid smell from the bodies of different animals which they had killed throughout the English lines but which they had not covered with turves or soil or thrown into the waters of the river so that they were forced to endure their decaying stench.[5] Among the dead special mention must be made of the venerable Richard Courtenay, bishop of Norwich, a most loyal supporter of the king. He was succeeded as bishop by John Wakering.[6] The earl of Suffolk, Michael de la Pole died of the same cause. So that his family should not be without a head, the king created his son earl of Suffolk in his place, but the over-savage Atropos cut the thread of the son's life also, at the battle I shall describe later.[7]

At the same time illness enforced the return to England of [Thomas] the duke of Clarence, the earl of March [Edmund Mortimer], the earl of Arundel,[8] the earl marshal[9] and many other victims of the dysentery. But the earl of Arundel, so it is said, was killed by poison soon after his return home.

---

[1]   The *Gesta* confirms this: FitzHugh and Erpingham were acting in the king's stead: *Gesta Henrici*, pp. 50–1.

[2]   According to the *Gesta* author a knight was sent to King Charles to advise him of the town's surrender. On 27 September the Sire de Gaucort and his remaining knights were also allowed to depart on condition that they surrendered themselves at Calais on 11 November: *Gesta Henrici*, pp. 50–1, 54–7.

[3]   According to the *Gesta* author, there were 64 hostages; Adam Usk records that they were held with ropes around their necks: *Usk*, p. 74. The anonymous chronicler in BL, Cotton MS Cleopatra C IV claims that Henry kept them waiting on their knees in an adjoining tent. See also Wylie, *Henry V,* i. 55.

[4]   Dorset had already been appointed admiral of England, Ireland and Aquitaine and captain of Calais. At Harfleur he commanded a force of 100 men-at-arms and 300 archers.

[5]   The Kenilworth chronicler John Streeche, writing shortly after Henry's death, recorded that it was the unripe grapes and other fruit and shellfish that had infected so many of Henry's soldiers: John Streeche, p. 152.

[6]   Courtenay died on 15 September. Wakering was elected on 24 November although he was not consecrated until May 1416.

[7]   De la Pole died on 18 September. His son (b. c.1395) was still a minor; he died at Agincourt barely a month later. Of the three fates of classical mythology, Clotho bears the distaff at birth, Lachesis spins the thread of life and Atropos cuts it at death.

[8]   Walsingham is in error: Thomas Fitzalan, earl of Arundel, died from dysentery at Harfleur: Wylie, *Henry V,* ii. 67.

[9]   John Mowbray (b.1392) younger son of Thomas Mowbray, 1st duke of Norfolk, who died in 1399. He had succeeded his elder brother Thomas after his execution for treason in 1405 (see above, p. 338).

[The king proceeds towards Calais]

When the king of England had settled matters at Harfleur as befitted a king and a victor, he decided to proceed by land towards Calais with quite a small force, not more, so it is said, than eight thousand archers and armed men, a great many of whom were hampered by the dysentery they had picked up at Harfleur, as I have described above.[1] It is remarkable that with this small band he dared to attack a thick forest of the French, and still more remarkable that he found a way through it, since it had been previously reinforced by a number of barriers. For throughout the whole time of the siege of the town of Harfleur the French had assembled a force of picked men from their own troops, the bravest and boldest men from surrounding districts and hired mercenaries from all quarters, the numbers of which, so it is said, had grown to one hundred and forty thousand soldiers.[2]

So these prepared themselves for a day, time and hour on which they would be able to attack the king and his tiny flock, now attenuated by famine, dysentery and fever. And when for almost twenty days the king had ridden over the kingdom of France with the enemy everywhere removing supplies from his path before he could reach a site for pitching camp, there was such a shortage of bread in his army that most of his men were eating horse meat or filbert nuts in place of bread, while for almost eighteen days the only drink for all the lesser ranks was water. It was on such luxuries and dainties that the champions of the king of England were nourished and fed, as they prepared to join battle with all those thousands of giants. Indeed it was a wonder that they were able to stand at all, when you add in that they were exhausted by their marches, hollow-eyed from keeping watch and weakened by the cold at night. But He who wished to destroy the strong by the weak put life in the feeble and gave strength to the infirm.[3]

[The armies encamp within sight of each other]

When King Henry, not without the greatest difficulty, had crossed the rivers in between him and the French, as the French had destroyed the bridges which could have shortened his route, the French at once massed together and hurried with all their troops to cut off the road which he would have to use to go past Calais, and on 24 October they halted at a certain little town.[4] King

---

[1] According to the *Gesta Henrici*, after he had taken possession of Harfleur, Henry dispatched his herald to the dauphin requesting that he come to Harfleur within the next eight days to ensure that further bloodshed be avoided. No such embassy was forthcoming and, apparently contrary to the advice of his captains, Henry chose to march towards Calais; whether he was confident he could lead his army to safety, or whether he wanted to draw the French into a pitched battle remains unclear. Certainly his army was much depleted. The *Gesta* author records that king gave permission to those 'direly afflicted and disabled' to return to England and he estimates that Henry's force was reduced to 5,000 archers and only 900 men-at-arms, significantly fewer than Walsingham's figure of 8,000 and almost half the number with which he had embarked. Henry left Harfleur between 6 and 8 October: *Gesta Henrici*, pp. 58–9; Wylie, *Henry V*, ii. 75–7.
[2] In common with all contemporary authorities, Walsingham exaggerates the size of the French forces; the *Scotichronicon* suggested as many as 200,000 took the field at Agincourt (viii. 85). Such figures are fanciful but the numerical superiority of the French was undeniable; when the armies did meet at Agincourt (see below, pp. 410–12) there may have been as many as 60,000, ten times as many as in Henry's army: *Gesta Henrici*, p. 82 n.
[3] The *Gesta* author, who was on the march, recalled that Henry was able to negotiate bread and wine from the towns through which they passed: *Gesta Henrici*, pp. 62–3.
[4] The greatest obstacle on the route to Calais was the river Somme and according to the *Gesta* author, the English expected the French to attack them as they attempted the crossing. Henry planned to take his army across the ford at Blanchetaque near Abbeville where Edward III had crossed on his way to Crécy in 1346. He reached the ford on Sunday 13 October but found it already staked and with French troops patrolling on the opposite bank; he moved down river to another possible crossing place at Pont-Remy but again found it staked. Finally on 18 October he reached an undefended ford near Voyennes and Béthencourt where, according to the French chronicler Lefèvre, his men improvised a pontoon using doors and window frames to ferry the soldiers and equipment across. The army faced three further tributaries of the Somme, the Ancre, Grouche and Ternoise, the last of which they crossed on 23 October. It was the day after, according to the *Gesta* author, that the English for the first time saw the full might of the French host gathered ahead of them (*Gesta Henrici*, pp. 76–7). Now they pitched camp in, or nearby Maisoncelles, the 'little town' Walsingham refers to here.

Henry was not dismayed. He proceeded steadily on the journey that he had undertaken and advanced so close to the French that on the very same night both armies encamped within a mile of each other. The two armies presented a different appearance and a dissimilar look.

The French were refreshed and with full stomachs. The English were exhausted, weak, worn out with hunger and lacked even supplies of water. But they knew for certain that they would be fighting the next day, and joining battle with all the nobility of France. And so not only did they keep awake all night attending to their bodies, but they also by prayer and confession showed concern for their individual souls, since the French had boasted of their intention to spare no one except the famous English lords and the king himself and to slay everyone else without pity, or at least to mutilate their limbs beyond repair. And so our men were the more keyed up. They worked themselves up to a pitch of anger and comforted one another to face all the chances of war.

[A battle between the English and the French]

And so in the king's camp

> The rising day the mountains scarce had spread
> With heaven's light, when sounded from afar
> The trumpet's brazen blare[1]

and our men hurried from all sides to fall in before their leader, doubly prepared with bold spirits and pure consciences to face the challenge of Mars.

After seeing his men arrive with such keenness, the king at once led out his troops on to a field recently sown with wheat, where the uneven softness of the ground made it very difficult to halt for a short time or to advance. The French at daybreak no less eagerly sent their vanguard towards this field, its ranks full of brave men and bright with gleaming armour, while on the flanks of both armies the cavalry rode in front on noble horses of good stock. To quote the poet

> Down from their breasts the golden trappings hung

while above

> Covered in gold, they champ between their teeth the yellow gold.[2]

Because the place was so muddy the French were not willing to advance far into the field.[3] They were deeply contemptuous of the small numbers of the English, and were waiting to see what they intended to do. The wide-open space that lay between the two armies was, so it is said, about a mile long, but it did not happen that

> Both lines advanced with equal charge to fight.[4]

The French stayed fixed in their first position, so that, if the English wished to engage with the enemy, they would have to cover the intervening space on foot while loaded down with weapons. Meanwhile King Henry, appreciating the cleverness of the French in staying thus fixed in one position to avoid tiring themselves marching over the muddy field,

> Along the ranks he flew, borne on his lofty steed,
> Encouraged leaders and strengthened minds for war[5]

And said

> O most faithful friends, for a mighty work of courage, highest task, on to the field we go.[6]

Look! Here is that very day which your valour has so often asked for. 'So put forth all your strength',[7] and see what lance, axe, sword and arrow can achieve in the hand of the powerful. Whoever longs for wealth, honours or rewards, will surely win them here. Indeed

---

[1]   Virgil, *Aeneid*, xii. 113–14; ix. 503.
[2]   Ibid., vii. 278, 279.
[3]   The *Gesta* author, who was not positioned on the battlefield, says nothing of the mud. For an account of the conditions see also Wylie, *Henry V*, ii. 140–77; Allmand, *Henry V*, pp. 87–102.
[4]   Lucan, *De bello civili*, vii. 385.
[5]   Balbus Italicus, *Ilias Latina*, 496–7.
[6]   Lucan, *De bello civili*, ix. 381–2.
[7]   Ibid., vii. 344.

'In this field's midst has God placed everything.'[1]

Having said this, he gave orders for the standards to be taken up, saying, 'Because the enemy are unjustly trying to keep us from our journey, let us advance against them in the name of the Trinity, and at the best hour of the whole year.' The standards were lifted on high, and King Henry gave the command to his men to advance in order, with the archers made to go in front on the right wing and on the left. And the archers, seeing before them the men who yesterday had sworn to kill or maim them, were inflamed with a burning anger. They forgot all their tiredness, their hardships and their weakness, and, as I might say, 'The glass-green bile rose up within their hearts,'[2] and anger 'provided strength and courage.'[3]

It was amazing how the archer who yesterday had been unable to draw a weak bow, was now strong enough to draw the toughest bow without difficulty just as he wished.

The French saw that our men had hard work in crossing the field and thought that the hour was now smiling upon them in which they could attack weary men, whom they thought they would have no trouble in taking prisoner. So with terrifying shouts they charged over the field, with the cavalry sent in front to knock down our archers with the iron-clad breasts of their warhorses and then to trample on them with the hooves of these same steeds. But, at the wish of God, things happened differently from their expectations. For our bowmen, meeting the cavalry all along the line, shot so many arrows in a single volley that the first hail storm scattered the French horsemen.[4] For, under the rule of God,

No missile sped without a wound, no hand its victim missed[5]

and there was no respite for the French from the arrows shot by English right hands, since

Each arrow in its target lodged, each strike a wound inflicted.[6]

But then, as soon as the horses were pierced by the arrows, their riders reined them round and rode headlong into their own ranks, and all the cavalry who had escaped death left the field. Then, as the battle lines clashed, the loud war cries of our men struck the stars on high, and the vast sky was somehow filled with their shouts. Then again on all sides there flew a cloud of arrows. Sword rang on sword, while the javelins, which were constantly hurled, struck helmets, armour and breastplates. So the French fell in great numbers as the arrows pierced them, here fifty, and there again sixty.

King Henry himself, fulfilling the role of soldier as well as of king, was the first to charge the enemy. He inflicted and received cruel blows, giving his men in his own person brave examples of daring as he scattered the enemy ranks with his ready axe. And in the same way the knights, emulating the acts of the king, strained with all their might to lay low with the sword that forest of shouting Frenchmen which opposed them, until at last force made a way and the French did not so much fall back as fall dead on the ground. And indeed when they saw those, whom they believed to be unconquerable, brought low in the clash of battle, at once

Their hearts were numbed; an icy tremor ran along the marrow of their bones[7]

so deeply that they stood there motionless and senseless while our men wrenched the axes from their hands and cut them down with them like cattle. From then on the killing lost all pattern and no sort of battle ensued.[8] The issue was decided by slaughtering, with our men lacking the energy to kill every one of the enemy that could have been killed.

---

1   Ibid., vii. 348.
2   Persius, *Satirae*, iii. 8.
3   Virgil, *Aeneid*, ix. 764.
4   The *Gesta* author reports that the French knights '. . . were forced to fall back under showers of arrows and to flee to their rearguard except for a very few who . . . rode through between the archers and the woodlands and . . . for the many who were stopped by the stakes driven into the ground'.
5   Statius, *Thebaid*, ix. 770–1.
6   Ibid., x. 656.
7   Virgil, *Aeneid*, ii. 120–1.
8   Lucan, *De bello civili*, vii. 532–35.

Thus then perished almost all the flower of French chivalry, cut down by the hands of a small band whom a short while before they had held in the greatest contempt. On that field fell the dukes of Alençon,[1] Brabant[2] and Bar[3] together with five counts[4] and the constable of France[5] and the seneschal of Hainault,[6] the king of France's master of artillery[7] and about one hundred other famous lords.[8] Three thousand and sixty nine knights and esquires are said to have been killed. The number of ordinary soldiers killed was not counted up by the reporters of the knights who were killed. Taken prisoner in the battle were the dukes of Orléans and Bourbon, the counts of Eu[9] and Vendôme,[10] Arthur, brother of the duke of Brittany who called himself 'earl of Richmond,'[11] a certain Boucicault, the most highly respected knight of the whole land of France who was also marshal of France,[12] and about seven hundred others, according to the reports.[13] The casualties on king Henry's side were Edward duke of York,[14] Michael earl of Suffolk,[15] four knights, one squire called David Gam,[16] and twenty-eight commoners.[17]

While the king and his men were occupied on the battlefield, fighting hand to hand against masses of Frenchmen, some French scum made an attack on his rear, pillaged the baggage that had been put on one side and made off with their loot. When they found the king's crown among it, they made their companions so happy with a baseless joy that they got the bells solemnly rung, and the canticle of praise 'We praise you, O Lord' sung over and over amid great stamping of feet.[18] For they had been told the false tale that King Henry had been taken prisoner and would be arriving any minute. But after a little while they learned the true result of the battle from a sad messenger and then their singing was turned to mourning, their joy to sorrow.

1 Jean, 1st duke of Alençon and son-in-law of Henry IV's queen, Joan of Navarre.
2 Antoine, duke of Brabant, son of Philip the Bold, duke of Burgundy and brother of John the Fearless.
3 Edward III, duke of Bar, brother of the duke of Alençon, grandson of Jean II of France.
4 The counts of Marle, Vaudemont, Blamont, Roucy and Fauquembergues. A further four were also killed in the battle, the counts of Nevers, brother of Duke John the Fearless of Burgundy, Grandpré, Dammartin and Vaucourt.
5 Charles d'Albret.
6 Jean de Verchin.
7 Jean de Bueil.
8 The king's maitre d'hôtel, Guichard Dauphin was also among the dead.
9 Charles d'Artois (b. c.1393/4), succeeded his father, Count Philip, in 1397. Henry V insisted that he was not freed before Henry VI came of age; he was finally freed in 1438.
10 Louis de Bourbon, count of Vendôme (b. c.1376), grand maître of Charles VI's household and a member of the final embassy to England before Henry embarked in August. He remained in captivity in England until 1424.
11 Correctly, Arthur, count of Richemont (b. c.1393), second son of Jean IV, duke of Brittany and Joan of Navarre, who subsequently married Henry IV. This connection may account for his early release from captivity, before Henry V's own death.
12 Jean le Meingre de Boucicault (b. c.1366), marshal of France. He died in captivity at Methley, Yorkshire, in 1421.
13 The French chroniclers claimed that as many as 1,500 prisoners were taken, and it may be a figure higher than 700 is accurate. The *Gesta* reports that on the point of victory it was feared that some French knights had regrouped for a renewed attack and the English responded by putting to the sword the majority of their prisoners, save for a handful of the nobility: *Gesta Henrici*, pp. 90–3. See also Wylie, *Henry V*, ii. 179–89.
14 Son of Edmund Langley, duke of York (d.1404).
15 The twenty-year-old heir of the earl of Suffolk who had died at Harfleur. See above, p. 408.
16 For David Gam, alias David ap Llewelyn, see above, p. 383.
17 The English casualties were surprisingly low; other chroniclers give even lower figures, the lowest being no more than a dozen; Shakespeare counted 25 commoners: *Henry V*, Act 4, Scene 8. This seems unlikely, but, reporting to parliament the following year, Bishop Beaufort maintained that the victory had been secured without great loss of life. See also Wylie, *Henry V*, ii. 186–9.
18 The *Gesta* author confirms this story, reporting that a sword, crown and other 'precious objects' were seized; the sword was presented to Philip, son of John the Fearless, and the other objects included a cross set with precious stones and valued at 13,000 crowns: *Gesta Henrici*, pp. 84–5 and n.

The aftermath of the battle

King Henry ascribed all these successes to God, as was right, and gave boundless thanks to Him who had given him an unexpected victory and crushed the fiercest of foes. So he stayed the night by the battlefield, and on the next day, a Saturday, he continued the journey which he had begun towards Calais. Then on 16 November he at last landed at Dover amid a great snowstorm.[1] On 23 November he came to London, bringing with him the dukes and counts he had recently captured in war, whose names have been recorded above. It is not within my powers to describe the great joy, celebration and triumph with which the people of London greeted his return, for the elaborate decorations and different spectacles put on at vast expense deservedly demand extended treatment.[2] As he approached the church of St Paul's, he was welcomed there by a solemn procession of twelve bishops wearing mitres,[3] who met him and led him to the high altar. Having completed his devotions, he returned to the churchyard, where the horses had been tethered in the meantime, and, mounting his warhorse, he made for Westminster, accompanied by the knights on horseback who had ridden with him through the middle of London. On his arrival at Westminster he was amazed to find himself met by a greater crowd of people than he had ever seen gathered in London before. All of this was not a pleasing sight for the French eyes. So the abbot and monks of Westminster received him with a magnificent procession and escorted him into the church. Having paid his vows to St Edward, he went to his royal palace, where he stayed for several days.

On 1 December at the order of the king the bishops and abbots were present in London in great numbers to attend the solemn funeral service for Edward, once duke of York, and Michael, earl of Suffolk, and for the others, both French and English, who had been killed on the continent. The king had given orders for these exequies to be royally carried out. The king's uncle, the earl of Dorset [Thomas Beaufort], came to this service from Harfleur, of which he was now governor. A short while before he had led a cavalry raid on the surrounding countryside, and drove back before him eight hundred captives, whom he put under close custody in the town.[4]

In this year the king of Portugal [João I], relying especially upon the help of English merchants and the Germans, fought a battle with the Saracens in the land of the king of Mauretania. He came off the winner, sending many thousands of the heathen down to the son-in-law of Ceres.[5] And he captured a very large town of theirs, situated on the sea and in their tongue called 'Ceuta'. It is said to be surrounded by a circle of strong, high walls twenty miles long.

[1416]

In 1416 the king kept Christmas near London at Lambeth. News was brought at this time of a battle fought between the English and the French near the town of Harfleur, in which many Frenchmen were killed.

---

1   Henry's ships were scattered in the storm and according to the French chronicler Monstrelet two of them foundered. After landing at Dover, Henry progressed to Canterbury where he remained for two days before moving on to the capital. See also Wylie, *Henry V*, ii. 253–6.

2   The *Gesta* author gives them such a treatment, describing in detail (*Gesta Henrici*, pp. 102–13) the pageant which incorporated allegorical tableaux comparable to those presented at the coronation of Richard II (see above, pp. 38–9). As was customary, on his entrance into the city the king was met by a delegation comprising the mayor and aldermen. He made offerings at the shrine of St Erkenwald at St Paul's before moving on to Westminster.

3   Others disagree: Thomas Elmham reported eighteen prelates and the London chronicler claims there were sixteen bishops and abbots.

4   According to the *Gesta* author this was a protracted skirmish with French forces that had attacked the English baggage train as it returned to Harfleur after provisioning.

5   i.e. Pluto, king of the Underworld. The capture of Ceuta on the Moroccan coast marked the beginning of a phase of Portuguese overseas expansion that continued to the close of the reign of João I in 1433. By that date the Portuguese had also annexed Madeira and the Azores. See A. de Sonsa, 'Portugal' I *The New Cambridge Medieval History VII. C. 1415–1500*, ed. C. T. Allmand (Cambridge, 1998), pp. 627–44.

Around the time of the feast of the Purification [2 February] seven dolphins sported in the Thames, of which four were killed. According to some people's interpretation, they foretold a huge tempest of wind and storm, which immediately followed.

[A battle between the earl of Dorset and the count of Armagnac][1]

On Ash Wednesday [4 March] at the beginning of Lent the earl of Dorset [Thomas Beaufort], governor of Harfleur, fought a battle with the count of Alençon,[2] that is of Armagnac, the leader of the French army, in which great numbers of men were killed on both sides, mainly because the count had made a surprise attack on our men. But the French were routed and on that day were put to flight by our men. Their one and only consolation was that, while the two sides were fighting, some French rascals stole the horses and baggage of the English, so that our men had to return to the town of Harfleur, a distance of many miles, on foot and still carrying their weapons. They marched along the coast, in order to keep the enemy always in front of their faces and not positioned in their rear. Weighed down by their arms they marched for the whole of Thursday and the following night. But on the Friday morning they looked up and saw the French troops massed on the hills together with their leader the count of Armagnac and ready to attack. So the count of Alençon sent an armed messenger to say to the earl, 'You can see that you are trapped between us and the sea and that you have no room for escape left you. So to avoid being killed by the swords in our hands, surrender yourselves to me. You will be treated with all the honour that your noble birth demands, and your ransom will be a reasonable one and not excessive. The earl replied to this, 'Report back to him who sent you that it has never been the English way of life to surrender to the enemy before the business of Mars and Bellona has even begun. Nor will he find me so insane as to hand myself over to the man whom God is able to deliver into my hands before nightfall.'

Having heard this reply [Bernard] the count of Armagnac, roused to fury, attempted to descend the slopes of the mountain with his cavalry at a rapid pace. But our archers were waiting for them and either turned them aside with their arrows or killed them. Then the battle waxed hot for those that remained, and for a long time both sides waged the contest of Mars with swords and axes. But at last God took pity and an army that was fasting, weary, hungry and worn out by a lack of food and sleep triumphed through a clear miracle from God. For there were not more than fifteen hundred English in this engagement, but they won a glorious victory and drove off in flight fifteen thousand of the French and almost captured their general. It is said that, despite its being forbidden by the holy time of Lent and by the inescapable fasting imposed by Ash Wednesday, the French roasted meat in their camp and brought in prostitutes, so that, after stuffing their stomachs, they could glut themselves with the filth of Venus.

About this time a ban was put on Genoese half-pence being used in buying or selling by English merchants, as these coins were too light and three of them were not equal in weight to one penny.

[1]   Dorset's garrison at Harfleur was under growing pressure during the winter of 1415 and the spring of 1416. Dorset lacked manpower and, increasingly, provisions, and was compelled to make forays into the surrounding country which became ever more dangerous as the French forces began to encircle the town. This particular engagement appears to have been the most serious of several skirmishes that occurred at this time. According to the *Gesta* author, whose account is somewhat clearer than Walsingham is here, the Harfleur garrison first encountered D'Albret at Valmont. D'Albret's forces were superior and the English were forced to make terms, but they escaped, only to encounter an equally substantial French force under the command of Marshal de Loigny at Cap de la Hève; in spite of the odds, the English successfully routed them. See *Gesta Henrici*, pp. 115–21; Wylie, *Henry V,* ii. 334, 341, 349.

[2]   Bernard D'Albret, who succeeded in the title at the death of his brother at Agincourt. See above, p. 412 and n.

The coming of the emperor to London

On 7 May in this year the Emperor Sigismund came to London.[1] He was escorted amid magnificent splendour by the king and the nobles of the land and lodged in the king's palace near Westminster, while the king himself stayed not far away from the emperor at Lambeth. Because a parliament was being held in London at this time, the emperor made a solemn entrance to its meeting and spoke for a very long time with effusive praise of the king, his brothers, the nobles of the kingdom and the whole land. He produced a statue of St George made of gold, whose 'workmanship excelled its material' and which he wished to be placed at Windsor where St George was served with particular devotion by the priests of the king. And in his wish to show the king of the Romans every consideration, King Henry suspended for the time being all sittings of parliament and took the emperor with him to Windsor for the feast of St George. There he honoured the emperor with the title of this great brotherhood and the noble attire of that order. And he put a royal collar round his neck, which the emperor ever afterwards wore at all public gatherings and important occasions.[2]

The duke of Holland

Before the feast of the Ascension the duke of Holland visited England with a great fleet of ships and stores of food to have discussions with our king and with the king of the Romans [i.e. Sigismund].[3] He had betrothed his daughter to the dauphin, younger son of the king of France, who, after the death of the first-born dauphin, was now seen as the heir apparent to the kingdom of France.[4]

Horrific thunderstorms

On 14 June on the feast of the holy Trinity [i.e. Trinity Sunday] and for two days and nights afterwards, terrifying thunderclaps were heard, which lasted without any letting up and broke all records. They were preceded by awesome flashes of continuous lightning that flattened and killed many people with their strikes, set fire to trees and destroyed buildings.[5]

[The duke of Bedford captures some French ships]

During the whole summer men thought that through the mediation of the emperor peace was about to be made between England and France. But peace negotiations were broken off through the dithering of the French, mainly because they had collected a fleet of large ships, carracks and galleys with which to make some sort of an attack on Harfleur or to invade the kingdom of England.[6] John, duke of Bedford and brother of the king, was sent against them with a strong

---

1   Sigismund had been engaged in negotiations for a resolution to the schism when news of the capture of Harfleur diverted him. He had hoped to intercept Henry at Calais on his return after Agincourt but had arrived too late. He landed at Dover on 1 May 1416. He progressed towards the capital and was met at Blackheath by a deputation of London citizens and then again a mile from the city by the king and his magnates. See also Wylie, *Henry V*, ii. 354–6, 365–6.
2   Sigismund was installed as a Knight of the Garter (on 20 May) and was also presented with the 'S S' collar, the badge of Lancastrian loyalty.
3   William VI (1366–1417), duke of Bavaria and count of Holland, Hainault and Zeeland reached London on 25 May, sailing up river on the Thames to meet the king at Lambeth. He came to England at the suggestion of Charles VI to intercede with Henry.
4   Count William was himself allied to the French through his own marriage to the sister of John the Fearless, duke of Burgundy. Now his daughter Jacqueline was betrothed to Jean de Touraine, heir apparent to Charles VI after the death of the Dauphin Louis on 18 December 1415.
5   Walsingham is the only authority to report this episode.
6   This is somewhat disingenuous. Henry had been planning another expedition to France at least since the beginning of the year. The embassies of Sigismund and Count William had persuaded him to postpone them temporarily, but the commons was pressuring for the campaign and opposed the terms of the settlement preferred by the emperor and the count, under which Harfleur would be surrendered into their joint custody. Henry announced his forthcoming arrival at Southampton to take command of his army, although a week

force, and on the day of the feast of the assumption of the blessed Virgin [15 August] he engaged in battle with them.[1] He had on his side the men belonging to Lord Henry Percy, whom the king had ransomed from the hands of the Scots and some time ago made earl of Northumberland. Percy's men played a large part in the battle and exposed themselves to danger more than the others. And thanks to the bravery and courage of the duke of Bedford, three carracks were captured and one large ship which we call a 'hulk' or 'cock-boat' and four other vessels of the sort we call 'sloops'.[2] Three other carracks, that could not face the attack of our men and the cloud of their arrows, got away. One of these before our men's eyes broke up upon a sandbank and sank. Two only, which were helped by the wind, got away. Nor must I suppress the fact that before our fleet left England another large carrack sank off Southampton with the loss of eighty well-armed men commonly known as 'light harneys'.

The title of the emperor[3]

Sigismund, by the grace of God always king Augustus of the Romans, and king of Hungary, Dalmatia, Croatia, Ravia, Servia, Gallicia, Lodomaria, Komaron, and king of Bulgaria and margrave of Brandenburg and Bohemia and heir to Luxembourg and Racia and emperor, being about to leave England, thus saluted her in published charters which contained these words, 'Farewell, and rejoice in your glorious triumph, O happy and blessed England. Rightly are you thus named, for with your almost angelic nature you give glory, praise and adoration to Jesus. And in such words do I give you the praise which you rightly and properly deserve.'

The emperor and the king of England made a joint alliance, which said that they themselves and their successors would be good, strong and stable friends for ever, bound and joined in alliance on behalf of themselves and their heirs and successors against all men of whatever rank, status, position or condition, and against all men who can live or die, with the exception of the holy Roman church and the pope of the Romans etc., as is written in another chronicle.[4]

[The king reconciles Sigismund and the duke of Burgundy]

In order to show that he genuinely wanted peace, the king of England crossed the Channel to Calais in person, in order not to supply any material for slander to the French, who had promised him that it would not be they who failed to open up a wide road to peace. But at a meeting at Calais with the emperor, after hearing from him that the French were producing nothing except their usual tricks and deceit, he poured scorn on the French lies and brought about reconciliation and peace between the emperor [Sigismund] and the duke of Burgundy [John the Fearless], who had been quarrelling.[5]

later under the eye of Sigismund he also sent commissioners to France to negotiate a truce. For their part, as Walsingham suggests, the French were no more committed to these negotiations; the encirclement of Harfleur continued throughout May and June and on 22 June French ships also began to blockade Portsmouth and the Isle of Wight. See also Wylie, *Henry V,* ii. 347–9.
1   Bedford was appointed supreme commander of the sea for three months on 22 July 1416, with Thomas, Lord Morley and Sir Walter Hungerford as his admirals. The aim of this expedition was to break the French blockade of Harfleur and to refresh and reinforce the garrison. Bedford engaged the French ships at the mouth of the Seine. According to the *Gesta* author the battle lasted for five or six hours and some 1,500 men were killed and four hundred of the enemy were captured. It is notable the *Gesta* does not record the role of Henry Percy in this engagement. See also *CPR, 1416–22,* p. 38; Wylie, *Henry V,* ii. 347–9.
2   The *Gesta* confirms the number of vessels captured noting that the larger vessel was 'the mother of them all': *Gesta Henrici,* pp. 130–1.
3   A heading that might suggest that the rubrics were simply added by the scribe and not devised by Walsingham himself. The interest in Sigismund's diplomatic style is perhaps another sign of Walsingham's service as precentor at St Albans. See above, p. 6.
4   The pact was signed at Canterbury on 15 August. Sigismund was depressed at the duplicity of the French and their assault on the English coast at the end of June, just at the point that Sigismund believed he had revived the peace negotiations, was the final straw. Under the treaty the emperor agreed to support Henry in pursuit of his rights in France, just as Henry would support him in the consolidation of his claim to the imperial crown and to the crown of Bohemia. See also Wylie, *Henry V,* ii. 365.
5   Sigismund left England for Calais on 25 August; Henry followed him on 4 September, leaving from Sand-

The reason for the quarrel was that the duke of Burgundy, while his father Philip was alive, had been taken prisoner in a war being fought against the Turks and the Tartars. The emperor, who was then king of Hungary, had ransomed the duke for a huge sum of money and sent him back to his country as a freed man, after the duke had sworn that he would faithfully pay back the king of Hungary the sum that had been spent for him. By now the duke's father had died, for ten years had gone by, and the king of Hungary had heard nothing from the duke about the sum that was owing. And so the king was extremely angry and was thinking about punishing the duke's crime of treachery. But it was now, although late in the day, that our king intervened and the two of them were made friends again. They came to an agreement and together fixed upon definite days for repayment. When this had been done, the duke paid homage to the emperor.[1]

Duke Humphrey escorts the emperor to the town of Dordrecht

After this Humphrey, the duke of Gloucester, the youngest brother of the king, with a large royal retinue magnificently escorted the emperor, who was now an ally of our king and kingdom, until he came to the town of Dordrecht.[2] Here the emperor rewarded in imperial fashion all the English from the highest to the lowest, so that all those who had chanced to be part of that escort counted themselves lucky.

A Lollard is beheaded

Benedict Woolman, a citizen of London and a Lollard, who had delivered tracts, full of errors, over a wide area, was taken prisoner, drawn, hung and beheaded on the day of the feast of St Michael [29 September].

A parliament

The parliament, which I have said was adjourned because of the presence of the king of the Romans, was continued in London during the feast of St Luke [18 October].[3] At this parliament Thomas Beaufort, earl of Dorset, was created duke of Exeter, and given a grant of £1,000 annually from the royal treasury and the £40 from the town of Exeter that had usually gone to the king.[4] When the nobles in the parliament were asked if they agreed with this, they replied it would have been very well done if the king's grant had not been so meagre and a bad match for the services and virtues of this great man. In this parliament the king was granted a two-tenths tax from the clergy, which was to be paid within the space of one year.[5]

---

wich to avoid interception by the French ships in the Channel. Although negotiation with the Armagnac faction had been abandoned, Henry remained willing to explore the possibility of an alliance with the duke of Burgundy. Their negotiations continued until 13 October and although no formal agreement was made it appears that Burgundy was now willing to give support to Henry at least covertly. At the same time as these negotiations, a French embassy had agreed a temporary truce with the English ambassadors ostensibly to continue until February 1417. See also Wylie, *Henry V*, ii. 366.

1   The ransom was only one part of their quarrel. Sigismund was also threatened by the expansion of Burgundian interests on the borders of the empire. Duke John's nephew had succeeded to Brabant and Luxembourg, annexed by his father (John's brother) Anthony, and his subsequent marriage to the heiress of William of Bavaria had increased the sense of Burgundian encirclement. Upper Alsace had also fallen under Burgundian influence through the marriage of Duke John's sister to a brother of Frederick of Austria.

2   Refused a ship by William of Holland, Sigismund left Calais under English escort on 24 October. Gloucester was accompanied by Sir John Tiptoft.

3   Writs were issued on 3 September and parliament met on 19 October. It sat until 18 November: *RP*, iv. 94, 96.

4   A reward for his efforts at Harfleur. The *Gesta* author records 'his distinguished efforts and great exertions' (*Gesta Henrici*, pp. 180–1). See also *CPR, 1416–22*, p. 53.

5   The commons showed some reluctance, and stipulated that no further subsidy should be requested until these taxes now granted were collected. Convocation met in the next month and granted two further tenths on condition that one granted at their previous meeting be postponed.

The king of Aragon

The king of Aragon [Ferdinand I], who had long been troubled by arthritis caused by gout, said goodbye to this world. His death greatly hindered the negotiations for the union of the church. For the emperor had made a personal visit to him and had so far made him a willing helper in the general crisis that he had promised to take away all his obedience from Peter de Luna [Benedict XIII]. But, alas, soon afterwards his life was cut short by the weaver's shears.[1] The result was that his youthful son ignored his father's promises and supported the party of the antipope, who was so hardened in crime that he got his cardinals to swear that immediately after his death, whenever it happened, they would choose a new pope from among themselves.

The cut-throats

In the same year three mendicant cut-throats kidnapped three citizens' small sons from the town of Lynn and mutilated them, as was their practice. They gouged out the eyes of one of them, broke the back of another and also cut out the tongues of these two. But the third was treated more leniently by his captor and allowed the use of his tongue. After a little while the father of the third lad, who was a merchant of London, came to the place where the mendicants were. When the lad saw him, he recognised his father and began to cry out, 'Here is my father.' The father indeed recognised his son, snatched him from out of the middle of the mendicants and immediately got them arrested. They confessed their crime and were strung up.

The celebration of orders in the monastery

The bishop of Cyrene[2] held a solemn service of ordination at St Albans in the chapel of the blessed Virgin on the 29 December, one of the Ember Saturdays.

[1417]

In 1417, the fourth year of the reign of King Henry V, the king kept Christmas at Kenilworth. At this time, so it is said, a plot was hatched against him by an esquire who was an accomplice of [Sir] John Oldcastle.

The day after Christmas Lollard tracts, full of malice and poison and attacking all the estates of the church, were delivered to almost every great house or hostelry in the towns of St Albans, Northampton and Reading. Nobody knew who was responsible.

The unjust vexation of Brother Robert Stoke, prior of Binham, over the collection of the clerical tenth[3]

James Child of Great Walsingham was in charge of the spiritualities of the Norwich diocese. He wanted to cause trouble to the prior of Binham, and so gave him the job of collector of the tithes that were granted to the king. This went against the wording of the privileges granted by kings Richard and Henry and the present king, which said that no abbot of St Albans or priors of the cells in his charge should be made collectors of these tithes against their will. But the king and the barons at the wool-sack noticed his malice against the prior, and turned his evil deed upon his own head by making him personally responsible for collecting the tithes or providing other collectors.

---

1   Ferdinand I, 'the Just' (b.1379), king of Aragon and Sicily from 1412, had come to support the conciliar solution to the schism. His heir was Alfonso V (b.1396) known as the magnanimous.
2   The Augustinian friar, John Alen, was suffragan bishop of the titular see of Cyrene.
3   Robert Stoke was prior of Binham from at least 1401: *Gesta abbatum*, ed. Riley, iii. 480. The exempt status – i.e. exemption from royal or episcopal jurisdiction – of the abbey and its dependent priories was frequently tested in the fourteenth and fifteenth centuries and a favourite weapon wielded by diocesans was the requirement for the collection of the clerical tenth. Binham had been targeted in this way several times before, as Walsingham himself recorded in the *Gesta abbatum*: *Gesta abbatum*, ed. Riley, iii. 282–3.

The decree of the council of Constance concerning the election of the future pope[1]

'In order that the election of the next high pontiff of the Romans, which is about to take place very soon, should be confirmed more securely by the authoritative assent of several people, to the praise, glory and honour of omnipotent God and to the peace and unity of the universal church and all Christian people, and in order that there may be no later qualifications or scruples left in the minds of men when the state of the church depends on this election, but that there may result from the election one certain, true, complete and perfect union, the holy general synod of Constance, having taken thought for the common good, ordains, decides and decrees, with the special, express consent and voluntary agreement of the cardinals of the holy Roman church present in person at this synod and of their college and of all nations present at this council, that at least for the election of the high Roman pontiff on this occasion, the cardinals shall be joined by six prelates and six other honourable ecclesiastics now in holy orders from each nation now listed as present at this synod of Constance, and each nation shall have taken thought to elect these prelates and ecclesiastics to represent them on this matter within ten days. This same holy synod gives the power of electing the Roman pontiff to all these people, according to the rules here set down as being essential, namely (a) that that person shall be held to be the pope at Rome by the whole church without any exception, who has been elected and received by the two groups of cardinals meeting in conclave and by two parties from each nation, chosen to be added to the cardinals and then added for that election; and (b) that the election shall not be valid nor the person elected be held to be pope unless the two groups of cardinals meeting in conclave and the two parties from the various nations chosen to be added to the cardinals and then added for that election shall agree on the election of the Roman pontiff and confirm their agreement.

'And the synod also ordains and decrees that the votes cast by the various people in this election shall have no validity unless, as said above, the two groups of the cardinals and the two groups elected by the various nations and then added to the cardinals as principals or subordinates shall be in agreement. There is also this point that the prelates and the others chosen to be added to the cardinals themselves for this election and then added are to be obliged to observe collectively and singly the rulings and the penalties set down for this papal election and the other customary rulings, just as the cardinals themselves are obliged to observe them and bind themselves to that observance. Also the electors, cardinals and others, before they proceed to the election, shall be obliged to swear and shall swear that, as they engage on the business of the election which is before them, when what is being discussed is the creation of someone to be the vicar of Jesus Christ, the successor of the blessed Peter, the ruler of the universal church and the shepherd of the flock of Christ, they will proceed with pure, unbiased minds, as they believe will be to the good and the general advantage of the universal church, setting aside all inordinate partiality for any person of a particular nation or any other kind of partiality, all hatred, favouritism or support, so that provision may be made by their efforts for a beneficial and suitable pastor for the universal church.

'The same holy synod also decrees and decides that ten days counted successively from now are fixed and assigned in which the cardinals of the holy Roman church, collectively and singly, present and absent, and the other electors mentioned above, are to go into conclave in this city of Constance in the mayoral building of the city's community now set aside for this business, the issue being the notorious interregnum in the Roman church. And the aforesaid electors, the cardinals and the others mentioned above, are to enter into the conclave itself to hold this election and to do, observe and carry out the other requirements, as laid down in the laws on other points besides the ones mentioned above affecting the cardinals and the others in this election of a Roman pontiff. The same holy Synod wishes all these requirements noted above to be observed in

---

[1]   The decree was issued during session 40 of the council on 30 October 1417. As with his account of the council's earlier proceedings, Walsingham appears to have worked directly from the documents themselves. See also *Constantiensis concilii acta et decreta*, ed. von der Hardt, iv. 1453–55.

all their fullness throughout the election. This is the format and this is the method approved, ordained and decreed for the election on this occasion.

'And to remove and eliminate all possible scruples, this synod qualifies each and every one of those now present at the synod and those who will arrive to join it as fit persons for all necessary lawful acts done by them as agents or observers in this synod. The other decrees of this same sacred council are to be valid for ever, (and this holy synod makes good all defects, if any by chance have occurred in the foregoing), not even taking into account any apostolic constitutions published at general councils of the church and other constitutions which say the contrary.'

The first statute[1]

The holy and general synod of the church at Constance has decided and decreed that the person who is next chosen as pope by the grace of God, together with this holy council or with people appointed by the individual countries is under the obligation of reforming the church at its head and in the Roman Curia according to equity and the good government of the church before this holy council is dissolved. They are to deal with the following matters which have been brought before their notice for reform by other nations.

1. The number, quality and origin of the lord cardinals.
2. The reservation of benefices by the apostolic see.
3. Common services and blood-lettings.
4. The bestowal of benefices and reversionary graces.
5. Confirmation of elections.
6. Which matters are to be dealt with in the Roman Curia and which not.
7. Appeals to the Roman Curia.
8. The offices of chancellor and confessor.
9. The exemptions and the associations made during the schism.
10. Commendations.
11. Revenues from the intervening time.
12. Not alienating the goods of the Roman church.
13. Why and how corrections and depositions can take place.
14. The rooting out of simony.
15. Dispensations.
16. The appointments made by pope and cardinals.
17. Indulgences.
18. Tithes.

It was added that when this assignment had been completed by the groups concerned, the others would be allowed by the permission of the pope freely to return to their homes.

Second statute[2]

The holy general synod of Constance noted the former agreements of the church of the province of Narbonne about admitting in the same synod the cardinals of Peter de Luna, once called in his obedience Benedict XIII. It also noted that after the notorious ejection of this Peter de Luna those same lord cardinals, who had long ago been summoned according to these same agreements and before this ejection of Peter, had not arrived, although they had been expected for three months and more since the day of the ejection. So the synod decided and decreed to move to the election of the Roman pontiff according to the decrees of the same synod, and to proceed with the authority of the same synod, notwithstanding the absence of the cardinals. But if they arrived before the election of the future pontiff had been completed and joined this same council

---

[1]   In the *acta* collected by Von der Hardt this and the statute following precede the decree on the election of the pope: *Constantiensis concilii acta et decreta*, ed. von der Hardt, iv. 1452–3.
[2]   Walsingham's text again reproduces that contained in the collection of Constance *acta*: *Constantiensis concilii acta et decreta*, ed. von der Hardt, iv. 1452–3.

according to the wording of the law and the decrees of the council, the synod declared that they would be admitted to the actual election together with the others.

Cardinal Colonna is chosen as pope[1]

On 31 October the bishop of Winchester [Henry Beaufort] arrived at the council. He was intending to go on a pilgrimage to Jerusalem after the election of the high pontiff was over. His eloquent persuasion had such an effect at the council that he spurred on all the lord cardinals to come to an agreement and to hurry with greater speed to hold the election of the high pontiff. So the house called the conclave was immediately got ready, with its splendidly covered couches for the lord cardinals and the electors who were to join them. For it had been ordained by decree of the council that six men should be chosen from each country present to enter the conclave with the cardinals, as explained above. And so the men who entered the conclave from England were the bishops of London,[2] Bath,[3] Norwich[4] and Lichfield,[5] the abbot of York[6] and Master Thomas Polton, dean of York.[7] And each nation wrote the names of their persons on a list, which was covered by and contained within a wax seal. So the selected persons entered the conclave on the day of the Four Kings [8 November]. After their entrance a layperson brought all the lists with their wax seals to the vice-chancellor in the conclave. And he, with his arms bare right up to the elbow, put all the lists on the table. Then a decision was made about how the inmates in the conclave should eat; and it was decided that they should have bread and wine, and on one day one kind of meat, and on another one kind of fish, and on each day one kind of drink, as the day required.[8]

Then the emperor [Sigismund] and the thirteen dukes and the leading citizens of the city of Constance swore on the Book that they would faithfully keep the conclave free from interruption, and not allow other foods to be sent in other than the ones decided upon. When this had been done, the emperor inspected the whole house in person, and shut the door behind him with two keys. A hole a foot square had been made in the door of that house, through which food for the inmates had to be passed. And the abbot of Bury St Edmunds[9] and the prior of St John of Clerkenwell [i.e. the Hospitallers][10] were assigned to taste beforehand the food for the English members every day that they were in the conclave. And as soon as the food had been served to the people within, the opening was closed with three keys.

So, as they conferred about the task laid upon them, some nominated the bishop of Winchester [Henry Beaufort], some the bishop of London [Richard Clifford], and some the cardinal of France.[11] Nothing was settled on the first day or on the second. Then on the day of St Martin [11 November], early in the morning, the bishop of London came and spoke these words among all the cardinals, 'I, Richard, bishop of London, propose my lord cardinal Colonna.' And having heard this speech, suddenly all those present, by the grace of God, agreed upon the same person. And straightaway they divested him of all his clothing and reclothed him with new

---

1   Walsingham's account of the election process follows closely the collected *acta* of the council to the extent that it must be conjectured that there was an early copy at St Albans. Compare *Constantiensis concilii acta et decreta*, ed. von der Hardt, iv. 1461–85.
2   Richard Clifford, bishop of London from 1407 (translated from Worcester) until his death in 1421.
3   Nicholas Bubwith, bishop of Bath and Wells from 1407 (translated from Salisbury) until his death in 1424.
4   John Wakeryng, bishop of Norwich from 1415 until his death in 1425.
5   John Catterick, bishop of Coventry and Lichfield from 1415 (translated from St David's) until his translation to Exeter in 1419.
6   Thomas Spofford, who held the abbacy from 1405 until he was translated to the see of Hereford in 1421.
7   Polton (d.1433) had passed much of his career in the papal curia where by 1417 he was a protonotary. He had been dean of York since 1416: Emden, *BRUO*, iii. 1494–5.
8   This was in compliance with the constitutions of Clement VI: *Constantiensis concilii acta et decreta*, ed. von der Hardt, iv. 1463–6.
9   William Exeter held the abbacy from 1415 until his death in 1429.
10   William Hulles was prior from 1417–33.
11   Pierre D'Ailly, bishop of Cambrai.

garments and placed him at the altar and kissed his hands and feet. Then the bishop of London gave the pope a ring worth eighty marks and put it on his finger, saying these words, 'Behold, holy father, I give your holiness in marriage to the holy Roman church.' When this had been done, one of those who had been enclosed speedily broke open the door in the wall and cried, 'We have a pope, Martin.' And then they all came out and went into the great church, and the cantors of the chapel of the pope sang the canticle 'We praise you God'.[1]

On the following day the pope was made a priest and on the next day he was consecrated as a bishop with ointment from the bishop of London, and wearing his bishop's mitre he celebrated his first Mass, at which one hundred and forty mitred bishops were present. On the following Sunday [14 November] at daybreak the pope went in solemn procession across the church from the southern part to the west, where was stationed a priest holding some hemp and tow in his hands, and, as the pope approached, he set fire to the hemp and the tow and burnt them saying, 'Look, holy father! This is how the glory of the world passes away.' After this on the same day a kind of balcony, twenty feet high, was made for the coronation of the pope.[2] The prior of St John at Clerkenwell [William Hulles] held the crown of the pope in the coronation service. On the same day after the midday meal the pope rode through the middle of the city of Constance, followed on horseback by all the bishops wearing mitres on their heads and by the abbots. The pope's horse had trappings of red scarlet, while the horses of all the bishops had trappings of white linen cloth, and during this cavalcade the emperor held the rein of the pope's horse. When the pope arrived at the town square, he was met there by all the Jews of the city, who handed to him, as was the custom, a book of their rites and their law. The pope received them and put them behind his back, saying, 'Let the old give place, all things are new.' The pope, so men say, was originally called Paulinus, as he was born of that noble and ancient tribe, the Paulina tribe at Rome.

[King Henry lands at Touques in Normandy]

In this year, towards the end of the month of July, King Henry with a large fleet cut a furrow through the sea and on the tenth day of his voyage landed safely in Normandy, in fact on the feast of St Peter ad Vincula [1 August], at a place called Touques.[3] This was a strong town with an imposing castle and which was accustomed to pay eight thousand crowns in taxes each year. Here five hundred horsemen joined battle with the king, wishing to prevent his passage. But once their captain had been killed by our archers and his deputy captured, the rest fled in fear. So the king sent messengers to the governor of the castle, instructing him to surrender the castle to him if he wished for his own safety or that of his men. The governor very humbly and courteously asked the king to grant him a truce of six days so that in this interval he could seek help from the king of France, and said that if no help came before the end of the period, he would surrender the castle to the king. And this the governor did.[4] Those who wished to remain were allowed by the king's grace to stay in the town, while those who wished to depart took with them of the king's grace their money and chattels, but leaving behind their weapons and instruments of war and their supplies in the castle. In the same manner the town of Auvillars with its castle was surrendered to the king.

---

[1] See also *Constantiensis concilii acta et decreta*, ed. von der Hardt, iv. 1482–5.

[2] Following the preparations described by Walsingham the coronation of Pope Martin took place on 21 November. See *Constantiensis concilii acta et decreta*, ed. von der Hardt, iv. 1486–90 at 1488–9.

[3] Henry embarked on 23 July 1417 with a force of 12,000 men and 1,500 vessels, twice as many men as had accompanied him on the Agincourt campaign. His crossing was facilitated by the defeat on 29 June of a large French force gathered in the Channel to intercept his ships. The French expected Henry to land again at Harfleur and thus the garrison at Touques lacked the reinforcements it might otherwise have expected. See also Wylie, *Henry V*, iii. 53; Allmand, *Henry V*, pp. 113–14.

[4] The castle was surrendered to Henry on 3 August; the dauphin was encamped at Rouen but did not come to the garrison's aid. The castle at nearby Deauville also capitulated at this time. See also Wylie, *Henry V*, ii. 53–5.

[The king protects the monks of the district from his troops][1]

At this time a monk who was wandering about on his own was captured and despoiled by one of the king's household. When the king discovered this, he had the monk summoned and anxiously asked him if he would recognise the person who had stolen his bits and pieces. When the monk replied that he would know the person well if he saw him, many people were led before him and at last he pointed to one of them and said that he was the one who had stolen his goods. The king was very angry and there and then he found the thief guilty, and said that death was the appropriate penalty for one who had laid his hands on the belongings of monks, when he could have satisfied his needs from other sources. If, however, he did nothing similar in the future, he could enjoy for the present the verdict of acquittal. And the king made the fellow give back to the monk the goods which he had previously taken, and instructed the monk to return to his house and fearlessly offer to God the customary services together with his brother monks. He declared that he had not come to Normandy as a robber bent on stealing the property of monks, but rather as a king determined to save their goods from theft. And at once he had a proclamation made throughout the army that no soldier should dare to rob any monk, cleric, priest or any obvious ecclesiastic, or molest them in any way or set hands on church property with a view to stealing it under pain of hanging and the noose.

When this proclamation became common knowledge among the country people, you might have seen them wandering here and there throughout our camp wearing clerical garb, engaged in the transactions of the marketplace, and coming and going as they pleased, with the English outwitted by their holy cunning. The English were unable to see the plain truth of the matter, as the country people had shaved their heads, so that the sight of these shaven heads would more effectively deceive the English. In consequence the king also had it proclaimed that no one should dare to rape any married woman, widow or virgin or to steal the goods of the people who had surrendered to the king under pain of the penalty mentioned above.

[The king besieges Caen]

On 13 August the king with his army withdrew from the town of Touques and spent the night at the town of St Sauveur de Dives.[2] On the next day, a Saturday, he spent the night at the town of Granville, where he also stayed on Sunday, the feast of the assumption of the blessed Mary [15 August]. On Monday he spent the night at the abbey of Fontenay [le Tesson][3] and on Tuesday he arrived at the town of Éterville. On Wednesday he encamped with his army just to the south of the town of Caen, next to the monastery of St Stephen [Thomas]. The duke of Clarence was to the north of the town, near the nunnery of the Holy Trinity. The earl marshal [John Mowbray] was encamped to the left of the king and Lord Maltravers[4] next to him. Next to Lord Maltravers were placed the Lords Talbot[5] and Umfraville,[6] and after them lords Neville and Willoughby.[7] To the right of the king were stationed the earl of Warwick and Sir John Grey, and next to them the earls of Huntingdon and Salisbury [Thomas Montagu] and Sir John Cornwall.

Such were the dispositions of the king's army. The French had barricaded themselves in the abbey of St Stephen, but when the Frenchmen forming the garrison in the abbey saw that they were not equal to the strength of the king, they hurried to abandon the place. Grabbing the food

---

1   With an obvious appeal for Walsingham, this story is not reported either by the other principal authorities.
2   As Henry advanced on Caen, Thomas, duke of Clarence was sent to occupy Lisieux. See also Wylie, *Henry V*, ii. 55–6; Allmand, *Henry V*, pp. 117–18.
3   The abbey of St Andrew, Fontenay.
4   John Fitzalan, lord Maltravers or Mautravers.
5   Gilbert, 5th Baron Talbot (b.1383). He had served with Henry in Wales during his father's reign and was appointed justice of Chester in 1413. He died at the siege of Rouen in 1418.
6   Sir Gilbert Umfreville (b.1390), a Northumbrian knight, son-in-law of Ralph Neville, 1st earl of Westmorland, who had been appointed a chamber knight to Henry V at his accession.
7   Robert II (d.1452), 6th baron Willoughby.

supplies and the other valuables in the building, they secretly transferred themselves to the town, thus getting a name for a clear act of sacrilege. Once safe in the town, they discussed among themselves how they could destroy the abbey by fire and level the towers of the church to the ground, as they were afraid that much damage could be done to the town from these towers.

But a monk named Gerard heard such plans being whispered among the French and, fearing the destruction of his monastery, he bravely took the risk and in the silence of that night he crawled on hands and knees past the campfires, weapons and swords of the enemy until he arrived at the place where the duke of Clarence, brother of the king, was keeping watch over his part of the siege. Having gained access to the duke's presence, he saw him resting on the grass in a garden, armed from top to toe, and with his head resting on a stone. He quickly fell to his knees and with tears besought him to save his abbey from the destruction that would immediately follow, unless he came to its help very speedily. 'It is especially suitable for you,' he said, 'to save our abbey, seeing that you are descended from the line of kings who founded, built and endowed it. So without delay use me as your leader to show you the way, and I will lead you inside it and make you glad that you have helped our abbey.'[1]

Without delay the duke did as the monk had advised, and, seizing scaling-ladders, he came to that part that the monk well knew was unfortified. For only a few invalids had been left behind, more for show than for actual defence. These were terrified by the duke's arrival, but he either took them prisoner or allowed them to depart, thinking that it was not worth killing such worthless rustics. He did order one of them to be beheaded who had confessed to stealing monastery property, namely the iron from the windows and other things of this kind. As the duke said to him, 'If we are justly punishing our own men with death for such sacrilege, you are much more deserving of this penalty, seeing that you are not frightened to sack the shrines of your own country.' So in this manner the duke captured the monastery and next day he brought in the king, who was overjoyed that he could see all that was happening in the town from the roofs and the towers of the monastery, and that he could fix and plant on them his guns, called 'cannons' by the French, which would enable him to attack the town more fiercely.

[The English capture Caen]

After these happenings the English soldiers were told the day and hour on which they must make their assault on the town. In the meantime, at the terrifying sound of the signal given by clarions and trumpets, the besieged rushed eagerly to the walls, encouraging each other and armed with weapons, swords and missiles, spears and stones to repel force with force. In King Henry's army, to quote the poet

> Each soldier clad his hostile breast with weapons,
> With which to fight and buy with blood a name,
> To last forever more.[2]

Among the knights Sir Edmund Springhouse,[3] who long ago together with others had been given the belt of knighthood before the walls of Caen, climbed these walls in full armour and

> With one hand, then the other, gave and took
> the wounds of battle.
> Just like a boar, driven far in woods by barks
> Of hounds, with flashing jaws scatters his speedy foes,
> But dies himself soon after.[4]

---

[1]   The historic connections between the English conquerors and the Norman *pays* was a feature of the English propaganda, and as the author of a history of Normandy, Walsingham was especially attracted to this theme. He is the only authority to recount the story of Gerard the monk. See also Wylie, *Henry V,* ii. 56–64.
[2]   Ovid, *Amores*, ii. x. 31, 32.
[3]   Sir Edmund Springhouse also known as Sprencheux had served throughout the Normandy campaign: *CCR, 1419–22,* p. 25; *CPR, 1416–22,* p. 46.
[4]   Ovid, *Fasti,* ii. 234, 231–2.

So also the noble Sir Edmund, while he was thrusting many from the walls and killing several with the sword as he performed the acts of Mars, slipped himself and fell on the ruins of the wall, where he sat and fought until he was himself killed. At once, armed as he was and still breathing, he was cremated by those inhuman French scum, who set flames around him.

But King Henry's soldiers did not cease their attack on the enemy. Rather their anger was aroused by the calamity that had befallen their doughty fellow-soldier, an outstandingly handsome young man and a model of behaviour, and they made their way up the walls still more fiercely, and blazed with anger as they came to grips with those wicked men who had seen to the cremation of Sir Edmund's body. They exhausted the French so much in that quarter that those who were guarding the town in another quarter thought it necessary to leave their own post and rush to the part where the king was attacking the town. So with there being few defenders in the abandoned quarter, [Thomas] the duke of Clarence placed his ladders at the very spot which had been thought to be the best protected, scaled the walls, and then, jumping down behind the French, caused such unexpected terror among them that they were not sure whether it was more use to advance against the king or to turn about and join battle with the duke. So there took place a widespread slaughter of the French, as the king's men stood firm against the French front while the duke of Clarence's men attacked their rear and took away all hope of safety from the French.

In this manner King Henry captured Caen, although the castle had not yet been cleared of rebels. And so the king battered the castle with such heavy gunfire that the garrison thought it was impossible to defend the place.[1] Then, granted a parley, they obtained from the king the freedom to depart themselves, but leaving behind in the castle their weapons, supplies, gold, silver and jewels. But so that they should not depart completely empty-handed and resourceless, the king kindly granted that the knights indeed could take away with them a fixed quantity of gold, while the esquires also were allowed to carry off a specified amount and others not more than a limited amount, under penalty of loss of the sums granted them and likewise of their lives. He also allowed the women to take with them their ornaments or whatever was moveable and to depart unhurt. And they, so it is said, carried away large sums of gold in bags. The ungrateful French troops made a poor response to all these kindnesses shown by the generous King Henry. They envied his success, and so they set fire to and burnt the gold and silver and all the property that had been carried into the castle for safe keeping. This became clear after their departure.

After the surrender of the castle at Caen, which had been promised to the king on condition that the French king or the dauphin or [Bernard] the count of Armagnac had not ended the siege by warfare by 19 September, the city and church of Bayeux and many other towns surrendered to the English under a similar agreement. Here I should note that I have been told that there are eighteen churches in Caen, if you include the churches of the monks.

[Scottish aid to the Lollards is repelled]

While this was happening in Normandy, the Lollards, led by [Sir] John Oldcastle, began their ravings again in England. Indeed Oldcastle with prayers and promises of money persuaded the Scots to invade a land that, so he claimed, could be easily conquered while the king was away in France. They say that Oldcastle spoke with the Scot, William Douglas,[2] at Pontefract and promised him a huge sum of gold if he would rouse his people to arms and get the man who in Scotland was falsely called King Richard to come with them and show himself as king. The Scot indeed, driven by 'sacred hunger for gold', soon got his fellow tribesmen with their loud war cries to come to lay siege to the castle and town of Roxburgh. On their arrival, the Scots sent in miners to work and to speed up the overthrowing of the walls.[3]

---

[1]   Caen capitulated on 4 September, barely two weeks after the siege began. See also Allmand, *Henry V,* pp. 117–18.

[2]   William Douglas, 2nd earl of Angus (1398–1437).

[3]   Whether or not they were incited to invasion by Oldcastle as Walsingham suggests, the Scots needed no encouragement to take advantage of Henry's absence in France; they had launched an earlier assault on the borders at the time of the Agincourt campaign. Archibald, 4th earl of Douglas, besieged Roxburgh whilst

It happened that the duke of Exeter, Lord Thomas Beaufort, had come on a pilgrimage to Bridlington at this time, and as soon as he heard the news of the attack, he hastened to the area, collecting soldiers and archers as he went along and losing no time in encountering the enemy. And from a different quarter the governor of the kingdom, John, duke of Bedford and brother of the king, with other nobles of the land collected a great force and came to the same town of Roxburgh. When the Scots discovered this through scouts, they did not dare to wait any longer, but 'to female flight they turned their shameful backs'.[1] This was not surprising as more than a hundred thousand men were said to have assembled to drive back the Scots. And so that the hundred thousand who had come with our heroes should not be thought raw rustics, that very venerable figure, the duke of Exeter [Thomas Beaufort], openly declared that he knew he had chosen of all that army forty thousand warlike soldiers of surpassing courage and spirit and equal to the nobler sort of the whole kingdom, notwithstanding the fact that such a huge army was serving with the king in Normandy.

[Defacement of books by the Lollards]

At that time the Lollard leader, [Sir] John Oldcastle, while on the lookout for hiding places in different parts, laid low for many days near St Albans in the home of a countryman who had a suitable mansion there on the lands of the abbot of St Albans.[2] When the abbot's people heard of this, they hurried to the place by night. They did not find Sir John there, but they did arrest some of his closest associates and took them off to prison. When the leader of these disbelievers heard this news, he groaned deeply and said that his grand scheme had had the stuffing knocked out of it, now that the closest partners in his wishes had been taken prisoner. There were also found at this place books written in English and some books that once had been handsomely decorated with pictures of different saints. But the wretches had scratched out the heads on these pictures, following the beliefs of their false doctrine, and in the Litanies they had removed the names of all the saints together with the mentions of the blessed Virgin down as far as the verse, 'Spare us, o Lord'. There were also found there some writings full of blasphemies against the blessed Mary, which horror compels me to omit from my history. One of these books, which had been defaced with such scratchings out, was sent by the abbot of St Albans [William Heyworth] to the lord our king together with some of the other works of the madmen found in the house, and the king sent the book on to the archbishop of Canterbury, so that he might show it in London when he was preaching sermons at St Paul's cross. In this way the citizens could not fail to know the depth of the frenzy actuating the Lollards, who did not allow (I pass over the pictures) even the names of the Saints to be inserted in their pages.[3]

[Appointments in Normandy. The king captures Falaise]

The king of England, showing tremendous energy at this time, captured on the continent more than a hundred cities and walled towns with their castles and defences. He entrusted the guarding of the town of Caen with its castle to lords Talbot [Gilbert, 5th lord] and [Sir Gilbert] Umfreville, the city of Bayeux to John Ashton,[4] and the city of Lisieux with its castle to Richard Woodville.[5] He gave the castle of Touques to [Thomas] the duke of Clarence, his brother, and the castle of Auvillars to the earl of Salisbury. He gave the Mirabelle castle, that is the castle of Marevyle to the duke of Clarence, who placed a governor in it. The castle of Creully was given by the king to Sir

---

Murdoch, duke of Albany attacked Berwick. Both attacks failed and the Scots, according to their own chronicler, 'returned home with dishonour': *Scotichronicon*, viii. 87.
[1]   Ovid, *Fasti*, vi. 522.
[2]   William Heyworth, abbot of St Albans from 1401 until 1420 when he was provided to the see of Coventry and Lichfield.
[3]   Walsingham provides here a rare and valuable witness to the production of Lollard texts.
[4]   John Ashton, a knight of the duchy of Lancaster, was appointed seneschal of Bayeux on 20 September 1417. See also *CCR, 1413–19*, pp. 302, 374.
[5]   Richard Woodville was an esquire of the king and subsequently chamberlain to John, duke of Bedford.

Brian de Stapleton,[1] but he was immediately deprived of his life by cruel fortune before his time. The king gave the castle of Courseulles to Sir Philip Leche,[2] the castle of Lingèvres to Sir William Talbot,[3] the castle of Tilly-sur-Seulles to Sir John Grey,[4] Troarn abbey to [   ][5] and the church with little fort at Estrennes to Sir William Bourchier.[6]

On 4 September this year came the death at Constance, where the council had not yet ended, of Robert Hallum, bishop of Salisbury.[7]

In the month of December King Henry began the siege of Falaise. It was a strongly fortified town with a large garrison, proud of its wealth, well equipped with engines of war, and so boastful of its walls that at the start it did not even think it worth the bother to shut its gates against the king. But the terror inspired by the king's guns meant that the town itself was surrendered to him after very little trouble. The defenders in the castle, however, with great contempt for the English, held out right until the feast of the Purification of the Blessed Virgin [2 February], with many insults being bandied to and fro in the meantime.[8] At last the stubbornness of the besieged crumbled, and, sorry that that they had persevered in their obstinacy for so long, they behaved like humble men and begged the king for mercy. For they could not endure the awesome volleys of stones, feared by everybody, which they saw launched into their midst time after time. And so they preferred to save their lives by making an agreement once on any terms than to die daily through their fear of death. So after certain conditions had been laid down, the citizens assured the king that they would repair at their own expense the damage done to the castle and the houses destroyed in the town, apart from those houses that they had handed over to the king as the price of their ransom. The king had imposed this obligation on them because the great destruction of the castle had been caused by the length of their own spirited defence of it.

[The capture and execution of Sir John Oldcastle]

About this time the capture took place in England on the lands of Lord Charlton of Powys of that boastful ancient of evil days, Lollard leader and prince of heretics, John Oldcastle, once called Lord Cobham.[9] His capture was not without danger and damage for those who took him prisoner, but nor did he himself get taken without suffering a wound. At this same time all the estates of the realm had been summoned to London for a parliament to discuss giving financial help to the king, who was toiling in lands beyond the sea. And when the nobles and other persons present at the parliament heard that their public enemy had been captured, they agreed unanimously that parliament should not be dissolved until he had been questioned before it and his replies heard. So the lord of Powys was sent to bring him in under a strong escort. He brought the wounded Oldcastle to London in a litter, accompanied by one priest who shared all his secrets.[10] As soon as he had been placed before the ruler of the kingdom, the duke of Bedford, and the estates of parliament, at once the indictment was read out in his hearing concerning his rebellion against the king in St Giles's fields and other treasonable offences, which have been partly described earlier as they

---

1   Sir Brian Stapleton, a Yorkshire knight, whose grandfather, also Sir Brian (d. 1394), had fought at Crécy. He was killed in action near Alençon, *CPR, 1416–22*, p. 331.
2   Sir Philip Leche, a Derbyshire knight, served with distinction in the Normandy campaign attracting the attention of the French chronicler Monstrelet. He died at Melun. See *CCR, 1413–19*, p. 184; Wylie, *Henry V*, iii. 210–11.
3   For Sir William Talbot see *CCR, 1413–19*, pp. 115, 376; *CPR, 1416–22*, pp. 84, 197, 203.
4   For Sir John Grey (d. 1421) see *CCR, 1413–19*, p. 475; *CPR, 1416–22*, p. 384.
5   There is a blank space here in the manuscript.
6   For Bourchier see above, p. 356 and n.
7   Hallum died on 4 September 1417.
8   The siege of Falaise lasted for at least two months, but Walsingham's dating is more than a month out; the town was surrendered before Christmas 1417 and the castle on 2 January.
9   For Oldcastle's earlier exploits see above, pp. 390–4, 405–6.
10   Oldcastle was arrested near Welshpool in late November 1417 by Edward, Lord Charlton of Powys. Adam Usk reported that he was 'handsomely rewarded for the capture' (*Usk*, pp. 266–7). See also *CPR, 1416–22*, p. 325.

happened. He was asked how he wished to excuse himself and to show why he did not deserve to be sentenced to death.

Oldcastle immediately sought a different avenue of escape, and, using a parable, he began to preach about the mercy of God and to say that all men who wished to be imitators of God should always exalt mercy above judgement. Punishment belonged to God alone and should be left to him alone and not be exercised by his worshippers. And he bought time by saying many other such things until the lord chief justice advised the king's deputy not to allow Oldcastle to waste their time to no purpose and annoy the nobles of the land sitting before him. So the ruler of the land ordered him to confine his replies to the charges brought against him. Sir John saw that he was being put under constant pressure. He meditated briefly, then, breaking silence, he replied at last, saying, 'It means absolutely nothing to me that I am being judged by you or put to death by men.' And he began again his impertinent prattlings until the chief justice ordered him to give his final answer and tell them, if he could, why he should not be put to death. With consummate arrogance and perversity he evaded the question and forthwith replied that he acknowledged no judge among then, while his liege lord, King Richard, was still alive in the kingdom of Scotland. Once they had received this reply, there was no need of witnesses, and they immediately ordered him to be drawn and hung from the gallows and then to be burnt while hanging from them. Present on this occasion was the ruler of the land together with many knights and honourable persons. Of these Oldcastle is said to have spoken his last words to Sir Thomas Erpingham, begging him, if he saw his victim rise again on the third day, to procure peace for his followers. The bigot was so far gone in his craziness that he actually thought he would rise again from the dead after three days.[1]

[1418]

Here begins the sixth year of Henry V

In 1418, the fifth year of the reign of King Henry V, the king kept Christmas in the city of Bayeux in Normandy. At this time the castle of Falaise was surrendered to the king, the town of Falaise having surrendered to him previously.[2] Also the city of the Abrinci, that is Avranches, was surrendered to the king.[3]

After the feast of Easter [27 March], the king sent his officers to besiege various places, Thomas duke of Clarence to the monastery of Bec Herluin which is seven miles from Rouen, Humphrey duke of Gloucester to the town of Cherbourg, Richard [Beauchamp] earl of Warwick to the castle of Domfront and Sir Gilbert Umfreville to Neuilly.[4]

On St George's day [23 April] the king kept solemn festival in the castle at Caen. There he created five new knights, Louis Robesart,[5] Roger Salvayn,[6] John Stewart, Robert Schotesbroke'[7] and John Montgomery, and dispatched them to the various sieges mentioned above.

At this time a friar of the order of preachers called Vincent, a doctor of theology and now more than sixty years old, preached sermons full of grace in Brittany and won many to his God and Lord.[8] His preaching had such attractiveness and sweetness that he bored none of his

---

1   Walsingham is the only authority to offer such a detailed account of Oldcastle's end. His execution on 14 December 1417 was extreme; he was drawn to St Giles's fields where he was chained and roasted.
2   Falaise castle was surrendered on 2 January; Allmand, *Henry V,* pp. 118–19.
3   Avranches surrendered on 16 February.
4   With the army of Duke John of Burgundy advancing on Paris, Henry now moved to consolidate his position in the Cotentin.
5   Louis Robesart, a Hainaulter, had been in the service of the king from the outset of the Normandy campaign. He had been employed on several occasions as an envoy and later, May 1420, was appointed Henry's standard bearer: *CPR, 1416–22,* pp. 27, 66, 337, 406; Wylie, *Henry V,* iii. 291 and n.
6   Salvayn had served as treasurer of Calais since 1413: *CPR, 1416–22,* pp. 135, 139.
7   Robert Schotesbroke had been an esquire of the king since 1413: *CCR, 1413–19,* pp. 45, 143.
8   This was Vincent Ferrier (d.1419). He had been present at the closing stages of the council at Constance, but began journeying westward in the winter of 1417 on what was to be his last evangelical tour. He entered Brittany at the invitation of the duke in February 1418 and it was at Rennes that he received an invitation

hearers, but charmed and refreshed all of them, even though a sermon of his could last for many hours. More than two hundred folk followed him around all the time, attracted by his honeyed words.

The king of England heard of his fame and sent highly respectable messengers to him, namely his confessor and the almoner of his household, to ask him to deign to visit him in Normandy. For he really wanted to see him and talk with him. So the friar came to the king on the Friday before the feast of Pentecost [15 May]. But because the king was busily engaged with his nobles at that time, he could not see the friar until the Monday. On that day in the presence of the king the friar celebrated the mass and preached with such wisdom and grace that the king marvelled greatly. In his sermon preached before the king he praised him for hounding down and putting to death that famous heretic [Sir] John Oldcastle, declaring that God had prepared seats in heaven for all who took part in his destruction. The king discussed many difficult questions with the friar, and he received such discriminating replies that he declared he had never found a man of such wisdom and intelligence.

It happened at that moment that there was brought before the king a dumb youth who it was said had not eaten or drunk anything for the last two years, although he looked so full of life and had such a good colour that you could have thought he had been fed entirely on tit-bits. The king ordered the youth to be taken to brother Vincent. And when he had stayed with Vincent for just one day, he was able to form and speak in his native tongue the words, 'Jesus mercy, mercy Jesus', and on another day, 'Jesus and Mary, blessed be they. Mary and Jesus, blessed be they.' It is also said of this Vincent that he had such a good memory that he could even have rewritten the whole bible if it had been destroyed. The king wrote about him to a friend of his as follows: 'Would to God that you had seen brother Vincent and had a conversation with him. And would that I could have two or three doctors of theology in England who were willing to listen to Vincent and follow his rule of life and preach to our English with the dash and fervour of Vincent in his sermons.'[1]

[The count of Armagnac murdered by men of the duke of Burgundy]

During the feast of the Trinity [22 May] at the order of the king, Thomas, duke of Exeter and the king's uncle, departed for Normandy with fifteen thousand soldiers, so it is said.

In the month of June the Burgundians entered Paris by night and helped by some of the citizens seized the count of Armagnac and butchered him to death in the most degrading fashion. For, so it is said, they cruelly flayed off his skin and, after he had been flayed, they rolled his bloody body in feathers and next hung him up by his own bootlaces. Then when he cooled down, they plucked him, taking out the feathers one by one, so that as the feathers were pulled out he just about suffered as many deaths as there were feathers pulled from his body before he actually died. Several nobles were murdered in that savage uprising, namely the cardinal de Bar[2] the archbishop of Rheims,[3] the bishops of Meaux,[4] Coutances[5] and Lisieux,[6] the abbots of St Denis[7] and

---

from Henry V. Ferrier met the king at Caen on or around 4 May, preached before him, performed a miracle (as recounted here by Walsingham) and was also said to have predicted the murder of the count of Armagnac, which took place the following month.

1   This may well be Walsingham's invention, but the enthusiasm for Ferrier's evangelism that he gives Henry here is not implausible in a king who had already demonstrated his support for religious reform through his promotion of the Brigittine and Celestine orders. See above, p. 398.
2   Louis de Bar.
3   Walsingham is in error: the archbishop of Rheims, Renaud de Chartres, was not amongst the prisoners killed.
4   Jean de Saints, bishop of Meaux from 1409.
5   Jean de Marle, bishop of Coutances from 1417.
6   Pierre Fresnel, bishop of Lisieux from 1417.
7   Philippe de Villette, abbot of St Denis.

Jormayle,[1] the chancellor of France,[2] the provost of Paris[3] and several others, amounting to four-teen thousand people. Nor could their tyrannical fury be satisfied by the slaughter of so many men. They attacked women as well, and five thousand women are said to have been killed.[4]

[Cherbourg and Louviers surrender to King Henry]

After a siege of six months the town of Cherbourg with its castle was surrendered to the duke of Gloucester.[5]

About the same time king Henry laid siege to the strongly fortified town of Louviers.[6] Many of the king's men were wounded by the gunners of the town and in his anger at this the king made such fierce assaults on the town that the citizens were thrown into dismay and humbly begged for peace. The duke of Clarence [Thomas] and the knights John Cornwall[7] and Ralph Cromwell,[8] were sent as the king's envoys to announce to the citizens the conditions of peace and to report back their wishes to the king. So the three estates of the town, clergy, knights and citizens together with the commons received from King Henry the following edict: the treaty did not apply to John Courall of Melun, the governor of Louviers. He was not to enjoy the grace and favour of King Henry, as once when governor of Bayeux he had sworn an oath to the king but had clearly been guilty of perjury. Another condition was that all three estates should totally surrender to the king their persons, lives, lands, inherited property, moveables and other possessions, and should surrender the town of Louviers into the hands of the king or his commissioners on the day or hour decided upon by the king. In return for their humble submission the king granted them their ancestral, inherited rights apart from the lands and inherited property given by the king before the present agreement. So the three estates and particularly soldiers and bowmen from other countries swore that for the future they would not take up arms against the king of France and of England nor would they be found as armed opponents in any war against him or any of his people.

---

1   The name of this abbey is corrupt; Galbraith suggested Cornille: *St Albans Chronicle*, ed. Galbraith, p. 120 n.

2   Henri de Marle, chancellor of France.

3   Provost, Tanneguy de Châtel, in fact escaped Paris with the dauphin; the office was then placed in the hands of Guy de Presles, sire de Bar, known as 'Le Veau de Bar'.

4   Here Walsingham conflates two events that were connected – indeed the one led directly to the other – but were separated by several weeks. A group of pro-Burgundian Parisians provoked an uprising on the night of 20/30 May, seizing the king from the Hôtel de St Pol, and massacred as many Armagnacs as they could find; the count of Armagnac himself evaded capture and the provost of Paris, Tanneguy de Châtel, placed the fifteen-year-old dauphin in his own custody in the Bastille. This Armagnac remnant attempted to recover the city on 1 June but was repelled and the dauphin withdrew to Bourges. Reprisals followed in Paris and on 12 July the Armagnac prisoners and the count of Armagnac himself were killed. For a full, first-hand account of the violence in Paris see *A Parisian Journal, 1400–49, Translated from the Anonymous Journal d'un Bourgeois de Paris*, ed. and trans., J. Shirley (Oxford, 1968), pp. 111–24.

5   Much of western Normandy had already submitted to Henry's forces, but a handful of fortifications continued to hold out, of which the fortified coastal town of Cherbourg was undoubtedly the strongest. The castle and town were garrisoned with as many as 1,000 men-at-arms, and the defensive walls were entirely encircled by the sea at every high tide. Gloucester's forces arrived in the early spring and established a blockade on land and sea; the garrison attempted several counter-attacks but as starvation threatened they were compelled to agree terms on 22 August for surrender on the feast of Michaelmas. Such a lengthy siege was costly to the English and there were many casualties: Wylie, *Henry V*, iii. 108–11; Allmand, *Henry V*, p. 120.

6   Henry reached Louviers on 8 June. The town was besieged for almost a fortnight before it capitulated; the settlement whose terms Walsingham transcribes here gives the date of surrender as 23 June, but the French chroniclers suggest 20 June: Wylie, *Henry V*, iii. 114 and n. Later accounts, such as that of the Kenilworth chronicler John Streeche (p. 163), report that Henry himself narrowly escaped injury during an assault from the garrison's guns and that as an act of revenge at the end of the siege the king hanged all but one of the gunners. See also Allmand, *Henry V*, p. 121.

7   For Cornwall see above, p. 342 and n.

8   Ralph, (c.1393–1456), 3rd baron Cromwell, who had served with Clarence in the expedition of 1412: *CCR, 1419–22*, p. 149.

And in return for this submission the duke of Clarence promised the above mentioned peoples that he would plead with the lord king to give them back their horses and weapons and all their other property, in return for which these peoples were to fight in arms for the king of France and England at their own expense in his wars from this time, the eve of the feast of John the Baptist [i.e. 23 June] until the feast of St Michael next following [29 September]. Also the three estates were bound by oath to set free to the lord king all the renegades from England, that is the Welsh, Irish, Normans who had taken the oath and Gascons. Also the three estates of the town swore that all the provisions that had been laid up for the defence of the town should stay there, together with stones and all other means of defence.[1]

So the town was surrendered to the king on the eve of the feast of St John Baptist [i.e. 23 June] and on the Monday following the king moved his army towards the Pont de L'Arche,[2] and at the same time the duke of Exeter [Thomas Beaufort] besieged and captured the city of Évreux.[3]

[Three English victories in one week]

In the octave of the assumption of the blessed Mary [26 August] in this year, Jesus Christ, so it is thought, out of honour for his glorious Mother, whom the king of England worships with special devotion gave him three miraculous victories in different places in the province of Normandy. The first was that a hundred of our Englishmen on Tuesday in that octave captured three great lords and eighty other people at a place called Quillebeuf and compelled three hundred other Frenchmen to take to flight.[4] The second victory was on Thursday, when quite four hundred of the enemy entered the outskirts of the city of Évreux and were put to flight by eleven Englishmen, who captured four of them, killed twelve and seized forty of their horses.[5] The third was on the following Saturday very early in the morning. The enemy indeed were set on retaking the town called Louviers, which King Henry had captured on his first expedition of the present year,[6] but the captain of the town with a hundred of our men marched bravely out against a thousand and by the will of God defeated them. Blessed be God, to whom be honour and glory and victory everlasting, for he delivered into the hands of our men, after many of the enemy had already been killed, one hundred and eighty well-born Frenchmen.[7]

---

[1] Quite why Walsingham gives a digest of the terms under which Louviers surrendered – as opposed to Cherbourg, or another town – is unclear; perhaps it was simply that for once these details were available to him. The terms were typical of those imposed on the conquered towns; Henry's priority was to secure the use of the towns' resources, military as well as alimentary.

[2] Where the River Seine meets the River Eure: Henry reached here on 27 June.

[3] Evreux surrendered to Exeter's forces on 20 May after only four days; it may be that the garrison wished to avoid the devastation which had attended the siege at the abbey of Bec three weeks before: Wylie, *Henry V*, iii. 112.

[4] Walsingham is the only contemporary authority to record this skirmish although it was elaborated upon by Tito Livio Frulovisi and other later writers. Quillebeuf was on the southern bank of the Seine and a small French force had established itself there to harry the English supply ships sailing upriver; on 16 August the troops were routed and as many as eighty of them were captured.

[5] Walsingham again is the only authority to record this incident which appears to have taken place on 18 August.

[6] For the capture of Louviers see above, p. 430.

[7] The counter-attack at Louviers is attested by other authorities, but only Walsingham reports the action of the English captain and the number of troops that supported him.

[The surrender of Rouen]

On 19 January in 1419 the city of Rouen was surrendered to the king.[1] On the day on which the siege began there were 270,000 people in the town, and 30,000 of these died of hunger.[2] Why, the citizens were even forced by their hunger to eat their horses, dogs and rats. Dogs with some flesh on them were sold for 10 pence, a rat for 6 pence, a thin horse for 20 pence, an egg for 13 pence, a quart of corn, that is the quarter of a gallon, for 10 shillings, and an apple for 40 pence.[3] The mercenaries of both the castle and the town were allowed to go away in their doublets, having sworn an oath that they would not bear arms against the king for the year next following. The citizens of Rouen were to give to our lord king three hundred thousand scudi in order to regain their possessions and peace with the king. The first payment was to be on the twenty-second day of the present month of January, and the second on the next feast of St Matthew [21 September] without there being any delay with the payment.[4] The wicked Alan Blanchart, who had hanged Englishmen from the walls of Rouen, and tied dogs to their necks, and put some in sacks with dogs tied to their beards and drowned them in the river Seine, was drawn and hanged.[5] Guy le Bouteiller was governor of Rouen

[The capture of Pontoise]

On 31 July the town of Pontoise near Paris was unexpectedly taken by the astuteness and the stout-hearted action of the Captal de Buch.[6] He had spent the night in hiding in the vineyards near the town with some of the king's household, and in the morning watch he suddenly, with the

---

1   According to the Kenilworth chronicler, John Streeche (pp. 168–78), Henry reached the eastern edge of Rouen on 29 July 1418 and on the following day deployed his captains to different stations surrounding the city walls and took the Carthusian monastery of Mont Gargane as his centre of command. The siege contin-ued for almost six months. The English were distracted by the need to defend their supply routes and it was not until the earl of Warwick had defeated the garrison at Caudebec, which had harried English vessels bearing equipment and provisions for the front, that they were able to place greater pressure on Rouen itself. The citizens attempted several counter-attacks and in October it appeared for a time that a vast army under John the Fearless was about to relieve them. But Burgundy's army advanced no further than Pontoise and by the beginning of the Christmas festival the onset of famine forced the Rouen authorities to sue for terms. Negotiations began on 31 December and were concluded on 13 January: it was agreed that the city would submit to Henry if no reinforcements had appeared by 19 January. None came, and on that day, the keys of the city were delivered to Henry at the Charterhouse. According to Tito Livio and the account of the English soldier John Page, the progress of Henry's procession into the city was hampered by the corpses of famine victims that littered the streets. See also Allmand, *Henry V,* pp. 123–7.
2   Perhaps because they did not anticipate a protracted siege the authorities admitted a large number of out-siders to the city before the gates were closed, although Walsingham's estimate for the besieged population is a great exaggeration.
3   The city's reserves of food had been exhausted by October 1381 and both English and French authorities record the privations into which the citizens were forced. Walsingham's claim that dogs and rats were now traded for food is corroborated by the eyewitness, John Page, who recalled that 'For xxx d went a ratte, for ii nobles went a catte': 'The Siege of Rouen' in *The Historical Collections of a Citizen of London in the Fifteenth Century,* ed. J. Gairdner, Camden Society, New Series, xvii (1876), pp. 1–54 at 18.
4   The citizens were rewarded for their compliance. The governor, Guy Le Bouteiller, was given Norman estates seized by the English. See Wylie, *Henry V,* iii. 144–5.
5   Under the terms of the surrender, nine of the besieged were excluded from the king's mercy, including the mayor, the archbishop's vicar general and several merchants, but the most notorious was Alain Blanchard, captain of the crossbowmen, who was accused of having treated savagely the handful of English prisoners he and his men had been able to seize. He was executed after Henry's entry into the town: the French authorities dispute the manner of execution, claiming that he was beheaded. See Wylie, *Henry V,* iii. 144 n.
6   Gaston de Foix, brother of Jean, count of Foix and the second son of Count Archambaud de Grailly of Foix. He held estates in Gascony from which he took the title Captal de Buch. Walsingham's date for this episode is correct although the manoeuvre to take the town began on the night of 30 July: two divisions of English troops, one under the command of Gaston de Foix the other under John Holland, earl of Huntingdon, approached Pontoise at night from either side of the town, with the aim of combining at the main gate to effect entry. However, Huntingdon's forces were waylaid by marshy ground and Foix's men

help of scaling ladders, climbed the walls. After a long struggle, in which many defenders were killed and several wounded, and when the citizens saw that the unconquered numbers of the enemy in their midst were ever increasing, they lost their heads, opened the gates and fled wherever chance took each man. There were a thousand particularly valiant men, carrying spears and shields stationed in that town for its defence and two thousand crossbowmen, but all of these, when they saw the town captured, hurried to flee to Paris as fast as they could.[1] But they were intercepted and their passage blocked by the earl of Huntingdon [John Holland]. He himself had been given the job in this assault of keeping the citizens occupied in one part of the town, while other English tried to scale the walls in another part, but he had been slowed down by the marshes and had not found a way out of them until sunrise. Almost all that crowd was killed by the earl, while the town was held by our men. They found there two years food supplies of every kind.[2] The king wrote in dispatches of the wealth and usefulness of this pleasant town and said that in all his exploits on the continent he had not done anything more valuable. The capture of Pontoise took place as the truce expired and on the day after the French had deceived and disappointed King Henry and refused the ways to peace that the king had offered.[3] Men say that the town had been stocked with food sufficient for two years.

On the next Monday after the feast of St Matthew [21 September], the apostle, the castle of Gisors was retaken by the English, and on the next Saturday after the same feast the English also recovered Chateau Gaillard.[4]

The slaying of the duke of Burgundy

On 16 June, the day after the feast of Corpus Christi, the council of the household of the French king and the queen of France and the duke of Burgundy [John the Fearless] met with our king at Mantes on the river Seine to discuss the matter of peace between the two kingdoms. But that meeting achieved nothing, as after a few days the duke of Burgundy was wickedly slain by the treachery of the dauphin.

The duke of Burgundy was treacherously slain, after being called to a meeting with the dauphin and his perfidious accomplices, even though they had all previously bound themselves by the same oath on both sides that no one would harm any other of those who came to the conference.[5] In his desire to avenge the murder of his father, the son and heir of the duke of

---

siezed the gate alone, taking advantage of the absence of the guard at the first Mass of the day. See also Allmand, *Henry V*, pp. 142–3.

1   Here Walsingham gives the garrison in classical clothing: there were 1,000 men-at-arms and 2,000 crossbowmen.

2   The supplies seized were said to be valued at two million crowns: Wylie, *Henry V*, iii. 179.

3   The French had opened peace negotiations with the English soon after the submission of Rouen in January 1419. Talks began at Rouen in mid-March between Henry's envoys, headed by the earl of Warwick, and the French delegation led by the duke of Brittany, and continued at Mantes and Vernon. The French at first demonstrated a willingness to concede to the English demands for the territories originally granted under the treaty of Bretigny, and for the duchy of Normandy, and a desire to secure a permanent peace sealed with the marriage of Henry to the daughter of their king. A meeting between Henry and Queen Isabel, deputising for her husband, was convened at Meulan on 29 May. But now the negotiations proved far less fruitful and although talks continued at intervals until the beginning of July, no final agreement between the parties could be found. A truce had been agreed until 29 July and it was on this day that preparations were made for the assault against Pontoise. See Wylie, *Henry V*, iii. 161–70.

4   Henry reached Gisors on 31 August and after treating on 11 September, the garrison finally surrendered on 23 September. Walsingham wrongly dates the defeat of Chateau Gaillard. The garrison was loyal to the dauphin and had withstood the siege for more than six months. It did not surrender until the end of November and the English did not enter it until 8 December.

5   With the fall of Pontoise an English advance on Paris seemed certain and on 2 August Thomas, duke of Clarence, arrived at the gates of the city to taunt the citizens although he did not attempt to gain entry. These events convinced Duke John of the urgent need to conclude a permanent peace with the dauphin although it was only after several weeks that a mutually acceptable meetingplace could be agreed. The meeting was at Montereau, at the confluence of the rivers Seine and Yonne on 10 September. It was arranged that the duke and the dauphin would greet one another on the covered bridge across the river but as John the Fearless

Burgundy humbly dispatched many honoured persons to our king and through them made an oath of loyal service to King Henry, becoming his liegeman.[1]

Balthazar Cossa, formerly known as Pope John XXIII, was deposed and imprisoned by a decree of the council of Constance. But after the humble submission which he made to Pope Martin, he was freed from prison and restored to the rank of cardinal.

The bishop of Surronensis, the suffragan of the bishop of Winchester, at the invitation of the abbot and the monks, presided over a solemn service of ordination at St Albans on 23 September.[2]

In this year the widow of the late King Henry, Queen [Jo]anna, was accused of an evil deed, namely of having plotted to harm the king. All her servants were taken from her and she was given into the custody of John Pelham. He allowed her nine serving women and took her into Pevensey castle that he might keep her guarded there under his care.[3]

Around the time of the feast of All Saints [1 November] the duchess of Clarence [Margaret, d.1439] with many other ladies crossed over the sea to Neustria [i.e. Normandy].

Humphrey, duke of Gloucester and youngest brother of the king, was made guardian of the realm in the place of his brother John, duke of Bedford, the middle brother of the king, who, at the summons of the king, sailed to Normandy after Easter [18 April] in the following year with a strong force of soldiers, after gloriously governing the country for two years.[4]

[1420]

In 1420, still in the seventh year of the reign of King Henry V, duke Humphrey, the youngest brother of the king, was made *locum tenens* and guardian of the kingdom, in the place of his brother John, duke of Bedford.

On 16 March in this year, during the siege of Fresnay-le-Vicomte by the earl of Salisbury [Thomas Montgu], a battle was fought between our men and the troops of the dauphin who had arrived to break up the siege. Our men won a glorious victory over seven thousand Frenchmen, even though they did not number more than two thousand. And with God's help it was brought about that about five thousand of the French were slain by our men, and six hundred of them taken prisoner, including the marshal, John de Rieux and also William de la Crosse with many other honourable men.[5] The captains in this battle were the earl of Huntingdon, the earl marshal,

---

entered the enclosure at the bridge's centre he was set upon by assassins. He was killed by an axe-blow to the head, probably struck from behind by Tanneguy du Châtel, the Armagnac Provost of Paris; the duke's Burgundian retainers fled in panic. See also Vaughan, *John the Fearless*, pp. 263–86.

1   Walsingham telescopes what were long and at times tortuous negotiations. Philip – later called 'the Good' – the heir to Duke John received the news of his father's death at Ghent. His first act was to secure the loyalty of his Flemish subjects but on 1 October he did appoint ambassadors to treat with the English. The talks began at Mantes on 26 October. The conditions Henry placed on any peace were uncompromising – that Duke Philip support Henry becoming regent of France while Charles VI lived and his succession as king after his death – and at first the envoys demurred. It was only after further discussion, and parallel talks with the representatives of Charles VI, that Philip made formal submission to Henry's terms at Arras on 2 December. The treaty, which incorporated a truce between Charles and Henry negotiated by the Burgundian envoys on Charles's behalf, was finally ratified on 5 January.

2   John Sewale was created bishop of Surronensis – a see *in partibus infidelium* – in 1405 and in this capacity served as a suffragan in the dioceses of St David's, London, Salisbury and Winchester. He died in 1426.

3   Joan of Navarre was suspected of having conspired to use witchcraft against the king in collusion with several members of her household, including a Franciscan friar, John Randolf. Her property was seized on 27 September and on 1 October she was placed under house arrest at Rotherhithe. On 15 December she was placed in the custody of John Pelham and remained in his care until 8 March 1420. See Wylie, *Henry V*, iii. 222–3.

4   Gloucester was appointed on 30 December 1419. The date of Bedford's departure for France is not recorded. See also *CPR, 1416–19*, p. 254.

5   This was a successful ambush that took place on 3 March. The force of French (and Scots) were from Le Mans and, as Walsingham observes, were aiming to relieve the garrison at Fresnay-le-Vicomte. As well as notable prisoners, the English also captured the Scots' war chest: Wylie, *Henry V*, iii. 216.

Sir John Cornwall and Sir Philip le Beche. Sir Philip with his archers cut off the fleeing French from the town of Le Mans to which they were hurrying, and with thick arrow fire did a lot of damage. In fact the fugitives were so jammed together at the gateway into the town that the French cavalry not only rode down their own foot-soldiers but also crushed and trampled upon their allies who were on horseback and escaping in haste. Many standards of nobles on the French side were captured in this battle including that of William Douglas,[1] who lost his standard and had more than a hundred of his Scots slain. The king gave orders for William Douglas's standard to be displayed in St Mary's church in Rouen.

At this time the duke of Burgundy [Philip the Good] tried very hard to bring about peace and concord between the two kings.[2] The proposed manner, form and conditions of peace and the articles which were drawn up and published, were as follows.[3]

'Firstly that our king should accept and have as his wife the Lady Katherine, the most beautiful daughter of Charles, king of France, and that through this marriage he should regard and have his illustrious relations, the king and queen of France, as his father and mother and thus venerate them before all other persons in the world. Secondly that he should not stop his kinsman, the king of France, from holding and possessing in his accustomed fashion, for as long as he lived, the crown and kingship of France with all its revenues for maintaining his position and carrying out the tasks laid upon him as king, and that his kinswoman, the most high queen of France [Isabel], the wife of this same king of France, should also for as long as she lived hold the rank and position of queen according to the customs of France.

The illustrious king of England offered to keep, carry out and fulfil these conditions, provided that the following conditions were similarly promised, agreed upon and carried out by the French king. Firstly, that immediately after the death of his relative, the king of France, and then successively, the crown and kingdom of France with all its laws and appurtenances should belong to and remain with Henry himself and his heirs for ever. Secondly, that as regards that which his most high kinsman of France is considered as possessing, because of his ill health so that he cannot be properly free to manage the business of the kingdom, for saving the life of his kinsman of France, the full authority to exercise rule over France should belong to and remain with King Henry himself, together with the council of the nobles and wise men of France who were loyal to his most high relative and who were lovers of the welfare and honour of France, so that, during any such regency, he might be able to rule and govern France as justice and equity demanded both through his own person and also through others whom he himself and the council of nobles mentioned above had thought should be sent to France for this purpose. Thirdly, that the lords,

---

1   Sir William Douglas of Drumlanrig.
2   The treaty concluded between Duke Philip and Henry on 5 January 1420 had also established a truce between the English king and Charles VI until March. This was now extended until April and both parties began preparations for securing a permanent peace under the terms Henry had already agreed with Duke Philip, that is his marriage to Charles's daughter Katherine and his appointment as regent. Negotiations began at Troyes where Charles and Isabel were already established and where Duke Philip and English envoys had arrived by 23 March. A treaty was drafted on 9 April although discussions continued with the envoys of Henry V for another month while the support of both the parlement and university of Paris was also secured. Meanwhile Henry departed from Rouen in the direction of Troyes, passing first around Paris, as Walsingham describes below.
3   Walsingham here focuses upon the implications of the peace for the persons of Charles, his daughter Katherine, Duke Philip and Henry, rather than its wider political ramifications. The treaty that was sealed at Troyes on 21 May established Henry as regent of France and heir to the kingdom; when Charles died, the crowns of England and France would be unified, although both kingdoms would continue to enjoy their own customs and laws. While the treaty required Burgundy to remain loyal to both England and France and not to pursue his own self-aggrandisement as his father had done, it also required Henry to undertake the defence of the kingdom of France from its enemies – meaning the dauphin and the remnants of the Armagnac cause – the potential costs of which alarmed the commons when they examined the treaty in the following parliament. Perhaps most importantly, the treaty ignored entirely the Dauphin Charles and his claims as King Charles's heir; the treaty forbade all parties from entering into negotiations with him or his supporters. See also Allmand, *Henry V,* pp. 144–9.

magnates and nobles and the estates both spiritual and temporal of France, the cities and the notable gentry, and the citizens and burgesses of the towns of France, who at the moment were in obedience to his kinsman, should swear the following oath:

Firstly, that they will humbly and submissively obey and attend to this same King Henry, as he exercises his power and authority of governing and ruling the kingdom of France, and to his orders in all things concerning his exercise of rule in France and in all matters whatsoever. Also, that in all respects and in every way, in matters which can affect them as a body and as individuals, the lords, magnates etc. themselves, shall well and faithfully observe and to the best of their ability get others to observe the treaty which has been agreed and settled on by the kinsman and kinswoman of King Henry and King Henry himself together with the council of those whom the kinsman and kinswoman and King Henry himself thought should be consulted in this matter.

Also, that from the moment of the death of his kinsman of France and ever afterwards, they will themselves be loyal liegemen of King Henry and his heirs, and without opposition, argument or scruples receive and acknowledge him as their supreme liege lord and king of France and obey him as such; and that, except for the said kinsman, they will never obey any one after this as king and regent of the kingdom of France except for King Henry and his heirs.

Also, that they will not advise, help or agree to any plot for King Henry to lose life or limb, or to undergo the evil fate of being taken prisoner, or for him to suffer any loss or diminution in person, position, honour or estate. But if they become aware of any such plots or schemes against him, they are to do all in their power to prevent them and to tell King Henry of them as quickly as possible, either in their own person or through messenger or letter.

Also, that on the foregoing points, both collectively and singly, and on any others agreed between his kinsman himself and King Henry on this issue, the king of France [Charles VI] will produce and give to King Henry, or get produced and given, his letters patent signed with his great seal, also the letters patent of confirmatory approval of the most high princess, his consort, and of his illustrious kinsman, the duke [Philip] of Burgundy, and of the other lords and magnates of France who are subjects of his kinsman of France now or in the future and whose letters patent King Henry shall wish to demand from his kinsman on this matter, with their content, layout and language as clear, open and unambiguous as the councils of both parties to the agreement shall be able to advise. The king of France shall also produce and give all kinds of reasonable securities that King Henry may wish to demand on this matter.

And King Henry undertakes that he for his part will in the same way produce and give on the same matters his own letters patent, those of confirmatory approval of his most noble brothers and of others of the blood royal, and of those magnates who are his subjects, and also all kinds of reasonable securities which his kinsman may wish to demand on this matter.'

At the urging of the duke of Burgundy, the French king and the queen, his consort, and the magnates and lords who attended them gratefully accepted the foregoing articles and promised faithfully to observe them.

[The treaty of Troyes]

And so the king of England on 8 May began to ride with his army towards the king of France, who was staying at Troyes in the territory of Ponthieu. He passed through the town of St Denis, where he offered up his prayers and made his devotions.[1] Then he passed near the moats surrounding Paris to the apparent great joy of the inhabitants who inspected him.[2] And he came to the bridge of Charenton, which has a very strong tower erected on it, and the bridge on both sides of the tower can be lifted up and withdrawn, so that nobody can get to the tower if these bridges are lifted up. Here the king dispatched Sir William Gascoigne[3] with a strong body of troops to guard the bridge until he should return, and he did the same in all places that had such bridges.

---

[1]   Henry visited the abbey of St Denis on the evening of 8 May.
[2]   The Parisians watched Henry's progress from the Porte St Martin.
[3]   Sir William Gascoigne, a Yorkshire knight, son of the celebrated chief justice of the same name. He was killed in action in 1422.

At last on 20 May he came to Troyes, where about a mile outside the town our king was met with great reverence by the bishops who were in the town, the chancellor of France, all the clergy, all who held any position in the French court, the duke of Burgundy and many lords and knights. On the morrow the parties assembled at St Peter's church,[1] the king of France coming with forty lords, knights and esquires specially assigned for this duty. The duchess of Clarence also entered the church together with our king. The queen of France arrived with the duke of Burgundy and forty persons of his council and with her came her daughter, the Lady Katherine, duchess of Baire, and the future queen of England.[2] The king and queen of France met in the middle of the church itself, and ascended the steps to the high altar side by side, where in the presence of both parties all the articles and points agreed upon in the treaty were read out.

These, with the agreement of the parties, were then sealed with the seals of both kings, and the parties took an oath to preserve harmony without deceit. When this had been done, King Henry and Katherine joined hands, plighted their troth, and pledged loyalty to one another.[3] After this the duke of Burgundy publicly swore an oath that he would be obedient to our king as regent of France, as long as the term of the life of the king of France should last, and that after his death, he would at once become the liegeman of our king. Then peace was straightway proclaimed, first on the part of the king of France in the French tongue and afterwards on the part of our king in our own tongue. Then the articles of this treaty were read out and published throughout the city of Troyes and the English army.

At the beginning of June the Scots captured Wark castle. Sir Gilbert Umfraville and Sir Robert Ogilvie offered a great sum of gold to get it back, but the Scots shilly-shallied, and the lords achieved nothing. So these angry heroes collected a force of two thousand tough troops and encircled and laid siege to the castle. They took it by force, made some of the Scots prisoner and beheaded the rest.[4]

The discovery of Joseph of Arimathea

The monks at Glastonbury were keen to find the remains of Joseph of Arimathea, but although they began the work they had no success.

In this year Hugh [of Morton], abbot of Gloucester, died. His place was taken by Richard, a monk of the same church, after a free election.[5] During the same days came the death of the abbot of Glastonbury, a man full of days and, while he was alive, a golden column of the monastic religion. His successor was Nicholas Frome, a monk of that monastery and religious order. Rising as a star in the east over the watchtower of that monastery, he took on the insignia of pastor.[6]

On 2 December in this year a parliament was held at Westminster, with Humphrey, duke of Gloucester, the own brother of the king, taking the place of the king. In this parliament to the smiles and joy of the whole English people it was publicly announced by the archbishop of Canterbury, speaking for his serene highness, by the grace of God the king, that his royal majesty was showing them mercy and had considered the peace of his subjects, since for the present he had no wish for a tenth or fifteenth tax to be imposed on either people or clergy.[7]

On 3 June, the day after the feast of Trinity, our King Henry took to wife the Lady Katherine,

---

1 Correctly, the cathedral church of St Peter.
2 Katherine of Valois (1401–37), the tenth child and sixth daughter of Charles VI.
3 The betrothal between Henry and Katherine occurred directly after the sealing of the treaty in the cathedral but their marriage did not take place until 2 June, when a grand procession was made through the streets of Troyes: Wylie, *Henry V,* iii. 205. Henry then progressed to Sens on 4 June to begin the siege there.
4 The castle of Wark was held by Sir Robert Ogle (not Ogilvie) a Northumberland knight. It was captured in 1419, according to the *Scotichronicon* by William Haliburton of Fast Castle. This authority also records the beheading of the Scots: *Scotichronicon,* viii. 112–13.
5 Hugh of Morton was in fact succeeded by John Morwent: *VCH Gloucestershire,* ii. 61.
6 Abbot John Chinnock of Glastonbury had ruled Glastonbury since 1375. His successor, Nicholas Frome, held the abbacy until his death in 1456. For Frome see also Emden, *BRUO,* ii. 730.
7 The commons had hoped that the king would have returned to England in time to attend this parliament in person and they now petitioned Gloucester to urge him to return as soon as possible.

and assigned to her as servants of her household some noble English women. Nor did any Frenchman remain in her service except for three women of good birth and two maidservants to serve their mistress.

On 14 June there was a solemn procession in London, during which a sermon was publicly preached at St Paul's cross concerning the happenings described above. It was also made public during the sermon that the seal of the king of England was being broken up and a new design made which had at its top the name of the king, with his title added underneath by which our king was called in the writing 'King of England', and 'Regent' or 'Ruler of France' and heir apparent to that kingdom.[1]

And so after the marriage between the king of England and the Lady Katherine had been solemnly celebrated, as I have described, and peace made again, the king of England, as ruler of France and heir to its kingdom, set about subduing with all his might the cities which were in rebellion against him and against the French crown. He took the towns of Sens and 'Botreus', which were immediately surrendered to him.[2] Then with his armies he turned his attention to the very strong city of Melun and encircled it with very powerful besieging forces. For there were present at the siege the kings of England, France and Scotland, the dukes of Bavaria [i.e. William, Count of Holland], Clarence, Bedford and Exeter, the earls of the March, Warwick, Huntingdon, Somerset etc., and other lords, barons, knights and esquires of noble birth and strong in battle, whose names I do not remember. The siege itself lasted for fourteen weeks and four days, from the feast of St Mary Magdalene [22 July] right up to the next feast of All Saints following [1 November].[3] It produced almost daily fierce struggles between besiegers and besieged, and very many were wounded, mutilated and killed. For it is claimed that more than one thousand seven hundred of the besiegers were killed, so that the siege did more harm to the English than any of their sieges that had preceded it. At length, when all the food supplies of the besieged were used up and ran out, they surrendered themselves to the mercy of the kings of England and France. More than four hundred of the more powerful were committed to the custody of different fortresses, but the rest were allowed to depart by the goodness of the king of England.[4] So after a glorious but costly victory over the rebels, the two kings with a great part of their armies marched to Paris, intending with due solemnity to celebrate the days of Christmas there and to hold a most important parliament.[5]

These things happened in 1420, the fortieth year of the reign of the king of France and the eighth of the king of England.

So ended a year of fertile corn crops and a rich harvest of fruit, but one in which there had been a desperate shortage and want of money. For our king on his overseas expeditions with his army had ordered such a stream of money to flow across the sea after him that even among the

1   Walsingham is the only contemporary authority to describe this in detail: the creation of a new seal was bound to catch the eye of this former precentor who had once presided over the chancery at St Albans.
2   Henry now undertook to fulfil the responsibility he had accepted under the terms of the treaty at Troyes, to defeat the remaining Dauphinist-Armagnac resistance. Sens was besieged on 2 June and had surrendered no more than a week later. 'Botreus' perhaps refers to Bray, the next town to be taken by the English forces (June 16); they moved on to Montereau before confronting Melun: Wylie, *Henry V*, iii. 208–10.
3   Walsingham's dates are close but not correct: the siege began on 13 July and the town finally surrendered on 18 November. In contrast to English experiences elsewhere, there was much skirmishing between the besiegers and the garrison at least until the town's food supplies were exhausted in mid-October. The siege represented something of a test for the terms of the Troyes treaty since Duke Philip of Burgundy and his forces worked in partnership with King Henry.
4   It was a savage form of goodness that saw Henry commit some 600 prisoners to custody in the Paris gaols where many of them, unable to raise ransom, subsequently died.
5   The so-called 'solemn parliament' which was convened at Paris on 23 December saw Kings Henry and Charles formally disinherit the Dauphin Charles in a special session of the *lit de justice*. The murder of Duke John of Burgundy was declared an act of treason and the estates and titles of the conspirators were declared forfeit. The English parliament also convened in December (2): *RP*, iv. 123.

ordinary people scarcely enough pennies remained for them to be able lay up sufficient supplies of corn.[1]

In 1421, the ninth year of Henry V, king of England and heir and regent of France, our famous king kept Christmas in Paris, in a very well fortified place which is called the district or castle of St Antoine.[2] This castle is built on one side of the city. Its walls are made of close-fitting stone and are very strong. From it you have a view of so much of the city that those who control it can easily stop all the citizens from rebelling. From here he was able to keep an eye on the city and easily squash any rebels, if this was necessary. His army kept watch and provided a powerful enough garrison.

[The king returns to England]

After the days of Christmas and the important parliament in Paris had been completed, the king of England moved on to Rouen, and there with his Norman and English liegemen he held another similar parliament.[3] Then having positioned what he thought were strong enough garrisons to keep secure the kingdom of France and the dukedom of Normandy, he hurried to England, passing through Picardy and Normandy, and arrived at Dover and then at Canterbury on the eve of the Purification of the blessed Mary [2 February], accompanied by his queen whom he had lately married and just a small household. He had with him only the duke of Bedford, the earl of Warwick [Richard Beauchamp] and the knight Sir John Cornwall, for everyone else was left behind overseas to guard his gains and the country.

Having also spent a few days at Canterbury, he arrived at London, where he was welcomed by a highly delighted clergy and people with plays and shows of different kinds, as befitted the occasion. And also on the first Sunday in the following Lent [23 February] the queen was escorted from the Tower of London to Westminster in a fitting procession with horsemen at its head, and there she was solemnly crowned in a service taken by the archbishop of Canterbury and other appropriate clerics.[4]

And so when the coronation of the queen had been celebrated with all fitting solemnity and joy, and a suitable retinue had been provided for herself and her household, the king and the queen made a tour of various holy places famous for their saints, and after they had performed this pilgrimage and made their vows the king kept Easter at Leicester.[5] He did not keep the feast of St George on its actual day [23 April], but postponed it until the Sunday after the Ascension of our Lord [16 May], so that it could be held in his castle at Windsor as usual.

---

[1]   As Walsingham suggests here, there is no doubt that the costs of Henry's campaigning were now being felt in England, as the commons would remind him in the next, and his last parliament.

[2]   Henry entered Paris on 1 December in grand procession, riding alongside Charles VI and flanked by Duke Philip of Burgundy. In the weeks that followed the Estates General were convened and the murderers of Duke John at Montereau were tried before the parlement in the presence of both Charles and Henry. Contrary to Walsingham's claim, Henry and Katherine passed Christmas at the Palais de Louvre.

[3]   Henry arrived at Rouen on 31 December 1420. He summoned the three estates to secure their assent to the terms of the Troyes treaty, to levy taxes and to make provision for the defence of the duchy during the visit to England that he now contemplated. He appears to have left Rouen on 19 January; Wylie, *Henry V*, iii. 234–64, 266.

[4]   Henry arrived in London alone on 8 February and Katherine followed on 21 February. As was customary, the mayor and aldermen met her at Blackheath and escorted her into the city, where a pageant reminiscent of the spectacle after Agincourt entertained her as she made her way to the Tower. She was crowned at Westminster Abbey on 23 February, which was the third Sunday in Lent and not the first as Walsingham claims here.

[5]   Walsingham must have been an eyewitness to this pilgrimage for the first place they visited was St Albans on 27 February. Then they progressed westwards to Bristol, and then northwards through the marches to Weobley and Shrewsbury. Henry and Katherine continued north to York from where Henry visited the shrine of St John of Bridlington and the minster at Beverley. It was there that news reached him of the death of Clarence at Baugé.

[Benedictine reforms]

At this time a parliament, which had been fixed by the king in the first place, was begun at London and finished successfully within a month.[1] For besides the grant to the king of a tenth tax from the clergy and of a fifteenth from the people as a subsidy for the carrying out of his wars, many other matters affecting clergy and people were reformed at the king's will. These reforms particularly affected the order of Black Monks [i.e. the Benedictines], who had gathered together there in great numbers at the king's edict. For there had assembled as many as sixty abbots and priors from the various houses, and also more than three hundred monks, scholars and proctors.[2] For various disloyal monks had informed the king's majesty that their abbots with their friends had wandered far from the pathway, that monastic religious life had fallen away from the standards of its original rule and observances, and that it necessarily followed that it could only be reformed by the king himself and no other.[3] This information was the more believable, as most of the senior, leading monks of this order had died, and their places then taken by the unbridled young.[4]

So the king, accompanied by only four nobles, very humbly went before the Benedictines where they were gathered together in the chapter house at Westminster, and after he had given them a respectful greeting, he took his seat to listen to a suitable sermon on the subject from the bishop of Exeter, Master Edmund Lacy, professor of theology.[5] When the sermon was ended, the king himself spoke to them about the religious life lived by the monks in olden days which had led to his predecessors and others showing their devotion by founding and endowing monasteries, and about the failure of men of his own day to show a similar devotion. He put before them certain matters which they were to put right and he earnestly pleaded with them to return to their former way of life and to pray without ceasing for himself and the well-being of his kingdom and of the church. With a great deal of warmth and goodwill he assured them that if they did this they need have no great fear of any enemy, and that he himself had the greatest confidence in their prayers.

When the king's points and various others had been carefully discussed and approved by the bishop and others of the king's party, by the abbot of St Albans,[6] professor of holy theology, and other men of marked authority and wisdom at the meeting, a reform of these matters was decided upon, as far as the times, circumstances and human weakness seemed to permit, and subject to the approval of the next chapter meeting of the province and to the confirmation of the pope.

---

[1]   The writs of summons to parliament had been issued as early as 27 February but the session did not open until 2 May: *RP,* iv. 129. The principal business of this parliament was to ratify the treaty of Troyes: the commons now proved less anxious about its terms than they had been the previous December and it was duly ratified.

[2]   On 25 March Henry summoned the abbots and priors of the Benedictine order to meet at the chapter house at Westminster Abbey on 5 May; Henry himself joined the discussions on 7 May. His aim was to effect a general and wide-ranging reform of the order, but his particular concern was to compel them to return to an *ad literam* adherence to the rule of St Benedict.

[3]   Henry's interest in religious, and in particular monastic reform, was well established but it may be that, as Walsingham here suggests, he was persuaded on this occasion to intervene in the affairs of the Benedictines by their rivals in religion. The anonymous chronicler of Crowland abbey corroborates Walsingham's story, claiming that in particular the prior of the Carthusian monastery at Mount Grace had convinced Henry that individual and institutional corruption was widespread in Benedictine cloisters and that monastic life was on the point of collapse. See also Pantin, *Chapters,* iii. 98–134.

[4]   This is not simply nostalgia on the part of the ageing Walsingham; for much of the second half of the fourteenth century England's greater Benedictine abbeys and priories had been led by prominent and politically astute abbots, such as William Colchester (d.1420) of Westminster Abbey and Walsingham's own pastor, Thomas de la Mare (d.1396), councillor and friend to Edward III and the queen mother, Joan of Kent.

[5]   Lacy was also bishop of Exeter. See also Emden, *BRUO,* ii. 1081–3.

[6]   John Wheathampstead, elected to the abbacy in September 1420. He had spent almost two decades at Oxford and had completed the doctorate in theology. He emerged at the council as a spokesman for the Benedictine order. Emden, *BRUO,* iii. 2032–4.

Anyone who wishes to see a copy of these reforms, can find them in the monastery at St Albans or in several other Benedictine monasteries.[1]

It was also decreed by the clergy at the same parliament on the very strong recommendation of the king, so it is said, that every third benefice in the gift and presentation of the abbots and their monasteries, which became vacant over a seven year period starting from then, should be presented to a clerk of the universities of Oxford or Cambridge, according to the form and manner in a statute where a fuller description is given.[2]

The right was also secured from a petition to the king that parts of the counties of Northamptonshire, Herefordshire and Essex, which the king himself held in hereditary right, should enjoy privileges equal to the other privileges that had originally been granted to the dukedom of Lancaster by King Edward III of England.

Death of the duke of Clarence

The next event was that Thomas, duke of Clarence and brother of the king, set off to France with a very strong English army,[3] and subduing rebels against his king and kingdom and taking their goods for the benefit of himself and his men, he came to a very strong castle in the district of Meyns called Beaufort.[4] Here he was informed by two Scots, who had been cut off by his scouts or spies, that the army of the dauphin, numbering about four thousand soldiers, was encamped near a town some four miles distant. The duke was unreasonably excited by the news and to a greater degree than was fitting for such a great general, and he hurriedly sent messengers to the captains of his army dispersed across the countryside to follow him without delay.[5] The duke himself also began marching with a few men more than a number [blank space in MS] not been calculated, and came to a river and a marshy area. He only got across with great difficulty and not without losses of men and horses, and he was marching along with his force in scattered attachments and no sort of fighting order when he fell into the hands of his enemies. The duke himself and several other nobles were slain by his foes, and very many were taken prisoner who would only be released after heavy ransoms. And many more still would have fallen, had not night stopped their battle.[6]

The enemy did not know which of their adversaries they had killed until two English heralds, captured for this very purpose and bound with a strict oath on this matter, made a scrutiny of the bodies of the slain and at once gave the French fuller information. Then they loaded the body of the duke on to a cart, to be taken with other prisoners to the dauphin who was then at Turon. But the bastard son of the duke[7] assembled the rest of the army, bravely snatched the body from the

---

[1] The king's proposals were subject to the scrutiny of a committee of thirty leading Benedictines, and were revised to the point that any novel or radical element was removed. Copies were distributed to the convents themselves but they did not inform the order's own on-going process of statute making through its General and Provincial chapters.

[2] This measure was agreed in the convocation that met from 5–27 May. There had been growing pressure from the chancellor and masters of Oxford for greater provision to be made for graduates of the university who struggled to secure suitable preferment.

[3] Walsingham is wrong: Clarence had remained in France.

[4] Following a resurgence of the Armagnac-Dauphinist remnant at the beginning of 1421, Clarence had mustered his forces at Bernay to make ready for a pursuit into Anjou. He advanced south into Maine crossing the River Loir at Luché. He attempted to besiege Angers but meeting greater resistance than expected he withdrew to Beaufort-en-Vallée, as Walsingham here reports, where he was on 22 March when the Scots prisoners brought him news of the Dauphinist force nearby at Baugé.

[5] Not all of Clarence's captains was convinced by the plan and there is a tradition in Hardyng's Chronicle (which is not contemporary) that Sir Gilbert Umfraville tried to persuade the duke to turn back.

[6] Clarence and his men surprised the Franco-Scottish force but encountering and engaging the Scots first they were unaware of the French nearby and soon found themselves to be surrounded and fatally outnumbered. According to the contemporary French authorities, Clarence was the first to fall, run through by the sword of Charles le Bouteiller, but, as might be expected, the *Scotichronicon* claimed that his killers were Scots, namely John, Lord Swinton of that Ilk and the earl of Buchan: *Scotichronicon*, viii. 118–21.

[7] John son of the duke, continued to serve as king's knight, receiving lands and revenues in Ireland: *CPR, 1429–36*, pp. 41, 122; Wylie, *Henry V*, iii. 308 and n.

hands of the French, and sent it to the duchess, the wife of the duke, in Normandy. It was after-wards buried in Christ Church in Canterbury. There also fell in this battle the Lord Roos and his brother, Sir Gilbert Umfreville, who had been made earl of Kyme, and Sir John Grey, who in the same way had been made earl of Tancerville by the duke of Clarence in Normandy. The earl of Huntingdon [John Holland], the earl of Somerset [Edmund Beaufort] and his brother Lord Fitzwalter[1] and Sir William Bower were also taken prisoner.[2]

[The king returns to France]

The enemies of King Henry in his absence now took a fortified town that had originally been surrendered to the English, killing with the sword its English governor and all the others.[3] The French were elated by these victories and were growing so bold that there was a fear that the other towns previously surrendered to the English would rebel and return to the French.[4] And so his faithful liegemen besought the king more earnestly to hurry with all speed to those parts with a strong band of armed men.

So the king, having arranged all matters concerning the kingdom of England and the wars against Scotland according to his pleasure, returned to French parts with a strong force of soldiers and archers, more than fifteen hundred in number,[5] in order to avenge with all his might the deaths of his brother and other Englishmen. But the dauphin refused to engage in combat with him, although he had told King Henry differently through his envoys and had, so it is said, the bigger army, and had bound himself with an oath that he was willing to fight with our king of England, if the chance was given him. But for the time being the dauphin remained in distant parts and ravaged the country all about, so that people said that the greater part of his hired troops left him, unwilling to serve him any longer.[6] So King Henry with great losses to his army fruitlessly chased the dauphin through territories first devastated by him.[7] Then with this force he laid siege to the town of Meaux, situated on a river in the lands of de Brie and full of rebels.[8] Here his great force suffered wastage and was weakened through fighting and lack of food, and a great part of it went back to England, with very little intention of returning to France again.

---

1   Walter, 5th baron Fitzwalter, who died in 1431.

2   Contemporary French chroniclers record exaggerated numbers of English dead, Monstrelet claiming as many as 3,000 casualties and 200 prisoners. In fact the force that engaged the French and Scots army was no larger than around 1,500 men of which it appears more than two-thirds were killed and the remainder captured. The battle passed into local mythology and amongst other legends it was claimed that the wheel of a nearby watermill turned three times with the flow of blood from the English dead: Wylie, *Henry V*, iii. 305–6 and n; Allmand, *Henry V*, pp. 158–61.

3   Walsingham is the only authority to report this; the town in question must be Le Mans from where the earl of Salisbury and the remains of Clarence's army retreated only hours after the disaster of Baugé. Beyond Le Mans, however, the Franco-Scottish force seem to have been disinclined to capitalise on their surprise victory: Wylie, *Henry V*, iii. 311–12.

4   Walsingham presents the battle as a purely French triumph but it was widely regarded as an equally signif-icant success for the Scots, often derided for their lack of martial skill. On receiving news of the battle, Pope Martin V is reported to have declared that 'Truly the Scots are the antidote to the English!': *Scotichronicon*, viii. 120–1.

5   Henry left England on 10 June and landed at Calais the following day. Walsingham drastically underesti-mates the force that accompanied him, which numbered approximately 900 knights and men-at-arms and 3,300 archers.

6   After Baugé, the first intention of the Dauphinists had been to attack Normandy from the south but the effectiveness of the raids led by the earl of Salisbury dissuaded them and instead they turned to the valley of the Loire and the region immediately to the south of the Île de France.

7   Henry had planned to spend time in Picardy but news of the northward advance of the Dauphinists – they were laying siege to Chartres when he landed at Calais – pushed him towards Paris from where he might plan his counterattack. His army advanced from Paris on 8 July and so began twelve months of continuous campaigning, which were to be the last twelve months of his life. The *Scotichronicon* reports that he passed through Melun, putting twenty Scotsmen to the sword as punishment for Baugé, but his chronology here is confused: *Scotichronicon*, viii. 122–3.

8   The English had begun the siege of Meaux by mid-October. The garrison held firm and the English suf-fered significant casualties; Henry supervised the siege but was not present throughout. It was almost eight months later, in May 1422, that the garrison finally made its submission to the king.

[The duke of Burgundy wins a victory]

About the same time, the duke of Burgundy [Philip] with English help encircled with siege works the very strong town of St Riquier, which had rebelled against him and the French crown.[1] But for the following reasons he did not obtain its surrender. For a force of men from Picardy and France assembled from all sides and tried to break the siege by attacking the duke of Burgundy [Philip] with a greater number of soldiers. The duke learned a little beforehand through scouts that they were coming, and burnt his tents and pretended that he was fleeing. His enemies were still more enraged by this and did not stop pursuing him. But they were caught between the duke and some men in ambush in different positions, and one thousand eight hundred of them were killed with others taken prisoner, while some escaped by fleeing. And so, after abandoning the siege, the duke himself returned thanks to God for his great victory, and immediately fulfilled the pilgrimages and vows that he had promised to fulfil if he won. For he was not able any longer to besiege the town with his army, as he had burnt his tents, as I described above, and a great part of his army had left him before the battle, while his enemies, having suffered such provocation, were able to put increasingly greater numbers than his in the field day by day.

[The emperor Sigismund wages war on the Lollards in Prague]

After Sigismund, that most Christian and excellent king of Hungary, Bohemia and the Romans, had been elected holy Roman emperor, and by his careful work as president had brought stability to the church of God at its general council by appointing Pope Martin V as the true vicar of Christ and the successor to Peter in that church, he returned to his own kingdoms and dominions. His intention was to use all his resources to wage war on the enemies of the faith, and to eliminate the Lollard heresy, which during the times of his elder brother [i.e. Wenzel IV, King of Bohemia] and through his support had grown strong in Bohemia.[2] So he collected a vast army of soldiers and encircled with massive siege-works the university city of Prague. It was in Prague, more than in any other city, that the heresy had started and put down its roots before spreading to other places. The city was also in rebellion against him. So the besieged, seeing that they could not resist such a power, surrendered totally to his authority, declaring that they would be his liegemen and would obey his decisions, orders and commands, provided that he sent away the greatest part of his army, which had devastated their whole country, and negotiated with them in a friendly fashion while keeping only his usual army. They sent him food supplies and gifts as a sign that they

---

[1]   St Riquier in Picardy had been taken by two Dauphinist captains, Guy de Nesle, the Sire d'Offemont and Poton de Saintrailles. Duke Philip laid siege to the town in late July but after a month he withdrew to confront what was believed to be the greater threat of a large Dauphinist force advancing from the south to reinforce the towns they already held to the north of the Somme. Duke Philip caught the advancing army at the riverbank near Mons-en-Vimeau and although his own force was small and he sustained losses of his own he did succeed in inflicting severe casualties upon them. Walsingham's somewhat garbled account of the battle that follows in this passage reflects the confused and contradictory reports that circulated not only in England but also in Paris in the aftermath: Wylie, *Henry V*, iii. 334–6; R. Vaughan, *Philip the Good. The Apogee of Burgundy* (London, 1970), pp. 12, 17.

[2]   Walsingham here is referring to the Hussite heresy, which in terms of its origins and the target of its teachings had much in common with Wyclifism. Its progenitor, the Bohemian theologian, Jan Hus, had been tried and executed at the council of Constance in 1415, but his ideas had already won wide support in Bohemia and Prague itself was in the hands of the Hussites. Emperor Sigismund had presided at Constance and had supported the council's elimination of Hus, whose heresy represented a threat not only to the success of the council but also to Sigismund's own claim on the kingdom of Bohemia. The incumbent ruler, Sigismund's elder brother Wenzel, initially had shown favour to Hus and his followers and they gained such a hold in the church and university of Prague that when Sigismund finally persuaded Wenzel to move against them in 1419 the city erupted in violent rebellion. Facing the prospect of civil war, Wenzel succumbed to a stroke on 16 August. Sigismund now sought to assert his claim to the kingdom but was repelled by Hussite forces in 1420. With the support of Martin V he gathered a crusading force against them. The conflict continued until Sigismund's death in 1437. See also H. Kaminsky, *A History of the Hussite Revolution* (Berkley and Los Angeles, 1967), pp. 265–309.

intended to keep their promise and received his envoys with honour. Sigismund believed their promises too easily and wishing to avoid the spilling of Christian blood he sent away the strongest part of his armies and with just his usual army remaining, as they had wished, stayed behind to settle matters finally.

So the deceitful, lying citizens, seeing that circumstances smiled upon their wishes, suddenly attacked his troops and killed a very great number of them before the emperor could come to the help of the remainder. But finally the emperor got a livelier spirit back in his troops and charged three times into the middle of the enemy, killing very many and forcing the remainder to return into the city. Then he went back home with the remainder of his army, intending to return again with a stronger force and avenge the injury done to him. And indeed he did assemble a very strong army of his princes, dukes and knights, and soldiers, archers and crossbowmen as well, and together with the archbishops of Cologne, Mainz and Trier[1] and others made into crusaders for this purpose by the urging and the authority of the pope, he did not cease to hunt down the heretics and to recall them to unity and the true faith and church or to hand them over to perish by fire or sword.

[The birth of Henry VI]

Also in this year the Lady Katherine, queen of England, gave birth to her firstborn son at Windsor castle on the feast of St Nicholas [6 December], bishop and confessor.[2] And he was called by the name of Henry. His godparents who received him from the sacred font were John, duke of Bedford, his uncle and at that time governor of England, Henry [Beaufort], uncle of the king and bishop of Winchester, and the lady Jacqueline [of Hainault], duchess of Holland who at that time was staying in England. The service was taken by Henry [Chichele], archbishop of Canterbury, with all due solemnity and to the especial joy of all the English. The prince was given impressive presents of great value for his baptism.

Also on 1 December of this year at the king's order a parliament assembled at Westminster under the presidency of the duke of Bedford, who was then governor of England.[3] At this parliament a fifteenth tax from the lay people was granted to the lord king to subsidise his wars, its payment being due on the feast of the purification of the blessed Virgin [2 February] and St Martin [11 November].[4] No tax from the clergy was granted on this occasion, because the tenth tax granted from it on similar terms in the last parliament had not yet been fully paid. The people's tax was also under the condition that the first half of it should be paid in saved money and other money which was then currency. For it had been laid down that such saved money should be common currency with the rest of the coinage right up to the feast of the Purification, provided that it was genuine gold or silver and had not been greatly devalued by clipping or washing.

Also in the April of this year the queen of England crossed the Channel to Normandy with a strong force, escorted by John, brother of the king and duke of Bedford. Duke Humphrey, his brother, took his place as governor of England.[5]

---

1   The archbishops were Theodoricus de Mörs, Conrad de Daun and Otto de Zeigenhain.
2   The birth occurred at 4p.m. The occasion was marked with the ringing of church bells in the city of London and the lighting of bonfires at Paris. Henry was still engaged in the siege of Meaux. See also Allmand, *Henry V,* pp. 167–8.
3   The date of its dissolution is not recorded.
4   The grant was justified on the grounds that it would be used for the defence of the realm, but few could have doubted that in reality it was needed to support the continuing conflict in France.
5   Walsingham's chronology is incorrect here: Bedford departed between 4 and 12 May, when Gloucester first appears as governor of the realm.

In 1422 the king of England and regent and heir to the kingdom of France, kept Christmas with the small army of Englishmen that was left to him at the siege of Meaux in the district of de Brie.[1] He had been besieging it since [blank space in MS] month in the previous year. And the siege actually lasted until 5 May in this following year. On this day the city with all things belonging to it was put into the hands and mercy of King Henry.[2] The king indeed bestowed his mercy on all the besieged except the Scots, the Irish, disloyal Englishmen and others who had previously sworn him an oath of allegiance. Some of the more important prisoners were sent across to England under the escort of the earl of Devonshire [Hugh Courtenay, 12th earl] and there put in different prisons, with large sums of money, it is believed, being necessary for their ransom. The king found that the weapons, food supplies and valuables in Meaux were completely undamaged.

Meanwhile the dauphin with the count of Armagnac and the Scots and other adherents to his cause and a very strong army besieged Cosne, a fortified town belonging to the duke of Burgundy [Philip]. So the inhabitants, put in a tight spot by their lack of food supplies, sent for help to the duke of Burgundy and also to the king of England, heir and regent of France; if no help came, they would be forced to surrender their city to the dauphin. So the king sent his armies there under the command of John, duke of Bedford, Thomas Beaufort his uncle, the duke of Exeter, the earls of the March and Warwick and other earls, barons and knights whose names I do not know, accompanied by the duke of Burgundy, the intention being to lift the siege by joining battle with the enemy. But in his usual fashion the dauphin took to his heels as soon as he learned of their arrival from scouts, and left his tents behind to be ransacked by the English.[3]

[Illness and death of king Henry]

In the meantime King Henry, who had been ill for a long time owing to his excessive, unceasing labours, was attacked by an acute fever and overpowering dysentery, which so wasted his strength that his doctors dared not apply any internal medicines, but were in great despair for his life. So the king, seeing that death was near and close at hand, summoned his dukes and others who could be present, and made wise dispositions for the kingdoms of England and France and the dukedom of Normandy, drew up his will, and decided to pay his debts from his treasuries and abundant stores of valuables. Then, having received the life-giving sacrament of our Lord's body and the other sacraments of a Christian, he said farewell to this world and his people, and in true penitence, with a sure and certain faith and hope, and with charity towards all and leaving good memories behind he handed back his soul to his creator on 30 August, after he had reigned for nine years, five months and fourteen days. He did not leave his like on earth among Christian kings or princes, so that not only the people of England and France but all Christendom mourned his death as he deserved.[4]

He had a pious mind and his words were few and well-judged. Far-sighted in his planning and

---

[1] In fact Henry celebrated Christmas at Paris with Charles VI and Queen Isabeau and joined his army at Meaux in mid-January.
[2] Walsingham's dates are again inaccurate: negotiations with the besieged began at the end of April and agreement on the terms of the surrender was reached on 2 May. The market was surrendered on 10 May and the prisoners were taken from the town on 15 May. For a full account see Allmand, *Henry V*, pp. 164–70.
[3] The Dauphinists reached Cosne in early August 1422: the Anglo-Burgundian army arrived on 11 August and prepared to engage the enemy the following day when it was discovered that they had fled.
[4] Henry's health had begun to fail even before the end of the siege at Meaux. He had returned to Paris and then removed to Senlis, moving subsequently to Corbeil and then finally to his castle at Bois de Vincennes, where he died. It was only when he attempted to join the Anglo-Burgundian army advancing on Cosne that it became clear that his condition was grievous. It was widely believed that he had contracted smallpox (although in Normandy the rumour-mongers favoured leprosy) but Walsingham's assessment that he was suffering from dysentery may be more accurate. After taking his leave of his most trusted captains and discussing the terms of his will, he died at 2a.m. on Monday 31 August 1422. See also Allmand, *Henry V*, pp. 173–4.

shrewd in judgement, he showed modesty in his bearing and magnanimity in his actions. He worked unceasingly, frequently went on pilgrimage and was a generous alms-giver. He was a devout Christian and supported and honoured the ministers and servants of the church. He was also a distinguished and fortunate leader in war, who in all his battles always came off the victor. His construction of new buildings and his foundation of monasteries were on a magnificent scale. He was a munificent giver of presents, and in all matters he hunted down and fought against the enemies of the faith and the church.

When his subjects reflected on these qualities and on his famous deeds, they felt great dread at the sudden, terrible change in their fortunes that the right hand of the Lord had brought about, and their sorrow cannot be described. Nor is this surprising, since instead of a puissant king and discerning lord who was splendidly equipped with all the characteristics of goodness, they were receiving for their king and lord his weak, infant son who was not yet a year old, and who would be the ruler of the numerous, vast kingdoms and dominions which were his by inheritance. They were afraid when they thought of the saying of Solomon, 'Woe to that land whose king is a boy' [Ecclesiastes 10:16], and their one hope was that they would be helped by the mercy of the good God who accomplishes his miracles equally with the small and with the big, and whose hand would not be stopped from doing good, provided that they, like their king, were humble and small in God's eyes and in their own, and all of one mind in their actions and in their counsels for the good.

[The death of Charles VI, king of France]

When Charles, king of France, heard of the death of his son-in-law of England, he celebrated solemn exequies and masses for his soul in his chapel. Then by edict he summoned the great number of his prelates and his lords as well, who a short time previously had agreed to the treaty made between the kingdoms of France and England. He had this treaty read through in their presence and confirmed a second time by an oath made by him and his lords on the body of our Lord and on the holy gospel of God. Then King Charles wasted away in sorrow and loneliness, and thirteen days later he too said farewell to the unstable light of this world.[1] But great grief and sorrow for King Henry was felt even by almost all Frenchmen, who, after the disturbing, wicked tyranny of others, had experienced the fair and thoughtful rule of the king of England. Especially sad were the people of Paris and Rouen. In return for his virtues they paid proper and extensive honour to his body with funeral services and prayers, and even offered vast sums of gold that they might be marked out by the honour and consolation of having his body buried among them. But this could not be, for King Henry had already recorded in his will his wish to be buried at Westminster. And this was later done with all due honours, as described below.[2]

[Provisions for the government of France]

Meanwhile at a great council of both kingdoms held at Paris and Rouen, John, brother of the king and duke of Bedford, was confirmed as governor of the dukedom of Normandy and the duke of

---

1   Walsingham's chronology is incorrect: Charles VI died at the Hôtel Saint-Pol in Paris six weeks after Henry V on 21 October 1422 at 6a.m. His body remained there for the remainder of that day as many distinguished visitors paid their respects. The corpse was embalmed on 22 October and the following day it was placed in the royal chapel where masses were celebrated by the king's confessor and representatives from each of the four orders of friars. The king's chancellor and councillors were uncertain as to whether to recognise Henry VI as Charles's heir as the treaty of Troyes required them and this, together with the absence of the English regent, John, duke of Bedford, caused the funeral to be delayed for over a fortnight. The funeral service itself took place at the cathedral of Notre Dame on 9 November and the next day the body was escorted out of the city to be buried at the abbey of St Denis.

2   Henry's body was flensed and his flesh and bones placed in a lead casket for their journey to England; his organs were interred at St Maur-des-Fossés. The funeral cortège made its ceremonial progress through St Denis, where a requiem Mass was celebrated at the abbey and at Rouen, where 220 burgesses, all dressed in black and carrying flaming torches, escorted the coffin from the outskirts of the city to the cathedral. After the Mass, the coffin was taken to the castle where it lay in state for more than a fortnight (19 September – 5 October). In spite of Walsingham's comments here, however, the funeral cortège did not pass through Paris.

Burgundy as regent for the king and kingdom of France, just as King Henry had arranged while he was alive. Also the earls of Salisbury [Thomas Montagu] and Suffolk[1] and several other lords were left in France to guard the castles and towns, while almost all the remaining earls and lords, together with the body of the king and with the queen, returned to Calais and then to London. The treasuries and valuables of the king had been sent ahead to be kept safe in the Tower of London.

[The funeral of king Henry V and a parliament]

When funeral services for King Henry had also been solemnly celebrated at Canterbury, St Paul's and Westminster, as befitted so great a prince,[2] a parliament was begun which had been previously summoned to Westminster on the authority and by the writs of King Henry VI of England, the son of the late king. The parliament was presided over by the king's uncle, Humphrey, duke of Gloucester, who had previously been commissioned by the king to be governor of England.[3] At this parliament solemn exequies for the king were celebrated by all the estates, as I describe below.

The furnishing of the dead king's funeral, if you would like to know about it, was as follows. On the coffin containing his corpse was placed a figure very like to the dead king in height and appearance, clad in a long, loose-fitting purple cloak edged with ermine, with the sceptre in one hand and a round, golden ball with a cross affixed in the other hand, and with a golden crown placed on its head over the royal cap, and slippers on its feet. And it was placed so high up on the carriage that it could be seen by individuals, so that the sorrow and grief might be increased, and so that the king's friends and subjects might pray to the Lord for his soul with deeper feeling. It is also said that a thousand large torches were carried around his body by men of standing, and that cloths of golden silk had been put upon it. And, as was the custom, three warhorses with their riders handsomely armed with the arms of the kings of England and of France, were led to the high altar at Westminster, where the riders were then stripped of their armour. The arms were taken off completely and carried together with banners in one long, unbroken line around the body of the dead man, the arms being those of St George, of England and of France and the banners being those of the holy trinity and St Mary.

And so in this fashion the body of the king was carried right into the abbey, and was honourably buried by the prelates and nobles of the land among the kings of England buried there, between the bier of St Edward and the chapel of the holy Virgin in the place containing the relics of the dead. And then the parliament continued.

In this parliament with the assent of all the estates the duke of Gloucester was appointed and named as the defender and protector of England in the absence of his elder brother, the duke of Bedford. And all the duties and rewards of the kingdom were committed to his care.

---

[1]   William de la Pole (1396–1450), 4th earl of Suffolk, and from 1448, 1st duke of Suffolk.
[2]   The funeral cortège made the crossing to Dover in early November; Archbishop Chichele met it at Dover and escorted the coffin to Canterbury; a requiem Mass was celebrated, first at Dover by Bishop Thomas Hatfield of Durham and then at Canterbury cathedral by the archbishop. The cortège then made its way to London, the mayor and aldermen making their way to Blackheath to meet it, all dressed in white. Another requiem was celebrated at St Paul's and then on 6 November the funeral procession was made to Westminster Abbey; the interment itself took place the following day. The tomb was made from Caen stone and Purbeck marble and bore an effigy of the king carved from oak and covered with silver. Under the terms of Henry's will a chantry chapel was built around the tomb although it took more than two decades to complete.
[3]   Parliament opened on 9 November and continued until 18 December: *RP*, iv. 169, 173. See also R. A. Griffiths, *The Reign of Henry VI. The Exercise of Royal Authority, 1422–61* (London, 1981), pp. 20–4.

Guide to Further Reading

Thomas Walsingham's *Chronica maiora* describes a period of crisis and change in the political, cultural, religious and social life of Britain and continental Europe. The following selection of studies provides an entry-point into this half-century of high drama and should enable the reader to set Walsingham's own reportage into a wider context.

England, 1376–1399

Crown and Nobility

A. Goodman, *John of Gaunt. The Exercise of Princely Power in Fourteenth-Century Europe* (London, 1992)

G. L. Harriss, *Shaping the Nation: England, 1360–1461* (Oxford, 2005)

W. M. Ormrod, *The Reign of Edward III: Crown and Political Society in England, 1327–77* (New Haven and London, 1990)

Politics and Crisis in Fourteenth-Century England, ed. J. Taylor and W. Childs (Gloucester, 1990)

Richard II: The Art of Kingship, ed. J. L. Gillespie and A. Goodman (Oxford, 1999)

N. Saul, *Richard II* (New Haven and London, 1997)

Government, War and Society

C. T. Allmand, *The Hundred Years War, England and France at War, c. 1300–1450* (Cambridge, 1988)

A. Dunn, *The Peasants' Revolt of 1381* (Stroud, 2001)

C. Given-Wilson, *The English Nobility in the Late Middle Ages* (London, 1987)

G. A. Holmes, *The Good Parliament* (Oxford, 1975)

W. M. Ormrod, *Political Life in Medieval England* (Basingstoke, 1995)

England, 1399–1422

Crown and Nobility

C. T. Allmand, *Henry V* (London, 1992)

J. L. Kirby, *Henry IV of England* (London, 1971)

Henry IV: The Establishment of the Regime, 1399–1406, ed. G. Dodd and D. Biggs (York, 2003)

Henry V: The Practice of Kingship, ed. G. L. Harriss (Oxford, 1985)

Government, War and Society

C. T. Allmand, *Lancastrian Normandy: The History of a Medieval Occupation, 1415–50* (Oxford, 1983)

A. Curry, *The Battle of Agincourt: Sources and Interpretations* (Woodbridge, 2000)

K. B. McFarlane, *Lancastrian Kings and Lollard Knights* (Oxford, 1972)

K. B. McFarlane, *England in the Fifteenth Century* (London, 1981)

P. M. McNiven, *Heresy and Politics in the Reign of Henry IV: The Burning of John Badby* (Woodbridge, 1987)

E. Powell, *Kingship, Law and Society: Criminal Justice in the Reign of Henry V* (Oxford, 1989)

Ireland, Scotland and Wales

A. D. M. Barrell, *Medieval Scotland* (Cambridge, 2000)

G. W. S. Barrow, *Scotland and its Neighbours in the Middle Ages* (London, 1992)

The Exercise of Power in Medieval Scotland, 1200–1500, ed. S. Boardman and A. Ross (Dublin, 2003)

J. F. Lydon, *Ireland in the Later Middle Ages* (London, 1973)

Medieval Ireland, 1169–1534, ed. A. Cosgrove (Oxford, 1993)

A. D. Carr, *Medieval Wales* (London, 1993)

R. R. Davies, *Conquest, Coexistence and Change: Wales, 1066–1415* (Oxford, 1987)

G. Williams, *Recovery, Reorientation and Reformation; Wales 1415–1642* (Oxford, 1993)

Continental Europe

Europe

B. Guenée, *States and Rulers in Later Medieval Europe* (London, 1981)

The New Cambridge Medieval History VI. 1300–1415, ed. M. Jones (Cambridge, 2000)

The New Cambridge Medieval History VII. 1415–1500, ed. C. T. Allmand (Cambridge, 1998)

France

R. C. Famiglietti, *Royal Intrigue: Crisis at the Court of Charles VI, 1392–1420* (New York, 1986)

J. B. Henneman, *Olivier de Clisson and Political Society in France under Charles V* (Philadelphia, 1994)

R. J. Knecht, *The Valois: Kings of France, 1328–1589* (London, 2004)

P. S. Lewis, *Late Medieval France* (London, 1968)

E. Perroy, *The Hundred Years War* (London, 1960)

M. G. A. Vale, *Charles VII* (London, 1974).

The French Dominions

M. Jones, *Ducal Brittany* (Oxford, 1980)

D. Nicholas, *Medieval Flanders* (London, 1992)

R. Vaughan, *Valois Burgundy* (London, 1974)

R. Vaughan, *Philip the Bold: The Formation of the Burgundian State* (London, 1962)

R. Vaughan, *John the Fearless: The Growth of Burgundian Power* (London, 1966)

R. Vaughan, *Philip the Good: The Apogee of Burgundy* (London, 1970)

Central and Southern Europe

F. R. H. Du Boulay, *Germany in the Later Middle Ages* (London, 1973)

Italy in the Age of the Renaissance, ed. D. Hay and J. E. Law (2nd edn., London, 1989)

J. E. Law, *The Lords of Renaissance Italy* (3rd edn., Oxford, 2002)

J. N. Hillgarth, *The Spanish Kingdoms, 1250–1516* (2 vols, Oxford, 1976–78)

B. F. Reilly, *The Medieval Spains* (Cambridge, 1993)

The Hundred Years War, 1337–1453

C. T. Allmand, *The Hundred Years War, England and France at War, c. 1300–1450* (Cambridge, 1988)

C. T. Allmand, *Lancastrian Normandy: The History of a Medieval Occupation, 1415–50* (Oxford, 1983)

J. Sumption, *The Hundred Years War I. Trial by Battle* (London, 1990)

J. Sumption, *The Hundred Years War II: Trial by Fire* (London, 1999)

M. G. A. Vale, *English Gascony, 1399–1453. A Study of War, Government and Politics during the Later Stages of the Hundred Years War* (Oxford, 1970)

International Relations

Britain, France, and the Empire, 1350–1500, ed. M. Kekewich and S. Rose (London, 2004).

C. M. D. Crowder, *Heresy, Unity and Reform: Conciliar Responses to the Great Schism, 1378–1460* (London, 1977)

M. Harvey, *England, Rome and the Papacy: The Study of a Relationship, 1414–64* (Manchester, 1993)

J. J. N. Palmer, *England, France and Christendom, 1377–99* (London, 1972)

J. A. F. Thomson, *Popes and Princes, 1417–1517: Politics and Polity in the Late Medieval Church* (London, 1980)

Church and Religion

M. Aston, *Lollards and Reformers: Images and Literacy in Late Medieval English Religion* (London, 1984)

A. Hudson, *The Premature Reformation: Wycliffite Texts and Lollard History* (Oxford, 1988)

A. Kenny, *Wyclif* (Oxford, 1990)

Lollardy and the Gentry in the Later Middle Ages, ed. M. Aston and C. Richmond (Stroud, 1997)

R. N. Swanson, *Church and Society in Late Medieval England* (Oxford, 1989)

S. Ozment, *The Age of Reform, 1250–1550: An Intellectual and Religious History of Late Medieval and Renaissance Europe* (New Haven and London, 1980)

Monasticism

J. G. Clark, *A Monastic Renaissance at St Albans: Thomas Walsingham and his Circle, c.1350-c.1440* (Oxford, 2004)

R. B. Dobson, *Durham Priory, 1400–1450* (Cambridge, 1973)

B. F. Harvey, *Westminster Abbey and its Estates in the Middle Ages* (Oxford, 1977)

B. F. Harvey, *Living and Dying in England: The Monastic Experience, 1100–1540* (Oxford, 1993)

D. Knowles, *The Religious Orders in England* (3 vols., Cambridge, 1948–59)

The Religious Orders in Pre-Reformation England, ed. J. G. Clark (Woodbridge, 2002)

J. H. Tillotson, *Monastery and Society in Late Medieval England: Selected Account Rolls from Selby Abbey, Yorkshire, 1398–1537* (Woodbridge, 1988)

Culture

J. A. Burrow, *Ricardian Poetry: Chaucer, Langland and the Gawain Poet* (London, 1992)

Chaucer's England: Literature in Historical Context, ed. B. Hanawalt (Minneapolis, 1992)

A. Cobban, *The Medieval English Universities: Oxford and Cambridge to 1500* (London, 1988)

Gothic: Art for England, 1400–1547, ed. R. Marks and P. Williamson (London, 2003)

A. Gransden, *Historical Writing in England II: c. 1307 to the Early Sixteenth Century* (London, 1982).

S. Justice, *Writing and Rebellion: England in 1381* (Berkeley and London, 1994)

G. Matthew, *The Court of Richard II* (London, 1968)

V. J. Scattergood and J. W. Sherborne, *English Court Culture in the Later Middle Ages* (London, 1983)

P. Ströhm, *England's Empty Throne: Usurpation and the Language of Legitimation, 1399–1422* (Oxford, 1998)

Index